Lecture Notes in Computer Science 8767

Commenced Publication in 1973
Founding and Former Series Editors:
Gerhard Goos, Juris Hartmanis, and Jan van Leeuwen

T0214887

Juergen Dingel   Wolfram Schulte Isidro Ramos
Silvia Abrahão   Emilio Insfran (Eds.)

Model-Driven Engineering Languages and Systems

17th International Conference, MODELS 2014
Valencia, Spain, September 28 – October 3, 2014
Proceedings

 Springer

Volume Editors

Juergen Dingel
Queen's University, Kingston, ON, Canada
E-mail: dingel@cs.queensu.ca

Wolfram Schulte
Microsoft Research, Redmond, WA, USA
E-mail: schulte@microsoft.com

Isidro Ramos
Silvia Abrahão
Emilio Insfran
Universitat Politècnica de València, Spain
E-mail: {iramos, sabrahao, einsfran}@dsic.upv.es

ISSN 0302-9743   e-ISSN 1611-3349
ISBN 978-3-319-11652-5   e-ISBN 978-3-319-11653-2
DOI 10.1007/978-3-319-11653-2
Springer Cham Heidelberg New York Dordrecht London

Library of Congress Control Number: 2014948734

LNCS Sublibrary: SL 2 – Programming and Software Engineering

Typesetting: Camera-ready by author, data conversion by Scientific Publishing Services, Chennai, India

Printed on acid-free paper

Springer is part of Springer Science+Business Media (www.springer.com)

Preface

Software and systems development based on modeling recognizes abstraction and automation as key principles to deal with the complexity of modern software. Model-based development approaches have the proven capability to deliver complex, dependable software efficiently and effectively.

The MODELS conference series brings together educators, practitioners, and researchers to solidify and extend the benefits of modeling for the development of current and future software and systems by providing the premier venue for the dissemination and discussion of high-quality work in the area of software and systems modeling. The scope of the conference series is broad, encompassing modeling languages, methods, tools, and applications considered from theoretical and practical angles and in academic and industrial settings.

For MODELS 2014, authors were invited to submit papers to a Foundations track and a Model-Driven Engineering in Practice track. The Foundations track provides a forum for new ideas, results, and insights that can advance the state-of-the-art and contains four paper categories: Technical papers present novel, scientifically rigorous solutions to significant model-based development problems. Exploratory papers describe new, unconventional research positions and approaches. Empirical evaluation papers assess existing problem cases or validate proposed solutions scientifically through, e.g., empirical studies, experiments, case studies, or simulations. Modeling pearls are polished, elegant, and insightful applications of modeling. For the first time, authors could submit supporting artifacts via the Repository for Model Driven Development (ReMoDD). For modeling pearls this was required and for empirical evaluation papers this was encouraged.

The MDE in Practice track challenges researchers and practitioners to discuss innovations and solutions to concrete software modeling problems and experiences related to the industrial adoption of modeling techniques. Authors were invited to submit original experience reports and case studies, both with clear take-away value by describing the context of a problem of practical, industrial importance and application and its solution.

Overall, 126 full papers were submitted to the Foundations track and 35 to the MDE in Practice track. Paper authors came from 33 different countries with Germany, USA, Norway, and France being the most frequent.

The MODELS 2014 review process was designed to ensure high-quality feedback to the authors and a high-quality program. As in the two previous years, a Program Board (PB) was used to assist the Program Committee (PC) chairs in the monitoring of the reviews and the online PC discussion period. After every submission had been reviewed by three PC members, authors had a chance to correct factual mistakes in the reviews in a response period. Papers, reviews, and author responses were discussed in detail by the PC and PB during a two-week online discussion period. On May 29, 2014, the PB meeting was held in Potsdam, Germany, with all PB members in attendance to discuss the papers for which the online discussion period had not resulted in a clear decision. At that meeting, 30 of 126 submissions to the Foundations track were accepted and three more were invited to resubmit after the correction of specific deficiencies; for the MDE in Practice Track, eight of 35 submissions were accepted and one was invited to resubmit. After review of the resubmissions by the PB, all of them were accepted, resulting in an acceptance rate of 26% for both the Foundations track and the MDE in Practice track.

The resulting program is broad and inclusive covering, e.g., the theory, practice, and pragmatics of modeling languages; model transformation; survey and vision papers; and experience reports and descriptions of the application of model-based development. Papers report on the use of modeling in a wide range of contexts ranging from domains in which modeling and model-based development have already become part of the recognized best practices (e.g., embedded devices, distributed systems, signal processing, mechatronic systems, and control systems), to domains in which the use of modeling is a growing trend (e.g., web and mobile applications, and cloud computing), to domains in which software modeling techniques traditionally have not been used (e.g., tax law and grant proposal writing). This diversity provides evidence for the increasing maturity and adoption of modeling.

The paper presentations in the Foundations and MDE in Practice tracks were complemented by three keynotes and two panels.

The keynotes nicely echoed the diversity and quality of the MODELS 2014 program: The benefits of formal, foundational work in modeling languages were explored by Jose Meseguer, Professor of Computer Science at the University of Illinois at Urbana-Champaign (UIUC), in his keynote on "Why Formal Modeling Language Semantics Matters". In his keynote on "Modeling: a Practical Perspective", Wolfgang Grieskamp, staff engineer at Google, reported on current uses and opportunities for modeling in industrial software engineering. In the third keynote, Nuria Oliver, Scientific Director and founder of the User, Data and Media Intelligence research areas at Telefonica Research in Barcelona, Spain, shared her thoughts on the use of models for improving the products and services of a large telecommunications company in her presentation "Towards Data-Driven Models of Human Behavior". We welcome these international leaders and experts to the MODELS community and thank them for enriching the conference with their keynotes.

The first panel on "Modeling Outside the Box" sought to break new ground in the use of modeling and encourage the audience to develop innovative, visionary ideas about new areas of application and uses. The second panel "What Practioners and Industry Really Want" reached out to industry and attempted to identify industrial needs and challenges. We thank all panel participants for sharing their time, expertise, and ideas with the community so generously.

MODELS 2014 would have been impossible without the hard work of many people. It starts with the authors who submitted papers to MODELS. We thank them for sharing their work with us and giving us the material of which high-quality conference programs are made. We are grateful to the PB, PC, and the additional reviewers for ensuring that MODELS remains a venue worth attenting and submitting to. Their efforts constitute a vital contribution to the research community which, unfortunately, often do not receive the recognition they deserve. On the more technical side, a big thank-you must go to Richard van de Stadt. His CyberChairPRO system and the prompt, reliable support Richard provided significantly facilitated many aspects of our work. Robert France provided help with the use of ReMoDD for artifact submission which we gratefully acknowledge. We thank Holger Giese and his staff for helping with the organization of the PB meeting in Potsdam and the subsequent MDE workshop at the Hasso-Plattner-Institute which featured a wide range of talks and provided a stimulating overview of the trends, challenges, and open problems in MDE. We also thank the members of the Steering and Organizing Committees for their support and efforts to make MODELS 2014 a success. Lastly, we gratefully acknowledge the assistance of our sponsors and supporting organizations including the Universitat Politècnica de València (UPV), which provided the venue and facilities for the conference and satellite events, the Escola Técnica Superior de Ingenieria Informática (ETSINF-UPV), and our society sponsors IEEE, IEEE Computer Society, ACM, and ACM SIGSoft.

August 2014

Juergen Dingel
Wolfram Schulte
Isidro Ramos
Silvia Abrahão
Emilio Insfran

Organization

General Chairs

Isidro Ramos   Universitat Politècnica de València, Spain
Silvia Abrahão   Universitat Politècnica de València, Spain

Local Organizing Chair

Emilio Insfran   Universitat Politècnica de València, Spain

Foundations Track Program Chair

Juergen Dingel   Queen's University, Canada

MDE in Practice Track Program Chair

Wolfram Schulte   Microsoft Research, USA

Steering Committee Chair

Gregor Engels   University of Paderborn, Germany

Tutorial Chairs

Juan de Lara   Universidad Autónoma de Madrid, Spain
Michel Chaudron   Chalmers University of Technology, Sweden

Workshop Chairs

Gabriele Taentzer   Philipps-Universität Marburg, Germany
Alfonso Pierantonio   University of L'Aquila, Italy

Panel Chair

Timothy C. Lethbridge   University of Ottawa, Canada

Demonstration Chairs

Tao Yue   Simula Research Laboratory, Norway
Benoit Combemale   University of Rennes 1/Inria, France

Poster Chairs

Manuel Wimmer   Vienna University of Technology, Austria
Stefan Sauer   University of Paderborn, Germany

Social Media Chairs

Jordi Cabot   École des Mines de Nantes, France
Dimitris Kolovos   University of York, UK

ACM Student Research Competition Chairs

Marcela Genero   University of Castilla-la Mancha, Spain
Shaz Qadeer   Microsoft Research, USA

Publicity Chairs

Alessandro Garcia   PUC-Rio, Brazil
Nelly Bencomo   Aston University, UK

Educators' Symposium Chairs

Birgit Demuth   TU Dresden, Germany
Dave Stikkolorum   Leiden University, The Netherlands

Doctoral Symposium Chair

Benoit Baudry   Inria, France

Financial Chairs

José Ángel Carsí   Universitat Politènica de València, Spain
Patricio Letelier   Universitat Politènica de València, Spain

Local Facilities Chair

Javier González-Huerta   Universitat Politènica de València, Spain

Student Volunteers Chair

M. Carmen Penadés   Universitat Politènica de València, Spain

Web Chair

Priscila Cedillo   Universitat Politènica de València, Spain

Program Board

Jean-Michel Bruel   CNRS/IRIT, Université de Toulouse, France
Gregor Engels   University of Paderborn, Germany
Martin Gogolla   University of Bremen, Germany
Øystein Haugen   SINTEF, Norway
Heinrich Hussmann   Ludwig-Maximilians-Universität München,
                                 Germany
Jean-Marc Jézéquel   IRISA, France
Gerti Kappel   Vienna University of Technology, Austria
Ana Moreira   Universidade Nova de Lisboa, Portugal
Richard Paige   University of York, UK
Andy Schürr   Technische Universität Darmstadt, Germany
Perdita Stevens   University of Edinburgh, UK

Program Committee: Foundations Track

Daniel Amyot   University of Ottawa, Canada
João Araújo   Universidade Nova de Lisboa, Portugal
Mira Balaban   Ben-Gurion University, Israel
Benoit Baudry   Inria, France
Nelly Bencomo   Aston University, UK
Xavier Blanc   University of Bordeaux, France
Ruth Breu   University of Innsbruck, Austria
Jordi Cabot   École des Mines de Nantes / Inria, France
Michel Chaudron   Chalmers University of Technology, Sweden
Marsha Chechik   University of Toronto, Canada
Siobhan Clarke   Trinity College Dublin, Ireland
Juan de Lara   Universidad Autonoma de Madrid, Spain
Zinovy Diskin   McMaster University and University of
                                 Waterloo, Canada
Alexander Egyed   Johannes Kepler University, Austria
Rik Eshuis   Eindhoven University of Technology,
                                 The Netherlands
Lidia Fuentes   Universidad de Malaga, Spain
Alessandro Garcia   PUC-Rio, Brazil

Sebastien Gérard   CEA List, France
Holger Giese   Hasso Plattner Institute,
                                  University of Potsdam, Germany
Jeff Gray   University of Alabama, USA
John Grundy   Swinburne University of Technology, Australia
Reiko Heckel   University of Leicester, UK
Constance Heitmeyer   Naval Research Laboratory, USA
Peter Herrmann   NTNU, Norway
James Hill   Indiana University, and Purdue University,
                                  USA
Zhenjiang Hu   National Institute of Informatics, and
                                  The Graduate University for Advanced
                                  Studies, Japan
Ferhat Khendek   Concordia University, Canada
Joerg Kienzle   McGill University, Canada
Thomas Kühne   Victoria University of Wellington, New Zealand
Yvan Labiche   Carleton University, Canada
Yves Le Traon   University of Luxembourg, Luxembourg
Timothy Lethbridge   University of Ottawa, Canada
Frederic Mallet   Université Nice Sophia Antipolis - I3S/Inria,
                                  France
Shahar Maoz   Tel Aviv University, Israel
Hong Mei   Peking University, China
Dragan Milicev   University of Belgrade, Serbia and Montenegro
Raffaela Mirandola   Politecnico di Milano, Italy
Henry Muccini   University of L'Aquila, Italy
Shiva Nejati   SnT Centre, University of Luxembourg,
                                  Luxembourg
Ileana Ober   IRIT Universite de Toulouse, France
Alfonso Pierantonio   University of L'Aquila, Italy
Gianna Reggio   DIBRIS - University of Genoa, Italy
Bernhard Rumpe   RWTH Aachen University, Germany
Ina Schaefer   Technische Universität Braunschweig,
                                  Germany
Friedrich Steimann   Fernuniversität in Hagen, Germany
Gabriele Taentzer   Philipps-Universität Marburg, Germany
Stavros Tripakis   UC Berkeley, USA
Antonio Vallecillo   Universidad de Málaga, Spain
Dániel Varró   Budapest University of Technology
                                  and Economics, Hungary
Andrzej Wasowski   IT University of Copenhagen, Denmark
Michael Whalen   University of Minnesota, USA
Tao Yue   Simula Research Laboratory, Norway
Steffen Zschaler   King's College London, UK

Program Committee: MDE in Practice Track

Shaukat Ali	Simula Research Laboratory, Norway
Balbir Barn	Middlesex University, UK
Fernando Brito e Abreu	DCTI, ISCTE-IUL, and CITI, FCT/UNL, Portugal
Andreas Graf	itemis AG, Germany
Wolfgang Grieskamp	Google Inc, USA
Pavel Hruby	CSC, Denmark
Tihamer Levendovszky	Vanderbilt University, USA
Pieter Mosterman	MathWorks, USA
Barbara Paech	Universität Heidelberg, Germany
Oscar Pastor	Universitat Politecnica de Valencia, Spain
Alexander Pretschner	Technische Universität München, Germany
Shaz Qadeer	MSR, USA
Bernhard Schaetz	Fortiss, Germany
Bran Selic	Malina Software Corp, Canada
Ketil Stolen	SINTEF, Norway
Stephan Thesing	Eurocopter Deutschland GmbH, Germany
Juha-Pekka Tolvanen	MetaCase, Finland
Mario Trapp	Fraunhofer IESE, Germany
Markus Völter	Independent/itemis, Germany

Steering Committee

Gregor Engels (Chair)	University of Paderborn, Germany
Lionel Briand (Vice Chair)	University of Luxembourg, Luxembourg
Silvia Abrahão	Universitat Politènica de València, Spain
Benoit Baudry	IRISA - Inria, France
Ruth Breu	University of Innsbruck, Austria
Jean-Michel Bruel	IRIT, France
Krzysztof Czarnecki	University of Waterloo, Canada
Laurie Dillon	Michigan State University, USA
Juergen Dingel	Queen's University, Canada
Geri Georg	Colorado State University, USA
Jeff Gray	University of Alabama, USA
Øystein Haugen	SINTEF, Norway
Jörg Kienzle	McGill University, Canada
Thomas Kühne	Victoria University of Wellington, New Zealand
Timothy C. Lethbridge	University of Ottawa, Canada
Ana Moreira	Universidade Nova de Lisboa, Portugal
Pierre-Alain Muller	University of Haute-Alsace, France
Dorina Petriu	Carleton University, Canada
Rob Pettit	The Aerospace Corp., USA
Gianna Reggio	University of Genoa, Italy

Bernhard Schätz   Technical University of Munich, Germany
Wolfram Schulte   Microsoft Research, USA
Andy Schürr   Technical University of Darmstadt, Germany
Steve Seidman   Texas State University, USA
Jon Whittle   Lancaster University, UK

Additional Reviewers

Mathieu Acher	Michalis Famelis
Omar Alam	Matthias Farwick
Shaukat Ali	Michael Felderer
Andre Almeida	Asbjørn Følstad
Eduardo Cunha de Almeida	Helena Galhardas
Mohamed Almorsy	Nadia Gamez
Anthony Anjorin	Achraf Ghabi
Michal Antkiewicz	Hamid Gholizadeh
Thorsten Arendt	Holger Giese
Svetlana Arifulina	Erik Gøsta Nilsson
Iman Avazpour	László Gönczy
Inmaculada Ayala	Miguel Goulao
Eiji Adachi Barbosa	Önder Gürcan
Bruno Barroca	Ábel Hegedüs
Andreas Bayha	Katrin Hoelldobler
Guillaume Becan	Sönke Holthusen
Klaus Becker	Jose-Miguel Horcas
Sana Ben Nasr	Ákos Horváth
Gábor Bergmann	Gang Huang
Thomas Beyhl	Christopher Hénard
Tegawendé Bissyandé	Lu Hong
Jan Olaf Blech	Paul Huebner
Benjamin Braatz	Ludovico Iovino
Hakan Burden	Ethan Jackson
Javier Canovas	Azadeh Jahanbanifar
Everton Cavalcante	Abhinaya Kasoju
Hyun Cho	Sahar Kokaly
Benoit Combemale	Carsten Kolassa
Jonathan Corley	Thomas Kurpick
Raphael de Aquino Gomes	Remo Lachmann
Julien DeAntoni	Leen Lambers
Alessio Di Sandro	Grischa Liebel
Aleksandar Dimovski	David Lindecker
Johannes Dyck	Lukas Linsbauer
Robert Eikermann	Hong Lu
Romina Eramo	Ivano Malavolta
Ramin Etemadi	Azzam Maraee

Jabi Martinez
Salvador Martinez
Kristin Mead
Thorsten Merten
Zarko Mijailovic
Jean-Vivien Millo
Amir Moin
Yupanqui Munoz Julho
Mina Nabi
Florian Noyrit
Rafael Olaechea
Pablo Oliveira Antonino
Aida Omerovic
Jose Ignacio Panach
Diego Perez-Palacin
Monica Pinto
Dimitri Plotnikov
Jean Quilbeuf
István Ráth
Deni Raco
Pedro Ramos
Edson Ramiro
Atle Refsdal
Raghava Rao Mukkamala
Jan Reineke
Markus Riedl
Alexander Roth

Margarete Sackmann
Rick Salay
Pablo Sanchez
Jesús Sánchez Cuadrado
Nicolas Sannier
Matthias Schöttle
Martina Seidl
Christian Sillaber
Bjørnar Solhaug
Hui Song
Stefan Stanciulescu
Harald Störrle
Arnon Sturm
Yu Sun
Robert Tairas
Massimo Tisi
Francisco Valverde
Thomas Vogel
Shuai Wang
Arif Wider
Sebastian Wilms
Andreas Wortmann
Laurent Wouters
Yingfei Xiong
Huihui Zhang
Tewfik Ziadi
Sergey Zverlov

Organizational Sponsors

Keynote Abstracts

Why Formal Modeling Language Semantics Matters

José Meseguer

University of Illinois at Urbana-Champaign, USA

Abstract. The point of modeling languages is not just modeling, but modeling as a powerful means of making software development much more reliable, reusable, automated, and cost effective. For all these purposes, model transformations, as a disciplined technique to systematically relate models within a modeling language and across languages, play a crucial role. In particular, automatic code generation from models is one of its great advantages.

As in the case of programming languages and compilers for such languages — which can be seen as a specific, special case of modeling languages and model transformations — there are two ways of going about all this: (i) the usual, engineering way of building and using practical tools, like parsers, compilers, and debuggers and, likewise, modeling tools and model transformations, where the semantics is implicit in the tools themselves and informal; and (ii) a formal semantics based approach, where the different languages involved are given a formal semantics and correctness issues, such as the correctness of programs and models, and of compilers and model transformers, can be addressed head-on with powerful methods. It seems fair to say that, both for programming and for modeling languages, the usual engineering approach is at present the prevailing one. But this should not blind us to the existence of intrinsically superior technological possibilities for the future. Furthermore, the reasons for taking formal semantics seriously are even more compelling for modeling languages than for programming languages. Specifically, the following crucial advantages can be gained:

1. Formal Analysis of Model-Based Designs to uncover costly design errors much earlier in the development cycle.
2. Correct-by-Construction Model Transformations based on formal patterns, that can be amortized across many instances.
3. Modeling-Language-Generic Formal Analysis tools that are semantics-based and can likewise be amortized across many languages.
4. Correct-by-Construction Code Generators, a burning issue for cyber-physical systems, and a must for high-quality, highly reliable implementations.

Although the full potential for enjoying all these advantages has yet to be exploited and much work remains ahead, none of this is some pie-in-the-sky day dreaming. There is already a substantial body of research, tools, and case studies demonstrating that a formal semantics based approach to modeling languages is a real possibility. For example, formal approaches to modeling language semantics based on: (i) type theory, (ii) graph transformations, and (iii) rewriting logic, all converge in giving strong evidence for the many practical advantages that can be gained.

Besides discussing in more detail the issues involved, the talk will give a report from the trenches based on my own personal involvement in advancing semantics-based approached to modeling and programming languages. In particular, I will discuss relevant advances within the rewriting logic semantics project, which explicitly aims at basing both programming and modeling languages on a formal executable semantics; and at developing language-generic, semantics-based formal analysis tool and methods.

Modeling: A Practical Perspective

Wolfgang Grieskamp

Google Inc, USA

Abstract. My talk will explore some of the basic ideas of the modeling approach as they apply to software engineering. I will use the domain of model-based testing, and discuss its foundations and adoption successes and pitfalls. A major focus will be on the bells and whistles which may help with getting modeling into mainstream. I will also discuss opportunities and challenges for model-based software development which arise from the cloud computing environment found in most of today's industry.

Towards Data-Driven Models of Human Behavior

Nuria Oliver

Telefonica Research, Spain

Abstract. We live in a world of data, of big data, a big part of which has been generated by humans through their interactions with both the physical and digital world. A key element in the exponential growth of human behavioral data is the mobile phone. There are almost as many mobile phones in the world as humans. The mobile phone is the piece of technology with the highest levels of adoption in human history. We carry them with us all through the day (and night, in many cases), leaving digital traces of our physical interactions. Mobile phones have become sensors of human activity in the large scale and also the most personal devices.

In my talk, I will present some of the work that we are doing at Telefonica Research in the area of modeling humans from large-scale human behavioral data, such as inferring personality, socio-economic status, attentiveness to messages or taste. I will highlight opportunities and challenges associated with building data-driven models of human behavior.

Table of Contents

MDE: Past, Present and Future

Formal Semantics, Specification and Verification

Models at Runtime

Feature and Variability Modeling

Composition and Adaptation

Practices and Experience

Modeling for Analysis

Pragmatics

Model Extraction, Manipulation and Persistence

Model Transformation 2

Querying

Model-Driven Development of Mobile Applications Allowing Role-Driven Variants[*]

Steffen Vaupel[1], Gabriele Taentzer[1], Jan Peer Harries[1],
Raphael Stroh[1], René Gerlach[2], and Michael Guckert[2]

[1] Philipps-Universität Marburg, Germany
{svaupel,taentzer,harries,strohraphael}@informatik.uni-marburg.de
[2] KITE - Kompetenzzentrum für Informationstechnologie,
Technische Hochschule Mittelhessen, Germany
{rene.gerlach,michael.guckert}@mnd.thm.de

Abstract. Rapidly increasing numbers of applications and users make the development of mobile applications to one of the most promising fields in software engineering. Due to short time-to-market, differing platforms and fast emerging technologies, mobile application development faces typical challenges where model-driven development can help. We present a modeling language and an infrastructure for the model-driven development (MDD) of Android apps supporting the specification of different app variants according to user roles. For example, providing users may continuously configure and modify custom content with one app variant whereas end users are supposed to use provided content in their variant. Our approach allows a flexible app development on different abstraction levels: compact modeling of standard app elements, detailed modeling of individual elements, and separate provider models for specific custom needs. We demonstrate our MDD-approach at two apps: a phone book manager and a conference guide being configured by conference organizers for participants.

Keywords: model-driven development, mobile application, Android.

1 Introduction

An infrastructure for model-driven development has a high potential for accelerating the development of software applications. While just modeling the application-specific data structures, processes and layouts, runnable software systems can be generated. Hence, MDD does not concentrate on technical details but lifts software development to a higher abstraction level. Moreover, the amount of standardization in code as well as in user interfaces is increased. A high quality MDD infrastructure can considerably reduce the time to market in consequence.

[*] This work was partially funded by LOEWE HA project no. 355/12-45 (State Offensive for the Development of Scientific and Economic Excellence).

J. Dingel et al. (Eds.): MODELS 2014, LNCS 8767, pp. 1–17, 2014.
© Springer International Publishing Switzerland 2014

Mobile application development faces several specific challenges that come on top of commonplace software production problems. Popular platforms differ widely in hardware and software architectural aspects and typically show short life and innovation cycles with considerable changes. Moreover, the market does not allow a strategy that restricts app supply to a single platform. Therefore multi-platform app development is a very time and cost-intensive necessity. It demands that apps have to be built more or less from scratch for each and every noteworthy target platform. Available solutions try to circumvent this problem by using web-based approaches, often struggling with restricted access to the technical equipment of the phone and making less efficient use of the device compared to native apps. Furthermore, web-based solutions require an app to stay on-line more or less permanently which may cause considerable costs and restricted usability.

Although there are already some approaches to model-driven development of mobile apps, our contribution differs considerably in design and purpose of the language. It allows a very flexible app design along the credo: "Model as abstract as possible and as concrete as needed." Data, behavior and user interfaces can be modeled on adequate abstraction levels meaning that behavior and UI design are modeled in more detail only if standard solutions are not used. Separating the model into an app model and one or several provider models, we achieve the possibility of a two stage generation and deployment process. While the app model defines the basic data structures, behavior and layout, these basic elements may be used in provider models to define specific custom needs. Hence, a provider model is an instance of the app model which in turn is an instance of the meta-model defining the overall modeling language. This approach suits very well to the kind of apps we consider here: While app models are developed by software developers, provider models are usually constructed by customers generally not being software experts. A typical example for such an app is a museum guide. Here, the app model contains information about objects, categories, events, and tours in museums in general. It specifies possible behavior like searching for museum objects, reading detailed information about them, and following tours. General page styles are also provided by that model. Customers may add one or more provider models containing information about objects being currently presented and additional categories to group objects semantically. Specific functionality also be added such as reading upcoming events of the next four weeks, reading details about a top object, and special page styles like one for the next exhibition. Changing a provider model does not lead to deploying the app anew. It only requires to make the modified instance model available. It integrates into the app model providing a refreshed application with up-to-date data and adapted functionality. Generated apps can work off-line without major restrictions.

The paper is structured as follows: In the next section, the kind of apps considered is presented. In particular, we explain the kind of mobile apps we consider. In Section 3, we present our language design and discuss it along typical design guidelines. Section 4 presents the developed MDD-infrastructure consisting of several model editors and a code generator for the Android operating system. Section 5 reports on a case example. Finally, Sections 6 and 7 discuss related work and conclude this paper.

2 The Mobile Applications Domain

Mobile apps are developed for very diverse purposes ranging from mere entertainment to serious business applications. We are heading towards a kind of business app where basic generic building blocks are provided for a selected domain. These building blocks can be used and refined by domain experts to customize them according to their specific needs. The fully customized app is then ready to be used by end users. Let's consider concrete scenarios as they occur in our collaboration with advenco, the industry partner of our project: *key2guide* is a multimedia guide that can be configured without programming. Its typical application lies in the context of tourism where visitors are guided through places of interest, e.g. a museum, an exhibition, a town or a region. Objects of interest (e.g. paintings, crafts and sculptures presented in a museum) are listed and explained by enriched information. Furthermore objects may be categorized and ordered in additional structures, i.e. tours that guide visitors through an exhibition. As the reader might expect, such an app is pretty data-oriented. This data usually changes frequently over time. In consequence, a typical requirement is to offer a possibility that domain experts (e.g. museum administrators or tourism managers) can refresh data regularly. Moreover, moving around in a region might lead to restricted Internet connections. Hence, web apps would not be preferred solutions. In contrast, apps shall typically run off-line but can download new provider information from time to time.

A second product by advenco, called *key2operate*, allows to define manual business processes with mobile device support to be integrated into a holistic production process. E.g. in order to inspect machines of a production plant, the worker gets a list of inspection requests that has to be executed sequentially. Such an execution might include the collection of critical data (e.g. pressure or temperature). Machines can be identified by scanning bar codes or reading RFID chips. Control values might be entered manually by the worker. Moreover start and end times of the execution may be taken. After finishing an inspection request, the app shall display the next request to be executed and direct the worker to the corresponding machine in line. Again, an app is required that may be configured by users being production managers here defining their intended business processes. As production processes have become very flexible nowadays, manual processes with mobile device support also have to be continuously adaptable. *key2operate* allows such process adaptations without newly deploying it. However, process definitions are pretty simple since they support simple data structures only. Both apps work with a web-based backend content management system to maintain configurations that are available for end users.

To summarize: We are heading towards model-driven development of mobile business apps that support the configuration of user-specific variants. In this scenario, there are typically several kinds of users, e.g. *providers* who provide custom content, and *end users* consuming a configured app with all provided information. Of course, the groups of providers and end users may be structured more elaborately such that different roles are defined. For example, a tourist guide for a town may cover sights in the town as well as several museums and exhibitions. The guiding information is typically given by several providers with different roles. Tourism managers of the town are allowed to edit information about sights in the category town only, while e.g. administrators of the history museum may edit all the information about objects in their museum. Role-specific app variants shall be developed.

Throughout our project work, the mobile apps described above (*key2guide* and *key2operate*) were used as reference applications for the development of an MDD infrastructure. In the beginning, we analyzed and optimized these apps in order to approximate a best practice solution in prototypical re-implementations. Thereafter, we used them to test the developed infrastructure by modeling them and comparing the generated apps with the original ones. Due to space limitations, we have chosen a smaller example to be used as demonstration object throughout this paper. This example shows a number of important features of our approach:

Example (A simple phone book app). *One of the core apps for smart phones are phone books where contacts can be managed. In the following, we show a simple phone book app for adding, editing, and searching contact information about persons. Moreover, phone numbers are connected to the phone app such that selecting a phone number starts dialing it. Figure 1 shows selected screen shots of the phone app, already generated by our infrastructure. Little arrows indicate the order of views shown. In the following section, we discuss selected parts of the underlying model.*

3   Language Design

The core of an infrastructure for model-driven development is the modeling language. In the following, we first present the main design decisions that guided us to our modeling language for mobile applications. Thereafter, we present the defining meta-model including all main well-formedness rules restricting allowed model structures. To illustrate the language, we show selected parts of a simple phone book app model. Finally, the presented modeling language is discussed along design guidelines for domain-specific languages.

3.1   Design Decisions

Due to our domain analysis, we want to support the generation of mobile apps that can be flexibly configured by providing users. This main requirement is reflected in our modeling approach by distinguishing two kinds of models: *app models* specifying all potential facilities of apps, and *provider models* defining

(a) Main Menu with *Manage Persons* Process (CRUD functionality)

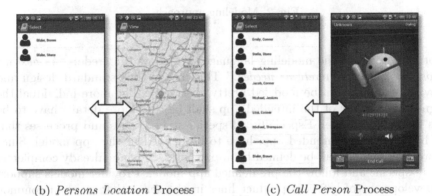

(b) *Persons Location* Process   (c) *Call Person* Process

Fig. 1. Screen shots of phone book app

the actual apps. In Figure 2, this general modeling approach is illustrated. While app models are used to generate Android projects (1) being deployed afterwards (2), provider models are interpreted by generated Android apps (3), i.e., can be used without redeploying an app. Instance models can be carried out in two ways: usually this will be done at runtime, because the instance model does not exist at build time, alternatively it can be done at build time, by adding the instance model to the resources of the generated android projects.

The general approach to the modeling language is component-based: An app model consists of a *data model* defining the underlying class structure, a *GUI model* containing the definition of pages and style settings for the graphical user interface, and a *process model* which defines the behavior facilities of an app in form of processes and tasks. Data and GUI models are independent of each other, but the process model depends on them. A provider model contains an *object model* defining an object structure as instance of the class structure in the data model, a *style model* defining explicit styles and pages for individual graphical user interfaces, and a *process instance model* selecting interesting processes and providing them with actual arguments to specify the actual behavior of the intended app. Similarly to the app model, object and style models are independent of each other but used by the process instance model.

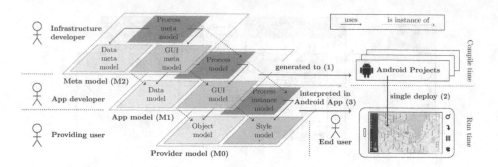

Fig. 2. Modeling approach

For the design of the modeling language, we follow the credo: *"As abstract as possible and as concrete as needed."* This means that standard design and behavior of an app can be modeled pretty abstractly. The more individual the design and behavior of the intended app shall be, the more details have to be given in the app model. Especially, all special styles, pages and processes that may be used in the intended app, have to be defined in the app model. Since the provider model shall be defined by app experts, they are already completely domain-specific and follow the pre-defined app model. Provider models support the development of software product lines in the sense that a set of common features are shared and some role-based variability is supported. Differences of considered apps are modeled separately by different provider models.

As far as possible, we reuse existing modeling languages which applies to the definition of data structures. Data modeling has become mature and is well supported by the Eclipse Modeling Framework (EMF)[22]. Hence, it is also used here to define the data model of an app. Specific information to the code generator (which is little up to now) is given by annotations.

The GUI model specifies views along their purposes as e.g. viewing and editing an object, searching objects from a list and showing them, doing a login and choosing a use case from a set. A GUI model is usually not intended to specify the inherent hierarchical structure of UI components as done in rich layout editors like the Interface Builder [20], Android Common XML Editor [12] and Android Studio [25]. However, the model can be gradually refined to obtain more specificity in the generated app. Style settings are specified independently of views and follow the same design idea, i.e. the more default look-and-feel is used, the more abstract the model can be.

Activities and services are modeled similarly along their purposes, i.e. different kinds of processes are available covering usual purposes such as CRUD functionality (create an object, read all objects, update or edit an object, delete an object) including searching, choosing processes as well as invoking GUI components, operations and processes. More specific purposes may be covered by the well-known concept of libraries, i.e. a basic language is extended by language components for different purposes as done for LabView [10].

To support the security and permission concepts of mobile platforms, the process model includes platform-independent permission levels. The permission concept is fine granular (i.e. on the level of single tasks), nevertheless some platforms like Android support only coarse granular permissions (i.e. on the level of applications). Another security-related feature is the user-specific instantiation of processes. Potentially, features of an application can be disabled by a restricted process instance model.

3.2   Language Definition

After having presented the main design decisions for our modeling language, we focus on its meta-model now. It is defined on the basis of EMF and consists of three separated Ecore models bundled in one resource set. While the data model is defined by the original Ecore model, two new Ecore models have been defined to model behavior and user interfaces of mobile apps.

Given a data model with Ecore, it is equipped with domain-specific semantics. Data models are not only used to generate the underlying object access but influence also the presentation of data at the user interface. For example, sub-objects lead to a tabbed presentation of objects, attribute names are shown as labels (if not overwritten) and attribute types define the appropriate kind of edit element being text fields, check boxes, spinners, etc. Furthermore, data models determine the behavior of pre-defined CRUD processes in the obvious way. Attribute names are not always well-suited to be viewed in the final app. For example, an attribute name has to be string without blanks and other separators while labels in app view may consist of several words, e.g. "Mobile number". In such a case, an attribute may be annotated by the intended label.

The meta-model for user interface models is shown in Figure 3. Different views in user interfaces of mobile apps are modeled by different kinds of pages (View Page, Edit Page,...) each having a pre-defined structure of UI components and following a purpose. Only custom pages allow an individual structure of UI components (not further detailed here). The indicated ones are considered basic and may be accomplished with special-purpose ones in the future. The look-and-feel of a user interface is specified in style settings.

Figure 4 shows the meta-model for behavior models of mobile apps. This meta-model is influenced by the language design of BPMN [6] and (WS)-BPEL [5]. The main ingredients of a behavior model are processes which may be defined in a compositional way. Especially the composition of existing processes promises a scalable effort for process modeling. Each process has a name and a number of variables that may also function as parameters. A parameter is modeled as a variable with a global scope, contrary to locally scoped variables. The body of a process defines the actual behavior consisting of a set of tasks ordered by typical control structures and potentially equipped with permissions. There is a number of pre-defined tasks covering basic CRUD functionality on objects, control structures, the invocation of an external operation or an already defined process as well as the view of a page. While task CrudGui covers the whole CRUD functionality with corresponding views, Create, Read and Delete just

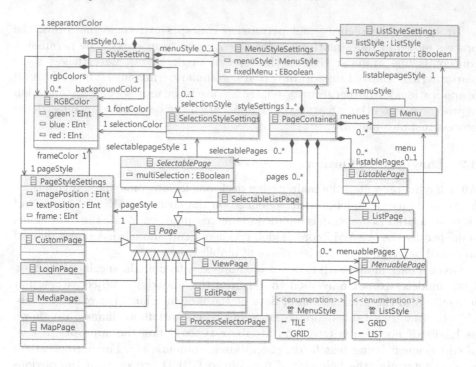

Fig. 3. Ecore model for defining graphical user interfaces of mobile apps

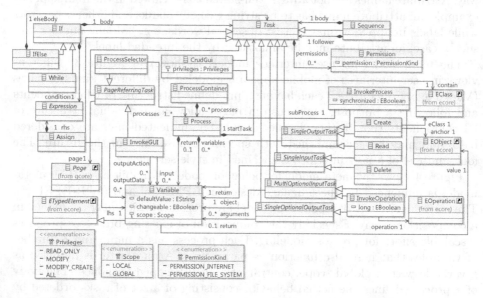

Fig. 4. Ecore model for defining mobile app behavior

cover single internal CRUD functionalities. When invoking a process, the kind of invocation - synchronous or asynchronous - has to be specified.

Since all three meta-model parts are Ecore models, each model element can be annotated to cover additional generator-relevant information or just comments.

To get consistent app models, we need a number of well-formedness rules in addition. Especially the consistency between model components has to be taken into account. The main ones are listed below formulated in natural language. The complete list of rules formalized as OCL constraints can be found at [4].

1. There is exactly one process with name *Main*. This process is the first one to be executed.
2. There is at least one task of type *ProcessSelector* in the *Main* process.
3. A *Process* being registered in a *ProcessSelector*, contains - potentially transitively - at least one task of type *InvokeGUI* or *CrudGui*.
4. Considering task *InvokeGUI*, number, ordering and types of input and output data as well as output actions has to be consistent with the type of page invoked. E.g. a *MapPage* gets two Double values as output data, a *Login-Page* gets two strings as input to show the user name and password and a Boolean value as output data representing the result of a login trial.

Example (App model of simple phone book app). *In the following, we present an instance model of the presented meta-model being the app model of the simple phone book app introduced in Section 2. We concentrate on selected model parts; the whole app model is presented at [4].*

The simple data model is an Ecore model depicted in Figure 5. The structuring of contact data in a Person *and* Address *seems to have advantages, since not too much information will be presented in one view.* PhoneBook *is just a container for* Persons *and not intended to be viewed.*

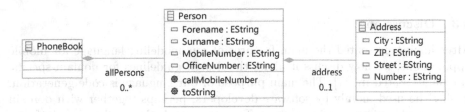

Fig. 5. Data model of simple phone book app

Next, the user interface of our phone book app is modeled. This part of the app model is pretty simple, it just contains a default style setting, a default menu, and four pages, namely a ProcessSelectorPage, *an* EditPage, *a* ViewPage*and a* SelectableListPage *for* Person *objects and a* MapPage *for* Address *objects. Note that we just add these pages to the model but do not specify their structures (see Figure 6).*

The behavior of the phone book app is modeled by a process selector as main process that contains processes for all use cases provided. Figures 7(a) and 7(b)

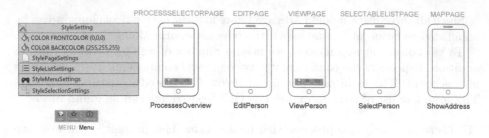

Fig. 6. User interface model of simple phone book app

show processes Main *being a process selector and* CRUDPerson *covering the whole CRUD functionality for contacts. Figure 7(c) shows the definition of a search process where first a search pattern is created that may be edited in an EditPage, then it is passed to a ReadProcess resulting in a list of persons being viewed in a SelectableListPage. If a person is selected from that list, its details are shown in a ViewPage. Figure 7(d) shows how to connect to the phone app to call a person. After searching for a person, operation* callMobileNumber *is invoked on the selected Person object. Just a few lines of code are needed to start the corresponding Android activity. I.e. the operation is implemented manually. At [4], process* NearToMe *is shown defining situation-dependent behavior in the sense that all persons of my phone book with an address near to my current position are displayed.*

An initial provider model *just contains an empty phone book as object model and the main process as process instance model. The object model changes whenever the list of contacts is modified by the user.*

3.3   Discussion

After having presented the main features of our modeling language for mobile applications, we now discuss it along the design guidelines for domain-specific languages stated in [17]. The main purpose of our language is code generation. It shall be used mainly by software developers, perhaps together with domain experts and content providing users. The language is designed to be platform-independent, i.e. independent of Android or other mobile platforms.

A decision whether to use a textual or graphical concrete syntax does not have to be taken since we design the language with EMF and therefore, have the possibility to add a textual syntax with e.g. Xtext [9] or a graphical one with e.g. the Graphical Modeling Framework (GMF) [13,21]. Currently, a graphical editor is provided as presented in the next section. The development of a textual one is less work and shall be added in the near future. We decided to reuse EMF for data modeling since it is very mature. Since we define our language with EMF, the Ecore meta-model can also be reused, together with its type system.

Next, we discuss the choice of language elements. Since all generated mobile apps shall share the same architecture design (being detailed in the next section),

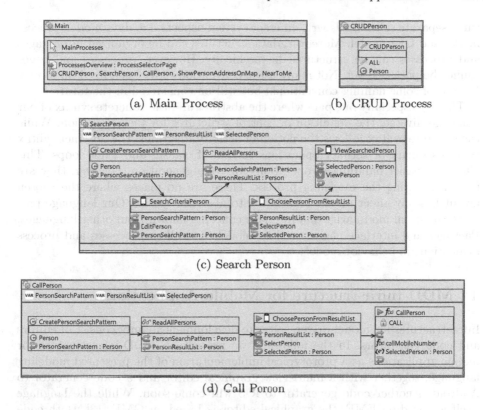

(a) Main Process   (b) CRUD Process

(c) Search Person

(d) Call Person

Fig. 7. Process model of simple phone book app

the modeling language does not need to reflect the architecture. However, data
structures, behavior and user interface design are covered. Since we want to raise
the abstraction level of the modeling language as high as possible, we have discussed each specific feature of mobile apps carefully to decide if it can be set automatically by the generator or if the modeler should care about it. For example,
asynchronous execution of an operation is decided indirectly if the operation is
classified as long-lasting but can also be set directly. Permissions are completely
in the hand of the modeler since they depend on the operations executed. The authors of [17] emphasize the simplicity of a language to be useful. Our language follows this guideline by avoiding unnecessary elements and conceptual redundancy,
having a very limited number of elements in the core language and avoiding elements that lead to inefficient code.

The concrete syntax has to be well chosen: For data modeling, we adopt
the usual notion of class diagrams since it has proven to be very useful. Process models adopt the activity modeling style to define control structures on
tasks since well-structured activity diagrams map usual control structures very
well. Notations for pages and tasks use typical forms and icons to increase their
descriptiveness and make them easily distinguishable. Models are organized in

three separate sub-models wrt. different system aspects, i.e. data model, process model and GUI model. Moreover, data structures can be organized in packages and processes can be structured hierarchically. However, processes and pages cannot be packaged yet. Not many usage conventions have been fixed up to now (except of some naming conventions) but will be considered in the future.

There is especially one part where the abstract and the concrete syntax of our language diverge, the definition of control structures for task execution. While the concrete syntax follows the notion of activity diagrams, the abstract syntax contains binary or ternary operations such as if clauses and while loops. This allows an easier handling of operations for code generation, however, they are unhandy during the modeling process. There are no places where the chosen layout has any affect on the translation to abstract syntax. Our language provides the usual modularity and interface concepts known from other languages: Packages and interface classes in data models as well as processes and process invocations in behavior models.

4   MDD-Infrastructure for Mobile Applications

Infrastructures for model-driven software development mainly consist of editors and code generators. In the following, we present an MDD-infrastructure for mobile applications as a prototypical implementation of the presented modeling language, together with a multi-view graphical editor and a code generator to Android. Another code generator to iOS will come soon. While the language itself is based on EMF, the graphical editor is based on GMF [13]. Both code generators are written in Xtend [9]. The editor and the code generator are designed as separate Eclipse plug-ins. They use the common implementation of the abstract language syntax including model validation, captured again in plug-ins.

Graphical editor for app models. The graphical editor for app models is designed as a graphical editor consisting of three different views for data modeling, process modeling and GUI modeling. The existing Ecore diagram editor has been integrated for data modeling. Figures 6 and 7 show screen shots of depicted processes and pages. As expected, changes in one view are immediately propagated to the other ones accordingly.

While the concrete syntax of control structures for task execution follows the notion of activity diagrams, the abstract syntax contains binary or ternary operations such as if clauses and while loops instead. This diversion between the abstract and the concrete syntax of our language cannot be covered directly by mapping concrete model elements to abstract ones. Therefore, a slight extension of the modeling language has been defined and is handled by the editor, i.e. concrete models are mapped to extended abstract models that are translated to non-extended ones by a simple model transformation. By application of the well-known generation gap pattern [23, p.85-101], the standard presentation of GMF-based editors has been adapted to special needs such as special labels and icons.

Code generation to Android. Having edited an app model, it has to be validated before code generation since the code generator is designed for correct models only. The code generator produces two projects: an Android project containing all the modeled activities, and an Android library project. Mobile apps shall be generated that can be flexibly configured by content providing users, of course without redeploying these apps. To realize this requirement, an Android library project is generated being based on EMF. This library project is able to interpret configurations written by providers. It is used by the main Android project. (See Figure 8.) The main Android project follows the usual model-view-controller architecture of Android apps. Packages **model** and **crud** form the data access layer with the usual CRUD functionality, while package **gui** contains controllers in form of activities, fragments, adapters, and services. Additionally, view components are generated as app resources.

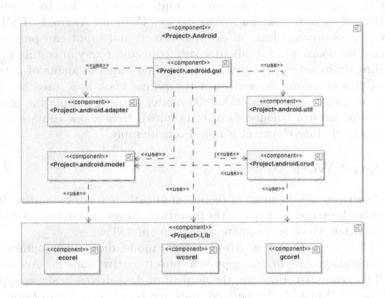

Fig. 8. Architecture of generated apps

All these projects are usually immediately compiled and then, ready to start. By default, the SD card of the mobile device contains an initial provider model consisting of an empty object model, i.e., without any data, and an initial process instance model containing the main process with all those processes assigned to the main process by the app model. This provider model can be extended during run time. After regeneration, it might become partly invalid, dependent on the kind of app model changes. If, e.g., the process model has changed but the data model has not, the object model is still readable, but the process instance model is not. It is up to future work, to support automated migration of provider models.

5   Case Study

Our major case study is a guide app for conferences being configured to guide participants through conferences like Models 2014. Depending on the user's role, i.e. provider or consumer, two different provider models are used leading to two different app variants: one for conference organizers with the full range of CRUD processes and one for participants with read and search processes only. Participants use the app as a conference guide with the look-and-feel of a native app. Besides searching for information, they may select sessions and add them to a list of favorites. These sessions may be transferred to the selected Android calendar so that reminders can be set. At [4], the interested reader can find additional information about how the guide app is modeled and how data can be entered. It shows a typical application of our two stage app development by showing how to generate an app and how to specialize it to variants for different custom needs. For a conference, quite some data has to be provided which is usually tedious using a mobile device. Using an Android HDMI stick, the app can be presented on an external screen and input can be given via an external keyboard which leads to a very convenient way of editing provider models directly by an app, suitable for providing larger amounts of data. The models of this guide app as well as of the phone book app (used as running example) are pretty small (less than 100 model elements) while the generated code is comprehensive (thousands of code lines). Hence, one can see that the abstraction level of development is raised considerably.

6   Related Work

The model-driven development of mobile applications is an innovative subject which has not been tackled much in the literature. Nevertheless, there are already some approaches which we compare to ours in the following.

MD^2 [14] is an approach to cross-platform model-driven development [7] of mobile applications. As in our approach, purely native apps for Android and iOS shall be generated. However, the domain of data-driven business apps, differs from ours: While MD^2-generated apps are based on a kind of app model only, our approach offers provider models in addition. Moreover, the underlying modeling languages differ in various aspects: The view specification by MD^2 is structure-oriented and pretty detailed, i.e. views are specified on an abstraction layer similar to UI editors. In contrast, the gcore language of our approach is purpose-oriented and thus, lifted to a higher abstraction level. MD^2-controller specifications show some similarities and some differences to our process specification. Similarly to our approach, action types for CRUD operations are provided. But it is not clear how additional operations (different from CRUD functionality) can be invoked, as e.g. starting a phone call by selecting a phone number. The generated Android apps follow the MVC-architecture pattern as well. While the data model is translated to plain (old) Java objects (POJOs) in MD^2 with serialization facilities for server communication as well as a JEE application to be run on a server, our approach also supports off-line execution.

Two further MDD approaches focusing on data-centric apps are *applause* [8,2] and *ModAgile* [3]. Both support cross-platform development for mainly Android and iOS. In contrast to our approach, behavior is nearly not modeled and user interfaces are modeled rather fine-grained.

Another kind of development tools for Android apps are event-driven approaches such as App Inventor [1] providing a kind of graphical programming language based on building blocks and Arctis [18] being based on activity diagrams. Both approaches focus on rather fine-grained behavior and/or UI specification and largely neglect the modeling of data structures.

Besides the generation of native apps, there are several approaches to the model-driven development of mobile Web apps being originated in the generation of Web applications. Although Web apps show platform independence by running in a Web environment, they have to face some limitations wrt. device-specific features, due to the use of HTML5 [19,24]. There are several approaches to MDD of Web apps, such as *mobl* [16,15] and a WebML-based solution by WebRatio [11]. Since we are heading towards apps being most of the time off-line as demanded by the domain considered, Web apps are not well-suited.

Our approach supports the model-driven development of native apps by high-level modeling of data structures, behavior and user interfaces. In addition, the role-based configuration of app variants is supported.

7 Conclusion

Model-driven development of mobile apps is a promising approach to face fast emerging technology development for several mobile platforms as well as short time-to-market with support for several if not all existing platforms. In this paper, a modeling language for mobile applications is presented that allows to model mobile apps as abstract as possible and as concrete as needed. Different user roles are not combined in one app but lead to several app variants that may be configured after code generation, i.e. by content providing users, for end users. The considered domain are business apps being data or event-driven such as tourist and conference guides as well as manual sub-processes in production processes. A selection of example apps being developed with our MDD-tool environment, can be found at [4]. Future work shall cover further platforms, a code generator to iOS is currently under development, and language extensions towards flexible sensor handling and augmented reality. Moreover, generated apps shall be evaluated wrt. software quality criteria, especially usability, data management, energy efficiency and security.

References

1. App Inventor, http://appinventor.mit.edu
2. Applause, https://github.com/applause/applause
3. ModAgile, http://www.modagile-mobile.de

4. PIMAR: Model-driven development of mobile apps, http://www.uni-marburg.de/fb12/swt/forschung/software/pimar/
5. Web Services Business Process Execution Language (WS-BPEL) Version 2.0 (2007), http://docs.oasis-open.org/wsbpel/2.0/OS/wsbpel-v2.0-OS.html
6. Business Process Model and Notation (BPMN) Version 2.0. (January 2011), http://www.omg.org/spec/BPMN/2.0
7. Allen, S., Graupera, V., Lundrigan, L.: Pro Smartphone Cross-Platform Development: iPhone, Blackberry, Windows Mobile and Android Development and Distribution. Apresspod Series. Apress (2010), http://books.google.de/books?id=JKpKrwtoWNAC
8. Behrens, H.: MDSD for the iPhone: Developing a domain-specific language and IDE tooling to produce real world applications for mobile devices. In: Cook, W.R., Clarke, S., Rinard, M.C. (eds.) SPLASH/OOPSLA Companion, pp. 123–128. ACM (2010)
9. Bettini, L.: Implementing Domain-Specific Languages with Xtext and Xtend. Packt Publishing Ltd. (2013)
10. Bishop, R.: Learning with LabVIEW. Pearson Education (2011)
11. Ceri, S., Fraternali, P., Bongio, A.: Web Modeling Language (WebML): A modeling language for designing Web sites. Computer Networks 33(1-6), 137–157 (2000)
12. Goadrich, M.H., Rogers, M.P.: Smart smartphone development: iOS versus Android. In: Proceedings of the 42nd ACM Technical Symposium on Computer Science Education, SIGCSE 2011, pp. 607–612. ACM, New York (2011)
13. Gronback, R.: Eclipse Modeling Project: A Domain-Specific Language (DSL) Toolkit. Eclipse Series. Pearson Education (2009), http://books.google.de/books?id=8CrCXVZXLjcC
14. Heitkötter, H., Majchrzak, T.A., Kuchen, H.: Cross-Platform Model-Driven Development of Mobile Applications with md^2. In: Proceedings of the 28th Annual ACM Symposium on Applied Computing, SAC 2013, Coimbra, Portugal, March 18-22, pp. 526–533. ACM (2013)
15. Hemel, Z., Visser, E.: Declaratively programming the mobile web with Mobl. In: Lopes, C.V., Fisher, K. (eds.) OOPSLA, pp. 695–712. ACM (2011)
16. Hemel, Z., Visser, E.: Mobl: the new language of the mobile web. In: Lopes, C.V., Fisher, K. (eds.) OOPSLA Companion, pp. 23–24. ACM (2011)
17. Karsai, G., Krahn, H., Pinkernell, C., Rumpe, B., Schneider, M., Völkel, S.: Design Guidelines for Domain Specific Languages. In: Rossi, M., Sprinkle, J., Gray, J., Tolvanen, J.P. (eds.) Proceedings of the 9th OOPSLA Workshop on Domain-Specific Modeling (DSM 2009), pp. 7–13 (2009)
18. Kraemer, F.A.: Engineering Android Applications Based on UML Activities. In: Whittle, J., Clark, T., Kühne, T. (eds.) MODELS 2011. LNCS, vol. 6981, pp. 183–197. Springer, Heidelberg (2011)
19. Oehlman, D., Blanc, S.: Pro Android Web Apps: Develop for Android using HTML5, CSS3 & JavaScript. Apresspod Series. Apress (2011), http://books.google.de/books?id=pZlF7lQY5SQC
20. Piper, I.: Learn Xcode Tools for Mac OS X and iPhone Development. IT Pro. Apress (2010)
21. Rubel, D., Wren, J., Clayberg, E.: The Eclipse Graphical Editing Framework (GEF). Eclipse (Addison-Wesley). Addison-Wesley (2011), http://books.google.de/books?id=GiKTAR9M-L4C
22. Steinberg, D., Budinsky, F., Paternostro, M., Merks, E.: EMF: Eclipse Modeling Framework, 2nd edn. Addison-Wesley, Boston (2009)

23. Vlissides, J.: Pattern hatching: design patterns applied. The software patterns series. Addison-Wesley (1998), http://books.google.de/books?id=4qRQAAAAMAAJ
24. Williams, G.: Learn HTML5 and JavaScript for Android. ITPro collection. Apress (2012), http://books.google.de/books?id=PRlytmflmhoC
25. Zapata, B.: Android Studio Application Development. Packt Publishing (2013)

A Model-Based System to Automate Cloud Resource Allocation and Optimization

Yu Sun[1], Jules White[1], and Sean Eade[2]

[1] Vanderbilt University, Nashville, TN 37212
{yu.sun.1,jules.white}@vanderbilt.edu
[2] Siemens Industry, Wendell, NC 27951
sean.eade@siemens.com

Abstract. Cloud computing offers a flexible approach to elastically allocate computing resources for web applications without significant upfront hardware acquisition costs. Although a diverse collection of cloud resources is available, choosing the most optimized and cost-effective set of cloud resources to meet the QoS requirements is not a straightforward task. Manual load testing, monitoring of resource utilization, followed by bottleneck analysis is time consuming and complex due to limitations of the abstractions of load testing tools, challenges characterizing resource utilization, significant manual test orchestration effort, and complexity of selecting resource configurations to test. This paper introduces a model-based approach to simplify, optimize, and automate cloud resource allocation decisions to meet QoS goals for web applications. Given a high-level application description and QoS requirements, the model-based approach automatically tests the application under a variety of load and resources to derive the most cost-effective resource configuration to meet the QoS goals.

Keywords: Cloud Computing, Resource Allocation, Resource Optimization, Model-Based System, Domain-Specific Language.

1 Introduction

Cloud computing shifts computing from local dedicated resources to distributed, virtual, elastic, multi-tenant resources. This paradigm provides end-users with on-demand access to computing, storage, and software services [1]. Amazon Web Services (AWS) [2] is a successful cloud computing platform that supports customized applications with high availability and scalability. Users can allocate, execute, and terminate the instances (i.e., cloud servers) as needed, and pay for the cost of time and storage that the active instances use based on a utility cost model [3].

In order to satisfy the various quality of service (QoS) requirements, such as response time and throughput, of a wide variety of application types, cloud providers offer a menu of server types with different configurations of CPU capacity, memory, network capacity, disk I/O performance, and disk storage size. Table 1 shows a subset of the server configurations provided by AWS as of 2014. For example, the *m1.small* server with 1 CPU and 1.7 GB memory costs $0.06/hour, while the more powerful

J. Dingel et al. (Eds.): MODELS 2014, LNCS 8767, pp. 18–34, 2014.

Table 1. A Subset of AWS EC2 Instance Types and Pricing [4]

Type	ECU	Memory (GB)	Storage (DB)	Price
t1.micro	< 1 (variable)	0.615	40	$0.02 / hour
m1.small	1	1.7	160	$0.06 / hour
m1.medium	2	3.75	410	$0.12 / hour
m1.large	4	7.5	840	$0.24 / hour
m2.2xlarge	13	34.2	850	$0.82 / hour
m2.4xlarge	26	68.4	1680	$1.64 / hour

m2.4xlarge server costs $1.6/hour. A key goal of cloud computing users is to determine the appropriate subset of these resource configurations that will run an application and meet its QoS goals.

A common use case of the cloud is to offer existing software products, particularly web-based applications, through a software as a service (SaaS) model. In a SaaS model, the application provider runs the web application in the cloud and customers remotely access the software platform, while the provider manages and maintains the software. SaaS providers typically provide service level agreements (SLAs) to their clients dictating the number of users they will support, the availability of the service, the response time, and other parameters. For example, a provider of a SaaS electronic medical records system will guarantee that a certain number of employees in a hospital can simultaneously access the system and that it will provide response times under 1 second.

An important consideration of SaaS providers is minimizing their operational costs while guaranteeing that the QoS requirements specified in their SLAs are met. For example, for the medical records system, the SaaS provider would like to minimize the cloud resources allocated to it, in order to reduce operational cost, while guaranteeing that the chosen cloud resources can support the number of simultaneous clients and response times agreed to in the client SLAs. Moreover, as new clients are added and the QoS requirements grown, particularly in terms of the number of supported clients, the SaaS provider would like to know how adding resources on-demand, which is called auto-scaling, will affect the application. Blindly allocating resources to the application to meet increasing load is not cost effective and needs to be guided by a firm understanding of how resource allocations impact QoS goals.

Problem. While cloud providers allow for simple and relatively quick resource allocation for applications, it is not an easy or straightforward task to decide the most optimized and cost-effective resource configuration to run a specific application based on its QoS requirements. For instance, if a custom web application is expected to support 1000 simultaneous users with a throughput of 1000 requests/minute, it is challenging to decide the type and minimum number of servers needed by simply looking at the hardware configurations. Complex experimentation and load testing with the application on a wide variety of resource configurations is needed. The most common practice is to deploy the application and perform a load stress test on each type of resource configuration, followed by analysis of the test results and selection of a resource configuration [5]. A number of load testing tools (e.g., jMeter [6][7], ApacheBench [8], and HP LoadRunner [9]) are available to automatically trigger a large amount of test requests and collect the performance data.

Despite the importance of selecting a cost optimized resource allocation to meet QoS goals, many organizations do not have the time, resources, or experience to derive and perform a myriad of load testing experiments on a wide variety of resource types. Instead, developers typically employ a trial and error approach where they guess at the appropriate resource allocation, load test the application, and then accept it if the performance is at or above QoS goals. Optimization is usually only performed months or years into the application's life in the cloud, when insight into the affect of resource allocations on QoS goals is better understood. Even then, the optimization is often not systematic.

The primary challenges that prevent early resource allocation optimization stem from the limitations of the load testing tools and a number of manual procedures required in the cloud resource optimization process. It is often difficult to specify the customized load tests and correlate load test configuration with the expected QoS goals. Besides, manually performing the load test with different cloud resources and deriving the optimized resource configuration are tedious and error-prone. Even when an optimized resource configuration is finally obtained, executing the allocation and deployment of all the resources requires extra manual operations as well. Although research works have been done to attack some of challenges separately (e.g., modeling realistic user test behavior to produce customized load test [25], monitoring target test server performance metrics for capacity planning [19]), a complete and fully automated approach designed specific to resource allocation and optimization in cloud is not available.

Solution Approach → Model-based Resource Optimization, Allocation and Recommendation System (ROAR). To address these challenges, this paper presents a model-based system - ROAR that raises the level of abstraction when performing load testing and automates cloud resource optimization and allocation in order to transparently converting users application-specific QoS goals to a set of optimized resources running in the cloud. A textual DSL is defined to specify the high-level and customizable load testing plan and QoS requirements without low-level configuration details, such as the number of threads to use, the concurrent clients, and the duration of keeping opened connections. The model built from the DSL can generate a test specification that is compatible with jMeter, which is a powerful and extensible load testing tool based on multithreading framework for measuring the performance of web applications. A plugin has been built for jMeter to include the performance metrics of the target server and automatically align the metrics with the test data in order to correlate the QoS with the cloud resource configuration, which is the key limitation of jMeter that presents it from analyzing and optimizing cloud resources. ROAR includes a resource optimization engine that is capable of deriving the appropriate cloud resource configurations to test and automatically orchestrating the tests against each resource allocation before using the results to recommend a cost-optimized resource allocation to meet the QoS goals.

2   Motiving Example: Cloud-Based Computer Vision

The example used in this paper is based on a web service built to support the Hybrid 4-Dimensional Augmented Reality (HD4AR) mobile/web platform [13][14].

HD4AR is a high-precision mobile augmented reality technology that allows users to snap photos of real world objects, such as a car engine, upload the photograph to a cloud-based server, and receive an augmented image back that visualizes relevant cyber-information on top of it. The project was commercialized as a startup company, called PAR Works with venture capital funding, and it exposes the core augmented reality functions through a HTTP-based web service and SDKs for mobile developers. PAR Works has won awards for this technology at the 2013 Consumer Electronics Show (CES) and the 2013 South by SouthWest (SXSW) conference.

The original HD4AR application was built as a stand-alone web application to be deployed in-house by organizations. However, based on customer requests, the platform was migrated to a SaaS model. A key requirement, therefore, was determining how to appropriately provision resources to meet the QoS requirements of the application. Determining how to provision cloud resources for HD4AR was non-trivial since it included complex structure-from-motion computer vision algorithms that were difficult to model and characterize with existing analysis-based approaches.

The initial SaaS platform was released in November 2012 and started to attract a large number of developers. With increased usage of the platform and the usage data collected, a new web service called *HD4ARWebDataService* was built to 1) provide runtime configurations for mobile apps to optimize their performance (e.g., the list of server endpoints to use, the HTTP dispatch rules for submitting augmentation requests, and the interval of refreshing the configuration), 2) provide a list of trending objects to augment (i.e., the most popular objects that were being photographed) that was based on usage data over the past 8 hours. The key APIs provided by this service are listed in Table 2.

Table 2. HTTP APIs from HD4ARWebDataService

API Purpose	HTTP Method	HTTP URI	Call Frequency Per Client	Throughput (2000 clients)
Get trending sites	GET	/v1/ar/site/trending	1 / 5 mins	400 / min
Update trending sites	POST	/v1/ar/site/trending	1 / 8 hours	1 / 8 hours
Get app configuration	GET	/v1/ar/app/config	1 / min	2000 / min
Update app configuration	POST	/v1/ar/app/config	1 / 5 hours	1 / 5 hours

By the time when *HD4ARWebDataService* was built, the platform needed to support roughly 2,000 active users per minute on Android and iOS. Based on the frequency of calling each API from the client, it was possible to predict the minimum throughput needed to support the clients, as shown in Table 2. The key goal from a SaaS deployment perspective was to derive a cost-effective cloud resource allocation to meet the target QoS throughput requirements.

3   Cloud Resource Optimization Challenges

Determining the most cost-effective set of resources to meet a web application's QoS requirements without over-provisioning resources is a common problem in transitioning web applications to a SaaS model. This section presents some of the key challenges to deriving cost-optimized cloud resource configurations for web applications.

Challenge 1 – Translating high-level QoS goals into low-level load generator configuration abstractions. In order to produce the huge amount of test traffic needed for QoS metrics, most tools use a multi-threaded architecture for load testing. The load test modeling abstractions from these tools are focused on the low-level threading details of the tooling rather than higher-level QoS performance specifications. For instance, jMeter, one of the most popular load testing tools, requires the specification of *Thread Groups* including the number of threads, the ramp-up period, and loop count. Wrk [10] takes command-line parameters to control the number of connections to keep open, the number of threads, and the duration of the test. All of these OS-level details on threads create an additional level of complexity for end-users to convert the expected throughput to test into the right threading configurations that can generate the appropriate load profile. Additionally, increasing the number of threads does not always increase the throughput linearly [11], which makes the translation of high-level QoS goals into low-level load testing tool configuration abstractions even more challenging. Developers have to manually analyze their needs in order to derive the appropriate threading and ramp up configurations, which is non-trivial in many cases.

Challenge 2 – Highly customized test flows are either not supported by load testing tools or difficult to verify. Most command-line based testing tools such as Wrk and ApacheBench only support testing on a single HTTP API each time. Customized testing scenarios with a sequence of HTTP APIs (e.g., first get data through an HTTP GET, then update the data through an HTTP POST, and finally GET the data again) cannot be handled by these tools. Some other tools like jMeter supports using logic controllers to enable the customized tests. However, the controllers provide low-level programmatic APIs with configuration elements such as for-each, loops, if statements, and switch statements, etc. It is often very challenging for developers to verify if the customized test flow they programmed is correct or not.

Challenge 3 – Resource bottleneck analysis is challenging because current tools do not collect or correlate this information with QoS metrics from tests. It is essential to understand resource utilization of allocated cloud resources in order to identify bottlenecks and make appropriate resource allocation decisions. Moreover, temporal correlation of these resource utilizations with QoS performance metrics throughout the tests is essential for: 1) when required QoS goals are not met, identifying the resource bottlenecks in order to adjust resource allocations (e.g., add more memory or switch to a more powerful CPU); 2) even if the required QoS goals are satisfied, deriving resource utilization in order to estimate and ensure resource slack to handle load fluctuation (e.g., ensure 20% spare CPU cycles); and 3) when QoS goals are satisfied, ensuring that there is not substantial excess capacity (e.g., CPU utilization is at 70% or less). The goal is to find the exact resource configuration where the QoS goals are met, there is sufficient resource slack for absorbing load fluctuations, there is not too much excess capacity, and there is no more efficient resource configuration that better fits the QoS and cost goals. Manual monitoring, collection, and temporal correlation of QoS metrics with resource utilization data is tedious and inaccurate.

Challenge 4 – Lack of model analysis to derive an appropriate resource configuration sampling strategy and termination criteria for tests. The resource configuration design space for an application has a huge number of permutations. A key task in optimizing resource allocations is selecting the appropriate points in the design space to sample and test in order to make resource allocation decisions. Moreover, developers must decide when enough data has been collected to stop sampling the configuration space and make a resource allocation recommendation. In order to find the most optimized set of cloud resources for running the application with the desired QoS, the same load test has to be run multiple times against the different samples of cloud resources. By comparing the different test data and performance metrics, the final decision on the required cloud resources can be made. Based on the different profiles (e.g., most cost-effective, fastest response), the decision may vary.

Challenge 5 – Lack of end-to-end test orchestration of resource allocation, load generation, resource utilization metric collection, and QoS metric tracking. Current load testing tools only focus on the generation of loads and the tracking of a few QoS metrics. However, other key aspects of a test, such as the automated allocation of different resource configurations sampled from the resource configuration space or the collection of resource utilization data from the allocated resources, are not managed by the tools. Allocating cloud resources for complex web applications such as multi-tier web architecture requires a number of system-level configurations (e.g., security groups, load balancers, DNS names, databases) that current tools force developers to manually manage. Although most cloud providers offer tools to automate the allocation and deployment of cloud resources, they mostly contain many low-level details to configure. For example, Cloud Formation, [12] provided by Amazon AWS, is an effective tool to automatically deploy an entire server stack with the cloud resources specified. However, it is a JSON-based specification that includes the configuration of over 50 resource types and hundreds of parameters, and is completely disconnected from current load testing tools. Moreover, once the resource allocations are made and tests launched, the resource utilizations on each cloud server need to be carefully remotely tracked, collected, and temporally correlated with QoS metrics tracked in the load testing tool.

4   Solution Approach → Model-Based Resource Optimization, Allocation and Recommendation System (ROAR)

To overcome the challenges presented in Section 3, we developed ROAR, an approach that combines modeling, model analysis, test automation, code generation, and optimization techniques to simplify and optimize the derivation of cloud resource sets that will meet a web application's QoS goals. A key component of the solution is the use of a high-level textual DSL to capture key resource configuration space and QoS goal information that is not currently captured in existing load generation tools. Moreover, the approach uses model analysis to automatically identify the correlation between the QoS performance and different resource configurations. The approach also uses code generation to automate the allocation and testing of resource configurations.

An overview of ROAR is shown in Figure 1. The textual DSL - the Generic Resource Optimization for Web applications Language (GROWL) is provided to enable developers to configure the high-level test plan specification and QoS goals without requiring low-level threading and logic controller configurations. GROWL is used to generate a jMeter compatible XML-specification for load testing and resource allocation sampling strategies for our resource optimization engine. The engine triggers the load test using a modified version of jMeter that intelligently samples and collects QoS and resource utilization data from varying cloud resource configurations, to derive a cost-optimized resource configuration to meet application QoS goals. Finally, a deployment template for the target cloud provider, such as an Amazon AWS Cloud Formation template, is generated automatically as the optimization engine output. The templates allow for automated deployment and redeployment of the web application in the derived resource configuration.

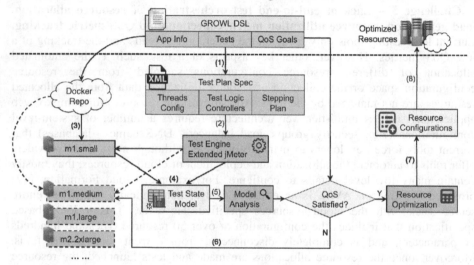

Fig. 1. Overview of ROAR

4.1   Addressing Challenges 1 and 2: High-Level DSL Aligned with the QoS Domain

Based on our experience using a variety of load testing tools, we determined key components of their typical abstractions that were not properly aligned with the domain of cloud resource allocation derivation: 1) the low-level test thread group configurations (e.g., the number of threads, thread ramp-up time, duration of open connections); 2) The complex test logic controllers based on procedural programming concepts.

To addresses these abstraction issues, a textual DSL - GROWL was developed to enable developers to specify web application QoS goals and automatically generate load testing plans without knowing of the underlying low-level jMeter-specific details, such as thread group or logic controllers. Figure 2 shows the specification of the test plan for our motivating example in GROWL. A GROWL specification contains three major sections. The *app* section describes the basic information about the application to test, with three attributes: 1) *name* is the identification of the application to test, which does not need to be unique; 2) *containerId* is a concept from Docker [16], specifying the ID of the target deployable and runnable web application stored in Docker repository, which our test engine will use to locate and load the applications in the cloud server. In order to automate the application deployment to different target servers for testing, we used a containerization approach, based on the Docker container mechanism, to ease the process. More details about Docker and our automated deployment process will be discussed in Section 4.4; 3) *port* is the port number that will be used by the web application.

The second section *tests* configures the details on what HTTP APIs to test and how to test them. The *tests* section contains a list of samplers. Each sampler represents a specific type of HTTP request that we want to include in the QoS specification. The typical HTTP request configurations, such as *HTTP Method* (e.g., GET, POST, DELETE), *HTTP URI*, *HTTP Headers/Parameters* (not shown in this example), *HTTP Request Body* can be provided for each sampler. The *percentage* attribute in each sampler controls the frequency of each sample in the overall test plan. For instance, the percentage 83.2 means that the test sampler will send 83.2% of all requests in the load test to this path. This attribute is the key to simplify the usage of traditional jMeter logic controllers. By default, all the samplers will be executed in random order with the given *percentage*. However, if the *ordered* attribute in tests is set to true, each sampler will be executed in the order as specified in the *tests* section.

The third section, *performance*, specifies the expected QoS goals we want to support. Currently, only *throughput* is supported. The example in Figure 2 shows a throughput requirement for 2402 requests/minute. GROWL has been implemented using xText [17]. An XML-based specification is generated (step (1) in Figure 1) from a GROWL model instance as the input to the cloud resource optimization engine through xTend [18].

```
app {
    name : test;
    containerId : parworks/webdataservice;
    port : 8080;
}
tests {
    ordered : false;
    sampler {
        method : GET;
        path : "/v1/ar/app/config";
        percentage : 83.2;
    }
    sampler {
        method : POST;
        path : "/v1/ar/app/config";
        percentage : 0.01;
        requestBody : "{\"interval\":60, \"endpoint\":\"http://us-east-1.ar.service.com\"]}";
    }
    ... ...
}
performance {
    throughput : 2402;
    timeunit : MINUTE;
}
```

Fig. 2. The Test Configuration Sample in GROWL

One part of the generated test specification, based on the *tests* section, is the XML-based jMeter test plan, which uses a series of jMeter logic controllers to construct a test that loads the various web application paths according to the percentages or ordering specified in GROWL. For instance, the two update APIs are not called very often, so the generated jMeter test plan uses an *OnceOnlyController* to send only one request for the entire test period. The two get APIs are put inside of a *ThroughputController* provided by jMeter to accurately control the execution frequency of their samplers. Finally, all four controllers are nested inside an *InterleaveController* that indicates to jMeter to alternate between each of the controllers in each loop iteration. Clearly, there is a significant amount of logic and associated abstractions that are specific to jMeter and disconnected from the domain of specifying desired web application QoS.

The standard jMeter test plan only allows developers to specify the number of concurrent threads to use and provides no guarantee that the test will sufficiently load the web application to assess if the QoS goal is met. If the number of threads configured is not sufficient, jMeter will not be able to test the full capacity of the target server; but if the number configured is too large and they ramp up too quickly, it will cause the server to run out of CPU or memory before exposing the actual throughput and server resource utilization under load. Developers must, therefore, rely on trial and error specification of these parameters to test each target throughput.

To overcome this issue, we developed a model analysis to determine the appropriate test strategy to assess the target throughput goal. In order to produce test loads with the desired throughput accurately, we developed a customized jMeter plugin [19] and throughput shaper that analyzes and operates on the GROWL model. The shaper is capable of dynamically controlling the number of threads being used in order to ensure that the test meets the GROWL goals. Based on the needed throughput, it automatically increases or decreases the number of threads to reach the throughput accurately, while simultaneously watching the resource utilization of the target server to ensure that it isn't overloaded too quickly. The shaper supports gradual throughput increments. A throughput stepping plan is automatically derived from the specified throughput QoS goals in GROWL. For instance, the generated test plan increases the throughput from 1 to 500 within the first 5 seconds and then keeps running at 500 for another 20 seconds before jumping to the next level at 1000. The test plan specification will be loaded to the extended jMeter engine to trigger the load test (Step (2) in Figure 1).

4.2   Addressing Challenge 3: Automated Temporal Correlation of Resource Utilization and QoS Metrics and Injection into the Test State Model

A key component of ROAR is a mechanism to collect and correlate server resource utilization with QoS goals. The throughput shaper discretizes the test epoch into a series of discrete time units with known QoS values. The QoS values at each discrete time unit are correlated with server resource utilization during the same time unit. To record the actual throughput in each moment, we modified the native jMeter SimpleReporter listener to be capable of automatically reporting the throughput every single second (the native SimpleReporter only reports the current aggregated throughput). To record the target server performance metrics, another customized jMeter plugin [19] is applied, which runs a web-based performance monitor agent in the target server. HTTP calls can be made from jMeter to retrieve the performance metrics at runtime and assign them to the appropriate time unit for correlation with QoS values. A list of detailed resource utilization metrics are supported, but we only record CPU, memory, network I/O and disk I/O, since we have found these to be the primary resource utilization metrics for making resource allocation decisions. The extensions we made to the plugin include 1) using a global clock that is consistent with the time used by the throughput records; 2) enabling the collection process in non-GUI jMeter mode; and 3) distributed resource utilization collection using the global clock.

Based on the global clock, the collected resource utilization and QoS metrics are aligned and stored in a test state model (Step (4) in Figure 1). The test state model is the input to the bottleneck analysis and resource optimization algorithms run later and can also be loaded in the performance viewer to display the results visually. As shown in Figure 3, based on the global clock, the correlation of QoS (throughput and latency) and resource utilization (CPU/memory/network/disk utilization) can be clearly seen.

4.3 Addressing Challenge 4: Model Analysis to Sample and Optimize the Resource Configuration with Smart Termination Strategies

The test state model containing the global clock-aligned QoS values and resource utilizations allows us to analyze resource bottlenecks and derive the best cloud resource configurations to meet the modeled QoS goals. One issue that has to be dealt with before resource configuration derivation is potential points of instability in the data, which show an inconsistent correlation between the QoS and the resource utilization with the values recorded during the rest of the test epoch. These periods of instability are due to jMeter's creation and termination of a larger number of threads in the beginning and end of the tests. A filtering step is used to eliminate any unstable data points (Step (5) in Figure 1). The resource allocation analysis can be performed with a variety of models and optimization goals [20][21][22]. ROAR uses an optimization engine to select the minimum number of servers N needed to run the web application in order to reach the expected throughput. Let Tex be the expected throughput specified in GROWL, Tp be the actual peak throughput we can get from a single server, then:

$$N = \lceil Tex / Tp \rceil$$

The key problem here is to find a reasonable Tp from all the data points in the test state model. Generally, when the peak throughput is reached, one or more resource utilizations will also approach 100% utilization (e.g., CPU or memory utilization goes to 100%, or network usage goes to 100%), and at the same time, the average latency of responses increases dramatically. We use these two conditions to determine Tp. Figure 3 shows a typical dataset collected during a test. The throughput shaper produces an increasing number of requests as indicated by the expected throughput (yellow line in Figure 3a), but the actual throughput fails to meet the QoS goal after about 30 seconds (blue line in Figure 3a). The throughput reaches its limit because the average latency (yellow line in Figure 3b) increases at the same time. Checking the performance metrics of the target server, it can be found that although CPU and memory have not been fully utilized (Figure 3c), the network bandwidth has reached capacity (Figure 3d), and therefore the peak throughput using this server is about 1500 requests/sec.

The same process needs to be repeated for each type of resource to get the different values for N. In Amazon EC2, resources can only be allocated in fixed configurations of memory, CPU, and network capacity – not in arbitrary configurations. There are over 20 different *instance types*, which are virtual machines with fixed resource configurations, provided by AWS, so it is challenging to manually sample the performance of all instance types. The optimization engine is capable of automating all the tests sequentially (Step (6) in Figure 1). In addition, as the test samples increasingly larger resource configurations, if the target QoS is met, the test can terminate after the next resource configuration is tested. The reason that the test can terminate is that any larger resource configurations will only have additional slack resources that are not needed to meet the desired QoS goals.

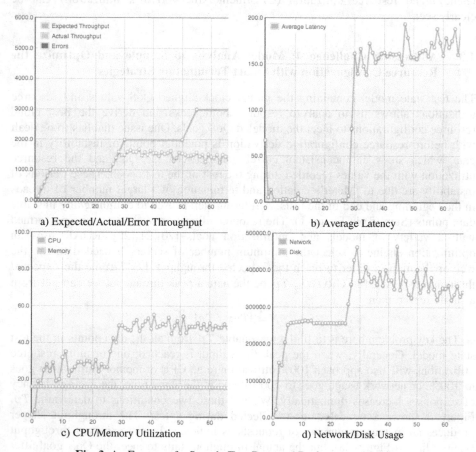

a) Expected/Actual/Error Throughput

b) Average Latency

c) CPU/Memory Utilization

d) Network/Disk Usage

Fig. 3. An Excerpt of a Sample Test Data and Performance Metrics

The final resource configuration is decided by comparing and analyzing the results (Step (7) in Figure 1). The most cost-effective solution is derived by finding the minimum total cost of using each type of server to reach the desired throughput. If P_i represents the cost of the server type i, the total cost is $C_i = P_i * N_i$, and the most cost-effective solution is $\min_i C_i$.

Besides finding the most cost-effective solution, knowing the solution that supports the fastest response time (i.e., the lowest response latency) is also essential for general web applications in practice. The fastest response time configuration is decided by the average latency measured for each type of server. We have not included latency as part of the QoS goals in GROWL with the current version, because the latency varies based on the testing environment (e.g., running the load test inside AWS would have a much lower latency than running the test outside of AWS). However, the comparison of the average latencies for different server types could produce a good indicator of the performance with which two different servers can handle the same request load. Thus, we choose the server type with the lowest average latency as the fastest response time configuration.

4.4   Addressing Challenge 5: End-to-End Test Orchestration

Using ROAR, developers only need to create the GROWL model - the rest of the testing and resource derivation process is automated for them. As shown in Figure 1, the basic workflow of the automated end-to-end test process is to first run the web application in the most resource constrained configuration, followed by using jMeter to trigger the load test based on the generated XML test plan specification. Once the test state model is generated, the optimization controller uses the test output data to choose the next resource configuration and then switches to a bigger type of server with more powerful hardware configuration if the resource bottlenecks were found. The entire testing process is repeated to derive a model of the QoS and resource utilization on the new resource configuration. This process is repeated until the most cost-effective and fastest response time configuration solution is found. A prototype of a web-based service has been implemented to take the GROWL as the input and generate the final cloud resource configurations ready for deployment.

Although allocating resources is easy, deploying different web applications can require setting up different software libraries and environment configurations, which makes it difficult to build a generic automated deployment engine. In order to solve this problem, we applied the container-based deployment tool - Docker. Docker is a tool that can package an application and its dependencies in a virtual process-based container that can run on any Linux server. Users only need to package their application in a Docker container and push the application to the Docker repository. The testing server will pull the container based on the ID specified in GROWL and run it automatically (Step (3) in Figure 1). With the flexibility and portability of GROWL containers, we can deploy a web application in any type of the target cloud server at anytime.

Another important capability of Docker is the ability to version containers in Git. Each change to a container can be tracked. GROWL models and the generated test state models can also be versioned along with Docker containers in order to understand how the performance and resource allocations change as the application evolves.

Once the cloud resource allocation needed to meet the QoS goals is derived, ROAR can then automatically allocate the resources and deploy the web application. Manually allocating resources with a fleet of servers in a cloud environment is not an easy task, particularly when optimized service architecture patterns and best practices are needed. For instance, in AWS, the best practice of deploying multiple servers to support the same web application is to use an Elastic Load Balancer (ELB) [23] as the entry point, which is capable of handling any amount of requests from users and balancing dispatching of the requests to each server behind it. A number of configuration parameters for security group, private keys, availability zones, server launch user data, and DNS names also have to be specified correctly.

In order to ease the resource allocation process, we use a generative approach to produce the configuration artifacts needed for each cloud provider. Currently, ROAR only supports artifact generation for AWS, but support for OpenStack is planned. The AWS artifact generator is built on top of the AWS Cloud Formation service, which provides an engine for automating the deployment of multi-server architectures via templates defined in JSON [12]. Based on the N and server type generated from the resource optimization engine, we fill the template with the appropriate configuration steps, resource types, and other parameters needed to launch the application. The generated template can be uploaded to the AWS Cloud Formation console, allowing developers to deploy the web application in the derived configuration with a single click (Step (8) in Figure 1).

5   Experiments

In this section, we present a case study based on the motivating example in Section 2. The actual required throughput of the application described in Section 2 is 2402 requests/min (40 requests/sec). In order to better illustrate the optimization process and different solutions generated using our model-driven framework, we present the model and analyses used to derive cloud resource configurations for target throughputs of 2400 requests/sec and 5000 requests/sec.

Table 3 shows the QoS values derived for the case study application when running on different cloud resource configurations. It can be seen that different peak throughputs were reached using different types of servers. The last 3 types in Table 3 can all satisfy the target throughput goal of 2400 requests/sec. Of course, their resource utilizations were different at the moment of peak throughput (e.g., the CPU utilization of *m2.2xlarge* was only 20% at the peak throughput point, while CPU utilization reached almost 80% in the *m1.medium* server). Based on the peak throughput, the engine calculated the minimum number of servers needed to reach the expected throughput, and the total cost of running the server fleet in AWS. Therefore, using 1 *m1.medium* or 2 *m1.small* servers is the most cost-effective solution. However, when it comes to the average latency, *m1.medium* obviously has a better performance, so the 1 *m1.medium* is the preferred most cost-effective solution in this case. Different solutions can be derived based on the criteria. If users would like to choose the fastest response solution, using a single *m1.large* would be the ideal choice.

Table 3. Resource Optimization Result based on Expected Throughput of 2400/sec

Instance Type	Peak Throughput (requests/sec)	Average Latency (ms)	Total Servers Required	Total Cost Per Hour
t1.micro	450	44	7	$0.14 / hour
m1.small	1560	20	2	$0.12 / hour
m1.medium	2400	7	1	$0.12 / hour
m1.large	2400	3	1	$0.24 / hour
m2.2xlarge	2400	3	1	$0.82 / hour

In the second experiment, we tested the same application with a larger QoS throughput goal of 5000 requests/sec. As shown in Table 4, *m1.medium* also reached its throughput limit at 3300 requests/sec. For *m1.large* and *m2.2xlarge*, they are both still powerful enough to support the expected top throughput. Thus, the most cost-effective solution in this case is to just use a single *m1.large* server instance. The other two solutions at the rate of $0.24/hours consist of 4 *m1.small* or 2 *m1.medium* servers. If the user selection criterion is the solution with the highest availability (i.e., the highest degree of redundancy in the servers), a user could use a multi-server solution rather than a single server. Moreover, they could precisely calculate the added cost of their solution and the impact of losing one or more servers on QoS properties.

Table 4. Resource Allocation Result based on Expected Throughput of 5000/sec

Instance Type	Peak Throughput (requests/sec)	Average Latency (ms)	Total Servers Required	Total Cost Per Hour
t1.micro	400	45	13	$0.26 / hour
m1.small	1500	20	4	$0.24 / hour
m1.medium	3300	8	2	$0.24 / hour
m1.large	5000	3	1	$0.24 / hour
m2.2xlarge	5000	3	1	$0.82 / hour

6   Related Works

Ferry et al. [32] summarized the state-of-the-art on cloud optimization and pointed out the need for model-driven engineering techniques and methods to aid provisioning, deployment, monitoring, and adaptation of multi-cloud systems. Revel8or [24] is a model-driven capacity planning toolsuite to solve the problems related to complex multi-tier applications with strict performance requirements. They use UML 2.0 to model and annotate design diagrams, and derive performance analysis models. However, Revel8or only supports applications developed in a model-driven approach from platform-independent model to platform-specific model to the final code, while our approach targets all web applications, including hand-written and legacy applications. Another DSL – TOSCA [31] was proposed by Binz et al. to specify the topology and orchestration configuration for cloud applications in order to ease the cloud management tasks.

A number of research projects have focused on model-based load testing. Draheim et al. [25] used a modeling approach to produce realistic load testing scripts for web applications. Their approach simplifies the creation of realistic usage models of individual user behavior based on stochastic models. However, they do not analyze the minimum required cloud resources. Wang et al. [26] present a Load Testing Automation Framework (LTAF), which offers usage models to simulate users' behavior in load testing and workflow models to generate the realistic testing load. Similar to the previous work, LTAF also focused on simplified creation of realistic load testing configurations for web applications, with detailed performance reports. Neither of these two frameworks takes the target server resource consumption into consideration since resource optimization is not their goal.

Cloud resource allocation and optimization has become one research area, but there is no related work being done from the single web application load testing perspective. Wei etl al. [27] applied game theory to solve cloud-based resources allocation problems using abstract resource and application mathematics models. Based on a specification of the application's QoS constraints, Binary Integer Mining and evolutionary algorithms are used to drive the optimization solution. This work differs from ours in that: 1) it focuses on resource allocation for multiple applications scheduling in large cloud environments and 2) it emphasizes abstract analysis rather than empirical testing of real applications. Li et al. [28] present a method for resource optimization in clouds by using performance models in the deployment and operations of the applications running in the cloud. An optimization algorithm is implemented to accommodate different goals, scopes and timescales of optimization actions, in order to minimize cost while meeting SLAs across a large variety of workloads. A recent work done by Chalsiri et al. [29] focused on the cloud resource optimization problem from a different perspective. They looked at provisioning algorithms to better utilize market-based resources that fluctuate in cost based on demand to reduce total cost. In order to handle the resource optimization for multiple applications, Frey et al. presented a search-based genetic algorithm to find the near-optimal solution that optimizes response times, costs, and number of SLA violations [30]. Their approach is based on the simulation tool – CDOSim to improve the search process, while our approach focuses on performing actual benchmarking to obtain the accurate data. Instead of using genetic algorithm, Catan et al. [33] enabled the specification of application dependencies and criteria, and applied external constraint solvers to reach the optimization configuration.

7   Conclusions and Future Work

In this paper, we present a model-based approach, called ROAR, to automate the testing and derivation of optimized cloud resource allocations for web applications. A textual DSL is used to hide the low-level configuration and analysis details of load testing. An optimization engine, guided by resource utilization data from the servers under tests, automates the load testing process and the sampling of resource configurations to test. Finally, an optimized resource configuration to meet the web application's QoS goals is produced and a deployment and configuration template is generated for the target cloud provider.

One of the major research directions in the future is to continue to enrich GROWL and expose more best practices in load testing and resource optimization as simple DSL language constructs, such as supporting complex test behaviors that are driven by the input parameters (e.g., generate random or variable parameters as test inputs), or time-based tests (e.g., send request *r1* during the period of *t1*, and request *r2* only during the period of *t2*). Furthermore, QoS goals are currently based on the aggregated throughput for the whole test plan only. Enabling other types of QoS goals to be expressed in GROWL, such as percentile latency, would be very practical as well. Supporting resource optimization for multi-tier web applications is our next key goal. The motivating example shown in this paper is a real web service used as a SaaS solution. However, the testing and optimization process currently focuses on each tier individually, which requires developers to derive the expected QoS values of each tier separately. Being capable of automatically testing and deriving resource configurations for an entire multi-tier web application, without specifying QoS requirements for each individual tier, would simplify the testing and resource optimization process for multi-tiered web applications.

References

1. Hayes, B.: Cloud computing. Communications of the ACM 51(7), 9–11 (2008)
2. Amazon Web Services (2014), http://aws.amazon.com/
3. Rappa, M.: The utility business model and the future of computing services. IBM Systems Journal 43(1), 32–42 (2004)
4. Amazon Elastic Computing Cloud (EC2) Pricing (2014),
   http://aws.amazon.com/ec2/pricing/
5. Menascé, D.: Load testing of web sites. IEEE Internet Computing 6(4), 70–74 (2002)
6. Halili, E.H.: Apache JMeter: A practical beginner's guide to automated testing and performance measurement for your websites. Packt Publishing Ltd. (2008)
7. Apache JMeter (2014), https://jmeter.apache.org/
8. Apache HTTP Server Benchmarking Tool (2014),
   http://httpd.apache.org/docs/2.2/programs/ab.html
9. HP LoadRunner (2014), http://www8.hp.com/us/en/software-solutions/loadrunner-load-testing/
10. Wrk – Modern HTTP Benchmarking Tool (2014), https://github.com/wg/wrk
11. Bacigalupo, D.A., Jarvis, S.A., He, L., Nudd, G.R.: An investigation into the application of different performance prediction techniques to e-commerce applications. In: Proceedings of 18th International Parallel and Distributed Processing Symposium, pp. 26–30 (2004)
12. AWS Cloud Formation (2014), http://aws.amazon.com/cloudformation/
13. Bae, H., Golparvar-Fard, M., White, J.: High-precision vision-based mobile augmented reality system for context-aware architectural, engineering, construction and facility management (AEC/FM) applications. Visualization in Engineering 1(1), 1–13 (2013)
14. PAR Works MARS (2014),
   https://play.google.com/store/apps/details?id=com.parworks.mars
15. Amazon Simple Storage Service (Amazon S3) (2014),
   http://aws.amazon.com/s3/
16. Docker (2014), https://www.docker.io/

17. Eysholdt, M., Behrens, H.: Xtext: implement your language faster than the quick and dirty way. In: Proceedings of the ACM International Conference Companion on Object Oriented Programming Systems Languages and Applications Companion, pp. 307–309 (2010)
18. Bettini, L.: Implementing Domain-Specific Languages with Xtext and Xtend. Packt Publishing Ltd. (2013)
19. Custom Plugins for Apache JMeter (2014), http://jmeter-plugins.org/
20. Lin, W.Y., Lin, G.Y., Wei, H.Y.: Dynamic auction mechanism for cloud resource allocation. In: Proceedings of 10th IEEE/ACM International Conference on Cluster, Cloud and Grid Computing (CCGrid), pp. 591–592 (2010)
21. Wei, G., Vasilakos, A.V., Zheng, Y., Xiong, N.: A game-theoretic method of fair resource allocation for cloud computing services. The Journal of Supercomputing 54(2), 252–269 (2010)
22. Warneke, D., Kao, O.: Exploiting dynamic resource allocation for efficient parallel data processing in the cloud. IEEE Transactions on Parallel and Distributed Systems 22(6), 985–997 (2011)
23. Amazon Elastic Load Balancing (2014),
http://aws.amazon.com/elasticloadbalancing/
24. Zhu, L., Liu, Y., Bui, N.B., Gorton, I.: Revel8or: Model driven capacity planning tool suite. In: Proceedings of 29th International Conference on Software Engineering (ICSE), pp. 797–800 (2007)
25. Draheim, D., Grundy, J., Hosking, J., Lutteroth, C., Weber, G.: Realistic load testing of web applications. In: Proceedings of the 10th European Conference on Software Maintenance and Reengineering, pp. 57–70 (2006)
26. Wang, X., Zhou, B., Li, W.: Model-based load testing of web applications. Journal of the Chinese Institute of Engineers 36(1), 74–86 (2013)
27. Wei, G., Vasilakos, A.V., Zheng, Y., Xiong, N.: A game-theoretic method of fair resource allocation for cloud computing services. The Journal of Supercomputing 54(2), 252–269 (2010)
28. Li, J., Chinneck, J., Woodside, M., Litoiu, M., Iszlai, G.: Performance model driven QoS guarantees and optimization in clouds. In: ICSE Workshop on Software Engineering Challenges of Cloud Computing, pp. 15–22 (2009)
29. Chaisiri, S., Lee, B.S., Niyato, D.: Optimization of resource provisioning cost in cloud computing. IEEE Transactions on Services Computing 5(2), 164–177 (2012)
30. Frey, S., Fittkau, F., Hasselbring, W.: Search-based genetic optimization for deployment and reconfiguration of software in the cloud. In: Proceedings of the 2013 International Conference on Software Engineering, pp. 512–521. IEEE Press, Piscataway (2013)
31. Binz, T., Breitenbücher, U., Kopp, O., Leymann, F.: TOSCA: Portable automated deployment and management of cloud applications. In: Advanced Web Services, pp. 527–549. Springer, New York (2014)
32. Ferry, N., Rossini, A., Chauvel, F., Morin, B., Solberg, A.: Towards model-driven provisioning, deployment, monitoring, and adaptation of multi-cloud systems. In: CLOUD 2013: IEEE 6th International Conference on Cloud Computing, pp. 887–894 (2013)
33. Catan, M., et al.: Aeolus: Mastering the Complexity of Cloud Application Deployment. In: Lau, K.-K., Lamersdorf, W., Pimentel, E. (eds.) ESOCC 2013. LNCS, vol. 8135, pp. 1–3. Springer, Heidelberg (2013)

An Evaluation of the Effectiveness
of the Atomic Section Model

Sunitha Thummala and Jeff Offutt

Software Engineering
George Mason University, Fairfax VA, USA
{sthumma3, offutt} @gmu.edu

Abstract. Society increasingly depends on web applications for business and pleasure. As the use of web applications continues to increase, the number of failures, some minor and some major, continues to grow. A significant problem is that we still have relatively weak abilities to test web applications. Traditional testing techniques do not adequately model or test these novel technologies. The atomic section model (ASM), models web applications to support design, analysis, and testing. This paper presents an empirical study to evaluate the effectiveness of the ASM. The model was implemented into a tool, WASP, which extracts the ASM from the implementation and supports various test criteria. We studied ten web applications, totaling 156 components and 11,829 lines of code. Using WASP, we generated 207 tests, which revealed 31 faults. Seventeen of those faults exposed internal information about the application and server.

Keywords: Web applications, Test criteria, Model based testing, Atomic section modeling.

1   Introduction

A web application is a program that is deployed on a server and accessible through the Internet. Web applications form an important part of our daily lives as we use them for business, e-commerce, and even paying bills. Most businesses use web applications to interact with customers and business partners. A major benefit of web applications is that they can be accessed anytime from anywhere. A previous paper explained why large web applications need to be reliable, secure, maintainable, usable, and available [1]. A 2013 comScore study reported that consumers spent $42.3 billion dollars online in 2012 during the holidays [2].

Unfortunately, web applications continue to have many failures. The London Olympics website in 2011 crashed due to the sudden increase in customers after it announced 2.3 million tickets were available for purchase [3]. According to a Forbes report in 2013, Amazon.com lost $66,240 per minute of downtime [4]. The US health care web application in 2013 had numerous failures that led to significant costs, both monetary and political [5]. Target also suffered a massive credit card breach in 2013. All of these examples highlight the fact that we still do not always build reliable and secure web applications.

J. Dingel et al. (Eds.): MODELS 2014, LNCS 8767, pp. 35–49, 2014.

Web applications use many different technologies, including interpretive languages (Perl), scripted page modules (JSPs and ASPs), compiled module languages (servlets and ASPs), programming language extensions (JavaBeans and EJBs), general-purpose programming languages (Java and C#), sequential databases (SQL), and data representation languages (XML). As will be described in section 2, web application software uses new forms of control couplings, including forward, redirect, and user-controlled buttons on browsers. They also use new state handling and variable scoping mechanisms, including objects stored in a session and in a context.

As described in detail in a previous paper [6], traditional models and analysis techniques are not sufficient to capture all of the nuances of web applications. This causes model-based testing techniques that rely on traditional models such as statecharts and collaboration diagrams to be inadequate to test web apps. The same paper introduced the atomic section model (ASM), which has explicit mechanisms to model the novel control connections and data handling mechanisms in web applications.

ASM addresses the following issues in web applications:

1. Distributed integration
2. Dynamic creation of HTML forms
3. Ability of users to directly control the potential flow of execution

This paper presents an empirical evaluation of using the ASM to test existing web applications. Tests were designed from the requirements as a traditional testing method, and compared with tests designed from the ASM.

The rest of the paper is organized as follows. Section 5 presents prior research related to this paper. Section 2 summarizes the atomic section model, and section 3 describes a tool that we developed to partially automate test generation using the ASM. Section 4 then presents an empirical evaluation of using the ASM to generate tests on ten web applications, and finally section 6 concludes the paper.

2   Modeling Web Applications

This study is based on prior work by Offutt and Wu [6]. Web applications are deployed on a server and users run them across the internet through a browser. Thus, web application UIs are in HTML, using static links and form inputs. For conciseness, we often shorten "web application" to simply *web app*.

Web apps are composed from independent, and often distributed, components built with diverse technologies such as Java servlets, JSPs, ASPs, and many others. Thus, key to a web app are the *interactions* among the software components. Users run web apps through browsers, which generate HTTP *requests* to web servers, which then activate the requested software components, which in turn interact with other components, and eventually return *responses* to the users.

Deploying software across the web brings two essential new design challenges. One is remembering who the user is across multiple requests to the same server, and another is keeping data persistent across those multiple requests. HTTP is a *stateless* protocol, so each request is independent and run as a separate execution thread. To solve the first challenge, web apps define a *session* to be a sequence of related HTTP requests from the same user. Session states are maintained in special state variables on the server that are indexed by *cookies* that are stored on the users' computers and submitted to the server with requests.

For the second challenge, web app technologies use new forms of data scoping. Web software components cannot share global variables or objects. But since components run as threads within a process, the server creates a special object called the "session object" to store persistent data. Session data are commonly scoped to be available to (1) the same software component on different requests, (2) different software components on the same request, (3) all requests from the same session, or (4) all applications running within the same web server[1].

These powerful new technologies are, in a sense, new language features. Although they are built on top of traditional languages (such as Java and C#), programmers use them as if they are basic parts of the language. Not surprisingly, traditional modeling languages do not fully model all aspects of these technologies. The remainder of this section summarizes the atomic section model from Offutt and Wu [6], and discusses how the model is used to design tests.

2.1 The Atomic Section Model

An *atomic section* (ATS) is a section of HTML that has the property that if part of a section is sent to a client, then the entire section is (the "all-or-nothing property"). Atomic sections are combined to form regular expressions called *component expressions* (CE). Let c be a component consisting of n atomic sections $p_1, p_2, ..., p_n$. CEs combine ATSs in one of four ways:

1. *Sequence*: ($CE \rightarrow p_i \bullet p_j$): The component expression is p_i followed by p_j.
2. *Selection* ($CE \rightarrow p_i \mid p_j$): The component expression is either p_i or p_j, but not both. A typical example could be a code block that is sent from an *if-else* construct. Only the HTML section in the block that gets executed is sent to the client.
3. *Iteration* ($CE \rightarrow p_i^*$): The component expression contains zero or more occurrences of p_i in sequence, usually because the HTML is in a loop.
4. *Aggregation* ($CE \rightarrow p_i\{p_j\}$): p_j is included as part of p_i when p_i is sent to the client. These come from function calls in p_i and from file *include* commands.

A complete component expression models all possible web pages that the component can generate, much as a control flow graph models all possible execution paths in a method.

Transitions. Web apps are inherently component-based, and connect the components in novel ways. The ASM identifies five kinds of transitions. In the following definitions, p and q are component expressions and c is a component that generates HTML. The arrows are used in pictorial representations to distinguish the different types of transitions.

1. *Simple Link Transition* ($p \longrightarrow c$): The anchor tag $\langle a \rangle$ causes a link transition from the client to a component c on the server. Note that p may have more than one simple link transition, and so more than one possible destination. Anchor tags are the only source for simple link transitions.

---

[1] This terminology is from the J2EE framework. Other frameworks use slightly different terminology and some have slightly different scopes.

2. *Form Link Transition* ($p \twoheadrightarrow c$): Submitting forms in p causes a transition to component c on the server.
3. *Component Expression Transition* ($c \multimap p$): A component c executes and causes a component expression p to be returned to the client. The same component can produce more than one component expression.
4. *Operational Transition* ($p \rightsquigarrow q$): The user can create new transitions out of the software's control by pressing the refresh button, the back button, the forward button, accessing the history menu, or directly modifying the URL in the browser (URL rewriting). This amounts to random control flow jumps in the software, which is not possible in traditional and desktop software
5. *Redirect Transition* ($p \rightarrowtail q$): A redirect transition is a server-side software transition that is **not** under control of the tester. Redirection sometimes goes through the browser, and sometimes remains on the server, but is normally not visible to the user. Form data from the request is usually sent to the new component, but there is no return (hence this differs from a traditional method call).

Component Interaction Model. A component expression describes all web pages that can be produced by a web software component. Component expressions are composed with transitions to model an entire web app. A *Component Interaction Model* (CIM) defines the start page of a web application, a set of atomic sections, component expressions, and a set of transitions to model the possible flows of control through a web app. When taken together with the set of variables that define the state of a web app, the CIM is called a web application transition graph (ATG).

ASM currently does not model data flow. An interesting future study would be to investigate whether adding data flow criteria to the ASM could help detect more faults.

2.2 Test Criteria

Abstract model-based tests are designed from the ATG using three coverage criteria. Using coverage criteria to design tests has several advantages, including fewer tests that reveal more faults, traceability, and direct guidance for when to stop testing.

1. **Prime path coverage:** A *simple path* is a path in a graph such that no nodes except the first and the last appear more than once. A *prime path* is a simple path that does not appear as a proper sub-path of any other simple path [7]. Prime path coverage requires all prime paths in the graph to be executed.
2. **Invalid Access Coverage:** Each non-start node in an ATG is accessed directly, as if a tester jumps into the middle of a program. Users might do this accidentally, may save a URL to a page purposefully to avoid going through the lengthy application logic, or as a malicious attack. Note that this is not possible in traditional software.
3. **Invalid Path Coverage:** Invalid paths are created by first traversing a prime path, then adding an operational transition (IP1). Each invalid path is then extended, when possible, by adding transitions to all nodes accessible from the end of the invalid path (IP2).

The original ASM paper by Offutt and Wu [6] used one experiment subject and very little automation. This paper presents a significantly stronger empirical evaluation using ten experiment subjects and a complete tool that constructs ASMs automatically from the source code.

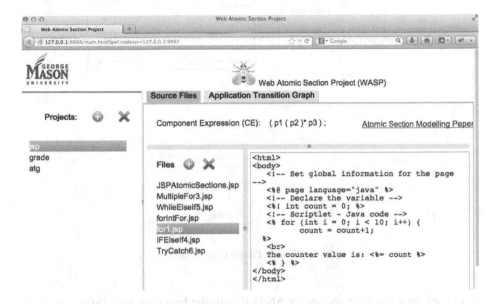

Fig. 1. Web Atomic Section Project Tool

3 The Web Atomic Section Project (WASP)

We developed the Web Atomic Section Project (WASP) to automate creation of the atomic section model. WASP was built as a web app. Users start by uploading source files. WASP then calculates the atomic sections and builds the web application graph. A screenshot of WASP is shown in figure 1.

Figure 1 shows the atomic section calculation for a simple JSP, *for1.jsp*. The expression shows sequence by concatenating the components rather than using the ● symbol. p_2 is the HTML produced within the *for* loop body ("$\langle br \rangle$*The counter value is: $\langle$% count %$\rangle$*").

Figure 2 shows a sample web application graph constructed by WASP. *Login* is the start component, and has a form link transition to *gradeServlet* and a simple link transition to *syllabus*. The servlet *gradeServlet* has a form link transition to itself and a simple link transition to *sendMail*.

The major components of WASP are the atomic section calculator and the application transition graph constructor. The atomic section calculator was built using ANTLR (ANother Tool for Language Recognition) [8]. ANTLR is used to construct compilers, recognizers, etc. It uses an input grammar for a language and develops the output source code based on semantic actions written by the user. Since servlets are special-purpose

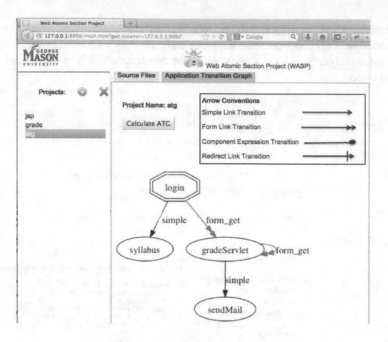

Fig. 2. Application Graph Construction

Java classes, they can be translated by ANTLR with the Java grammar. JSPs consist of HTML mixed with Java code and so are required to be pre-processed. A JSP is pre-processed by converting into its corresponding servlet by using the Jasper library of Tomcat.

The second major component, the application transition graph constructor parses Java servlets, JSPs and HTML files (for simple links, form links, forward transitions, redirect transitions) and uses the open source tool Graphviz [9] to construct the web application transition graph. WASP has some limitations. First, it is a static analysis tool, so dynamic references in the source code cannot be processed. Second, JSPs containing tag libraries are not processed. WASP extracts atomic sections and creates the application transition graph, but does not directly generate test values.

4   Empirical Evaluation

For this study, we used WASP to generate atomic sections and web application graphs for ten web applications. Our goal was to evaluate the usefulness of the ASM for testing. Specific research questions were:

1. RQ1: Can the ASM be computed with sufficient speed and usability to be effectively used by engineers?
2. RQ2: Can the ASM help find faults in web applications?
3. RQ3: What kinds of faults does ASM help identify?

4.1 Experimental Design

For experimental subjects, we used ten web applications that were built with the J2EE framework (servlets and JSPs) by graduate students in a graduate component-based software engineering course.

Two web apps (subjects one and two) were developed by the first author; the first web app is used to help students find internships, and the second allows customers to buy books online. Four web apps (subjects three, four, five and six) let users fill out surveys after visiting a campus and also see survey results from other visitors. Two web apps (subjects seven and eight) let users create events, create other users, assign them to a group, and make events available to everybody in a group. Two web apps (subjects nine and ten) store information about employees and provide access to employers.

All the web apps had been tested lightly by the developers. The programmers had considerable freedom in their designs, thus the programs written to the same requirements were quite different. This was intentional—we wanted to investigate the ability to find naturally occurring faults, but not trivial faults.

We generated test sets according to four different criteria. First, as a control, we generated requirements-based tests to represent the kinds of tests that are typically used in industry. We gave the requirements documents to a professional software tester with eight years of experience system testing, who generated tests for each subject. The professional tester was free to make any assumptions based on the requirements document. The tests were based purely on the requirements document and the tester allocated eight hours to design the tests. The requirements document did not mention things such as URL manipulation and browser controls, so the tester did not design tests for such actions. Then the first author ran the tests and recorded failures by hand.

Next we generated tests for the three test criteria in section 2. We used WASP to generate the CEs and ATGs, then the graph coverage web application [7] associated with Ammann and Offutt's book to generate the prime paths and test paths [10]. The graph coverage web app generated 73 prime path test requirements. The remaining 205 tests (41 invalid access and 164 invalid path) were generated by hand based on the ATG generated by WASP. We then created values by hand to satisfy all the 278 test paths. No tool is available to automatically generate test inputs to tour test paths. The manual work involved in setting up the system environment and database, deploying the executable web archive files, generating test case inputs, running tests, evaluating test outputs, and calculating coverage took around 60 hours over a period of ten days.

4.2 Experimental Results

The subject programs and experimental results are summarized in table 1. The second, third, and fourth columns summarize statistics about the web apps–the number of software components, the number of lines of code[2], and the number of atomic sections created by WASP. The software components were Java servlets, JSPs, and plain Java classes. The final eight columns give data from the tests. For each of our four test sets, the table gives the number of tests and the number of tests that failed. Recall that the

---

[2] Counted by loc-calculator (https://code.google.com/p/loc-calculator/)

Table 1. Experimental results of applying four test sets to ten web applications

Sub-ject	Comp-onents	LOC	Atomic Sections	Tests							
				Requirements		Prime Path		Invalid Access		Invalid Path	
				Tests	Failures	Tests	Failures	Tests	Failures	Tests	Failures
1	15	825	22	20	1	9	0	4	1	24	3
2	14	927	12	20	0	4	0	6	2	12	2
3	14	1485	8	20	1	9	1	5	2	20	1
4	18	1327	15	20	0	9	0	5	2	25	2
5	14	986	9	19	1	10	1	2	1	7	1
6	20	1473	19	12	0	3	0	2	0	7	1
7	9	782	7	13	1	2	0	2	0	7	1
8	9	688	8	9	0	2	0	2	0	11	1
9	19	1758	30	20	1	16	0	7	2	30	1
10	24	1578	45	16	0	9	0	6	3	21	3
Total	156	11,829	175	169	5	73	2	41	13	164	16

invalid path tests are extended versions of the prime path tests. The bottom row gives the sum of each column.

The requirements-based tests found a total of five failures with 169 tests. Thus, around 3% of the tests detected failures. The failures produced by the requirements-based tests are documented in table 2.

Table 2. Summary of failures found by requirements-based tests

Failure Type	Failure Description	Number found of this type
1	Did not display expected messages for invalid input	3
2	Allowed user to check out when total was $0	1
3	List of events not displayed, threw exception	1
	Total	**5**

We generated a total of 278 tests from the ASM (prime paths, invalid access, and invalid path). The prime path tests found two failures, the invalid access tests found 13, and the invalid path tests found 16.

Four of the five failures the requirements-based tests found were also found by the invalid access and invalid path tests. The failure not found by ASM in table 2 is of failure type 3. This exception occurs only when a file that needs to be updated is locked by another process (for example, when the file is open in an editor).

Thus, around 16% of the ASM tests found faults, a number that most testers would consider to indicate very efficient testing. These 31 failures are summarized in table 3.

Finally, we analyzed each failure to determine the underlying fault. Each failure was found to represent a distinct fault. The faults are summarized in table 4.

4.3   Atomic Section Coverage

Atomic section coverage requires each atomic section to be covered at least once [6]. After the above study was complete, we measured the ATS coverage of the tests.

Table 3. Types of failures found by ASM tests

Failure Type	Failure Description	Number of failures found by ASM tests
1	Duplicate records added	2
2	Unhandled software exception	7
3	Irrelevant error message	4
4	Runtime exception	11
5	Empty student record displayed due to URL rewriting	1
6	Displayed incorrect information	3
7	Displayed blank page	1
8	Allowed to check out when total was $0	1
9	Doubled the number of items in cart when page refreshed	1
	Total	31

Table 4. Types of faults found by ASM tests

Fault Type	Fault Description	Number of faults found by ASM tests
1	Allowing double submit form action	2
2	Not checking for null object	11
3	Resource URL not mapped correctly	3
4	Did not check for invalid input values such as empty or incorrect syntax	8
5	Did not have code to check for error scenario	2
6	Did not check if value being inserted is already present in the DB (duplicate item)	2
7	Did not check if value is greater than zero for enabling submit button	1
8	doGet() method not implemented	1
9	Search function for when only one parameter was given was incorrect	1
	Total	31

The ASM tests (prime paths, invalid access, and invalid path) covered 170 of the 175 atomic sections (ATS). We hand-designed tests to cover two of the remaining ATSs, but the other three were in unreachable code. The additional two tests reached atomic sections that handled unexpected behavior and abnormal database conditions, and each resulted in an additional failure. The first of the three unreachable ATSs was in a JSP component. One JSP checks for a null value, and if the value is not null, passes control to another JSP. The second JSP also checks for a null value. Redundant checks such as this are usually considered to be sound engineering practice. The other two were in code that printed messages if a variable had a particular value. However, that variable was not given a value in the back-end code. These probably represent faults in the program—either the message is not needed, or the back-end code should set a value for the variable.

This is additional evidence of the strength of the atomic section model. Simply covering atomic sections helped reveal faults that were not revealed by previous tests.

4.4 Discussion

It is telling to note that the requirements-based tests found only five faults, and four of those were also found by the ASM tests. Four sets of tests were derived from the ASM. The prime path criterion is the most traditional, and is defined on arbitrary graphs, yet it only found two faults. Most of the faults were found by tests that were only generated as a result of the atomic section model, and would be unlikely to be generated if the ASM were not used.

Of the 31 failures found by the ASM tests, 17 revealed information about the components or server where the web app was deployed. These failures are not only distressing to users, but also potential security vulnerabilities.

IP coverage of ASM requires an operational transition (back button, forward button, refresh button or URL rewriting) to be added to each prime path. We classified the failures found by ASM into failures that could potentially be discovered by a user using normal interaction sequences (such using the back button, the forward button, the refresh button, or by entering invalid data in forms) versus failures produced using IA or IP-URL rewriting. Of the 31 failures, 13 could have been found by users using normal interaction sequences, and 18 could only be found using IA or IP-URL rewriting.

Our study started with three research questions. We were able to successfully use WASP to generate CEs and ATGs, and then successfully design and create tests. The CEs and ATGs were calculated by WASP for each experiment subject in less than a minute, and the users were easily able to turn those into tests. Thus, the answer to RQ1 is clearly yes. Among the failures found using this study, the majority of the failures were found with the ASM tests, but not the requirements-based test. Thus, we conclude the answer to RQ2 is also yes. We explore RQ3, the kinds of faults identified, in the following subsection.

4.5 Example Failures

We already mentioned several failures that could be security vulnerabilities. Another common problem we found was web apps that assumed all requests would be HTTP POST requests. The invalid access tests called components directly with GET requests, and some components that did not expect to be called directly had runtime exceptions.

Several invalid path tests caused session variables to be accessed incorrectly, thus causing inconsistencies in the program state. This is a common problem in commercial web apps that we see regularly, so the ability to identify such flaws during pre-release testing can be quite helpful.

We also found several instances of the "double submit form problem," where if a user clicks on a back or refresh button after a form is submitted, the form is submitted again. This sometimes can lead to two orders being placed. The many commercial web apps that warn users to "not click the back button" indicate that this kind of fault is common, often known, but seldom corrected.

These faults are usually found after the software is completed, and not corrected because changing the design would be too difficult. They might be easier to correct if found earlier during testing.

One fault in the bookstore application was revealed by an invalid access test, causing a blank page to be returned to the user. When given an invalid ID through URL rewriting, the bookstore application also crashed with a generic "application error" message, as opposed to correctly telling the user that the ID was invalid. This was a case where the programmer assumed the component would only be accessed through normal channels, and the ID would always be valid.

One of the additional tests added to cover the remaining ATS discovered an interesting fault. The code was:

```
RequestDispatcher dispatcher = getServletContext().getRequestDispatcher ("/banner");
if (dispatcher != null)
    dispatcher.include (request, response);
```

The atomic section model places HTML generated by the statement inside the *if* block into one atomic section. The *if*-block does not have an *else* clause, but a blank atomic section is created in the component expression as a selection. Thus, a test was created to take the (null) *else* clause by making the banner servlet unavailable. This test resulted in an HTTP 505 internal server error, revealing a flaw in the program.

An invalid access test for the internship app revealed a null pointer exception because a session variable was accessed without being set. Another resulted in the message "You are applying for internship id: *null*." Again, the id variable had not been given a value prior to being used.

4.6   Statistical Analysis of Experiment Results

Hypothesis Testing: The null hypothesis for this experiment states that the ASM is not effective in revealing faults (number of faults that can be found is zero). The alternate hypothesis states that ASM is effective in finding faults (number of faults that can be found is greater than zero).

$$H_0: \mu \leq 0;$$
$$H_A: \mu > 0 \text{ (research hypothesis)};$$
Sample size N = 10
Sample mean X = 3.1
Standard deviation S = 1.66
DF = 9

Referring to the experiment results found in table 5, the test will be conducted at 0.05 level of significance ($\alpha = 0.05$). Assuming a normal distribution of faults found using ASM over all programs, we use a T distribution with nine degrees of freedom. Based on our null and alternate hypothesis, this will be a one tailed test.

Table 5. Number of faults found by ASM tests in each test subject

Experiment Subject	1	2	3	4	5	6	7	8	9	10	Total
No. of faults	4	4	4	4	3	1	1	1	3	6	31

The critical value for α of 0.05 and 9 degrees of freedom is (t_α) 1.83. The test statistic $t = X - \mu \div [\, S \div \sqrt{N} \,]$

The test statistic is 5.96, which is greater than 1.83 (t_α), and so we reject the null hypothesis. Thus, our alternate hypothesis that ASM is effective in finding faults holds.

Confidence Interval Analysis: Our experiment used ten experiment subjects. The number of faults found in each test subject is shown in table 5. Given the small random sample size of 10 experiment subjects, assuming a normal distribution of the average number of faults found using ASM over all the programs, we use a T distribution with nine Degrees of Freedom (DF).

$$CI = X \pm T_{0.05} \times S \div \sqrt{N}$$
$$CI = 3.1 \pm 1.83 \times 1.66 \div \sqrt{10}$$
$$CI = 3.1 \pm 0.96$$
$$CI = [2.14, 4.06]$$

Assuming a 90% confidence interval, the estimate of the average mean is in the range between 2.14 and 4.06. We are 90% confident that the average number of faults found by using ASM can be between 2 and 4 (by rounding to the nearest whole number).

4.7   Threats to Validity

Although the results strongly indicate that the ASM is an effective way to design tests, the study has some limitations. As usual with most software engineering studies, there is no way to show that the selected subjects are representative. This is true both for the web apps and the human programmers. In particular, the programmers were graduate students who may make different mistakes than experienced programmers. Because of the amount of work involved, we could only get one professional tester to participate in the requirements based tests. If more testers had participated, the results could have been different. A threat to internal validity is that manual analysis was used for various activities, including running tests, calculating coverage, and calculating the atomic sections. Finally, we cannot be sure that the tools used worked perfectly.

5   Related Work

Research into testing web applications can be split into static techniques, which analyze HTML and other static aspects of websites, and dynamic techniques, which test web application software. Dynamic techniques can be further divided into external techniques, which use only the URLs to access the program, and internal techniques, which can access the source code or the server. Our research analyzes the source code to design tests, thus is dynamic and internal.

Most static research has focused on client-side validation and static server-side validation of links. An extensive listing of existing web test support tools is on a web site maintained by Hower [11]. The list includes link checking tools, HTML validators, capture/playback tools, security test tools, and load and performance stress tools. These are all static validation and measurement tools, none of which support functional testing of programs deployed on the web, as our research does.

Kung et al. [12,13] developed a model to represent web sites as a graph, and provided preliminary definitions for developing tests based on the graph in terms of web page traversals.

Their model includes static link transitions and focuses on the client side with only limited use of the server software. They did not model application transitions, as the ASM does.

Halfond and Orso [14] studied the problem of finding web app user interface screens. These screens are created dynamically, thus the problem of finding all screens is undecidable. They used static analysis to find more of the screens than previous techniques. Instead of focusing on individual screens, the ASM technique is internal and identifies atomic sections that represent all possible screens.

The closest research to this paper was by Di Lucca and Di Penta [15]. They proposed testing sequences through a web application that incorporate some of the operational transitions in this paper, specifically focusing on the back and forward button transitions. Di Lucca and Di Penta's model focused on some browser capabilities, but not server-side software or web pages generated by the software.

Andrews et al. [16,17] modeled web applications as hierarchical finite state machines, and generated tests as paths through the FSMs. This approach was pure system level and focused on behavioral aspects of web applications, as opposed to the structural aspects the atomic section model represents. Benedikt, Freire, and Godefroid [18] presented VeriWeb, a dynamic navigation testing tool for web applications. VeriWeb explores sequences of links in web applications by exploring "action sequences" [18]. Values are provided by the tester. VeriWeb only follows explicit HTML links, as opposed to the many transitions the atomic section model uses.

Finding input values is a difficult problem that we do not address. Elbaum, Karre, and Rothermel [19] proposed the use of "user session data," which are values supplied by previous users in log files. Alshahwan and Harman [20] introduced a technique that supports web application regression testing by repairing user session data when the software changes. Lee and Offutt [21] used a form of mutation analysis to generate test values from previously existing XML messages. Jia and Liu [22] also generated test values using XML.

In related research, we have developed *bypass testing* [23,24] to send invalid data to web applications, bypassing some of the input validation. This is a stress testing approach that does not explore the kinds of interaction paths that ASM explores.

6   Conclusions and Future Work

This paper makes two contributions. First, the atomic section model has been implemented in a tool that analyzes web app source files, extracts atomic sections and computes component expressions, then identifies transitions and constructs web application
transition graphs. Second, the ATSs and ATGs were used to design three different types
of tests, and compared with requirements-based tests, which are typical of those used
for system testing, on the basis of how many naturally occurring faults they detected.
Because the ASM test generation process is incomplete and imperfect, we did not compare cost.

We generated a total of 278 ASM tests (73 PP, 41 IA, and 164 IP), which revealed
31 failures. The two tests that were added to cover additional atomic sections revealed
two more failures, and the analysis to cover the remaining atomic sections uncovered
two more. This contrasts with the 169 requirements-based tests, which only revealed
five failures. Thus, we conclude that the ASM tests are much more effective at detecting failures than the requirements-based tests. This should not be surprising; the atomic
section model captures elements of the design and implementation that are not captured
in the requirements, and some of those elements are commonly misused and misunder-
stood by software engineers.

In the future, we hope to extend WASP to handle more technologies such as GWT,
AJAX, JSF, etc. The atomic sections are less visible in some of these technologies, so
computing the component expressions could be quite different. We also hope to include
JavaScript in our analysis, including the concurrency aspects. Finally, we would like to
explore other uses of the ASM. It captures fundamental aspects of the integration and
execution of web applications, and could be used to support design modeling, program
slicing, and change impact analysis.

References

1. Offutt, J.: Quality attributes of Web software applications. IEEE Software: Special Issue on
   Software Engineering of Internet Software 19(2), 25–32 (2002)
2. comScore: 2012 U.S. online holiday spending grows 14 percent vs. year ago to 42.3 billion
   dollars (January 2013), http://www.comscore.com/ (last access: June 2014)
3. LogiGear: The seven most stunning website failures of 2011 (2012),
   http://www.logigear.com/magazine/issue/past-articles/
   the-seven-most-stunning-website-failures-of-2011/ (last   access:
   June 2014)
4. Clay, K.: Amazon.com goes down, loses $66,240 per minute (2013),
   http://www.forbes.com/sites/kellyclay/2013/08/19/
   amazon-com-goes-down-loses-66240-per-minute/ (last   access: March
   2014)
5. Ford, P.: The obamacare website didn't have to fail. How to do better next time. Bloomberg
   Businessweek Technology (October 2013), http://www.graphviz.org/ (last access:
   June 2014)
6. Offutt, J., Wu, Y.: Modeling presentation layers of web applications for testing. Software and
   Systems Modeling 9(2), 257–280 (2010)

7. Ammann, P., Offutt, J.: Introduction to Software Testing. Cambridge University Press, Cambridge (2008) ISBN 978-0-521-88038-1
8. Parr, T.: Antlr parser generator (2003), http://www.antlr.org/ (ast access: June 2014)
9. Software, O.S.: Graphviz, http://www.graphviz.org/ (last access: March 2014)
10. Ammann, P., Offutt, J., Xu, W., Li, N.: Graph coverage web applications (2008), http://cs.gmu.edu:8080/offutt/coverage/GraphCoverage (last access: March 2014)
11. Hower, R.: Web site test tools and site management tools (2002), http://www.softwareqatest.com/qatweb1.html
12. Kung, D., Liu, C.H., Hsia, P.: An object-oriented Web test model for testing Web applications. In: 24th Annual International Computer Software and Applications Conference (COMPSAC 2000), Taipei, Taiwan, pp. 537–542. IEEE Computer Society Press (October 2000)
13. Liu, C.H., Kung, D., Hsia, P., Hsu, C.T.: Structural testing of Web applications. In: Proceedings of the 11th International Symposium on Software Reliability Engineering, San Jose CA, pp. 84–96. IEEE Computer Society Press (October 2000)
14. Halfond, W.G.J., Orso, A.: Improving test case generation for web applications using automated interface discovery. In: Proceedings of the Foundations of Software Engineering, Dubrovnik, Croatia, pp. 145–154 (2007)
15. Lucca, G.A.D., Penta, M.D.: Considering browser interaction in web application testing. In: 5th International Workshop on Web Site Evolution (WSE 2003), Amsterdam, The Netherlands, pp. 74–84. IEEE Computer Society Press (September 2003)
16. Andrews, A., Offutt, J., Alexander, R.: Testing Web applications by modeling with FSMs. Software and Systems Modeling 4(3), 326–345 (2005)
17. Andrews, A., Offutt, J., Dyreson, C., Mallery, C.J., Jerath, K., Alexander, R.: Scalability issues with using FSMWeb to test web applications. Information and Software Technology 52(1), 52–66 (2010)
18. Benedikt, M., Freire, J., Godefroid, P.: VeriWeb: Automatically testing dynamic Web sites. In: Proceedings of 11th International World Wide Web Conference (WWW 2002) – Alternate Paper Tracks (WE-3 Web Testing and Maintenance), Honolulu, HI, pp. 654–668 (May 2002)
19. Elbaum, S., Rothermel, G., Karre, S., Fisher, M.: Leveraging user-session data to support web application testing. IEEE Transactions on Software Engineering 31(3), 187–202 (2005)
20. Alshahwan, N., Harman, M.: Automated repair of session data to improve web application regression testing. In: 1st IEEE International Conference on Software Testing, Verification and Validation (ICST 2008 Industry Track), Lillehammer, Norway, pp. 298–307 (April 2008)
21. Lee, S.C., Offutt, J.: Generating test cases for XML-based Web component interactions using mutation analysis. In: Proceedings of the 12th International Symposium on Software Reliability Engineering, Hong Kong China, pp. 200–209. IEEE Computer Society Press (November 2001)
22. Jia, X., Liu, H.: Rigorous and automatic testing of Web applications. In: 6th IASTED International Conference on Software Engineering and Applications (SEA 2002), Cambridge, MA, pp. 280–285 (November 2002)
23. Offutt, J., Wu, Y., Du, X., Huang, H.: Bypass testing of web applications. In: 15th International Symposium on Software Reliability Engineering, Saint-Malo, Bretagne, France, pp. 187–197. IEEE Computer Society Press (November 2004)
24. Offutt, J., Papadimitriou, V., Praphamontripong, U.: A case study on bypass testing of web applications. Springer's Empirical Software Engineering 1–36 (July 2012) (Published online), doi:10.1007/s10664-012-9216-x

Parsing in a Broad Sense

Vadim Zaytsev[1] and Anya Helene Bagge[2]

[1] Universiteit van Amsterdam, The Netherlands
vadim@grammarware.net
[2] Universitetet i Bergen, Norway
anya@ii.uib.no

Abstract. Having multiple representations of the same instance is common in software language engineering: models can be visualised as graphs, edited as text, serialised as XML. When mappings between such representations are considered, terms "parsing" and "unparsing" are often used with incompatible meanings and varying sets of underlying assumptions. We investigate 12 classes of artefacts found in software language processing, present a case study demonstrating their implementations and state-of-the-art mappings among them, and systematically explore the technical research space of bidirectional mappings to build on top of the existing body of work and discover as of yet unused relationships.

Keywords: Parsing, unparsing, pretty-printing, model synchronisation, technical space bridging, bidirectional model transformation.

1 Introduction

Parsing is a well established research field [1] — in fact, its maturity has already become its own enemy: new results are specialised refinements published at a handful of venues with a critical mass of experts to appreciate them. Unparsing is a less active field, there are no books on *unparsing techniques* and there is no general terminological agreement (printing, pretty-printing, unparsing, formatting), but this family of mappings has nevertheless been studied well [2,3,4,5,6,7,8,9,10,11]. Parsing research concerns recognising grammatically formed sentences, providing error-correcting feedback, constructing graph-based representations, as well as optimising such algorithms on time, memory and lookahead. Research questions in the domain of unparsing include conservatism (in BX related to hippocraticness [12] and resourcefulness [13]), metalanguage completeness and designing a universal way to specify pretty-printers. It was suggested that unparsing in a broad sense should comprise advanced techniques like syntax highlighting [14, §3.8.3] and adjustment to screen width [11, §2.1]. Methods have been proposed to infer parsers from unparsers [11], unparsers from parsers [15,16] or both from annotated syntactic definitions [17,18,19]. Our attempt is about *modelling parsing and unparsing together as bidirectional transformation*, essentially by breaking up big step parsing into smaller steps for the sake of bidirectionalisation [20] and analysis. There are no general BX frameworks [12] to give a solution. This modelling approach can provide useful insights

J. Dingel et al. (Eds.): MODELS 2014, LNCS 8767, pp. 50–67, 2014.

in bridging the gap between structural editors and text-based IDEs, which is known to be one of the open problems of software language engineering [21].

2 Motivation

Bidirectional transformations are traditionally [12] useful for situations when we need consistency restoration among two or more entities that share information in such a way that if one is updated, the other(s) need to coevolve. For example, a language instance (the term we use to avoid committing to "model", "program", "table", etc) can be expected to be defined in a specific way (i.e., to belong to an algebraic data type), but its concrete implementation can take a form of a textual file, or a graph, or an XML tree — one can think of scenarios when we would like to freely choose which instance to update so that the rest get co-updated automatically. (This can be seen correponding to the classic PIM/PSM distinction in MDA or to Ast/Cst from the next sections).

When two instances represent the same information in different ways, the mapping between them is bijective, and the solution is trivial. However, it is often the case that each kind of an instance is only a "view" on the complete picture. In the database technical space, this complete picture is formally defined, and we know exactly what the view is lacking. This allows an asymmetrical view/update or get/putback solution with one function taking just one argument and replacing its target with a new result, and one function taking two arguments and updating one of them [22,13,23]. However, in software language engineering we often end up having bits of specific locally significant information scattered among many artefacts. For example, a text of a program (Str) can contain indentation preferred by programmers, while the graphical model of the same instance (Dra) can contain colours and coordinates of its visualisation, and the abstract internal representation (Ast) can have precalculated metrics values cached in its nodes. Solving the problem by creating one huge structure to cover everything is undesirable: this solution is neither modular nor extendable.

In our endeavour to stay unbiased, we adopt a symmetrical approach that treats all views uniformly, as will be described in detail in § 3. To model all existing work we will also need a more demanding definition than the one used for lenses [22], since many techniques in the grammarware technological space are error-correcting, and thus can update both entities for consistency.

In § 4, we will propose a megamodel of mappings between strings, tokenised strings, layout-free lists of tokens, lexical source models, parse forests, parse trees, concrete syntax trees, abstract syntax trees, pictures, graphs and models of different kinds. We will also give examples of such mappings and argue how they fit our framework and what can we learn from it, leading to § 5 where a case study is presented with all types and mappings from Figure 1 implemented in Rascal [24], a metamodelling/metaprogramming language.

The main contribution of the paper is the structured megamodel of activities that can be viewed as either "parsing" or "unparsing"; the case study demonstrates its otherwise non-apparent aspects; the rest of the paper revisits and catalogues common software language engineering processes. The reader is expected to be familiar with modelling and megamodelling; background on parsing and bidirectionality is appreciated but not required: the necessary explanations and literature references are provided.

3   Bidirectionality

In this section we will recall some of the kinds of bidirectional mappings covered by previously existing research, in order to establish the background needed to appreciate and comprehend the main contribution of the paper (the megamodel on Figure 1). To simplify their comparison, we take the liberty of reformulating the definitions in a way that leaves them equivalent to their corresponding originals. We will also put a dot above a relation to account for undefined cases: e.g., the sign "$\dot{=}$" will denote "if all subformulae are defined, then equals".

The simplest form of a bidirectional mapping is a reversible function [25]:

Definition 1 (reversible function). *For a relation $\Psi \subseteq L \times R$, a reversible function f is a pair of functions for its forward execution $\overrightarrow{f} : L \to R$ and reverse execution $\overleftarrow{f} : R \to L$, such that*

$$\forall x \in L, \ \langle x, \overrightarrow{f}(x) \rangle \dot{\in} \Psi \tag{1}$$

$$\forall y \in R, \ \langle \overleftarrow{f}(y), y \rangle \dot{\in} \Psi \tag{2}$$

If it is bijective, then also

$$\forall x \in L, \ (\overleftarrow{f} \circ \overrightarrow{f})(x) \dot{=} x \tag{3}$$

$$\forall y \in R, \ (\overrightarrow{f} \circ \overleftarrow{f})(y) \dot{=} y \tag{4}$$

A lens [22] is a more complex bidirectional mapping defined asymmetrically such that one of its components can observe both the "old" value being updated and the changed one. We will call them "Foster BX" here to avoid confusion with many variations of lenses (for the purpose of this paper, we only need well-behaved lenses).

Definition 2 (Foster BX). *A get function $\nearrow : L \to R$ and a putback function $\searrow : R \times L \to L$ form a well-behaved lens, if*

$$\forall x \in L, \ \searrow (\nearrow(x), x) \dot{=} x \tag{5}$$

$$\forall x \in L, \forall y \in R, \ \nearrow (\searrow(y, x)) \dot{=} y \tag{6}$$

If a reversible function f exists, then constructing a lens is trivial: $\nearrow \equiv \overrightarrow{f}$ and $\forall x \in L, \searrow (y, x) \equiv \overleftarrow{f}(y)$. The inverse construction of a reversible function from a lens is only possible if both $\nearrow$ and $\searrow$ are bijective (Eq. 3 and Eq. 4 hold).

As an example of symmetric bidirectional mapping, we recall the notation by Meertens [26], with terms for properties inherited from Stevens [12]:

Definition 3 (Meertens BX). *A* bidirectional mapping *is a relation Ψ and its* ***maintainer,*** *which is a pair of functions* $\triangleright : L \times R \to R$ *and* $\triangleleft : L \times R \to L$ *that are* correct:

$$\forall x \in L, \forall y \in R, \langle x, x \triangleright y \rangle \dot{\in} \Psi, \langle x \triangleleft y, y \rangle \dot{\in} \Psi \qquad (7)$$

and hippocratic:

$$\forall x \in L, \forall y \in R, \langle x, y \rangle \in \Psi \Rightarrow x \triangleright y = y, x \triangleleft y = x \qquad (8)$$

Intuitively, correctness means that the result of either function is according to the relation Ψ. Hippocraticness means that no modification happens if the two values are already properly related (i.e., the transformation is guaranteed to "do no harm"). In other words, a maintainer $\triangleright$ and $\triangleleft$ can *maintain* the relation Ψ either by leaving their arguments unchanged if the relation is already respected or by massaging one of them with the data from the other one, until they do.

Constructing a trivial Meertens maintainer from a lens is straightforward:

$$x \triangleright y \equiv \nearrow (x)$$
$$x \triangleleft y \equiv \searrow (y, x)$$

Obviously, the inverse operation is only possible when the right semi-maintainer does not require y for computing its result.

While the symmetry of the definition allows us to research scenarios of two or more views of equal importance and comparable expressiveness, semi-maintainers always assume one side to be correct, which especially in the context of parsing only models straightforward precise parsing [1] or noncorrecting recovery strategies [27]. For more complicated scenarios, we introduce the following kind of bidirectional transformations:

Definition 4 (Final BX). *A* final bidirectional mapping *is a relation Ψ and its* ***sustainer,*** *which is a pair of functions* $\blacktriangleright : L \times R \to \Psi$ *and* $\blacktriangleleft : L \times R \to \Psi$ *that are* hippocratic:

$$\forall x \in L, \forall y \in R, \langle x, y \rangle \in \Psi \Rightarrow x \blacktriangleright y = \langle x, y \rangle, x \blacktriangleleft y = \langle x, y \rangle \qquad (9)$$

Final BX is also *correct* in the sense of the codomain of $\blacktriangleright$ and $\blacktriangleleft$ being Ψ. Constructing a sustainer from a Meertens BX or a Foster BX is trivial:

$$x \blacktriangleright y \equiv \langle x, x \triangleright y \rangle \equiv \langle x, \nearrow (x) \rangle$$
$$x \blacktriangleleft y \equiv \langle x \triangleleft y, y \rangle \equiv \langle \searrow (y, x), y \rangle$$

Correctness of this construction is a direct consequence of the (rather strict) properties we have demanded in Def. 2 and Def. 3. For example, if maintainer functions were allowed to violate correctness, we would have needed to construct a sequence of updates until a fixed point would have been reached.

The inverse operation is only possible for noncorrecting sustainers:

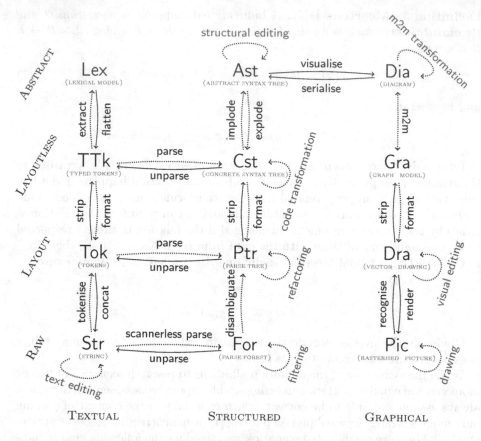

Fig. 1. Bidirectional megamodel of parsing. Dotted lines denote mappings that rely on either lexical or syntactic definitions; solid lines denote universally defined mappings. The loops are examples of transformations.

Definition 5 (noncorrection property). *A sustainer is* noncorrecting, *if*

$$\forall x \in L, \forall y \in R \quad x \blacktriangleright y = \langle x, y' \rangle \tag{10}$$

$$\forall x \in L, \forall y \in R \quad x \blacktriangleleft y = \langle x', y \rangle \tag{11}$$

Noncorrecting sustainers are equivalent to maintainers.

4   Artefacts and Mappings

Let us first introduce the kinds of artefacts we will use for the remainder of the paper:

- Str — a string.
- Tok — a finite sequence of strings (called *tokens*) which, when concatenated, yields Str. Includes spaces, line breaks, comments, etc — collectively, *layout*.

- TTk — a finite sequence of typed tokens, with layout removed, some classified as numbers of strings, etc.
- Lex — a lexical source model [28,29] that addes grouping to typing; in fact a possibly incomplete tree connecting most tokens together in one structure.
- For — a forest of parse trees, a parse graph or an ambiguous parse tree with sharing; a tree-like structure that models Str according to a syntactic definition.
- Ptr — an unambiguous parse tree where the leaves can be concatenated to form Str.
- Cst — a parse tree with concrete syntax information. Structurally similar to Ptr, but without layout.
- Ast — a tree which contains only abstract syntax information.
- Pic — a picture, which can be an ad hoc model, a natural model [30] or a rendering of a formal model.
- Dra — a graphical representation of a model (not necessarily a tree), a drawing in the sense of GraphML or SVG, or a metamodel-indepenent syntax but metametamodel-specific syntax like OMG HUTN.
- Gra — an entity-relationship graph or any other primitive "boxes and arrows" level model.
- Dia — a figure, a graphical model in the sense of EMF or UML, a model with an explicit advanced metamodel.

Figure 1 shows a megamodel of all the different artefacts and the mappings between them. The artefacts in the left column of the megamodel are *textual* (examples of these can be seen in Figure 2), the ones in the middle are *structured* (examples of these can be seen in Figure 3), and the ones on the right are *graphical* (Figure 4). Going "up" the megamodel increases the level of details in annotations: in Str we have one monolithic chunk, in Tok we know the boundaries between tokens, in TTk some tokens have types, in Lex some are grouped together (and similarly for other columns).

For example, classic parsing (e.g., using yacc [31]) is TTk → Cst or Tok → Ptr; layout-sensitive generalised scannerless parsing is Str → For (and possibly Str → For → Ptr). Going from TTk or Cst to Tok or Ptr is code formatting.

An interesting and important detail of those mappings for us is whether they are defined generally or parametric with a language specification of some kind (usually a grammar, a metamodel, a lexical definition, a regexp). For example, Ptr → Tok unparsing can be done by traversing a tree and collecting all its leaves from left to right. However, in order to construct a meaningful Cst tree from a TTk sequence, we need to rely on the hierarchy of linguistic categories (i.e., a grammar). Especially for the case of Ast ⇌ Cst there are fairly complicated mapping inference strategies from (annotated) language specifications [32,33].

4.1 Fundamental Operations

Tokenisation. A tokeniser $tokenise_L : Str \rightarrow Tok$ for some lexical grammar L, maps a character sequence $c_1, \ldots, c_n$ to a token sequence $w_1, \ldots, w_k$ in such a

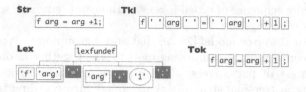

Fig. 2. Textual representations of a simple program. Clockwise from top left, Str (initial string), Tok (including layout), TTk (tokenised), Lex (lexical model).

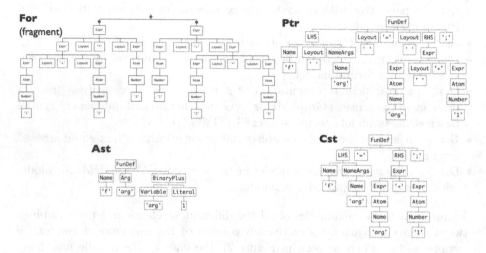

Fig. 3. Structured representations of a simple program. Clockwise from top left, For (forest of ambiguous interpretations), Ptr (parse tree including layout), Cst (concrete syntax), Ast (abstract syntax).

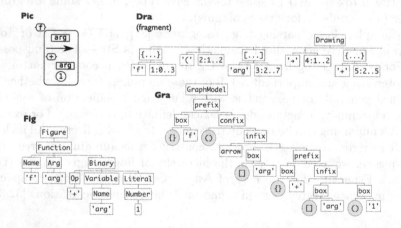

Fig. 4. Graphical representations of a simple program. Clockwise from top left, Pic (rasterised picture), Dra (vector picture), Gra (specific graphical model), Dia (abstract model).

way that their concatenations are equal (i.e., $c_1 + \cdots + c_n = w_1 \cdots + w_k$). We call the reverse operation concat:

$$\forall x \in \mathsf{Str}, \mathsf{concat}(\mathsf{tokenise}_\mathsf{L}(x)) \doteq x \qquad (12)$$

$$\forall y \in \mathsf{Tok}, \mathsf{tokenise}_\mathsf{L}(\mathsf{concat}(y)) \doteq y \qquad (13)$$

Note that concat can be defined independently of the lexical grammar.

Adding/Removing Layout. The strip operation removes layout; format introduces it. While stripping of layout is grammar independent, format is not. We can apply stripping and formatting to sequences (strip : $\mathsf{Tok} \to \mathsf{TTk}$, format$_\mathsf{L}$: $\mathsf{TTk} \to$ Tok), trees (strip : $\mathsf{Ptr} \to \mathsf{Cst}$, format$_\mathsf{G}$: $\mathsf{Cst} \to \mathsf{Ptr}$) and models (strip : $\mathsf{Dra} \to \mathsf{Gra}$, format$_\mathsf{M}$: $\mathsf{Gra} \to \mathsf{Dra}$).

Stripping has the following property (shown for format$_\mathsf{M}$, defined similarly for the other two variants):

$$\forall x \in \mathsf{Gra}, \mathsf{strip}(\mathsf{format}(x)) \doteq x \qquad (14)$$

Bidirectional stripping/formatting is at least a Foster BX: without knowing what the original input looked like prior to stripping, it is generally impossible to format it in the same way. With a Final BX we can model error correcting formatting as well. For example, if an arc is added to a Gra model, the visual formatter can suggest to add the target node to the model because it knows that drawing an edge always ends in a vertex. However, it is often desirable that such a sustainer is deterministic in the sense of Eq. 14 or close to it — i.e., reformatting a model will not result in a totally alien graph.

Layout preservation and propagation through transformations remains a challenging research topic even without considering error correction [34,19].

Parsing/Unparsing. Parsing recovers the implicit structure in the input sequence, representing it explicitly in a tree. The forward operations parse$_\mathsf{G}$: $\mathsf{Tok} \to \mathsf{Ptr}$ and parse$_\mathsf{G}$: $\mathsf{TTk} \to \mathsf{Cst}$ uncover the grammatical structure (defined in a grammar G) of a sequence (with or without layout). Parsing is readily reversible, with universally defined reverse operations unparse : $\mathsf{Ptr} \to \mathsf{Tok}$ and unparse : $\mathsf{Cst} \to \mathsf{TTk}$:

$$\forall x \in \mathsf{Tok}, \mathsf{unparse}(\mathsf{parse}_\mathsf{G}(x)) \doteq x \qquad (15)$$

$$\forall x \in \mathsf{TTk}, \mathsf{unparse}(\mathsf{parse}_\mathsf{G}(x)) \doteq x \qquad (16)$$

$$\forall y \in \mathsf{Ptr}, \mathsf{parse}_\mathsf{G}(\mathsf{unparse}(y)) \doteq y \qquad (17)$$

$$\forall y \in \mathsf{Cst}, \mathsf{parse}_\mathsf{G}(\mathsf{unparse}(y)) \doteq y \qquad (18)$$

Unparsing may be implemented by, for instance, collecting the leaves of the tree into a sequence.

Implosion/Explosion. For conversion to and from abstract syntax trees, we have implode$_\mathsf{G}$: $\mathsf{Cst} \to \mathsf{Ast}$ and explode$_\mathsf{G}$: $\mathsf{Ast} \to \mathsf{Cst}$. The explode mapping is non-trivial and requires knowledge of the intended syntax; implode can be defined in multiple ways, including the straightforward uniform mapping of Stratego/XT's implode-asfix [35] or Rascal's implode [24]. The explosion is harder to implement, and therefore it is rarely found in standard libraries.

Tree disambiguation. Earlier approaches to parsing always tried to burden the grammar with additional information to guide the parsing (and sometimes also the unparsing) process [1]. The state of the art in practical source code manipulation usually relies on a relatively uniform parsing algorithm (SGLR, GLL or Packrat) that yields a For structure which is then filtered according to extra information [36,24]. In such a decoupled scenario this additional knowledge can come from the grammar, from a separate specification, from a classifying oracle, etc, which gives more flexibility to the language engineer. Thus, we must add the disambiguate operation both as a (metamodel-specific) mapping from For to Ptr, and as a For → For refinement. There is no currently available research results on bidirectionalising this mapping, even though many recommenders can possibly be implemented as Ptr → For transformations.

Rendering/Recognising. Image recognition techniques can be applied to extract structured graph information from a picture, identifying (with some degree of certainty) model elements, their positioning and relationships. Of course, some natural models are never meant to be recognised this way [30]. The reverse mapping is much more trivial and present in most visual editors.

4.2 Familiar Operations Decomposed

We can now decompose common operations into the fundamental components of the previous section; either single-step mappings $L \to R$ from one representation to another, or transformations $L \to L$ within the same representation.

For example, *code reindentation* is a transformation at the layout level, indent : Tok → Tok (or Ptr → Ptr), modifying the layout of the input while preserving the property:

$$\forall x \in \mathsf{Tok}, \mathsf{strip}(\mathsf{indent}(x)) \doteq \mathsf{strip}(x) \tag{19}$$

That is, changes in indentation make no difference at the layoutless level.

A compiler can be similarly decomposed, with the crucial transformation being, for example, $\mathsf{Ast_C} \to \mathsf{Ast_{ASM}}$. A full C compiler might be a pipeline $\mathsf{Str_C} \to \mathsf{Tok_C} \to \mathsf{Ptr_C} \to \mathsf{Cst_C} \to \mathsf{Ast_C} \to \mathsf{Ast_{IR}} \to \mathsf{Ast_{ASM}} \to \mathsf{Cst_{ASM}} \to \mathsf{TTk_{ASM}} \to \mathsf{Tok_{ASM}} \to \mathsf{Str_{ASM}}$.

Examples

- A traditional lexer does Str → Tok → TTk in a single integrated step.
- Classic compiler textbook parsing is TTk → Cst [1]; though the resulting tree is often implicit (e.g., syntax-directed compilation).
- Layout-sensitive parsing is Tok → Ptr [37].

- Scannerless parsing is, in effect, parsing with Tok = Str or TTk = Str [38].
- The crucial steps of the PGF code formatting framework [9] are Ptr →
  Tok →* Tok → Str, with tokens being annotated with extra information,
  and additional information from the parse tree appearing as control tokens.
- Code refactoring is, for instance, Ptr → Ptr [19], lowered to Str → Str.
- A structural editor does user-directed Ast → Ast transformation internally,
  while maintaining a Str representation for the user's benefit [39]. An IDE
  editor does user-directed Str → Str transformation, while maintaining an
  internal Ast representation.
- Wadler's prettier printer [5] does Cst → Ptr → Tok in single integrated step.

4.3 Discussion

Source-to-Source Transformations and Lowering. From the user's perspective, a transformation such as reindentation is an operation $\text{indent}_{\text{Str}} : \text{Str} \rightarrow \text{Str}$ on text, rather than on tokens. It has the property:

$$\forall x \in \text{Str}, \text{tokenise}(\text{indent}_{\text{Str}}(x)) \doteq \text{indent}_{\text{Tok}}(\text{tokenise}(x)) \qquad (20)$$

An implementation of $\text{indent}_{\text{Str}}$ may be obtained by applying concat to both sides and reducing:

$$\text{concat}(\text{tokenise}(\text{indent}_{\text{Str}}(x))) \doteq \text{concat}(\text{indent}_{\text{Tok}}(\text{tokenise}(x))) \iff$$
$$\text{indent}_{\text{Str}}(x) \doteq \text{concat}(\text{indent}_{\text{Tok}}(\text{tokenise}(x))) \qquad \text{by Eq. 12}$$

This is called the *lowering* (to an operation on more concrete representations) of indent. A transformation lowered to Str → Str is usually called a *source-to-source* transformation. Given the operations in § 4.1 we may lower any transformation, as we please.

Transformation tools often allow the use of concrete syntax when specifying transformations – in effect, specifying transformation rules at the Str or Pic level. The rules are then *lifted* to the representation where the transformation actually takes place. For example; Stratego/XT [35] allows concrete syntax in transformation rules. Such rules are then parsed, disambiguated, stripped and imploded (and optionally desugared) into transformations on Ast.

In general, given a series of converting transformations from artifact A to B and back, we may implement any transformation on A by a transformation on B. Further explorations are needed to determine the required properties of such conversions.

Model-to-Model Transformation. There are models that have an advanced metamodel and many relations like "inherits from" or "conforms to" (i.e., Dia), which are apparently distinct from a simple view on the same models (i.e., Gra). Such a simplified view, a "concrete visual syntax" so to speak, can concern itself with the fact that we have nodes of various kinds (boxes, tables, pictures) which are connected by edges (lines, arrows, colours), all of them possibly labelled. If such distinction was to be made, we could see the difference between model-to-model transformations that refine and evolve the baseline model, and model-to-model transformations that "downgrade" it to one of the possible forms suitable for rendering. Then, Gra → Dia is a model-to-model transformation that can also be seen as "parsing" of the visual lexems to a model in a chosen language (a diagram).

Ast → Dia mappings are often viewed as *visualisations* and Dia → Ast ones as *serialisations*, even though in general they are glorified tree-to-graph transformations and graph-to-tree ones. So far we could not spot any research attempts to investigate mappings between lower levels of the central and the right column of Figure 1, except for idiosyncratic throwaway visualisations that are not meant to be edited and not meant to be transformed.

Layout Preservation. Layout preservation is an important requirement in certain grammarware applications, such as for instance automated refactoring. A *layout-preserving transformation* is one where all layout is intact, except for layouts in the parts that have been changed by the transformation. In essence, a transformation on an abstract representation is reflected in the concrete representation.

A layout-preserving transformation on a Cst is a transformation $t : \text{Cst} \to \text{Cst}$, lowered to $u : \text{Ptr} \to \text{Ptr}$, using a Foster BX with $\nearrow = \text{strip}$:

$$u(x) = \searrow (t(\nearrow (x)), x), \quad x \in \text{Ptr} \tag{21}$$

Lowering all the way to Str is simple, and gives us $r : \text{Str} \to \text{Str}$:

$$r(x) = \text{concat}(\text{unparse}(u(\text{parse}(\text{tokenise}(x))))), \quad x \in \text{Str} \tag{22}$$

Incrementality. Suppose that we have a concrete and an abstract representation (e.g., a Str and a Cst), and a change in the concrete one should be reflected in the abstract one (this could be seen as the dual of layout preservation).

Again, we can use Foster BX. For example, for incremental parsing, we define editing edit_{Ptr} of parse trees as follows, where edit_{Str} is the user's editing transformation:

$$\text{edit}_{\text{Ptr}}(x) = \text{parse}_{\text{inc}}(\text{edit}_{\text{Tok}}(\text{unparse}(x)), x) \tag{23}$$

$$\text{edit}_{\text{Tok}}(y) = \text{tokenise}_{\text{inc}}(\text{edit}_{\text{Str}}(\text{concat}(y)), y) \tag{24}$$

The unparse and concat operation corresponds to the $\nearrow$ of Foster BX, while $\text{parse}_{\text{inc}} : \text{Tok} \times \text{Ptr} \to \text{Ptr}$ and $\text{tokenise}_{\text{inc}} : \text{Str} \times \text{Tok} \to \text{Tok}$ corresponds to $\searrow$. While the former two operations are trivial (defined in § 4.1), the latter two would be somewhat more challenging to implement.

We consider incremental parsing as a function taking the changed source and the original parse tree as input. In practice incremental parsing could hardly be constructed in this way as we still need to at least scan the source, which takes $O(n)$ time. It is more often that the incremental transformation takes the *change* directly as input [40], which is better formalised as *delta lenses* [41,42] or *edit lenses* [43].

Multiple Equitable Views. Foster BX inherently prefers one view over the other(s), which is acceptable for any framework with a clear baseline artefact and ones derived from it. However, there are cases when we want to continuously maintain relations among several views of the same "importance", and that is where we switch to Meertens BX. Imagine an IDE-enabled textual DSL with a built-in pretty-printing functionality. In that case, we have Str which is being edited by the user, whose typing actions can be mapped to incremental transformations on Ptr, since the grammar is known to the tool. However, an automated pretty-printing feature is a mapping from Cst to Ptr. In both cases we would like to retain the information present the the "pre-transformation" state of both Cst and Ptr entities, for the sake of optimisation (incremental parsing makes IDE much more responsive) and usability (a user should be able to pretty-print a fragment of code without destroying the rest of the program).

Correcting Updates. By using Final BX, we can perform correcting updates, where a change in one of the views can trigger a negotiation sequence ultimately resulting in multiple updates possibly at all other views, including the initially changed one. For example, a parse error (e.g., " ' ; ' expected") during incremental parsing may result in a corrective measure being taken (e.g., "insert ' ; '") in order for the parsing to continue [44]. Final BX pushes this change back to the input, so that the error can be corrected at the source, most likely by some kind of user interaction, such as Eclipse's *Quick Fix* feature.

5   Case study

In order to demonstrate the main ideas of this paper, we have prepared an open source prototype available at http://github.com/grammarware/bx-parsing. This section will introduce it briefly, all interested readers are invited to investigate the code, illustrations and documentation at the repository. The language for the implementation is Rascal [24], which is a one-stop-shop language workbench suitable for rapid prototyping of grammarware, defining data types, specifying program analyses and visualising results. Most figures on pages of this paper were automatically generated by it. All type definitions include a validation and a visualisation function. All types and mappings contain test cases.

The following twelve algebraic data types are defined in our prototype:

- Str — a string;
- Tok — a list of strings;
- TTk — a list of strings non-empty modulo whitespace stripping;
- Lex — a lexical model: left hand side tokens, right hand side tokens; tokens are typed (alphabetic, numeric, special);
- For — a parse forest defined by an ambiguous grammar;
- Ptr — a parse tree with explicit layout;
- Cst — a parse tree with layout discarded;
- Ast — an abstract data type;
- Pic — a multiline string representing a textual drawing;

- Dra — a list of visual elements such as symbols and labels, with coordinates;
- Gra — a hierarchical structure of prefix/infix/confix operators with implicit positioning;
- Dia — an abstract graphical model.

The mappings within the left ("textual") column of Figure 1 are mostly string manipulations on regular language level: since Rascal's default parsing algorithm is GLL, we implemented an explicit DFA tokeniser for Str → Tok; a library function `trim()` is used for Tok → TTk; pattern matching with regular expression-based for TTk → Lex. Going down on the diagram is even easier: Lex → TTk does not rely on the structure of Lex, it just grabs all the tokens from it sequentially; TTk → Tok intercalates tokens with one space between any adjacent ones; Tok → Str uses a standard concatenation function.

In the default setup of Rascal, For → Ptr is called disambiguation and/or filtering [36], and Ptr ⇌ Cst is provided automatically. In order to separate bijective mapping between instances of one equivalent type to another, from the actual adjustments, we defined For, Ptr and Cst with three different grammars. Traditional concrete syntax matching does not work on ambiguous grammars (since the query of the match is also ambiguous), so For → Ptr is the longest and the ugliest of the mappings since it relies on low level constructions. Ptr → Cst is a top-down traversal that matches all layout and reconstructs a tree without it. Cst → Ast is very similar, it traverses a tree and constructs an ADT instance.

In general, Pic → Dra involves some kind of image recognition, and in our prototype indeed we scan the lines of the textual picture to identify elements, and convert them to Dra elements with appropriate coordinates. (Avoiding true image recognition algorithms outweighing illustrative code was one of the reasons we opted for drawing with text instead of pixels). In Dra → Gra we make some assumptions about the structure of the drawing: for example, we expect parenthesis to match.(Parentheses in our textual picture correspond to box containers in pixel visualisations, and the parenthesis matching thus corresponds to checking whether other elements fit inside the box or are placed outside it). Gra ⇌ Dia are m2m transformations between domains of graph models (boxes and arrows) and of function definitions (arguments and expressions).

Horizontal mappings are easier, since one of the main design concerns behind Rascal is EASY [24] parsing and fact extraction. We provide both Ast/Dia bridges (which are not uncommon in modern practice) and Lex/Ast (which are non-existent) bridges. There are several bonus mappings illustrating technological shortcuts, which we will not describe here due to space constraints. For example, there is a Gra → Pic mapping using Rascal string comprehensions to avoid low level coordinates arithmetic.

Now let us consider Ptr ⇌ Dra: a bidirectional mapping between a parse tree and a vector drawing. As we know, a parse tree contains structured information about the instance, including textual indentation; a drawing is similar to that, but contains information about graphical elements comprising the picture. We have prepared several implementations of Ptr ⇌ Dra:

- Reversible.rsc (Def. 1): $\overrightarrow{f}$ is ptr2dra, $\overleftarrow{f}$ is dra2ptr, and a problem with obtaining a valid final or intermediate instance is modelled by throwing an exception. From the tests we can see that $\overleftarrow{f} \circ \overrightarrow{f}$ is not always an identity function, which breaks Eq. 3 — hence, this mapping is reversible, but not bijective.

- Foster.rsc (Def. 2): $\nearrow$ is still ptr2dra, but $\searrow$ is a superposition of dra2ptr on an updated Dra instance and a balancing function that traverses two Ptr instances (the old one and the updated one) and in its result saves all the element information from the new instance with as much as possible from the indentation of the old one. This ensures the GetPut law (Eq. 5). However, this mapping disregards repositioning of graphical elements, which breaks the PutGet law (Eq. 6). Hence, the well-behavedness of the mapping is only preserved if the elements of the vector drawing do not move frome their default locations.

- Meertens.rsc (Def. 3): both $\triangleright$ and $\triangleleft$ implemented in the same way $\searrow$ was explained above — $\triangleright$ traverses two Dra instances and $\triangleleft$ traverses two Ptr instances. There are two lessons to learn here: first, since we have achieved correctness and hippocraticness in all desired scenarios, this is probably the BX that we want to have for Ptr $\rightleftharpoons$ Dra; second, both Dra and Ptr traversals needed to be programmed separately, which leads to duplicated effort and error-proneness.

- Final.rsc (Def. 4): $\blacktriangleright$ and $\blacktriangleleft$ behave similarly to $\triangleright$ and $\triangleleft$ resp., with two major differences: they fix some mistakes in Ptr (referencing undeclared variables) and in Dra (unbalanced brackets). This error recovery is motivated by the fact that the main purpose of bidirectional model transformation is consistency restoration [12]. However, Final BX can also be used to detect certain properties of instances and consistently enforce them at all ends.

The entire prototype is around 3000 lines, well tested and documented.

6   Related Work

Danvy [45] was the first one to propose a type-safe approach to unparsing by using embedded function composition and continuations. More recent research resulted in both embedding of this approach, referred to as string comprehensions, in modern metaprogramming languages [24] and development of the counterpart solution for pattern-driven selective parsing, referred to as "un-unparsing" [46].

Matsuda and Wang [11] propose a way to derive a (simplified) grammar from an unparser specification, which allowed them to focus on unparsing and infer a parser automatically.

Rendel and Ostermann [18] and Duregård and Jansson [16] independently define collections of Haskell ADTs to represent invertible syntax definitions, which can be used together with compatible combinator libraries to infer both parser (with Alex and Happy) and unparsers.

Brabrand et al [15] propose XSugar language that is used to provide a readable non-XML syntactic alternative to XML documents while retaining editability of both instances and preserving schema- conformance on the XML side.

For quasi-oblivious lenses [13], where the put function ignores differences between equivalent concrete arguments, we can say that $\forall x \in L, \forall y \in R, \langle x, y \rangle \in \Psi \Rightarrow x \triangleleft y = \langle x', y \rangle$, where $x \sim x', \langle x', y \rangle \in \Psi$. In general, the vision expressed in this paper, can be conceptually viewed as establishing several equivalence relations specific for the domain of parsing/unparsing. Moreover, our research is not limited to *dictionary lenses* of Bohannon et al [13], since it concerns Final BX (Def. 4) and allows to continue expanding the bidirectional view on *semi-parsing* methods [47], especially Lex $\rightleftharpoons$ Ast mappings that are entirely avoided in the current state of the art.

The distinction we draw between textual, structured and graphical representations on Figure 1 and Figures 2–4, relates to the concept of a technical space [48]. We admit not having enough knowledge to add another column related to ontologies [49] and perhaps other spaces.

Obviously, the landscape of bidirectional model transformation [12] is much broader than just introducing or losing structure. The topics our work is the most close to, are model driven reverse engineering [50,51,52] for the parsing part and an even bigger one of model driven generation for the unparsing part.

7 Concluding Remarks

In this paper, we have considered parsing, unparsing, formatting, pretty-printing, tokenising, syntactic and lexical analyses and other techniques related to mapping between textual, structured data and visual models, from the bidirectional transformation perspective. We have proposed a uniform megamodel (Figure 1) for twelve classes of software artefacts (Figures 2–4) involved in these mappings, and given a number of examples from existing software language processing literature. We were able to find a place for all the mappings that we have considered, even though some explicitly or implicitly "skip" a step. The framework that was introduced, can be used to study such mappings in detail and assess actual contributions, weaknesses and compatibility. For example, with such an approach, we can take a seemingly monolithic Ast $\rightleftharpoons$ Str mapping of Ensō [32] and decompose it in easily comprehensible stages of Str $\rightleftharpoons$ Tok which is bijective because of fixed lexical syntax; Tok $\rightleftharpoons$ Ptr $\rightleftharpoons$ Cst which relies on the Wadler algorithm [5]; and Cst $\rightleftharpoons$ Ast inferred by the authors' own interpreter relying on annotations in Ast specifications ("schemas"). Another example is clear positioning of techniques such as rewriting with layout [34] which provide data structures that work like Cst in some cases and like Ptr in others.

Detailed investigation of lowering/lifting operations deserves much more attention than we could spare within this paper, because these concepts can help us seek, understand and address cases of lost information due to its propagation through the artefacts of Figure 1. We have also not touched upon the very related topic of model synchronisation [53] as a scenario when both bidirectionally linked artefacts change simultaneously, and the system needs to evolve by incorporating both changes on both sides — it would be very interesting to see how the existing methods work on Final BX, especially on their compositionality, which requires termination proofs.

After introducing a megamodel for (un)parsing mappings in § 4, we have explained the difference between general mappings (the ones defined universally, like concatenation) and language-parametric (roughly speaking, the ones requiring a grammar), and presented a case study in § 5. This work will serve as a foundation for us to answer research questions not only like "how to map X to Y, given specifications for all involved syntaxes?", but also like "how to map X to some Y?" and "how to find the best Y to map from X?".

References

1. Aho, A.V., Sethi, R., Ullman, J.D.: Compilers: Principles, Techniques and Tools. Addison-Wesley (1985)
2. Hughes, J.: The Design of a Pretty-printing Library. In: AFP, pp. 53–96 (1995)
3. van den Brand, M.G.J., Visser, E.: Generation of Formatters for Context-Free Languages. ACM TOSEM 5(1), 1–41 (1996)
4. Ruckert, M.: Conservative Pretty-Printing. SIGPLAN Notices 23(2), 39–44 (1996)
5. Wadler, P.: A Prettier Printer (1997), http://homepages.inf.ed.ac.uk/wadler/papers/prettier/prettier.pdf
6. de Jonge, M.: Pretty-Printing for Software Reengineering. In: ICSM. IEEE (2002)
7. van den Brand, M.G.J., Kooiker, A.T., Veerman, N.P., Vinju, J.J.: An Architecture for Context-sensitive Formatting. In: ICSM 2005 (2005)
8. Arnoldus, B., van den Brand, M., Serebrenik, A.: Less is More: Unparser-Completeness of Metalanguages for Template Engines. In: GPCE, pp. 137–146 (2011)
9. Bagge, A.H., Hasu, T.: A Pretty Good Formatting Pipeline. In: Erwig, M., Paige, R.F., Van Wyk, E. (eds.) SLE 2013. LNCS, vol. 8225, pp. 177–196. Springer, Heidelberg (2013)
10. Danielsson, N.A.: Correct-by-construction Pretty-printing. In: DTP. ACM (2013)
11. Matsuda, K., Wang, M.: FliPpr: A Prettier Invertible Printing System. In: Felleisen, M., Gardner, P. (eds.) ESOP 2013. LNCS, vol. 7792, pp. 101–120. Springer, Heidelberg (2013)
12. Stevens, P.: A Landscape of Bidirectional Model Transformations. In: Lämmel, R., Visser, J., Saraiva, J. (eds.) GTTSE 2007. LNCS, vol. 5235, pp. 408–424. Springer, Heidelberg (2008)
13. Bohannon, A., Foster, J.N., Pierce, B.C., Pilkiewicz, A., Schmitt, A.: Boomerang: Resourceful Lenses for String Data. In: POPL 2008, pp. 407–419. ACM (2008)
14. Zaytsev, V.: The Grammar Hammer of 2012. ACM CoRR 1212.4446, 1–32 (2012)
15. Brabrand, C., Møller, A.: Dual Syntax for XML Languages. In: Bierman, G., Koch, C. (eds.) DBPL 2005. LNCS, vol. 3774, pp. 27–41. Springer, Heidelberg (2005)
16. Duregård, J., Jansson, P.: Embedded Parser Generators. In: Haskell. ACM (2011)
17. Boulton, R.: Syn: A Single Language for Specifying Abstract Syntax Trees, Lexical Analysis, Parsing and Pretty-printing. University of Cambridge (1996)
18. Rendel, T., Ostermann, K.: Invertible Syntax Descriptions: Unifying Parsing and Pretty Printing. In: Haskell 2010, pp. 1–12. ACM (2010)

19. de Jonge, M., Visser, E.: An Algorithm for Layout Preservation in Refactoring Transformations. In: Sloane, A., Aßmann, U. (eds.) SLE 2011. LNCS, vol. 6940, pp. 40–59. Springer, Heidelberg (2012)
20. Zaytsev, V.: Case Studies in Bidirectionalisation. In: TFP 2014, pp. 51–58 (2014)
21. Bagge, A.H., Zaytsev, V.: Workshop on Open and Original Problems in Software Language Engineering. In: WCRE 2013, pp. 493–494. IEEE (2013)
22. Foster, J.N., Greenwald, M.B., Moore, J.T., Pierce, B.C., Schmitt, A.: Combinators for Bidirectional Tree Transformations: A Linguistic Approach to the View-Update Problem. ACM TOPLAS 29 (May 2007)
23. Czarnecki, K., Foster, J.N., Hu, Z., Lämmel, R., Schürr, A., Terwilliger, J.F.: Bidirectional Transformations: A Cross-Discipline Perspective. In: Paige, R.F. (ed.) ICMT 2009. LNCS, vol. 5563, pp. 260–283. Springer, Heidelberg (2009)
24. Klint, P., van der Storm, T., Vinju, J.: EASY Meta-programming with Rascal. In: Fernandes, J.M., Lämmel, R., Visser, J., Saraiva, J. (eds.) GTTSE 2009. LNCS, vol. 6491, pp. 222–289. Springer, Heidelberg (2011)
25. McCarthy, J.: The Inversion of Functions Defined by Turing Machines. In: Automata Studies, pp. 177–181 (1956)
26. Meertens, L.: Designing Constraint Maintainers for User Interaction (June 1998)
27. Richter, H.: Noncorrecting Syntax Error Recovery. ACM TOPLAS 7(3), 478–489 (1985)
28. Cox, A., Clarke, C.: Syntactic Approximation Using Iterative Lexical Analysis. In: IWPC 2003, pp. 154–163 (2003)
29. Murphy, G.C., Notkin, D.: Lightweight Lexical Source Model Extraction. ACM TOSEM 5(3), 262–292 (1996)
30. Zarwin, Z., Sottet, J.S., Favre, J.M.: Natural Modeling: Retrospective and Perspectives an Anthropological Point of View. In: XM 2012, pp. 3–8. ACM (2012)
31. Johnson, S.C.: YACC—Yet Another Compiler Compiler. Computer Science Technical Report 32, AT&T Bell Laboratories (1975)
32. van der Storm, T., Cook, W.R., Loh, A.: The Design and Implementation of Object Grammars. SCP (2014)
33. Wile, D.S.: Abstract Syntax from Concrete Syntax. In: ICSE. ACM (1997)
34. van den Brand, M.G.J., Vinju, J.J.: Rewriting with Layout. In: RULE (2000)
35. Bravenboer, M., Kalleberg, K.T., Vermaas, R., Visser, E.: Stratego/XT 0.17. A Language and Toolset for Program Transformation. SCP 72(1-2), 52–70 (2008)
36. Basten, H.J.S., Vinju, J.J.: Faster Ambiguity Detection by Grammar Filtering. In: LDTA (2010)
37. Erdweg, S., Rendel, T., Kästner, C., Ostermann, K.: Layout-Sensitive Generalized Parsing. In: Czarnecki, K., Hedin, G. (eds.) SLE 2012. LNCS, vol. 7745, pp. 244–263. Springer, Heidelberg (2013)
38. Salomon, D.J., Cormack, G.V.: Scannerless NSLR(1) Parsing of Programming Languages. In: PLDI 1989, pp. 170–178. ACM (1989)
39. Völter, M., Benz, S., Dietrich, C., Engelmann, B., Helander, M., Kats, L.C.L., Visser, E., Wachsmuth, G.: DSL Engineering. dslbook.org (2013)
40. Wang, M., Gibbons, J., Wu, N.: Incremental Updates for Efficient Bidirectional Transformations. In: ICFP 2011, pp. 392–403. ACM (2011)
41. Diskin, Z., Xiong, Y., Czarnecki, K.: From State- to Delta-Based Bidirectional Model Transformations: The Asymmetric Case. JOT 10, 1–25 (2011)
42. Diskin, Z., Xiong, Y., Czarnecki, K., Ehrig, H., Hermann, F., Orejas, F.: From State- to Delta-Based Bidirectional Model Transformations: The Symmetric Case. In: Whittle, J., Clark, T., Kühne, T. (eds.) MODELS 2011. LNCS, vol. 6981, pp. 304–318. Springer, Heidelberg (2011)

43. Hofmann, M., Pierce, B., Wagner, D.: Edit Lenses. In: POPL. ACM (2012)
44. de Jonge, M., Kats, L.C.L., Visser, E., Söderberg, E.: Natural and Flexible Error Recovery for Generated Modular Language Environments. ACM TOPLAS 34(4), 15:1–15:50 (2012)
45. Danvy, O.: Functional unparsing. JFP 8(6) (1998) 621–625
46. Asai, K., Kiselyov, O., Shan, C.-C.: Functional un|unparsing. Higher-Order and Symbolic Computation 24(4), 311–340 (2011)
47. Zaytsev, V.: Formal Foundations for Semi-parsing. In: CSMR-WCRE (2014)
48. Bézivin, J., Kurtev, I.: Model-based Technology Integration with the Technical Space Concept. In: MIS. Springer (2005)
49. Parreiras, F.S., Staab, S., Winter, A.: On Marrying Ontological and Metamodeling Technical Spaces. In: ESEC-FSE, pp. 439–448. ACM (2007)
50. Bruneliére, H., Cabot, J., Jouault, F., Madiot, F.: MoDisco: A Generic and Extensible Framework for Model Driven Reverse Engineering. In: ASE (2010)
51. Ramón, Ó.S., Cuadrado, J.S., Molina, J.G.: Model-driven Reverse Engineering of Legacy Graphical User Interfaces. In: ASE, pp. 147–150. ACM (2010)
52. Rugaber, S., Stirewalt, K.: Model-Driven Reverse Engineering. IEEE Software 21(4), 45–53 (2004)
53. Diskin, Z.: Algebraic Models for Bidirectional Model Synchronization. In: Czarnecki, K., Ober, I., Bruel, J.-M., Uhl, A., Völter, M. (eds.) MODELS 2008. LNCS, vol. 5301, pp. 21–36. Springer, Heidelberg (2008)

Streaming Model Transformations
By Complex Event Processing*

István Dávid[1], István Ráth[1], and Dániel Varró[1,2,3]

[1] Budapest University of Technology and Economics,
Department of Measurement and Information Systems,
Magyar tudósok krt. 2., 1117 Budapest, Hungary
davidi@inf.mit.bme.hu, {rath,varro}@mit.bme.hu
[2] DIRO, Université de Montréal, Canada
[3] MSDL, Dept. of Computer Science, McGill University, Montréal, Canada

Abstract. Streaming model transformations represent a novel class of
transformations dealing with models whose elements are continuously
produced or modified by a background process [1]. Executing streaming
transformations requires efficient techniques to recognize the activated
transformation rules on a potentially infinite input stream. Detecting a
series of events triggered by compound structural changes is especially
challenging for a high volume of rapid modifications, a characteristic of
an emerging class of applications built on runtime models.

In this paper, we propose a novel approach for streaming model transformations by combining incremental model query techniques with complex event processing (CEP) and reactive (event-driven) transformations.
The event stream is automatically populated from elementary model
changes by the incremental query engine, and the CEP engine is used
to identify complex event combinations, which are used to trigger the
execution of transformation rules. We demonstrate our approach in the
context of automated gesture recognition over live models populated by
KINECT sensor data.

Keywords: Streaming model transformations, complex event processing, live models, change-driven transformations.

1   Introduction

Scalability of models, queries and transformations is a key challenge in model-
driven engineering to handle complex industrial domains such as automotive,
avionics, cyber-physical systems or ubiquitous computing. The maintenance and
manipulation of large models identifies unique scenarios addressed by a novel
class of model transformations (MT) to overcome the limitations or extend the
capabilities of traditional (batch or incremental) MT approaches.

Change-driven transformations [2] consume or produce changes of source and
target models as their input or output models to enable transformations over

---

* This work was partially supported by the CERTIMOT (ERC_HU-09-01-2010-0003)
and MONDO (EU ICT-611125) projects partly during the third author's sabbatical.

J. Dingel et al. (Eds.): MODELS 2014, LNCS 8767, pp. 68–83, 2014.

partially materialized models and to reduce traceability information. Streaming transformations are defined [1] as a "special kind of transformation in which the whole input model is not completely available at the beginning of the transformation, but it is continuously generated." An additional class of streaming transformations aims to tackle huge models by feeding a transformation process incrementally (keeping only a part of the model in memory at any time).

In the current paper, we identify and address a novel class of streaming transformations for live models where the models themselves are not necessarily huge or infinite, but they change or evolve at a very fast rate (for instance, 25 times per second), and it is the stream of model changes that requires efficient processing. We propose a novel technique for streaming transformations to process these event streams in order to identify a complex series of events and then execute model transformations over them in a reactive way.

Our contribution includes a domain-specific event processing language for defining atomic events classes (from elementary or compound model changes using change patterns [2]) and combining these events into complex patterns of events. We also propose a general, model-based complex event processing architecture with a prototype engine VIATRA-CEP to process rapidly evolving event streams. We also include an initial scalability assessment of the framework on a live model transformation scenario.

Our approach keeps the advantages of change-driven transformation as models can be partially materialized, since the processed event stream carries over only few relevant contextual model elements but not the models themselves. Instead, incremental model queries observe the model and publish relevant structural changes as atomic events in an event stream. Then this stream is processed by integrating known techniques from *complex event processing* (CEP) [3] to identify and handle a complex series of events.

In the rest of the paper, in Section 2, we introduce a case study of gesture recognition over live models used as a running example. The core ideas of our approach are presented in Section 3 while Section 4 presents an integrated tool set as a proof-of-concept. We carry out an initial performance of the approach in Section 5. Finally, related approaches and tools are described in Section 6 and Section 7 concludes our paper.

2   Case Study: Gesture Recognition by Live Models

Our approach will be demonstrated on a gesture recognition case study. The use case is based on our preliminary work [4], presented earlier at EclipseCon Europe 2012, but without using the framework described in this paper.

In the case study, a human body is observed by optical sensors. The stream of data from the sensors (Microsoft KINECT [5] in our case) carries the spatial position of the hands, wrists, knees, etc. This stream is continuously processed and its data is stored in a *live model*, technically, an EMF model maintained via a Java based API [6]. Every time the optical sensors capture a new frame, the model is updated with the appropriate spatial data. The sensors process 25 frames per second, resulting in 25 model update transactions each second. The complexity of the scenario arises from the frequent changes the model undergoes. Executing model transformations on such a model poses several problems, since it would become obsolete quickly after being loaded into the memory. Moreover, model update transactions affect multiple model elements.

Figure 1 shows an excerpt from the domain metamodel [6], containing the head and the right arm. Similar metamodel elements describe the other three limbs of the body.

In this case study, we aim at recognizing a gesture in order to control a PowerPoint presentation with it. On the recognized gesture, the presentation advances to the next slide, therefore the gesture is referred to as the *forward gesture*. In our presentation [4] there is also a *backward gesture* to move back to the previous slide.

As illustrated in Figure 2, the *forward gesture* consists of two postures: the *forward start* and the *forward end*. To recognize the gesture, the series of these two postures needs to be identified. Postures are considered as certain *states* of the body, which are de-

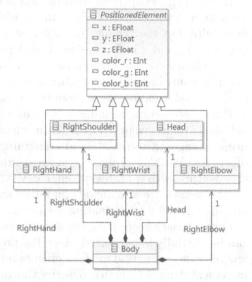

Fig. 1. Excerpt from the domain metamodel [6]

scribed with a *range* or interval of spatial data. For example, the *forward start* posture is defined by the right arm being approximately stretched roughly to the height of the shoulder. Determining whether the arm is stretched is achieved by continuously measuring the angle between the upper and lower arm and smoothing the resulting stream of spatial data by a moving average transformation [7].

Processing a series of postures could be interpreted as a state machine, in which the states represent postures and transitions are triggered if a body leaves the valid range of the state and enters another. For instance, the body initiates the *forward start* posture by first entering the posture (*forward start found*), then leaving it (*forward start lost*) after a certain amount of time.

3   Overview of the Approach

First, in Section 3.1, we provide a taxonomy (illustrated in Figure 3) on structural model changes and events (Section 3.1). In Section 3.2 we propose a novel approach for modeling and processing these changes as complex events in order to support streaming transformations. In Section 3.3, the detection of complex event processing is briefly discussed.

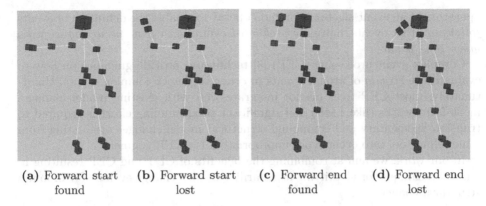

(a) Forward start   (b) Forward start   (c) Forward end   (d) Forward end
found   lost   found   lost

Fig. 2. Body postures with the key context of the human body highlighted

3.1 A Taxonomy of Structural Model Changes

Elementary and compound structural model changes. We define *elementary* changes as the most basic modifications applied on the model which cannot be refined into multiple modification steps. For example, in the case study in Section 2, such an elementary change would be moving the body's right hand on the x-axis, since it would require changing only one attribute of a `PositionedElement`. (See Figure 1.) Elementary model changes in this case are handled by the Eclipse Modeling Framework (EMF) [8] and its notifier/adapter techniques enabled by the EMF Notification API.

On the other hand, *compound* changes consist of multiple elementary changes between two states (snapshots) of the model (called the pre-state and the post-state). For example, if the whole right arm is moved, the elbow, the wrist and the hand are moved consequently, i.e. the change affects multiple model elements. The techniques of change-driven transformations (CDT) [2] are capable of identifying compound structural changes by using *change patterns* [2,9,10]. Change patterns observe the delta between the pre-state and the post-state irrespective of how those states were reached, thus they abstract from the actual trajectories in the state space.

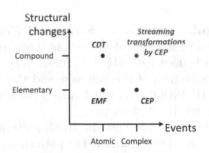

Fig. 3. Structural changes vs. events

Atomic and Complex Events. In our work, we consider both atomic and compound structural changes as *atomic events* in the event stream. This setup allows the use of events of different granularity. An atomic event is specified by its *type*, a set of model elements passed as *parameters* and a *timestamp*. Complex events are built up from sequences of atomic events and other complex events, using operators of an event algebra. Common operators enable the definition of events *following* other events, mutually *prohibited* events, or events *occurring within a given time window*.

Complex event processing (CEP) [3] techniques provide guidance on how to evaluate the stream of atomic events in order to detect complex events. Unfortunately, most CEP tools do not integrate well with existing model management frameworks (like EMF) and significant programming effort is required to translate elementary and compound structural model changes originating from a modeling tool into event types appropriate for a CEP engine.

In our work, we aim at combining the benefits of CDT and CEP resulting in a novel technique for identifying arbitrarily complex change events of compound structural changes.

3.2 Structural Changes, Events and Streaming Transformations

In this section, we demonstrate how streaming transformations can be defined by building upon well-established model query and transformation languages by elaborating the case study of Section 2. First, model queries will be used to identify the current state of the model and automatically publish notifications on relevant state changes in the form of atomic events. Then these atomic events will be combined into complex events using operators of an event algebra. Finally, we define transformation rules that are activated by a complex event.

Model Queries for Structural Constraints. Model queries capture structural constraints of a model. In this paper, we employ the graph pattern language IQPL used by EMF-INCQUERY [11]. This choice is motivated by the high expressiveness of the language and the incremental query evaluation strategy of EMF-INCQUERY, which allows the sending of notifications upon the change of the result set of queries.

Listing 1 presents the graph pattern depicting the *Forward start* posture, as presented in Figure 2a. The pattern is parameterized with the spatial data of the right arm (consisting of the right hand, the right elbow and the right shoulder); the head; and the body the previous parts belong to. Accordingly, joins over the model are defined to describe this relationship in Lines 8-11. The *Forward start* posture requires a stretched right arm to be detected, but the arm shall not be held higher than head level (see Lines 13-14 and 16-17, respectively).

The latter one is a negative pattern call, which prohibits the occurrence of the `rightHandAboveHead` pattern presented in Listing 2. The pattern compares the spatial coordinates of the right hand and the head by their y coordinate. In Lines 8-9, the y coordinate of the right hand and the head is bound to the `RHy` and `Hy` variables, respectively. The variables are evaluated in a *check* block in Lines 11-18 by invoking a Java based `MovingAverageCalculator` using Xbase syntax [12]. The details of the `rightHandAboveHead` pattern are omitted for space consideration.

```
 1 pattern ForwardStart(              1 pattern rightHandAboveHead(
 2 B: Body,                           2 B: Body,
 3 RH: RightHand,                     3 RH: RightHand,
 4 RE: RightElbow,                    4 H: Head)
 5 RS: RightShoulder,                 5 {
 6 H: Head)                           6 Body.RightHand(B, RH);
 7 {                                  7 Body.Head(B, H);
 8 Body.Head(B, H);                   8 RightHand.y(RH,RHy);
 9 Body.RightHand(B, RH);             9 Head.y(H,Hy);
10 Body.RightElbow(B, RE);           10
11 Body.RightShoulder(B, RS);        11 check(
12                                   12 MovingAverageCalculator::
13 find                             13 getCalculator("HY").
14 stretchedRightArm(B, RH, RE, RS);  14 addValue(Hy).movingAvg <
15                                   15 MovingAverageCalculator::
16 neg find                         16 getCalculator("RHY").
17 rightHandAboveHead(B, RH, H);    17 addValue(RHy).movingAvg
18                                   18 );
19 }                                19 }
```

Listing 1. ForwardStart posture   **Listing 2.** rightHandAboveHead

Defining Atomic Events. In order to define atomic events, we propose an event processing language called the VIATRA-CEP Event Processing Language (VEPL). We built upon the result set of model queries to identify relevant structural changes, i.e. we identify when a new match is found for a model query or when an existing match is lost. These compound changes constitute the atomic events in our approach. Formally, an atomic event is specified as $a = (t, \mathcal{P}, d)$ where $a.t$ denotes the type, $a.\mathcal{P}$ is a list of parameters and $a.d$ is a timestamp of the event.

```
 1 IQPatternEvent ForwardStartFound(B: Body)
 2 {
 3     iqPatternRef:
 4         ForwardStart(B, _RH, _RE, _RS, _H)
 5     iqChangeType:
 6         NEW_MATCH_FOUND
 7 }
 8
 9 IQPatternEvent ForwardStartLost(B: Body)
10 {
11     iqPatternRef:
12         ForwardStart(B, _RH, _RE, _RS, _H)
13     iqChangeType:
14         EXISTING_MATCH_LOST
15 }
```

Listing 3. Atomic event types

Listing 3 presents two atomic events reusing the graph pattern from Listing 1. Pattern FSFound describes the event when the *Forward start* posture is found (Figure 2a), while pattern FSLost describes the event when the *Forward start* posture is lost (Figure 2b).

Both atomic events are parameterized with a Body parameter (Line 1, Line 8), evaluated at execution time. This enables collecting atomic events per body, i.e. to distinguish between atomic events based on their source.

Referring to IQPL patterns is a special feature of our language aiming to seamlessly integrate a language for graph patterns with a language for event patterns in VEPL. This reference to the IQPL pattern is supported by the iqPatternRef attribute (Line 2-3, Line 9-10). The parameter list after the IQPL pattern reuses the input parameter (B: Body). The other parameters are not specified, as designated by their names augmented with an underscore character. (A notation similar to Prolog's anonymous predicates.) Two similar atomic events describe the cases in which the *Forward end* posture is found and lost.

Defining Complex Events. In the next step, atomic events are combined into a complex event. In Listing 4, the `definition` part contains the constraints for the complex event, consisting of atomic events in this specific case. The atomic events connected with the *ordered* operator (denoted with an arrow). Therefore, this pattern defines a complex event, in which the referred atomic events are observed in the specific order. Since atomic events carry information about the appropriate structural changes, this complex event will occur exactly on the series of postures depicted in Figure 2. The input parameter of the complex event (`B: Body`) and its usage in the `definition` part ensures that only atomic events originating from the same body are combined in a single complex event instance.

```
1  ComplexEvent ForwardGesture(B: Body){
2      definition : ForwardStartFound(B) -> ForwardStartLost(B)
3                      -> ForwardEndFound(B) -> ForwardEndLost(B)
4  }
```

Listing 4. A complex event pattern reusing atomic events from Listing 3

Complex events are built up from sequences of atomic events and other complex events, using operators of an event algebra. The event algebra of the VEPL language offers three *operators* to formalize complex event patterns: the *ordered*, the *unordered* and the *timewindow* operator. The **ordered** operator (o) prescribes strict ordering between the events the complex event pattern consists of. The **unordered** operator (u) allows the corresponding atomic events to occur in arbitrary order. The **timewindow** operator defines an upper limit for the complex event to be detected, starting from the first atomic event observed in the particular complex event pattern.

Formally, a complex event pattern C is built inductively from a set $\mathcal{A}$ of atomic events using three operators $\{o, u, tw\}$ as follows:

- **Atomic events:** Every atomic event a is a complex event $e \in C$.
- **Ordered operator:** If c_1 and c_2 are complex events then $o(c_1, c_2)$ is a complex event
- **Unordered operator:** If c_1 and c_2 are complex events then $u(c_1, c_2)$ is a complex event
- **Timewindow operator:** If c is a complex event and d is a timestamp then $tw(c, d)$ is a complex event

A complex event pattern C is evaluated against a timestamp ordered stream of observed events denoted as $\vec{E}_0^n : e_0 \ldots e_n$ with $e_i = (t_i, P_i, d_i)$ and $\forall j > i : d_j > d_i$. Initially, all e_i are atomic event instances. However, during evaluation, when a complex event instance c_j is detected after processing event e_i, then c_j is inserted into the stream (with d_i as the timestamp of the detection) to allow the detection of depending complex events later. The semantics of the operators in the event algebra is defined as follows:

- **Ordered operator:** $\vec{E}_0^n \models \mathfrak{o}(c_1, c_2)$ iff two events with types corresponding to c_1 and c_2 are present in the stream in the given order with the same parameter binding, i.e. $\exists i, j : c_1.t = e_i.t \wedge c_2.t = e_j.t \wedge e_j.d > e_i.d \wedge e_i.\sigma(P_i) = e_j.\sigma(P_j)$. The timestamp of $\mathfrak{o}(c_1, c_2)$ becomes $e_j.d$.
- **Unordered operator:** $\vec{E}_0^n \models \mathfrak{u}(c_1, c_2)$ iff both c_1 and c_2 are present in stream in an arbitrary order $\vec{E}_0^n \models \mathfrak{o}(c_1, c_2)$ or $\vec{E}_0^n \models \mathfrak{o}(c_2, c_1)$; The timestamp of $\mathfrak{o}(c_1, c_2)$ is $max(e_i.d, e_j.d)$.
- **Timewindow operator:** $\vec{E}_0^n \models \mathfrak{w}(c_1, d_1)$ iff exists an event e_i in the stream with timestamp value less then d_1, i.e. $\exists i : c_1.t = e_i.t \wedge e_j.d < d_1$.

Defining Transformation Rules. As the final step to our approach, the actual streaming transformations are defined. VEPL enables defining model transformations and organizing them into rules guarded by the previously defined complex event patterns. In principle, an arbitrary transformation language can be used as an action language (e.g. Xtend as in our example). All variables are bound when the trigger event is instantiated are accessible in the action part. Listing 5 shows a rule containing a model transformation which executes the action defined within the **action** block on the appearance of the **ForwardGesture** pattern, referenced in the **event** block.

```
1  Rule transactionRule {
2      event : ForwardGesture(B: Body)
3      action {
4          //acquiring the complex event
5          val observedComplexEvent = activation.observableEventPattern
6          //extracting the parameter
7          val body = observedComplexEvent.B
8          // additional operation to be executed
9      }
10 }
```

Listing 5. A streaming transformation rule

3.3 Detecting Complex Events

The event processing algebra, its operators and logical structures are mapped to a *deterministic finite automaton* (DFA) based representation, to keep track of partially and fully matched complex event patterns. As highlighted in Figure 4, exactly one automaton is generated for every complex event pattern at compile time. *States* in the automaton represent the relevant phases of detecting the complex event pattern, i.e. the different states of the pattern matching process. *Transitions* of the automaton identify how the matching process can evolve from one state to another in accordance with the operators used in the complex event pattern and the triggering event.

During execution time, *tokens* represent the (partial or complete) complex event pattern *instances* which are stored in the states of the automaton. If there is a token at a state of the DFA, and the next event in the event stream corresponds to the trigger event of an outgoing transition, then the token is passed along the

transition to the next state, thus the
detection of the complex event enters
a new phase. There may be multiple
tokens flowing in the same automaton at a time since the next event in
the stream may contribute to different
parts of the same complex event pattern according to its context. When a
complex event is detected, a new complex event instance is placed to the
event stream with corresponding type
and timestamp.

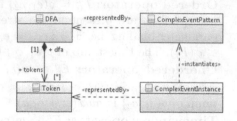

Fig. 4. Mapping between complex event
patterns and the semantic model

Event processing contexts specify constraints on how occurrences may be selected when looking for occurrence patterns that match the operator semantics
[13]. Due to space restrictions, the reader is referred to [14] for the details of
complex event pattern detection in VEPL. There we also prove that the automaton representing the detection cycle of complex events is always finite and
deterministic.

4 Architecture and Use of the Prototype Tooling

In this section, we give an overview of the technological aspects and the tooling
of our approach. First, in Section 4.1 we present an architecture and a prototype
tool VIATRA-CEP[1] for processing complex events and supporting streaming
transformations. We also present the tool in action along a sample execution
scenario of our case study in Section 4.2.

4.1 Architectural Overview

Figure 5 presents the architecture of our streaming transformation framework.
The *Model* is continuously queried by an *Incremental query engine* with queries
that are defined using the *Query language*. This enables not only to efficiently
obtain the match sets of a query, but it also continuously tracks changes of the
model.

Changes in the model are continuously propagated to the query engine through
a notification API, where callback functions can be registered to instance model elements that receive notification objects (e.g. ADD, REMOVE, SET etc.) when an
elementary model manipulation is carried out. The framework internally stores
and maintains the partial pattern matches as notifications arrive.

As a query evaluates successfully, it produces a tuple of elements as the match
set. This data is wrapped into atomic *change events* and published on the *Event
stream*. The *Event stream* is continuously processed by a reactive *Rule engine*,
which handles the triggering of the predefined model transformations.

---

[1] https://incquery.net/publications/viatra-cep

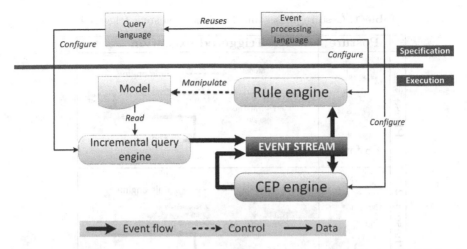

Fig. 5. Conceptual overview of the approach with our key contributions highlighted

In order to activate streaming transformation rules guarded by complex event patterns, the *Event stream* is also processed by a *CEP engine*. The engine continuously evaluates the complex event patterns based on the processed atomic events. If a complex event pattern is matched, a complex event instance is generated, published on the event stream and eventually processed by the Rule engine, which would trigger the appropriate model transformation.

In our prototype tool, a dedicated general purpose CEP engine (called VIATRA-CEP) was developed to support the VEPL language. However, the architecture can also incorporate the integration of an external CEP engine (such as ESPER [15]) as demonstrated in our preliminary work [4]. The case studies in [4] highlighted that significant programming overhead is required to translate structural changes to appropriate events and define complex event patterns accordingly, which requires further investigations. Our VIATRA-CEP prototype seamlessly integrates with advanced EMF-related technologies such as EMF models, the EMF-INCQUERY framework [11] for incremental queries and existing transformation languages and tools.

4.2 Sample Execution of the Case Study

Table 1 summarizes the execution steps triggered by four consecutive snapshots of the forward gesture.

- **Phase #1.** The *ForwardStart* pattern (Listing 1) is found *(1)* in the model by the query engine. This results in a new tuple of model elements as a match set, which data is wrapped into an atomic event by the query engine and passed to the event stream *(2)*. In *Step (3a)* the Rule engine processes the atomic event and if a transformation rule is activated, the appropriate transformation gets executed. However, since no transformation rules are associated with event *ForwardStart*, no transformation rules are activated

Table 1. Gesture phases and the execution steps triggered

at this point. In *Step (3b)* the CEP engine processes the atomic event as well and updates the complex event candidates, i.e. the partially matched complex events.

– **Phase #2 and #3.** In the next phase, we detect that a match of the *ForwardStart* pattern is lost. The same steps are executed as above, only this time an atomic event of type *ForwardStartLost* is published on the event stream and processed by the Rule engine and the CEP engine. In Phase #3, a *ForwardEndFound* atomic event is identified and placed on the stream.

- **Phase #4.** The *ForwardEnd* pattern is lost and a *ForwardEndLost* atomic event is published on the event stream consequently. Now there will be additional steps triggered after *Step (3b)*. After having processed the *ForwardEndLost* atomic event, the CEP engine detects the *ForwardGesture* complex event, instantiates the appropriate complex event instance consequently and publishes it on the event stream *Step (4)*. In *Step (5)* the Rule engine processes the complex event and checks for activated transformation rules. The rule defined in Listing 5 will be activated and the appropriate action will be executed in *Step (6)*.

5   Evaluation

To estimate the performance and scalability of our tool, we had to design a semi-synthetic benchmark based on the use case of Section 2. The reason for this is that Microsoft KINECT can only detect at most two bodies, and the refresh rate is a fixed 25 frames per second (FPS), which is easily processed by our CEP engine.

Evaluation Setup. The core of the simulation is a previously recorded real execution sequence in which the right arm is rotated. A full arm cycle consists of 12 positions, i.e. 12 frames. Every cycle yields exactly one *Forward gesture* (Figure 2) composed of the sequence of 4 atomic events; and every cycle also yields two atomic events considered as noise. This makes 6 atomic events generated for each cycle.

Our simulations aim at stress testing our CEP prototype, which is carried out by multiplying this sequence along a different number of bodies in the model. This part of the benchmark scenario is artificial in the sense that KINECT can handle at most two bodies, but the actual positions of the bodies remain realistic.

After starting the simulations, we primarily measure the *number of detected complex events per second*. From this rate, we calculate the effective processing rate (i.e. the theoretical upper limit) of the CEP engine measured in *frames per second* (FPS). This value is compared to the original FPS rate of the KINECT sensor. We continue increasing the number of bodies up to the point when the processing rate is greater than the recording rate.

Summary of Results. Table 6 summarizes our results. Rows represent the individual measurements with respect to the increasing number of bodies *Body count*. The next two columns present the throughput of *complex events* (1/s) and *atomic events* (1/s), respectively. The latter is calculated from the former, since for every complex event to be detected, 6 atomic events are observed (as discussed above). The number of *atomic events in the model* denotes how many atomic events are triggered by elementary or compound model changes *per cycle*, i.e. while the right arm makes a circle. This is the number of atomic events *required* to be processed in order to achieve the frames-per-second (FPS) ratio the KINECT sensors work with. Finally, *processing speed* summarizes the FPS of our prototype compared to the basic FPS value of KINECT (25). This value is calculated as the ratio of the *Atomic event throughput* and the *Atomic events in the model*. This ratio is acceptable if it is above 1, otherwise the processing rate of complex events falls short to the data production rate of the KINECT sensor.

Body count	Complex event throughput	Atomic event throughput	Atomic events in the model	Processing speed
#	[1/sec]	[1/sec]	[1/cycle]	[x 25 FPS]
1	69.041	414.248	6	69.041
2	63.458	380.749	12	31.729
4	66.094	396.562	24	16.523
8	41.907	251.442	48	5.238
16	35.003	210.017	96	2.188
24	24.220	145.322	144	1.009
25	20.611	123.664	150	0.824

Fig. 6. Throughput and the highest processing speed

As a summary, our measurements show that our approach scales up to 24 bodies in the model (the lowest processing speed above 1) at 25×1.009 FPS. In order to interpret this value, we need to recall that one body consists of 20 control points each of them containing 6 attributes (see *PositionedElements* in Figure 1), from which 2 are actually modified in the simulations. Therefore, for each body, 40 elementary model changes are triggered in every frame (assuming that the limbs are not reattached to different bodies).

Handling 24 bodies at a rate of 25×1.009 FPS yields approximately 24000 complex events per second. Based on our measurements (which were carried out using a 2.9GHz CPU), we conclude that our proof-of-concept implementation offers promising performance and scalability while it integrates smoothly with Eclipse based tooling. It should be noted, however, that because of the rather simple movement profile (only a few coordinates are manipulated), the results cannot be trivially extrapolated for data streams of real KINECT devices.

6   Related Work

We give an overview of various approaches related to our work.

Streaming Model Transformations. In [1] the authors present streaming transformations working on a stream of model fragments and elements. In contrast to this technique, our approach leverages derived information regarding the model in the form of change events, which decouples the execution from the actual model. Consequently, the issues discussed in [1] (e.g. dealing with references among model elements and transformation scheduling) are not present in our case.

The concept of change-driven transformations is proposed in [2] for executing transformations on change models as input or output. Our approach extends this approach since identifying complex model changes enables CDTs of higher granularity and also enables the integration of complex event processing. Live models used in the current paper are different from living models [9], while the change pattern formalism is reused from [2] while similar formalisms were proposed in [9,10]. A formal foundation of infinite models is presented in [16] by redefining OCL operators over infinite collections. This is complementary problem as the models themselves are finite in our case, but their lifeline is infinite due to high frequency model changes.

Complex Event Processing. ESPER [15] is an open source event processing engine. It has been employed in our preliminary work [4], presented at the EclipseCon Europe 2012. Despite being a high-end CEP engine concerning its performance and the descriptive power of its language, supporting the scenarios like those presented in [1] is cumbersome and infeasible.

Other open CEP engines (e.g. StreamBase, Drools Fusion) can also be considered but integration into an existing MDE tooling remains a significant technical challenge since defining change patterns and feeding model (change) information into the engine requires significant programming effort. The integrated approach presented in this paper (classified as a detection-oriented CEP) overcomes this issue by providing a language supporting directly referencing graph patterns and organizing them into complex event patterns.

Processing Runtime Models. Processing of runtime models may introduce somewhat related challenges. Incremental model transformations are used in [17] for efficient runtime monitoring. Song et al. introduced incremental QVT transformations [18] for runtime models. However, these techniques primarily focus on obtaining a faithful model of the running system, while they do not consider event streams or complex event processing over live models.

Context-aware systems [19] introduce novel challenges for model transformations where not only business-relevant data needs to be processed, but also data from the context or environment of the system. Our approach could be a feasible solution to execute model-transformations in a context-aware fashion, e.g. in cyber-physical systems where environmental data gathered by the sensors could affect the overall transformation process.

7   Conclusions and Future Work

In this paper, we identified and addressed a novel class of streaming transformations [1] for live models where the models themselves are available, but they evolve at a very fast rate (resulting in thousands of changes in every second). Elementary model changes (e.g. EMF notifications) as well as derived compound changes of match sets of change patterns [2] are encapsulated into a stream of atomic events. This event stream is consumed by complex event processing techniques to identify complex series of events (appearing within a timeframe) and execute streaming transformations upon their detection.

We proposed a language built as an extension of an existing query and transformation language with execution semantics, and presented an integrated model-based complex event processing engine VIATRA-CEP to a proof-of-concept prototype. Initial experimental evaluation over a complex gesture recognition case study demonstrates the practical feasibility of our approach.

A main advantage of our framework is that models are not required to be kept in memory during transformation as only the stream of events is processed. Elementary and compound structural changes are first encapsulated into atomic changes by incremental model queries. Atomic events contain only the few relevant contextual model elements required to identify complex events and trigger related transformations for complex event processing. As a result, the time and structural dimension of changes is kept separated both from a conceptual and a tooling viewpoint.

Future Work and Potential Applications. In the future, we plan to apply the framework in various domains. *Models at runtime* (M@RT) [20] aim at representing the prevailing state of the underlying system. Processing streams of changes or change events arising from these models, instead of approaching them with batch or incremental transformations seems to be a natural fit.

Increasing the number of source models might introduce issues regarding the scalability of a transformation engine, especially when *distributed and federated data sources* are required to be handled. Dealing with change events instead of keeping model fragments from different models in memory, may significantly simplify this task.

As a primary direction for technical future work, we plan several enhancements to the change pattern modeling language, which currently lacks desirable features, such as branching patterns [21], negative patterns and temporal algebraic structures [22]. We envisage a general *canonical form* of event pattern definitions, which every event pattern could be translated into and would enable optimization steps prior to the execution.

References

1. Sánchez Cuadrado, J., de Lara, J.: Streaming model transformations: Scenarios, challenges and initial solutions. In: Duddy, K., Kappel, G. (eds.) ICMB 2013. LNCS, vol. 7909, pp. 1–16. Springer, Heidelberg (2013)
2. Bergmann, G., Ráth, I., Varró, G., Varró, D.: Change-driven model transformations. change (in) the rule to rule the change. Software and Systems Modeling 11, 431–461 (2012)
3. Luckham, D.C.: The Power of Events: An Introduction to Complex Event Processing in Distributed Enterprise Systems. Addison-Wesley Longman Publishing Co., Inc., Boston (2001)

4. Dávid, I., Ráth, I.: Realtime gesture recognition with Jnect and Esper. Tech demo at EclipseCon Europe (2012), http://incquery.net/incquery/demos/jnect (Accessed: July 1, 2014)
5. Microsoft Corp.: Microsoft Kinect official website, http://www.microsoft.com/en-us/kinectforwindows/ (Accessed: July 1, 2014)
6. Helming, J., Neufeld, E., Koegel, M.: jnect – An Eclipse Plug-In providing a Java Adapter for the Microsoft Kinect SDK, http://code.google.com/a/eclipselabs.org/p/jnect/ (Accessed: July 1, 2014)
7. Box, G., Jenkins, G., Reinsel, G.: Time Series Analysis: Forecasting and Control. Wiley Series in Probability and Statistics. Wiley (2008)
8. Eclipse Foundation: Eclipse Modeling Framework Project (EMF), http://www.eclipse.org/modeling/emf/ (Accessed: July 1, 2014)
9. Breu, R., Agreiter, B., Farwick, M., Felderer, M., Hafner, M., Innerhofer-Oberperfler, F.: Living Models - Ten Principles for Change-Driven Software Engineering. Int. J. Software and Informatics 5(1-2), 267–290 (2011)
10. Yskout, K., Scandariato, R., Joosen, W.: Change patterns: Co-evolving requirements and architecture. Software and Systems Modeling (2012)
11. Ujhelyi, Z., Bergmann, G., Hegedüs, Á., Horváth, Á., Izsó, B., Szatmári, Z., Varró, D.: An Integrated Development Environment for Live Model Queries. Science of Computer Programming (2013)
12. Eclipse Foundation: Xtext 2.6.0 Documentation, http://www.eclipse.org/Xtext/documentation/2.6.0/Xtext%20Documentation.pdf (Accessed: July 1, 2014)
13. Carlson, J.: An Intuitive and Resource-Efficient Event Detection Algebra (2004), http://citeseerx.ist.psu.edu/viewdoc/summary?doi=10.1.1.3.9957 (Accessed: July 1, 2014)
14. Dávid, I.: Complex Event Processin in Model Transformation Systems. Master's thesis, Department of Measurement and Information Systems, Budapest University of Technology and Economics (2013)
15. EsperTech Inc.: Esper Official Website, http://esper.codehaus.org (Accessed: July 1, 2014)
16. Combemale, B., Thirioux, X., Baudry, B.: Formally Defining and Iterating Infinite Models. In: France, R.B., Kazmeier, J., Breu, R., Atkinson, C. (eds.) MODELS 2012. LNCS, vol. 7590, pp. 119–133. Springer, Heidelberg (2012)
17. Vogel, T., Neumann, S., Hildebrandt, S., Giese, H., Becker, B.: Incremental Model Synchronization for Efficient Run-Time Monitoring. In: Ghosh, S. (ed.) MODELS 2009. LNCS, vol. 6002, pp. 124–139. Springer, Heidelberg (2010)
18. Song, H., Huang, G., Chauvel, F., Zhang, W., Sun, Y., Shao, W., Mei, H.: Instant and Incremental QVT Transformation for Runtime Models. In: Whittle, J., Clark, T., Kühne, T. (eds.) MODELS 2011. LNCS, vol. 6981, pp. 273–288. Springer, Heidelberg (2011)
19. Baldauf, M., Dustdar, S., Rosenberg, F.: A Survey on Context-Aware Systems. Int. J. Ad Hoc Ubiquitous Comput. 2(4), 263–277 (2007)
20. Blair, G., Bencomo, N., France, R.: Models@ run.time. Computer 42(10), 22–27 (2009)
21. Ben-Ari, M., Manna, Z., Pnueli, A.: The Temporal Logic of Branching Time. In: Proceedings of the 8th ACM SIGPLAN-SIGACT Symposium on Principles of Programming Languages. POPL 1981, pp. 164–176. ACM, New York (1981)
22. Gabbay, D.M.: Temporal Logic: Mathematical Foundations and Computational Aspects. Clarendon Press, Oxford (1994)

On the Use of Signatures for Source Incremental Model-to-text Transformation

Babajide Ogunyomi, Louis M. Rose, and Dimitrios S. Kolovos

Department of Computer Science, University of York
Deramore Lane, Heslington, York, YO10 5GH, UK
{bjo500,louis.rose,dimitris.kolovos}@york.ac.uk

Abstract. Model-to-text (M2T) transformation is an important model management operation, used to implement code and documentation generation, model serialisation (enabling model interchange), and model visualisation and exploration. Despite the importance of M2T transformation, contemporary M2T transformation languages cannot be used to easily produce transformations that scale well as the size of the input model increases, which limits their applicability in practice. In this paper, we propose an extension to template-based M2T languages that adds support for signatures, lightweight and concise proxies for templates, which are used to reduce the time taken to re-execute a M2T transformation in response to changes to the input model. We report our initial results in applying signatures to two existing M2T transformations, which indicate a reduction of 33-47% in transformation execution time.

1 Introduction

Model-Driven Engineering (MDE) often involves the application of different types of model management operations including model-to-model transformation, model-to-text transformation, model validation, model merging, model comparison and model refactoring. As MDE is increasingly applied to larger and more complex systems, achieving greater scalability of contemporary MDE processes, practices and technologies is of increasing importance.

Scalability in software engineering has different dimensions, including but not limited to: the number of software engineers; the size of engineering artefacts; the size and complexity of languages used; and the size of engineering tasks that are carried out. In this paper, we focus on assessing and improving the scalability of model-to-text transformation with respect to the increasing size of engineering artefacts (i.e., models).

Our work is motivated by our recent participation in an EC FP7 project (INESS, grant #218575), which involved applying model-to-text transformation to generate (from UML models) code that was amenable to model checking. In our work on this project, we found that code generation would take around 1 hour for the largest models provided by our industrial partners. Often the results of model checking would necessitate small changes to these large models, and hence re-execution of the code-generating transformation was necessary to

J. Dingel et al. (Eds.): MODELS 2014, LNCS 8767, pp. 84–98, 2014.

verify the new models. Each new version of a model would result in an hour of code generation, irrespective of the proportion of the source model that had changed. Ideally, the execution time of the code-generating transformation would have been directly proportional to the magnitude of the change to the source model: small changes to the model would have resulted in significantly reduced execution time of the code-generating transformation. This ideal is realised with a *source incremental* transformation engine [1].

In this paper, we present and evaluate the use of *signatures*, which are lightweight mechanisms for determining which subset of a M2T transformation must be re-executed in response to a change to its input model(s). By reducing the number of templates (and, consequently, expressions) that must be evaluated by the transformation engine in order to propagate changes from input models to generated text, signatures contribute to increasing the scalability of M2T transformation by providing source incrementality. This paper makes the following contributions:

- A brief review of existing contemporary M2T languages and their support for incrementality (Section 2).
- A design for signatures, an extension for template-based M2T languages that can be used to implement source incremental M2T transformations (Section 3).
- An empirical evaluation and discussion of the benefits of the use of signatures based on our experiences with introducing source incrementality to two existing M2T transformations (Section 4).

2 Background: Model-to-text Transformation

Model-to-text (M2T) transformation is a model management operation that involves generating text (e.g., source code, documentation, configuration files, reports, etc.) from models. Historically, M2T transformations have been implemented using either a visitor-based or a template-based approach [1]. A visitor-based approach traverses the source model, generating text for a subset of the elements encountered during the traversal. A template-based approach (Listing 1.1) involves specifying templates whose structure more closely resemble the generated text. Any portions of generated text that vary over model elements are replaced with dynamic (executable) sections, which are evaluated with respect to the model. Any portions of generated text that remain the same are termed static sections. Many contemporary M2T transformation languages use the template-based rather than the visitor-based approach. This is likely to be partly due to OMG's standardisation of a M2T language in 2008, MOFM2T 1.0, which proposes a template-based M2T language.

2.1 M2T Transformation Languages

Over the past decade, many M2T transformation languages have been developed, including T4, JET, Acceleo, Xpand and the Epsilon Generation Language (EGL)

[2]. We now briefly compare these languages and discuss the extent to which they are in use today.

JET and MOFScript were among the first implementations of usable M2T transformation languages for MDE. JET is used to generate text from EMF-based models. JET templates can contain any Java code, and the JET engine translates JET templates into pure Java code prior to transformation execution. MOFScript was a direct result of the OMG RFP for a M2T transformation language. MOFScript works with any MOF based model, and is heavily influenced by QVT. It is essentially an imperative language which supports all primitive data types and abstract data types such as collections, lists etc. Development and maintenance of JET and MOFScript appears to have ceased in 2008 and in 2009, respectively (according to http://www.eclipse.org/modeling/m2t/downloads/).

T4, Acceleo, Xpand and EGL are more recent M2T transformation languages. The T4 transformation engine is largely dependent on the .NET framework and thus targeted towards Microsoft's Visual Studio developers. Transformation control logic is written as fragments of program code in C# or Visual Basic. Acceleo, Xpand and EGL are template-based languages which integrate with the Eclipse development environment. They generally provide similar core capabilities, although each language also has a few unique features (e.g., Acceleo provides an editor that can be used to quickly parameterise a text file to form a template; Xpand provides aspect-oriented programming constructs for enhanced modularity and reusability of templates; and EGL can generate text from many different types of model including EMF, plain XML, Google Drive spreadsheets, etc.).

2.2   Incrementality in M2T Transformation

Incrementality in software engineering refers to the process of reacting to changes in an artefact in a manner that minimises the need for redundant re-computations. In 2006, Czarnecki and Helsen [1] identified 3 types of incrementality for M2T transformation: user edit-preserving incrementality, target incrementality, and source incrementality. In previous work, we have reviewed contemporary M2T transformation languages, identifying that whilst user-edit preserving incrementality and target incrementality are widely supported, source incrementality is not supported at all, to the best of our knowledge [3]. In this paper, we focus on source incrementality and argue that it is an essential feature for providing scalable M2T transformation capabilities.

```
1   [template public helloWorld(name : String)]
2   Hello [name/]!
3   [/template]
```

Listing 1.1. Example of a template-based M2T transformation, in OMG MOFM2T syntax. Line 2 contains a static section ("Hello"), a dynamic section (that outputs the value of the name variable) and another static section ("!").

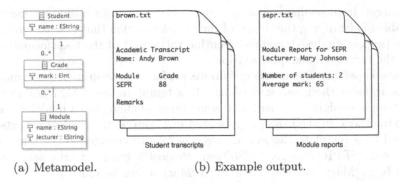

(a) Metamodel.   (b) Example output.

Fig. 1. Artefacts for a M2T transformation that generates reports

Source incrementality is the capability of a M2T transformation engine to respond to changes in its source models in a way that minimises (ideally eliminates) the need for recomputations that will not eventually have an impact on its output. Achieving a high degree of source incrementally can significantly improve the efficiency of complex transformations, especially when they operate on large and/or complex source models (with many cross-references between model elements and/or inter-dependencies between source models).

3   Signatures for Source Incremental M2T Transformation

Arguably, a combination of precise model differencing and static analysis could be used to achieve source incrementality: static analysis could be used to identify the set of templates that need to be re-executed in response to changes identified via model differencing. However, this approach to source incrementality is very challenging to achieve in practice as the majority of contemporary M2T languages are not amenable to static analysis at the required level of precision. More specifically, contemporary M2T languages are normally dynamically-typed and support features, such as dynamic dispatch and first-order logic functions, that inhibit precise static analysis.

This section proposes an alternative approach that uses *signatures*: concise and lightweight proxies for templates that indicate whether or not a change to an input model will alter the output of a template. Signatures provide some support for source incrementality for contemporary template-based M2T languages, without relying on model differencing and static analysis. This section summarises the approach, discusses the way in which existing template-based M2T languages can be extended with support for signatures, and briefly describes a prototypical implementation of signatures.

3.1   Overview

A source-incremental transformation engine seeks to reduce the amount of transformation execution time necessary to propagate changes from the source model to the target. In providing source incrementality, a transformation engine must be capable of identifying the subset of the transformation that is sensitive to the changes (impact analysis), and re-executing the subset of the transformation to update the target (change propagation).

Of these capabilities, as mentioned above, performing accurate impact analysis presents arguably the greatest challenge. In a template-based M2T transformation, a template might be sensitive to some types of change to a model element, but not to others. In the example presented in Figure 1, the student reports are generated by a template that, clearly, is sensitive to changes to the name of a module (e.g., "SEPR" changes to "Software Project"), but not to the name of the lecturer (e.g., "Mary Johnson" changes to "Mary Johnson-Smith").

Signatures, as discussed below, provide a lightweight mechanism for describing the changes to which a template is sensitive. When a transformation is first executed, signatures are calculated and written to non-volatile storage. When a transformation is re-executed in response to changes to the source model, the signatures are recomputed and compared to those from the previous execution. A template is re-executed only if its current signature differs from its previous signature.

3.2   Design

Before discussing our proposed extension to support signatures in template-based M2T languages, we must first consider the way in which transformation execution is implemented in typical template-based M2T languages. To avoid specialising the discussion to a specific transformation language or engine, we use the terminology and execution model described in the OMG MOFM2T standard.

A M2T transformation is specified using a *Module*, which comprises one or more *Templates*. A *Template* comprises a set of *Parameters*, which specify the data on which a template must be executed; and a set of *Expressions*, which specify the behaviour of the template. In addition to the typical types of expression used for model management (e.g., accessing or updating the properties of a model element, iterating over associated model elements, etc.), M2T transformation languages provide two further types of expressions: *TemplateInvocations*, which are used for invoking other templates; and *FileBlocks*, which are used for redirecting generated text to a file. A *TemplateInvocation* is equivalent to in situ placement of the text produced by the *Template* being invoked.

Consider, for example, the M2T transformation in Listing 1.2, which produces student transcripts of the form shown on the right-hand side of Figure 1. This M2T transformation comprises three templates: *generateReports* (lines 3-10), *studentToTranscript* (lines 12-22), and *courseToReport* (lines 24-32). All of the templates accept one parameter (a *University* object, a *Student* object and a *Course* object, respectively). The first template invokes the second (third) template on line 5 (line 8) by passing an instance of Student (Course). Note that the second and third templates both redirect their output to a file named after the *Student* or *Course* on which they are invoked (lines 13 and 25).

```
 1  [module generateReports(University)]
 2
 3  [template public generateReports(u : University)]
 4  [for (s : Student | u.students)]
 5  [studentToTranscript(s)/]
 6  [/for]
 7  [for (c : Course | u.courses)]
 8  [courseToReport(c)/]
 9  [/for]
10  [/template]
11
12  [template public studentToTranscript(s : Student)]
13  [file (s.name)/]
14  Academic Transcript
15  Name: [s.name/]
16  Module  Grade
17  [for (g : Grade | s.grades)]
18  [g.course.name/]  [g.mark/]
19  [/for]
20  Remarks
21  [/file]
22  [/template]
23
24  [template public courseToReport(c : Course)]
25  [file (c.name)/]
26  Course Report for [c.name/]
27  Lecturer: [c.lecturer/]
28
29  Number of students: [c.grades->size()/]
30  Average mark: [c.grades->collect(mark)->sum() / c.grades->size()/]
31  [/file]
32  [/template]
```

Listing 1.2. Example of a template-based M2T transformation, specified in OMG MOFM2T syntax.

Execution of a M2T transformation specification (i.e., a *Module*) is performed by a transformation engine. A transformation engine takes as input a source model and a *Module*, and outputs text. Execution begins by creating a *TemplateInvocation* from an initial *Template* and *Parameter Values*. The *TemplateInvocation* is executed by evaluating the expressions of its *Template* in the context of its *Parameter Values*. During the evaluation of a *TemplateInvocation*, additional *TemplateInvocations* can be created and evaluated in the same manner, and any *FileBlocks* are evaluated by writing to disk the text generated when evaluating the expressions contained within the *FileBlock*.

For example, execution of the of the M2T transformation in Listing 1.2 would proceed as follows:

1. Load the source model.
2. Create and evaluate a *TemplateInvocation* for the primary template, *generateReports* (see line 1), passing the only *University* object in the source as a parameter value.
3. For each of the *Students* contained in the *University*:
   (a) Create and evaluate a *TemplateInvocation* for the *studentToTranscript* template, passing the current *Student* object as a parameter value.

(b) Emit the text for the student transcript (lines 14-20) to a text file with the same name as the *Student*.
4. For each of the *Courses* contained in the *University*:
   (a) Create and evaluate a *TemplateInvocation* for the *courseToReport* template, passing the current *Course* object as a parameter value.
   (b) Emit the text for the course report (lines 26-30) to a text file with the same name as the *Course*.

In a typical M2T transformation engine, execution involves creating and evaluating *TemplateInvocations*. In a source incremental M2T transformation engine, execution additionally involves identifying the subset of *TemplateInvocations* that need to be evaluated to propagate changes from the source model to the generated text. In other words, a source incremental M2T transformation engine identifies but, crucially, does not evaluate *TemplateInvocations* for which the generated text is known due to a previous invocation of the transformation.

3.2.1 Extending M2T Transformation Languages with Signatures. Given a template-based M2T language with the execution model described above, an extension to provide source incrementality via signatures involves the addition of the following three concepts:

– A **Signature** is a value that is isomorphic with the text generated by a *TemplateInvocation*, and is used by a source incremental transformation engine to determine whether or not a *TemplateInvocation* needs to be re-evaluated.
– A **SignatureCalculator** is a strategy for computing a *Signature* from a *TemplateInvocation*. The choice of algorithm for calculating signatures is left to the implementor, but we discuss two suitable algorithms in Section 3.2.2. Note that any algorithm for calculating a signature must be less computationally expensive than executing the *TemplateInvocation* (i.e., producing the generated text from the template).
– A **SignatureStore** is responsible for storing the *Signatures* calculated during the evaluation of a M2T transformation, and makes these *Signatures* available to the transformation engine during the next evaluation of M2T transformation on the same source model. The way in which Signatures are stored is left to the implementor, but some possible solutions are flat files, an XML document, or a database. A *SignatureStore* must be capable of persisting *Signatures* between invocations of a M2T transformation (in non-volatile storage). Moreover, a *SignatureStore* must be performant: any gains achieved with a source incremental engine might be negated if the *SignatureStore* cannot efficiently read and write *Signatures*.

Adding support for signatures to a template-based M2T language involves extending the transformation engine with additional logic that invokes a *SignatureCalculator* and a *SignatureStore* (Figure 2). During initialisation, the transformation engine requests that the *SignatureStore* prepares to access any existing

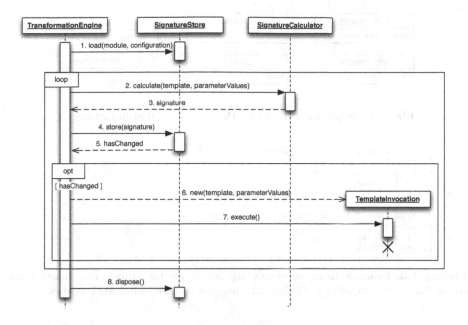

Fig. 2. UML sequence diagram describing how Signatures are used to determine whether or not a TemplateInvocation should be executed

Signatures for the current M2T transformation (*Module*) and the current *Configuration* (i.e., source model, file system location for the generated files, etc). Whenever the transformation engine would ordinarily create a *TemplateInvocation* from a *Template* and a set of *ParameterValues*, it instead asks the *SignatureCalculator* to calculate a **Signature** from the *Template* and *ParameterValues* (step 2). The transformation engine stores the *Signature* using the *SignatureStore* (step 4). The *SignatureStore* returns a Boolean value (*hasChanged*) which indicates whether or not the *Signature* differs from the *Signature* already contained in the *SignatureStore* from any previous evaluation of this M2T transformation (step 5). If the *Signature* has changed, a *TemplateInvocation* is created and executed (steps 6 and 7). The transformation engine informs the *SignatureStore* (step 8) when the transformation completes, so that it can write the *Signatures* to non-volatile storage.

3.2.2   Signature Calculation Strategies. As discussed briefly above, a *SignatureCalculator* is a strategy for computing a *Signature*. The remainder of this section describes two calculation strategies: *automatic* and *user-defined*. In both cases, *Signature* values comprise (i) data obtained from the *ParameterValues* and *Template* (as discussed below), and (ii) a hash of the *Template*. The latter is included to ensure that the transformation engine can detect and re-execute templates that have been modified by the transformation developer.

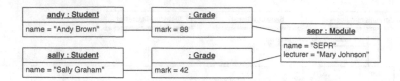

Fig. 3. Example input model for the transformation in Listing 1.2

```
1   // Signature for studentToTranscript(s : Student)
2   [s.name/],
3   [for (g : Grade | s.grades)]
4   [g.course.name/],[g.mark/],
5   [/for]
6
7   // Signature for courseToReport(c : Course)
8   [c.name/],
9   [c.lecturer/],
10  [c.grades->size()/],
11  [c.grades.collect(mark)->sum() / c.grades->size()/]
```

Listing 1.3. Example using automatic signatures for the studentToTranscript and courseToReport templates in Listing 1.2, specified in OMG MOFM2T syntax.

Automatic Signatures. A straightforward algorithm for calculating signatures is to concatenate the text generated by evaluating only the dynamic sections of a template, ignoring any static sections and any file output blocks. This algorithm is likely to be less computationally expensive than a typical evaluation of the template because fewer statements are evaluated and no disk access is required. For example, suppose the M2T transformation in Listing 1.2 is evaluated on the model in Figure 3. The automatic signature calculation strategy would compute signatures equivalent to the code in Listing 1.3 for the *studentToTranscript* and *courseToReport* templates in Listing 1.2. Consequently, the following signatures will be computed:

1. For *studentToTranscript* on *Andy Brown*: Andy Brown,SEPR,88
2. For *studentToTranscript* on *Sally Graham*: Sally Graham,SEPR,42
3. For *courseToReport* on *SEPR*: Mary Johnson,2,65

Suppose that mark of the Grade associated with Sally Graham and SEPR is changed from 42 to 54. When the M2T transformation is next executed, the following new signatures will be computed:

1. For *studentToTranscript* on *Andy Brown*: Andy Brown,SEPR,88
2. For *studentToTranscript* on *Sally Graham*: Sally Graham,SEPR,54
3. For *courseToReport* on *SEPR*: Mary Johnson,2,74

The second and third *Signatures* differ, and hence the transformation engine will create and evaluate *TemplateInvocations* to recompute the generated text

```
1  [template public voterStatus(p : Person)]
2  [if (person.age >= 18)]
3    [person.forename/] [person.surname/] should complete a voting form.
4  [else]
5    [person.forename/] [person.surname/] is ineligible to vote.
6  [/if]
7  [/template]
```

Listing 1.4. Use of a dynamic section to control the flow of execution, which causes our straightforward signature calculation strategy to produce a non-isomorphic signature.

```
1  [template public voterStatus(person : Person)]
2  [signature person.age + person.forename + person.surname/]
3  ...
4  [/template]
```

Listing 1.5. Enhancement to the template in Listing 1.4, which adds a user-defined signature on line 2.

for these templates and parameter values. The first *Signature* remains the same and so the transformation engine takes no further action.

Despite reducing the execution time of transformations, this algorithm does not always produce *Signatures* that are isomorphic with the text generated by their corresponding *TemplateInvocations*. For example, consider Listing 1.4. Here, the *person.age* attribute indirectly contributes to the generated text. The *Signature* calculated by the automatic algorithm would be equivalent to evaluating the expression *person.forename + person.surname*, which is not sensitive to changes to the *person.age* attribute.

User-defined Signatures. An alternative strategy, which addresses the shortcomings of the automatic strategy, is to allow users to specify the expressions that are used to calculate *Signatures*. This can be achieved by adding a new construct to the M2T template language. For example, Listing 1.5 demonstrates the way in which a user-defined signature could be used to calculate signatures for the template that the automatic strategy finds problematic. In addition to addressing the primary shortcoming of the automatic strategy, the user-defined strategy is also likely to be more performant, because no analysis or invocation of a template is necessary to calculate signatures.

A drawback of the user-defined strategy is that the transformation developer must ensure that signature expressions are consistent with the template. For large or complicated templates, user-defined signatures are likely to be both difficult to specify initially and difficult to maintain. A hybrid strategy in which a transformation developer can add to the automatically generated signature might be an acceptable compromise. For example, the developer would be able to add the *person.age* attribute to the automatically generated signature for the template in Listing 1.4. As discussed in Section 6, we are currently investigating structures that assist developers in identifying and maintaining user-defined signatures.

4 Evaluation and Experience Report

We now report the results of an empirical evaluation of the signature-based approach, which compared transformation execution times in incremental and non-incremental modes and investigated the threshold after which incremental transformation no longer outperformed non-incremental transformation. The evaluation shows that source incremental transformations can be more efficient than non-incremental transformations, particularly for frequent or relatively small changes to models.

The automatic signature calculation strategy (rather than the user-defined strategy) was used for the evaluation, for two reasons. Firstly, the automatic strategy was sufficient for generating accurate signatures for the selected M2T transformations. Secondly, we have not yet developed structures to assist in identifying and testing user-defined signatures, and hence adding user-defined signatures to larger and more complicated M2T templates would have been time consuming and error-prone. The use of the automatic strategy does not threaten the validity of our results, because the user-defined strategy is more performant than the automatic strategy. In other words, the results presented in this section are an underestimate of the efficacy of our approach, and would be improved by application of the user-defined signature calculation strategy.

4.1 Empirical Evaluation

We applied our extensions to EGL to two M2T transformations (Pongo and GraphitiX) to investigate the comparative execution times of using and not using signatures to provide source incrementality. When measuring execution times for transformation invocations that did not use signatures, we used our modified version of EGL but disabled source incrementality (by substituting dummy implementations of the *SignatureCalculator* and *SignatureStore*). We elected not to use the larger and more complicated M2T transformation from INESS (Section 1) until we have developed structures for assisting in the identification and testing of the user-defined signature calculation strategy, as discussed in Section 4.2.

4.1.1   Pongo. Pongo[1] is a M2T transformation, implemented in EGL, that generates data mapper layers for MongoDB, a non-relational database. Pongo consumes an Ecore model that describes the types and properties of the objects to be stored in the database, and generates Java code that can be used to interact with the database via the user-defined types and properties (without needing to use the MongoDB API). Pongo was developed by one of the authors (Kolovos). The results presented below use Pongo v0.5, which was released prior to our implementation of source incrementality in EGL.

To replicate the effects of using a source incremental transformation engine throughout the lifetime of a development project, we used Pongo to generate

---

[1] https://code.google.com/p/pongo/

Table 1. Results of using non-incremental and incremental M2T transformation for the Pongo M2T transformation, applied to 11 historical versions of the GMFGraph Ecore model

Version	Elements Changed (#)	Non-Incremental		Incremental	
		Invocations (#)	Time (s)	Invocations (#)	Time (s; %)
1.23	-	67	1.51	67	1.83 (121%)
1.24	1	67	1.85	1	0.78 (42%)
1.25	1	68	1.71	2	0.67 (39%)
1.26	1	69	1.54	1	0.70 (45%)
1.27	10	69	1.55	44	0.77 (50%)
1.28	10	69	1.64	44	0.62 (38%)
1.29	14	69	1.69	14	0.53 (31%)
1.30	24	72	1.58	35	0.61 (39%)
1.31	1	72	1.53	0	0.57 (37%)
1.32	1	72	1.53	0	0.46 (30%)
1.33	3	74	1.58	3	0.45 (28%)
			17.71		7.99 (45%)

Java code from the 11 versions the GmfGraph Ecore model obtained from the Subversion repository[2] of the GMF team. We selected GmfGraph due to the availability of historical versions, and because it was not developed at York.

The results (Table 1) show the difference in number of template invocations and total execution time between non-incremental and incremental execution modes of execution, for each of the 11 versions of the GmfGraph model. For the first invocation of the transformation (version 1.23), the incremental mode of execution took slightly longer to execute than the non-incremental mode because the former incurs an overhead as it must calculate and store signatures for every template invocation. In every subsequent invocation of the transformation, the incremental mode of execution required between 28% and 50% of the execution time required by the non-incremental mode. In a project for which Pongo was applied once for each version of the GMF project, the incremental mode would require 45% of the execution time of the non-incremental mode. The overall reduction in execution time (9.72s) is modest, but that is partly explained by the relatively small size of the Pongo transformation (6 EGL templates totalling 329 lines of code), and of the GmfGraph model (averaging 65 classes).

4.1.2 GraphitiX.
GraphitiX [3] is a code generator, implemented in EGL, that generates Java code for a graphical editor from a description of the concrete and abstract syntax of a domain-specific modelling language. Compared to the Pongo transformation, GraphitiX is much larger (23 EGL templates totalling 1689 lines of code). GraphitiX was developed by one of the authors (Ogunyomi). The results presented below use Subversion revision 1 of GraphitiX, which was developed prior to our implementation of source incrementality in EGL.

To examine how the reduction of execution time varies as the magnitude of change in a model increases, we applied GraphitiX to a large model, changed a

---

[2] https://git.eclipse.org/c/gmf-tooling
[3] https://code.google.com/p/graphiti-x/

proportion of the model, and re-executed GraphitiX. We wished to determine the proportion of the model that needed to change after which the incremental mode of execution became more costly than non-incremental mode with respect to the total transformation time. (Recall that incremental mode incurs the overhead of calculating and storing signatures). The input models were constructed via a script that generated classes with identical structure (a constant number of attributes and no associations). At every iteration, a subset of all classes were modified (by renaming one attribute).

As shown in Table 2, the results highlight the impact that the magnitude of change on an input model can have on an incremental transformation. The results suggest that source incremental transformation requires less computation than non-incremental transformation until a significant proportion of the source model is changed. In this case, source incremental transformation outperforms non-incremental transformation until 300 (30% of) classes in the input model were changed.

Table 2. Results of using non-incremental and incremental M2T transformation for the GraphitiX M2T transformation, applied to increasingly larger proportions of changes to the source model

Change (# Elements)	Non-Incremental		Incremental	
	Template Invocations (#)	Time (s)	Template Invocations (#)	Time (s; %)
-	4012	49.97	4012	76.04 (152.17%)
1	4012	45.02	3	38.99 (86.61%)
4	4012	43.86	6	36.51 (83.24%)
5	4012	43.38	7	36.40 (83.91%)
10	4012	43.99	12	36.56 (83.11%)
20	4012	43.75	22	36.73 (83.95%)
100	4012	44.44	102	39.29 (88.41%)
300	4012	44.39	302	44.71 (100.72%)
600	4012	44.02	602	53.57 (121.69%)

4.2   Discussion

Our initial experiments have indicated that the use of signatures for providing source incrementality is promising: we have demonstrated that a reduction in execution time is observed both for realistic changes to a model (e.g., the changes made to GmfGraph Ecore model) and until a significant proportion of a model is changed (e.g., renaming an attribute in around 30% of the classes in a model used as input to the GraphitiX transformation). The results also indicate that source incrementality using our approach is more efficient than non-incremental transformations when frequent, small changes are made to a model throughout the lifetime of a project.

Further performance improvements are likely to be achievable via the application of user-defined signatures, particularly to templates that have been identified as bottlenecks. We will extend our empirical investigations along these lines once we have developed structures that assist in the identification and testing of user-defined signatures. In particular, we anticipate extending our evaluation to include the larger and more complicate M2T transformation used in the INESS project (Section 1), for which the automatic signature calculation strategy will not always be sufficient.

5   Related Work

Source incrementality has been previously explored in the context of model-to-model (M2M transformation). PMT [4] is a M2M transformation language that synchronises models via trace links, which contain information relating to the provenance of target model elements with respect to source model elements [5]. PMT is a rule-based M2M transformation language and the transformation engine uses identifiers to match source model elements to target model elements. PMT has two source incremental execution modes. In fully conservative mode, changes made to a source model that do not affect any elements of the existing target model (e.g., the addition of a new element to the source model), a matching target element is created in the target model. In semi-conservative mode, changes made to a source model element that replace elements of the existing target model are permitted.

Hearnden et al. [6] describes a source incremental M2M transformation engine, in which a tree is used to represent the trace of a transformation execution. Each node in the tree represents either a source or target element, while the edges represent the transformation rules. An important feature of this approach is that the entire transformation context is maintained throughout all transformation executions. As changes are made to the source model, the changes are propagated to the tree and, in turn, to the target model.

6   Conclusion

Notwithstanding the potential productivity and portability gains of MDE, scalability – the ability for MDE tools, techniques and practices to be applied to larger and more complex systems – remains an open research challenge. In this paper, we have explored an approach to reducing the execution time of M2T transformations in the response to changes to large models. We have contributed a design for an extension to M2T transformation languages that will enable support for source incrementality via the application of *signatures*, concise and lightweight proxies for templates that are used to perform impact analysis on a model with respect to a transformation. We have demonstrated the potential efficacy of signatures via an empirical evaluation.

In future work, we will develop structures that can assist developers in the identification and testing of user-defined signatures (which will outperform automatic signatures). In particular, we will apply dynamic analysis techniques to determine the data that is accessed by a template. The results of the dynamic analysis will be compared to any user-defined signature for a template to determine whether the data used to calculate the signature is necessary and sufficient. Once we have automated support for developing user-defined signatures, we will also extend our empirical evaluation to investigate incrementality for larger and more complicated M2T transformations (such as the INESS M2T transformation described in Section 1), for which user-defined signatures will be required to ensure correctness of the incremental transformation.

Acknowledgements. This work was partially supported by the European Commission, through the Scalable Modelling and Model Management on the Cloud (MONDO) FP7 STREP project (grant #611125). The motivating example discussed in this paper was taken from Rose's work on the INESS project, which was supported by the European Commission and co-funded under the 7th Framework Programme (grant #218575).

References

1. Czarnecki, K., Helsen, S.: Feature-based survey of model transformation approaches. IBM Systems Journal 45(3), 621–645 (2006)
2. Rose, L.M., Paige, R.F., Kolovos, D.S., Polack, F.A.C.: The Epsilon Generation Language. In: Schieferdecker, I., Hartman, A. (eds.) ECMDA-FA 2008. LNCS, vol. 5095, pp. 1–16. Springer, Heidelberg (2008)
3. Ogunyomi, B.: Incremental Model-to-Text Transformation (Qualifying Dissertation). PhD thesis, University of York (2013)
4. Tratt, L.: A change propagating model transformation language. Journal of Object Technology 7(3), 107–126 (2008)
5. Winkler, S., von Pilgrim, J.: A survey of traceability in requirements engineering and model-driven development. Software and System Modeling 9, 529–565 (2010)
6. Hearnden, D., Lawley, M., Raymond, K.: Incremental model transformation for the evolution of model-driven systems. In: Wang, J., Whittle, J., Harel, D., Reggio, G. (eds.) MoDELS 2006. LNCS, vol. 4199, pp. 321–335. Springer, Heidelberg (2006)

Modeling Systemic Behavior by State-Based Holonic Modular Units

Luca Pazzi

University of Modena and Reggio Emilia
DIEF-UNIMORE
Via Vignolese 905, I-41125 Modena, Italy
luca.pazzi@unimore.it

Abstract. The paper explores a vision in modeling the behavior of complex systems by modular units hosting state machines arranged in part-whole hierarchies and communicating through event flows. Each modular unit plays at the same time the double role of part and whole, i.e. it is inspired by the philosophical idea of holon, providing both an interface and an implementation by which other component state machines may be controlled in order to achieve a global behavior. It is moreover observed that it is possible to assign a formal characterization to such state modules, due to their part-whole arrangement, since higher-level behaviors can derive formally their meaning from lower-level component behaviors. Such a way of arranging behavioral modules allows to establish directly correct-by-construction safety and liveness properties of state-based systems thus challenging the current approach by which state machines interact at the same level and have to be model-checked for ensuring correctness.

Keywords: state-based modeling, holons, component-based modeling, model checking, correctness by construction.

1 Introduction

Holons, in the terminology of Arthur Koestler in his 1967 book *The Ghost in the Machine* [1] are entities which are, at the same time, both parts and wholes. Accordingly, complex phenomena and entities can be decomposed into part/whole hierarchies, named *holarchies*, with *holon* nodes at each level. The main interest in the holonic approach lies in the fact that it reconciles both the reductionist and the holistic view in systems analysis.

By the reductionistic view, which dates back to Descartes and is sometimes referred to as *divide and conquer* or more formally *analytic reduction*, a complex system can be analyzed by "reduction" into distinct parts so that they can be analysed separately. Such decomposition allows to deal effectively with systems complexity, by recursively confining it into less complex and distinct parts, namely *subsystems*. In order to be effective, analytic reduction implies the following assumptions: the division into parts will not distort the phenomenon being studied and the behavior of the components is the same when examined

J. Dingel et al. (Eds.): MODELS 2014, LNCS 8767, pp. 99–115, 2014.
© Springer International Publishing Switzerland 2014

apart as when playing their part in the whole system. Additionally a third fundamental assumption is that it is possible to draw a clear boundary between the interactions among the subsystems and the behavior of the subsystems themselves [2][3].

While it is easy to discover and model standalone entities and systems, difficulty arises in assembling more complex systems using such entities as components, since there is no agreement on a composition model which allows full composability of abstractions. By full composability we mean that the *same exact* component should work in the whole without having to modify it in order to adapt it to any composition context (*off the shelf* approach), thus fully satisfying the second assumption of the reductionistic program reported above.

The current approach consists essentially of the composition model implicit in the object-oriented paradigm, by which systems modeled by objects interact and synchronize by invoking procedural methods on other objects, typically, albeit not only, by direct message exchange through object-valued attributes, called references. In other words, since there are no specific constructs for modeling the composition of objects as a whole, the object-oriented paradigm is inherently "component-oriented". As stated by Rumbaugh, it may be therefore observed that *"in the current object-oriented paradigm interactions are buried in the instance variables and methods of the classes, so that the overall structure of the system is not readily apparent"* [4]. A construct for modeling the overall structure of systems is missing in the object-oriented paradigm. Such a "missing" construct should be able to emphasize such a structure and to model its overall dynamics as a *whole*, thus correcting its tendency to be component-oriented.

Finally, such a construct should be moreover able to act as a standalone component into more complex wholes without further modifications. In other words, it is desirable, for elegance and simplicity, not only to have an additional modular construct for implementing wholes from components, but to have a single constructs playing both roles seaminglessy.

1.1 The "Missing Whole" Problem

The major difficulty in achieving effective object composition lies in missing the semantic distinction between *intra-* and *inter-*object behavior. While the former pertains naturally to the object itself, the latter acts as some sort of glue in the assembly of object components into more complex wholes.

Current object-oriented modeling techniques do not make any semantic distinction amongst the two kinds of behavior, since both are modeled by the same object construct, that is by mutual object references and remote method invocation through message passing. In this way, as observed, most of current modeling object oriented development methodologies and formalisms in analysis and implementation make the object construct semantically overloaded, since it hosts both its endogenous behavior as a component and, at the same time, the exogenous behavior of the system being assembled, resulting in the tight coupling of abstractions and implementations.

The "missing whole" problem has been moreover partially dealt with by means of different external mechanisms patched to the object-oriented paradigm in order to enhance it. for example, by specific object patterns and communication mechanisms, like the Mediator and the Observer design pattern [5] as well as the Model View Controller (MVC) mechanism [6]. The Mediator pattern decouples interacting classes by gathering their interacting portion of behavior within a single "mediator" class, thus improving the overall understandability and self-containment of the original classes. The role and the meaning of such "mediator" class has interesting interpretations beyond its immediate pragmatic one, which consists in laying a bridge among different behaviors. Such a bridging role is achieved by prescribing changes to other classes in reaction to other changes happening in the original classes. In other words such a bridging class hosts, as a matter of fact, a behavior on its own.

On the other hand, any systemic behavior can be seen abstractly as a reactive, coordinating behavior: it must in fact specify which actions have to be undertaken in reaction to specific changes in system components in order to prescribe additional changes to other system components. In other words a systemic behavior links different behaviors, and it can be modeled either by a specific modular construct of the language or it may be embedded within the original behaviors. The two approaches in modeling systemic behavior can be named respectively "explicit" versus "implicit" [7][8] depending on whether or not the system dynamics is hosted within a *single* modular unit of behavior. By the implicit approach an aggregate is modeled through a web of references by which the component objects refer one to another. This way the associative knowledge between the component objects is modeled directly (by object-valued attributes), hiding the structure and the behavior of the aggregate which is therefore not identified as a relevant object. By the explicit approach, an explicit additional object is inserted in the modeling instead, holding part-of relationships to the component objects. The two approaches bear consequences on software quality factors, for example implicit modeling tends to produce software artifacts which are tightly coupled and not self contained, thus producing software which is difficult to maintain, reuse, understand, and so on.

By adopting the explicit view, communication among systems has moreover to be revised accordingly, due to the presence of an additional centralized unit of behavior. In other words, components, which are no more tightly coupled one with another are now tightly coupled with the mediator class itself. The original tightly coupled modules have in fact to maintain static references to the class implementing the centralized behavior in order to notify them of changes in their internal status, allowing the mediator class to react appropriately through other static references. The Observer design pattern and the MVC mechanism may then be used in order to patch a reactive event-based communication framework to the object paradigm, with the aim of decoupling components classes from such specialized controller classes.

Object-oriented methodologies in the last two decades presented different approaches to the joint modeling of structural and behavioral aspects, essentially by encapsulating behavior around already discovered structures, with the result that not readily apparent systems and wholes were often missing in the final design. In other words, since components are self-evident while systems are often not, such methodologies provided very few support in discovering enclosing wholes, thus committing themselves towards the implicit modeling approach. A slightly different approach may be found instead in the Object Modeling Technique (OMT) by Rumbaugh [4] and in the Fusion method by Coleman et al. [9] which emphasized the role played by mutual relationships in discovering new encapsulating classes. Most of such work eventually merged into the UML [10] and the UML 2 [11] standards, which partly corrected the implicit tendency by a wealth of modeling constructs, for example by distinguishing between "weak" aggregation and "strong" composition relationships and introducing suitable "association" classes, albeit missing, in some sense, a unifying and comprehensive theoretical framework.

The aim of this paper is to show that a different paradigm may be pursued by going beyond the existing, partial, solutions towards a vision of the object paradigm which coherently combines components and wholes through a revised communication mechanism. The paper employs the Part-Whole Statecharts (PWS) formalism [12] in order to illustrate the more general idea of holonic modeling. Part-Whole Statecharts have already been used in pioneering the feasibility of holarchies of unmanned vehicles and of multiagent systems [13][14][15]. The same formalism has been endowed recently [16] with a formal syntax and semantics which allows, by construction, to build correct modules without using model checking techniques.

1.2   Structure of the Work

Section 2 discusses and compares general principles of behavioral composition, interaction and synchronization. Section 3 presents a modular construct which implements the general idea of holon and Section 4 discusses the feasibility of modeling real-world cases through Part-Whole Statecharts.

2   Behavioral-Driven Composition

It may be observed that entities which exhibit a peer to peer coordinated behavior act, globally, as a new aggregated entity. This is true both of entities communicating and coordinating through exchange of signals as well as of entities having a mechanical connection which trivially constrains them to behavioral coordination. Process algebras [17][18] furnish an interesting example in Hoare's CSP seminal work, where a customer CUST is modeled by a process which interact with a vending machine VM, the interaction becoming a new single process P = CUST||VM, with || being the concurrency operator in CSP. In the rest of the paper we will use, with no loss of generality with respect to process algebras, a state-based formalism which lends itself to a very readable, albeit formal, diagrammatic form through the concepts of states and state transitions.

Focusing directly on entities without considering their joint behavior, a practice inspired by common-sense real-world observation, may be misleading in finding higher level, more complex entities and systems. A system is in fact assembled from a set of physical components, which exercise physical control one upon another and exhibit individual state changes induced by mutual and direct physical interactions. The point is that local state changes can be seen, alternatively, as a global single state change at the system level, since an aggregate of coordinated entities moves from one global state to the another as its distinct components move from one state to the another.

The final step consists in hypothesizing that *since each entity hosts a behavior, each behavior implies the existence of a suitable entity which hosts it.* Looking at behavioral aggregation represents therefore a challenging clue in developing new modeling paradigms and constructs built according to the principle of explicit modeling of associative behavior.

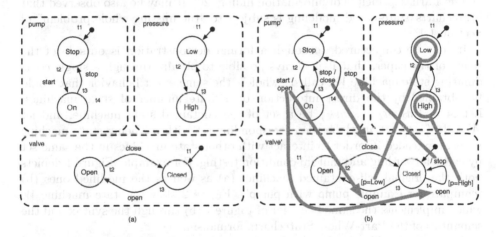

Fig. 1. The behavioral assemblage of three standalone Statecharts (a), into a complex system (b), obtained by modifying their behavior through direct event forwarding and mutual state condition testing. Grey arrows emphasizing mutual interactions and dependences visually depict the global systemic behavior.

2.1   The Explicit Modeling Conjecture

Statecharts, by David Harel [19], allow to model compound behaviors by a set of interacting parallel state machines, each state machine hosted within an AND-decomposed state, each single state of the machine being an XOR-decomposed state. Statecharts may then be used in a straightforward way to represent single behaviors. Such behaviors in turn may be composed into more complex ones through mutual coordination and synchronization, by forwarding command events from one machine to the another as well as by requiring state conditions to be satisfied before a transition is taken. As an example consider Figure 1 where three Statecharts automata taken in isolation in (a) form, globally, a system in (b) once automata are modified in order to mutually implement the following behavior:

"The pump may be started and stopped, and the valve is opened and closed accordingly in order to allow the flow of liquid into tank. A sensor detects tank pressure and inhibits valve opening when the pressure is too high, in order to avoid reflux from the tank. When the opening of the valve is not permitted, a stop signal is sent back to the pump."

Behavioral interdependences which implement the behavior above are depicted in Figure 1 (b) by grey arrows: it may be easily observed that in such a form, the whole behavior is hardly understandable, modifiable, testable and not easily amenable to be checked for safety analysis. In other words, the Statecharts construct requires to modify the internal behavior of components, thus contravening Parnas' principle of information hiding [20]. It may be also observed that Statecharts' state-based modeling is subject to "the missing whole problem" of Section 1.1.

It may be conjectured, although a formal demonstration is outside of the scope of the paper, that it is always possible to obtain, through a single coordinating state machine W, called "whole", the same exact behavior that would be obtained by the direct interaction of a finite number of state machines. Let $\mathcal{A} = \{m_1, m_2, \ldots, m_N\}$ be a set of self contained state machine, and let $\mathcal{A}' = \{m'_1, m'_2, \ldots, m'_N\}$ be the corresponding set with m'_i being state machine $m_i \in \mathcal{A}$ extended in order to interact with other state machines in the same set by event forwarding and mutual condition testing. For example, Figure 1 depicts both the original self-contained machines (a) as well as the modified ones (b) (compare for example pump with pump'). Figure 2 shows a state machine W which implements the same behavior of Figure 1 (b) through the syntax and the semantics of the Part-Whole Statecharts formalism.

State machine W plays a coordination role towards the original interacting state machines, by labeling its state transitions with coordination commands directed to state machines belonging to the set $\mathcal{A}$ and reacting to state changes coming from the machines in the same set. Additionally, a definite semantics can be assigned to the states in W as shown in [16].

3   Holons

Holons are modular units which host a behavioral construct, in the case at hand a state machine, playing, at the same time, a twofold role:

1. the state machine coordinates the behavior of other component holons through their state machine interface;
2. the state machine provides an interface to other holons which coordinate the holon.

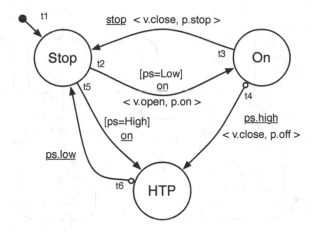

Fig. 2. The complex behavior of Figure 1 (b) modeled through a coordinating state machine, obtained as the "whole" section of an extend PW Statecharts machine (adapted from [21]). The automaton coordinates the behavior of the pump (p) and of the valve (v) depending on the pressure sensor (ps). State HTP denotes the exceptional case of "high tank-pressure". Transitions t_4 and t_6 are taken automatically as the tank pressure changes.

The two points match the general notion which stands behind the holonic paradigm (the so called "Janus", i.e., *double face*, paradigm). Holons are at the same time both whole (i.e., coordinating) and part (i.e., coordinated) entities. Holons are arranged in part-whole hierarchies called *holarchies* by the recursive pattern of composition depicted in Figure 3 (b). In such a pattern holon W coordinates the joint behavior of its component holons A, B, C.

The proposed holonic pattern of composition is *asymmetrical*, since wholes know their parts, but parts are forbidden to know the whole in order to maximize self containment and reusability.

Such an asymmetry is achieved by having two typologies of signals which travel from parts to whole and viceversa, as shown in Figure 3 (b):

1. the (whole section of the) holon has to *prescribe* coordinated behavior to each of its component holons: this is depicted by grey arrows in the picture;
2. the holon has to *react* to changes happening in its component parts: this is depicted by white arrows in the same picture.

Such a feature heavily relies on a suitable communication mechanism which implements both event delivery from the whole to a recipient (grey arrows) as well as a notification mechanism of any change happening within a component towards the whole (white arrows in the picture). Aim of the mechanism is, beyond carrying events, to decouple component holons from their coordinating counterparts, since the holon interface does not contain any reference to them. If, on one hand, such a holon implementation is tightly coupled to its component

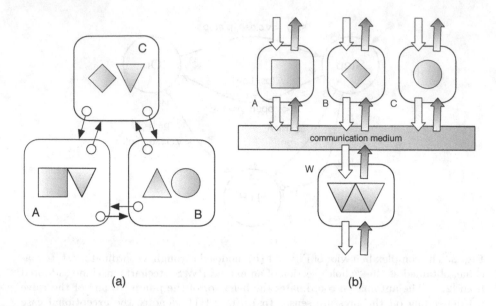

Fig. 3. The implicit modeling of three interacting entities through the reference construct (a) and the correspondent explicit modeling through four holons (b). The picture suggests that triangle-shaped associative behavior may be gathered within holon W thus freeing holons A, B and C from unnecessary details.

parts, holon interface does not contain any reference to any other holon in order to achieve loose coupling among them. Parts do not know the whole, since they have to be composed in many different, not foreseeable, contexts. The whole does know its parts, instead, in order to achieve a useful composition.

For example, state transitions in the Part-Whole Statecharts formalism (chosen for illustrating holons' features in the paper) contain event commands of the form $\langle c.e \rangle$: once the transition is triggered, event e is delivered to component c whose interface contains a transition which has e as trigger (Figure 4 (a)). Vice versa, any change in a component holon, say d, is "notified" to the holon which has d as component, where a transition may have d.f as trigger, meaning that holon W has to react to event f from holon d (Figure 4 (b)).

4   Formal Specification and Semantics

It is possible to annotate state-based holons at design time in such a way that the behavior implemented at each level of composition can be formally specified and verified. Part-Whole Statecharts, as observed, already provide the formal instruments for performing formal specification of the semantics of state-based holons. This marks an evolutionary advantage with respect to traditional object-oriented and state-based modeling, where interacting and mutually referring modules have no semantics, as observed in the Statecharts case [22].

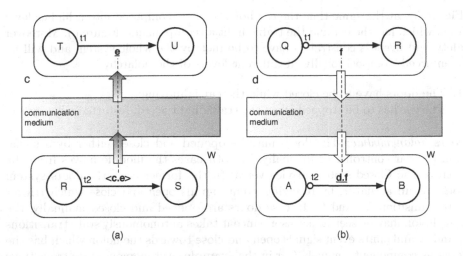

Fig. 4. The double role played by a communication medium among holons. (a) The "delivery" role, by which a command c.e is dispatched, by the occurrence of state transition t_2, from the whole automaton of holon W to component holon c, activating, through its interface, state transition t_1 triggered by e. (b) The reverse "notification" role, by which the occurrence of state transition t_1, labelled by f in the interface of component holon d, is notified to the whole section of holon W activating state transition t_2 triggered by d f (Figure 4 (b)).

It is presumable that part-whole arrangement of modules in combination with hierarchical rules of control are at the basis of this important property of holons. Coordinating state-based holons, each referring to a finite and fixed number of component holons, allows in fact to map each of its states at a given composition level to a well defined configuration of states belonging to the next composition level. Such configurations can be equivalently expressed by a propositional formula in a suitable boolean algebra [16].

Correctness, and consequently safety and liveness, may thus be achieved by construction, by computing such propositions state by state as already shown in Part-Whole Statecharts. It can be hypothesized that checking correctness of each holon by construction may be also achieved by employing other formalisms for expressing holons dynamics, for example by procedural languages, since any state automaton may be deterministically translated into plain code. It may be finally observed that state based specifications and models may be directly executed.

4.1   Example

An automated car has to be controlled in order to start and stop depending on a traffic light on a track. The same car has a system of automated doors which can be operated either by a controller or manually. The car can be therefore seen as a holon having the automated doors and the engine as component holons

(Figure 5); at the same time the car holon can be composed into a higher level holon which has the car and the traffic light as components (Figure 6). Moreover safety and liveness constraints have to be met by the whole system and will be be enforced, compositionally, at different levels of the holarchy:

1. The doors have to be closed while the car is moving;
2. The car has to be stopped when the traffic light is red, restarted when green.

Doors holon module: The doors may be opened and closed either by a signal from the car controller or manually. In both cases the module moves from the Open to the Closed state and vice versa. In the former case, the doors system works as an actuator, by receiving event signals open and close which trigger state transitions t_3 and t_4. In case doors are opened and closed manually, the same holon may be seen as a sensor, since it takes autonomously state transitions t_2 and t_5 and emits event signals open and close towards the holon which has the doors as components, namely Car in the example. Autonomous state transitions such as t_2 and t_5 are denoted by a small white circle near the starting state.

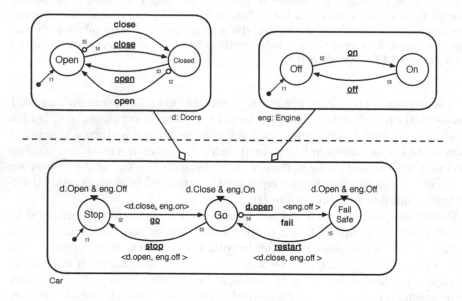

Fig. 5. A holarchy controlling a safe automated car on a track

Engine holon module: The car engine may be simply turned on and off by receiving event signals on and off which trigger state transitions t_2 and t_3 and move the holon into the corresponding states On and Off.

Car holon module: this holon has two regular working states, Stop and Go. An additional FailSafe state takes into account the exceptional behavior resulting from the manual opening of the doors while the car is moving. As in PW State-charts, states are annotated by state propositions which are guaranteed to hold when the system is within that state. For example, d.Open & eng.Off associated to state Stop means that when in such a state the doors have to be opened and the engine must be turned off. State proposition d.Close & eng.On associated to state Go means conversely that when the car is moving the doors have to be closed and the engine turned on. Transitions t_2 and t_3 are externally trig-gerable by events go and stop which will be part of the interface of the holon (see holon Car in the context of the holarchy in Figure 6). Transitions t_2 and t_3, once triggered, propagate respectively command events $\langle$d.close, eng.on$\rangle$ and $\langle$d.open, eng.off$\rangle$ towards component holons Doors and Engine. It can be easily verified that both transitions agree with the state propositions of the starting and arrival states. Finally, when in the Go state, the manual opening of the doors causes event open belonging to transition t_2 of holon Doors to be sent towards holon Car. This in turn triggers transition t_4, which sends an off command event $\langle$eng.off$\rangle$ to the Engine holon which then moves to state FailSafe. Since transition t_4 is triggered by an event coming from a component, the resulting transition t_4 will be seen by external contexts as autonomously triggered (see the interface of Car in Figure 6). The system may be restarted by sending a restart event from external composition contexts (such as holon GlobalTrackMonitor of Fig-ure 6) which triggers transition t_5 which in turns closes the doors and restarts the engine by commands $\langle$d.close, eng.on$\rangle$.

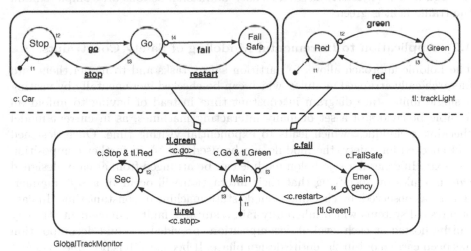

Fig. 6. The holarchy coordinating the automated car of Figure 5 and a traffic light which enables either a main (Main) or a crossing secondary (Sec) road. Holon Car is now employed in the model through its interface, obtained by simply hiding its components' holons as well as any reference to them from the implementation of Figure 5.

Once holon Car has been designed and verified against the first of the two safety constraints listed above, its interface may be employed in higher level composition contexts without any concern for safety. In other words, any of the go-, stop- and restart-triggered state transitions may asked to be taken in holon Car without having doors opened while the car is moving. We then model a global monitor for the track system, which has in charge both the automated car and a traffic light in order to stop it when a secondary road is enabled (Figure 6). Since it employs the holon Car which has been already verified for safety, it now suffices to employ it for implementing the final behavior checking only for the second safety constraint.

Traffic Light holon module: the state machine is the interface of a sensor which detects the current color of the lights from the main road, by changing state (Red and Green) by taking the two autonomous transitions t_2 and t_3. The traffic light device enables and prevents access to the secondary road accordingly.

Global Track Monitor holon module: as red and green events are emitted by the Traffic Light, autonomous transitions t_2 and t_3 are triggered, which in turn send actions go and stop to the car ($\langle$c.go$\rangle$ and $\langle$c.stop$\rangle$). It may be easily verified that state propositions c.Stop & tl.Red c.Go & tl.Green, associated respectively to states Sec and Main are trivially verified by such state transitions. When in state Main the event unsafe signaling that a a door has been opened while the car is moving, brings the system to state Emergency where additional actions can be taken (not shown in the example): the car is restarted by transition t_4 through action $\langle$c.restart$\rangle$ as soon as such additional actions are completed and the traffic light is green.

4.2   Application to Incremental Modeling of Safety Constraints

The holonic approach allows to partition safety tasks and to model them into hierarchically arranged modules, which can be checked incrementally by visiting a single finite state diagram in constant time instead of having to unfold all feasible behaviors of a set of many interacting machines, as in current model checking techniques, which leads to exponential visiting time. Once designed and checked for safety, the module can be used "as is" in further composition contexts. In general a *safe* holon module can be arranged from already-designed *safe* modules by specifying that their interaction will occur in a *safe* manner, that is, as observed, by checking a single state machine in constant time. In case of physical systems which inherently fail, a suitable fault management strategy can be hosted at each level of decomposition, provided a sound decomposition has been carried out in the entire design phase. It becomes thus possible to defeat the overall complexity given by the concurrent modeling of operating modes and failure management policies. For example, fail silently sub-devices may be used as components for assembling a device behavior, which is able, at the higher level to *reduce* the fail silent behavior to a more tractable fail explicit behavior. The latter, in turn, may be used, at the next composition level, to obtain a fail safe or fail operational behavior. Examples of such hierarchical arrangement of failure modes and related devices are given in [23][24][25] and are summarized in Figure 7.

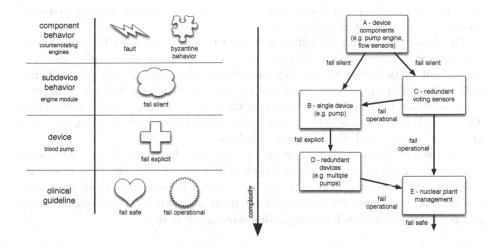

Fig. 7. Fault management strategies and devices tend to be placed at different levels of complexity in hierarchically decomposed behavior(adapted from [24])

5   Conclusions and Further Research

The paper main thesis is that an unifying paradigm may be founded upon different empirical and theoretical evidences, among which already existing improvements to the current OO paradigm.

Interacting modules synchronize system behavior by message exchange. Such messages, however, denote different kinds of information. Typically, systems communicate either by "peer to peer" or "part to whole" message exchange, the latter case pertaining to systems composed of other systems. The problem consists, at the ontological level, in determining whether two systems stand in the former or in the latter relationship. The object oriented paradigm, for example, do not distinguish amongst the two cases, thus giving rise to the "semantic overloading" of the reference mechanism.

As observed, vertical, part-whole, system composition is asymmetrical in nature and preserves model reusability. On the other hand, horizontal, peer to peer message exchange hinders model reusability, since it forces system modelers to introduce exogenous details within systems being modeled, bringing severe limitations to the overall software quality of the modeled systems. Physical interactions among physical systems denote in fact conceptual structures, not evident at first sight, which are well suited in order to host the overall interaction and synchronization knowledge among the component parts. By introducing additional system entities with the aim of lodging such a knowledge in a localized and compact manner, we obtain a part-whole hierarchy of systems, called holarchy. Such systems are, at the same time, both parts and wholes within a holarchy, thus giving a formal characterization to the notion of holon [26][27] which may give, in turn, further impulse to use of holarchies in distributed agent-based manufacturing systems[28][29][30][31].

The paper presents an explicit construct for the recursive modeling of systems. The approach forces the modeler to express the behavior of composition by a single unit of behavior. Such a behavioral unit plays the double role of being both a specification of the behavior of the system of interacting parts, as well as an interface for further composition of the entire assembled system as whole. This double side, "Janus"-like feature makes such kind of construct suitable for modeling, as observed, the behavior of holons.

The presented approach may be finally used in order to partition safety tasks into hierarchically arranged modules, each checked incrementally. Real-time critical systems, for example, may benefit from the approach since it allows to decompose a single, monolithic, control program into smaller, safe, reusable and composable systems, each hosting a different safety policy.

5.1 Further Research

Peer-to-peer (P2P) direct modeling is of paramount importance in expressing mutual interaction among entities and systems. Peer-to-peer interacting entities may be seen in many cases as playing specific roles within an implicit whole/holon. For example, "husband" and "wife" are both entities playing the respective roles in a P2P cooperation. Peer-to-peer modeling however does not allow to compute an exact state semantics, while part-to-whole (P2W) modeling instead does, as suggested by the paper. It seems evident that any peer-to-peer modeling corresponds to a specific part-to-whole modeling. For example, wife and husband are both part of a "family", which may be represented by an explicit entity/holon having two "humans" as components playing the "husband" and "wife" roles as components of the family holon.

As observed in the paper, it may be conjectured that it is always possible to obtain through the holonic P2W approach the same exact behavior that would be obtained by the direct P2P interaction of a finite number of state machines. It would then be interesting to investigate further whether an equivalence theorem between P2P and P2W modeling could be show to hold. Any P2P cooperation could then be checked by transforming it in a P2W holonic model for the sake of verification, and back for the sake of readability.

Another point which is worth further investigating and is not covered in the paper deals with inheritance. It is worth noting that the more we model state constraints within single modules the more we restrict the resulting global cartesian automaton [32]. A starting point towards a novel notion of holonic inheritance should therefore take into account, among possible other aspects, adding or removing behavioral restrictions to state machines in moving along inheritance hierarchies.

Finally, more research is needed in order to move towards more complex composition structures albeit retaining the part-whole hierarchical arrangement. For example, what if the same component is part of two different holons? Figure 8-(a) shows two different cross road controllers (CrossRoad1 and CrossRoad2) which share traffic light main1:TLight1. In order to avoid race conditions, the idea is to restrict control of main1 to a single holon (CrossRoad1 in the picture) through triggerable transitions t_2 and t_3 by command events go and stop (b). The rule, to be further investigated, is that transitions controlled by a given holon become simply observable by other holons in the composition graph. In this way, holon CrossRoad2 would acquire the same traffic light with transitions t_2 and t_3 seen as autonomous and non controllable (c), i.e. by simply "sensing" its state changes and taking decisions accordingly. Holarchies, by such a perspective, may be thus thought as acyclic direct graphs instead of simple partonomic trees, thus gaining more flexibility in modeling complex scenarios.

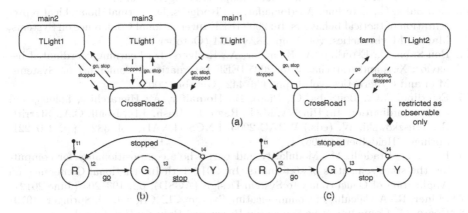

Fig. 8. (a) The same traffic light holon main1:TLight1 may be shared by two crossroad controller holons, with the restriction that at most one is allowed to trigger its transitions in order to avoid race conditions. (b) The interface of main1 as seen by CrossRoad1 with transitions t_2 and t_3 triggerable by events go and stop. (c) The interface of main1 as seen by CrossRoad2 with autonomous transitions t_2 and t_3 emitting events go and stop.

References

1. Koestler, A.: The ghost in the machine. Hutchinson, London (1976)
2. Leveson, N.: Engineering a Safer World: Systems Thinking Applied to Safety. Engineering Systems. MIT Press (2011)
3. Weinberg, G.M.: An introduction to general systems thinking. Behavioral Science 21(4), 289–290 (1976)
4. Rumbaugh, J., Blaha, M., Premerlani, W., Eddy, F., Lorensen, W.: Object-Oriented Modeling and Design. Prentice Hall (1991)
5. Gamma, E., Helm, R., Johnson, R., Vlissides, J.: Design patterns: elements of reusable object-oriented software. Addison-Wesley Longman Publishing Co., Inc., Boston (1995)
6. Krasner, G.E., Pope, S.T.: A cookbook for using the model-view controller user interface paradigm in smalltalk-80. J. Object Oriented Program. 1(3), 26–49 (1988)

7. Pazzi, L.: Implicit versus explicit characterization of complex entities and events. Data & Knowledge Engineering 31, 115–134 (1999)
8. Wand, Y., Storey, V.C., Weber, R.: An ontological analysis of the relationship construct in conceptual modeling. ACM Trans. Database Syst. 24, 494–528 (1999)
9. Coleman, D., Arnold, P., Bodoff, S., Dollin, C., Gilchrist, H., Hayes, F., Jeremaes, P.: Object-Oriented Development: The Fusion Method. Prentice-Hall, Inc., Upper Saddle River (1994)
10. Rumbaugh, J., Jacobson, I., Booch, G.: The Unified Modeling Language Reference Manual. Addison-Wesley (1998)
11. Rumbaugh, J., Jacobson, I., Booch, G.: Unified Modeling Language Reference Manual, The 2nd edn. Pearson Higher Education (2004)
12. Pazzi, L.: Extending statecharts for representing parts and wholes. In: Proceedings of the EuroMicro 1997 Conference, Budapest, Hungary (1997)
13. Bou-Saba, C., Esterline, A., Homaifar, A., Rodgers, D.: Formal, holarchical representation of tactical behaviors. In: 2005 IEEE International Conference on Systems, Man and Cybernetics, vol. 4, pp. 3828–3834 (October 2005)
14. Bou-Saba, C., Esterline, A., Homaifar, A., Rodgers, D.: Learning coordinated behavior: Xcss and statecharts. In: 2005 IEEE International Conference on Systems, Man and Cybernetics, vol. 1, pp. 436–442 (October 2005)
15. Esterline, A.C., BouSaba, C., Pioro, B., Homaifar, A.: Hierarchies, holons, and agent coordination. In: Hinchey, M.G., Rago, P., Rash, J.L., Rouff, C.A., Sterritt, R., Truszkowski, W. (eds.) WRAC 2005. LNCS (LNAI), vol. 3825, pp. 210–221. Springer, Heidelberg (2006)
16. Pazzi, L., Pradelli, M.: Modularity and part-whole compositionality for computing the state semantics of statecharts. In: 2012 12th International Conference on Application of Concurrency to System Design (ACSD), pp. 193–203 (June 2012)
17. Milner, R.: A Calculus of Communicating Systems. LNCS, vol. 92. Springer (1979)
18. Hoare, C.: Communicating Sequential Processes. Prentice-Hall (1985)
19. Harel, D.: Statecharts: A visual formalism for complex systems. Science of Computer Programming 8, 231–274 (1987)
20. Parnas, D., Clements, P., Weiss, D.: The modular structure of complex systems. IEEE Transactions on Software Engineering SE-11(3), 259–266 (1985)
21. Pazzi, L., Pradelli, M.: A state-based systemic view of behavior for safe medical computer applications. In: 21st IEEE International Symposium on Computer-Based Medical Systems, CBMS 2008, pp. 108–113 (2008)
22. Von der Beek, M.: A comparison of statecharts variant. In: Langmaack, H., de Roever, W.-P., Vytopil, J. (eds.) FTRTFT 1994 and ProCoS 1994. LNCS, vol. 863, pp. 128–148. Springer, Heidelberg (1994)
23. Pazzi, L., Pradelli, M.: Part-whole hierarchical modularization of fault-tolerant and goal-based autonomic systems. In: 2nd IFAC Symposium on Dependable Control of Discrete Systems, DCDS 2009, pp. 175–180 (2009)
24. Pazzi, L., Pradelli, M.: Using part-whole statecharts for the safe modeling of clinical guidelines. In: 2010 IEEE Workshop on Health Care Management, WHCM (2010)
25. Pazzi, L., Interlandi, M., Pradelli, M.: Automatic fault behavior detection and modeling by a state-based specification method. In: 2010 IEEE 12th International Symposium on High-Assurance Systems Engineering (HASE), pp. 166–167 (November 2010)
26. Hilaire, V., Koukam, A., Rodriguez, S.: An adaptative agent architecture for holonic multi-agent systems. ACM Trans. Auton. Adapt. Syst. 3(1), 2:1–2:24 (2008)
27. Mella, P.: The Holonic Revolution. Holons, Holarchies and Holonic Networks. The Ghost in the Production Machine. Pavia University Press (2009)

28. van Leeuwen, E., Norrie, D.: Holons and holarchies (intelligent manufacturing systems). Manufacturing Engineer 76(2), 86–88 (1997)
29. Sabaz, D., Gruver, W., Smith, M.: Distributed systems with agents and holons. In: 2004 IEEE International Conference on Systems, Man and Cybernetics, vol. 2, pp. 1958–1963 (October 2004)
30. Giret, A., Botti, V.: Identifying and specifying holons in manufacturing systems. In: 7th World Congress on Intelligent Control and Automation, WCICA 2008, pp. 404–409 (June 2008)
31. Dominici, G., Palumbo, F.: Decoding the japanese lean production system according to a viable systems perspective. Systemic Practice and Action Research 26(2), 153–171 (2013)
32. Arnold, A.: Finite Transition Systems: Semantics of Communicating Systems. Prentice-Hall International Series in Computer Science. Masson/Prentice Hall (1994)

Semantic Model Differencing Utilizing Behavioral Semantics Specifications

Philip Langer, Tanja Mayerhofer, and Gerti Kappel

Business Informatics Group, Vienna University of Technology, Vienna, Austria
{langer,mayerhofer,gerti}@big.tuwien.ac.at

Abstract. Identifying differences among models is a crucial prerequisite for several development and change management tasks in model-driven engineering. The majority of existing model differencing approaches focus on revealing syntactic differences which can only approximate semantic differences among models. Significant advances in semantic model differencing have been recently made by Maoz *et al.* [16] who propose semantic diff operators for UML class and activity diagrams. In this paper, we present a generic semantic differencing approach which can be instantiated to realize semantic diff operators for specific modeling languages. Our approach utilizes the behavioral semantics specification of the considered modeling language, which enables to execute models and capture execution traces representing the models' semantic interpretation. Based on this semantic interpretation, semantic differences can be revealed.

1 Introduction

The identification of differences among independently developed or consecutive versions of software artifacts is not only a crucial prerequisite for several important development and change management tasks, such as merging and incremental testing, but also for enabling developers to efficiently comprehend an artifact's evolution. As in model-driven engineering the main software artifacts are models, techniques for identifying *differences among models* are of major importance.

The challenge of model differencing has attracted much research in the past years, which lead to significant advances and a variety of approaches. The majority of them use a *syntactic differencing* approach, which applies a fine-grained comparison of models based on their abstract syntax representation. As shown by Alanen and Porres [1] and later by Lin *et al.* [14], syntactic differencing algorithms can be designed in a generic manner—that is, they can be applied to models conforming to any modeling language. The result of such a differencing approach is a set of syntactic differences, such as model elements that only exist in one model. Although syntactic differences constitute valuable and efficiently processable information sufficient for several application domains, they are only an approximation of the *semantic differences* among models with respect to their meaning [10]. In fact, few syntactic differences among models may induce many semantic differences, whereas also syntactically different models may still exhibit the same semantics [16]. The identification of semantic differences is crucial for understanding the evolution of a model, as it enables to reason about the meaning of a change. Compared to syntactic differencing, semantic differencing enables several

J. Dingel et al. (Eds.): MODELS 2014, LNCS 8767, pp. 116–132, 2014.
© Springer International Publishing Switzerland 2014

additional analyses, such as the verification of the semantic preservation of changes like of refactorings and the identification of semantic conflicts among concurrent changes.

Significant advances towards *semantic model differencing* have been recently made by Maoz *et al.* [16]. They propose semantic diff operators yielding so-called *diff witnesses*, which are interpretations over a model that are valid in only one of the two compared models. The semantic diff operator has to be realized specifically for each modeling language by transforming models into an adequate semantic domain, performing dedicated analyses within this semantic domain, translating the results of the analyses back again, and representing them in the form of diff witnesses. Following this procedure, Maoz *et al.* presented dedicated diff operators for UML activity diagrams [17] and class diagrams [18]. Developing such diff operators for a specific modeling language, however, still remains a major challenge, as one has to develop often non-trivial transformations encoding the semantics of the modeling language into a semantic domain, perform analyses dedicated to semantic differencing in this semantic domain, and translate the results into diff witnesses on the level of the modeling language—notably, this challenging process has to be repeated for every modeling language.

To mitigate this challenge, we present a *generic* semantic differencing approach that can be instantiated to realize semantic diff operators for specific modeling languages. This approach follows the spirit of *generic* syntactic differencing, which utilizes metamodels to obtain the necessary information on the syntactic structure of the models to be compared. Accordingly, we propose to utilize the behavioral semantics of a modeling language to support the semantic model differencing. In particular, we exploit the executability of the behavioral semantics to obtain execution traces for the models to be compared. These traces are considered as semantic interpretations over the models and, thus, act as input to the semantic comparison. The actual comparison logics is specified in terms of dedicated match rules defining which differences among these interpretations constitute semantic differences. Semantic diff operators defined with our approach are enumerative yielding diff witnesses, which constitute manifestations of semantic differences among models and enable modeler's to reason about a model's evolution. Hence, the diff operators constitute a crucial basis for supporting collaborative work on models as well as for carrying out model management activities, such as model versioning and refactoring, which can be supported by an automated analysis of diff witnesses for identifying conflicting changes and causes of semantic differences.

In Section 2, we discuss existing work in the area of model differencing, before we introduce our semantic differencing approach in Section 3. Subsequently, we show in Section 4 how semantic diff operators can be implemented by applying our approach to an existing semantics specification approach. In Section 5, we address the issue of generating model inputs relevant to semantic differencing. Finally, we present an evaluation of the feasibility of our approach in Section 6 and draw conclusions in Section 7.

2   Related Work

Most of the existing model differencing approaches compare two models based on their *abstract syntax* representation (e.g., [1,2,14,25,26,31]). In particular, a match between two models is computed yielding the correspondences between their model elements, before a fine-grained comparison of all corresponding model elements is performed. The result of this syntactic differencing is the set of model elements present in only one model and a description of differences among model elements present in both models.

However, to determine whether two syntactically different models also differ in their meaning, the semantics of the modeling language they conform to has to be taken into account [10]. Few *semantic model differencing* approaches have been proposed in the past. Generally, we can distinguish enumerative and non-enumerative approaches. *Enumerative* approaches calculate semantic interpretations of two compared models called *diff witnesses*, which are only valid for one of the two models and, hence, provide evidence about the existence of semantic differences among the models. *Non-enumerative* approaches do not calculate and enumerate diff witnesses directly, but instead compute an aggregated description of the semantic difference among the compared models [8].

Significant advances in semantic differencing have been achieved by Mazo *et al.*, who propose an approach for defining enumerative semantic diff operators [16]. In this approach, two models to be compared are translated into an adequate semantic domain whereupon dedicated algorithms are used to calculate semantic differences in the form of diff witnesses. Following this approach, they define the diff operators CDDiff [18] and ADDiff [17], for UML class diagrams and UML activity diagrams, respectively. CDDiff translates UML class diagrams into an Alloy module to generate object diagrams that are valid instances of one class diagram but not of the other. ADDiff translates two UML activity diagrams into SMV modules to identify execution traces which are possible only in one of the two activity diagrams. Gerth *et al.* [9] developed an enumerative semantic diff operator similar to ADDiff for detecting semantic differences among process models. Therefore, the process models are translated into process model terms, which are subsequently compared to identify execution traces valid only for one of the two compared models. Another approach for defining enumerative semantic diff operators was presented by Reiter *et al.* [28]. In their approach, two models that shall be compared are translated into a common semantic domain. The resulting so-called *semantic views* of the two models are subsequently compared by syntactic differencing techniques to identify semantic differences.

Unlike the approaches discussed so far, Fahrenberg *et al.* [8] propose an approach for defining non-enumerative semantic diff operators. Therefore, the models to be compared are mapped into a semantic domain having an algebraic structure that enables to define the difference among two models in the form of an operator on the semantic domain. Thereby, the difference is captured in the form of a model conform to the same modeling language as the two compared models. Fahrenberg *et al.* applied this approach for defining semantic diff operators for feature models as well as automata specifications [8], and later also for UML class diagrams [7].

3   Overview

Developing semantic diff operators using the discussed existing semantic differencing approaches poses a major challenge, because one has to develop non-trivial transformations encoding the semantics of the modeling language into an adequate semantic domain, in which then specific semantic comparison algorithms have to be imple-

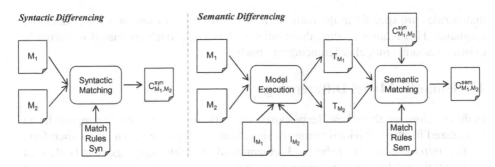

Fig. 1. Overview of semantic differencing approach

mented. To mitigate this challenge, we propose a *generic* semantic differencing approach that can be instantiated to realize semantic diff operators for specific modeling languages. Therefore, we utilize the *behavioral semantics specification* of a modeling language, which can be defined using existing semantics specification approaches, such as xMOF [20], Kermeta [22], or DMM [5]. Such semantics specifications can be used for various application domains, ranging from model simulation, verification, through to validation. In this work, we aim at reusing such semantics specifications also for semantic model differencing. In particular, we exploit the fact that behavioral semantics specifications enable the execution of models and that the identification of semantic differences among models is possible based on *execution traces*, since they reflect the models' behavior and, hence, constitute the semantic interpretation of the models.

Figure 1 depicts an overview of our semantic model differencing approach consisting of three steps: syntactic matching, model execution, and semantic matching. In the *syntactic matching* step, syntactically corresponding elements of the two compared models M_1 and M_2 are identified based on syntactic match rules $MatchRulesSyn$ for establishing syntactic correspondences C_{M_1,M_2}^{syn} between the models. In the *model execution* step, the models M_1 and M_2 are executed for relevant inputs I_{M_1} and I_{M_2} based on the behavioral semantics specification of the modeling language. During model execution, the traces T_{M_1} and T_{M_2} are captured, which constitute the semantic interpretation of the executed models M_1 and M_2. We assume that the model execution is deterministic, meaning that the model execution yields for a given input always the same execution trace, and that the number of possible traces is finite. In the *semantic matching* step, the captured execution traces T_{M_1} and T_{M_2} are compared based on semantic match rules $MatchRulesSem$, which define the semantic equivalence criteria, to establish semantic correspondences C_{M_1,M_2}^{sem} between the models M_1 and M_2. Thereby, two models M_1 and M_2 are semantically equivalent, if the traces captured during their execution T_{M_1} and T_{M_2} match according to the semantic match rules. In the semantic matching, also the syntactic correspondences of the examined models C_{M_1,M_2}^{syn} may be taken into account.

Our semantic model differencing approach is *generic*, because it enables to implement semantic diff operators for any modeling languages whose behavioral semantics is defined such that conforming models can be executed and execution traces can be obtained. From all artifacts involved in the semantic differencing, only the semantic match rules are specific to the realization of a semantic diff operator for a modeling language. This is an important differentiator of our approach compared to currently existing semantic model differencing approaches.

4 Semantic Model Differencing

In this section, we show how the proposed semantic model differencing approach can be realized for the behavioral semantics specification language xMOF [20]. Therefore, we first introduce how the behavioral semantics of modeling languages can be defined with xMOF and how this definition is used to execute models. Second, we present which trace information is needed for semantically differencing models. Third, we show how semantic match rules can be defined for semantically comparing models based on execution traces. For illustrating the presented techniques, we use the Petri net language as a running example throughout the paper.

4.1 Behavioral Semantics Specification with xMOF

The semantics specification language xMOF integrates existing metamodeling languages, in particular Ecore, with the action language of UML [23]. This enables the definition of the behavioral semantics of the concepts of a modeling language by introducing operations for the respective metaclasses and defining their behavior with UML activities. UML's action language for defining activities provides a predefined set of actions for expressing the manipulation of objects and links (e.g., CreateObject-Action) and the communication between objects (e.g., CallOperationAction), as well as a model library of primitive behaviors (e.g., IntegerPlus). xMOF enables the execution of models by executing the activities defined in the modeling language's semantics specification based on the fUML virtual machine. fUML [24] is a standard of the OMG, which defines the semantics of a subset of UML activity diagrams formally and provides a virtual machine enabling the execution of fUML-compliant models.

Example. In the upper left part of Figure 2, the *Ecore-based metamodel* of the Petri net language is depicted. A Petri net (Net) consists of a set of uniquely named places (Place) and transitions (Transition), whereas transitions reference their input and output places (input, output). The initial marking of the Petri net is captured by an Integer attribute (initialTokens) of the Place metaclass.

In xMOF, the behavioral semantics of a modeling language is defined in an *xMOF-based configuration*. This xMOF-based configuration contains for each metaclass in the metamodel a *configuration class*, which extends the respective metaclass with its behavioral semantics by introducing additional attributes and references for capturing runtime information, as well as additional operations and activities for defining behavior. In the lower left part of Figure 2, the configuration classes contained by the xMOF-based configuration of the Petri net language are shown. To capture the number of held tokens of a Petri net during its execution, the Integer attribute tokens is introduced in the configuration class PlaceConfiguration. The main() operation of NetConfiguration serves as entry point for executing a Petri net model. It first calls the operation initializeMarking(), which initializes the tokens attribute of each Place instance with the value of the

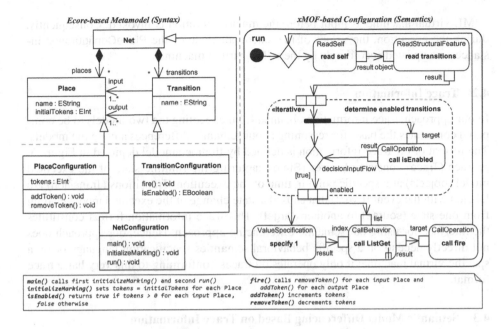

Fig. 2. Petri net language specification

initialTokens attribute, before the operation run() is invoked. The activity defining the behavior of run() is depicted in the right part of Figure 2. It determines in a loop the set of enabled transitions (ExpansionRegion "determine enabled transitions"), selects the first enabled transition (CallBehaviorAction "call ListGet"), and calls the operation fire() (CallOperationAction "call fire") for this transition. Subsequently, the operation fire() calls for each input place of the transition the operation removeToken() to decrement its tokens value and addToken() for each output place to increment its tokens value.

Based on this behavioral semantics specification, a Petri net model can be executed. Therefore, the configuration classes are instantiated for each model element in the Petri net model and the resulting instances are initialized according to the attribute values and references of the respective model element. These instances are then provided to the

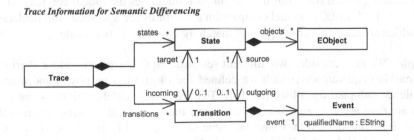

Fig. 3. Trace information format specification

fUML virtual machine as input before the main() operation is invoked. Consequently, during the execution, the values of the tokens attribute of the PlaceConfiguration instances are updated accordingly by the fUML virtual machine.

4.2   Trace Information

In our approach, trace information obtained from executing the two models to be compared constitutes the basis for reasoning about semantic differences among the models. The format of the trace information is defined by the metamodel depicted in Figure 3. A trace (Trace) consists of states (State) capturing the runtime state of the executed model (objects) at a specific point in time of the execution. Transitions (Transition) are labeled with the event (Event) that caused a state change of the executed model leading from one state (source) to another (target). This trace information format constitutes the interface for using our semantic differencing approach. Hence, our approach does not directly depend on a specific behavioral semantics specification language or on a specific virtual machine; it only operates on traces conforming to this very basic trace format.

4.3   Semantic Model Differencing Based on Trace Information

For semantically differencing two models, the trace information captured by executing these models are compared according to semantic match rules. These match rules decide based on the states of the compared models and based on the events causing state transitions which model elements semantically correspond to each other and whether the two models are semantically equivalent. The semantic match rules are specific to the considered modeling language as well as to the relevant semantic equivalence criteria. Thereby our approach is flexible in the sense that match rules can be expressed for different equivalence criteria. This is an important property because, depending on the usage scenario of a modeling language, different equivalence criteria for models may apply. For Petri nets, for instance, different equivalence criteria are *marking equivalence*, *trace equivalence*, and *bisimulation equivalence* [6]. If Petri nets are used to define production processes, where the tokens residing in places represent production resources, the marking equivalence criteria might be the most suitable equivalence criteria. However, if Petri nets are used to define business processes, the trace equivalence criteria might be more adequate.

For defining match rules, our implementation integrates the model comparison language ECL [12]. In ECL, model comparison algorithms are specified with declarative rules which are used to identify pairs of matching elements in two models.

Example. We now consider two different semantic equivalence criteria for Petri nets: final marking equivalence (which we defined for illustration purposes) and marking equivalence (adopted from literature [6]). Two Petri net models with the same set of places are *final marking equivalent* if they have the same final marking, whereas they are *marking equivalent*, if they have the same set of reachable markings. The example Petri net models $PN1$ and $PN2$ depicted in Figure 4 are not final marking equivalent because their final markings $M_{2,PN1}$ and $M_{2,PN2}$ are different. However, they are marking equivalent, as they have the same set of reachable markings ($M_{0,PN1}$ matches with $M_{1,PN2}$, $M_{1,PN1}$ with $M_{2,PN2}$, and $M_{2,PN1}$ with $M_{0,PN2}$).

Listing 1 shows the semantic match rules expressed in ECL for determining whether two Petri net models are final marking equivalent. The semantic match rule *Match Trace* (lines 1-8) is responsible for matching the traces captured for the execution of two compared Petri net models. If the models are final marking equivalent, this rule has to return true, otherwise false. Therefore, the respective final states of the two traces *markingStatesLeft* and *markingStatesRight* are obtained using the operation *getMarkingStates()* (lines 10-12). These retrieved final states are then matched with each other (line 6) and if they match, the Petri net models are final marking equivalent and true is returned. The two final states are matched by the rule *MatchState* (line 14-22). Therefore, the final runtime states of the PlaceConfiguration instances from the respective final state are retrieved by calling the operation *getPlaceConfigurations()* (lines 24-30) and true is returned if the PlaceConfiguration instances match (line 20). The PlaceConfiguration instances are matched by the rule *MatchPlaceConfiguration* (lines 32-37), which defines that two PlaceConfiguration instances match, if they match syntactically (this is checked by the extended syntactic match rule *MatchPlace* not shown here, which defines that two Place instances match if they have the same name) and if they contain the same amount of tokens (line 36). Thus, in the end, the match rule *MatchTrace* returns true, if the two compared Petri net models have the same markings in the end of the execution and are, hence, final marking equivalent.

For realizing the marking equivalence criteria, the operation *getMarkingStates()* has to be adapted as shown in Listing 2. It retrieves the state after the initializeMarking activity has been executed for the NetConfiguration instance (line 3) and after each execution of the fire activity for any TransitionConfiguration instance (line 4). Therefore, the operation *getStatesAfterEvent()* provided by the trace is used, which retrieves the states caused by an event corresponding to the provided qualified name. Thus, the operation *getMarkingStates()* returns the runtime states of the compared models after initializing the marking of the net and after each transition firing, i.e., each state after reaching a new marking. These sets of states *markingStatesLeft* and *markingStatesRight* match (cf. line 6 in Listing 1), if each state in *markingStatesLeft* has a corresponding state in *markingStatesRight* and vice versa; that is, if each marking reachable in $PN1$ is also reachable in $PN2$ and vice versa. Please note that we restrict ourselves in this example to conflict-free and terminating Petri nets.

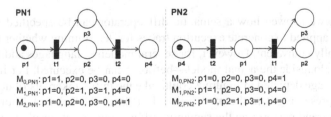

PN1
p3
p1 t1 p2 t2 p4
$M_{0,PN1}$: p1=1, p2=0, p3=0, p4=0
$M_{1,PN1}$: p1=0, p2=1, p3=1, p4=0
$M_{2,PN1}$: p1=0, p2=0, p3=0, p4=1

PN2
p3
p4 t2 p1 t1 p2
$M_{0,PN2}$: p1=0, p2=0, p3=0, p4=1
$M_{1,PN2}$: p1=1, p2=0, p3=0, p4=0
$M_{2,PN2}$: p1=0, p2=1, p3=1, p4=0

Fig. 4. Example Petri net models

```
1  rule MatchTrace
2      match left : Left!Trace with right : Right!Trace {
3        compare {
4              var markingStatesLeft : Set = left.getMarkingStates();
5              var markingStatesRight : Set = right.getMarkingStates();
6              return markingStatesLeft.matches(markingStatesRight);
7        }
8      }
9
10  operation Trace getMarkingStates() : Set {
11      return self.states.at(self.states.size() − 1).asSet();
12  }
13
14  @lazy
15  rule MatchState
16      match left : Left!State with right : Right!State {
17        compare {
18              var placeConfsLeft : Set = left.getPlaceConfigurations();
19              var placeConfsRight : Set = right.getPlaceConfigurations();
20              return placeConfsLeft.matches(placeConfsRight);
21        }
22      }
23
24  operation State getPlaceConfigurations() : Set {
25      var placeConfs : Set = new Set();
26      for (object : Any in self.objects)
27          if (object.isKindOf(PlaceConfiguration))
28              placeConfs.add(object);
29      return placeConfs;
30  }
31
32  @lazy
33  rule MatchPlaceConfiguration
34      match left : Left!PlaceConfiguration with right : Right!PlaceConfiguration
35      extends MatchPlace {
36        compare : left.tokens = right.tokens
37      }
```

Listing 1. Semantic match rules for Petri net final marking equivalence

```
1  operation Trace getMarkingStates() : Set {
2      var markingStates : Set = new Set();
3      markingStates.addAll(self.getStatesAfterEvent("petrinetConfiguration.NetConfiguration.
          ↪initializeMarking"));
4      markingStates.addAll(self.getStatesAfterEvent("petrinetConfiguration.
          ↪TransitionConfiguration.fire"));
5      return markingStates;
6  }
```

Listing 2. Adaptation of semantic match rules for Petri net marking equivalence

5   Input Generation Using Symbolic Execution

In Section 4, we showed how a semantic diff operator can be specified with match
rules that are applied to concrete execution traces for determining whether two models
are semantically equivalent. However, for several modeling languages additional input
is required—alongside the actual model—before it can be executed. For instance, the
Petri net language depicted in Figure 2 could take the initial token distribution as input
instead of representing it in the model directly (Place.initialTokens). Enumerating all
possible inputs and performing the semantic differencing for all resulting traces is not
feasible for several scenarios, as the number of possible inputs may quickly become

large or even infinite. In fact, we are interested only in inputs that cause *distinct and for the semantic differencing relevant execution traces*. Having obtained such inputs, the models to be compared can be executed for these inputs and the semantic match rules can be applied on the captured traces for semantically differencing the models. Thereby, two models are semantically equivalent, if they exhibit the same behavior for the same inputs as defined by the semantic match rules. If they behave differently for the same input, they differ semantically and the respective input constitutes a diff witness.

For *automatically* generating relevant inputs from the semantics specification of the modeling language for the two models to be compared, we apply an adaptation of symbolic execution [3]. The basic idea behind symbolic execution, as introduced by Clarke [4], is to execute a program—in our case, the semantics specification for a specific model—with *symbolic values* in place of concrete values and to record a *path constraint*, which is a quantifier-free first-order formula, for each conditional statement that is evaluated over symbolic values along an execution path. For each symbolic value, a symbolic state is maintained during the symbolic execution, which maps symbolic values to symbolic expressions. After executing a path symbolically, we obtain a sequence of path constraints, which can be conjuncted and solved by a constraint solver to obtain concrete inputs. An execution with these inputs will consequently exercise the path that has been recorded symbolically. If a conjunction of path constraints is unsatisfiable, the execution path can never occur. Using backtracking and negations of path constraints, we may further obtain *all feasible paths* represented as an *execution tree*, which is a binary tree, where each node denotes a path constraint and each edge a Boolean value.

More recently, several extensions and flavors of traditional symbolic execution have been proposed (cf. [3] for a survey). For this work, we apply a combination of concolic execution [29] and generalized symbolic execution [11]. *Concolic execution* significantly decreases the number of path constraints by distinguishing between concrete and symbolic values. The program is essentially executed as normal and only statements that depend on symbolic values are handled differently. As we execute the semantics specification with a concrete model (to be compared) and additional input, we may consider only the additional input as symbolic values—statements that interact with the executed model itself are executed as normal. One of the key ideas behind *generalized symbolic execution* also used in this work is to use lazy initialization of symbolic values. Thus, we execute the model as normal and initialize empty objects for symbolic values only when the execution accesses the object for the first time. Similarly, attribute values of objects are only initialized on their first access during the execution with dedicated values to induce a certain path during the execution.

Example: Initial tokens as input. Before we discuss how we apply symbolic execution on our running example, we have to slightly modify the Petri net language depicted in Figure 2 such that it takes the initial token distribution as input. Therefore, we add a class Token, which owns a reference named place to Place denoting the token's initial place. Additionally, we change the operation NetConfiguration.main() and add a parameter initialTokens of type EList<Token> to this operation. The activity specifying the behavior of the operation main() passes the list of initial tokens to the operation initialize-Marking(), which in turn sets the number of tokens for each place p to p.tokens = initialTokens->select(t | t.place = p).size(); note that we define

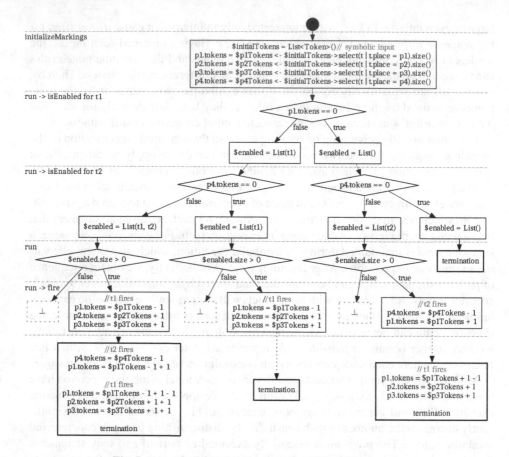

Fig. 5. Excerpt of the execution tree for $PN2$ (cf. Figure 4)

this assignment here in OCL syntax for the sake of brevity, in an operational semantics specification, this assignment is specified in terms of an action language, such as fUML.

Example: Symbolic execution. To derive input values that cause all distinct execution traces, we symbolically execute the operational semantics of the Petri net language with both models to be compared, whereas the input of the execution—that is, the parameter initialTokens of type EList<Token>—is represented as a symbolic value. Figure 5 shows an excerpt of the resulting execution tree for $PN2$ (cf. Figure 4). Note that we bound the symbolic execution to at most one initial token per place in this example. We depict path constraints as diamonds and the symbolic states of symbolic values in boxes; symbolic values are prefixed with a $ symbol. The uppermost box shows the symbolic states after executing the operation initializeMarking(initial-Tokens). As this operation assigns the number of tokens based on the symbolic input initialTokens to the tokens attribute of each place, also the values assigned to this attribute are handled symbolically. The initial symbolic values for this attribute are mapped to the symbolic expression `$initialTokens->select(t | t.place`

= pX) . size (). In Figure 5, this expression is abbreviated with $pXTokens. After the markings are initialized, the operation run() is called (cf. Figure 2). This operation iterates through the transitions of the net and checks whether they are enabled. Therefore, in the first iteration, isEnabled() is called on transition t1, which in turn iterates through all of its incoming places (p1 in our example) and checks whether there is an incoming place without tokens. Therefore, the symbolic value p1.tokens is accessed and the condition p1 . tokens == 0 is evaluated. We do not interfere with the concrete execution except for the access of the symbolic value and the evaluation of the condition in order to record the path condition, update the execution tree (cf. Figure 5), and solve the constraint to compute concrete values for the involved symbolic values inducing the true branch and the false branch, respectively. After that, we continue with the concrete execution with the respective concrete values for both branches. Depending on which branch is taken (i.e., t1 is enabled or not), t1 is added to the output expansion node enabled of the expansion region in the activity run (cf. Figure 2). In the symbolic execution of activities, we handle expansion nodes as list variables. As the addition of t1 to the expansion node depends on symbolic values, we also consider the list variable, denoted with $enabled, as symbolic. In the next iteration of run, the same procedure is applied to transition t2 and its input place p4; thus, the execution tree is updated accordingly. Next, the execution checks whether the list of enabled transitions contains at least one element with the condition $enabled.size > 0. As this condition accesses $enabled, which is considered as symbolic value, we record it in the execution tree and try to produce values for the true and false branch. However, the constraint solver cannot find a solution for the false branch, denoted with $\perp$ in Figure 5, because in three paths $enabled will always contain at least one transition according to the path conditions and symbolic states. Thus, in three of the six branches, fire() is called for the first transition in the list $enabled causing changes in the tokens attribute of the incoming and outgoing places. As the tokens attribute is considered as symbolic, we update their symbolic states. Finally, the execution proceeds with iterating through transitions again and firing them, if they are enabled. As we bound the symbolic execution to at most one initial token per place, all branches either terminate eventually or lead to an unsatisfiable state (e.g., violating the bound condition).

The final execution tree contains four satisfiable execution paths. The path conditions of these paths represent symbolically all relevant initial token markings for this net inducing all distinct execution traces. Using a constraint solver, we can generate Token objects with corresponding links to the places in the net such that the initial markings of the four inputs are: $\{p1 = 1\}$, $\{p1 = 1, p4 = 1\}$, $\{p4 = 1\}$, and $\{\}$ (no tokens at all). When repeating the symbolic execution for the Petri net $PN1$ in Figure 4, we obtain two additional inputs: $\{p1 = 1, p2 = 1\}$ (or p3 instead of p2), and $\{p1 = 1, p2 = 1, p3 = 1\}$. With this total of six inputs, we invoke the semantic differencing based on the semantic match rules to obtain all diff witnesses (cf. Section 4).

6   Evaluation

We evaluated our approach regarding three aspects. First, we investigate whether our generic approach is powerful enough to specify semantic diff operators equivalent to those specifically designed for particular modeling languages. Second, we examine the performance of applying semantic diff operators realized with our approach. Third, we evaluate the feasibility of realizing symbolic execution of models based on an operational semantics specification, in particular, using fUML.

Expressive power of generic semantic differencing. To assess whether our generic approach provides the necessary expressive power to define non-trivial semantic diff operators, we carried out two case studies, in which we implemented diff operators for UML activity diagrams and class diagrams according to ADDiff [17] and CDDiff [18] developed by Maoz *et al.* This allows us to evaluate whether our generic approach is powerful enough to compare to one of the most sophisticated language-specific approaches in the semantic differencing domain. Therefore, we implemented the same semantics of UML activity diagrams and class diagrams as defined by Maoz *et al.* using xMOF. While the focus of the evaluation lies on the expressive power of our approach regarding the definition of diff operators, the following figures shall indicate, that the semantics specifications developed for the case studies are of high complexity. The semantics specification of activity diagrams comprises 38 configuration classes consisting of 60 activities in total, which contain altogether 380 activity nodes. The semantics specification of class diagrams comprises 56 configuration classes, 119 activities, and 1003 nodes. For realizing the semantic diff operators we implemented semantic match rule corresponding to the semantic differencing algorithms defined by Maoz *et al.* They enabled us to detect the same diff witnesses as Maoz *et al.* among their case study example models published in [17,18]. The interested reader can find our case studies at our project website [21]. For brevity, we discuss only the results of the case studies in the following.

From the case studies, we conclude that the expressive power of our generic semantic differencing approach is sufficient for defining non-trivial semantic diff operators. Implementing the semantic match rules requires besides knowledge about model comparison languages, such as ECL, knowledge about the behavioral semantics specification of the considered modeling language. Hence, defining semantic diff operators is a task that has to be performed by someone experienced with language engineering.

Performance of applying the semantic matching. We measured the performance of the implemented diff operators in terms of time needed for evaluating whether the example models are semantically different for a given set of input values. This experiment was performed on a Intel Dual Core i5-2520M CPU, 2.5 GHz, with 8 GB RAM, running Windows 7. Table 1 shows the time needed for syntactic matching ($SynMatching$), model execution ($Execution$), and semantic matching ($SemMatching$), as well as the total time needed ($Total$). Please note that these figures do not include the time needed for generating all relevant inputs because an implementation of symbolic model execution for fUML is not integrated yet with our semantic differencing prototype. For activity diagrams, Table 1 also provides the number of activity nodes ($\#Nodes$), as well as the number of input values to consider ($\#Inputs$), as they have a significant influence on the execution time. For class diagrams, we provide the number of objects ($\#Objects$) as well as links ($\#Links$) of the input object diagram. The performance results indicate that the model execution is the most expensive step in the semantic model differencing as it takes around 95% of the overall time. Thus, the main reason

Table 1. Performance results for semantically differencing example models

UML activity diagram

Example	#Nodes	#Inputs	SynMatching	Execution	SemMatching	Total
Anon V1/V2	15/15	2	51 ms	7905 ms	341 ms	8297 ms
Anon V2/V3	15/19	1	72 ms	7374 ms	246 ms	7692 ms
hire V1/V2	14/15	1	47 ms	5259 ms	283 ms	5589 ms
hire V2/V3	15/15	1	47 ms	5745 ms	304 ms	6096 ms
hire V3/V4	15/15	1	48 ms	2011 ms	95 ms	2154 ms
IBM2557 V1/V2	18/16	3	85 ms	25889 ms	1159 ms	27133 ms

UML class diagram

Example	#Objects	#Links	SynMatching	Execution	SemMatching	Total
EMT V1/V2	2	1	17 ms	1203 ms	119 ms	1339 ms
EMT V1/V2	4	3	16 ms	6790 ms	275 ms	7081 ms
EMT V1/V2	6	5	15 ms	26438 ms	543 ms	26996 ms

for the weaker performance result compared to the approach of Maoz *et al.* [17,18] is the performance of the model execution carried out by the fUML virtual machine.

Symbolic execution of fUML. An important prerequisite for realizing symbolic execution is the identification of conditional executions, as well as the extraction of the condition in terms of a quantifier free path constraint. Therefore, we analyzed the feasibility of identifying and mapping conditional language concepts of fUML's action language to corresponding OCL path constraint templates. In this analysis, we faced several challenges, since the execution flow is driven by offering and accepting object tokens through input and output pins of actions; if an action, e.g., a ReadStructural-FeatureValueAction, reads a non-existing value, no token is placed on its output pin, which in turn prevents the execution of the action that waits for the token. Thus, actions that take inputs from actions reading symbolic values, have to be considered as conditional and, therefore, a dedicated path constraint has to be generated. Besides, we have to map the different ways of using DecisionNodes to path constraints, which was, however, mostly straightforward. Nevertheless, we were able to map the fUML concepts used in the case studies to corresponding path conditions. Moreover, in the semantics specifications of our two case studies, we only used the standardized primitive operators and behaviors of fUML, such as greater than, logical AND, list size, etc. As all of these operators and behaviors are supported in OCL, it is straightforward to represent the symbolic state of symbolic variables entirely in OCL, which enabled us to avoid suffering from symbolic imprecision. For realizing generalized concolic execution [29,11] of fUML, it is moreover crucial to distinguish among concrete and symbolic values and, therefore, to extract a value dependency graph for determining whether a value depends directly or indirectly on a symbolic value. Therefore, we performed an experimental implementation for analyzing the dependencies of values, which is, in comparison to usual programming languages, easily possible thanks to the explicit representation of the object flow in fUML. The support for explicating data dependencies has been integrated in our execution trace for fUML [19].

Constraint solving with symbolic execution paths. To enable finding concrete objects and links that satisfy a sequence of path conditions, we implemented an integration of xMOF and fUML with the model validator plug-in for USE [13] by Kuhlmann *et al.*

Therefore, we translate the (configuration) metamodel of the modeling language into a UML class diagram in USE, transform the models to be compared into object diagrams, and represent path constraints as OCL invariants. Now, we may start the model validator plug-in, which internally translates those diagrams and the constraints into the relational logics of Kodkod [30] to apply an efficient SAT-based search for an object diagram that satisfies all constraints. Note that constraint solving is an inherently computation-intensive task. Although our experiments showed that this plug-in of USE is comparably efficient, the constraint solving took up to several seconds in our case studies, which may impair the runtime of symbolic execution drastically. Nevertheless, the runtime of the constraint solving significantly depends on the bounds (e.g., number of objects per class, range of Integer values); thus, there is a large potential for optimizing the constraint solving by extracting heuristics from the operational semantics specification to limit the bounds automatically. Moreover, a feature of this plug-in that significantly improved its application for our purpose is its support for *extending* specified object diagrams *incrementally* for validating additional constraints.

7 Conclusion

We proposed a generic semantic model differencing approach that—in contrast to existing approaches—makes use of the behavioral semantics specifications of modeling languages for supporting the semantic comparison of models. Thus, non-trivial transformations into a semantic domain specifically for enabling semantic differencing can be avoided. Instead, the behavioral semantics specifications of modeling languages, which may also be employed, e.g., for simulation, are reused to enable semantic differencing.

We showed how our approach can be realized for the operational semantics specification approach xMOF to enable the implementation of semantic diff operators. Furthermore, we presented a solution for generating relevant inputs required for the underlying model execution based on symbolic execution. The evaluation of our approach with two case studies revealed that our approach is expressive enough to define different semantic equivalence criteria for specific modeling languages. However, it also turned out that we face serious performance issues caused by the slow model execution, but also by the inherently time-consuming constraint solving task in the symbolic execution. To address this issue we plan to improve the virtual machine for executing models, but also envision an adaptation of *directed and differential symbolic execution* [15,27] for generating relevant inputs more efficiently. One idea behind those symbolic execution strategies is to consider syntactic differences in the models to be compared and direct the symbolic execution towards those differences, whereas unchanged parts are pruned, if possible. Moreover, we will investigate whether it is possible to avoid the generation of concrete inputs at all and, instead, analyze the symbolic representations of the execution trees of both models directly for reasoning about semantic differences.

Acknowledgments. This work is partly funded by the European Commission under the ICT Policy Support Programme grant no. 317859 and by the Austrian Federal Ministry of Transport, Innovation and Technology (BMVIT) under the FFG BRIDGE program grant no. 832160.

References

1. Alanen, M., Porres, I.: Difference and union of models. In: Stevens, P., Whittle, J., Booch, G. (eds.) UML 2003. LNCS, vol. 2863, pp. 2–17. Springer, Heidelberg (2003)
2. Brun, C., Pierantonio, A.: Model Differences in the Eclipse Modeling Framework. UP-GRADE, The European Journal for the Informatics Professional 9(2), 29–34 (2008)
3. Cadar, C., Sen, K.: Symbolic Execution for Software Testing: Three Decades Later. Communications of the ACM 56(2), 82–90 (2013)
4. Clarke, L.A.: A Program Testing System. In: Proceedings of the 1976 Annual Conference (ACM 1976), pp. 488–491. ACM (1976)
5. Engels, G., Hausmann, J.H., Heckel, R., Sauer, S.: Dynamic Meta Modeling: A Graphical Approach to the Operational Semantics of Behavioral Diagrams in UML. In: Evans, A., Caskurlu, B., Selic, B. (eds.) UML 2000. LNCS, vol. 1939, pp. 323–337. Springer, Heidelberg (2000)
6. Esparza, J., Nielsen, M.: Decidability Issues for Petri Nets. Technical Report, BRICS RS948, BRICS Report Series, Department of Computer Science, University of Aarhus (1994), http://www.brics.dk
7. Fahrenberg, U., Acher, M., Legay, A., Wasowski, A.: Sound Merging and Differencing for Class Diagrams. In: Gnesi, S., Rensink, A. (eds.) FASE 2014. LNCS, vol. 8411, pp. 63–78. Springer, Heidelberg (2014)
8. Fahrenberg, U., Legay, A., Wasowski, A.: Vision Paper: Make a Difference (Semantically). In: Whittle, J., Clark, T., Kühne, T. (eds.) MODELS 2011. LNCS, vol. 6981, pp. 490–500. Springer, Heidelberg (2011)
9. Gerth, C., Küster, J.M., Luckey, M., Engels, G.: Precise Detection of Conflicting Change Operations Using Process Model Terms. In: Petriu, D.C., Rouquette, N., Haugen, Ø. (eds.) MODELS 2010, Part II. LNCS, vol. 6395, pp. 93–107. Springer, Heidelberg (2010)
10. Harel, D., Rumpe, B.: Meaningful Modeling: What's the Semantics of "Semantics"? Computer 37(10), 64–72 (2004)
11. Khurshid, S., Păsăreanu, C.S., Visser, W.: Generalized Symbolic Execution for Model Checking and Testing. In: Garavel, H., Hatcliff, J. (eds.) TACAS 2003. LNCS, vol. 2619, pp. 553–568. Springer, Heidelberg (2003)
12. Kolovos, D., Rose, L., García-Domínguez, A., Paige, R.: The Epsilon Book (March 2014), https://www.eclipse.org/epsilon/doc/book/
13. Kuhlmann, M., Hamann, L., Gogolla, M.: Extensive Validation of OCL Models by Integrating SAT Solving into USE. In: Bishop, J., Vallecillo, A. (eds.) TOOLS 2011. LNCS, vol. 6705, pp. 290–306. Springer, Heidelberg (2011)
14. Lin, Y., Gray, J., Jouault, F.: DSMDiff: A Differentiation Tool for Domain-Specific Models. European Journal of Information Systems 16(4), 349–361 (2007)
15. Ma, K.-K., Yit Phang, K., Foster, J.S., Hicks, M.: Directed Symbolic Execution. In: Yahav, E. (ed.) SAS 2011. LNCS, vol. 6887, pp. 95–111. Springer, Heidelberg (2011)
16. Maoz, S., Ringert, J.O., Rumpe, B.: A Manifesto for Semantic Model Differencing. In: Dingel, J., Solberg, A. (eds.) MODELS 2010. LNCS, vol. 6627, pp. 194–203. Springer, Heidelberg (2011)
17. Maoz, S., Ringert, J.O., Rumpe, B.: ADDiff: Semantic Differencing for Activity Diagrams. In: Proceedings of the 19th ACM SIGSOFT Symposium and the 13th European Conference on Foundations of Software Engineering (ESEC/FSE 2011), pp. 179–189. ACM (2011)
18. Maoz, S., Ringert, J.O., Rumpe, B.: CDDiff: Semantic Differencing for Class Diagrams. In: Mezini, M. (ed.) ECOOP 2011. LNCS, vol. 6813, pp. 230–254. Springer, Heidelberg (2011)

19. Mayerhofer, T., Langer, P., Kappel, G.: A Runtime Model for fUML. In: Proceedings of the 7th Workshop on Models@run.time (MRT) co-located with the 15th International Conference on Model Driven Engineering Languages and Systems (MODELS 2012), pp. 53–58. ACM (2012)

20. Mayerhofer, T., Langer, P., Wimmer, M., Kappel, G.: xMOF: Executable DSMLs Based on fUML. In: Erwig, M., Paige, R.F., Van Wyk, E. (eds.) SLE 2013. LNCS, vol. 8225, pp. 56–75. Springer, Heidelberg (2013)

21. Moliz project, http://www.modelexecution.org

22. Muller, P.-A., Fleurey, F., Jézéquel, J.-M.: Weaving Executability into Object-Oriented Meta-languages. In: Briand, L.C., Williams, C. (eds.) MODELS 2005. LNCS, vol. 3713, pp. 264–278. Springer, Heidelberg (2005)

23. Object Management Group. OMG Unified Modeling Language (OMG UML), Superstructure, Version 2.4.1 (August 2011), http://www.omg.org/spec/UML/2.4.1

24. Object Management Group. Semantics of a Foundational Subset for Executable UML Models (fUML), Version 1.0 (February 2011), http://www.omg.org/spec/FUML/1.0

25. Ohst, D., Welle, M., Kelter, U.: Differences Between Versions of UML Diagrams. SIGSOFT Software Engineering Notes 28(5), 227–236 (2003)

26. Oliveira, H., Murta, L., Werner, C.: Odyssey-VCS: A Flexible Version Control System for UML Model Elements. In: Proceedings of the 12th International Workshop on Software Configuration Management (SCM 2005), pp. 1–16. ACM (2005)

27. Person, S., Dwyer, M.B., Elbaum, S.G., Pasareanu, C.S.: Differential Symbolic Execution. In: Proceedings of the 16th ACM SIGSOFT International Symposium on Foundations of Software Engineering (FSE 2008), pp. 226–237. ACM (2008)

28. Reiter, T., Altmanninger, K., Bergmayr, A., Schwinger, W., Kotsis, G.: Models in Conflict – Detection of Semantic Conflicts in Model-based Development. In: Proceedings of the 3rd International Workshop on Model-Driven Enterprise Information Systems (MDEIS) co-located with the 9th International Conference on Enterprise Information Systems (ICEIS 2007), pp. 29–40 (2007)

29. Sen, K.: Concolic Testing. In: Proceedings of the 22nd IEEE/ACM International Conference on Automated Software Engineering (ASE 2007), pp. 571–572. ACM (2007)

30. Torlak, E., Jackson, D.: Kodkod: A relational model finder. In: Grumberg, O., Huth, M. (eds.) TACAS 2007. LNCS, vol. 4424, pp. 632–647. Springer, Heidelberg (2007)

31. Xing, Z., Stroulia, E.: UMLDiff: An Algorithm for Object-oriented Design Differencing. In: Proceedings of the 20th IEEE/ACM International Conference on Automated Software Engineering (ASE 2005), pp. 54–65. ACM (2005)

Formalizing Execution Semantics of UML Profiles with fUML Models

Jérémie Tatibouët, Arnaud Cuccuru, Sébastien Gérard, and François Terrier

CEA, LIST, Laboratory of Model Driven Engineering for Embedded Systems,
P.C. 174, Gif-sur-Yvette, 91191, France
{jeremie.tatibouet, arnaud.cuccuru, sebastien.gerard,
francois.terrier}@cea.fr

Abstract. UML Profiles are not only sets of annotations. They have semantics. Executing a model on which a profile is applied requires semantics of this latter to be considered. The issue is that in practice semantics of profiles are mainly specified in prose. In this form it cannot be processed by tools enabling model execution. Although latest developments advocate for a standard way to formalize semantics of profiles, no such approach could be found in the literature. This paper addresses this issue with a systematic approach based on fUML to formalize the execution semantics of UML profiles. This approach is validated by formalizing the execution semantics of a subset of the MARTE profile. The proposal is compatible with any tool implementing UML and clearly identifies the mapping between stereotypes and semantic definitions.

Keywords: fUML, Alf, Profile, Semantics, Execution, MARTE.

1 Introduction

A model of a system relies on a particular language. This language (i.e. its abstract syntax) may support syntactic constructs enabling engineers to describe structure and/or behavior. Choices made by engineers at design time usually have an important impact on how the future system behave at runtime. The interest for them is to put confidence in their modeling choices [19]. Model execution is a solution to help obtaining such confidence. By enabling engineers to have a direct insight in the models at runtime, it enables them to evaluate impact of their modeling choices. This approach by execution is complementary with formal technics. For instance, in the context of a large applicative model, it can be used to run a set of well identified scenarios to ensure about correctness of a particular behavior instead of trying to explore a huge state space.

Executability of a language is a property provided both by the way a language semantics is formalized and by the language chosen to formalize it. The semantics in itself only defines the meaning of a language [8] regardless of the form (e.g. operational, axiomatic, translational) it is formalized. Interest of having well-formalized semantics for our languages is widely admitted by the model-driven engineering (MDE) community. Beyond executability, the semantic formalization

J. Dingel et al. (Eds.): MODELS 2014, LNCS 8767, pp. 133–148, 2014.

ensures language users share a common understanding of artifacts (e.g. models) built with the language and that verification techniques can be applied to assess correctness of the semantics.

Since 2010 and the release of foundational UML [1] (fUML) a subset of UML limited to composite structures, classes (structure) and activities (behavior) has a precise execution semantics. This semantics is formalized as a class model called semantic model. Application models designed with this subset of UML are de-facto executable. However if these models have applied profiles, semantics of these latter have no influence in the execution. There are two reasons for that. First fUML is agnostic of stereotypes. Next, most of the time profiles semantics remain specified in prose (at the best). For instance, this is the case for MARTE [3] and SysML [4] which are widely used profiles. This observation is highlighted by [6] and confirmed by Pardillo in [7]. In this systematic review of UML profiles, the author identifies reasons that may lead language designers to keep semantic definitions informal. The lack of guidelines and tool support to assist language designers in this task are the main reasons. This considerably limits interest of profiles and their practical usability in a context in which engineers look for rapid prototyping and evaluation of their modeling choices at early stages of their design flows.

Although latest developments advocate [9] for a standard way to formalize semantics of profiles, no such approach could be found in the literature. This paper addresses this issue with a systematic approach based on fUML to formalize the execution semantics of UML profiles. The central idea is that if a profile has execution semantics, it can be specified as a fUML model being an extension of the fUML semantic model. The approach aims to guide language designer to designing semantics with fUML. It is completely model-driven and compatible with any tools implementing UML.

This paper is organized as follows. In section 2 we provide key points to understand fUML and the architecture of its semantic model. Next, in section 3 we review the approaches proposing to formalize language semantics and especially those related to UML profiles. According to this analysis, we define the objectives a systematic approach to define profile semantics must fulfill. Section 4 describes the process of extending the fUML semantic model and semantics relationships with the profile. In section 5 we validate our approach by defining the execution of semantics of a subset of MARTE [3]. Benefits and limitations of the approach are discussed. Finally, section 6 presents the tooling built to support the methodology and section 7 concludes the paper.

2   fUML Background

This section provides an overview of the fUML semantic model and identifies its extension points. The fUML semantic model defines a hierarchy of semantic visitors specified by UML classes. There are three fundamental types of visitors: *Value*, *Activation* and *Execution*.

- Visitors defined as sub-classes of *Value* define how instances of UML structural elements are represented and handled at runtime. For instance, *Object* is a visitor which captures the execution semantics of *Class* (cf. Figure 1). This means *Object* is the representation of an instance of *Class*. It is extended by *CS_Object* in the context of composite structures to capture a wider semantics.
- Visitors defined as sub-classes of *ActivityNodeActivation* implement the execution semantics of activity nodes. For instance, *AcceptEventActionActivation* (cf. Figure 1) captures the semantics of *AcceptEventAction* which is an action node and so an activity node.
- Visitors defined as sub-classes of *Execution* are not related to a particular element of the abstract syntax considered by fUML. Instead, they are in charge of managing a set of activation nodes capturing a behavior.

In fUML, each semantic visitor (associated or not to an element of the UML abstract syntax subset) captures execution semantics through its operations. Extending the execution semantics captured in the fUML semantic model can be realized by extending (i.e. inheriting) one or more visitors.

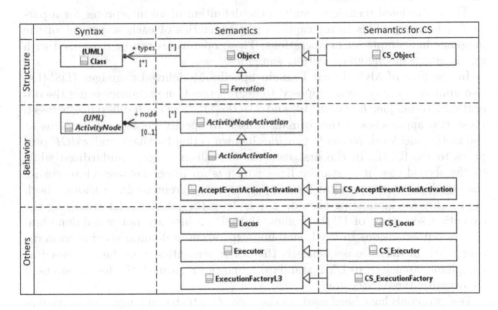

Fig. 1. foundational UML background

The fUML semantic model also provides key classes (i.e. *Locus*, *Executor* and *ExecutionFactory* shown in Figure 1) that are responsible for instantiation and storage of semantic visitors.

- *Locus* defines a virtual memory keeping track of values created at runtime. It is reponsible for instantiation of classifiers. This formalizes the semantic mapping exisiting between *Class* and *Object*.

- *Executor* defines the entry point of an execution in the fUML semantics.
- *ExecutionFactory* is responsible for the instantiation of visitors inheriting from *Execution* and *ActivityNodeActivation*. The instantiation strategy formalizes the relation between visitors (e.g. *AcceptEventActionActivation*) and abstract syntax elements (e.g. *AcceptEventAction*).

Providing these key classes with extensions enables integration of new semantic visitors and specification of their instantiation rules. Details on fUML architecture can be found in [1] and [2].

3   Related Works Analysis

Language semantics can be specified with different techniques: operational, axiomatic, denotational or translational. Although it is possible to execute models from axiomatic semantics as shown in [12], in practice languages requiring to be executable have a semantics defined using either the operational technique or the translational technique.

The operational technique enables the definition of an interpreter for a particular language. This latter captures the semantics of each statement of the language in a simple set of operations. These operations can be expressed with any language having an execution semantics.

In the area of MOF-based Domain Specific Modeling Languages (DSMLs) two approaches have been proposed to define execution semantics using the operational technique: *Kermeta* [10] and *xMOF* [11]. The main difference between these two approaches is the formalism used to specify behavioral concerns at the metamodel level. *Kermeta* provides its own action language and *xMOF* proposes to use fUML. In the first case the formalism is not standardized while in the second case it is standardized which is an important aspect to ensure the semantic description can be supported by different tools. Although both approaches are interesting they do not address the problem of formalizing the execution semantics of UML profiles. Indeed, profiles are not standalone languages but extensions to UML enabling expression of domain specific concerns over UML models. Consequence is that their semantics must be expressed as compliant extensions to UML standard semantics regardless the formalism used to formalize these extensions.

Few proposals have been made in the area of UML-based languages to systematize the way execution semantics are described. According to what we found in the litterature, proposed approaches rely on translational semantics. The translational technique aims to map a language abstract syntax to another language abstract syntax which is intented to have a formalized semantics. It exists different solution to implement the translational approach. Contributions trying to provide UML semantics with an execution semantics seem to focus on code generation and model transformation.

Code generation approaches (e.g. the one presented in [13]) have the drawback to encapsulate the semantics of the language within the code generator. The consequence is that UML profile users have to study the implementation to understand its semantics [9]. In addition, during generated code analysis a strong technical effort will be required to distinguish what represents the semantics and what represents the model.

The probably most complete approach proposing to use model tranformations for specifying UML profiles execution semantics is the one presented in [15]. Authors proposal is to represent UML abstract syntax and its extensions (i.e. stereotypes) as an ASM [14] domain whose semantics is then described operationally using abstract state-machines (i.e. extended Finite State Machines). The ASM language seems to be a good target to express equivalent UML models. It has formal basis, it is known by the community and supported by tools. However the approach implies models produced by users are transformed into equivalent ASM representations. Therefore the execution is performed on transformed models and not on the users models. The consequence is that users will have to investigate the transformation program to understand the impacts of their modeling choices in terms of execution.

According to the analysis of the related works, our working context and experience, we derive a set of objectives a systematic approach to formalize the execution semantics of UML profiles must provide. In addition we motivate our choice to use fUML as semantic pivot.

1. Semantic designed through the methodology must be tool agnostic. *Rationale*: To enable language users to share a common understanding of the semantic, the description must be compatible between different tools. The best way to achieve this goal is to rely on a standard.
2. Semantic specification must be based on standard UML semantics. *Rationale*: Profiles are UML based languages. Extensions made to UML have impacts on its semantics. This latter is formalized by fUML therefore profiles semantics should be extensions to fUML.
3. Effort required to understand the semantics must be minimized. *Rationale*: Translational approach increases the technical effort to understand a semantic specification. Indeed, they introduce intermediate steps (e.g. model transformations) to obtain an executable model from the source model. This step must be investigated in addition to the semantics of the target language to enable the designer to understand impact of his modeling choices at runtime.
4. Clear relationships between stereotypes and semantics definitions must be defined. *Rationale*: Providing a language with a semantics means the abstract syntax elements of this language are mapped to their semantic definitions (i.e. meanings). Profiles do not escape the rule. It must possible to identify elements of the specification capturing the semantic of a stereotype.
5. Verification techniques must be applicable to ensure the correctness of the semantic specification. *Rationale*: Languages used to describe critical systems (e.g. real-time systems) may have to demonstrate their conformance to a specific semantics. UML base semantics is based on mathematical foundations which ensures verification techniques are applicable.

4 Extending fUML Semantic Model: A Model-Driven Approach

This section presents the process of extending the fUML semantic model to formalize profile execution semantics. In sub-section 4.1 we present the relationships existing between a profile, the fUML semantic model and its extensions. Next, in section 4.2, we provide a detailed description of the methodology enabling the construction of a semantic model formalizing profile execution semantics. To improve readability of this section, fUML concepts or extensions are followed by quote *SV* (i.e. semantic visitor) while UML concepts are followed by quote *MC* (i.e. meta-class).

4.1 Concepts

Guidelines to define profile abstract syntax are identified by Selic in [16]. The profile design process starts with the construction of a domain model capturing the concepts of the domain under study. Then, this model is projected on the UML metamodel. The projection consists in selecting the metaclasses that will be extended to support domain concepts over UML. Extensions are defined as stereotypes with an expressiveness limited to what the domain must support.

In rectangle number 1 of Figure 2, a profile specified through this methodology is represented. It provides the *Broadcast* concept which is formalized as a stereotype only applicable on action nodes of type *SendSignalAction (MC)*. Here starts the specification of the profile execution semantics.

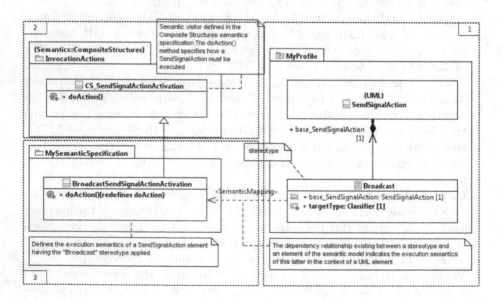

Fig. 2. Conceptual Approach

```
activity doAction() {
    UML::SendSignalAction action = (UML::SendSignalAction)this.node;
    UML::Stereotype stereotype = action.getAppliedStereotype("MyProfile::Broadcast");
    UML::Property p = null;
    UML::Class targetType = null;
    fUML::Semantics::CommonBehaviors::Communications::SignalInstance signalInstance = null;
    fUML::Semantics::Loci::LociL1::Locus locus = this.getExecutionLocus();
    if(stereotype!=null){
        targetType = (UML::Class) action.getValue(stereotype, "targetType");
        for(extent in locus.getExtent(targetType)){
            signalInstance = new fUML::Semantics::CommonBehaviors::Communications::SignalInstance();
            signalInstance.type = action.'signal';
            ((fUML::Semantics::Classes::Kernel::Object)extent).send(signalInstance);
        }
    }
}
```

Fig. 3. Execution semantics captured by *BroadcastSendSignalActionActivation*

Formalizing the Execution Semantics of Stereotypes. In the fUML semantic model *SendSignalAction (MC)* has a formalized execution semantics which states "*When all the prerequisites of the action execution are satisfied, a signal instance of the type specified by the signal property is generated from the argument values and this signal instance is transmitted to the identified target object*". This execution semantics is captured by *CS_SendSignalActionActivation (SV)* through the behavior specified for its *doAction* operation (cf. rectangle 2 of Figure 2). Applying the stereotype *Broadcast* on a *SendSignalAction (MC)* changes its execution semantics. Indeed the semantics associated to such stereotype could be "*When all the prerequisites of the action execution are satisfied, a signal instance of the type specified by signal is generated from the argument values and this signal instance is transmitted concurrently to every object classified under the type specified by the argument targetType*".

If we want the application of the stereotype to be reflected at runtime, the fUML semantics model must be extended. An extension is the formalization of the execution semantics associated to each stereotype of a profile. It is a fUML model (i.e. a class model) that can be used to parameterize the standard semantic model.

The general process of formalizing the execution semantics of a stereotypes consists in extending visitors defined in the fUML semantic model using standard object oriented mechanisms (e.g. inheritance, polymorphism). Visitors that can be extended have been identified in Section 2. As an exemple, The formalization of the *Broadcast* stereotype is presented in the rectangle 3 of Figure 2.

1. We identify the semantic visitor (cf. rectangle 2) capturing the execution semantics of *SendSignalAction (MC)*.
2. In a new model this semantic visitor is specialized (cf. *BroadcastSendSignalActionActivation (SV)* in rectangle 3).
3. The new semantic visitor implements the execution semantics by redefining behaviors associated to its generalization (cf. Figure 3). This can be realized using Alf [5] (i.e. the textual notation for fUML) or activity models. Both are equivalent.

4. The stereotype is linked with its semantic definition using a *Dependency (MC)* stereotyped *SemanticMapping*. This is illustrated in Figure 2.

Dependencies and Instantiation. The role of dependencies stereotyped *SemanticMapping* is also to indicate the context in which a new semantic visitor can be instantiated in the fUML runtime. A stereotype can depend on multiple semantic visitors. This is the case when a stereotype is defined as being applicable on an abstract UML element (i.e. an abstract UML metaclass). For example, if a stereotype is applicable on any action nodes (i.e. *Action (MC)*).

Depending on the concrete action this stereotype is applied on, the execution semantics can be different. As an example if the stereotype *Trace* is applied on a *CallBehaviorAction (MC)* we will trace the call to a specific behavior. Meanwhile if it is applied on an *AcceptEventAction (MC)* we will trace the signals that are received. This implies that the stereotype has two associated visitors extending the basic execution semantics defined for these kinds of action nodes in the extended semantic model.

Core Extensions of the fUML Semantic Model. Specific classes of the fUML semantic model are in charge of organizing the instantiation of semantic visitors, their execution and the management of runtime values. These classes are *Locus*, *Execution* and *ExecutionFactory*. They have been introduced in Section 2. Extensions to these classes are usually implied by the definition of new semantic visitors. This sub-section identifies cases in which these classes need to be extended.

– Extension to *Locus* class and its *instantiate* operation is implied by the specification of a specialization of *CS_Object (SV)* which is a particular type of *Value*. This case occurs when the profile has a stereotype defining a new semantics for *Classifier (MC)*. An extension to this class and its associated behaviors can be automatically derived from the dependencies stereotyped *SemanticMapping* specified in the extended semantic model.
– Extension to *Execution (SV)* class and its *execute* operation can be required by the definition of a stereotype targeting *Behavior (MC)* or any of its subclasses. Likewise it can be implied by the contextual visitor requiring an *Execution (SV)* to be instantiated (e.g. *Object (SV)*).
– *ExecutionFactory* is responsible for instantiating any other semantic visitors. Extension to this class is required as soon as one ore more semantic visitors have been defined in the semantic specification. As for *Locus*, a full extension to this class can be automatically derived from dependencies stereotyped *SemanticMapping*.

4.2   Semantic Model Extension: Detailed Construction Process

In the previous section, we have presented how we formalize stereotypes semantics with fUML and the implications on core classes defined in the standard semantic model. In this section, we define a fine grained process to formalize the execution semantics of a UML profile.

S1 The first step consists in selecting the definition of one stereotype of a profile.

(a) If the meta-class extended by the stereotype does not have sub-meta-classes and is not abstract then the designer of the semantic model can start step 2.

(b) If the meta-class extended by the stereotype has concrete sub-meta-classes this implies the stereotype can be applied on every syntax element defined from that meta-class. Consequently, the designer of the semantic model must select every concrete sub-meta-classes of that meta-class for which an execution semantics should be formalized. Note that if the base meta-class is not abstract then it belongs to the set of selected meta-classes. For this set the step 2 must be applied.

S2 The second step describes how to extend a semantic visitor existing in the fUML semantic model and to link this extension to a particular stereotype defined in the profile. It consists in the following tasks.

(a) The designer must select in the standard fUML semantic model the visitor defining the execution semantics of the current meta-class.

(b) To capture the execution semantics related to the stereotype application the designer must create a new class extending that semantic visitor.

(c) Operation(s) of the newly created visitor must be defined using activities (specified textually using Alf[5]) in order to perform the expected behavior when interpreting the profiled element.

(d) Finally the relationship between the current stereotype and the semantic visitor is formalized using a dependency link. The stereotype plays the *client* role while the opposite end (i.e. the semantic visitor) plays the *supplier* role.

S3 Steps *S1* and *S2* must be repeated for every stereotype of the profile. When all stereotypes have been considered, then the specification of extensions related either to the management or the instantiation strategy of the semantic visitors must be defined.

5   Formalizing the Execution Semantics of a Subset of the HLAM MARTE Sub-profile

Based-on the concepts presented in section 4, we validated our approach on a subset of the MARTE profile [3]: HLAM (i.e. High-Level Application Modeling). This case study has been chosen by the OMG in the context of composite structures semantic specification (cf. annex A of [2]). It is representative to validate our approach. Indeed, it implies extensions to all visitors of the fUML semantic model except to *ActivityNodeActivation* which has already been extended in Figure 2.

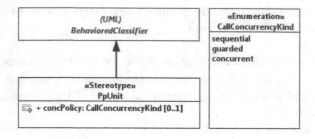

Fig. 4. The sub-profile under consideration

5.1   Presentation of the HLAM Subset

HLAM is a sub-profile of MARTE. It provides high-level modeling concepts to deal with real-time and embedded feature modeling. An excerpt of this sub-profile is shown on Figure 4. It contains the definition of the stereotype *PpUnit* and an enumeration *CallConcurencyKind*.

The stereotype *PpUnit* (i.e. protected passive unit) can be applied on syntactic elements inheriting from *BehavioredClassifier (MC)* (e.g. *Class (MC)*). A protected passive unit is used to represent shared information among execution threads. It provides protection mechanisms to support concurrent accesses from these latter. This implies to capture an execution semantics that is different than for regular *Class (MC)*. We can distinguish three different cases :

1. If the *concPolicy* value is *sequential*, only one execution thread can access a feature (e.g. property) of a *PpUnit*. In this case the *PpUnit* does not own the access control mechanism. Each client of this object must deal with concurrent conflicts.
2. If the *concPolicy* value is *concurrent* then multiple execution threads at a time can access a *PpUnit*.
3. If the *concPolicy* value is *guarded* then only one execution thread at a time can access a feature of a *PpUnit* while concurrent ones are suspended.

Among the three semantics presented above, the second is already captured by fUML. No assumption is made in the execution semantics to avoid concurrent access to features of a particular instance. With respect to the two other semantics (i.e. *sequential* and *guarded*) they are extensions of the fUML standard execution semantics. In the case study we will define required extensions to handle the *guarded* semantics.

5.2   Construction of the Semantic Model

This section describes the construction of the semantic model formalizing the execution semantics of the HLAM subset shown in Figure 4.

The first step (cf. item S1 of sub-section 4.2) consists in selecting a stereotype of the profile. We select *PpUnit*. It can be applied on *BehavioredClassifier*

(MC) which is abstract. Step S1-b applies: we search in fUML syntactic subset all concrete meta-classes of *BehavioredClassifier (MC)*. We obtain the set $\varphi = \{Class, Activity, OpaqueBehavior\}$.

Each meta-class in φ requiring a specific execution semantics must have its corresponding semantic visitor extended (cf. item S2 of sub-section 4.2). Here we only consider *Class (MC)* which semantics is captured by *Object (SV)* because MARTE profile [3] does not define semantics when stereotype *PpUnit* is applied on *Activity (MC)* or *OpaqueBehavior (MC)*.

Object (SV) captures the access semantics to feature values through the operations *getFeatureValue* and *setFeatureValue*. Semantics captured in these operations does not constrain concurrent access to features. Constraining access control to the features requires *Object (SV)* to be extended. Using standard object oriented inheritance mechanism we define *PpUnitObject (SV)* as a subclass of *CS_Object* (cf. Figure 5). One can notice the extension is done over *CS_Object (SV)* instead of *Object (SV)*. This makes the extension usable in the composites structures context. To enable *PpUnitObject (SV)* class to provide access control to its features values we add a property guard representing a mutex. The mutex library is itself an fUML model.

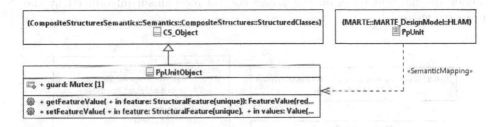

Fig. 5. Definition of a PpUnitObject as an extension of CS_Object

The next step of the methodology (cf. item S2-c of sub-section 4.2) consists in formalizing the behavioral part of the execution semantics captured by *PpUnitObject*. Semantic limitations where identified in *getFeatureValue* and *setFeatureValue* operations. Both are extended to implement an access control mechanism based on the property: *guard*. Figure 6, shows the behavior specification of the operation *getFeatureValue*. This specification clearly states that if the *concPolicy* of a class is guarded then only one active object at a time can access a feature of the *PpUnitObject*. The same pattern applies for the specification of the operation *setFeatureValue*.

PpUnitObject (SV) extension is not sufficient to ensure that operations that are also features of a *Class* will not be executed concurrently. In fUML runtime when an operation is called, an *ActivityExecution (SV)* is produced. This visitor is in charge of executing the behavior associated to an operation and encapsulates informations about the execution context. In the standard fUML semantics, two active objects can execute operations concurrently.

```
activity getFeatureValue(in feature: UML::Feature): fUML::Semantics::Classes::Kernel::FeatureValue{
    UML::Stereotype ppUnit = this.types[0].getAppliedStereotype("MARTE::MARTE_DesignModel::HLAM::PpUnit");
    MARTE::MARTE_DesignModel::HLAM::CallConcurrencyKind concPolicy =this.types.getValue(ppUnit, "concPolicy");
    fUML::Semantics::Classes::Kernel::FeatureValue featureValue = null;
    if(concPolicy==MARTE::MARTE_DesignModel::HLAM::CallConcurrencyKind::guarded){
        this.guard.lock();
        featureValue = super.getFeatureValue(feature);
        this.guard.unlock();
    }else{
        featureValue = super.getFeatureValue(feature);
    }
    return featureValue;
}
```

Fig. 6. Behavioral specification of getFeatureValue operation

Formalizing this constraint implies the definition of a new semantic visitor capturing how operations must be executed in the context of a *PpUnitObject (SV)*. This is typical application of derived semantic visitor definition as explained in sub-section 4.1. Figure 7 shows the definition of the *MarteGuardedExecution (SV)* extending *ActivityExecution (SV)*. Behavioral extension to the execution semantics is defined in the *execute* operation of the new visitor. Again the behavior specification relies on the access control mechanism introduced by the property guard.

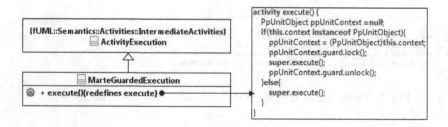

Fig. 7. Constrain concurrency between operation call

The last part of the methodology (cf item S3 in sub-section 4.2) consists in specifying under which conditions the semantic visitors defined in the context of the MARTE HLAM profile will be instantiated. As presented in sub-section 4.1, classes instantiation is handled by the *Locus*. A *PpUnitObject (SV)* is the representation at runtime of a instance of *Class* stereotyped *PpUnit*. Consequently its instantiation must be handled by the *Locus*. Therefore we define *MarteLocus* (cf. Figure 8) as an extension of *CS_Locus*. The instantiation logic is then captured in the behavior of the *instantiate* operation.

Visitors capturing execution semantics of behavioral specifications (e.g. *ReadSelfActionActivation (SV)*) or controlling execution of other semantic visitors (e.g. *Execution (SV)*) are instantiated by the *ExecutionFactory*. We defined *MarteGuardedExecution (SV)* which falls into this category. This implies the

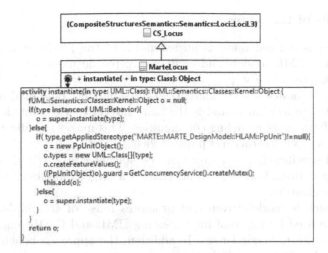

Fig. 8. Definition of MarteLocus as an extension of CS_Locus

Fig. 9. Definition of MarteExecutionFactory as an extension of CS_ExecutionFactory

extension of the regular *ExecutionFactory*. Instantiation rule is expressed in Alf [5] in the operation *instantiateVisitor*. This rule is: a *MarteGuardedExecution (SV)* can only be instantiated when an operation is called in the context of a *PpUnitObject (SV)* constraining the concurrency with a guarded semantics. Figure 9 shows the specification.

5.3   Benefits of the Approach

The semantics is defined once as an extension of the fUML semantic model expressed with fUML models and enables any profile models to be executed without any intermediate step.

The semantic model is a standard UML class model. This kind of model is known by UML practicioners and is the main interface of communication with stakeholders from other modeling communities. This makes specifications easily understandable from a structural point of view.

Behavioral specification of visitors can be specified in *Alf* [5] which is close to c-like programming languages. This enables a large community to read and verify the specification.

Our approach is model-driven and promotes reuse of standards. Semantic models can be used by any tool implementing UML and fUML (e.g., Papyrus, Entreprise Architect, Magic Draw). In addition, the approach benefits from an integration within Papyrus (cf. Section 6).

fUML has formal foundations. As stated in [17], these foundations can be used to verify properties of fUML models "applying the theorem proving approach". Since the semantic model is a fUML model verification techniques can be applied to check semantic consistency.

The specification provides a clear separation between syntax and semantics and identifies the relations between stereotypes and semantic definitions.

5.4   Limitations of the Approach

The approach requires a background in fUML to be usable. This implies a technical effort to realize the first specification.

The semantic specification does not handle cases were multiple stereotypes are applied over the same modeling construct. This mean there are no rules to compose the execution of multiple semantic visitors for the same model element.

The problem of semantic consistency is not adressed since we do not have mechanisms to ensure a profile semantics does not contradict fUML semantics. However it may be possible to develop automatic consistency check based on the axiomatic foundations of fUML.

The current version of tools supporting the methodlogy does not support automated generation of extensions to *ExecutionFactory* and *Locus*.

6   Tool support

Papyrus modeler provides an fUML engine called MOKA (cf. Figure 10). This latter implements the standard fUML semantics. What we have added to MOKA is the possibility to be parameterized by an fUML model implementing the semantics of a particular profile (inspired from [18]). Thus on requesting a fUML profiled model to be executed a designer can choose the adequate semantic extension. Contributions found in the extension are dynamically injected at runtime

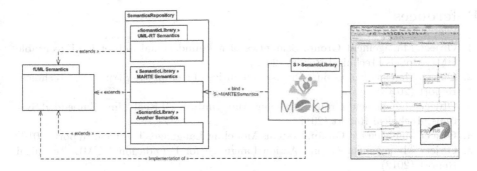

Fig. 10. Make use of formalized execution semantics through MOKA

to reflect the execution semantics applied by stereotype application. Portions of
the extended semantic model injected at runtime are executed as fUML models.

Although our approach advocates for specifying the entire semantics of a profile as a fUML model, we also let the opportunity to the designer to define extensions as implementations. An eclipse plugin can be generated from a semantic
specification placed in a fUML model. This plugin will contains glue classes required to interface the model execution and an implementation of fUML. Other
semantic contributions can be placed as regular Java classes in the plugin.

7   Conclusions and Future Works

In this paper, we have presented a methodology to formalize UML profiles semantics. Our approach relies on the fUML standard. It proposes to specify the
semantics of a particular profile as an extension of the semantic model defined
by fUML.

Our approach is entirely model-driven. An extension to the semantic model is
formalized by the definition of new semantic visitors extending those considered
by fUML. New visitors are UML classes which override behaviors provided in
their parent classes using standard object oriented mechanisms. The semantic
specification is an fUML model which is by construction compliant with the
design of the standard.

Models using profiles with a semantics formalized using our approach are
directly executable and observable executions reflect the semantics introduced
by the profile. This enables engineers to evaluate impacts of their modeling
choices by executing their profiled models at early stages of their design flows.

For future works, we plan to support the automatic generation of extensions
related to classes responsibles for instantiating visitors specified in a extended
semantic model. Next, the main challenge is to consider cases were a single model
element can have multiple stereotypes applied. This implies multiple semantic
visitors to be defined and composed at runtime which actually not supported by
fUML. Furthermore, to ensure a consistent execution, semantic compatibility of
these visitors will have to be evaluated.

References

1. Object Management Group. Semantics of a Foundational Subset for Executable UML Models. Technical Report (2010)
2. Object Management Group. Precise Semantics of Composite Structures. Technical Report (2010)
3. Object Management Group. Modeling And Analysis Of Real-Time Embedded Systems. Technical Report (2011)
4. Object Management Group. Systems Modeling Language. Technical Report (2012)
5. Object Management Group. Action Language for Foundational UML. Technical Report (2012)
6. Partsch, H., Dausend, M., Gessenharter, D.: From Formal Semantics to Executable Models: A pragmatic Approach to Model-Driven Development. International Journal of Software and Informatics 5, 291–312 (2011)
7. Pardillo, J.: A Systematic Review on the definition of UML profiles. Model Driven Engineering Languages and Systems, 407–422 (2010)
8. Harel, D., Rumpe, B.: Meaningful Modeling: What's the Semantics of "Semantics". Computer 37, 64–72 (2004)
9. Graph, S., Ober, I.: How useful is the UML profile SPT without Semantics? In: International Workshop on Model, Design and Validation (2004)
10. Muller, P.A., Fleurey, F., Jezequel, J.M.: Weaving Executability into Object-Oriented Meta-languages. Model Driven Engineering Languages and Systems 8, 264–278 (2005)
11. Mayerhofer, T., Langer, P., Wimmer, M.: Towards xMOF: Executable DSMLs based on fUML. In: Proceedings of the 2012 Workshop on Domain-Specific Modeling, vol. 12, pp. 1–6 (2005)
12. Wouters, L., Gervais, M.-P.: xOWL: An Executable Modeling Language for Domain Experts. International Entreprise Distributed Object Computing 15, 215–222 (2011)
13. Mraidha, C., Tanguy, Y., Jouvray, C., Terrier, F., Gerard, S.: An Execution Framework for MARTE-based Models. Engineering of Complex Computer Systems 13, 222–227 (2008)
14. Borger, E.: The ASM Method for System Design and Analysis. A Tutorial Introduction. Frontiers of Combining Systems, 264–283 (2005)
15. Riccobene, E., Scandurra, P.: An Executable Semantics of the SystemC UML profile. Abstract State Machines, Alloy, B and Z, 75–90 (2010)
16. Selic, B.: A Systematic Approach to Domain-Specific Language Design Using UML. In: International Symposium on Object and Component-Oriented Real-Time Distributed Computing, pp. 2–9 (2007)
17. Romero, A., Schneider, K., Ferreira, M.: Using the Base Semantics given by fUML for Verification. MODELSWARD (2014)
18. Cuccuru, A., Mraidha, C., Terrier, F., Gérard, S.: Enhancing UML Extensions with Operational Semantics. In: Engels, G., Opdyke, B., Schmidt, D.C., Weil, F. (eds.) MODELS 2007. LNCS, vol. 4735, pp. 271–285. Springer, Heidelberg (2007)
19. Selic, B.: Elements of Model-Based Engineering with UML2: What They Don't Teach You About UML, Technical Report (2009)

Who Knows/Uses What of the UML: A Personal Opinion Survey

Gianna Reggio, Maurizio Leotta, and Filippo Ricca

DIBRIS, Università di Genova, Italy
{gianna.reggio,maurizio.leotta,filippo.ricca}@unige.it

Abstract. UML is a comprehensive notation, offering a very large set of diagrams and constructs covering any possible modelling need. As consequence, on one hand, it is difficult and time consuming to master it, and on the other hand, people tend, naturally, to consider only a part of it. In practice, many UML diagrams/constructs seem scarcely used or even their existence is not known. By means of a study covering any possible source of information (e.g. UML books and tools), we started to assess which part of the UML is considered and used in practice. Here, we present some results about knowledge and usage of the UML diagrams by means of a personal opinion survey with 275 participants from both industry and academy, analysing also the influence of different factors: working environment (academia vs. industry), working role, seniority, education, and gender.

Keywords: UML Usage and Knowledge, Personal Opinion Survey, Empirical Study.

1 Introduction

UML is a comprehensive notation grown up during the years; it is general purpose and so it has a very large number of constructs to cover any possible modelling need in any possible context. Here we report some data to illustrate the size of UML: (1) the specification document for version 2.4.1 (superstructure only) [22] has 732 pages, (2) there are 14 different types of diagrams (the latest, profile diagram, has been added in version 2.1), and (3), each diagram offers a large number of constructs (e.g. 47 for the activity diagram).

Being a so big notation has some drawbacks hindering its acceptance, its adoption and its usage; see, e.g. as this feeling is quite strongly expressed on the SEI (Software Engineering Institute) Architecture Technology User Network blog[1] *"UML is too complex. UML has increased in complexity and size over the years. Today there are 14 different types of diagrams! That's too much for a human being to grasp. Some people shy away from UML because they judge that the effort to climb the learning curve will not pay off"*. Trivially, printing the UML specification requires a large number of paper sheets, but it also requires many hours to read and understand it, not to mention maintaining and evolving it by the designers of the notation, and of course learning and teaching the whole UML is a difficult task [25].

---

[1] http://saturnnetwork.wordpress.com/2010/10/22/five-reasons-developers-dont-use-uml-and-six-reasons-to-use-it/

J. Dingel et al. (Eds.): MODELS 2014, LNCS 8767, pp. 149–165, 2014.

It is worthwhile noticing that this feeling has been also acknowledged by the OMG[2], indeed the next version (2.5) waiting for the formal release is the result of the "UML Simplification" initiative [19], but in this case the simplification will cover only the way UML is defined without any impact on its constructs; nevertheless as stated by Steve Cook in his blog[3] *"the work done in 2.5 provides an excellent foundation for future simplifications and improvements"*.

However, to the best of our knowledge, only few studies have addressed the extent to which UML diagrams are known and used in practice [2,4,8,18], and neither examined why professionals choose to use some diagrams and ignore others. Our research seeks to address the first issue by surveying the UML usage in practice.

UML is so huge that it is not possible to investigate the knowledge and usage level of the whole notation in "only one shot". So we decided to start considering only the UML diagrams and the constructs of use case and activity diagrams.

We have decided to investigate all the possible sources providing information on the knowledge/usage of the UML. Precisely, the considered sources are: books (guides about the UML and books using the UML as a notation, i.e. books where UML is not the primary subject), university courses, tutorials, tools, people (academics and professionals), web resources and model repositories, e.g. ReMoDD[4]. We think to have taken into account all sensible, accessible, and non-biased sources; for example research papers on the UML are not a good choice, since they usually cover the newest and most problematic features; whole models produced in industry are wonderful, but it is extremely difficult to get a sensible number of them, and in many cases it is impossible to examine them, since they have been produced with tools not available to the authors.

We have already published the results of our first survey concerning static sources (only UML books, courses, tutorials and tools) [14,15,16]. Here, we present the results of a novel personal opinion survey with 275 respondents from both academia and industry aimed to understand: (1) which UML diagrams are known/used, and (2) whether the working environment (academia versus industry), the working role, the UML seniority (years of UML knowledge), the UML education (how the UML was learned), and the gender influence the results. Then, we briefly compare the personal opinion survey results with those of the previous survey on the static sources. The results of our investigations will be useful to anyone that for various reasons has to consider only a part of the UML, for example teachers and instructors with a fixed number of teaching hours, people engaged in self learning and developers of model transformations interested to understand which diagrams/constructs are neglected and why.

We present in Section 2 the design and the procedure of the conducted personal opinion survey, and in Section 3 some results and possible threats to validity. Related works are in Section 4, followed by conclusions and future works in Section 5.

---

[2] http://www.omg.org

[3] http://searchsoa.techtarget.com/feature/Steve-Cook-on-what-architects-can-expect-from-UML-25-revision

[4] http://www.cs.colostate.edu/remodd/v1/

2 Study Definition, Design, and Procedure

The main aim of this work is to collect information on the knowledge and usage of the UML in the industrial and academic reality. In particular, the survey focuses on UML diagrams and on the constructs of the use case and activity diagrams. In this paper, for space reason, we focus only on the results about the UML diagrams. To implement this survey, we: (*i*) used the same framework of [20,21] (based on [6]), (*ii*) followed as much as possible the suggestions given in [7], and (*iii*) adopted an on-line questionnaire to collect information.

The **goal** of the survey is *taking a snapshot of UML knowledge and usage in the industry and academy* taking the perspective of:
- **teachers and instructors**: allowing to offer courses and/or tutorials concentrating on a smaller language made out of the most used UML diagrams/constructs;
- **tool builders/users**: interested to focus the tools on the most used UML diagrams/constructs, since the tools covering a smaller number of diagrams/constructs will be simpler to implement and to use;
- **notation designers**: interested in discovering scarcely used constructs, and understanding for which reasons they have been added to the UML. Moreover, other interesting questions could arise: are the scarcely used constructs derived[5] or primitive? Can the scarcely used constructs be applied only in specific cases? It will be interesting to investigate whether the metamodel (and subsequently the UML specification) may be easily simplified, without losing expressive power, to cover only the most used parts.

The context consists of a sample of 275 professionals and academics having at least a basic UML knowledge.

Research Questions. Given the above goal, the survey aimed at addressing the following *research questions*:
RQ1: *Which of the UML diagrams are the most/less known?*
RQ2: *Which of the UML diagrams are the most/less used in practice?*
RQ3: *Have Professionals and Academics the same level of knowledge and use of UML?*
RQ4: *Have the working role, UML seniority, UML education type, and gender any kind of influence on the level of knowledge and use of the UML?*

Target Population and Sample Identification. The target population is the set of individuals to whom the survey applies. In our case the population consists of professionals and academics having at least a basic UML knowledge. Our sample consists of university professors, researchers, students (mainly PhD), and professionals (mainly, project managers, business analysts, software architects, designers, and developers) who work (1) in companies of the IT field; their skills are related to the production, maintenance or management of software systems (the larger part); (2) in companies that do not directly belong to the IT field (a smaller part) but that use information systems to carry out and support the company's business activities; (3) for public agencies, government enterprises; the remainder of the sample perform other kinds of activities.

The sample was obtained in two ways: (1) by convenience, i.e. relying on the network contacts of our research group, and (2) by sending invitation messages on mailing lists

---

[5] A derived construct may be replaced by a combination of other constructs.

and Web groups concerning UML, MD and software engineering. In particular, we have used some lists available at the university (such as former students or people who have participated in previous surveys about other topics) and international professional groups (e.g. LinkedIn). We opted for non-probabilistic sampling methods even if we know all the problems of this sampling (e.g. the risk of using a sample not representative of the target population) [7] because this survey is exploratory and because we thought that the target population was hard to identify and of limited availability.

In total, we received 275 complete responses to our survey. Unfortunately, we do not know exactly how many people have been reached by our invitation messages and advertisements, so we cannot calculate the response rate. The same problem is present also in other software engineering surveys (e.g. in [10]).

Data Collection. Data were collected through the creation of an on line questionnaire. The use of a web-based tool simplifies and speeds up the completion of the questionnaire with clear advantages in terms of the number of responses obtained [6]. The online questionnaire has been developed and published using LimeSurvey[6].

Questionnaire Design. The questionnaire is organized into four sections each of them implemented as a Web page. The first section contains the questions designed to get information about the survey participants, while the 2nd, 3rd, and 4th sections contain a series of questions designed to assess the knowledge and usage of the UML, respectively focusing on UML diagrams, use case diagram constructs and activity diagram constructs. This division was necessary to create different paths to complete the questionnaire depending on the type of response given by the participants (e.g. the activity diagram section is skipped if a participant states that (s)he does not know that kind of diagram). Thus, the total number of questions to compile is variable depending on the responses given to previous questions. A partial list of questions (i.e. the "Personal Data" and "UML Diagrams" sections) is shown in Table 1. Some of them are not mandatory (e.g. questions 1.1 and 1.2).

We have decided to formulate the questions about the knowledge and usage of a diagram/construct in terms of "having seen a model containing it" and "having produced a model containing it", to avoid misunderstandings or personal interpretations by the respondents. For example "I know diagram/construct X" may be interpreted as "I know its existence" or "I know its syntax and semantics"; similarly, instead of "I have used diagram/construct X" we have preferred the most precise "I have produced a model containing diagram/construct X". Furthermore, to avoid that someone that knows or has used a diagram/construct but perhaps (s)he is not able to remember its precise name (e.g. composite structure diagram used to represent structured classes and collaborations) we have added an example to the question (see, e.g. Fig. 1).

We have chosen to force the participants to answer all the questions in each section of the questionnaire using a special option provided by LimeSurvey; in this way it was possible to get all the questionnaires filled out correctly. The only optional questions concern full name and email (i.e. questions 1.1 and 1.2); so we allowed the participants to complete the questionnaire anonymously (some studies have shown that the response rate is affected by the anonymity policy of a study [24]).

---

[6] http://www.limesurvey.org

Table 1. Questionnaire (only "Personal Data" and "UML Diagrams" sections reported)

ID	Conditional	Question
1.1		What is your full name? *(optional)*
1.2		Please provide a valid personal email address. *(optional)*
1.3		What is your gender?
1.4		How old are you?
1.5		What is your nationality?
1.6		What is your current occupation?
1.7	Yes[a]	What legal entity does your company fit?
1.8	Yes[a]	What is the main business activity of your company?
1.9	Yes[a]	Are modelling and/or MD* techniques used in your company?
1.10		Are you currently using UML for your (business) activity?
1.11		How did you learn UML?
1.12		How many years have you been using UML?
1.13	Yes[a]	Do you use software tools to produce UML models?
1.14	Yes[a]	List all the software modelling tools you have used.
1.15		Have you read the OMG UML specifications?
1.16		Are you active in OMG?
1.17		Did you take part in OMG UML definition?
1.18		Which one of the following OMG UML certifications do you have?
2.1		Class Diagram[b]
2.2		Object Diagram[b]
2.3		Activity Diagram[b]
2.4		Use Case Diagram[b]
2.5		State Machine[b]
2.6		Sequence Diagram[b]
2.7		Communication Diagram[b]
2.8		Component Diagram[b]
2.9		Composite Structure Diagram[b]
2.10		Deployment Diagram[b]
2.11		Package Diagram[b]
2.12		Timing Diagram[b]
2.13		Interaction Overview Diagram[b]
2.14		Profile Diagram[b]

[a] Shown only if a condition on the previous answers is satisfied

[b] *I have never seen it, I examined a model containing it, I produced a model containing it*
For each question in this group an image depicting a sample diagram is shown (see Fig. 1)

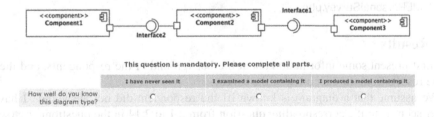

Component Diagram

This question is mandatory. Please complete all parts.

	I have never seen it	I examined a model containing it	I produced a model containing it
How well do you know this diagram type?			

Fig. 1. A question (Q 2.8) from the "UML Diagrams" questionnaire section

To harvest more answers, we decided that the questionnaire should take no longer than approximately 15 minutes to complete (long questionnaires get fewer answers than short questionnaires [24]) and we designed it accordingly.

The questionnaire was introduced with a brief statement about the purpose of our research (as suggested in [7]), and we added a sentence to clarify that all the collected information had to be considered highly confidential[7].

Survey Execution. The data presented in this paper have been collected since 1st of October 2013 until the 10th of March 2014 (about 5 month and half). Approximately every month, we sent to different mailing lists and groups an invitation to participate to the survey. The procedure followed to prepare, administer, and collect the questionnaire data is made up of the following five main steps:

1. *Preparation and Design of the Questionnaire.* Starting from similar questionnaires [20,21] and tailoring them to our objectives, an initial set of questions was agreed among us.
2. *Pilot Study.* A pilot study was performed before executing the survey (i) to tune the questionnaire and (ii) to reduce the ambiguities contained in the questions. An industrial IT professional and a university professor filled a preliminary version of the questionnaire and provided their judgment on it. Following the suggestions of the two contacted experts, minor changes to the questionnaire were made. After this pilot study we concluded that the survey was well suited for IT professionals and academics and that the questions were clear enough.
3. *On-line Deployment.* Once the questionnaire was refined after the pilot study, it was deployed on-line by using LimeSurvey as explained before.
4. *Monitoring.* During the data capture phase, our research group monitored the progress of the questionnaire submission. A few people reporting difficulties about the questions asked us for clarifications.
5. *Data Analysis.* After questionnaires have been collected, simple analyses were performed with the aim of answering the research questions. Given the nature of this survey, that is mainly descriptive (it describes some conditions or factors found in a population in terms of its frequency and impact [7]), we applied quite exclusively descriptive statistics and showed our findings by means of charts. For space reasons, we employed line charts instead of the more common/adapt column charts. Anonymized raw data are available at: http://sepl.dibris.unige.it/2014-UMLPersonalSurvey.php

3   Results

We first present some information about the background of the respondents, and then some results from the execution of the survey.

We assume that a diagram is known iff the respondent did not answered "I have never seen it" to the corresponding question from 2.1 to 2.14 in the questionnaire (see Table 1), and thus if (s)he has either just examined or produced a model containing it.

3.1   Respondents' Background

From the answers to the first section of the questionnaire we have found that: (Q1.3) the majority (83%) of the respondents are male, and (Q1.4) the most common age groups are 28-37 and 38-47 with respectively the 43% and 30% of the respondents.

---

[7] In conformity with privacy Italian law: "D.lgs. n. 196/2003".

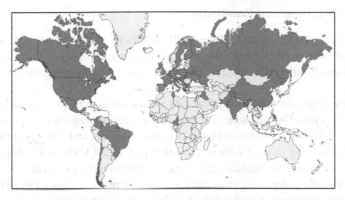

Fig. 2. Nationalities of the Respondents (dark grey means that in our sample we have at least one respondent for that Nation) – (Q1.5)

We have respondents from many different nationalities (Q1.5, see Fig. 2) with 231 participants from Europe (mainly from Italy with about the half of the survey's respondents, and then Germany and France), 32 from Americas (mainly from US, Brazil and Canada), 10 from Asia, and 2 from Africa. The majority of the respondents are professionals (60%) while the remaining are from the academia (40%). For what concerns the role of the respondents (Q1.6), the most frequent are software developer, professor, PhD student, and university researcher, see Fig. 3.

MD*[8] techniques (Q1.9) are used in the company of the 61% of the respondents, while the 54% of the respondents is using UML in their current activities (Q1.10). The majority of the respondents learned UML in university courses 50% or by self-study 38% (Q1.11). The 39% of the respondents use UML by less than 5 years, 35% by 5-10 years, 17% by 10-15 years and the remaining (9%) by more than 15 years (Q1.12). The 80% of the respondents create UML models using specific tools (Q1.13). The 49% of the respondents have read the OMG UML specifications (Q1.15). Only 2 respondents are active in the OMG, and only 7 took part in the OMG UML definition. Finally, only the 6% of the respondents have an OMG UML certification (Q1.18).

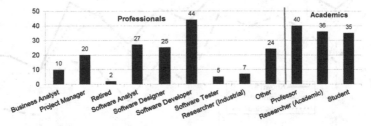

Fig. 3. Current Roles and number of the Respondents – (Q1.6)

---

[8] A common name for several model driven approaches and methodologies, such as MDD, MDSD, MDE, MDA [23].

3.2 RQ1: UML Diagrams Knowledge

The results about the knowledge of the UML diagrams of all the respondents can be seen in Fig. 4 (straight dark line). The chart shows that the level of knowledge of the various diagrams is quite different, and that we can distribute the diagrams in three main groups.

(K1) They are diagrams that are without any doubt *widely known*, precisely use case diagram (97%), class diagram, state machine and sequence diagram (96%), and activity diagram (92%). The most known one is the use case diagram, and this it is not surprising, since this diagram may be used without any other part of the UML, and it is truly useful to complement classical textual use case based requirements specifications, offering a nice way to visually summarize use cases, actors and relationships among them. Also the authors have proposed a method for building "disciplined use case specifications" where only this part of the UML is used [17]. All the diagram types in this group were already present in UML version 1.

(K2) Other diagrams are *known* with good percentage: package diagram (86%), component diagram (82%), object diagram (81%), deployment diagram (77%), and communication diagram (73%).

(K3) The remaining diagrams are *scarcely known*: composite structure diagram (59%), profile diagram (52%), interaction overview diagram (51%), and timing diagram (42%).

The answer to **RQ1** is then that some UML diagrams are very widely known **(K1)**, others are known **(K2)**, and the remaining ones are scarcely known **(K3)**. The least known is the timing diagram.

In Fig. 4 we have also presented the combined results of the previous survey [14] (dotted line) covering static sources about the UML (books, tools, university courses and tutorials). In this case the percentage is relative to the number of sources in which the various diagram types were considered. The lines in Fig. 4 are slight different but their trend is very similar (the Pearson's correlation coefficient between the two poly-lines is really high, 0.92), thus the most/less known diagrams are more or less the same, and so we have a confirmation of the soundness of the above answer to **RQ1**. The only

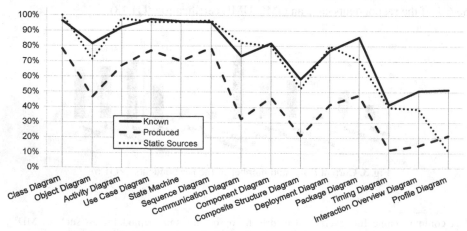

Fig. 4. UML diagrams knowledge and usage whole survey population

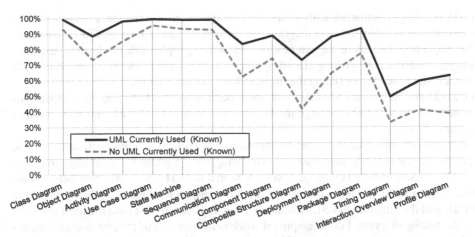

Fig. 5. UML diagrams knowledge: people currently/not currently using UML for their job

real visual difference between the two polylines concerns the profile diagram, where people knowledge seems better than its consideration by the static sources. However, it is the newest diagram (indeed it was introduced only in UML version 2.1), and it is sensible to assume that books/tools/courses take more time to integrate the novelties than people. A possible confounding factor about this comparison could be that our previous survey on static sources [14] has been performed about one year ago.

Finally, we have partitioned the knowledge level of the UML diagrams considering question Q1.10 (Are you currently using UML for your business activity?). Fig. 5 clearly shows that the current usage of the UML in the respondents' job activities is correlated with a higher level of UML knowledge. The difference about the two distributions (used/not used) is clear-cut for all the UML diagrams with the exception of the four most known diagrams where it is really small.

It is interesting to note that: (1) using currently UML implies a better knowledge of all the diagrams and not of only a subset of them, and (2) with the reduction of the UML diagrams knowledge increases the difference between the two distributions, in other words, diagrams in group K1 are known by everyone while specific diagrams (groups K2 and K3) are more known by those who are currently using UML in the everyday activities.

3.3 RQ2: UML Diagrams Usage

The data about the real usage of the various UML diagrams are also shown in Fig. 4 (dashed line). We can see that obviously the usage figures are lower than those referring to the knowledge of the various diagrams (on average of about 30%), but the distance is greater for the less known diagrams (e.g. for the composite structure diagram). This fact may be interpreted as either less known are less used because they are less "useful" or they are less used because people do not know them. However, they follow the same trend: most/less known diagrams are also the most/less used ones. This is confirmed by the Pearson's correlation coefficient between the two polylines that is really high (0.96). Thus we can again distribute the diagrams in three groups:

(U1) The diagrams that are without any doubt *widely used* are: sequence diagram (79%), class diagram (78%), use case diagram (77%), state machine diagram (70%), and activity diagram (67%). Here we can observe that some people have produced a sequence diagram without a supporting class diagram (thus they have made an inconsistent UML model, since the classes typing the lifelines have not been defined).

(U2) Other diagrams are *used* but with lower percentage: package diagram (48%), component diagram and object diagram (47%), deployment (42%), and communication diagram (32%).

(U3) The remaining diagrams can be considered *scarcely used*: composite structure and profile diagram (21%), interaction overview diagram (15%), and timing diagram (12%).

The answer to **RQ2** is then quite similar to that to **RQ1** (the correlation between the two RQs is really strong): some UML diagrams are widely used **(U1)**, other are used **(U2)**, and the remaining **(U3)** are scarcely used; and also in this case the least used one is the timing diagram. Future empirical work is needed to understand in which niches of the industry the diagrams in **(U3)** are really used, and whether they could be also useful elsewhere.

3.4   RQ3: Professionals vs. Academics

Fig. 6 presents the data about knowledge and usage of the UML partitioning the sample by category of occupation: professionals vs. academics. For what concerns the knowledge level, academics (straight dark line) seems to know a little more than professionals (dashed light line) — average less than 7%. Only in two cases professionals seem to know a slightly more than academics: for composite structure diagram (+6%), and timing diagram (+10%). Probably, this is due to a specific use of these two types of diagrams in industrial niches (e.g. timing diagrams are heavily used in avionics industries to model guidance and control systems).

The data about the usage of the various UML diagrams are also shown in Fig. 6 (see the dashed polylines). We can see that obviously the usage figures are lower than those referring to the knowledge of the various diagrams, but the distance between industry

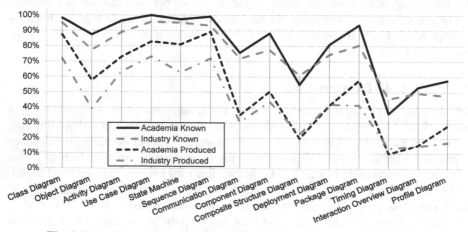

Fig. 6. UML diagrams knowledge and usage: Professionals versus Academics

and academic usage — on average of about 10% — is greater in some cases (e.g. for class, object, state machine, sequence and package diagrams). We believe that this is due to the different nature of the produced models containing the considered diagram type: relative to a real project for professionals and to a toy model used for teaching in the case of academics.

Thus, we can answer to question **RQ3** simply saying that UML is slightly more known and used by the academics than by the professionals except for composite structure diagrams and timing diagrams.

3.5 **RQ4**: Working Role, Seniority, Education, and Gender

Fig. 7 (upper part) shows the data about the knowledge of the UML diagrams distinguishing the different working roles. To keep the charts readable we do not report the data about the roles with a very low number of respondents (e.g. software tester, see Fig. 3).

In the case of the professionals, we can see that there is a visual difference between the developer and the other roles in the majority of the diagrams; it seems that developers are those with the less knowledge of the UML diagrams. These results seem to suggest that UML is less relevant for the last software development phases. For the aca-

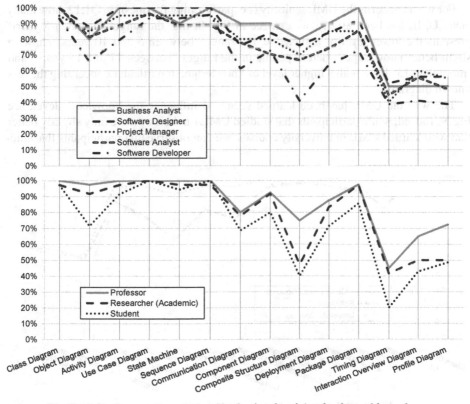

Fig. 7. UML diagrams knowledge: Professional and Academic working roles

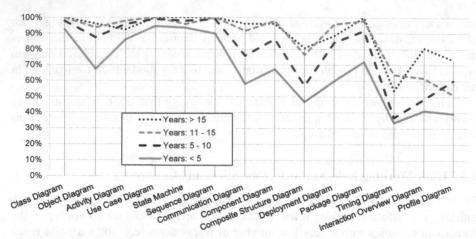

Fig. 8. UML diagrams knowledge: How many years have you been using UML?

demics, we can see — always in Fig. 7 (lower part) — that, as expected, students (86% of them are PhD) have slightly lower knowledge of the UML with respect to the other academic roles. This is more marked for object and timing diagrams.

For what concerns the UML seniority (i.e. partitioning for question Q1.12, how many years UML has been used?), we can see in Fig. 8, that the range "less than 5 years" presents the lower level of knowledge, the range "between 5 and 10 years" shows a slight better knowledge, whereas people in the ranges "between 11 and 15 years" and "more than 15" have both a higher level of knowledge, in particular concerning the less known diagrams.

The way the UML has been learned seems to influence the knowledge level, see Fig. 9. Indeed, while participants that studied UML on their own are only slightly better that who learned UML in university courses, we can observe that participants that stud-

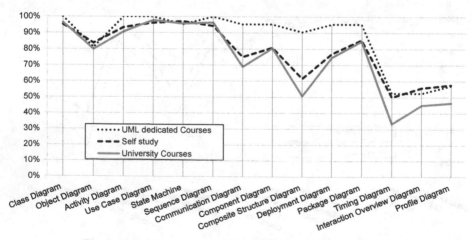

Fig. 9. UML diagrams knowledge: How did you learned UML?

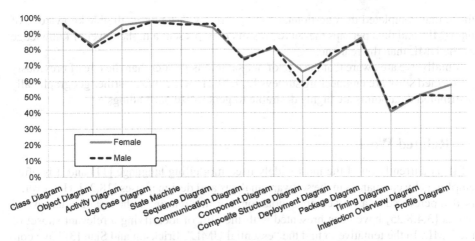

Fig. 10. UML diagrams knowledge: Male versus Female

ied UML in dedicated courses have a better knowledge in particular for communication, component, composite structure, deployment and package diagrams.

Finally, there is almost no difference in the UML knowledge if we consider the gender of the survey respondents (see Fig. 10).

Thus, we can answer to question **RQ4** saying that the factors we have considered (working role, seniority, education, and gender) do not have an influence on the UML knowledge.

3.6 Threats to Validity

In our opinion the main threats to validity of this study are the following: (1) non-probabilistic sampling method, (2) possible self-exclusion from participants not interested in our survey, (3) possible non representativeness of the sample, and (4) sample size and not uniform geographic distribution of the data points.

We opted for non-probabilistic sampling methods, even if we know very well all the problems of this sampling, for two reasons. First, this survey is exploratory. Second, we thought that the target population was hard to identify and reach (especially non-Italian people), and of limited availability (this is often true in software engineering surveys). This should be carefully considered when interpreting the results we obtained: with this kind of sampling it is difficult to generalize the results to the entire population.

We cannot exclude that some participants could have avoided to answer because they have already a well-defined opinion about the UML (e.g. "it is not useful" and "there is nothing to discuss about it"). Self-exclusion is a well-known problem in Internet surveys, in particular when advertised by means of mailing lists and groups as we did.

We were expecting the questionnaire to be filled by people with at least minimal knowledge of the UML. Examining the collected data, we discovered that eight respondents answered "I have never seen it" at all the questions about UML diagrams and thus we decided to delete them from the sample. Moreover, we received 22 incomplete questionnaires. We contacted some of these respondents to understand the drop out reason. In several cases the motivation was little knowledge of UML. So we can conjecture that those that completed the questionnaire are people with a non-negligible knowledge of the UML, and thus perhaps the survey results may present a higher level of knowledge of the UML than the real one.

Finally, we are aware that the size of our sample is greater than the one of previously performed software engineering surveys [2,9,20,21]. Of course, further geographically distributed data points are highly desirable to generalize our findings.

4   Related Work

UML is currently on of the most widely used modelling language [11] and it is often employed by companies in the software analysis and design phases [18,21]. However, it is also perceived as a very complex notation. For this reason, in the last decade, several works [3,4,8,25] have been presented with the aim of identifying a relevant subset of the UML. In the tentative to find the "essential UML", Erickson and Siau [3] have conducted a Delphi study[9] with the goal of identifying a UML kernel for three well-known UML application areas: Real-Time, Web-based, and Enterprise systems. The participants to the study were asked to rate the relative importance of the various UML diagrams in building systems. UML overall results (i.e. non-domain specific) were: 100% for class and state machine diagrams, 95.5% for sequence diagrams, 90.9% for use case diagrams. All the others diagrams received a percentage lower than 50%, e.g. 27.3% for activity diagrams. This last finding is in contrast with our results where the activity diagrams are well-known (92%) and used (67%). Another personal opinion survey by Grossman et al. [4] about UML confirms the results of Erickson and Siau. Results indicate that the three most important diagrams are use case diagram, class diagrams and sequence diagrams. Wrycza and Marcinkowski [25], in another personal opinion survey, have tried to downsize the UML finding the most useful diagrams. The participants perceived use case, class, activity, and sequence diagrams as the most useful.

In comparison to these works, our survey is quite different for several reasons: (1) we invited very different categories of UML users to participate, from academia and industry, while, for instance, the sample used by [25] is composed only by students (180 in total) with a very homogeneous background (e.g. they have all studied UML on the same book), and Grossman et al. focused their study only on developers; (2) we tried to get a remarkable number of participants (i.e. 275) compared for instance to the 131 of Grossman et al. [4] and the 44 of [3].

Another personal opinion survey about UML (171 professionals in total), by Dobing and Parsons [2], points out another strong statement: "regular usage of UML components were lower than expected". The authors of [2] suggest that the difficulty of understanding many of the notations "support the argument that the UML may be too complex". The same claim, in more or less different forms, is present in several blogs, where many proposals of UML simplification are arising[10]. Maybe, the most authoritative is the one of Ivar Jacobson entitled "Taking the temperature of UML" [5], where

---

[9] It attempts to form a reliable consensus of a group of experts in specialized areas.

[10] e.g. http://www.devx.com/architect/Article/45694 and http://blogs.msdn.com/b/sonuarora/archive/2009/11/02/simplify-uml.aspx

he wrote: *"Still, UML has become complex and clumsy. For 80% of all software only 20% of UML is needed. However, it is not easy to find the subset of UML which we would call the 'Essential' UML. We must make UML smarter to use"*. The need to simplify the UML is also shown by the recently released OMG draft proposal about this topic [19]. Moreover, the complexity of the UML seems to be one of the factors that limit its diffusion and usage in the industry [13].

The work in [8] shares our opinion on the importance to determine " which parts of UML are extensively used, which are scarcely or never used" (using their own words); however, differently from us they decided to analyse models publicly available on the web. Moreover, in their paper the frequency of use refers to the *concrete metaclasses* appearing in the metamodel (that should correspond to modelling concepts), and to *language units* (groups of tight-coupled modelling concepts), whereas we consider UML diagrams and visual constructs, that it is a user-view of the UML. The result of this study is that class, use case, and interaction are the most used language units, which roughly correspond to class, use case, sequence and interaction overview diagrams.

The main conclusion from a systematic literature review by Budgen et al. [1] is: while there are many studies that use the UML in some way, there are relatively few for which the UML is itself the object of study; there is a need to study the UML and its elements much more rigorously and to identify which features are valuable, and which could be discarded. Our work can be considered a first attempt in this direction.

5 Conclusions and Future Work

In this paper we have presented some results from a personal opinion survey, with respondents being both members of the academia and professionals, performed to investigate the level of knowledge and usage of the various UML diagrams, and to understand whether the working context, the working role, the education, the seniority (both obviously referring to the UML), and the gender influence the answer. This survey is part of a wider study aimed to gain information on the knowledge and usage of the UML diagrams and of the constructs of use case and activity diagrams, that includes a survey of static informative sources on the UML [14,15] (an extended version of [15], including also the constructs of use case diagram will appear in [16]).

The found results show that the level of knowledge and of usage of the various types of diagrams is quite different, and that these differences are quite stable also when considering different categories of peoples, for example the timing diagram is almost always the less known/used. Furthermore, these differences among the diffusion of the various diagram types are consistent with those found by the survey on the static sources.

The UML diagram types may be placed in three different groups. In the first group there are the widely known and used diagrams. They cover the basic modelling functionalities: structural (class diagram) and behavioural (state machine, sequence diagram and activity diagram), while use case diagram has a specific role for the requirement specifications based on use cases (and it seems to be used also without any other UML diagram). All of them were already present in the UML version 1. In the second group there are diagrams useful for representing more specific aspect of systems/software (e.g. communication and object diagrams) or useful in specific cases (e.g. component and deployment diagram) or needed only to structure a model in packages (package diagram). They are known and used but at a less extent than those in the first group. The third group contains diagrams covering very specific aspects of a system (e.g. interaction overview and timing diagrams) or having a very specific role (profile diagram), while composite structure diagram has two different forms, one for modelling structured classes and one for collaborations (the latter are quite useful for example for modelling SOA based systems, see e.g. SoaML [12]). All these diagrams have been introduced in UML version 2, and the profile diagram only in UML 2.1.

As future work we would like: (1) to extend our personal opinion survey in several directions (e.g. adding more data points, extending the survey to other nations and extending the goal of our survey, for example for understanding why professionals choose to use some diagrams and ignore others), (2) to extend the static sources considering also web resources and model repositories, e.g. ReMoDD.

References

1. Budgen, D., Burn, A.J., Brereton, O.P., Kitchenham, B.A., Pretorius, R.: Empirical evidence about the UML: A systematic literature review. Software Practice and Experience 41(4), 363–392 (2011)
2. Dobing, B., Parsons, J.: How UML is used. Communications of the ACM 49(5), 109–113 (2006)
3. Erickson, J., Siau, K.: Can UML be simplified? Practitioner use of UML in separate domains. In: Proceedings of 12th International Workshop on Exploring Modeling Methods for Systems Analysis and Design. EMMSAD 2007, vol. 365, pp. 81–90. CEUR Workshop Proceedings (2007)
4. Grossman, M., Aronson, J.E., McCarthy, R.V.: Does UML make the grade? Insights from the software development community. Information and Software Technology 47(6), 383–397 (2005)
5. Jacobson, I.: Taking the temperature of UML. Web site (2009), http://blog.ivarjacobson.com/taking-the-temperature-of-uml/
6. Jedlitschka, A., Ciolkowski, M., Denger, C., Freimut, B., Schlichting, A.: Relevant information sources for successful technology transfer: A survey using inspections as an example. In: Proceedings of 1st International Symposium on Empirical Software Engineering and Measurement, ESEM 2007, pp. 31–40. IEEE Computer Society (2007)
7. Kitchenham, B.A., Pfleeger, S.L.: Personal opinion surveys. In: Shull, F., Singer, J., Sjoberg, D.I.K. (eds.) Guide to Advanced Empirical Software Engineering, pp. 63–92. Springer, London (2008)
8. Langer, P., Mayerhofer, T., Wimmer, M., Kappel, G.: On the usage of UML: Initial results of analyzing open UML models. In: Modellierung 2014, Wien, Österreich, März 19-21. LNI, vol. 225, pp. 289–304. GI (2014)
9. Leotta, M., Ricca, F., Ribaudo, M., Reggio, G., Astesiano, E., Vernazza, T.: An exploratory survey on SOA knowledge, adoption and trend in the Italian industry. In: Proceedings of 14th International Symposium on Web Systems Evolution, WSE 2012, pp. 21–30. IEEE (2012)
10. Lethbridge, T.C.: A Survey of the Relevance of Computer Science and Software Engineering Education. In: Proceedings of the 11th Conference on Software Engineering Education and Training, CSEET 1998, pp. 56–66. IEEE (1998)
11. Mohagheghi, P., Dehlen, V., Neple, T.: Definitions and approaches to model quality in model-based software development - a review of literature. Information and Software Technology 51(12), 1646–1669 (2009)

12. OMG. Service oriented architecture Modeling Language (SoaML) Specification Version 1.0.1 (2012), http://www.omg.org/spec/SoaML/1.0.1/PDF
13. Petre, M.: UML in practice. In: Proceedings of 35th International Conference on Software Engineering, ICSE 2013, pp. 722–731. IEEE (2013)
14. Reggio, G., Leotta, M., Ricca, F., Clerissi, D.: What are the used UML diagrams? A preliminary survey. In: Proceedings of 3rd International Workshop on Experiences and Empirical Studies in Software Modeling (EESSMod 2013), vol. 1078, pp. 3–12. CEUR Workshop Proceedings (2013)
15. Reggio, G., Leotta, M., Ricca, F., Clerissi, D.: What are the used activity diagram constructs? A survey. In: Proceedings of 2nd International Conference on Model-Driven Engineering and Software Development, MODELSWARD 2014, pp. 87–98. SciTePress Digital Library (2014)
16. Reggio, G., Leotta, M., Ricca, F., Clerissi, D.: What are the used UML diagram constructs? A document and tool analysis study covering activity and use case diagrams. In: Hammoudi, S., Pires, L.F., Filipe, J., das Neves, R.C. (eds.) Model-Driven Engineering and Software Development. CCIS. Springer (in press); (Revised Selected Papers of 2nd International Conference on Model-Driven Engineering and Software Development)
17. Reggio, G., Ricca, F., Leotta, M.: Improving the quality and the comprehension of requirements: Disciplined use cases and mockups. In: Proceedings of 40th Euromicro Conference on Software Engineering and Advanced Applications, SEAA 2014. IEEE (in press, 2014)
18. Scanniello, G., Gravino, C., Tortora, G.: Investigating the role of UML in the software modeling and maintenance - A preliminary industrial survey. In: Proceedings of 12th International Conference on Enterprise Information Systems, ICEIS 2010, pp. 141–148. SciTePress (2010)
19. Seidewitz, E.: UML 2.5: Specification simplification. Presented at "Third Biannual Workshop on Eclipse Open Source Software and OMG Open Specifications" (May 2012)
20. Torchiano, M., Di Penta, M., Ricca, F., De Lucia, A., Lanubile, F.: Migration of information systems in the Italian industry: A state of the practice survey. Information and Software Technology 53, 71–86 (2011)
21. Torchiano, M., Tomassetti, F., Ricca, F., Tiso, A., Reggio, G.: Relevance, benefits, and problems of software modelling and model driven techniques: A survey in the Italian industry. Journal of Systems and Software 86(8), 2110–2126 (2013)
22. UML Revision Task Force. OMG Unified Modeling Language (OMG UML), Superstructure, V2.4.1 (2011)
23. Völter, M.: MD* best practices. Journal of Object Technology 8(6), 79–102 (2009)
24. Walonick, D.S.: Survival Statistics. StatPac, Inc. (1997)
25. Wrycza, S., Marcinkowski, B.: A light version of UML 2: Survey and outcomes. In: Proceedings of the Computer Science and IT Education Conference, CSITEd 2007 (2007)

Assessing the State-of-Practice of Model-Based Engineering in the Embedded Systems Domain

Grischa Liebel[1], Nadja Marko[2], Matthias Tichy[1], Andrea Leitner[2], and Jörgen Hansson[3]

[1] Software Engineering Division, Chalmers | University of Gothenburg, Sweden
grischa@chalmers.se|matthias.tichy@cse.gu.se
[2] Virtual Vehicle Research Center, Graz, Austria
nadja.marko@v2c2.at|andrea.leitner@v2c2.at
[3] School of Informatics, University of Skövde, Sweden
jorgen.hansson@his.se

Abstract. Model-Based Engineering (MBE) aims at increasing the effectiveness of engineering by using models as key artifacts in the development process. While empirical studies on the use and the effects of MBE in industry exist, there is only little work targeting the embedded systems domain. We contribute to the body of knowledge with a study on the use and the assessment of MBE in that particular domain. We collected quantitative data from 112 subjects, mostly professionals working with MBE, with the goal to assess the current State of Practice and the challenges the embedded systems domain is facing. Our main findings are that MBE is used by a majority of all participants in the embedded systems domain, mainly for simulation, code generation, and documentation. Reported positive effects of MBE are higher quality and improved reusability. Main shortcomings are interoperability difficulties between MBE tools, high training effort for developers and usability issues.

Keywords: Model-Based Engineering, Model-Driven Engineering, Embedded Systems, Industry, Modeling, Empirical Study, State-of-Practice.

1 Introduction

Model-Based Engineering (MBE)[1] has a long history in the embedded systems domain. For example, the first version of Matlab/Simulink has been released exactly 30 years ago and by now, it is one of the standard development tools in the automotive domain. MBE aims to increase the effectiveness and efficiency of Software Development [4]. However, empirical evaluation of MBE in industry is scarce [12]. The few existing empirical studies in this field suggest that MBE can have positive effects such as reduction of defects and productivity improvements [3, 12], or increased understandability [10]. Nevertheless, they also report

---

[1] We use the terms Model-Based Engineering and Model-Driven Engineering interchangeably for a process in which models are used as the primary artifacts.

J. Dingel et al. (Eds.): MODELS 2014, LNCS 8767, pp. 166–182, 2014.

challenges such as insufficient tool support [3,12,13], need for additional training [10] or the use of MBE with legacy software [10,12]. However, existing studies
are not explicitly targeted at the embedded systems domain [3,9,10,12–14], target only UML [2,5,8], limit themselves to the Brazilian embedded industry [1], or
collect only qualitative data from the automotive domain [11]. We contribute to
the body of knowledge with a survey on the use of MBE in the embedded systems
domain. The goal of the survey was to get an overview about the SoP and challenges the industry is faced with in order to understand industrial needs. More
precisely, with the study we want to answer the following research questions:

– **RQ1:** What is the current state of practice and the assessment of Model-
  Based Engineering in the embedded systems domain?
– **RQ2:** How does the use and the assessment of Model-Based Engineering
  differ between different demographic subgroups in the embedded systems
  domain?

RQ1 aims to capture the SoP of MBE in the embedded systems domain,
which includes the used modeling environments, modeling languages, types of
notations, purposes models are used for and how much activities concern MBE
compared to non-MBE. Moreover, we are interested in the introduction reasons and the effects, both positive and negative, after introduction of MBE as
well as current shortcomings of this method. With **RQ2**, we want to find out
whether there are substantial differences in the SoP between different groups in
the embedded systems domain, e.g., differences in the automotive domain and
the avionics domain or between new MBE users and highly experienced users.

In order to answer the research questions, we developed a web survey consisting of 24 questions. The survey was distributed to partners taking part in
five industrially driven European research projects (between 22 and 100 project
partners) as well as to personal contacts of which most are professionals working
with MBE. Finally, we have got 121 completed surveys from which 112 are used
for the data analysis.

In this paper, we focus on the presentation of the reported positive and negative effects of MBE, shortcomings of MBE, reasons for introducing MBE and
purposes models are used for in the development process. Overall, the survey answers show that many survey participants think that the positive effects predominate the negative effects of MBE. Nevertheless, they mention also
that interoperability challenges between tools exist and that it causes high efforts to train the developers. More detailed results will be discussed in Section
4. The complete data sample together with the questionnaire is published at
`www.cse.chalmers.se/~tichy/models14_LMTLH_dataset.zip`[2].

The remainder of this paper is structured as follows. In the following section,
we discuss related work. Section 3 contains the research methodology. This includes the process of study design, data collection, threats of validity. In Section
4, the key results of the survey are discussed. Finally, conclusions and future
work are discussed in Section 5.

---

[2] Password: mbe_usage14

2   Related Work

While industrial evaluation of MBE in research is limited [10], there are a number of recent publications addressing this topic. With respect to the embedded systems domain, we are only aware of two reported studies, [1] and [11], presenting the SoP of MBE in this particular domain. Other publications, such as [3,12] and [9], also include cases from the embedded systems domain, but do not explicitly address this domain as their target.

In [1], Agner et al. present the results of a survey on the use of UML and model-driven approaches in the Brazilian embedded software development industry. The participants come from a variety of different sub-domains, with industrial automation, information technology, telecommunications and electronic industry being the biggest groups. Key findings are that 45% of the 209 participants use UML. Of these 45%, the majority are experienced developers working at medium-sized companies. The subjects report increases in productivity and improvements in quality, maintenance and portability as key advantages of model-driven practices. According to the participants, the use of UML is mostly hindered by short lead times, lack of knowledge regarding UML and a limited number of employees with expert UML knowledge. Additionally, it is stated that models are mainly used for documentation with only little use of code generation or model-centric approaches in general. In contrast to [1], we do not limit ourselves to a region but include a wide range of subjects from global companies based in Europe.

Kirstan and Zimmermann report a case study within the automotive domain [11]. Their interviewees report positive effects of MBE like an earlier detection of errors, a higher degree of automation and cost savings during the initial phases of development. On the negative side, they state that large function models can become too complex and that interoperability between tools is difficult. The study is limited to qualitative data from a single sub-domain of the embedded systems domain, namely automotive.

Baker et al. present experiences with MBE at Motorola over a time span of almost 20 years in [3]. On the positive side, they report a defect reduction and an improvement in productivity. However, a number of challenges regarding MBE are named as well, such as lack of common tools, poor tool and generated code performance, lack of integrated tools, and lack of scalability.

Mohagheghi and Dehlen published a literature review on the industrial application of MBE [12]. The evidence collected during the review suggests that the use of MBE can lead to improvements in software quality and productivity. However, studies which report productivity losses are also quoted in the review. Insufficient tool chains, modeling complexity, and the use of MBE with legacy systems are reported as challenges. Additionally, the maturity of tool environments is stated to be unsatisfactory for a large-scale adoption of MBE. Generally, the authors conclude that there is too little evidence in order to generalize their results.

In a later publication by Mohagheghi et al., experiences from three companies in a European project "with the objective of developing techniques and tools for applying MDE" are reported [13]. According to the experiences at the studied companies, advantages of using MBE include the possibility to provide abstractions of complex systems, simulation and testing, and performance-related decision support. However, the authors also state that the development of reusable solutions using MBE requires additional effort and might decrease performance. Moreover, transformations required for tool integration can increase the complexity and the implementation effort according to the authors. Furthermore, the user-friendliness of MBE tools and means for managing models of complex systems is described as challenging.

Hutchinson et al. report industrial experiences from the adoption of MBE at a printer company, a car company and a telecommunications company in [9]. The authors conclude that a successful adoption of MBE seems to require, among others, an iterative and progressive approach, organizational commitment, and motivated users. The study is focused mainly on organizational challenges of MBE.

A further assessment of MBE in industry by Hutchinson et al. based on over 250 survey responses, 22 interviews, and observational studies from multiple domains is presented in [10]. From their survey, the authors report that significant additional training is needed for the use of MBE, but that MBE in turn can speed up the implementation of new requirements. Furthermore, the survey indicates that code generation is an important aspect of MBE productivity gains, but integrating the code into existing projects can be problematic. The majority of survey participants states that MBE increases understandability. From their interviews, the authors conclude that people's ability to think abstractly can have a huge impact on their ability to model. Hence, this ability influences the success of MBE.

According to a survey of 113 software practitioners reported by Forward and Lethbridge, common problems with model-centric development approaches are, among others, inconsistency of models over time, model interchange between tools and heavyweight modeling tools [7]. Code-centric development approaches, on the other hand, make it difficult to see the overall design and hard to understand the system behavior.

Torchiano et al. present findings from a survey on the State of Practice in model-driven approaches in the Italian software industry [14]. From the 155 subjects, 68% report to always or sometimes use models. The subjects who do not use models commonly state that modeling requires too much effort (50%) or is not useful enough (46%). Further findings are that models are used mainly in larger companies and that a majority of all the subjects using models (76%) apply UML.

Further empirical evaluations on the application of UML in particular can be found in [2, 5, 8]. These publications are related to our survey with respect to some aspects, such as UML notation types. However, they do not address MBE, or any approach where models are the primary artifact, in particular. Therefore, they are not discussed here in detail.

In conclusion, commonly reported problems in industry are insufficient tool support or tool chains, using MBE together with legacy systems, and the complexity of MBE and modeling in general. On the positive side, productivity gains, defect reductions and increased understandability are reported. However, there is a lack of empirical evidence and reported industry evaluations on the use of MBE within the embedded systems domain. Existing work is either not targeted at the embedded systems domain in particular [3, 9, 10, 12–14], is limited to the Brazilian market [1], or lacks quantitative data [11].

3   Research Methodology

This section outlines the research methodology, consisting of the study design, an outline of the data collection and threats to validity.

3.1   Study Design

The study was designed by three researchers from two different institutions and three practitioners from two different companies as part of the CRYSTAL project.

We decided to perform a survey in order to reach a larger sample size compared to other empirical strategies and, thus, get an overview of the embedded systems domain.

The survey questionnaire consisted of 24 closed-ended and open-ended questions. The first part of the questionnaire contained 13 questions gathering demographic data. Hereby, we asked for company size, position in the value chain, domain, experience with MBE, product size, working tasks, and the attitude towards MBE. The second part, consisting of the remaining eleven questions, addressed **RQ1**. Due to space limitations, we only use questions for the data analysis in this paper regarding the positive and negative effects of MBE, shortcomings of MBE, reasons for introducing MBE and purposes models are used for. The answers for all four questions were scored on a 5-level likert scale. Both parts of the questionnaire were considered together for answering **RQ2**.

The survey was piloted by eleven colleagues in academia and industry. Given their feedback and the time they needed to fill out the survey, the questionnaire was refined. The revised survey was reviewed a second time by one colleague not included in the pilot survey.

Furthermore, we derived a list of 24 hypotheses from the related work discussed in Section 2 (see Table 1) in order to guide the data analysis for **RQ1**. These were then evaluated based on our collected data. The descriptions of hypotheses **H1.1** through **H1.9** are summaries of the actual statements in the related work, based on our understanding. This is due to the fact that similar statements are present in multiple sources. For instance, Hypothesis **H1.5** describes tool quality in general, while Baker et al. talk about poor tool performance [3], Mohagheghi and Dehlen report lack of maturity of third-party tool environments [12], Mohagheghi et al. report challenges with the user-friendliness of tools [13], and Forward et al. report that heavyweight modeling tools are problematic [7]. While we lose the exact statements for **H1.1** through **H1.9** from related work, we argue that this summary is helpful for getting an overview over the findings in the area of MBE. We do not claim that this list of hypotheses is complete. However, we believe that it can guide future research in this area. Additionally, we derived a list of eight hypotheses in order to answer **RQ2**. We

Table 1. Hypotheses from related work

Hypoth.	Description	Reported by
H1.1	MBE leads to a reduction of defects/improvements in quality.	[1,3,12]
H1.2	MBE leads to improvements in productivity.	[1,3,12]
H1.3	MBE increases understandability.	[10], partly [13]
H1.4	Using MBE with legacy systems is challenging.	[10,12]
H1.5	Current MBE tools are insufficient.	[3,7,11–13]
H1.6	Significant additional training is needed for using MBE.	[1,10]
H1.7	UML is the preferred modeling language employed in MBE.	[1,14]
H1.8	Managing models of complex systems is challenging.	[11,13]
H1.9	Tool integration is challenging.	[7,11,13]
H1.10	Code generated from models has poor performance.	[3]
H1.11	MBE lacks scalability.	[3]
H1.12	The complexity of modeling is challenging.	[12]
H1.13	Advantages of MBE are simulation and testing, and performance-related decision support.	[13]
H1.14	MBE leads to an earlier detection of errors.	[11]
H1.15	MBE can speed up the implementation of new requirements.	[10]
H1.16	Code generation is an important aspect of MBE productivity gains.	[10]
H1.17	Companies which consider software development their main business seem to find the adoption of MBE more challenging than other companies.	[10]
H1.18	Modeling requires too much effort.	[14]
H1.19	Handling the consistency of models over time is challenging.	[7]
H1.20	Modeling is not useful enough.	[14]
H1.21	Models are used mainly in larger companies.	[14]
H1.22	UML is mostly used by experienced developers working at medium-sized companies.	[1]
H1.23	There is little use of code generation or model-centric approaches.	[1]
H1.24	MBE leads to a higher degree of automation.	[11]

derived these hypotheses after designing our questionnaire from our own view on MBE. That is, we elicited the hypotheses based demographic subgroups which we were able to distinguish in our survey. The alternative hypotheses that there are significant differences between the subgroups are listed in Table 2. The corresponding null hypotheses are that there are no significant differences between the subgroups.

Table 2. Hypotheses defined for RQ2

Hypoth.	Description
H2.1	Users of in-house tools report more positive and less negative effects of MBE than users who do not use in-house tools.
H2.2	Supporters of MBE report more positive effects than subjects opposed to or neutral towards MBE.
H2.3	Subjects who are still using MBE report more positive and less negative effects than subjects who stopped using MBE.
H2.4	Subjects who only use models for means of information/documentation report less positive than negative effects.
H2.5	Subjects who do not see many usability issues with MBE tools report fewer negative effects.
H2.6	Highly experienced users of MBE report less problems with MBE tools than users with less experience.
H2.7	Large companies have more tool integration problems than small or medium-sized enterprises.
H2.8	MBE promoters use more MBE tools in comparison to subjects neutral or opposed to MBE.

3.2   Data Collection

The theoretical target population of the survey are all people involved with systems engineering from the embedded systems domain, e.g. software architects, software developers, project managers, system engineers. We distributed the survey to partners taking part at the Artemis projects Crystal (70 partners), VeTeSS (22 partners), MBAT (38 partners), nSafeCer (29 partners), and EMC^2(100 partners), as well as to personal contacts of which most are professionals working with MBE. This can be described as a convenience sample. However, we also encouraged recipients to distribute the survey to colleagues or partners. We used an online survey[3] in order to keep administration costs low and facilitate the distribution.

The final version of the survey was published on 18th October 2013 for a time period of six weeks. Out of 196 started surveys, 121 were completed corresponding to a completion rate of 61.73%. The survey data was automatically coded and enhanced with additional quality data by the survey tool, such as completed answers and time to fill out the survey. We cleaned the remaining 121 surveys based on degradation points computed from missing answers and the time to fill out each survey page. As we did not use compulsory questions, it could happen that subjects lost interest but still navigated through the entire survey until the end or simply looked at the survey without filling in data. Therefore, we argue that this data cleaning process is necessary in order to ensure data validity as discussed in [15]. We excluded nine surveys based on a threshold of 200 degradation points proposed by the survey tool for a light data filtering. This left us with 112 answered surveys for data analysis. We made adaptations to the

---

[3] Through www.soscisurvey.de

demographic data in cases where free-text answers clearly corresponded to one of the given answering options.

3.3 Validity Threats

In the following, we discuss the four different aspects of validity as discussed in Wohlin et al. [15].

Construct Validity. Construct validity reflects whether the studied measures are generalizeable to the concept underlying the study. We collected data from different sources in order to avoid mono-operation bias. Hypothesis guessing, the participants guessing what the researchers are aiming for and answering accordingly, can not be ruled out completely. We tried, however, to formulate the questions in a neutral way and improved the questionnaire based on obtained feedback from the pilot study in order to address this threat. Finally, answers were treated completely anonymous in order to avoid biased answers due to evaluation apprehension.

Internal Validity. Internal validity reflects whether all causal relations are studied or if unknown factors affect the results. Instrumentation was improved by using a pilot study. The survey took approximately 15 minutes to fill out and was intended to be filled out once by every participant. This reduces the likelihood for learning effects and, hence, maturation effects. Additionally, the completion rate of 61.73% indicates that the majority of participants was interested in finishing the survey. Selection threats can not be ruled out as participants volunteered to fill out the survey.

External Validity. External validity is concerned with the generalizeability of the findings. The CRYSTAL project and other projects, to which the survey was distributed, consist of partners from all major sub-domains of the embedded systems domain. Additionally, demographic data was collected in order to confirm this aspect. Therefore, we are confident that we have reached subjects with a variety of different backgrounds representative for the embedded systems domain. While CRYSTAL is a project on European level, many of the involved partners are global companies. Hence, we argue that this does not limit the validity of our results and that it is possibile to generalize them to other cases on non-EU level.

Conclusion Validity. Conclusion validity is concerned with the ability to draw correct conclusions from the studied measures. We involved three researchers and three practitioners with different background into the study design. Therefore, the survey was designed by multiple people with different aims and backgrounds, which should reduce the risk for "fishing" for results. A standard introduction e-mail was designed to be distributed with the link to the online survey.

Hence, reliability of treatment implementation is given. Reliability of measures was increased through a survey pilot filled out by eleven people and then, after improvements, reviewed by one more researcher. The detailed questionnaire is furthermore published in order to enable replications and an assessment of the validity of our study. Significance tests were only performed based on our hypotheses. That is, we did only perform a fixed number of statistical tests and did not randomly search for significant results.

4 Results

This chapter summarizes the results of the survey. First, demographic data about the subjects participating in the survey is illustrated in order to get information about their company and experiences. Then, **RQ1** is addressed and, where possible, compared to hypotheses **H1.1** to **H1.24** in order to show our survey results and compare it to related work. Finally, we discuss **RQ2** based on hypotheses **H2.1** to **H2.8** and evaluate validity of the hypotheses.

4.1 Demographic Data

The first part of the survey contained context questions providing demographic data. Mainly, two kinds of background information have been asked; first, some context questions concerning the company and secondly, questions about the personal MBE experiences of the participants. With the company related questions we wanted to get an idea of the work environment such as domain, company size or company position. Questions about the personal experiences such as daily working tasks, usage of MBE or whether the participant is a supporter for MBE or not should help to better understand answers and opinions of the surveyed subjects.

Company context. From the 112 surveys a bit more than the half stated the company they worked for; consequently, at least 30 different companies could have been identified that participated in the online survey. About three-fourths of all respondents (87) work in large companies with more than 250 employees, 14 persons are employed in small and medium enterprises (SME) and 11 at university. Hence, the main percentage of answers represent opinions of large companies. 50 of the companies are first-tier supplier, 40 OEMs, 25 second-tier supplier and 18 have other positions in the value chain such as research institutes, consultants or technology/software provider. More than a half of the respondents (60) work in the automotive industry, 31 in avionics, 25 in health care, 15 in defense, 11 in rail and 4 in telecommunications. 16 companies work domain independently and 9 operate in other domains such as semiconductor or industrial automation industry. Asking the participants the point in time their company introduced MBE, 37 say that their company started 10 or more years ago, 56 state 1-10 years ago and 4 started in the last 12 months. 8 companies still do not apply MBE, the rest (10 participants) does not know the introduction time. Accordingly, most companies have experiences with MBE for quite some time. 73 companies use MBE for developing a commercial product, 46 therefrom for large scale series production (more than 1000 pieces), 19 for medium scale production and 8 for small scale production (less than 10 pieces). 23 use MBE for research demonstration, 9 use it for non-commercial products and 7 for other purposes such as teaching or developing methods and tools.

Personal experiences. In order to understand for which activities the participants use MBE, we asked for their main working tasks. The answers, multiple answers were possible, are: 60 of the participants implement software, 56 are responsible for architecture definition, 55 for testing, 53 for design definition, 49 specify requirements, 39 are project managers, 24 are safety managers, 16 are quality managers, 14 are responsible for customer support and 12 work in general management. 14 participants execute other activities than the mentioned, such as process improvement, consulting or tool engineering. Hence, we cover a diversity of subjects working in different functions. Concerning the MBE experience, many participants (46) are well experienced with more than 3 years of usage. 40 persons state that they have moderate experience and only 26 are new in the field of MBE. 72 of the participants are still using MBE, 15 have used MBE the last time 1 month to 1 year ago and 16 have used MBE the last time more than 1 year ago. Only 9 people state that they have never used MBE; thus, a large percentage of the survey participants are experienced. 86 of subjects are promoters for MBE, 25 have a neutral attitude for MBE and 0 are opponents.

4.2 RQ1: State of Practice

The key results of the survey should offer valuable clues to industrial needs concerning MBE. Mainly, reasons for applying MBE, effects of using it, shortcomings of MBE and model purposes represent interesting outcomes of the survey.

Modeling tools and languages. Even though we do not focus on presenting the answers about modeling tools and languages in this paper, we present a summary about the most used tools and languages as context for the following results. Regarding the technical aspects of MBE, we asked the participants which languages and notation types they use for modeling and which functional aspects of their system they describe using models. Most survey participants use Matlab/Simulink (50 answers) or Eclipse-based (34 answers) MBE tools. As for notations, Finite State Machines are used by 74 participants, followed by sequence-based models (64 participants) and block diagrams (61 participants). Finally, we asked for which functional aspects of a system participants already use models. Here, structure (68 participants), discrete state specifications (48 participants) and static interfaces (47 participants) are most common.

Needs for introducing MBE. One interesting issue is the motivation why companies decide to use models for developing their systems. Reasons for introducing MBE will give information about companies' opinions regarding the advantages of MBE as well as challenges they are faced with. Therefore, the survey contains one question asking about the needs for introducing MBE. The results are summarized in Figure 1.

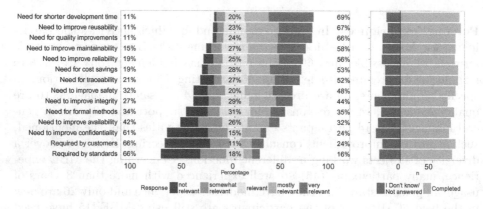

Fig. 1. Reasons for introducing MBE

On the left side of the figure the needs, which have been stated in the questionnaire, and the responses concerning the needs are listed. The three percentage declarations in the figure show on the left side the percentage of the answers with 'not relevant' and 'somewhat relevant', in the middle the percentage of the neutral 'relevant' answers and on the right side the percentage of answers with 'mostly relevant' and 'very relevant'. The second part of the figure located on the right side gives information about the amount of participants who filled in the grade (completed) and the number of participants who did not fill in a grade or do not know it (Not answered/I don't know). The figures in the following sections can be read equally but with adapted questions, responses and response types. As the figure shows, most participants (69%) think that their company adopted MBE because they had a need for shorter development time. Further, more than 50% say that needs for reusability, quality, maintainability and reliability improvements as well as cost savings and traceability are reasons for applying MBE. Least important for the respondents are needs to improve availability and confidentiality and that MBE is required by customers or standards.

Purpose of models. Further, we wanted to know for which purposes models are used for. The results for this question are illustrated in Figure 2. According to the responses, models are mainly used for simulation, code generation, opposing **H1.23**, and for information/documentation; hence, the automation of activities in the development process seems to be an important function. In contrast, timing analysis, safety compliance checks, reliability analysis and formal verification have not as much application as the other mentioned purposes.

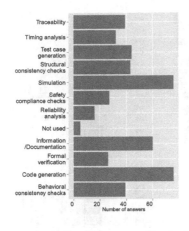

Fig. 2. Model purpose

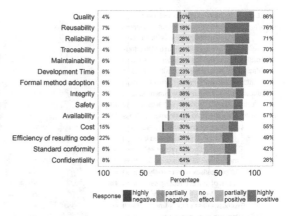

Fig. 3. Positive and negative effects of MBE

Positive and negative effects of MBE. In addition to the needs for introduction, the effects of the actual use of MBE are interesting. There are positive and negative effects when applying MBE; hence, we asked 'What were the effects of introducing MBE in your division/department?'. Figure 3 shows the answers for this question. For this question, between 5 and 9 people did not answer each item and between 30 and 53 did not know the effects. Accordingly, quality, reusability, reliability, traceability, maintainability, development time, formal method adoption, integrity, safety, availability, cost and efficiency of resulting code are rated highly or partially positive by most participants. Standard conformity and confidentiality have no effect according to more than 50% of the surveyed subjects. Thus, most survey participants think that MBE has more positive effects than negatives. From related work, **H1.1** (quality improvements) is supported by the data. **H1.2** (productivity improvements) and **H1.15** (increased development speed of new requirements) are supported with respect to development times. Other aspects of these hypotheses, such as productivity improvements due to increased efficiency, are not captured by our questionnaire. Finally, **H1.3** is supported with respect to maintainability.

Shortcomings of MBE. In order to identify potential improvements, subjects were asked about current shortcomings of MBE. Figure 4 shows the answers for this question which range from does not apply at all to fully applies. Many survey participants think that difficulties with interfaces to inter-operate with other tools is a shortcoming that fully or mostly applies. This is in line with survey results in [7], supporting **H1.9**. Moreover, more than one third of the people thinks that MBE requires a high effort to train developers (supporting **H1.6**), that there are usability issues with tools (supporting **H1.5** with respect to usability) and that benefits require high efforts (supporting **H1.18** and supporting **H1.20** with respect to the required effort). Even though **H1.18** is supported by

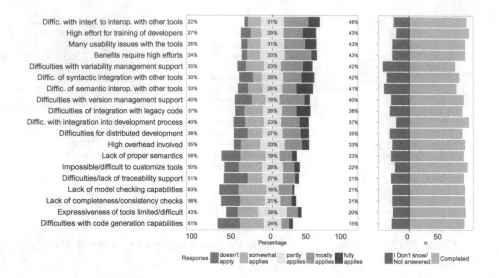

Fig. 4. Shortcomings of MBE

"benefits require high efforts", opinions about whether high overhead is involved with the usage of MBE vary. No shortcomings according to the responses are difficulties to customize tools and limitations on what can be expressed within tools what is in opposite to **H1.5** with respect to customization aspects and **H1.5** with respect to expressiveness. Hence, although the interoperability between tools seems to be a main shortcoming, capabilities of single methods and tools are satisfactory for many surveyed subjects.

MBE tool usage. In order to judge how familiar subjects are with MBE tooling, we asked how much they use MBE tools in comparison to non-MBE tools. Here, 5 subjects stated to not use any MBE tools, 26 answered that they use less MBE tools than non-MBE tools, 46 use more MBE tools than non-MBE tools and 11 use only MBE tools. Finally, 8 answered that they do not perform any engineering activities. Hence, the majority of all participants use mainly MBE tools during their work.

All in all it can be said that many survey participants think that the positive effects predominate the negative effects of MBE. However, the interoperability between tools and the usability of them, the effort to train developers as well as that the benefits require high efforts are considered as the main shortcomings of MBE.

4.3 RQ2: Differences by Subgroups

In the following, we discuss the results on research question 2 with respect to our hypotheses about differences in answers of subgroups of survey participants (cf.

Table 2). As shown in the previous section, the answers of the survey participants are ordinal scaled, e.g., a likert scale in the question about positive and negative effects of MBE. Thus, we have to use a statistical test which supports ordinal scaled data to assess whether the differences are significant. We use Fisher's exact test [6] (two-tailed) with a level of significance $\alpha \leq 0.05$. This test is a non-parametric statistical test for contingency tables. In our case, the contingency table consists of the answers of the participants in the columns and the different subgroups in the rows.

The hypotheses **H2.1**, **H2.2**, **H2.3**, **H2.4**, and **H2.5** address the full list of positive and negative effects as presented in Section 4.2. We check and report significance for each effect (e.g., cost, quality) individually.

For hypothesis **H2.4**, we do not have enough data for each subgroup in order to compare the groups. Hypotheses **H2.1**, **H2.6** and **H2.7** did not show any significant differences (i.e. $p \geq 0.05$) between the subgroups. Hence, here we can not reject the null hypotheses.

It is common that supporters of a paradigm or a methodology perceive its advantages much more positively than subjects who do not support it. Therefore, we tested this hypothesis for the case of MBE supporters and MBE opponents or neutral participants (**H2.2**). Traceability ($p = 0.00017$), safety ($p = 0.018$), and reusability ($p = 0.019$) yielded significant differences. That is, supporters of MBE perceive the effects of MBE on these three aspects significantly more positive than subjects opposed to or neutral towards MBE (See Fig. 3 for the complete sample). On traceability, 80% of MBE supporters report partially or highly positive effects, in contrast to only 27% for the opponents and neutral participants. Note that in our sample there are no opponents of MBE.

Similarly, it could be expected that participants who still use MBE also see more positive effects of MBE than participants who stopped using MBE (**H2.3**). However, significant differences exist only for cost ($p = 0.016$) and traceability ($p = 0.006$). That means that participants who are still using MBE report in total more positive effects on cost and traceability than participants who stopped using MBE. For instance, 79% of the participants still using MBE report partially or highly positive effects on traceability, while participants who stopped using MBE report only 48%. A possible explanation for the few significant differences might be that participants who stopped using MBE did so because they moved to a different position, e.g. in management, and not because they did not see the benefits of MBE.

Tooling in MBE is often reported to be insufficient. We would expect that usability issues with tools also influence other aspects such as productivity or quality negatively. Therefore, we investigated whether subjects who see many usability issues with MBE tools also report more negative effects than other subjects (**H2.5**). However, there is only a significant difference with respect to quality ($p = 0.011$). Participants who reported that many usability issues with tools mostly or fully applies rated the effects on quality slightly less positive (10% highly or partially negative, 13% no effect, and 77% partially or highly positive) than participants who reported that usability issues apply at most partly (0%, 7% and 93%).

Supporters of MBE also use more MBE tools in comparison to subjects who are opposed to or neutral towards MBE (**H2.8**) ($p = 0.00046$, less-than Fisher test). Here, 51 supporters of MBE reported to use MBE tools more than non-MBE tools or only MBE tools, and 18 reported to use less MBE tools than non-MBE tools or no MBE tools at all. This contrasts with a score of 5 and 13 answers on the opponent/neutral side.

In total we performed 72 significance checks resulting in seven significant differences. While the number of found significances is low for this amount of significance checks, we believe that our results could be used as indicators for future studies.

5   Conclusions and Future Work

The presented results strongly confirm that indeed Model-Based Engineering is widespread in the embedded domain. Models are clearly not only used for informative and documentation purposes; they are key artifacts of the development processes, and they are used for, e.g., simulation and code generation. Other widespread uses of significant importance are behavioral and structural consistency checking, as well as test case generation, traceability and timing analysis. While survey respondents reported mostly positive effects of Model-Based Engineering, the data also suggests some common and major challenges for MBE that need further attention. These include effective adoption among developers to reduce effort-intensive activities currently needed to realize benefits of MBE. Furthermore, some challenges concern the specific tools adopted and their interoperation.

In the future, we plan on following-up the results of this study by replicating the survey with a different target group in the embedded domain to validate the identified results. Furthermore, a validation of some effects of the introduction of Model-Based Engineering can be performed by collecting quantitative data in a company which introduces a MBE approach. Tool interoperability was mentioned as one of the key shortcomings, which fits well with the goals of the research project CRYSTAL where we focus on interoperability.

Acknowledgments. The research leading to these results has received partial funding from the European Union's Seventh Framework Program (FP7/2007-2013) for CRYSTAL-Critical System Engineering Acceleration Joint Undertaking under grant agreement No 332830 and from Vinnova under DIARIENR 2012-04304. Further, the authors gratefully acknowledge financial support from FFG Austria for the project in which the above presented research results were achieved. We would also like to thank Aleksander Lodwich, Jos Langen and Leon Bouwmeester for participating in the survey design and contributing to the final study.

References

1. Agner, L.T.W., Soares, I.W., Stadzisz, P.C., Simão, J.M.: A brazilian survey on UML and model-driven practices for embedded software development. Journal of Systems and Software 86(4), 997–1005 (2013), http://www.sciencedirect.com/science/article/pii/S0164121212003160; SI : Software Engineering in Brazil: Retrospective and Prospective Views
2. Anda, B., Hansen, K., Gullesen, I., Thorsen, H.: Experiences from introducing uml-based development in a large safety-critical project. Empirical Software Engineering 11(4), 555–581 (2006), http://dx.doi.org/10.1007/s10664-006-9020-6
3. Baker, P., Loh, S.C., Weil, F.: Model-driven engineering in a large industrial context - motorola case study. In: Briand, L.C., Williams, C. (eds.) MoDELS 2005. LNCS, vol. 3713, pp. 476–491. Springer, Heidelberg (2005)
4. Brambilla, M., Cabot, J., Wimmer, M.: Model-Driven Software Engineering in Practice. Synthesis Lectures on Software Engineering, Morgan & Claypool Publishers (2012)
5. Dobing, B., Parsons, J.: Dimensions of uml diagram use: A survey of practitioners. Journal of Database Management 19(1), 1–18 (2008), http://search.proquest.com/docview/199606166?accountid=10041
6. Fisher, R.A.: On the interpretation of χ^2 from contingency tables, and the calculation of p. Journal of the Royal Statistical Society 85(1), 87–94 (1922), http://www.jstor.org/stable/2340521
7. Forward, A., Lethbridge, T.C.: Problems and opportunities for model-centric versus code-centric software development: A survey of software professionals. In: Proceedings of the 2008 International Workshop on Models in Software Engineering, MiSE 2008, pp. 27–32. ACM, New York (2008), http://doi.acm.org/10.1145/1370731.1370738
8. Grossman, M., Aronson, J.E., McCarthy, R.V.: Does UML make the grade? insights from the software development community. Information and Software Technology 47(6), 383–397 (2005)
9. Hutchinson, J., Rouncefield, M., Whittle, J.: Model-driven engineering practices in industry. In: 2011 33rd International Conference on Software Engineering (ICSE), pp. 633–642 (2011)
10. Hutchinson, J., Whittle, J., Rouncefield, M., Kristoffersen, S.: Empirical assessment of mde in industry. In: 2011 33rd International Conference on Software Engineering (ICSE), pp. 471–480 (2011)
11. Kirstan, S., Zimmermann, J.: Evaluating costs and benefits of model-based development of embedded software systems in the car industry–results of a qualitative case study. In: Proceedings Workshop C2M: EEMDD "From Code Centric to Model Centric: Evaluating the Effectiveness of MDD" ECMFA (2010)
12. Mohagheghi, P., Dehlen, V.: Where is the proof? - a review of experiences from applying mde in industry. In: Schieferdecker, I., Hartman, A. (eds.) ECMDA-FA 2008. LNCS, vol. 5095, pp. 432–443. Springer, Heidelberg (2008), http://dx.doi.org/10.1007/978-3-540-69100-6_31
13. Mohagheghi, P., Gilani, W., Stefanescu, A., Fernandez, M., Nordmoen, B., Fritzsche, M.: Where does model-driven engineering help? experiences from three industrial cases. Software & Systems Modeling 12(3), 619–639 (2013), http://dx.doi.org/10.1007/s10270-011-0219-7

14. Torchiano, M., Tomassetti, F., Ricca, F., Tiso, A., Reggio, G.: Preliminary findings from a survey on the md* state of the practice. In: 2011 International Symposium on Empirical Software Engineering and Measurement (ESEM), pp. 372–375 (September 2011)
15. Wohlin, C., Runeson, P., Höst, M., Ohlsson, M.C., Regnell, B., Wesslén, A.: Experimentation in Software Engineering: An Introduction. Kluwer Academic Publishers, Norwell (2000)

The Relevance of Model-Driven Engineering
Thirty Years from Now

Gunter Mussbacher[1], Daniel Amyot[2], Ruth Breu[3], Jean-Michel Bruel[4],
Betty H.C. Cheng[5], Philippe Collet[6], Benoit Combemale[7], Robert B. France[8],
Rogardt Heldal[9], James Hill[10], Jörg Kienzle[1], Matthias Schöttle[1],
Friedrich Steimann[11], Dave Stikkolorum[12], and Jon Whittle[13]

[1] McGill University, Canada
[2] University of Ottawa, Canada
[3] University of Innsbruck, Austria
[4] University of Toulouse, France
[5] Michigan State University, USA
[6] Université Nice-Sophia Antipolis, France
[7] University of Rennes / INRIA, France
[8] Colorado State University, USA
[9] Chalmers University of Technology, Sweden
[10] Indiana University-Purdue University Indianapolis, USA
[11] Fernuniversität Hagen, Germany
[12] Leiden University, The Netherlands
[13] Lancaster University, UK
{gunter.mussbacher,joerg.kienzle}@mcgill.ca,
damyot@eecs.uottawa.ca, Ruth.Breu@uibk.ac.at, bruel@irit.fr,
chengb@cse.msu.edu, philippe.collet@unice.fr,
benoit.combemale@irisa.fr, france@cs.colostate.edu,
heldal@chalmers.se, hillj@cs.iupui.edu,
matthias.schoettle@mail.mcgill.ca, steimann@FernUni-Hagen.de,
d.r.stikkolorum@liacs.leidenuniv.nl, whittle@comp.lancs.ac.uk

Abstract. Although model-driven engineering (MDE) is now an established approach for developing complex software systems, it has not been universally adopted by the software industry. In order to better understand the reasons for this, as well as to identify future opportunities for MDE, we carried out a week-long design thinking experiment with 15 MDE experts. Participants were facilitated to identify the biggest problems with current MDE technologies, to identify grand challenges for society in the near future, and to identify ways that MDE could help to address these challenges. The outcome is a reflection of the current strengths of MDE, an outlook of the most pressing challenges for society at large over the next three decades, and an analysis of key future MDE research opportunities.

Keywords: Model-driven engineering, challenges, research opportunities.

J. Dingel et al. (Eds.): MODELS 2014, LNCS 8767, pp. 183–200, 2014.
© Springer International Publishing Switzerland 2014

1   Introduction

Model-driven engineering (MDE) is now an established approach for developing complex software systems and has been adopted successfully in many industries including the automotive industry, aerospace, telecommunications, and business information systems [26][27][38]. However, MDE is arguably still a niche technology [51]. It has not been adopted as widely as popular programming languages such as Java and C#, and, whilst some modeling languages like the Unified Modeling Language (UML) have become widespread [19], they are often not used to their full potential [43] and the use of models to automatically generate systems is still relatively rare [51]. One could argue that now is a good time to reflect on the successes of MDE as well as its shortcomings. It is a little over ten years since OMG published the first Model Driven Architecture (MDA; http://www.omg.org/mda/) specification, almost 20 years since it adopted UML, and many decades since the first Computer-Aided Software Engineering (CASE) tools were introduced. In all that time, MDE has *not* become the de-facto way to develop software systems. It is perhaps time, then, to examine the barriers to MDE adoption as well as to look for opportunities where MDE can make a difference in the future.

Towards this end, this paper reflects on the last twenty years of MDE research and practice, makes a candid assessment of where we believe MDE has succeeded and failed, and highlights key research and application opportunities for MDE in the next 30 years. Our intent is to bring fresh impetus to the MDE community and to define a roadmap for future research in this area, particularly in areas that remain largely unexplored by the community. The paper provides an opportunity for MDE researchers to consider their current MDE research within the broader context of grand societal challenges, with the aim to stimulate novel modeling research, techniques, and tools.

To put together this roadmap, we followed an approach loosely based on design thinking [15]. Design thinking is a well-established, brainstorming-oriented approach to problem solving that attempts to understand a problem from diverse perspectives, applies creativity techniques to generate as many solutions as possible without pre-filtering, and then down-selects and refines a smaller number of solutions based on well-defined criteria. In essence, design thinking is a process for tackling a problem by first *diverging* (pushing the envelope, envisioning novel ideas) and then *converging* (consolidating the results). Design thinking is based around a number of guiding principles that aim to take a diverse set of participants, each with differing views and experiences, and shape them towards a common and transformative solution: listening is favored over dominating, quantity of ideas over filtering, being positive over saying "No"; participation; seeking wild ideas; and trusting the process.

In our case, the "problem" to which we applied design thinking was how to increase the adoption of MDE and change the perception that MDE might not yet be a solution for the grand societal challenges of today. We brought together 15 junior and senior MDE researchers for a week-long design thinking exercise. Participants performed a series of activities, inspired by design thinking and creativity literature, that promoted thinking outside the box, including external provocations.

The result is a reflection of the current strengths of MDE and an analysis of key future research opportunities for MDE. This exploratory paper first gives an overview of the key accomplishments of the MDE community over the last 20 years (Section 2.1), and then summarizes major current problems in MDE (Section 2.2). Before continuing, the employed methodology based on design thinking is explained in more detail, including a description of specific activities and their rationale (Section 3). The paper then re-examines MDE through the lens of what are the most pressing challenges for society at large over the next three decades (Section 4.1). By focusing on four fictitious future software systems (Section 4.2), the paper unravels how MDE does or does not address the future challenges of society. Based on this analysis, the paper suggests four grand challenges for MDE (Section 5), which we hope will stimulate new research directions in this area. Section 6 concludes the paper and proposes action items that can be initiated immediately.

2   The Last 20 Years

MDE has made significant progress in addressing software engineering challenges over the past 20 years. The major areas of advancement include: modeling languages, model analysis techniques, model-based verification and validation, and model transformations. Each of these areas has developed foundational theories, tool support, bodies of empirical evidence, and, to varying degrees, has been used in industrial settings. For each area, we identify the key research challenges being addressed, highlight the key accomplishments, and give a few representative examples.

2.1   Major Areas of Advancement

Modeling Languages. Researchers working in the area of modeling languages have focused on two key challenges [21]: (i) *Abstraction Challenge:* What kind of modeling constructs and underlying foundation is needed to support the development of domain- or problem-level abstractions that are considered first-class modeling elements in a language? (ii) *Formality Challenge:* What characteristics and/or properties of a modeling language are necessary to enable automated processing and rigorous analysis? Furthermore, what aspects of a language should be formalized?

To address these challenges, a complementary set of strategies has evolved [21].

Extensible General-Purpose Modeling Languages. The abstraction challenge is addressed by providing a general-purpose language that has support for customizing the language to a specific domain. Example customizations are profiles (e.g., UML profiles), domain-specific modeling processes, and, at a fine-grained level, the use of specialized syntactic forms and constraints on specific modeling elements. The formality challenge can be handled by either mapping the modeling language to a formal language, or annotations can be added to the modeling language at the meta-model level to constrain properties that should hold between language elements.

Domain-Specific Modeling Languages (DSMLs). In order to create a modeling language for a given problem domain, meta-metamodeling mechanisms, such as OMG's

MOF [33] and its Ecore implementation have been extensively used. Intelligent textual and graphical editors, together with debuggers and code generators, can now be built (and even modeled) for DSMLs with relatively little effort.

General-purpose modeling languages are relatively more popular in the research, industrial, and educational arenas. Furthermore, the use of modeling has become sufficiently mature such that modeling standards have emerged. UML has been the de facto standard for object-oriented modeling [40]. Furthermore, commercial tools are also available for commonly used modeling languages, such as the Object Constraint Language (OCL), the Systems Modeling Language (SysML), and the Business Process Model and Notation (BPMN). Recently, numerous studies have been performed to study the impact of modeling on various aspects of software development [23][40], for use in specific domains, such as embedded systems [1], and to study the impact of the use of modeling languages in industry [43].

While initially DSMLs were created on a limited basis by individual organizations mostly in the research sector, numerous industrial organizations have witnessed the significant advantages of using DSMLs, particularly when considering automatic code generation and domain-specific analysis as objectives. As such, the field of modeling language engineering has emerged as an important area of research to enable a broader community to systematically develop DSMLs for their respective domain and organization. Example frameworks to support DSML development include MOF (http://www.omg.org/spec/MOF), EMF (http://www.eclipse.org/modeling/emf), VisualStudio [14], JetBrains/MPS (http://www.jetbrains.com/mps), Kermeta [29], GME (http://www.isis.vanderbilt.edu/Projects/gme), Epsilon [31], and Xtext (http://www.eclipse.org/Xtext). A popular DSMLs in relatively wide use is MATLAB's Simulink (http://www.mathworks.com/products/simulink).

Model Analysis. While the process of modeling facilitates a better understanding of system requirements, design constraints, and user needs, the value of models increases significantly with the ability to automatically process the models and analyze the models for various properties. Significant progress has been made to formally analyze models for behavioral properties [21][34][37]; analyze models for structural properties [6], both within a given diagram type [12], and across multiple types of diagrams [8]. Within the embedded systems domain, model analysis is achieved by executing models in simulation environments, such as Simulink [21][30] or USE [35]. Also models may be queried using standardized model query languages [32]. Finally, model understanding can be achieved through animation and visualization [13][22][44][46]. In some cases, production-quality tools have been built from research tools (e.g., Microsoft's Static Driver Verifier is based on a model-based approach to find errors in device drivers using the model checker SLAM [4]).

Model-Based Analysis. Models have also been an enabling technology used to facilitate numerous software and systems development tasks. For example, model-based testing has long been used in industry [7][17][18][48], and for specific domains, such as reactive and embedded systems [9]. Enterprise architecture models are among the modeling approaches settled in practice ([28], also see The Open Group Architecture Forum at http://www.opengroup.org/subjectareas/enterprise/togaf). The major goal of these models is to document actual elements of an organization's IT infrastructure, and to interrelate these elements as a basis for further analysis and decision support. Since enterprise architecture models usually get very large, visualization aspects have been considered for several years [10]. Similarly, business process and workflows models have been adopted by industry for many years. Business process models are both applied in a pure organizational context and within IT management to analyze organizational processes and their IT support [45]. In addition, workflow models are used to configure workflow engines, thus they have been precursors of using models at runtime [49]. Model-based testing applies implementation-independent models and code generation to the area of testing [41]. The manifold approaches in this area have not only addressed theoretical considerations of generating models and test cases, but yielded also practice-oriented methods and tools [48] and standardization efforts [3].

Model Transformations (Management). A model transformation establishes a relationship between two sets of models, and itself may even be model-based. Several categories of model transformations have been defined, as well as the intent for model transformations [39]. An operational transformation takes a source set of models to produce a target set of models that are a refinement, abstraction, or refactoring of the source. Emerging techniques in this category focus on the composition of multiple views to form a single integrated model, the decomposition of a single model into multiple models, each representing a different aspect of a system, and the translation of models to a format amenable to automated analysis, including static analysis, model checking, and other types of behavioral and performance analyses.

Synchronization transformations enable model traceability and synchronization between a model and its related artifacts. Examples include transformations to support code generation and code updates to reflect changes to models. The OMG Query/View/Transformation (QVT) standard [32] defines several languages that can be used to define such transformations at different levels of abstraction. To facilitate their use and development, Czarnecki and Helsen developed a survey of features used for transformation languages [16]. Successful tools for model transformations include ATL (http://www.eclipse.org/atl/), Epsilon (http://www.eclipse.org/epsilon/), and several tools based on Triple Graph Grammars [25].

Other contributions have gained traction, but are not as well established as the above, including model repositories (e.g., REMODD: http://www.remodd.org), patterns, aspects, features, models at run-time, and MDA/MDE processes.

2.2   Major Current Problems in Model-Driven Engineering

While much progress has been made in MDE over the last 20 years, the MDE community also has recognized many problems that it still must face. This subsection summarizes the main current problems in the field of MDE (in no particular order) as identified by the workshop participants.

Shortcomings of MDE to Address Increasing Demands on Software. Software has to respond to an ever-increasing number of demands. The explosion of stringent functional requirements and qualities is complemented by the ever-increasing need to customize and tailor software to specific usage contexts. Many software systems are tightly connected with their environment, are distributed, need to support heterogeneous platforms, and/or are open in nature. Software needs to adapt to rapidly changing hardware and implementation platforms, and is developed in a context that requires developers to shorten time-to-market to a minimum. In such context, the inherent complexity of the problems that we are trying to solve with software keeps growing.

Current modeling approaches, techniques and tools do not live up to the challenge. Often, mature tools provide techniques that can successfully cope with software systems that we were building a decade ago, but fail when applied to model complex systems like the ones described above. Some academic techniques propose interesting ways of addressing these shortcomings, but the prototypical nature of academic tools often prohibits their application to the development of real-world software systems.

Obstacles for Tool Usability and Adoption. The proliferation of modeling languages, tools, and techniques makes it hard for users to commit to using MDE. Even after a suitable language and tool have been identified, the users face significant usability challenges [24][42][52], e.g., steep learning curves, arduous user interfaces, and difficulty with migrating models from one version of a tool to the next. Despite the fact that software development is a team activity, there is little effective tool support for collaborative modeling. In general, tools do not support the fundamentally creative side of the modeling process due to their inflexibility and complexity. Far fewer MDE community or interactive forums on the web can be consulted to find solutions to problems when compared to programming-based forums. Finally, model transformations, which are essential in order for MDE to be effective, are difficult to maintain and adapt to changing requirements and implementation platforms [50].

MDE Is Not Considered "Cool". Even though MDE has been around for over 10 years, it is currently not as widespread in industry as the modeling community has hoped for [51]. As bluntly illustrated in Table 1, MDE is simply not considered cool. Why this is the case needs to be investigated. Maybe, the bad experience with CASE tools decades ago still casts a dark shadow on MDE. Maybe, the effects of the so-called UML Fever [5] are continuing to hurt the perception of MDE by people outside the community. Some even argue that there is a stronger need to investigate people's perception of MDE than to research new MDE technologies [11].

Table 1. Results of six queries (with quotes) on Google Search, February 12, 2014

	"Agile"...	"MDE"...	"Model-Driven Engineering"...
..."is cool"	4,250	10 (*)	0
..."is not cool"	1	41	10

(*) The first two results actually linked to Cabot's article entitled "Model driven engineering is not cool" [11], and 7 links had nothing to do with MDE.

Inconsistencies between Software Artifacts. A number of companies are using software modeling languages such as UML in their architecture development. The problem is that these models are often ignored as soon as one moves on to coding. Changes are made in the code but not in the models, leading to inconsistencies between software models and code. Synchronization of models between different levels of abstraction is not the norm. Good tool support is lacking to keep these models in sync today. A complicating factor is that often a system is modeled with multiple views using different models and modeling notations, thus further increasing the likelihood of introducing inconsistencies between these models. Even when additional information is overlaid onto an existing view (as is the case, for example, in UML, when stereotypes define non-functional properties), there are no guarantees that the resulting system is consistent or correctly functioning.

Models Are Still Not Valued as Much as Code. The advantage of code is that it is a product on its own. It is often quite motivating to work directly on the product. It permits a software engineer to point out, e.g., that this part is due to her programming. In addition, one can obtain constant feedback when programming by executing the code, allowing one to easily experiment with the code and test its behavior. Unfortunately, for many people, modeling is considered a superfluous activity that becomes an activity in itself not necessarily for the benefit of the software development. This concern makes it hard to see both the short and long time benefits of using models to specify the product and creates a lack of trust in the technology.

Lack of Fundamentals in MDE. Unlike most other fields of engineering, model-driven engineering does not have a Body of Knowledge (BoK) as such. Some recent initiatives such as SWEBOK (http://www.computer.org/portal/web/swebok) and SEMAT (http://semat.org/) aim at filling this gap, but the required effort is huge. This deficiency also hampers the support for reuse. Programming languages have libraries. Modeling libraries are emerging (e.g., [2], also see REMODD) but the lack of common representations, query mechanisms, and critical mass pose obstacles.

Education Issues. There is a large mismatch between modeling examples found in books and the ones used in the real world. For example, small and unrealistic state-chart diagrams are often used. It is relatively easy to teach the syntax of a modeling language such as UML, but we still struggle with how to teach design principles using modeling. For students, it is difficult to learn to use their abstraction abilities [36][47], which have been shown to closely relate to software design skills. For effective teaching, students need to be motivated by the benefits of modeling (e.g., solution complexity can only be managed by models instead of simple coding problems).

Uncertainty in Environments, Requirements, and Systems. It is not that hard to create a model if the problem fits one's mental picture. That usually depends on the modeler's domain knowledge and well-defined, stable domain abstractions. However, nowadays software more and more adapts (and sometimes self-adapts) to its environment. The inherent uncertainty in many such problem domains (such as human science, social issues, etc.) and environments makes software very complex. In the face of uncertainty, actual modeling techniques neither ease the integration of multiple concerns nor support problem domain modeling.

Lack of (Industrial) Evidence of Benefits. There have been a number of empirical papers in the last few years that address the lack of industrial proofs of benefits [20][50]. These papers give a good status of the use of MDE in industry, but they do not let us understand why MDE projects fail or succeed. We are still lacking knowledge on factors that make MDE successful, also considering that model-based approaches are regularly used in the hardware industry (e.g., model checking to analyze hardware designs instead of testing).

3   Methodology

In this section, we describe our methodology for defining the MDE roadmap presented in this paper. The method is loosely based on principles of design thinking [15], which aims to approach a problem from as many angles as possible (i.e., problem understanding), generate as many ideas as possible (i.e., ideas generation), and then only finally consolidate those ideas into a small number of workable solutions (i.e., ideas selection). This section describes how we applied design thinking in terms of the concrete activities (see Table 2) that our participants undertook.

Table 2. Activities of the Design Thinking Workshop

(Phase) Activities	Rationale
(1) Put Aside Personal Interests. Each participant was given an opportunity to talk about their own research agenda.	The aim was NOT to look for research overlaps or to build on existing research strengths. Since the workshop aimed at getting people to think differently, participants needed to put aside their own research interests for the week. By providing a forum to air their research first, participants feel content that their research has been articulated, and also feel happy to step outside their boundaries.
(2) Think Beyond MDE and Software Engineering. Participants were asked to identify the grand challenges of the population at large in the next 30 years. This was done by asking participants to describe two futuristic scenarios: a perfect day and a hellish day in 2030. (*)	One way to reach genuinely novel and different ideas is to change context completely. By asking participants to temporarily not think about software engineering, but instead think about societal challenges, we created an environment in which new thinking could blossom and participants could engage with issues that they feel passionate about.
(3) External Influences. Two external speakers from outside the software engineering community were invited to talk to participants: one was an expert on environmental sustainability, the other was an expert on robotics in marine environments.	External speakers were introduced at key points as a nudge to make sure participants continued to think differently: these speakers were introduced to provide inspiration from a perspective traditionally not considered in MDE research.
(4) Ideas Generation. Participants self-organized into small groups and generated ideas for future systems that could address grand challenges identified in phase 2.	Participants were provided with a safe, supportive environment to generate ideas. Ground rules were put in place to ensure that any idea could be heard. Participants were told to value listening over dominating in conversations, quantity of ideas rather than pre-filtering, being positive over being critical, to seek wild ideas, and to fully engage with the process.

Table 2. (*Continued*)

(5) Consolidation of Ideas. The participant groups were taken through a series of iterative cycles where they presented their ideas to an external mentor and their peers, received constructive feedback, and then were asked to re-present the evolving idea at regular intervals.	Through this process, the most promising ideas were nurtured to ensure that they satisfied the criteria of: novelty, feasibility (within 30 years), relevance to MDE, and a different way of thinking.
(6) Documentation of Results. During the workshop, the participants began writing this paper, which was then completed after the workshop.	The ideas developed in phase 5 were used as driving exemplars to identify new areas for MDE research, which are the ultimate result of the design thinking exercise.

(*) Not included for space reasons, see http://www.cs.mcgill.ca/~joerg/SEL/motb-day.html.

Setup and Participant Selection. We brought together 15 participants for a week-long design thinking workshop at McGill University's Bellairs Research Institute. Participants were required to devote themselves fully to the workshop for the whole week so that outside distractions could be minimized. The approach to participant selection was largely "curated" in that the organizers made a prioritized list of potential participants with the aim of maximizing diversity in terms of seniority, gender, and research area. In the case that an invited potential participant could not attend, the organizers went down the prioritized list trying to maintain diversity. The final set of 15 participants included 2 women and 13 men, who came from thirteen academic institutions from across 8 countries and covered research in a wide spectrum of the software lifecycle from early requirements to implementation. (It was of course disappointing to not maintain a better gender balance. Despite best efforts, we were constrained by the heavy skew towards male MDE researchers.)

Activities. Table 2 summarizes the activities of the design thinking workshop. Activities were designed to avoid tunnelled thinking so that genuinely fresh ideas could emerge. This was achieved in a number of ways: (1) Move people away from their own research areas so that they are open to fresh ideas; (2) Move people away from software engineering by having them discuss grand challenges of society today; (3) Introduce external speakers at key points to inject fresh ideas from a completely different perspective; (4) Encourage unfettered ideas generation, where "anything goes" and pre-filtering of ideas is discouraged; (5) Consolidate ideas by down-selecting and/or refining them according to well-defined criteria; and (6) Document the results. All of these activities are tried and tested, and are based on well-accepted techniques in design thinking and/or creativity theory.

Rationale. Table 2 gives the rationale for each phase of the design thinking exercise. Each phase was carefully designed so that, taken as a whole, the phases would lead to new ways of thinking about MDE and MDE research. It is important to understand that many of the activities in phases 1-5 are not an end by themselves, but are either ways of moving the group of participants towards the end goal, or ways of generating useful by-products. The ultimate end-result comes in phase 6, where the roadmap is defined. The ideas selected in phase 5, for example, were example futuristic systems where MDE could have an influence. Rather than proposing that the community should start developing these systems, we see these systems as useful driving ideas to help understand where the current gaps are in MDE research.

4   Grand Challenges for the Next 30 Years

Through several iterations of group brainstorming activities, prioritization activities, and the perfect/hellish-day-in-2030 session (phase 2 of our methodology), we identified six grand challenges for society at large to be addressed over the next three decades. They are introduced here in Section 4.1, in no particular order of importance. We also provide examples of futuristic software systems in Section 4.2 to illustrate potential solutions to some of these challenges and highlight the characteristics of such systems that may have to be addressed by new modeling solutions (phases 4 and 5 of our methodology).

4.1   Six Grand Challenges

1) Resource Affordability and Availability. Many kinds of resources exist, including health, food, knowledge, and energy. Yet, they are not available and affordable to all in equitable ways, even for primary needs. There is a need to substantially improve the management of resources, including their Creation, Access, Distribution, Usage, and Disposal (collectively referred to as CADUD), in order to improve resource availability and affordability for everyone. Additional threats to mitigate include costs, corruption, greed, wrong incentives, lack of basic infrastructures and data, and the use of local optimizations instead of more sensible global optimizations.

2) Sustainability. Many resources such as energy and food are not easily renewable without control and efforts, and we are now facing many sustainability issues that demand more precise, trustable, and timely information for decision making. In particular, there is much room for better trade-offs between economic growth and responsible use of resources, for education and understanding of cause and effects of CADUD-like resource management, and for ways to avoid misinformation of sustainability factors by special interest groups. There is a vicious cycle where the need for comfort often leads to growth, which in turn requires more energy, leading to pollution (and global warming) that stresses our level of comfort. Attitudes need to change at all levels of granularity (from the individual level to city-wide, regional, national, continental, and planetary levels).

3) Disaster and Crisis Management. There is a strong need to improve the predictability of natural disasters such as storms and earthquakes, as well as of human-triggered crises related to economy, health, and social tensions. Where predictions are impossible or fail, societies should be enabled to react in a timely way.

4) Steady-State Economy. Global and local economies are still based on a growth model that cannot be sustained forever. Mechanisms are needed to bring economies of any scale to a "steady-state" that would no longer rely on continuous growth, exploiting resources and people in all areas of the world.

5) Life Balance. Individuals are subject to many extrinsic factors such as peer pressure and demand for performance that are difficult to balance with real intrinsic motivation and a sustainable lifestyle. They are also bombarded with an ever-growing amount of information that strains the individual's abilities to cope with life's challenges. Support is needed to help understand, manage, and control extrinsic factors and information to avoid getting caught in a pernicious "rat race" and, instead, to achieve a healthy balance in life.

6) Common Sense. Current governance structures are often subject to bureaucracy and abusive lobbying. There is an opportunity to bring back common sense in governance and better balance the weight of individual/common needs versus the interests of special interest lobbying groups.

4.2   Four Examples of Futuristic Systems

1) Model-Experiencing Environments (MEEs). Facing the vicious cycles that hamper sustainable solutions development and effective resource management, we believe that any person, community, decision maker, or company should be able to play, analyze, and "experience her personalized *Model-Experiencing Environments (MEEs)*. Those *MEEs* are very "sophisticated and highly tuned *"what-if"* impact models, but with a simplified and adaptive user interface. Each *MEE* consists of combinations of interconnected models based on open data, enabling one to play, run, and see evidence on the impact over resource consumption chains.

We envision different kinds of *MEEs*. In any *MEE*, the user can adjust the level or amount of different properties she is interested in, e.g., impact on health, employment, economy, amount of waste, gas, water, or even taxes. Then, she is able to specify and assemble certain criteria in a *do-it-yourself* way for the scenario she is interested in. The selection is automatically propagated to the outcome view where the different impacts are shown. The impacts are visualized in graphs, charts, or any adapted interfaces such as personalized virtual reality ones. Finally, deployed *MEEs* feed back into underlying open models to improve accuracy or user confidence.

The following list overviews the different kinds of *MEEs*:

- *MEE* for Game-Based Learning: allows children to learn about impacts in a playful way (tackling challenge 5 (life balance)).
- Crowd-Sourcing *MEE* Use: permits several people to see impacts if they do something together (tackling challenges 1 (resources affordability and availability), 2 (sustainability), and 5).
- *MEE*-Enabled Community Decisions: informed decisions can be made by community members (tackling challenges 1, 2, 5, and 6 (common sense)).
- *MEE*-Driven Policy Analysis: enables policy makers to understand impacts of their decisions (tackling challenges 1, 2, 3 (disaster and crisis management), 4 (steady-state economy), 5, and 6).

In addition, *MEEs* are likely to be useful in broader domains than just resource impact models. Any kind of experiencing can benefit from *MEEs*: personal health companion, family expenses habits monitoring, etc. This ultimately allows models to be part of everybody's life and usage, making them trusted daily objects that enable everyone to learn, think, and act on her own.

2) Making Zense. Imagine relaxing yoga music... "Do you feel like you are in a rat race? Do you need to make personal decisions, but can't evaluate their short term and long term impact? Do you have trouble balancing work, family, and personal activities?" *Making Zense* helps you find a healthy balance. Humans are unique; modeling a human being is too complex. A human story captures important events and facts, accomplishments, failures, health records, nutrition history, sleep patterns, and social connections. A human story is completely personal and confidential, i.e., it is not possible to identify a living person from her human story, but there is a way to assess happiness levels throughout a person's life.

Billions and billions of human stories make up the *Human-esZense* – a vast collective wisdom, the essence of the human race. It does not stop there. Cities and countries are also unique, and their stories are also found in the *Human-esZense*. From time to time, a role model emerges from human stories. It is shaped by societal forces at play. A role model displays characteristics that are beneficial to achieve happiness.

Making Zense feeds your human story continuously into the *Human-esZense* and compares it with similar human stories. Based on this collective knowledge, personal trajectories are continuously presented, possible outcomes of one's life with varying probabilities and happiness levels, and role models are used to characterize these possible paths along your road to happiness. Once a role model you would like to aspire to is selected, the *Human-esZense* enables the assessment of what-if scenarios by comparing the proposed changes to your life based on the role model against the *Human-esZense*, addressing challenge 5 (life balance)).

3) Models4 △○△⁝⁝ (Modeling for the Illiterate). Most modeling languages and tools target highly-educated experts. Yet, many complain that models are difficult to create and use. One reason is that we have not yet fully understood what modeling is, and the intuition needed to make it effective. In addition, a global trend nowadays is to invite the population at large to learn programming (e.g., see the `code.org` effort), as programming and configuration will become pervasively required. *Models4△○△⁝⁝* is an application that enables anyone to create and use models needed to configure their daily lives and long-term goals, for example with the *MEE* and *Making Zense* systems. It is so intuitive that illiterate people can use it as effectively as domain experts, hence confronting the education portion of challenge 1 (resources affordability and availability). Note that by targeting illiterate people as a primary audience, the development of *Models4△○△⁝⁝* helps us truly understand what modeling really is, which in turn enables us to transfer this knowledge to a much broader set of modeling approaches, including those for software and systems development.

4) Have You Thought of ... (HYTo). Too often, projects are cancelled at very late stages. Political, cultural, or other factors can play a role in these decisions. For example, after the election of a local government, the political leaders decide to stop the creation of a promised 'very green' park, because of the intense lobbying of other parties, such as influential contractors who plan to develop the space into lucrative real-estate projects. 'Have you thought of the coming elections, which could possibly be won by the opposition party?', the *HYTo* application will ask you – along with 'Have you thought of the increase in tourist revenue because of the park?' and 'Have you thought of the increased CO_2 emissions because of reduced green space and increased traffic to the real-estate project?'. *HYTo* helps you make decisions while taking the predictions of other (external) factors into account. Consequently, *HYTo* is applicable to all challenges identified in the previous sub-section.

5   Grand Challenges of Model-Driven Engineering

As a community, we have made substantial progress in the areas of modeling languages, processes, quality, and automated integration of models (across domains and at different levels of abstraction). In addition, we now have, or are very close to having, good modeling techniques for tackling complexities related to scalability, forecasting/predictions, data/knowledge-awareness, personalized adaptation, usability, real-time, and perceived intelligence. However, these techniques are currently not capable of supporting the modeling needs required to realize the kinds of systems outlined in the previous section. While the MDE community tends to cope well with only one of these dimensions of complexity at a time, existing and future systems will face many of these dimensions at the same time, for example:

- Real-time, knowledge-aware forecasting at the personal level (as exemplified by *MEE*, *Making Zense*, and *HYTo*, which all try to predict future events and behaviors based on gathered knowledge),
- Personalized, ubiquitous access for uneducated users (obviously applicable to *Models4△○◌⁚⁚* but also to a certain degree to all other identified systems as they are deployed on a massive scale to users without expert knowledge),
- Ultra-large scale, intelligent, near-future predictions (which is an essential part of *MEE*, *HYTo*, as well as *Making Zense* not just at the personal level but also at the level of whole communities or even countries), and
- Knowledge-aware shaping of usable models, i.e., the tailoring of models to stakeholders' immediate needs based on knowledge accumulated at the individual, community, and global levels (as required for *Making Zense*, *HYTo*, and *MEE* because the power of these systems lies in the fact that contextual models are provided at the right level of abstraction for each stakeholder).

In the final phase of our design thinking-inspired methodology, we more closely looked at the grand societal challenges, futuristic systems and scenarios, and iterative refinements of our ideas through the lens of the MDE community and distilled them into common threads to highlight the following four grand modeling challenges and new research areas for MDE for the next 30 years.

I) Cross-Disciplinary Model Fusion. One grand challenge is to better take advantage of modeling knowledge *across* disciplines. Our MDE community has focused much on software and systems modeling, without much interaction with modeling activities in areas such as artificial intelligence, databases, the semantic web, or human-computer interactions. This lack of interaction and awareness is even worse when we consider entirely different fields, e.g., biology, economics, arts, law, medicine, and social sciences. We need to study more rigorously what other communities do and learn from their modeling experience and challenges. This will help us improve our modeling approaches to better deal with multiple dimensions of complexity, while at the same time enabling us to provide modeling approaches that better fit the needs of other disciplines. The MDE community has a lot to offer in terms of language, process, quality, and automation expertise that can be leveraged in these other disciplines. All of the challenges identified in the previous section require models from different disciplines to be *fused* into models that are usable by stakeholders. Solutions to challenges 2 (sustainability), 3 (disaster and crisis management), 4 (steady-state economy), and 6 (common sense) must, for example, make use of models from economics, physics, biology, and politics to adequately address these problems. Consequently, solution systems for these challenges (e.g., the highly sophisticated what-if scenarios of *MEE* and the context-aware questions of *HYTo*) rely on cross-disciplinary model fusion.

II) Personal Model Experience. A second grand challenge of MDE is to make modeling and the use of models directly benefit the *individual*. Nowadays, access to sophisticated models and model analysis is restricted to a select few. We need to find ways to provide individual end users with straightforward access to models that encode global information relevant to their particular situation. Furthermore, individuals must be allowed and able to customize these models to their particular context and needs, and feel confident that the customization is trustworthy and accurate. While some default models may be used as starting points, the high individuality of these personalized models presents new challenges for model reuse. Furthermore, innovative model analysis algorithms and tools have to be developed, that based on the global information and the individual's personal context, can produce valuable, timely insight, which the individual can then use to make decisions on a local scale in accordance to personal beliefs. Solutions to challenges 1 (resource affordability and availability), 2 (sustainability), and 5 (life balance), and hence solution systems for these challenges (i.e., *Making Zense*, *MEE*, and *HYTo*), depend on such a personal model experience to demonstrate to the individual the consequences of local/global and individual/communal actions. *Models4△○△∴∴* on the other hand, highlights the need to pay close attention to non-expert users.

III) Flexible Model Integration. An additional grand challenge is to determine how software models should be structured to provide value when developing systems that *flexibly* address *many* concerns *simultaneously*, as seen in the four types of systems described at the beginning of this section. This challenge is complementary to the first one that seeks for cross-fertilization with radically different disciplines to MDE, but it focuses on heterogeneous concern integration *within* an application field. This integration is already happening in the industry today. For example in the automotive industry, mechanical parts, electronic parts, and software are now extremely integrated. Furthermore, telecommunication plays an important role, as cars start to communicate more and more with each other and the surrounding environment. Software modeling can play an important role in integrating these large and complex systems. Tackling this integration challenge also means to be able to dynamically use and reuse models as well as integration strategies with better confidence in and pre-dictability of the result. To this aim, means must be devised that allow modelers to specify assumptions and limitations of models explicitly, as well as the contexts in which a model can successfully be applied, and how to apply it. Solutions to any of the identified societal challenges require flexible model integration, which can be observed most prominently in the *MEE* and *HYTo* solution systems where models for differing concerns need to be assembled on the fly depending on the user's context.

IV) Resemblance Modeling – From Models to Role Models. Last but not least, modeling, and object-oriented modeling in particular, has traditionally adopted an Aristotelian view according to which individuals (objects) are classified by universals (classes). These classes introduce a very convenient level of abstraction in that they allow forgetting the myriads of individuals that, from the viewpoint of the modeler, are all more or less the same. In particular, the introduction of classes allows the re-duction of a potentially infinite domain to a finite (and usually also rather small) one.

However, this abstraction is not without a price. In complex systems, the differenc-es between objects may be more important than their commonalities, and if traditional class-based modeling is used, one quickly ends up with one class per object. While this is not a problem per se, it does question the usefulness of class-based modeling in these contexts. The real problem surfaces however when the number of significantly differing individuals becomes so vast that mapping them to classes boosts models to an ultra-large scale. In that case, it may make sense to resort to a *prototype-based classification of individuals*, defined by the similarity and differences of one individu-al from another. Certain individuals, the prototypes, then serve as *role models* for others, which characterize themselves by stating their role models and the differences from them. Interaction between individuals is first defined at the prototype level; in-dividuals may choose to override wherever deemed apt. Models of this kind may never reach perfect accuracy; yet, they may trade precision for manageability which, at the ultra-large scale, may be the higher good.

The need for highly individualized models is most obvious in the *Making Zense* system (with its billions of unique human, city, and country models) and for the grand societal challenges where the individual is key (e.g., challenges 1 (resource afforda-bility and availability), 2 (sustainability), 5 (life balance), and 6 (common sense)).

6   Conclusion and Proposed Action Items

This paper formulates a roadmap by describing four grand MDE challenges that need to be addressed by the MDE community over the next 30 years. *Cross-Disciplinary Model Fusion* highlights the need to investigate modeling in radically different discip-lines. *Personal Model Experience* points out that the power of modeling and model analysis needs to be made available at an individual's level. *Flexible Model Integra-tion* advocates looking inward at software models to find ways to capture and conso-lidate heterogeneous application concerns. Finally, *Resemblance Modeling* questions the applicability of class-based modeling for systems with large numbers of highly unique individuals.

The six societal and four MDE challenges are an opportunity for the reader to put her modeling research into the perspective of the broader context of grand societal challenges, possibly stimulating her to apply modeling research, techniques, and tools to new areas, to different disciplines, or to bridge the gap and connect fields that have traditionally been isolated. The intermediate workshop results (summary of MDE success stories, current MDE problems, six pressing challenges for society at large, the perfect/hellish day in 2030, and the examples of futuristic systems) provide a rich frame of reference that allows the reader to look at the relevance of her research, and the research of the MDE community as a whole, from a different angle.

The roadmap intends to inspire the MDE community. It is our hope that the ideas presented here will incite new research directions and new technologies, which eventually partake in the creation of systems, similar to the ones envisioned in this paper, that considerably improve the quality of life of mankind.

While the main purpose of this paper is to explore an MDE research roadmap for the next 30 years, there are two immediate action items that emerged through intense discussions throughout the workshop. First, there is a need in the MDE community to more actively look outward instead of inward and invite other disciplines to join the dialog. Perhaps, a cross-disciplinary or extra-disciplinary track at the MODELS conference (e.g., a *Models OUtside Software Engineering* (MOUSE) track) may be a promising start. Second, the Artificial Intelligence, Analytics, and Natural-Language Processing communities had a coup d'éclat when IBM's Watson won Jeopardy. The MDE community should look for a similar demonstration of MDE capabilities that helps solve a significant societal problem, captivates informed insiders and general audiences, and makes everyone understand the value of modeling.

References

1. Agner, L.T.W., et al.: A Brazilian survey on UML and model-driven practices for embedded software development. J. of Systems and Software 86(4), 997–1005 (2013)
2. Alam, O., Kienzle, J., Mussbacher, G.: Concern-Oriented Software Design. In: Moreira, A., Schätz, B., Gray, J., Vallecillo, A., Clarke, P. (eds.) MODELS 2013. LNCS, vol. 8107, pp. 604–621. Springer, Heidelberg (2013)
3. Baker, P., Dai, Z.R., Grabowski, J., Haugen, Ø., Schieferdecker, I., Williams, C.: Model-Driven Testing – Using the UML Testing Profile. Springer, Berlin (2008)
4. Ball, T., Cook, B., Levin, V., Rajamani, S.K.: SLAM and Static Driver Verifier: Technology Transfer of Formal Methods inside Microsoft. In: Boiten, E.A., Derrick, J., Smith, G.P. (eds.) IFM 2004. LNCS, vol. 2999, pp. 1–20. Springer, Heidelberg (2004)
5. Bell, A.E.: Death by UML Fever. Queue 2(1), 72–80 (2004)
6. Berenbach, B.: The evaluation of large, complex UML analysis and design models. In: 26th International Conference on Software Engineering. IEEE Computer Society (2004)
7. Briand, L., Labiche, Y.: A UML-based approach to system testing. In: Gogolla, M., Kobryn, C. (eds.) UML 2001. LNCS, vol. 2185, pp. 194–208. Springer, Heidelberg (2001)
8. Briand, L.C., Labiche, Y., O'Sullivan, L.: Impact analysis and change management of UML models. In: IEEE International Conference on Software Maintenance (2003)
9. Broy, M., Jonsson, B., Katoen, J.-P., Leucker, M., Pretschner, A. (eds.): Model-Based Testing of Reactive Systems. LNCS, vol. 3472. Springer, Heidelberg (2005)

10. Buckl, S., et al.: Generating Visualizations of Enterprise Architectures using Model Trans-
    formations. Enterprise Modelling and Information Systems Arch. 2(2), 3–13 (2007)
11. Cabot, J.: Model driven engineering is not cool (November 08, 2012),
    http://modeling-languages.com/mde-is-not-cool/
12. Cheng, B.H.C., Stephenson, R., Berenbach, B.: Lessons learned from automated analysis
    of industrial UML class models (an experience report). In: Briand, L.C., Williams, C.
    (eds.) MoDELS 2005. LNCS, vol. 3713, pp. 324–338. Springer, Heidelberg (2005)
13. Combemale, B., et al.: Introducing simulation and model animation in the mdetopcased
    toolkit. In: 4th European Congress Embedded Real Time Software, ERTS (2008)
14. Cook, S., Jones, G., Kent, S., Wills, A.C.: Domain-specific development with visual studio
    DSL tools. Pearson Education (2007)
15. Cross, N.: Design Thinking: Understanding How Designers Think and Work. Berg, Ox-
    ford UK (2011)
16. Czarnecki, K., Helsen, S.: Classification of model transformation approaches. In: 2nd
    OOPSLA Wksh. on Generative Techniques in the Context of the MDA (2003)
17. Dalal, S.R., Jain, A., Karunanithi, N., Leaton, J.M., Lott, C.M., Patton, G.C., Horowitz,
    B.M.: Model-based testing in practice. In: 21st ICSE, pp. 285–294. ACM (March 1999)
18. Dias Neto, A.C., et al.: A survey on model-based testing approaches: a systematic review. In:
    Wksh. on Empirical Assessment of Softw. Eng. Lang. and Techn., pp. 31–36. ACM (2007)
19. Dobing, B., Parsons, J.: How UML is Used. Communications of the ACM 49, 109–113 (2006)
20. Farias, K., Garcia, A., Whittle, J., Lucena, C.: Analyzing the Effort of Composing Design
    Models of Large-Scale Software in Industrial Case Studies. In: Moreira, A., Schätz, B.,
    Gray, J., Vallecillo, A., Clarke, P. (eds.) MODELS 2013. LNCS, vol. 8107, pp. 639–655.
    Springer, Heidelberg (2013)
21. France, R., Rumpe, B.: Model-driven development of complex software. A research road-
    map. In: Future of Software Engineering. IEEE Computer Society (2007)
22. Goldsby, H.J., Cheng, B.H.C., Konrad, S., Kamdoum, S.: A visualization framework for
    the modeling and formal analysis of high assurance systems. In: Wang, J., Whittle, J.,
    Harel, D., Reggio, G. (eds.) MoDELS 2006. LNCS, vol. 4199, pp. 707–721. Springer,
    Heidelberg (2006)
23. Grossman, M., et al.: Does UML make the grade? Insights from the software development
    community. Information and Software Technology 47(6), 383–397 (2005)
24. Hill, J.H.: Measuring and reducing modeling effort in domain-specific modeling languages
    with examples. In: IEEE Eng. of Computer Based Systems (ECBS), pp. 120–129 (2011)
25. Hildebrandt, S., et al.: A Survey of Triple Graph Grammar Tools. Electronic Communica-
    tions of the EASST 57, 1–17 (2013)
26. Hutchinson, J., Rouncefield, M., Whittle, J.: Model Driven Engineering Practices in Indus-
    try. In: ICSE 2011, pp. 633–642 (2011)
27. Hutchinson, J., Whittle, J., Rouncefield, M., Kristoffersen, S.: Empirical Assessment of
    MDE in Industry. In: ICSE 2011, pp. 471–480 (2011)
28. Inmon, W.H., Zachman, J.A., Geiger, J.G.: Data Stores, Data Warehousing, and the Zach-
    man Framework: Managing Enterprise Knowledge. McGraw-Hill (1997)
29. Jézéquel, J.-M., Barais, O., Fleurey, F.: Model driven language engineering with Kermeta.
    In: Fernandes, J.M., Lämmel, R., Visser, J., Saraiva, J. (eds.) GTTSE 2009. LNCS,
    vol. 6491, pp. 201–221. Springer, Heidelberg (2011)
30. Kawahara, R., et al.: Verification of embedded system's specification using collaborative
    simulation of SysML and simulink models. In: MBSE 2009, pp. 21–28 (2009)
31. Kolovos, D.S., Paige, R.F., Polack, F.A.: Eclipse development tools for epsilon. In: Ec-
    lipse Summit Europe, Eclipse Modeling Symposium, vol. 20062 (2006)

32. Kurtev, I.: State of the art of QVT: A model transformation language standard. In: Schürr, A., Nagl, M., Zündorf, A. (eds.) AGTIVE 2007. LNCS, vol. 5088, pp. 377–393. Springer, Heidelberg (2008)

33. Lédeczi, Á., Bakay, A., Maroti, M., Volgyesi, P., Nordstrom, G., Sprinkle, J., Karsai, G.: Composing domain-specific design environments. Computer 34(11), 44–51 (2001)

34. Lilius, J., Paltor, I.P.: Formalising UML state machines for model checking. In: France, R.B. (ed.) UML 1999. LNCS, vol. 1723, pp. 430–444. Springer, Heidelberg (1999)

35. Martin, G., Büttner, F., Richters, M.: USE: A UML-based specification environment for validating UML and OCL. Science of Computer Programming 69(1), 27–34 (2007)

36. Mayart, F., Bruel, J.-M.: Psychological Requirements for Software Engineers: A Reverse Engineering Approach. In: IEEE C3SEE, pp. 137–146 (2004)

37. McUmber, W.E., Cheng, B.H.C.: A general framework for formalizing UML with formal languages. In: 23rd ICSE, pp. 433–442. IEEE Computer Society (2001)

38. Mohagheghi, P., Dehlen, V.: Where is the Proof? – A Review of Experiences from Applying MDE in Industry. In: Schieferdecker, I., Hartman, A. (eds.) ECMDA-FA 2008. LNCS, vol. 5095, pp. 432–443. Springer, Heidelberg (2008)

39. Moussa, A., et al.: Towards a model transformation intent catalog. In: First Workshop on the Analysis of Model Transformations, pp. 3–8. ACM (2012)

40. Nugroho, A., Chaudron, M.R.V.: A survey into the rigor of UML use and its perceived impact on quality and productivity. In: ESEM 2008, pp. 90–99. ACM (2008)

41. Offutt, J., Abdurazik, A.: Generating Tests from UML Specifications. In: France, R.B. (ed.) UML 1999. LNCS, vol. 1723, pp. 416–429. Springer, Heidelberg (1999)

42. Pati, T., Feiock, D.C., Hill, J.H.: Proactive modeling: auto-generating models from their semantics and constraints. In: Wksh. on Domain-Spec. Modeling, pp. 7–12. ACM (2012)

43. Petre, M.: UML in practice. In: 2013 International Conference on Software Engineering (ICSE 2013), pp. 722–731. IEEE Press (2013)

44. Radfelder, O., Gogolla, M.: On better understanding UML diagrams through interactive three-dimensional visualization and animation. In: AVI. ACM (2000)

45. Scheer, A.-W., Nüttgens, M.: ARIS Architecture and Reference Models for Business Process Management. In: van der Aalst, W., Desel, J., Oberweis, A. (eds.) Business Process Management. LNCS, vol. 1806, pp. 376–389. Springer, Heidelberg (2000)

46. Sol, E., Harel, D., Cohen, I.R.: Reactive animation: Realistic modeling of complex dynamic systems. Computer 38(1), 38–47 (2005)

47. Stikkolorum, D.R., Stevenson, C.E., Chaudron, M.R.V.: Assessing software design skills and their relation with reasoning skills. In: EduSymp 2013. CEUR, vol. 1134, paper 5 (2013)

48. Utting, M., Pretschner, A., Legeard, B.: A taxonomy of model-based testing approaches. Journal on Softw. Testing, Verification & Reliability 22(5), 297–312 (2006)

49. van der Aalst, W.M.P., van Hee, K.M.: Workflow Management: Models, Methods, and Systems. MIT Press (2002)

50. Whittle, J., Hutchinson, J., Rouncefield, M., Burden, H., Heldal, R.: Industrial Adoption of Model-Driven Engineering: Are the Tools Really the Problem? In: Moreira, A., Schätz, B., Gray, J., Vallecillo, A., Clarke, P. (eds.) MODELS 2013. LNCS, vol. 8107, pp. 1–17. Springer, Heidelberg (2013)

51. Whittle, J., Hutchinson, J., Rouncefield, M.: The State of Practice in Model-Driven Engineering. IEEE Software 31(3), 79–85 (2014)

52. Wu, Y., Hernandez, F., Ortega, F., Clarke, P.J., France, R.: Measuring the effort for creating and using domain-specific models. In: Wksh. on Domain-Spec. Mod., p. 14. ACM (2010)

Model-Driven Verifying Compilation
of Synchronous Distributed Applications*

Sagar Chaki and James Edmondson

Carnegie Mellon University, Pittsburgh, USA
{chaki,jredmondson}@sei.cmu.edu

Abstract. We present an approach, based on model-driven verifying compilation, to construct distributed applications that satisfy user-specified safety specifications, assuming a "synchronous network" model of computation. Given a distributed application P_d and a safety specification φ in a domain specific language DASL (that we have developed), we first use a combination of sequentialization and software model checking to verify that P_d satisfies φ. If verification succeeds, we generate an implementation of P_d that uses a novel barrier-based synchronizer protocol (that we have also developed) to implement the synchronous network semantics. We present the syntax and semantics of DASL. We also present, and prove correctness of, two sequentialization algorithms, and the synchronizer protocol. Finally, we evaluate the two sequentializations on a collection of distributed applications with safety-critical requirements.

1 Introduction

Distributed applications (i.e., software implementing distributed algorithms) play a critical, often silent, role in our day-to-day lives. Increasingly, they are being used in safety-critical domains. For example, Cyber-Physical intersection protocols [4] have been developed for ground-based vehicles that rely on vehicle-to-vehicle (V2V) communication. Safety-critical distributed applications must be subjected to rigorous verification & validation (V&V) before deployment. Indeed, incorrect operation of such applications can lead to damage or destruction of property, personal injury, and even loss of life.

The state-of-the-art in V&V of distributed applications relies heavily on testing. This has two problems. *First*, testing has poor coverage. This is particularly severe for distributed applications, since concurrency enables a large number of possible executions . *Second*, safety-critical applications are often produced via model-driven development (MDD), e.g., using Simulink in the automotive domain. While some form of testing is applied at each level of MDD, the assurance obtained at one level is not transferred to the next. In this paper, we

---

* This material is based upon work funded and supported by the Department of Defense under Contract No. FA8721-05-C-0003 with Carnegie Mellon University for the operation of the Software Engineering Institute, a federally funded research and development center. This material has been approved for public release and unlimited distribution. DM-0001118

J. Dingel et al. (Eds.): MODELS 2014, LNCS 8767, pp. 201–217, 2014.
© Springer International Publishing Switzerland 2014

present and empirically evaluate an approach, called DIVER, for producing verified distributed applications, that addresses both these challenges. Specifically, DIVER uses software model checking, an exhaustive and automated technique, for verification. It also uses a single "model" of the application to perform both verification and code generation, thus transferring the results of one to the other.

DIVER targets the *synchronous network* model of computation [16], or SN-MOC, where each node executes in rounds. Nodes communicate via single-writer-multiple-reader shared variables[1]. The final value of a variable at its writer node in any round (i) becomes visible to its reader nodes in the next round $(i + 1)$. SNMOC makes both programming and verification simpler, and is used in safety-critical domains, e.g., it reduced [17] verification time of an active-standby protocol (used in avionics systems) from 35 hours to 30 seconds.

DIVER is a *verifying compiler* [11]. The input to DIVER is a program P_d written in a domain specific language we have developed called Distributed Application Specification Language (DASL). P_d describes both a distributed application *App* and its correctness specification φ. DIVER outputs an executable for each node of *App* but only if it satisfies φ. It works in two steps:

1. *Verification*: Verify whether *App* satisfies φ. The verification is automated and exhaustive, and consists of two sub-steps:
   (a) *Sequentialization*: Construct a sequential (i.e., single threaded) program P_s that is semantically equivalent to *App* w.r.t. φ. Specifically, P_s is a C program containing an assertion α such that $P_s \models \alpha \iff P_d \models \varphi$, i.e., all legal executions of P_s satisfy α iff P_d satisfies φ.
   (b) *Model Checking*: Verify whether $P_s \models \alpha$ using software model checking [13] (SMC). We chose C and assertions for expressing P_s and α since these are the de-facto standards for describing SMC problems, and supported by state-of-the-art SMC engines. If SMC successfully verifies that $P_s \models \alpha$ then proceed to Step 2, otherwise declare $App \not\models \varphi$ and abort.
2. *Code Generation*: Generate C++ code for each node of *App* that relies on the MADARA [8] middleware for communication. We choose MADARA due to prior expertise, and our ability to implement SNMOC on top of its primitives. However, DIVER is compatible with other middleware that either support SNMOC natively, or provide an API on top of which SNMOC is implementable.

Our ultimate goal is to verify distributed applications running on mobile robots communicating over wireless networks. Such networks are not only asynchronous but have unbounded message delay. Therefore, we have also developed a protocol, called 2BSYNC, that implements SNMOC over asynchronous networks without relying on clock synchronization. To our knowledge, it is a new synchronizer protocol for wirelessly connected systems, and of independent interest.

The rest of this paper is organized as follows. After surveying related work (Sec. 2), we focus on our specific contributions. In Sec. 3, we present the syntax and semantics of DASL. The semantics leads immediately to a sequentialization we call SEQSEM. However SEQSEM produces a program with $\mathcal{O}(n^2)$ variables

---

[1] A version of SNMOC based on message-passing also appears in the literature.

(where n = number of nodes). This is undesirable from a verification perspective since the statespace of a program grows exponentially with the number of variables. Therefore, in Sec. 4 we develop, and prove correctness of, a more sophisticated sequentialization, called SEQDBL, that only requires $\mathcal{O}(n)$ variables. In Sec. 5, we present and prove correctness of our synchronizer protocol 2BSYNC. In Sec. 6, we present code generation from DASL to MADARA/C++. In Sec. 7, we compare SEQSEM and SEQDBL on a collection of distributed applications. Our results indicate that while SEQDBL is clearly better overall, for some applications, SEQSEM produces programs that are verified more quickly despite having many more variables. Finally, Sec. 8 concludes the paper.

2   Related Work

This work spans multiple disciplines – verification, distributed systems, middleware technology and code generation – which we briefly survey.

Verification. Most work in model checking concurrent software [2] use an asynchronous model of computation, based on either shared memory [1] or message-passing [7]. Some of these projects are also based on sequentialization [14,24]. Synchronous programming languages, such as Lustre [5], are not suitable for distributed applications, since they can only describe systems with a fixed number of nodes. DIVER is a verifying compiler for synchronous distributed applications that does both model-driven verification and code generation from a single DASL program. Humphrey et al. [12] use LTL to specify and synthesize correct multi-UAV missions. In contrast, our approach is based on verification. Process calculi, such as CCS [18] and CSP [10], use asynchronous message-passing communication and are verified via refinement checking. DASL uses synchronous shared-variable based communication, and its verification is based on model checking user-specified assertions. The synchronous programming language Lustre [5] differs from DASL in that there can be no cyclic-dependency (i.e., causality loops) between nodes, and each Lustre program has a fixed number of nodes. Note, however, that every "instance" of a DASL program can be represented in Lustre using unit-delay nodes to break causality.

Distributed Systems. Distributed algorithms are typically verified at the pseudo-code level manually using invariants and simulation relations [16]. Distributed systems are also heavily simulated [23] and tested, which are incomplete. DIVER is based on model checking, which is automated and exhaustive. Synchronizer protocols [3] have also been widely studied. Many rely on clock synchronization [17] – which is inappropriate for wireless communication – or direct message passing. 2BSYNC uses barriers, which is more appropriate for middleware, like MADARA [8], that provide a shared memory abstraction.

Middleware and Code Generation. For our code generation target, we chose MADARA [8]. There are multiple middleware solutions that provide infrastructure support for control and communication between distributed applications. CORBA [22] is an OMG standard for component-based distributed application development, but requires definition of component interactions and precise management of transportation options. OMG has another standard called the Data

Distribution Service [19] which facilitates quality-of-service contracts between publishers and subscribers and a complex but robust networking feature set. Tripakis et al. [25] have also explored implementing synchronous models via reduction to Kahn Process networks.

Several toolkits – e.g., COSMIC [20], AUTOSAR [9], and OCARINA [15] – provide verification and code generation for distributed applications, often with requirements of real-time support from underlying hardware, network connections, and operating systems. They force component paradigms or complex deployment configurations and metadata that is unnecessary for synchronous application specification and hinders verification. MADARA provides a more direct mapping for distributed algorithm logic, specializes in wireless communication – which is more appropriate for our target domain – and enforces Lamport clock-based consistency which provides a clean semantics and supports verification.

3   The DASL Language

A DASL program P_d describes a distributed application *App*, as well as its specification. The application consists of a number of nodes communicating via global variables over a synchronous network. Recall that each node executes in rounds. Formally, P_d is a 5-tuple $(GV, LV, \rho, n, \varphi)$ where: (i) GV is the set of global variables; (ii) LV is the set of node-local variables whose values persist across rounds; (iii) ρ is a function executed by each node in every round; (iv) n is the number of nodes; and (v) φ is the specification defined by a pair of functions *Init* and *Safety* that, respectively, establish a valid initial state, and check for violations of the desired safety property. The specification φ is used for verification only. The rest of P_d is used both for verification and code generation.

Syntax of DASL. Let TV be a set of temporary variables, IV be a set of id variables, and id be a distinguished variable such that GV, LV, TV, IV and $\{id\}$ are mutually disjoint. The body of ρ is a statement. The "abstract" syntax of statements, lvalues and expressions is given by the following BNF grammar:

(Statements) $stmt := skip \mid lval = exp \mid \text{ITE}(exp, stmt, stmt) \mid \text{WHILE}(exp, stmt)$
$\mid \text{ALL}(IV, stmt) \mid \langle stmt ; \ldots ; stmt \rangle \mid \nu(TV, stmt)$

(LValues) $lval := GV[exp] \mid LV \mid TV$

(Expressions) $exp := \mathbb{Z} \mid lval \mid id \mid IV \mid \sim exp \mid exp \diamond exp$

Intuitively, *skip* is a nop, $l = e$ is an assignment, ITE is an "if-then-else", WHILE is a while loop, ALL(v, st) executes st iteratively by substituting v with the id of each node, $\langle st_1 ; \ldots ; st_k \rangle$ executes st_1 through st_k in sequence, $\nu(v, st)$ introduces a fresh temporary variable v in scope of st, $\sim \in \{-, \neg\}$ is an unary operator, and $\diamond \in \{+, -, *, /, \wedge, \vee\}$ is a binary operator. ALL enables iteration over all nodes of *App* without knowing the exact number of such nodes a-priori.

Scoping and Assumptions. All global variables are arrays. We assume that: (i) each element of a global array has a single writer node; the mechanisms to enforce this are discussed later; (ii) variables in $GV \cup LV \cup \{id\}$ are always in

```
1   CONST OUTSIDE = 0;                      28   PROGRAM = node(0) || node(1);
2   CONST TRYING = 1;                       29
3   CONST INSIDE = 2;                       30
4                                           31   void INIT()
5   NODE node(id) {                         32   {
6     GLOBAL _Bool lock[#N];                33     FORALL_NODE(id) {
7     LOCAL unsigned char state;            34       ND(state.id); ND(lock[id]);
8                                           35       ASSUME(state.id == OUTSIDE &&
9     void ROUND() {                        36       lock[id] == 0 ||
10      _BOOL c;                            37       state.id == INSIDE &&
11      if(state == OUTSIDE) {              38       lock[id] == 1);
12        c = should_enter();               39     }
13        if(c) {                           40     FORALL_DISTINCT_NODE_PAIR
14          if(EXISTS_LOWER(idp,lock[idp])) 41       (id1,id2) {
15          return;                         42       ASSUME(state.id1 != INSIDE ||
16          lock[id] = 1; state = TRYING;   43           state.id2 != INSIDE);
17        }                                 44     }
18      } else if(state == TRYING) {        45   }
19        if(EXISTS_HIGHER(idp,lock[idp]))  46
20        return;                           47   void SAFETY()
21        state = INSIDE;                   48   {
22      } else if(state == INSIDE) {        49     FORALL_DISTINCT_NODE_PAIR
23        if(in_cs()) return;               50       (id1,id2) {
24        lock[id] = 0; state = OUTSIDE;    51       ASSERT(state.id1 != INSIDE ||
25      }                                   52           state.id2 != INSIDE);
26    }                                     53     }
27  }                                       54   }
```

Fig. 1. Example DASL program with 2 nodes using an id-based mutex protocol

scope; (iii) for each statement ALL(v, st) and $\nu(v, st)$, variable v is in scope of st; (iv) scoping is unambiguous, and only variables in scope are used in expressions; (v) id and id variables do not appear on the LHS of assignments, i.e., they are read-only; (vi) in any execution of ρ, a global array element is written atmost once. Note that these assumptions do not limit expressivity.

Init and Safety. The body of *Init* is a statement whose syntax is the same as *stmt* except that *lval* and *exp* are defined as:

$$\textbf{(LValues)} \ lval := GV[exp] \mid LV.IV \mid TV$$

$$\textbf{(Expressions)} \ exp := \mathbb{Z} \mid lval \mid IV \mid \sim exp \mid exp \diamond exp$$

Thus the key differences of *Init* with ρ are: (i) variable id is no longer in scope; and (ii) it is able to refer to local variables of nodes – specifically, the lvalue $v.i$ refers to local variable v of node with id i. Function *Safety* is the same as *Init* except: (i) it cannot access global variables; and (ii) it cannot modify local variables. Formally, the body of *Safety* is a statement whose syntax is the same as *stmt* except that *lval* and *exp* are defined as:

$$\textbf{(LValues)} \ lval := TV$$

$$\textbf{(Expressions)} \ exp := \mathbb{Z} \mid lval \mid LV.IV \mid IV \mid \sim exp \mid exp \diamond exp$$

Concrete Syntax. The "concrete" syntax of P_d consists of declarations for GV and LV, definitions of ρ, *Init*, and *Safety*, and the value of n. For example,

Figure 1 shows a DASL program with 2 nodes that use a protocol based on their ids to ensure mutual exclusion. The program consists of constant definitions (lines 1–3), the nodes and their ids (line 28), definition of function *Init* (lines 31–45), function *Safety* (lines 47–54), declarations of *GV* (line 6), *LV* (line 7), and the definition of function ρ (lines 9–26). Note that:

1. The concrete syntax is similar to C. This provides familiarity to practitioners, and simplifies sequentialization and code generation.
2. Constant definitions (lines 1–3) are allowed for readability.
3. Multi-dimensional global arrays are supported. Dimension #N denotes the number of nodes. Thus, there is one element of lock for each node. This supports a programming pattern where a node always writes to a global array element whose index equals its id (lines 16 and 24), ensuring that every global array element has one writer node.
4. Function ρ is called ROUND, and variable *id* is called id.
5. A node can invoke external functions (e.g., should_enter on line 12 and in_cs on line 23) as needed. External functions are assumed to be "pure" (i.e., they do not modify global, local, or temporary variables) and to return integer values non-deterministically.
6. There are three built-in functions to aid specification: (i) ND(v) sets variable v to a value non-deterministically; (ii) ASSUME(e) blocks all executions where e is FALSE; and (iii) assert(e) aborts all executions where e is FALSE. ASSUME and ND help specify legal initial states (lines 34, 35 and 42). ASSERT helps (line 51) to check for a violation of the safety property.
7. Iterators are available to: (i) execute a statement over all nodes (FORALL_NODE at line 33), all pairs of distinct nodes (FORALL_DISTINCT_NODE_PAIR at line 40 and 49), etc.; and (ii) evaluate an expression disjunctively over nodes that have a lower id (EXISTS_LOWER at line 14), a higher id (EXISTS_HIGHER at line 19), etc. They are all "syntactic sugar" defined formally using ALL in a natural manner.

Example 1. The DASL program in Figure 1 uses global variable lock to ensure mutual exclusion. Specifically, the node with id id enters the critical section (CS) if id is the largest index for which lock[id] is TRUE. To enter the CS, a node first checks (line 14) if the CS is available (i.e., not occupied by another node with smaller id). If this is not the case, it retries in the next round (line 15). Otherwise, it requests the CS (line 16). In the next round, the node checks (line 19) if it can enter the CS. If not, it retries (line 20) in the next round. Otherwise, it enters the CS (line 21). Once in the CS, the node performs arbitrary computation (line 23), releases the lock and exits (line 24). Note that since in_cs (line 23) returns a non-deterministic value, the node remains in the CS for arbitrary many rounds. *Init* ensures that initially each node is either inside or outside the CS (lines 33–39) with atmost one node being inside (lines 40–44). Function *Safety* aborts (lines 49–53) if multiple nodes are in the CS simultaneously.

Semantics of DASL. Consider a DASL program $P_d = (GV, LV, \rho, n, \varphi)$. We define the semantics of P_d in terms of a "sequential" (i.e., single-threaded) pro-

$$\Delta(\epsilon_1, \epsilon_2, skip) \equiv skip \qquad \Delta(\epsilon_1, \epsilon_2, l = e) \equiv \epsilon_1(l) = \epsilon_2(e)$$

$$\Delta(\epsilon_1, \epsilon_2, \text{ITE}(e, s, s')) \equiv \text{ITE}(\epsilon_2(e), \Delta(\epsilon_1, \epsilon_2, s), \Delta(\epsilon_1, \epsilon_2, s'))$$

$$\Delta(\epsilon_1, \epsilon_2, \text{WHILE}(e, s)) \equiv \text{WHILE}(\epsilon_2(e), \Delta(\epsilon_1, \epsilon_2, s))$$

$$\Delta(\epsilon_1, \epsilon_2, \text{ALL}(v, s)) \equiv \langle \Delta(\epsilon_1 \oplus (v, 0), \epsilon_2 \oplus (v, 0), s); \ldots; \Delta(\epsilon_1 \oplus (v, n-1), \epsilon_2 \oplus (v, n-1), s) \rangle$$

$$\Delta(\epsilon_1, \epsilon_2, \langle s; s' \rangle) \equiv \langle \Delta(\epsilon_1, \epsilon_2, s); \Delta(\epsilon_1, \epsilon_2, s') \rangle \qquad \Delta(\epsilon_1, \epsilon_2, \nu(v, s)) \equiv \nu(v, \Delta(\epsilon_1, \epsilon_2, s))$$

Fig. 2. The statement transformer mapping Δ

gram. Recall that P_d consists of n nodes executing concurrently and communicating via the shared variables GV. Each node is assigned a unique id between 0 and $n-1$, with N_i denoting the node with id i. We first create n copies of GV and LV, one for each node. For any $v \in GV \cup LV$, let v_i denote its copy made for N_i. Next, for each node N_i we create a copy of ρ, denoted ρ_i, by: (i) replacing each $v \in GV \cup LV$ with v_i; and (ii) expanding out each statement of the form $\text{ALL}(v, st)$ appropriately. We now define this formally.

ID Instantiation. An id instantiation is a partial mapping from $id \cup IV$ to $\mathbb{Z}$. Let $IdInst$ be the set of id instantiations. Let $\mu_\perp$ denote the empty id instantiation, i.e., $Domain(\mu_\perp) = \emptyset$. Given an id instantiation μ, a variable $v \notin Dom(\mu)$ and an integer z, $\mu \oplus (v, z)$ is the id instantiation that extends μ by mapping v to z.

Expression Transformer. An expression transformer is a mapping from expressions to expressions. Let $ExpTrans$ be the set of all expression transformers. Every id instantiation induces an expression transformer as follows.

Definition 1. *Define a mapping* $\epsilon : IdInst \mapsto ExpTrans$ *such that for any* $\mu \in IdInst$ *and* $e \in exp$, $\epsilon(\mu, e)$ *is obtained from* e *by replacing: (i) each* $v \in GV \cup LV$ *with* $v_{\mu(id)}$; *and (ii) each* $v.i \in LV.IV$ *with* $v_{\mu(i)}$.

A pair of expression transformers (ϵ_1, ϵ_2) induces a statement transformer that uses ϵ_1 to transform lvalues, ϵ_2 to transform expressions, and expands ALL statements. Formally, this defined as follows.

Definition 2 (Statement Transformer). *Define a mapping* $\Delta : ExpTrans \mapsto ExpTrans \mapsto stmt \mapsto stmt$ *as shown in Figure 2.*

Often, the two expression transformer arguments of Δ are equal. Therefore, for simplicity we write $\Delta(\epsilon, s)$ to mean $\Delta(\epsilon, \epsilon, s)$. Let the body of any function f be denoted by the statement $f()$. Then the semantics of node N_i in each round is given by the function ρ_i such that:

$$\rho_i() = \Delta(\epsilon(\mu_\perp \oplus (id, i)), \rho())$$

Thus, the body of ρ_i is obtained by transforming the body of ρ, starting with an id instantiation that maps id to i. Also, define functions $\tilde{Init}$ and $\tilde{Safety}$ as:

$$\tilde{Init}() = \Delta(\epsilon(\mu_\perp), Init()) \qquad \tilde{Safety}() = \Delta(\epsilon(\mu_\perp), Safety()) \qquad (1)$$

Thus, when transforming $Init$ and $Safety$, variable id is not in scope. Also, every lvalue $v.i$ is transformed to $v_{\mu(i)}$ since it refers to the local variable v of node N_i.

Semantics of P_d. The semantics of P_d is the sequential program that: (i) initializes variables by executing $\tilde{Init}()$; and then (ii) executes rounds. Each round consists of the following steps: (a) for every global array element $v[j]$, copy its value at its writer node to all its reader nodes; (b) check the property by executing *Safety*(); and (c) execute the sequence of statements $\langle \rho_0(); \ldots; \rho_{n-1}()\rangle$.

Recall that every global variable is an array. For a global variable $v \in GV$, let $Dim(v)$ denote its size. For each $j \in [1, Dim(v)]$, let $\mathcal{W}(v, j)$ denote the index of the node that writes to the element $v[j]$. Note that $\mathcal{W}(v, j)$ is well-defined due to our assumption that all global variables have a single writer node.

Definition 3 (Semantics). *The semantics of a* DASL *program $P_d = (GV, LV, \rho, n, \varphi)$, denoted $[\![P_d]\!]$, is the sequential program:*

$$[\![P_d]\!] = \langle \tilde{Init}(); \text{WHILE}(\text{TRUE}, Round)\rangle, \text{ where}$$
$$Round = \langle CopyGlobals; \tilde{Safety}(); \rho_0(); \ldots; \rho_{n-1}()\rangle, \text{ where}$$
$$CopyGlobals = \forall v \in GV \cdot \forall j \in [1, Dim(v)] \cdot \forall i \in [0, n) \cdot v_i[j] = v_{\mathcal{W}(v,j)}[j]$$

Note that the quantifiers in the definition of CopyGlobals are finitely instantiable. Hence, CopyGlobals expands to a finite sequence of assignments.

The semantics of P_d (Definition 3) is a sequential program. Thus, the procedure to construct $[\![P_d]\!]$, denoted SEQSEM, is a valid sequentialization for DASL. Note that $[\![P_d]\!]$ has $\mathcal{O}(n^2)$ global variables since there are $\mathcal{O}(n)$ global arrays, and each global array has $\mathcal{O}(n)$ elements. In Sec. 4 we present a more advanced sequentialization, SEQDBL, that produces programs with $\mathcal{O}(n)$ global variables.

4   Sequentializing DASL Programs

SEQDBL uses only two copies of GV, GV^1 and GV^0, where: (i) GV^1 is used as input in odd rounds and output in even rounds, while (ii) GV^0 is used as input in even rounds and output in odd rounds. More specifically, SEQDBL constructs the program P_s that: (i) initializes GV^1 and LV by executing $Init()$; and (ii) executes rounds. An odd round consists of the following steps: (a) check the property by executing *Safety*(); (b) copy GV^1 to GV^0; (b) execute the sequence of statements $\langle \rho_0(); \ldots; \rho_{n-1}()\rangle$, reading from GV^1 and writing to GV^0. An even round is the same as an odd round except that the roles of GV^1 and GV^0 are reversed. We now define P_s formally. For a global variable $v \in GV$, let v^1 and v^0 be its copy in GV^1 and GV^0, respectively. We begin with two expression transformers, ϵ^1 and ϵ^0. Then, we use them to transform functions *Init*, *Safety*, and $\rho_0, \ldots, \rho_{n-1}$. Finally, we define P_s in terms of these transformed functions.

Definition 4. *Define a mapping $\epsilon^1 : IdInst \mapsto ExpTrans$ such that for any $\mu \in IdInst$ and $e \in exp$, $\epsilon^1(\mu, e)$ is obtained from e by replacing: (i) each $v \in GV$ with v^1; (ii) each $v \in LV$ with $v_{\mu(id)}$; and (iii) each $v.i \in LV.IV$ with $v_{\mu(i)}$. Define mapping $\epsilon^0 : IdInst \mapsto ExpTrans$ to be the same as ϵ^1, except that every $v \in GV$ is replaced by v^0.*

Note that the only difference between ϵ^1 and ϵ^0 is in the treatment of global variables. For $i \in [0, n)$ define functions ρ_i^1 and ρ_i^0 such as:

$$\rho_i^1() = \Delta(\epsilon^0(\mu_\perp \oplus (id, i)), \epsilon^1(\mu_\perp \oplus (id, i)), \rho()) \\ \rho_i^0() = \Delta(\epsilon^1(\mu_\perp \oplus (id, i)), \epsilon^0(\mu_\perp \oplus (id, i)), \rho()) \tag{2}$$

Note that ρ_i^1 uses GV^0 for LHS of assignments, and GV^1 for other expressions. Thus, ρ_i^1 reads GV^1 and modifies GV^0. Similarly, ρ_i^0 reads GV^0 and modifies GV^1. Also, define functions $\ddot{Init}$, $Safety^1$ and $Safety^0$ as:

$$\ddot{Init}() = \Delta(\epsilon^1(\mu_\perp), Init()) \qquad Safety^1() = \Delta(\epsilon^0(\mu_\perp), \epsilon^1(\mu_\perp), Safety()) \\ Safety^0() = \Delta(\epsilon^1(\mu_\perp), \epsilon^0(\mu_\perp), Safety()) \tag{3}$$

Note that, $\ddot{Init}$ reads and modifies GV^1, $Safety^1$ reads GV^1 and modifies GV^0, while $Safety^0$ reads GV^0 and modifies GV^1. We now define P_s formally.

Definition 5 (Sequentialization). *The sequentialization of a* DASL *program* $P_d = (GV, LV, \rho, n, \varphi)$*, denoted* P_s*, is the sequential program:*

$$P_s = \langle \ddot{Init}(); \text{WHILE}(\text{TRUE}, \langle Round^1; Round^0 \rangle) \rangle, \text{ where}$$
$$Round^1 = \langle Safety^1(); CopyFwd; \rho_0^1(); \ldots; \rho_{n-1}^1() \rangle, \text{ where}$$
$$CopyFwd = \forall v \in GV . \forall j \in [1, Dim(v)] . v^0[j] = v^1[j], \text{ and}$$
$$Round^0 = \langle Safety^0(); CopyBwd; \rho_0^0(); \ldots; \rho_{n-1}^0() \rangle, \text{ where}$$
$$CopyBwd = \forall v \in GV . \forall j \in [1, Dim(v)] . v^1[j] = v^0[j]$$

Note that CopyFwd and CopyBwd expand to a finite sequence of assignments.

Correctness of SEQDBL. We now show that $[\![P_d]\!]$ and P_s are semantically equivalent, i.e., there is an execution of $[\![P_d]\!]$ that aborts iff there is an execution of P_s that aborts. For brevity, we only give a proof sketch. First, recall that $[\![P_d]\!]$ has n copies of GV, while P_s has just two. For simplicity, let $\mathbb{D}$ be the domain of values of all variables. Given a set of variables X, let $\mathcal{V}(X)$ be the set of mapping from X to $\mathbb{D}$. We write $\mathcal{V}_d$ to mean $\mathcal{V}(GV_1 \cup \cdots \cup GV_n)$, $\mathcal{V}^1$ to mean $\mathcal{V}(GV^1)$, $\mathcal{V}^0$ to mean $\mathcal{V}(GV^0)$, and $\mathcal{V}_l$ to mean $\mathcal{V}(LV)$. Thus, for example, an element of $\mathcal{V}_l$ maps local variables to values.

To relate $[\![P_d]\!]$ and P_s, we relate valuations of global variables of one to global variables of the other. Formally, we define a relation $\approx \subseteq \mathcal{V}_d \times (\mathcal{V}^1 \cup \mathcal{V}^0)$ as follows:

$$V \approx V' \iff \forall v \in GV . \forall j \in [1, Dim(v)] . V(v_{\mathcal{W}(v,j)}[j]) = V'(v[j])$$

In other words, V and V' are related iff for every global array element $v[j]$, the value of $v[j]$ at its writer node $\mathcal{W}(v, j)$ according to V is the same as the value of $v[j]$ according to V'. A state of $[\![P_d]\!]$ is a pair $(v_g, v_l) \in \mathcal{V}_d \times \mathcal{V}_l$. Similarly, a state of P_s is a triple $(v^1, v^0, v_l) \in \mathcal{V}^1 \times \mathcal{V}^0 \times \mathcal{V}_l$. Then, the following holds.

Theorem 1. *For every* $i \geq 1$*, state* (v_g, v_l) *is reachable at the start of the i-th execution of* $\tilde{Safety}()$ *in* $[\![P_d]\!]$ *iff: (a) i is odd and state* (v^1, v^0, v_l) *is reachable* at the start of the $\lceil \frac{i}{2} \rceil$-th execution of $Safety^1()$ in P_s such that $v_g \approx v^1$; or (b) i is even and state (v^1, v^0, v_l) is reachable at the start of the $\frac{i}{2}$-th execution of $Safety^0()$ in P_s such that $v_g \approx v^0$.

Proof. The proof is by induction over i. For brevity, we only give an outline. The base case ($i = 1$) follows from the definitions of $Init()$, $CopyGlobals$ (cf. (1)) and $\widetilde{Init}()$ (cf. (3)). For the inductive step, suppose i is odd and (v_g, v_l) is reachable at the start of the i-th execution of $\widetilde{Safety}()$ in $[\![P_d]\!]$. By inductive hypothesis, (v^1, v^0, v_l) is reachable at the start of the $\lceil \frac{i}{2} \rceil$-th execution of $Safety^1()$ in P_s such that $v_g \approx v^1$. Since, $Safety$ does not modify global or local variables, $[\![P_d]\!]$ next executes statement $X_d = \langle \rho_0; \ldots; \rho_{n-1}; CopyGlobals \rangle$ from state (v_g, v_l). Suppose it reaches state (v'_g, v'_l). Also, from the definition of $CopyFwd$, we know that P_s next executes statement $X_s = \langle \rho^1_0(); \ldots; \rho^1_{n-1}() \rangle$ from state (v^1, v^1, v_l). It can be shown that after executing X_s, P_s can also reach a state (v^1, v'^1, v_l) such that $v'_g \approx v'^1$. Similarly, suppose that after executing statement X_s, P_s reaches state (v^1, v'^1, v_l). Again it can be shown that after executing statement X_d, $[\![P_d]\!]$ can also reach state (v'_g, v'_l) such that $v'_g \approx v'^1$. This establishes the result for $i + 1$. By a symmetric argument, we can show that the result holds for the case when i is even as well. □

Correctness of SEQDBL. Recall that function $Safety$ reads local variables only. Thus, $\widetilde{Safety}() = Safety^1() = Safety^0()$. By Theorem 1, $[\![P_d]\!]$ executes $\widetilde{Safety}$ from a state (v_g, v_l) iff P_s executes $Safety^1$ or $Safety^0$ from a state (v^1, v^0, v_l). Hence, $[\![P_d]\!]$ aborts iff P_s also aborts, proving that SEQDBL is correct.

Note that both SEQSEM and SEQDBL rely crucially on our assumption of SN-MOC. However, in practice, networks in our domain of interest are asynchronous with unbounded message delays, and SNMOC must be implemented on top of it in order to deploy DASL applications. This is the topic of Section 5.

5   Implementing SNMOC

The synchronous network abstraction (SNMOC) is implemented on top of an asynchronous network via a "synchronizer" [3] protocol. In the literature, several synchronizers [16] have been proposed. Many, such as PALS [17], rely on clock synchronization. However, this is not appropriate for our target domain where networks have unbounded latency. To address this challenge, we have developed a new synchronizer that does not rely on any clock synchronization. Instead, our protcol, called 2-Barrier-Synchronization (2BSYNC), uses global variables to enforce a *barrier* before and after each round, thereby synchronizing rounds across all the application nodes. We now present 2BSYNC in more detail.

Consider a DASL program $P_d = (GV, LV, \rho, n, \varphi)$. Let W_i be the set of global variables written by node N_i, i.e., $W_i = \{v[j] \mid \mathcal{W}(v, j) = i\}$. We introduce n additional global "barrier" variables – $b_0, \ldots, b_{n-1}$ – each initialized to 0. For any set of global variables X, let $(X)!$ denote the *atomic broadcast* of the current value of all variables in X to other nodes. This means that the broadcasted values are received by other nodes atomically, i.e., at any point in time, either all of them are visible to a recipient node or none of them are. The atomic broadcast capability is crucial for implementing 2BSYNC, and we discuss it further later. Then, node N_i is implemented by the program $Node_i$ defined as follows (b_i++ is a shorthand for $b_i = b_i + 1$):

$$Node_i = \text{WHILE}(\text{TRUE}, Round_i), \text{ where}$$
$$Round_i = \langle b_i\text{++}; (W_i, b_i)!; Barr_i(); \rho_i(); b_i\text{++}; (b_i)!; Barr_i()\rangle, \text{ where} \quad (4)$$
$$Barr_i = \text{WHILE}(b_0 < b_i \vee \cdots \vee b_{n-1} < b_i, skip)$$

Note that $Barr_i$ implements a barrier since it forces $Node_i$ to wait till the values of the barrier variables at all other nodes have "caught up" with the value of its own barrier variable b_i.

Correctness of 2BSYNC. For any global array element $v[j]$, let $r(v[j], i, k)$ and $w(v[j], i, k)$ be the value of $v[j]$, before and after respectively, the execution of $\rho_i()$ during the k-th iteration of the outermost WHILE loop of $Node_i$. Let $\mathcal{I}(v[j])$ be the initial value of global array element $v[j]$ at its writer node. Thus, 2BSYNC is correct iff the following two conditions hold:

$$\forall v[j] \centerdot \forall i \in [0, n) \centerdot r(v[j], i, 1) = \mathcal{I}(v[j]) \quad (5)$$
$$\forall v[j] \centerdot \forall i \in [0, n) \centerdot \forall k > 1 \centerdot r(v[j], i, k) = w(v[j], \mathcal{W}(v, j), k - 1) \quad (6)$$

Let $\mathcal{B}(v[j], i, k)$ be the value of $v[j]$ broadcast atomically during the k-th iteration of the outermost WHILE loop of $Node_i$ in (4). Note that $\mathcal{B}(v[j], i, 1) = \mathcal{I}(v[j])$ and $\forall k > 1 \centerdot \mathcal{B}(v[j], i, k) = w(v[j], i, k - 1)$. Thus, (5) and (6) hold iff:

$$\forall v[j] \centerdot \forall i \in [0, n) \centerdot \forall k \geq 1 \centerdot r(v[j], i, k) = \mathcal{B}(v[j], \mathcal{W}(v, j), k) \quad (7)$$

Then, (7) follows from two observations. Due to the first $Barr_i$:

$$\forall v[j] \centerdot \forall i \in [0, n) \centerdot \forall k \geq 1 \centerdot r(v[j], i, k) = \mathcal{B}(v[j], \mathcal{W}(v, j), k') \implies k \leq k'$$

Again, due to the second $Barr_i$, we have:

$$\forall v[j] \centerdot \forall i \in [0, n) \centerdot \forall k \geq 1 \centerdot r(v[j], i, k) = \mathcal{B}(v[j], \mathcal{W}(v, j), k') \implies k' < k + 1$$

This completes the proof. Note that the 2BSYNC protocol must be implemented over a middleware that supports global variables as well as atomic broadcast. For this research, we use MADARA [8], a middleware developed for distributed AI applications. The support for global variables was already available in MADARA. We augmented it by implementing the atomic broadcast capability. In Section 6 we describe the process of generating C++ code for each node of a DASL program against the MADARA API.

6   Code Generation: From DASL to MADARA/C++

Once a DASL program P_d has been successfully verified, it is converted into an equivalent MADARA application P_m. MADARA is an open-source[2] middleware

---

[2] http://madara.googlecode.com

developed for distributed AI applications. It has been ported to a variety of real-world platforms and architectures (e.g., ARM and Intel) and operating systems (e.g., Linux, Windows, Android and iOS). MADARA applications can communicate via IP-based protocols like UDP, IP broadcast and IP multicast or the Data Distribution Service (DDS). These advantages are inherited by P_m by virtue of its use of MADARA. MADARA ensures consistency of global variables (GV) within P_m through a distributed context that maps variables to values, with each $v \in GV$ controlled by a private Lamport clock v_t, which enforces temporal consistency. This type of consistency is inherent in the underlying MADARA subsystems, and is useful for encoding the 2BSYNC protocol into the P_m program.

MADARA has two additional features crucial for implementing 2BSYNC. First, as part of this research, we augmented MADARA with a sendlist mechanism that allows application nodes to dynamically specify, at runtime, which variables in GV are disseminable immediately, and which variable disseminations should be delayed until later. This sendlist mechanism maps directly to the requirements of the 2BSYNC protocol (cf. Sec. 5). Specifically, we use it to enable barrier variable updates while actively suppressing the dissemination of other values written by node N_i until the time is appropriate. This is required to perform the atomic broadcast operation $(b_i)!$ in (4). Second, MADARA allows an application node to broadcast values of multiple context variables to other nodes as a "packet". MADARA ensures that the packet is received by other nodes "atomically", i.e., at any point in time, either all the values in the packet are observed by a receiver node, or none is. This is required to perform the atomic broadcast operation $(W_i, b_i)!$ in (4).

The generated program P_m preserves the semantics of the DASL program P_d that has been verified via sequentialization to P_s. The differences between P_m and P_d revolve around the following limitations and features of MADARA:

1. MADARA supports several first class types like strings, doubles, raw binary, and images but only one type of integer (a 64 bit integer). Consequently, Booleans and integers in P_d are encoded as 64 bit integers in P_m.
2. MADARA includes an efficient scripting environment for manipulating global variables (GV). It also provides classes – $Integer$, $Array$, $Array\_N$, etc. – that allow direct access to GV. We use the scripting environment wherever applicable, such as in the implementation of the 2BSYNC protocol. However, for user-defined functions, we generate code that uses the classes. This leads to a more direct mapping from P_d to P_m, especially for control statements such as if/then/else and switch statements. The MADARA equivalents of these control structures use logical operators like && and ||, and the class facades into the MADARA context yields P_m code that is easier to debug and modify, without requiring expertise about MADARA internals.
3. The MADARA context is appropriate for storing GV and LV but does not contain primitives that allow a node to perform omniscient variable accesses (i.e., to variables of other nodes) present in DASL programs, specifically in the $Init$ and $Safety$ functions (cf. Fig. 1). Because each node of P_m only has access to its own local variables, P_m does not contain code for $Init$ or

```
                                         3   // Generated code in (*$P_m$*)
0   // Source model in P_d                4   (id == 1 && lock[0]) ||
1   EXISTS_LOWER(idp,lock[idp])           5   (id == 2 && (lock[0] ||  lock[1])) ||
2   ...                                   6   (id == 3 && (lock[0] ||
                                             lock[1] || lock[2]))
```

```
                                         13  while (1)
0   // Source model in P_d                14  {
1   2BSYNC for 2 processes                15    knowledge.evaluate("++B.{.id}");
2   ...                                   16    if (id == 0)
3                                         17      knowledge.wait("B.1 >= B.0");
4   // Generated code in P_m              18    else
5   if (id == 0)                          19      knowledge.wait("B.0 >= B.1");
6     settings.send_list ["B.0"]          20
7       = true;                           21    ROUND ();
8   else                                  22
9     settings.send_list ["B.1"]          23    knowledge.evaluate("++B.{.id}");
10      = true;                           24    if (id == 0)
11                                        25      knowledge.wait("B.1 >= B.0",settings);
12  // Continued on the right             26    else
                                         27      knowledge.wait("B.0 >= B.1",settings);
                                         28  }
```

Fig. 3. P_m code generated from: (top) EXISTS_LOWER; (bottom) 2BSYNC

Safety. This makes sense since these two functions are meant for verification only. Still, for verification results to be valid, the initial state of P_m must be consistent with that constructed by *Init*. Currently, this is ensured manually.

4. Unlike the sequentialized program P_s, MADARA allows us to build a P_m that is *id*-neutral at compilation time. Through the usage of MADARA's object-oriented facades into the GV and LV contexts, a more direct mapping of the source P_d to P_m takes place. While the sequentialized program P_s contains separate code for each node of P_d, the application P_m consists of code for a single node whose *id* is supplied via a command line argument.

Fig. 3 illustrates examples of the code generation from sections of the P_d defined in Fig. 1. The examples outline the code unrolling of EXISTS_LOWER (top) and 2BSYNC (bottom), respectively. Note that variables B.0 and B.1 in Fig. 3 correspond to variables b_0 and b_1 in (4).

7   Empirical Evaluation

We implemented DIVER in a verifying compiler called DASLC, and used it to compare SEQSEM and SEQDBL on a set of synchronous distributed applications. All our experiments were done on a 8 core 2GHz machine running Ubuntu 12.04 with a time limit of 1 hour and a memory limit of 16GB. The parser for DASL programs was generated using flex/bison. The rest of DASLC was implemented in C++. DASLC generates ANSI C code – the safety property is encoded by assertions – which we verify using the model checker CBMC [6] v4.7. CBMC converts the target C program *Prog* and assertion *Asrt* into a propositional formula φ such that *Prog* violates *Asrt* iff φ is satisfiable. It then solves φ using an off-the-shelf SAT solver. We use the parallel

	MUTEX-OK						MUTEX-BUG1						MUTEX-BUG2					
R	T_S	T_D	T_S	T_D	T_S	T_D	T_S	T_D	T_S	T_D	T_S	T_D	T_S	T_D	T_S	T_D	T_S	T_D
	$n=6$		$n=8$		$n=10$		$n=6$		$n=8$		$n=10$		$n=6$		$n=8$		$n=10$	
60	406	396	1116	1051	2388	2268	184	175	517	439	1068	959	233	216	637	553	1292	1167
80	850	806	2268	1967	4525	4249	402	372	1013	925	2203	1812	500	462	1218	1112	2602	2139
100	1404	1381	3584	3452	7092	6764	734	686	1726	1566	3513	3287	890	838	2056	1860	4216	3742
	μ=1.040 σ=0.038						μ=1.056 σ=0.060						μ=1.065 σ=0.056					

	3DCOLL-OK-4x4						3DCOLL-OK-7x7						3DCOLL-BUG-4x4						3DCOLL-BUG-7x7					
R	T_S	T_D	T_S	T_D	T_S	T_D	T_S	T_D	T_S	T_D	T_S	T_D	T_S	T_D	T_S	T_D	T_S	T_D	T_S	T_D	T_S	T_D	T_S	T_D
	$n=2$		$n=4$		$n=6$		$n=2$		$n=4$		$n=6$		$n=2$		$n=4$		$n=6$		$n=2$		$n=4$		$n=6$	
10	13	10	59	40	219	96	31	35	323	148	1099	323	8	9	49	36	123	96	22	23	194	114	–	–
20	37	31	351	123	1014	480	73	72	1262	401	–	–	24	36	119	101	410	210	57	76	–	–	–	–
30	48	48	406	202	–	–	142	113	–	–	–	–	42	44	206	155	–	–	117	134	–	–	–	–
	μ=2.213 σ=0.715						μ=2.294 σ=0.763						μ=1.615 σ=0.425						μ=1.514 σ=0.344					

	2DCOLL-OK-4x4						2DCOLL-BUG1-4x4						2DCOLL-BUG2-4x4					
R	T_S	T_D	T_S	T_D	T_S	T_D	T_S	T_D	T_S	T_D	T_S	T_D	T_S	T_D	T_S	T_D	T_S	T_D
	$n=2$		$n=4$		$n=6$		$n=2$		$n=4$		$n=6$		$n=2$		$n=4$		$n=6$	
10	17	25	87	262	280	831	3	2	12	11	30	22	4	3	13	11	30	29
20	123	271	1474	2754	–	–	8	7	36	29	80	75	8	9	33	33	76	66
30	863	1301	–	–	–	–	12	15	57	51	144	105	16	21	57	77	150	120
	μ=0.446 σ=0.118						μ=1.282 σ=0.264						μ=1.056 σ=0.266					

	2DCOLL-OK-7x7						2DCOLL-BUG1-7x7						2DCOLL-BUG2-7x7					
R	T_S	T_D	T_S	T_D	T_S	T_D	T_S	T_D	T_S	T_D	T_S	T_D	T_S	T_D	T_S	T_D	T_S	T_D
	$n=2$		$n=4$		$n=6$		$n=2$		$n=4$		$n=6$		$n=2$		$n=4$		$n=6$	
10	74	146	395	1016	1707	–	7	7	32	24	101	70	5	10	26	36	188	113
20	1726	3096	–	–	–	–	15	22	94	55	345	150	19	22	71	113	207	166
30	–	–	–	–	–	–	40	35	180	91	–	223	46	68	124	295	416	235
	μ=0.598 σ=0.202						μ=1.382 σ=0.517						μ=0.906 σ=0.393					

Fig. 4. Experimental Results; T_S, T_D = verification time with SEQSEM, SEQDBL; n = no. of nodes; R = no. of rounds; $G \times G$ = grid size; μ, σ = mean, standard deviation of T_S/T_D for all experiments in that category; – denotes out of time/memory.

SAT solver PLINGELING (http://fmv.jku.at/lingeling) to utilize multiple cores. Since CBMC only verifies bounded programs, we fixed the number of rounds of execution of the target application for each verification run. Due to lack of space, we only present a subset of results that suffice to illustrate our main conclusions. Our tools, benchmarks, and complete results are available at http://www.contrib.andrew.cmu.edu/~schaki/misc/models14.zip . We verified several applications, varying number of nodes (n) and rounds (R), and using both SEQSEM and SEQDBL. We now present our results in detail.

Mutual Exclusion. The first application implemented a distributed mutual exclusion protocol. The DASL program for the correct version of this protocol is in Fig. 1. We also implemented two buggy versions of this protocol by omitting important checks (at lines 14–15 and lines 19–20 in Fig. 1). Results of verifying all three versions are shown in Fig. 4. As expected, verification time increases both with n and R. However, it is almost the same between SEQSEM and SE-QDBL for a fixed n and R, as shown by the values of μ and σ. This indicates that the techniques implemented in CBMC and PLINGELING effectively eliminate the complexity due to additional variables produced by SEQSEM.

3-Dimensional Collision Avoidance. The next application implemented a collision avoidance protocol where nodes (denoting robots flying over an area demarcated by a two-dimensional grid) are able to change their height to avoid colliding with each other. We implemented a correct and a buggy version of this protocol. The results of verifying the two versions are shown in Fig. 4. Again, verification time increases with n, R, and G (where grid-size $= G \times G$). In addition, programs generated by SEQDBL are verified faster (over 100% for the correct version and 50% for the buggy version) than those generated by SEQSEM, for a fixed n, R and G. This supports our intuition that the $\mathcal{O}(n)$ variables used by SEQDBL is better for verification.

2-Dimensional Collision Avoidance. The final application implemented a collision avoidance protocol where nodes can only move in two dimensions. We implemented a correct and two buggy versions of this protocol. The results of verifying them are shown in Fig. 4. Again, verification time increases with n, R, and G. However, the difference between SEQDBL and SEQSEM is subtle. For the BUG2 version, they are almost identical. For BUG1, SEQDBL leads to over 30% faster verification. However, for the correct version, SEQSEM allows verification to be 40% faster, even though it generates programs with more variables.

In summary, while SEQDBL is clearly the better option overall, there are cases where SEQSEM is more efficient. We believe that the optimizations and symbolic algorithms used by modern model checkers means that verification time is not just determined by the number of variables. While these results were obtained using CBMC, we believe that they are representative of symbolic model checkers. For example, similar non-monotonic performance has also been observed in other contexts, e.g., when comparing [21] BDD and SAT-based LTL model checkers. Note that, in general, model checking a buggy application is easier than a correct one since the latter requires complete statespace exploration.

8 Conclusion

We presented an approach for model-driven verifying compilation of distributed applications written in a domain-specific language, called DASL, against user-provided safety specifications. We assume a "synchronous network" model of computation. Our verification is based on sequentialization followed by software model checking. We develop two sequentialization techniques – SEQSEM and SE-QDBL– and compare them on a set of applications. SEQDBL produces programs with fewer variables, and empirically is more efficient for verification in most cases. We also develop a protocol to implement a synchronous network abstraction over an asynchronous network. This protocol does not require clock synchronization and is of independent interest. We believe that extending our approach to handle asynchronous and fault-tolerant programs, and proving correctness of code generation and middleware, are important directions to pursue.

References

1. Alglave, J., Kroening, D., Tautschnig, M.: Partial Orders for Efficient Bounded Model Checking of Concurrent Software. In: Sharygina, N., Veith, H. (eds.) CAV 2013. LNCS, vol. 8044, pp. 141–157. Springer, Heidelberg (2013)

2. Andrews, T., Qadeer, S., Rajamani, S.K., Rehof, J., Xie, Y.: Zing: A model checker for concurrent software. In: Alur, R., Peled, D.A. (eds.) CAV 2004. LNCS, vol. 3114, pp. 484–487. Springer, Heidelberg (2004)
3. Awerbuch, B.: Complexity of Network Synchronization. Journal of the ACM (JACM) 32(4), 804–823 (1985)
4. Azimi, S.R., Bhatia, G., Rajkumar, R., Mudalige, P.: Reliable intersection protocols using vehicular networks. In: Lu, C., Kumar, P.R., Stoleru, R. (eds.) Proceedings of the 4th International Conference on Cyber-Physical Systems (ICCPS 2013), pp. 1–10. Association for Computing Machinery, Philadelphia (2013)
5. Caspi, P., Pilaud, D., Halbwachs, N., Plaice, J.: Lustre: A Declarative Language for Programming Synchronous Systems. In: Proceedings of the 14th ACM SIGPLAN-SIGACT Symposium on Principles of Programming Languages (POPL 1987), pp. 178–188. Association for Computing Machinery, Munich (1987), http://doi.acm.org/10.1145/41625.41641
6. Clarke, E., Kroning, D., Lerda, F.: A Tool for Checking ANSI-C Programs. In: Jensen, K., Podelski, A. (eds.) TACAS 2004. LNCS, vol. 2988, pp. 168–176. Springer, Heidelberg (2004)
7. Cobleigh, J.M., Giannakopoulou, D., Păsăreanu, C.S.: Learning Assumptions for Compositional Verification. In: Garavel, H., Hatcliff, J. (eds.) TACAS 2003. LNCS, vol. 2619, pp. 331–346. Springer, Heidelberg (2003)
8. Edmondson, J., Gokhale, A.: Design of a Scalable Reasoning Engine for Distributed, Real-Time and Embedded Systems. In: Xiong, H., Lee, W.B. (eds.) KSEM 2011. LNCS, vol. 7091, pp. 221–232. Springer, Heidelberg (2011)
9. Fürst, S., Mössinger, J., Bunzel, S., Weber, T., Kirschke-Biller, F., Heitkämper, P., Kinkelin, G., Nishikawa, K., Lange, K.: AUTOSAR–A Worldwide Standard is on the Road. In: Proceedings of the 14th International VDI Congress Electronic Systems for Vehicles. Baden-Baden, Germany (2009)
10. Hoare, C.A.R.: Communicating Sequential Processes. Prentice Hall, London (1985)
11. Hoare, C.A.R.: The verifying compiler: A grand challenge for computing research. Journal of the ACM (JACM) 50(1), 63–69 (2003)
12. Humphrey, L., Wolff, E., Topcu, U.: Formal Specification and Synthesis of UAV Mission Plans. In: Proc. of AAAI Symposium, Baden-Baden, Germany (November 2014)
13. Jhala, R., Majumdar, R.: Software model checking. ACM Computing Surveys (CSUR) 41(4) (2009)
14. Lal, A., Reps, T.: Reducing Concurrent Analysis Under a Context Bound to Sequential Analysis. In: Gupta, A., Malik, S. (eds.) CAV 2008. LNCS, vol. 5123, pp. 37–51. Springer, Heidelberg (2008)
15. Lasnier, G., Zalila, B., Pautet, L., Hugues, J.: Ocarina: An Environment for AADL Models Analysis and Automatic Code Generation for High Integrity Applications. In: Kordon, F., Kermarrec, Y. (eds.) Ada-Europe 2009. LNCS, vol. 5570, pp. 237–250. Springer, Heidelberg (2009)
16. Lynch, N.A.: Distributed Algorithms. Morgan Kaufmann (1996)
17. Miller, S.P., Cofer, D.D., Sha, L., Meseguer, J., Al-Nayeem, A.: Implementing logical synchrony in integrated modular avionics. In: Proceedings of the 28th Digital Avionics Systems Conference (DASC 2009), pp. 1.A.3-1–1.A.3-12. IEEE Computer Society, Orlando (2009)
18. Milner, R.: Communication and Concurrency. Prentice-Hall International, London (1989)

19. Pardo-Castellote, G.: OMG Data-Distribution Service: Architectural Overview. In: Proceedings of the 23rd International Conference on Distributed Computing Systems Workshops (ICDCS 2003 Workshops), pp. 200–206. IEEE Computer Society, Providence (2003)

20. Schmidt, D.C., Gokhale, A., Natarajan, B., Neema, S., Bapty, T., Parsons, J., Gray, J., Nechypurenko, A., Wang, N.: CoSMIC: An MDA generative tool for distributed real-time and embedded component middleware and applications. In: Proceedings of the OOPSLA 2002 Workshop on Generative Techniques in the Context of Model Driven Architecture, Seattle, WA, USA (2002)

21. Schuppan, V., Darmawan, L.: Evaluating LTL Satisfiability Solvers. In: Bultan, T., Hsiung, P.-A. (eds.) ATVA 2011. LNCS, vol. 6996, pp. 397–413. Springer, Heidelberg (2011)

22. Siegel, J.: CORBA 3 fundamentals and programming, vol. 2. John Wiley & Sons, Chichester (2000)

23. Sulistio, A., Yeo, C.S., Buyya, R.: A taxonomy of computer-based simulations and its mapping to parallel and distributed systems simulation tools. Softw., Pract. Exper. 34(7), 653–673 (2004)

24. La Torre, S., Madhusudan, P., Parlato, G.: Reducing Context-Bounded Concurrent Reachability to Sequential Reachability. In: Bouajjani, A., Maler, O. (eds.) CAV 2009. LNCS, vol. 5643, pp. 477–492. Springer, Heidelberg (2009)

25. Tripakis, S., Pinello, C., Benveniste, A., Sangiovanni-Vincentelli, A.L., Caspi, P., Natale, M.D.: Implementing Synchronous Models on Loosely Time Triggered Architectures. IEEE Transactions on Computers (TC) 57(10), 1300–1314 (2008)

Environment-Centric Contracts
for Design of Cyber-Physical Systems

Jonas Westman[1] and Mattias Nyberg[1,2]

[1] Royal Institute of Technology (KTH), Stockholm, Sweden
jowestm@kth.se
[2] Scania, Södertälje, Sweden

Abstract. A contract splits the responsibilities between a component and its environment into a guarantee that expresses an intended property under the responsibility of the component, given that the environment fulfills the assumptions. Although current contract theories are limited to express contracts over interfaces of components, specifications that are not limited to interfaces are used in practice and are needed in order to properly express safety requirements. A framework is therefore presented, generalizing current contract theory to *environment-centric contracts* - contracts that are not limited to the interface of components. The framework includes revised definitions of properties of contracts, as well as theorems that specify exact conditions for when the properties hold. Furthermore, constraints are introduced, limiting the ports over which an environment-centric contract is expressed where the constraints constitute necessary conditions for the guarantee of the contract to hold in an architecture.

Keywords: Environment-Centric, Contracts, Architecture.

1 Introduction

The notion of contracts was first introduced in [1] as a pair of pre- and post-conditions [2–5] to formally specify the interface of software components. However, in more recent work [6–9] where the use of contracts is extended to the design of Cyber-Physical Systems (CPS) [10], the conceptual idea of a contract is rather described as: *"a component model that sets forth the assumptions under which the component may be used by its environment, and the corresponding promises that are guaranteed under such correct use"* [6], which indicates that contracts must not necessarily be limited to the interfaces of components.

However, in current contract theories [1,5–9,11–20], contracts are indeed limited to the interface of components, e.g. as shown in Fig. 1a where a contract for a controller $\mathbb{C}_1$ is limited to its interface. In this case, the guarantee G expresses that the desired output signal v to another controller $\mathbb{C}_2$ is a function of the voltage u at an input pin connected to a sensor $\mathbb{S}$. However, the guarantee G can only be assured to hold, given that the assumption A is fulfilled where A expresses constraints on the input u. In contrast to Fig. 1a, Fig. 1b shows another contract for $\mathbb{C}_1$ where both the guarantee G' and the assumption A' are

J. Dingel et al. (Eds.): MODELS 2014, LNCS 8767, pp. 218–234, 2014.

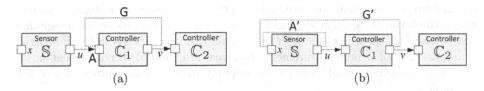

Fig. 1. Two contracts for a controller $\mathbb{C}_1$ are shown in (a) and (b), where the contract in (a) is limited to the interface of $\mathbb{C}_1$ and the contract in (b), is not

not limited to the interface of $\mathbb{C}_1$. In this case, the guarantee G' expresses that the output signal v shall correspond to a physical quantity x, as sensed by the sensor $\mathbb{S}$, given the assumption A that sensor $\mathbb{S}$ is functioning correctly.

In order to support specifications that are not limited to component interfaces, e.g. the one shown in Fig. 1b, the present paper generalizes current contract theories [1,5–9,11–20] to contracts that are not limited to interfaces of components. Inspired by [21,22], a contract that is not limited to the interface of a component, will in the following be referred to as an *environment-centric contract.*

It could be argued that the environment-centric contract in Fig. 1b is not needed since the interface of $\mathbb{C}_1$ could be extended to include the port x, which would allow the contract in Fig. 1b to be a contract for $\mathbb{C}_1$. However, in this case, the interface of the component $\mathbb{C}_1$ would not match the interface of the real world object that it models and would hence require the use of ambiguous representations of the real world.

Although environment-centric contracts are not supported by current contract theories [1,5–9, 11–20], there are at least two reasons why a generalization of current contract theories to environment-centric contracts is strongly needed.

The first reason is that a specification that is not limited to the interface of a component, e.g. the one shown in Fig. 1b, is capable of expressing that the responsibility of the component is to achieve an overall intended property of a system, instead of being restricted to express only its intended behavior. The same need, but in the context of functions, has been identified in [21, 22]. An example of when a specification such as the one shown in Fig. 1b is used in an industrial case-study, can be found in [23] where ModelicaML [24] is used to specify and verify requirements on a subsystem of a fuel management system where the requirements express the end-to-end functionality of the fuel management system in general. Another example can be found in [25] where SysML [26] is used to specify requirements on an engine knock controller and where the requirements allocated to the controller explicitly refer to parts, such as e.g. the piston, of the environment of the controller.

The second reason why environment-centric contracts are needed is that, in the area of functional safety [27, 28], the associated risk of a component, is assessed in the context of how it affects its environment, and not just by its immediate behavior. In order to properly express safety requirements on a component, there is hence a need to refer to parts in the environment that the component is to be deployed in. For example, in ISO 26262 [28], top-level safety requirements for an item, i.e. a system, are formulated in order to prevent or mitigate hazards, where the hazards *"shall be defined in terms of the conditions or behaviour that can be observed at the vehicle level"* [28]. This can be observed in the industrial examples [29, 30], where requirements that are not limited to component interfaces are necessarily used in order to properly express safety properties of the components.

The two reasons above explain the importance of allowing assumptions and guarantees to be expressed, not only over the interface, but also over ports in the environment. This motivates the main contribution of this paper, namely a framework that generalizes current contract theories to environment-centric contracts.

At the core of the framework is a corollary that, given an environment-centric contract, separates the respective conditions that a component and its environment need to meet in order to ensure seamless integration into a final product where the guarantee of the environment-centric contract holds. Considering such conditions, necessary constraints on the set of ports, i.e. *the scopes*, over which guarantees and assumptions can be expressed, are introduced. The constraints serve as a sanity check in order to determine that an environment-centric contract is not an unreasonable specification for a component in an architecture.

The framework includes revised definitions of the contract properties *consistency* [6, 7, 19], *compatibility* [6, 7, 19], and *dominance* [8, 20] as defined in current contract theories, as well as two theorems that specify necessary and sufficient conditions of consistency and compatibility. As a basis for structuring contracts in parallel to an architecture, a graph, called a *decomposition structure*, is introduced. Based on a decomposition structure, a theorem is presented with sufficient conditions of dominance.

Out of an extensive literature study of contract theories [1, 5–9, 11–20], no previous contract theories were found to explicitly support contracts that are not limited to the interface of components. Although both [19, 20] do allow assumptions that extend outside of the interface, both are, however, limited to express guarantees over the interface of components. Even though the abstract definition of a contract in [8] does not exclude that assumptions and the guarantees are limited to the interface of components, it is not treated explicitly. Moreover, [8] does not address compatibility and consistency issues between interfaces. In contrast to [8, 19, 20], the present paper focuses on fully generalizing contract theories by revising properties of contracts and providing theorems to support practical application.

Although the work in the present paper is a generalization of current contract theories [1, 5–9, 11–20] in general, due to the numerous contract theories that exist, the text is limited to discuss properties of contracts as presented in contract theories [6–8, 20] that can be traced back to the FP6 project SPEEDS [31]. This means that, e.g. the quotient operator [9, 19], is not discussed. The work is further confined to representing assumptions and guarantees as sets of runs, which means that neither modalities [8, 18] nor probabilities [17], are considered.

2   Assertions, Elements and Architectures

This section establishes a theoretical framework in order to model a CPS and its parts, and to be able to describe the notion of environment-centric contracts and its properties in Sec. 3 and 4. The framework mainly draws inspiration from the contract theory of the FP6 project SPEEDS [31] as described in [6, 7].

2.1   Assertions and Runs

Let $X = \{x_1, \ldots, x_N\}$ be a set of variables. Consider a trajectory of values of a variable x_i over a time window starting at a certain time t_0, e.g. as shown in Fig. 2a. A tuple of such trajectories, one for each variable in X, sorted according to a global ordering with respect to the identifiers of the variables, is called a *run* for X, and denoted ω_X. For example, a run $\omega_{\{x_i,x_j\}}$ is shown in Fig. 2b as a solid line, consisting of the trajectory shown in Fig. 2a and another trajectory of values of x_j, both represented as dashed lines.

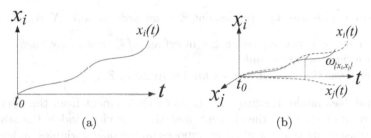

(a)   (b)

Fig. 2. A trajectory of values of x_i is shown in (a) and a run $\omega_{\{x_i,x_j\}}$ is shown in (b)

Given a set of variables X', an *assertion* W over X' is a possibly empty set of runs for X'. This notion corresponds to similar definitions in [6, 7, 30]. Note that, in the examples in the present paper, assertions will be specified by equations. The assertion is then the set of runs that are solutions to the equation.

Given an assertion W over $X = \{x_1, \ldots, x_N\}$, and another set of variables $X' \subseteq X$, the *projection* [6, 19, 20, 30] of W onto X', written $proj_{X'}(W)$, is the set of runs obtained when the trajectory of values of each variable $x_i \notin X'$ is removed from each run in W. Using notation of relational algebra [32], it holds that $proj_{X'}(W) = \pi_{X'}(W)$. For example, consider an assertion $\{\omega_{\{x_i,x_j\}}\}$ consisting of the run in Fig. 2b, $proj_{\{x_i\}}(\{\omega_{\{x_i,x_j\}}\})$ is the assertion containing only the trajectory in Fig. 2a.

Given an assertion W' over X' and another set of variables X, $\widetilde{proj}_X(W')$ denotes the set of runs where each run in W' is first extended with all possible runs for $X \setminus X'$, prior to applying the operation of projection. That is, $\widetilde{proj}_X(W') = proj_X(\{\omega_{X \cup X'} | proj_{X'}(\{\omega_{X \cup X'}\}) \subseteq W'\})$.

In the following, the symbols $\widehat{\cap}, \widehat{\cup}, \widehat{\subset}, \widehat{\subseteq}$, etc. will be used to denote that prior to using operations and relations on assertions over *dissimilar sets of variables*, the assertions are first extended to the union of the sets of variables involved using the operator $\widehat{proj}$. For example, given two assertions W and W' over the set of variables X and X' respectively, $W \widehat{\cap} W' = \widehat{proj}_{X \cup X'}(W) \cap \widehat{proj}_{X \cup X'}(W')$.

Let Ω_X denote the set of all possible runs for a set of variables X. An assertion W over X *constrains a set of variables* X' if for each $x' \in X'$, it holds that

$$\begin{cases} W \widehat{\subset} proj_{X \setminus \{x'\}}(W) & X \setminus \{x'\} \neq \emptyset \\ W \subset \Omega_{\{x'\}} & \text{otherwise.} \end{cases} \tag{1}$$

where $\subset$ denotes a proper subset.

2.2 Elements and Architectures

This section starts by introducing the concept of *elements*, corresponding to Heterogeneous Rich *Component* (HRC) in [6,7], in order to model any entity of a CPS, such as software, hardware, or physical entities, as well as to serve as a functional or logical design entity in general, e.g. as a SysML block [26].

Definition 1 (Element). *An* element $\mathbb{E}$ *is an ordered pair* (X, B) *where:*

a) X *is a set of variables, called the* interface *of* $\mathbb{E}$ *and where each* $x \in X$ *is called a* port variable; *and*
b) B *is an assertion over* X, *called the* behavior *of* $\mathbb{E}$.

Port variables model tangible quantities of the element from the perspective of an external observer to the element, and the behavior models the static and dynamic constraints that the element imposes on the port variables, independent of its surroundings. For example, consider a potentiometer $\mathbb{E}_{pot} = (X_{pot}, \mathsf{B}_{pot})$ where $X_{pot} = \{v_{ref}, v_{branch}, v_{gnd}\}$. The port variables v_{ref}, v_{branch}, and v_{gnd} model the reference, branch, and ground voltages, respectively. Furthermore, h models the position $(0 - 100\%)$ of the 'slider' that moves over the resistor and branches the circuit. Given a simplified model where currents are neglected, the behavior B_{pot} can be specified by the equation $h = \frac{v_{branch} - v_{gnd}}{v_{ref} - v_{gnd}}$.

The following describes how a set of elements can be structured in order to model a CPS, its parts, and its surroundings. Similar to e.g. [28,33], such a structure will be referred to as an *architecture*, which, in the present paper, will be denoted with the symbol $\mathscr{A}$. Prior to presenting the formal definition of an architecture, the concept is introduced informally by describing an architecture $\mathscr{A}_{LM-sys}$ of a "Level Meter system" (LM-system) $\mathbb{E}_{LM-sys}$, as shown in Fig. 3a where an element is represented as a rectangle filled with gray with white boxes on its edges that symbolize its port variables and in Fig. 3b where the hierarchical structure of the LM-system is shown as a tree.

As shown in Fig. 3a, the LM-system $\mathbb{E}_{LM-sys}$ consists of a tank $\mathbb{E}_{tank}$ and an electric-system $\mathbb{E}_{E-sys}$. The electric-system $\mathbb{E}_{E-sys}$ consists of the potentiometer $\mathbb{E}_{pot}$ as described in Sec. 2.2, a battery $\mathbb{E}_{bat}$ and a level meter $\mathbb{E}_{lMeter}$ where the

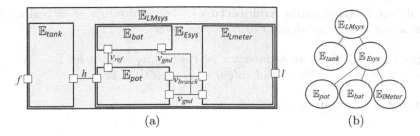

Fig. 3. An architecture $\mathscr{A}_{LM-sys}$ of a "Level Meter system"

behaviors B_{bat} and B_{Lmeter} of $\mathbb{E}_{bat}$ and $\mathbb{E}_{lMeter}$ are specified by the equations $v_{ref} - v_{gnd} = 5V$ and $l = \frac{v_{branch} - v_{gnd}}{5}$, respectively. The slider h is connected to a "floater", trailing the level f in the tank. In this way, the potentiometer $\mathbb{E}_{pot}$ is used as a level sensor to estimate the level in the tank. The estimated level is presented by the level meter $\mathbb{E}_{lMeter}$ where l denotes the presented level.

Notably, since each part of the electric-system $\mathbb{E}_{Esys}$ will have quantities that may not be perceivable when the parts are integrated with each other, e.g. v_{ref}, a port variable x of a child of $\mathbb{E}_{Esys}$ where $x \notin X_{Esys}$ cannot be a member of an interface of a non-descendant of $\mathbb{E}_{Esys}$, e.g. $\mathbb{E}_{tank}$. In order to further relate the individual behaviors of the children of $\mathbb{E}_{Esys}$ with the behavior of $\mathbb{E}_{Esys}$, the individual behaviors are first combined with each other using the intersection operator and subsequently restricted to the interface of $\mathbb{E}_{Esys}$ using the projection operator, in accordance with the Sec. 2.1, i.e., $B_{Esys} = \widehat{proj}_{X_{Esys}}(B_{pot} \widehat{\cap} B_{bat} \widehat{\cap} B_{Lmeter})$.

The formal definition of an architecture now follows:

Definition 2 (Architecture). *An architecture $\mathscr{A}$ is a set of elements organized into a rooted tree, such that:*

(a) *for any non-leaf node $\mathbb{E} = (X, B)$, with children $\{(X_i, B_i)\}_{i=1}^{N}$, it holds that*
$$B = \widehat{proj}_X(\widehat{\bigcap}_{i=1}^{N} B_i); \text{ and}$$
(b) *if there is a child $\mathbb{E}' = (X', B')$ and a non-descendant $\mathbb{E}'' = (X'', B'')$ of $\mathbb{E} = (X, B)$, such that $x \in X'$ and $x \in X''$, then it holds that $x \in X$.*

For convenience, in the context of an architecture, the *environment of an element* $\mathbb{E}$ is considered to be the set of elements in the surroundings of $\mathbb{E}$. That is, as shown in Fig 3, the elements $\mathbb{E}_{bat}$, $\mathbb{E}_{tank}$, and $\mathbb{E}_{lMeter}$ are elements in the environment of the potentiometer $\mathbb{E}_{pot}$.

Definition 3 (Environment of Element). *Given an architecture $\mathscr{A}$, the environment of an element $\mathbb{E} = (X, B)$ in $\mathscr{A}$, denoted $Env_{\mathscr{A}}(\mathbb{E})$, is the set of elements $\{\mathbb{E}_i\}_{i=1}^{N}$ such that $\mathbb{E}_i = (X_i, B_i)$ is either a sibling or a sibling of a proper ancestor of $\mathbb{E}$. Let $B_{Env_{\mathscr{A}}(\mathbb{E})} = \widehat{\bigcap}_{i=1}^{N} B_i$ denote the behavior of $Env_{\mathscr{A}}(\mathbb{E})$.*

Given that an assertion is possibly the empty set (See Sec. 2.1), a realizable architecture $\mathscr{A}$ is defined:

Definition 4 (Realizable Architecture). *An architecture $\mathscr{A}$ is* realizable *if the behavior of the root element of $\mathscr{A}$ is non-empty.*

Proposition 1. *Given an architecture $\mathscr{A}$ containing an element $\mathbb{E} = (X, \mathsf{B})$, it holds that $\mathscr{A}$ is realizable, if and only if $\mathsf{B}_{Env_{\mathscr{A}}(\mathbb{E})} \widehat{\cap} \mathsf{B} \neq \emptyset$.*

The proof of Proposition 1 can be found in [34].

3   Environment-Centric Contracts

As mentioned in Sec. 1, the notion of contracts was first introduced in [1] as a pair of pre and post-conditions, to be used as a specification in object-oriented programming. The principles behind contracts can, however, be traced back to early ideas on proof-methods [2–4] and compositional reasoning/verification [5, 11, 12]. Since then, several frameworks for compositional reasoning [13, 14] have emerged and also techniques to automate the approach have been proposed, see e.g. [35] or [36] for a survey. The work in [1] has been extended to e.g. component-based design [15] and analog systems [16].

In more recent work [6–8, 20], inspired by e.g. [37–40], the use of contracts is extended to serve as a central design philosophy in systems engineering to support the design of CPS. As mentioned in Sec. 1, in a context of CPS design, the conceptual idea of a contract does not prescribe that a contract must necessarily be limited to the interface of an element, thus allowing *environment-centric contracts*. Considering this, an environment-centric contract will, in the following, simply be referred to as a *contract* unless further distinction is necessary.

Definition 5 (Contract). *A contract $\mathcal{C}$ is a pair $(\mathcal{A}, \mathsf{G})$, where*

i) G is an assertion, called guarantee; *and*
ii) $\mathcal{A}$ is a set of assertions $\{A_i\}_{i=1}^{N}$ where each A_i is called an assumption.

The set of variables over which an assumption $A_i \in \mathcal{A}$ or a guarantee G is expressed, is called the *scope* of A_i or G, denoted X_{A_i} and X_{G}, respectively. For the sake of readability, let $A_{\mathcal{A}} = \widehat{\bigcap}_{j=1}^{N} A_i$ and $X_{A_{\mathcal{A}}} = \bigcup_{i=1}^{N} X_{A_i}$.

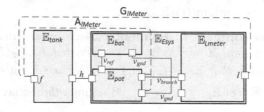

Fig. 4. A contract $\mathcal{C}_{lMeter} = (\{A_{lMeter}\}, \mathsf{G}_{lMeter})$

As an illustrative example, consider the architecture $\mathscr{A}_{LMsys}$ as shown in Fig. 3 and a contract $\mathcal{C}_{lMeter} = (\{A_{lMeter}\}, G_{lMeter})$ for the level meter $\mathbb{E}_{lMeter}$ as shown in Fig. 4 where the dashed lines represent the scopes of A_{lMeter} and G_{lMeter}, respectively. The assertion G_{lMeter}, specified by the equation $l = f$, expresses that the responsibility of $\mathbb{E}_{lMeter}$ is to guarantee that the presented fuel level l, shown by the meter, shall correspond to the level f in the tank. However, in order for the level meter $\mathbb{E}_{lMeter}$ to be able to ensure that G_{lMeter} holds, the voltage measured between v_{branch} and v_{gnd} on $\mathbb{E}_{lMeter}$ must map to a specific level in the tank. That is, the assumption A_{lMeter} is specified by the equation $f = \frac{v_{branch} - v_{gnd}}{5}$.

While contracts in current contract theories [1, 5–9, 11–20] are limited to express the intended behavior of $\mathbb{E}_{lMeter}$ as a relation between the voltage connections v_{branch} and v_{gnd}, and the presented level l, Definition 5 allows assigning the responsibility of achieving the guarantee G_{lMeter} to $\mathbb{E}_{lMeter}$ where G_{lMeter} has a scope that extends outside of the interface of $\mathbb{E}_{lMeter}$.

3.1 Conditions on Element and Environment

In this section, conditions on an element and the environment of the element are presented, where the conditions ensure that the overall property expressed by the guarantee of a contract is met. As previously indicated, a guarantee of a contract $\mathcal{C} = (\mathcal{A}, G)$ expresses an intended property under the responsibility of an element $\mathbb{E}$, given that the environment of the element fulfills the assumptions in an architecture $\mathscr{A}$. Formulated differently, the responsibility of the element is to ensure that the relation $B_{Env_{\mathscr{A}}(\mathbb{E})} \widehat{\cap} B \subseteq G$ holds, given that $B_{Env_{\mathscr{A}}(\mathbb{E})} \subseteq A_{\mathcal{A}}$.

Notably, if $A_{\mathcal{A}} \widehat{\cap} B \subseteq G$, which means that $\mathbb{E}$ *satisfies* $\mathcal{C}$ [6–8, 19, 20], and if $B_{Env_{\mathscr{A}}(\mathbb{E})} \subseteq A_{\mathcal{A}}$, then it follows that $B_{Env_{\mathscr{A}}(\mathbb{E})} \widehat{\cap} B \subseteq G$. Hence, the conditions for the relation $B_{Env_{\mathscr{A}}(\mathbb{E})} \widehat{\cap} B \subseteq G$ to hold in a given architecture, can be partitioned into the relations $A_{\mathcal{A}} \widehat{\cap} B \subseteq G$ and $B_{Env_{\mathscr{A}}(\mathbb{E})} \subseteq A_{\mathcal{A}}$ that express conditions on $\mathbb{E}$ and the environment of $\mathbb{E}$, respectively.

However, these conditions do not ensure that $B_{Env_{\mathscr{A}}(\mathbb{E})} \widehat{\cap} B \neq \emptyset$, which, according to Proposition 1, implies that the architecture is realizable. Since this is a necessary property in order to develop the product in practice, additional conditions must hence be imposed on the environment and on the element in order to ensure that not only the guarantee holds, but also that the architecture is realizable, i.e. that

$$\emptyset \subset B_{Env_{\mathscr{A}}(\mathbb{E})} \widehat{\cap} B \subseteq G. \tag{2}$$

Proposition 2. *Consider a contract $\mathcal{C} = (\mathcal{A}, G)$ and an element $\mathbb{E} = (X, B)$. If $\mathscr{A}$ is an architecture containing $\mathbb{E}$ where $\emptyset \subset B_{Env_{\mathscr{A}}(\mathbb{E})} \widehat{\cap} B \subseteq G$, then it holds that $B_{Env_{\mathscr{A}}(\mathbb{E})} \widehat{\cap} G \neq \emptyset$.*

The proof of Proposition 2 can be found in [34]. Proposition 2 expresses that $B_{Env_{\mathscr{A}}(\mathbb{E})} \widehat{\cap} G \neq \emptyset$ is a necessary condition for the relation (2), which means that it is not enough to simply require that the environment fulfills the assumptions in order for the relation (2) to hold. Now that this necessary condition on the environment has been identified, the following theorem expresses a complementary condition on the element in order for the relation (2) to hold.

Theorem 1. *Consider a contract* $C = (\mathcal{A}, G)$ *and an element* $\mathbb{E} = (X, B)$ *where* $A_{\mathcal{A}} \widehat{\cap} B \widehat{\subseteq} G$. *It holds that* $A_{\mathcal{A}} \widehat{\cap} G \widehat{\subseteq} B$, *if and only if* $\emptyset \subset B \widehat{\cap} B_{Env_{\mathcal{A}}(\mathbb{E})} \widehat{\subseteq} G$ *for each architecture* $\mathcal{A}$ *containing* $\mathbb{E}$ *where* $B_{Env_{\mathcal{A}}(\mathbb{E})} \widehat{\cap} G \neq \emptyset$ *and* $B_{Env_{\mathcal{A}}(\mathbb{E})} \widehat{\subseteq} A_{\mathcal{A}}$.

The proof for Theorem 1 can be found in [34]. The findings in Proposition 2 and Theorem 1 are now summarized in the following central corollary:

Corollary 1. *Given a contract* $C = (\mathcal{A}, G)$ *and an architecture* $\mathcal{A}$ *containing an element* $\mathbb{E} = (X, B)$, *it holds that* $\emptyset \subset B \widehat{\cap} B_{Env_{\mathcal{A}}(\mathbb{E})} \widehat{\subseteq} G$ *if*

i) $A_{\mathcal{A}} \widehat{\cap} B \widehat{\subseteq} G$ *and* $A_{\mathcal{A}} \widehat{\cap} G \widehat{\subseteq} B$, *and*
ii) $B_{Env_{\mathcal{A}}(\mathbb{E})} \widehat{\subseteq} A_{\mathcal{A}}$ *and* $B_{Env_{\mathcal{A}}(\mathbb{E})} \widehat{\cap} G \neq \emptyset$.

Corollary 1 cleanly separates the respective conditions that an element $\mathbb{E}$ and the environment of $\mathbb{E}$ need to meet with respect to a contract C, in order to obtain a realizable architecture where the guarantee of C holds.

3.2   Scoping Constraints

This section presents necessary constraints on the structural properties of a contract in order for the conditions (i) and (ii) of Corollary 1 to hold. The constraints serve as a sanity check in order to determine that a contract is not an unreasonable specification for an element in an architecture.

Consider two contracts C'_{Esys} nor C''_{Esys} for $\mathbb{E}_{Esys}$, as shown in Fig. 5a and 5b, respectively, in the context of the architecture $\mathcal{A}_{LMsys}$ as shown in Fig 3. Since v_{branch} is in both A'_{Esys} and G'_{Esys}, but neither in the interface of an element in the environment of $\mathbb{E}_{Esys}$ nor on the interface of $\mathbb{E}_{Esys}$, the environment of $\mathbb{E}_{Esys}$ cannot fulfill A'_{Esys} and $\mathbb{E}_{Esys}$ cannot satisfy C''_{Esys} in the generic case. This hence means that $\mathbb{E}_{Esys}$ and $Env_{\mathcal{A}_{LMsys}}(\mathbb{E}_{Esys})$ cannot meet the respective conditions (i) and (i) of Corollary 1 with respect to neither C'_{Esys} nor C''_{Esys}.

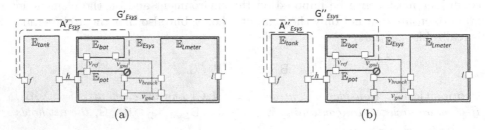

(a)   (b)

Fig. 5. Two contracts C'_{Esys} and C''_{Esys} for $\mathbb{E}_{Esys}$ where the conditions (i) and (ii) of Corollary 1 do not hold in the generic case

Theorem 2. *Given a contract $\mathcal{C} = (\mathcal{A}, \mathsf{G})$, if $\mathcal{A}$ is an architecture containing an element $\mathbb{E}$ where: i) $\mathsf{A}_{\mathcal{A}} \cap \mathsf{B} \subseteq \mathsf{G}$ and $\mathsf{A}_{\mathcal{A}} \cap \mathsf{G} \hat{\subseteq} \mathsf{B}$; and ii) $\mathsf{B}_{Env_{\mathcal{A}}(\mathbb{E})} \hat{\subseteq} \mathsf{A}_{\mathcal{A}}$ and $\mathsf{B}_{Env_{\mathcal{A}}(\mathbb{E})} \cap \mathsf{G} \neq \emptyset$, then it holds that*

a) $X'_{\mathsf{A}_{\mathcal{A}}} \subseteq X_{Env_{\mathcal{A}}(\mathbb{E})}$; and
b) $X'_{\mathsf{G}} \subseteq X_{Env_{\mathcal{A}}(\mathbb{E})} \cup X$,

where $X'_{\mathsf{A}_{\mathcal{A}}} \subseteq X_{\mathsf{A}_{\mathcal{A}}}$ and $X'_{\mathsf{G}} \subseteq X_{\mathsf{G}}$ are the sets of variables constrained by $\mathsf{A}_{\mathcal{A}}$ and G, respectively, and $X_{Env_{\mathcal{A}}(\mathbb{E})}$ denotes the union of the interfaces of the elements in the environment of $\mathbb{E}$ in $\mathcal{A}$.

The proof of Theorem 2 can be found in [34]. The relations (a) and (b) of Theorem 2 express necessary conditions on the structural properties of a contract $\mathcal{C} = (\mathcal{A}, \mathsf{G})$ in order for an element and its environment to meet the conditions (i) and (ii) of Corollary 1 in the context of an architecture. Considering Theorem 2, a contract $\mathcal{C}$ is said to be *scope-compliant* for $\mathbb{E} = (X, \mathsf{B})$ in an architecture $\mathcal{A}$, if the respective scopes of $\mathsf{A}_{\mathcal{A}}$ and G are subsets of $X_{Env_{\mathcal{A}}(\mathbb{E})}$ and $X_{Env_{\mathcal{A}}(\mathbb{E})} \cup X$.

Definition 6 (Scope-Compliant Contract for Element). *A contract $(\mathcal{A}, \mathsf{G})$ is* scope-compliant *for an element $\mathbb{E} = (X, \mathsf{B})$ in an architecture $\mathcal{A}$, if*

a) $X_{\mathsf{A}_{\mathcal{A}}} \subseteq X_{Env_{\mathcal{A}}(\mathbb{E})}$; and
b) $X_{\mathsf{G}} \subseteq X_{Env_{\mathcal{A}}(\mathbb{E})} \cup X$.

Under the assumption that the scopes of $\mathsf{A}_{\mathcal{A}}$ and G are equal to the set of variables which they constrain, relations (a) and (b) of Definition 6 hold for all cases where the relations (i) and (ii) of Theorem 2 also hold. This includes all of the practical cases since the relations (i) and (ii) of Theorem 2 still hold regardless of the inclusion of all variables that are not constrained by $\mathsf{A}_{\mathcal{A}}$ and G in $X_{\mathsf{A}_{\mathcal{A}}}$ and X_{G}, respectively.

Regarding the examples shown in Fig. 5a and 5b, since $X_{\mathsf{A}'_{Esys}} \not\subseteq X_{tank}$ and $X_{\mathsf{G}''_{Esys}} \not\subseteq X_{tank} \cup X_{Esys}$, in accordance with Definition 6, neither $\mathcal{C}'_{Esys}$ nor $\mathcal{C}''_{Esys}$ is scope-compliant for $\mathbb{E}_{Esys}$ in $\mathcal{A}_{LMsys}$. Definition 6 hence provides a means to detect that both the contracts $\mathcal{C}'_{Esys}$ and $\mathcal{C}''_{Esys}$ are unreasonable specifications for $\mathbb{E}_{Esys}$ in $\mathcal{A}_{LMsys}$ considering the scopes of the assumptions and the guarantees.

4   Properties of Environment-Centric Contracts

Since contracts in current contract theories [1, 5–9, 11–20] are limited to element interfaces, definitions that specify whether a contract or a set of contracts has a certain property or not, are also limited to the cases where contracts are limited to the interfaces of elements. Hence, in order to support the use of environment-centric contracts, this section presents revised definitions of the properties *consistency* [6, 7, 19], *compatibility* [6, 7, 19], and *dominance* [8, 20] of contracts as defined in current contract theories, as well as conditions for when such properties hold.

4.1   Consistency and Compatibility

In order to get a better understanding of when the properties *consistency* [6,7,19] and *compatibility* [6,7,19] are relevant, a scenario is examined where a contract is used to outsource the development of an element $\mathbb{E}$ with an interface X. Specifically, the scenario can be described in three phases:

1) a contract $(\mathcal{A}, G)$ and an interface specification X are handed from the client to a supplier;
2) an element $\mathbb{E} = (X, B)$ is delivered to the client that meets the condition (i) of Corollary 1; and
3) the client integrates the element $\mathbb{E}$ with a set of elements to form an architecture where the environment of $\mathbb{E}$ meets the condition (ii) of Corollary 1.

As expressed in phases (1-2), the client would expect the supplier to deliver an element that meets the condition (i) of Corollary 1 with respect to the contract $\mathcal{C}$. However, in order for the supplier to be able to meet the demands from the client, the supplier would expect that the contract is such that there actually exists an element that meets the condition (i) of Corollary 1. If such an element exists, then the contract will be referred to as a *consistent* contract.

Furthermore, in order for the client to be able to complete phase (3), at least one architecture containing an element $\mathbb{E} = (X, B)$ where the environment of $\mathbb{E}$ meets the condition (ii) of Corollary 1, needs to exist. If such an architecture exists, then the contract will be referred to as a *compatible* contract.

Now that the concepts of consistency and compatibility have been introduced in the context of a scenario, formal definitions follow.

Definition 7 (Consistent Contract). *A contract $(\mathcal{A}, G)$ is consistent with respect to a set of variables X if there exists an element $\mathbb{E} = (X, B)$ such that $A_{\mathcal{A}} \widehat{\cap} B \widehat{\subseteq} G$ and $A_{\mathcal{A}} \widehat{\cap} G \widehat{\subseteq} B$.*

Definition 7 is essentially a revision of the definition of consistency in [19] by considering the condition (i) of Corollary 1. Definition 7 is also closely related to definitions in [6,7], but where Definition 7, in contrast to the definitions in [6,7], allows contracts that are not limited to the interface and are further not limited to elements with defined inputs and outputs.

Theorem 3. *A contract $(\mathcal{A}, G)$ is consistent with respect to a set of variables X, if and only if $A_{\mathcal{A}} \widehat{\cap} \widehat{proj}_X(A_{\mathcal{A}} \widehat{\cap} G) \widehat{\subseteq} G$.*

The proof of Theorem 3 can be found in [34]. Given a contract $\mathcal{C} = (\mathcal{A}, G)$, Theorem 3 supports a way of verifying that $\mathcal{C}$ is consistent with respect to X or not, without having to go through all possible elements with an interface X in order to determine whether there exists an element $\mathbb{E} = (X, B)$ that meets the conditions (i) of Corollary 1.

Corollary 2. *Given a consistent contract $\mathcal{C} = (\mathcal{A}, G)$ with respect to a set of variables X, it holds that $X'_G \subseteq X_{A_{\mathcal{A}}} \cup X$, where $X'_G \subseteq X_G$ is the set of variables constrained by G.*

The proof of Corollary 2 can be found in [34]. Similar to Theorem 2, Corollary 2 expresses a structural property of $\mathcal{C}$ that constitutes a necessary condition in order for $\mathcal{C}$ to be consistent with respect to X. In the generic case, i.e. when $X'_\mathsf{G} = X_\mathsf{G}$, the scope of G must be a subset of $X_{\mathsf{A}_\mathcal{A}} \cup X$.

Definition 8 (Compatible Contract). *A contract $(\mathcal{A}, \mathsf{G})$ is compatible with respect to a set of variables X if there exists an architecture $\mathcal{A}$ containing an element $\mathbb{E} = (X, \mathsf{B})$, such that $\mathsf{B}_{Env_\mathcal{A}(\mathbb{E})} \widehat{\cap} \mathsf{G} \neq \emptyset$ and $\mathsf{B}_{Env_\mathcal{A}(\mathbb{E})} \widehat{\subseteq} \mathsf{A}_\mathcal{A}$.*

Definition 8 is essentially a revision of the definitions of compatibility in [19] by considering the condition (ii) of Corollary 1. Definition 8 is also closely related to the definitions of compatibility in [6,7], but where Definition 8, in contrast to the definitions in [6,7], allows contracts that are not limited to the interface and are further not limited to elements with defined inputs and outputs.

Theorem 4. *A contract $(\mathcal{A}, \mathsf{G})$ is compatible with respect to a set of variables X if and only if $\mathsf{A}_\mathcal{A} \widehat{\cap} \mathsf{G} \neq \emptyset$.*

The proof of Theorem 4 can be found in [34]. Given a contract $(\mathcal{A}, \mathsf{G})$ and a set of variables X, Theorem 4 supports a way of verifying that $(\mathcal{A}, \mathsf{G})$ is compatible with respect to X or not, without having to go through each architecture $\mathcal{A}$ containing an element $\mathbb{E} = (X, \mathsf{B})$ in order to determine whether there exists an architecture $\mathcal{A}$ where the condition (ii) of Corollary 1 hold.

4.2 Dominance

Prior to formally presenting the definition of dominance, a scenario is presented in the context of an Original Equipment Manufacturer (OEM)/supplier chain in order to provide an understanding of when the property is relevant:

1) a contract $\mathcal{C} = (\mathcal{A}, \mathsf{G})$ is decomposed into a set of contracts $\{\mathcal{C}_i\}_{i=1}^N$ where each contract $\mathcal{C}_i$ and an interface specification X_i is handed from the OEM to either a development team within the organization or to a supplier;
2) each development team or supplier develops an element $\mathbb{E}_i = (X_i, \mathsf{B}_i)$ that meets the condition (i) of Corollary 1 with respect to $\mathcal{C}_i$; and
3) the OEM integrates the set of elements $\mathbb{E}_i$ with each other to form an element $\mathbb{E}$ that meets the condition (i) of Corollary 1 with respect to $\mathcal{C}$.

As expressed in phase (3), the overall intent is to obtain an element $\mathbb{E}$ that meets the condition (i) of Corollary 1 with respect to $\mathcal{C}$. In order to achieve this, the intent is hence to decompose the contract $\mathcal{C}$ into the set $\{\mathcal{C}_i\}_{i=1}^N$ such that if each $\mathbb{E}_i$ meets the condition (i) of Corollary 1 with respect to $\mathcal{C}_i$, then $\mathbb{E}$ meets the condition (i) of Corollary 1 with respect to $\mathcal{C}$. If such a property holds, then $\mathcal{C}$ is said to *dominate* the set of contracts $\{\mathcal{C}_i\}_{i=1}^N$.

Notably, regardless of whether each child $\mathbb{E}_i$ of $\mathbb{E}$ meets the condition (i) of Corollary 1 or not, it might not be possible for $\mathbb{E}$ to meet the condition (i) of Corollary 1 with respect to $\mathcal{C}$. Specifically, this happens if G constrains variables on the interface of an element $\mathbb{E}_i$ that are not on the interface of $\mathbb{E}$. In accordance with Definition 6, if C is scope-compliant for $\mathbb{E}$ in $\mathscr{A}$, then G is not allowed to constrain any subset of $\bigcup_{i=1}^{N} X_i \setminus X$.

Definition 9 (Dominance of Contracts). *Given a set of variables X, a contract C and a set of contracts $\{C_i\}_{i=1}^{N}$, the contract C dominates $\{C_i\}_{i=1}^{N}$ if for any architecture $\mathscr{A}$ where C is scope-compliant for an element $\mathbb{E} = (X, B)$ in $\mathscr{A}$ and where $\{\mathbb{E}_i = (X_i, B)\}_{i=1}^{N}$ is the set of children of $\mathbb{E}$, it holds that*

$$A_{\mathscr{A}_i} \cap B_i \subseteq G_i \text{ and } A_{\mathscr{A}_i} \cap G_i \subseteq B_i \text{ for each } i \implies A_{\mathscr{A}} \cap B \subseteq G \text{ and } A_{\mathscr{A}} \cap G \subseteq B.$$

Definition 9 is essentially a generalization of the definitions of dominance presented in [8,20] by relying on the notion of scope-compliance as presented in Definition 6 and by considering the condition (i) of Corollary 1.

Decomposition Structures. This section introduces a graph, called a *decomposition structure*, in order to find a decomposition of a contract C into a set of contracts $\{C_i\}_{i=1}^{N}$ to achieve the property as expressed in Definition 9. Prior to presenting the formal definition of a decomposition structure, the concept is introduced informally by structuring a decomposition of a contract C_{Esys} into a set of contracts $\{C_{pot}, C_{bat}, C_{lMeter}\}$. The contracts represent the specifications of the parts of an electric-system of an LM-system, e.g. the one shown in Fig. 3.

Consider that the assumptions and the guarantees of each contract in the set $\{C_{Esys}, C_{pot}, C_{bat}, C_{lMeter}\}$ are organized as nodes in a directed graph, as shown in Fig. 6 where the boxes with rounded corners and dashed edges represent an hierarchical structure of contracts. The set of incoming arcs to a guarantee G from a set of assumptions $\mathscr{A}$, represents that $\mathscr{A}$ and G are in the same contract, e.g. the arc from A_{Esys} to the guarantee G_{Esys} represents the contract $(\{A_{Esys}\}, G_{Esys})$.

The set of incoming arcs to an assumption A from a set of assertions $\{W_i\}_{i=1}^{N}$ where W_i is either an assumption or a guarantee, represents the intention of $\bigcap_{i=1}^{N} W_i \subseteq A$. For example, the arc to A_{pot2} from the assumption A_{Esys}, represents the intent of $A_{Esys} \subseteq A_{pot2}$. The set of incoming arcs to a guarantee G from a set of guarantees $\{G_j\}_{j=1}^{M}$ represents the intent of $\bigcap_{j=1}^{M} G_j \subseteq G$. For example, the arc from the guarantee G_{lMeter} to G_{Esys}, represents the intent of $G_{lMeter} \subseteq G_{Esys}$.

The formal definition of a decomposition structure now follows:

Definition 10 (Decomposition Structure). *A decomposition structure $\mathfrak{D}$ of a contract $(\mathscr{A}, G)$ into a set of contracts $\{(\mathscr{A}_i, G_i)\}_{i=1}^{N}$ is a Directed Acyclic Graph (DAG), such that:*

a) *the guarantees G_i, the assumptions in each set $\mathscr{A}_i$, the assumptions in $\mathscr{A}$, and the guarantee G are the nodes in $\mathfrak{D}$;*

b) *G has no successors and at least one G_i is a direct predecessor of G;*

c) *G_i is the only direct successor of each assumption in $\mathscr{A}_i$; and each assumption in $\mathscr{A}_i$ has at least one predecessor;*

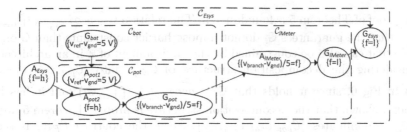

Fig. 6. A decomposition structure of $\mathcal{C}_{Esys}$ into $\{\mathcal{C}_{pot}, \mathcal{C}_{bat}, \mathcal{C}_{lMeter}\}$

d) each G_i has a direct successor that it is either an assumption in $\mathcal{A}_k$ where $k \neq i$ or G;

e) G is a direct successor of each assumption in $\mathcal{A}$; and if an assumption in $\mathcal{A}$ has a direct successor that is not G, then it is an assumption in $\mathcal{A}_i$.

Sufficient Conditions of Dominance. As previously indicated, a decomposition structure represents the intended dependencies between the assumptions and guarantees of a set of contracts. Given that the intended dependencies are, in fact, true, a decomposition structure will be referred to as *proper*.

Given a decomposition structure $\mathfrak{D}$, let $dPred()$ denote a function that takes a node W in $\mathfrak{D}$ as input and returns the direct predecessors of W.

Definition 11 (Proper Decomposition Structure). *A decomposition structure of a contract $(\mathcal{A}, G)$ into a set of contracts $\{(\{A_{ij}\}_{j=1}^{M_i}, G_i)\}_{i=1}^{N}$ is proper if:*

$$\bigcap_{\substack{W \in dPred(G), \\ W \in \{G_i\}_{i=1}^{N}}} W \,\widehat{\subseteq}\, G \text{ and } \bigcap_{W \in dPred(A_{ij})} W \,\widehat{\subseteq}\, A_{ij}, \text{ for each } i, j.$$

For example, since the relations $G_{bat} \,\widehat{\subseteq}\, A_{pot1}$, $A_{Esys} \,\widehat{\subseteq}\, A_{pot2}$, $G_{pot} \,\widehat{\subseteq}\, A_{lMeter}$, and $G_{lMeter} \,\widehat{\subseteq}\, G_{Esys}$ holds in Fig. 6, the decomposition structure is proper according to Definition 11.

However, even if a decomposition structure of a contract $(\mathcal{A}, G)$ into a set of contracts $\{(\mathcal{A}_i, G_i)\}_{i=1}^{N}$ is proper, it does not mean that $(\mathcal{A}, G)$ dominates $\{(\mathcal{A}_i, G_i)\}_{i=1}^{N}$. The reason for this is that a guarantee G_i can impose harder constraints on a variable than G and this variable can also be constrained by the environment of an element $\mathbb{E} = (X, B)$ in an architecture $\mathscr{A}$. This means that even if each element $\mathbb{E}_i$ meets the condition (i) of Corollary 1 with respect to $(\mathcal{A}_i, G_i)$, it cannot be ensured that it holds that $A_{\mathcal{A}} \cap G \,\widehat{\subseteq}\, B$ where $\mathbb{E}$ is the parent of each $\mathbb{E}_i$ in $\mathscr{A}$.

Now that the need for another condition, in addition to the decomposition being proper, has been introduced, sufficient conditions for dominance follow.

Theorem 5. *Given a set of variables X, a contract $\mathcal{C}$ and a set of contracts $\{\mathcal{C}_i\}_{i=1}^{N}$, the contract $\mathcal{C}$ dominates $\{\mathcal{C}_i\}_{i=1}^{N}$, if $G \,\widehat{\subseteq}\, \widehat{proj}_{X_{A_{\mathcal{A}}} \cup X}(\bigcap_{i=1}^{N} G_i)$ and there exists a proper decomposition structure of $\mathcal{C}$ into $\{\mathcal{C}_i\}_{i=1}^{N}$.*

The proof of Theorem 5 is found in [34]. The relation $G \widehat{\subseteq} \widehat{proj}_{X_{A_a} \cup X}(\widehat{\bigcap}_{i=1}^{N} G_i)$ ensures that the guarantees G_i do not impose harder constraints than G on any variable that can also be constrained by the environment of $\mathbb{E}$ in an architecture.

Considering the decomposition structure of C_{Esys} into $\{C_{pot}, C_{bat}, C_{lMeter}\}$ shown in Fig 6, since it holds that $G = \widehat{proj}_{X_{A_a} \cup X}(\widehat{\bigcap}_{i=1}^{N} G_i)$ and it has been previously shown that the decomposition structure is proper, Theorem 5 implies that C_{Esys} dominates $\{C_{pot}, C_{bat}, C_{lMeter}\}$. Since the contract C_{Esys} is scope-compliant for $\mathbb{E}_{Esys}$ in the architecture shown in Fig. 3 according to Definition 6, and each child $\mathbb{E}_i$ of $\mathbb{E}_{Esys}$ meets the condition (i) of Corollary 1 with respect to $C_i \in \{C_{pot}, C_{bat}, C_{lMeter}\}$, in accordance with Definition 9, it can be inferred that $\mathbb{E}_{Esys}$ meets the condition (i) of Corollary 1 with respect to C_{Esys}.

Remark 1 (Circular Reasoning). Since a decomposition structure is an *acyclic* graph, the use of circular argumentation [13, 20, 41] is avoided.

5   Conclusion

As discussed in Sec. 1, in order to be able to express that the responsibility of an element is to achieve an overall intended property of a system, current contract theories need to be generalized to *environment-centric contracts*. In order to achieve this, a theoretical framework was first introduced in Sec. 2 where the concepts *element* and *architecture* model a CPS and its parts.

Building on the theoretical framework, in Sec. 3, the constraint that a contract must be specified over the interface of an element was relaxed and Corollary 1 explicitly declares what conditions an element and an environment need to meet, respectively, in order to achieve a realizable architecture where the guarantee holds. Furthermore in Sec. 3, the notion of a *scope-compliant* contract was introduced that serves as a sanity check that a contract is not an unreasonable specification for an element in an architecture.

Building on Corollary 1, revised definitions of *consistency*, *compatibility*, and *dominance* were presented in Sec. 4. Complementing the definitions, Theorems 3 and 4 express necessary and sufficient conditions of consistency and compatibility, respectively, and Theorem 5 expresses sufficient conditions of dominance based on a graph, called a *decomposition structure*.

By providing revised definitions of properties of contracts and complementary theorems and definitions for practical application, the present paper fully generalizes current contract theories to environment-centric contracts. As mentioned in Sec. 1, such a generalization provides a much needed support for practical engineering and a necessary capability to properly express safety requirements.

References

1. Meyer, B.: Applying "Design by Contract". IEEE Computer 25, 40–51 (1992)
2. Misra, J., Chandy, K.M.: Proofs of networks of processes. IEEE Transactions on Software Engineering SE-7(4), 417–426 (1981)

3. Hoare, C.A.R.: An Axiomatic Basis for Computer Programming. Commun. ACM 12(10), 576–580 (1969)
4. Dijkstra, E.W.: Guarded Commands, Nondeterminacy and Formal Derivation of Programs. Commun. ACM 18(8), 453–457 (1975)
5. Jones, C.B.: Specification and Design of (Parallel) Programs. In: Mason, R.E.A. (ed.) Information Processing 1983. IFIP Congress Series, Paris, France, vol. 9, pp. 321–332. North-Holland (1983)
6. Benveniste, A., Caillaud, B., Ferrari, A., Mangeruca, L., Passerone, R., Sofronis, C.: Multiple Viewpoint Contract-Based Specification and Design. In: de Boer, F.S., Bonsangue, M.M., Graf, S., de Roever, W.-P. (eds.) FMCO 2007. LNCS, vol. 5382, pp. 200–225. Springer, Heidelberg (2008)
7. Sangiovanni-Vincentelli, A.L., Damm, W., Passerone, R.: Taming Dr. Frankenstein: Contract-Based Design for Cyber-Physical Systems. Eur. J. Control 18(3), 217–238 (2012)
8. Bauer, S.S., David, A., Hennicker, R., Guldstrand Larsen, K., Legay, A., Nyman, U., Wąsowski, A.: Moving from specifications to contracts in component-based design. In: de Lara, J., Zisman, A. (eds.) FASE 2012. LNCS, vol. 7212, pp. 43–58. Springer, Heidelberg (2012)
9. Chen, T., Chilton, C., Jonsson, B., Kwiatkowska, M.: A compositional specification theory for component behaviours. In: Seidl, H. (ed.) ESOP 2012. LNCS, vol. 7211, pp. 148–168. Springer, Heidelberg (2012)
10. Lee, E.: Cyber Physical Systems: Design Challenges. In: 11th IEEE Int. Symp. on Object Oriented Real-Time Distributed Computing (ISORC), pp. 363–369 (2008)
11. Pnueli, A.: Logics and models of concurrent systems, pp. 123–144. Springer-Verlag New York, Inc., New York (1985)
12. Shurek, G., Grumberg, O.: The modular framework of computer-aided verification. In: Clarke, E.M., Kurshan, R.P. (eds.) CAV 1990. LNCS, vol. 531, pp. 214–223. Springer, Heidelberg (1991)
13. Abadi, M., Lamport, L.: Composing specifications. ACM Trans. Program. Lang. Syst. 15(1), 73–132 (1993)
14. Alur, R., et al.: Mocha: Modularity in model checking. In: Hu, A.J., Vardi, M.Y. (eds.) CAV 1998. LNCS, vol. 1427, pp. 521–525. Springer, Heidelberg (1998)
15. Giese, H.: Contract-based Component System Design. In: Thirty-Third Annual Hawaii Int. Conf. on System Sciences (HICSS-33). IEEE Press, Maui (2000)
16. Sun, X., et al.: Contract-based System-Level Composition of Analog Circuits. In: 46th ACM/IEEE Design Automation Conf., DAC 2009, pp. 605–610 (July 2009)
17. Delahaye, B., Caillaud, B., Legay, A.: Probabilistic contracts: A compositional reasoning methodology for the design of systems with stochastic and/or non-deterministic aspects. Form. Methods Syst. Des. 38(1), 1–32 (2011)
18. Goessler, G., Raclet, J.-B.: Modal contracts for component-based design. In: Proc. of the 2009 7th IEEE Int. Conf. on Software Eng. and Formal Methods, SEFM 2009, pp. 295–303. IEEE Computer Society, Washington, DC (2009)
19. Benveniste, A., et al.: Contracts for System Design. Rapport de recherche RR-8147, INRIA (November 2012)
20. Quinton, S., Graf, S.: Contract-based verification of hierarchical systems of components. In: Sixth IEEE International Conference on Software Engineering and Formal Methods, SEFM 2008, pp. 377–381 (November 2008)
21. Chandrasekaran, B., Josephson, J.R.: Function in device representation (2000)
22. Umeda, Y., et al.: Function, behaviour, and structure. Applications of Artificial Intelligence in Engineering 1, 177–194 (1990)

23. Liang, F., et al.: Model-based requirement verification: A case study. In: Proc. of the 9th Int. Modelica Conf. (2012)
24. Schamai, W., et al.: Towards unified system modeling and simulation with modelicaml: Modeling of executable behavior using graphical notations. In: 7th Modelica Conference 2009. University Electronic Press (2009)
25. Boulanger, J.-L., Dao, V.Q.: Requirements engineering in a model-based methodology for embedded automotive software. In: IEEE Int. Conf. on Research, Innovation and Vision for the Future, RIVF 2008, pp. 263–268 (July 2008)
26. Friedenthal, S., Moore, A., Steiner, R.: A Practical Guide to SysML: Systems Modeling Language. Morgan Kaufmann Publishers Inc., San Francisco (2008)
27. IEC 61508: Functional safety of electrical/electronic/programmable electronic safety-related systems (2010)
28. ISO 26262: Road vehicles-Functional safety (2011)
29. Westman, J., Nyberg, M.: A Reference Example on the Specification of Safety Requirements using ISO 26262. In: Roy, M. (ed.) Proc. of Workshop DECS of SafeComp., France, NA (September 2013)
30. Westman, J., Nyberg, M., Törngren, M.: Structuring Safety Requirements in ISO 26262 Using Contract Theory. In: Bitsch, F., Guiochet, J., Kaâniche, M. (eds.) SAFECOMP. LNCS, vol. 8153, pp. 166–177. Springer, Heidelberg (2013)
31. SPEEDS: SPEculative and Exploratory Design in Sys. Eng. (2006-2009)
32. Codd, E.F.: A Relational Model of Data for Large Shared Data Banks. Commun. ACM 13(6), 377–387 (1970)
33. ISO/IEC/IEEE 42010: System and software eng. - Architecture description (2011)
34. Westman, J., Nyberg, M.: Environment-Centric Contracts for the Design of Cyber Physical Systems. Technical Report urn:nbn:se:kth:diva-143401, KTH (2014)
35. Păsăreanu, C.S., et al.: Learning to divide and conquer: Applying the l* algorithm to automate assume-guarantee reasoning. Form. Methods Syst. Des. 32(3), 175–205 (2008)
36. Cobleigh, J.M., Avrunin, G.S., Clarke, L.A.: Breaking up is hard to do: An evaluation of automated assume-guarantee reasoning. ACM Trans. Softw. Eng. Methodol. 17(2), 7:1–7:52 (2008)
37. Back, R.-J., Wright, J.V.: Contracts, Games and Refinement. In: Information and Computation, p. 200. Elsevier (1997)
38. Dill, D.L.: Trace Theory for Automatic Hierarchical Verification of Speed-Independent Circuits. In: Proceedings of the Fifth MIT Conference on Advanced Research in VLSI, pp. 51–65. MIT Press, Cambridge (1988)
39. de Alfaro, L., Henzinger, T.A.: Interface Theories for Component-based Design. In: Henzinger, T.A., Kirsch, C.M. (eds.) EMSOFT 2001. LNCS, vol. 2211, pp. 148–165. Springer, Heidelberg (2001)
40. Negulescu, R.: Process Spaces. In: Palamidessi, C. (ed.) CONCUR 2000. LNCS, vol. 1877, pp. 199–213. Springer, Heidelberg (2000)
41. Cofer, D., Gacek, A., Miller, S., Whalen, M.W., LaValley, B., Sha, L.: Compositional verification of architectural models. In: Goodloe, A.E., Person, S. (eds.) NFM 2012. LNCS, vol. 7226, pp. 126–140. Springer, Heidelberg (2012)

Removing Redundancies and Deducing Equivalences in UML Class Diagrams

Azzam Maraee[1,2]* and Mira Balaban[1]

[1] Computer Science Department, Ben-Gurion University of the Negev, Israel
[2] Deutsche Telekom Laboratories, Ben-Gurion University of the Negev, Israel
mari@cs.bgu.ac.il, mira@cs.bgu.ac.il

Abstract. The emerging Model-driven Engineering approach puts models at the heart of the software development process. The Class Diagram language is central within the UML. Automated support for class diagrams involves identification and repair of *correctness* and *quality* problems.

This paper presents methods and rules for improving class diagram quality. The paper introduces formal semantics for class diagrams, which distinguishes between *existential* to *universal* constraints, and defines redundancy of existential constraints. It provides and analyzes algorithms for removing redundancy of multiplicity and generalization-set constraints in class diagrams with class hierarchy, qualifier, association class, aggregation/composition, and inter-association constraints, and presents inference rules for deducing element equivalence. All methods are under implementation in the *FiniteSatUSE* tool.

1 Introduction

The central role of models in the emerging *Model-driven Engineering* approach calls for deep formal study of models, so that tools can provide an inclusive support to users. It is essential to have precise, consistent and correct models. Models should provide reliable support for the designed systems, and be subject to stringent quality verification and control criteria.

Class Diagrams are probably the most important and best understood model among all UML models. The Class Diagrams language allows complex constraints on its components. But the interaction among these constraints can create correctness and quality problems that users cannot observe without assistance. For example, the class diagram in Figure 1a includes (redundant) multiplicity constraints that cannot be realized, i.e., are not used in any legal instance (a system state). The minimum cardinalities of properties fm_1, tr, ca and the maximum cardinalities of properties cr, ev, htr_2, are redundant. Figure 1b presents an equivalent class diagram without redundancy of multiplicity constraints: All multiplicity constraints are either increased to meet the corresponding maximum, or decreased to meet the corresponding minimum. In order to develop tool support for class diagrams there is a need for a formal detailed study of the constraints and their interactions.

---

* Supported by the Lynn and William Frankel Center for Computer Sciences.

J. Dingel et al. (Eds.): MODELS 2014, LNCS 8767, pp. 235–251, 2014.
© Springer International Publishing Switzerland 2014

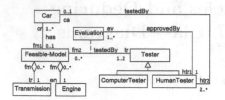
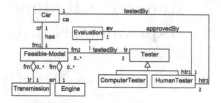

(a) A class diagram with redundancy of multiplicity constraints

(b) A tight class diagram, equivalent to Figure 1a

Fig. 1. A class diagram with its tightened equivalent version

Detection of redundant constraints and deduction of implied element equivalence are of utmost importance for model based software. Yet, although correctness of class diagrams has been studied in quite a few works, there is very little research on class-diagram constraints [1,2,3,4,5]. In [6] we started research in this direction with a complete method for removing redundant boundary cardinalities in a simple subset of UML class diagrams.

In this paper we develop methods for removing wider constraint redundancy and embark on equivalence deduction. We prove gap properties for multiplicity constraints, provide a complete wide extension for the previous method, remove redundancy in generalization-set constraints and suggest inference rules for element equivalence. For this purpose we present, in Section 2, formal semantics for class diagrams, with distinguishing between *existential* to *universal* constraints, and define redundancy of existential constraints. Section 3 introduces methods for removal of redundancy of multiplicity constraints; Section 4 handles redundancy of generalization-set constraints, and Section 5 introduces and analyzes basic inference rules. Section 6 shortly summarizes related work and concludes the paper.

2   Abstract Syntax and Semantics of Class Diagrams

We provide a formal set-based semantics, following the OMG specification [7,8]. Due to scope limitations we omit reference to class attributes, n-ary associations and to the constraints *association-class hierarchy, non-unique associations, redefinition, union* and *XOR*. Operations are not discussed since without contracts (OCL [9,10]) or other models, their effect on the semantics is not defined.

Abstract syntax:
A class diagram is a tuple $\langle \mathcal{C}, \mathcal{A}, \mathcal{P}, \mathcal{M}, \mathcal{Q}, \mathcal{DT}, \mathcal{Mappings}, \mathcal{Constraints} \rangle$, where $\mathcal{C}$ is a set of *class* symbols, $\mathcal{A}$ is a set of *association* symbols, $\mathcal{P}$ is a set of *property (association end)* symbols, $\mathcal{M}$ is a set of *multiplicity* symbols, $\mathcal{Q}$ is a set of *qualifier* symbols, and $\mathcal{DT}$ is a set of *data type* symbols.
The $\mathcal{Mappings}$ **are:**

- **Association mappings:** $prop_1, prop_2 : \mathcal{A} \to \mathcal{P}$ are injections that satisfy $prop_1(\mathcal{A}) \cap prop_2(\mathcal{A}) = \emptyset$ and $prop_1(\mathcal{A}) \cup prop_2(\mathcal{A}) = \mathcal{P}$ (where $prop_i(\mathcal{A}) = \{prop_i(a) | a \in \mathcal{A}\}$).
  Notation: For $a \in \mathcal{A}$ $props(a) = \langle prop_1(a), prop_2(a) \rangle$; for $p \in \mathcal{P}$ $assoc(p)$ denotes its unique association, and for $props(a) = \langle p_1, p_2 \rangle$, $assoc(p_1, p_2) = a$.
- **Property (association end) mappings:**
  1. $inverse : \mathcal{P} \to \mathcal{P}$ is a bijective mapping such that for $p \in \mathcal{P}$, $inverse(p) = p'$, where $assoc(p) = a$ and $props(a) = \langle p, p' \rangle$ or $props(a) = \langle p', p \rangle$. That is, $inverse(p)$ assigns to every property p its unique dual in its association. Note that $inverse$ is well defined since for each property p $assoc(p)$ is defined and maps p to a single association a, and $props(a)$ identifies exactly two properties, one of which is p.
     Notation: $inverse(p)$ is denoted p^{-1}. It satisfies $p = (p^{-1})^{-1}$, $p \neq p^{-1}$.
  2. $source : \mathcal{P} \to \mathcal{C}$ and $target : \mathcal{P} \to \mathcal{C}$ are mappings of properties to classes such that for a property $p \in \mathcal{P}$, $target(p) = source(p^{-1})$.
     Notation: For $a \in \mathcal{A}$, $class_1(a) = target(prop_1(a))$, $class_2(a) = target(prop_2(a))$, and $classes(a) = \langle class_1(a), class_2(a) \rangle$.
  3. $domain\_size : \mathcal{DT} \to \mathbb{N} \cup \{\infty\}$ is a size (cardinality) mapping for the data type symbols. The default data type cardinality is ∞.
  4. $qualifier : \mathcal{P} \to \mathcal{Q} \times \mathcal{DT}$ is a multi-valued mapping that assigns a (possibly empty) set of qualifier data type pairs to a property. The assigned property is called a *qualified property* and its association is a *qualified association*.
     For a property p, with $min(p) > 0$, for every qualifier $\langle q, Dt \rangle \in qualifier$ (p), $domain\_size(Dt) \neq \infty$.
     In Figure 1a, cr is fm_1^{-1}, $target(fm_1) = source(cr) = Feasible\text{-}Model$, $source(fm_1) = target(cr) = Car$, $props(has) = \langle fm_1, cr \rangle$, $assoc(cr) = assoc(fm_1) = assoc(fm_1, cr) = has$, and $classes(has) = \langle Car, Feasible\text{-}Model \rangle$. In Figure 2, $qualifier(p_2) = \{\langle q_1, D_1 \rangle, \langle q_2, D_2 \rangle\}$, and $domain\_size(D_1) = domain\_size(D_2) = \infty$.

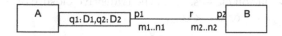

Fig. 2. A qualified association

- **Multiplicity mappingss:** $mul : \mathcal{P} \to \mathcal{M}$ is an injection that assigns a unique multiplicity to every property symbol. A multiplicity symbol is associated with a minimum and a maximum cardinalities: $min\_cardinality : \mathcal{M} \to \mathbb{N} \cup \{0\}$ and $max\_cardinality : \mathcal{M} \to \mathbb{N} \cup \{*\}$, such that if $max\_cardinality(mul(p)) \neq *$, then $min\_cardinality(mul(p)) \leq max\_cardinality(mul(p))$. A compact notation for the minimum and maximum cardinalities of a property: $min(p) = min\_cardinality(mul(p))$, $max(p) = max\_cardinality(mul(p))$. The natural numbers in the interval $[min(p), max(p)]$ (consider $*$ as ∞) are termed *cardinalities* of p, and $min(p), max(p)$ are the *boundary cardinalities*.

For simplicity we use a compact symbolic notation that captures all symbols related to an association. For example, the association *has* in Figure 1a is denoted $has(cr : Car[1..*], fm_1 : Feasible\text{-}Model[0..1])$. For qualified properties the qualifiers and their domains and sizes are added. The compact notation of the qualified association in Figure 2 is: $r(p_1 : A[m_1..n_1], p_2 : B\{q_1 : D_1(\infty), q_2 : D_2(\infty)\}[m_2, n_2])$ (recall that ∞ is the default domain size). Note that the qualifier of a property p is visualized on the side of its $source(p)$, i.e., on the opposite side of the visualization of p.

The *Constraints* **are:**

- **Association class:** A predicate on $\mathcal{C}$ that singles out the association classes within $\mathcal{C}$. Association classes are marked C^{AC}, and $\mathcal{AC}$ denotes the subset of association classes in $\mathcal{C}$.

  An injection $assoc_{ac}\colon \mathcal{AC} \to \mathcal{A}$ identifies every association class with a unique association. Visually, an association class is denoted as a class that is connected by a dashed line to its association line.

  For simplicity, we overload the mapping notations such that $assoc(C^{AC})$, $props(C^{AC})$, $props_1(C^{AC})$, $props_2(C^{AC})$, denote the association of an association class C^{AC} and its properties. The association class of an association a (if exists) is denoted $ac(a) = assoc_{ac}^{-1}(a)$. For example, in Figure 1a, $assoc_{ac}(Evaluation) = testedBy$, $props(Evaluation) = \langle fm_2, tr \rangle$ and $ac(testedBy) = Evaluation$.

- **Aggregation and Composition:** Predicates on $\mathcal{P}$, such that composition is a refinement of aggregation, i.e., for $p \in \mathcal{P}, composition(p) \Rightarrow aggregation$ (p). Aggregate/composite properties are denoted p^a and p^c respectively. Visually, aggregate/composition properties are marked by diamonds, with an empty diamond for aggregation and a solid diamond for composition. Restriction: For a composition property p^c, $max(p^c) = 1$.

- **Class hierarchy:** A non-circular binary relationship $\prec$ on the set of class symbols: $\prec\ \subseteq\ \mathcal{C} \times \mathcal{C}$. Henceforth $C_1 \prec C_2$, stands for C_1 is a subclass of C_2. The classes in a class hierarchy are either both association classes or both non-association classes. $\prec^*$ is the transitive closure of $\prec$, and $C_1 \preceq^* C_2$ stands for $C_1 = C_2$ or $C_1 \prec^* C_2$.

- **Generalization-set** *(GS)*: An $(n + 1)$-ary $n \geq 2$ relationship on $\mathcal{C}$. Its elements $\langle C, C_1, \ldots, C_n \rangle$, called *GS* constraints, must satisfy: For $i, j = 1..n$ (1) $C \neq C_i$; (2) $C_i \neq C_j$; (3) $C_i \prec C$. C is called the *superclass* and the C_i-s are called the *subclasses*. *GS* constraints are associated with at least one of the *disjoint/overlapping* and *complete/incomplete* constraints. A *GS* constraint is denoted $GS(C, C_1, \ldots, C_n; Const)$.

- **Subsetting:** A binary relation $\prec$ [1] on the set of property symbols: $\prec\ \subseteq\ \mathcal{P} \times \mathcal{P}$. $p_1 \prec p_2$, stands for "p_1 subsets p_2", where p_1 is *the subsetting property*, and p_2 is *the subsetted property*. The UML specification requires that $source(p_1) \prec^* source(p_2), target(p_1) \prec^* target(p_2)$ and $max(p_1) \leq max(p_2)$.

---

[1]   We use the same symbol as in class hierarchy. Distinction is made by context.

Similarly to class hierarchies, $\prec^*$ is the transitive closure of $\prec$, and $p_1 \preceq^* p_2$ stands for $p_1 = p_2$ or $p_1 \prec^* p_2$.

Semantics:

The standard set theoretic semantics of class diagrams associates a class diagram with *instances (states, interpretations)* $I = \langle D, \bullet \rangle$, that consists of a *semantic domain* D and an *extension mapping* $\bullet$, that maps syntactic symbols to elements over the semantic domain. Classes are mapped to sets of objects in the domain, properties are mapped to multi-valued functions over these sets, and associations are mapped to relationships between these sets. The sets denoted by classes and associations are called *extensions*. For a symbol x, $\bullet(x)$, its denotation in I, is shortened into x^I. The specification of symbol denotation and constraint semantics appears online in [11], and is not repeated here due to lack of space.

An instance I of a class diagram might or might not satisfy the constraints in the class diagram. For a constraint γ, the notation $I \models \gamma$ stands for "γ holds in I". A *legal instance* of a class diagram is an instance that satisfies all constraints; it is *empty* if all class extensions are empty, and is *infinite* if some class extension is not finite. A class diagram CD' is a *logical consequence* of a class diagram CD, denoted $CD \models CD'$, if all legal instances of CD are legal instances of CD'. They are *equivalent*, denoted $CD \equiv CD'$, if $CD \models CD'$ and $CD' \models CD'$. A class diagram is *satisfiable* if it has an instance in which all class and association extensions are not empty, and is *finitely satisfiable* if all the class and association extensions in this instance are also finite.

Existential constraints: UML class diagram constraints are *universal* in the sense that they impose restrictions on all intended instances. Constraints that specify inter-relationships that **might** hold in an intended instance are termed *existential constraints*. These are the GS-constraints *overlapping* and *incomplete*, and the multiplicity constraints, which in addition to the universal semantics have also an existential one. The existential constraints can be interpreted *demandingly* – requiring that the existential constraint is satisfied (realized) in some legal instance, or *permissively* – impose no constraint. For the class diagram existential constraints, the demanding approach means:

(1) *Overlapping GS constraint:* There exists an instance I such that for some i, j, $C_i^I \cap C_j^I \neq \emptyset$;

(2) *Incomplete GS constraint*: There exists an instance I such that $\bigcup_{i=1}^{n} C_i^I \neq C^I$.

(3) Multiplicity constraints: For every cardinality n of a property p, i.e., $min(p) \leq n \leq max(p)$, there exists a legal instance I, and an object $e \in source(p)^I$, such that $|p^I(e)| = n$. That is, n is realized by some object in some legal instance.

An existential constraint that does not hold under the demanding semantics is *redundant* and can be removed, since it has no effect on the set of states of a class diagram. Moreover, redundancy of an *overlapping* constraint implies a *disjoint* constraint, and redundancy of an *incomplete* constraint implies a *complete* constraint. Redundancy of boundary cardinalities implies tightening of multiplicity intervals, and redundancy of non-boundary cardinalities implies splitting of a multiplicity interval into several intervals.

A class diagram is *existentially satisfiable* if it is satisfiable and satisfies the demanding semantics, and is *existentially finitely satisfiable* if it is finitely satisfiable and satisfies the demanding semantics. In the following sections we investigate methods for removing redundancies in order to achieve existential finite satisfiability.

3 Removing Redundant Multiplicity Constraints

A property that has a redundant cardinality can be *tightened* by removing the redundant cardinality from its multiplicity interval (which might split the interval). We say that a *property is boundary tight* if its boundary cardinalities are not redundant, and is *tight* if all of its cardinalities are not redundant. A *class diagram is boundary tight* if all of its properties are boundary tight, and is *tight* if all of its properties are tight.

In [6] we presented a method for tightening boundary cardinalities of properties in class diagrams with binary associations and class hierarchy constraints (the set of such class diagrams is denoted $\mathcal{CD}_{mul,\prec}$). The method, termed **multiplicity-tightening** has three steps: (1) Construct an *identification graph* whose nodes correspond to classes and directed edges are labeled by property pairs and have weights that result from their multiplicities; (2) Identify cycles with weight 1 in the graph (where the weight of a path is the product of its edge weights); (3) Based on edge weights, tighten redundant multiplicities of properties in such cycles into point intervals, i.e., increase redundant minimum boundary cardinalities to meet their maximum ones, and decrease redundant maximum boundary cardinalities to meet their minimum ones.

The results in [6] show that this method handles all cases of redundancy of boundary cardinalities in class diagrams in $\mathcal{CD}_{mul,\prec}$. That is:

1. **Baoundary tight properties:** In a finitely satisfiable class diagram CD, with identification graph $graph(CD)$, a property p with $min(p) \neq max(p)$ is boundary tight if and only if all cycles in $graph(CD)$ through an edge labeled $\langle p, \_ \rangle$ or $\langle \_, p \rangle$ (_ being a wild card) have weight greater than 1.
2. **Completeness of multiplicity-tightening:** For a class diagram CD, **multiplicity-tightening** is an equivalent boundary tight class diagram.

Cardinality gaps: The above results ensure that application of the **multiplicity-tightening** method removes redundancy of boundary cardinalities. However, it is possible that a boundary tight property p with $min(p) \neq max(p)$ has a redundant cardinality, implying that its multiplicity interval has gaps, and should be split[2]. The following theorem shows that for class diagrams in $CD \in \mathcal{CD}_{mul,\prec}$, boundary tightness implies tightness. Therefore, the **multiplicity-tightening** method yields a tight class diagram.

---

[2] Note that the abstract syntax introduced in Section 2 does not include multiplicity constraints with gaps.

Theorem 1 (No cardinality gaps in $CD_{mul,\prec}$). *For a finitely satisfiable class diagram in $CD_{mul,\prec}$, if a property is boundary tight then it is also tight.*

Proof. In the appendix.

Corollary 1. *For a class diagram $CD \in CD_{mul,\prec}$, multiplicity-tightening (CD) is an equivalent tight class diagram.*

3.1 Extension to Class Diagrams with Qualifier, Aggregation/Composition, and Association Class Constraints

The results for tightening class diagrams in $CD_{mul,\prec}$ can be extended to class diagrams including also qualifier, aggregation/composition, and association class (without association class hierarchy) constraints (denote the set of such class diagrams $CD_{mul,\prec,Agg/Com,Qua,AC}$). The extension to $CD_{mul,\prec,Agg/Com,Qua,AC}$ is obtained by translating a class diagram in $CD_{mul,\prec,Agg/Com,Qua,AC}$ into a tagged class diagram in $CD_{mul,\prec}$, so that tightness is preserved (reduction of the "is tight?" problem). That is, we define a bijective translation Tr from $CD_{mul,\prec,Agg/Com,Qua,AC}$ to $CD_{mul,\prec}$, and show that it preserves tightness: For every $CD \in CD_{mul,\prec,Agg/Com,Qua,AC}$, CD is tight *iff* $Tr(CD)$ is tight. The overall multiplicity tightening method for $CD \in CD_{mul,\prec,Agg/Com,Qua,AC}$ is:

$$\text{multiplicity-tightening}(CD) = Tr^{-1}(\text{multiplicity-tightening}(Tr(CD))).$$

The Tr Translation
For a class diagram $CD \in CD_{mul,\prec,Agg/Com,Qua,AC}$, denote $CD' = Tr(CD)$. CD' is a class diagram in $CD_{mul,\prec}$, with additional *tags* that mark the original roles of the changed elements. The marks are used by the inverse construction. The Tr translation appears in the appendix. Figures 3b and 4b present the Tr translation of the class diagrams in Figures 3a, and 4a receptively.

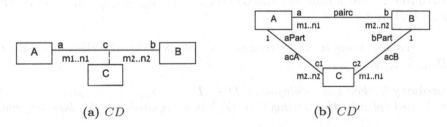

(a) CD (b) CD'

Fig. 3. The Tr translation of an association class constraint

Example (Multiplicity tightening in $CD_{mul,\prec,Agg/Com,Qua,AC}$): Figure 1a presents a non-tight class diagram with an association class: The minimum cardinalities of properties fm_1, tr, ca and the maximum cardinalities of properties cr, ev, htr_2, are redundant. Figure 1b presents a tight class diagram, equivalent to the one

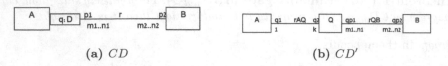

(a) CD (b) CD'

Fig. 4. The Tr translation of a qualifier constraint

in Figure 1a. It is obtained by applying the **multiplicity-tightening** method described above: First, Figure 1a is translated, using Tr into a class diagram in $CD_{mul,\prec}$ (Figure 5a), then this class diagram is tightened into an equivalent tight class diagram, still in $CD_{mul,\prec}$ (Figure 5b), which is then translated back, using Tr^{-1}, into the tight equivalent class diagram in Figure 1a.

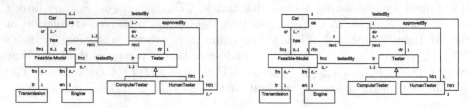

(a) A non-tight class diagram in $CD_{mul,\prec}$: The Tr translation of Figure 1a

(b) A tight class diagram, equivalent to the class diagram in Figure 5a

Fig. 5. Tightening steps for the class diagram in Figure 1a

Correctness of the Tr translation
The translation is proved correct in the appendix. The results are:

Corollary 2. *For a class diagram $CD \in CD_{mul,\prec,Agg/Com,Qua,AC}$, CD is tight iff $Tr(CD)$ is tight.*

This corrolary leads to an extension of corollary 1 for the class diagrams in $CD_{mul,\prec,Agg/Com,Qua,AC}$:

Corollary 3. *For a class diagram $CD \in CD_{mul,\prec,Agg/Com,Qua,AC}$, $Tr^{-1}(\textbf{multiplicity-tightening}(Tr(CD)))$ is an equivalent tight class diagram.*

Cardinality gaps: The results showing that there are no cardinality gaps in $CD_{mul,\prec}$ can be extended to cardinality gaps in $CD_{mul,\prec,Agg/Com,Qua,AC}$:

Theorem 2 (No cardinality gaps in $CD_{mul,\prec,Agg/Com,Qua,AC}$). *For a finitely satisfiable class diagram in $CD_{mul,\prec,Agg/Com,Qua,AC}$, if a property is boundary tight then it is also tight.*

3.2   Extension to Class Diagrams with Inter-association Constraints

The semantics of inter-association constraints is not local – it involves multiple associations and their end classes. The previous methods do not handle such global interaction. Our approach is to strengthen the **multiplicity-tightening** method with additional rules for removing redundant boundary cardinalities in inter-related associations. Due to space limitations we present only a rule for the *subsetting* constraint:

Subsetting-hierarchy: For every property p, set $max(p) := min\{max(p')|p \preceq^* p'\}$, where $\preceq^*$ is the reflexive transitive closure of $\prec$.

Example: Figures 6a and 6b present a non-tight class diagram (a) and an equivalent tight version (b), obtained by applying **multiplicity-tightening**, followed by application of the **Subsetting-hierarchy** rule. Figure 6a is not tight since applying **multiplicity-tightening** shows that property p is not boundary tight ($max(p)$ is set to 2), and $p_1 \preceq p$ implies that in every legal instance I, for each object $e \in A_1^I$, $p_1^I(e) \subseteq p^I(e)$, and hence $|p_1^I(e)| \leq 2$. Therefore, property p_1 should be tightened into $max(p_1) := 2$.

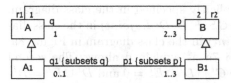
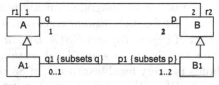

(a) Redundancy due to interaction of subsetting and multiplicity constraints

(b) An tight class diagram equivalent to 6a

Fig. 6. Removing redundancy that involves the subsetting constraint

4   Removing Redundant *Overlapping* and *Incomplete* Constraints

The demanding semantics for the *overlapping* and *complete* constraints requires that they are realized in some legal instances. Figures 7a and 7b show *overlapping* and *incomplete* constraints that do not satisfy this requirement. In 7a, the *overlapping* constraint is redundant since in every legal instance I, $B^I \cap C^I = \emptyset$ and $D^I \subseteq C^I$. Therefore, $B^I \cap D^I = \emptyset$. In 7b, the *incomplete* constraint is redundant since in every legal instance I, $B^I \subseteq A^I$, $C^I \subseteq A^I$, $A^I \subseteq D^I$ and $D^I = B^I \cup C^I$, implying $A^I = B^I \cup C^I$. Identification of these redundancies can meaningfully improve class diagram quality since redundancy of an *overlapping* constraint implies a *disjoint* constraint, and redundancy of an *incomplete* constraint implies a *complete* constraint. Due to space limitations, we focus only on *overlapping* constraints.

4.1   Redundancy of *Overlapping* Due to Interaction with *Disjoint* Constraints

A *disjoint* constraint, being universal, is stronger than the existential overlapping constraint. Therefore, when applied to the same GS, i.e., $GS(C, C_1, \ldots, C_n;$

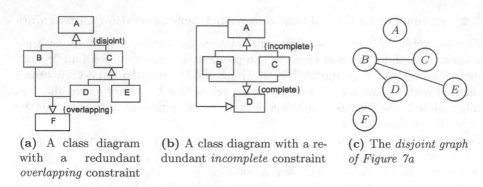

(a) A class diagram with a redundant *overlapping* constraint

(b) A class diagram with a redundant *incomplete* constraint

(c) The *disjoint graph* *of Figure 7a*

Fig. 7. Redundant *overlapping* and *incomplete GS* constraints

disjoint, overlapping), *disjoint* overrides *overlapping*, turning it redundant. Such cases can be immediately detected, and are syntactically forbidden. But what about implied *disjoint* constraints, i.e., constraints that hold in every legal instance of a class diagram, but are not explicitly specified in the class diagram. Examples for such *disjoint* constraints are $GS(F, B, D; disjoint)$ in the class diagram of Figure 7a, and $GS(A, B, C; disjoint)$ in the class diagram in Figure 8a. The first holds in every legal instance of 7a as explained above. The second holds in every legal instance I, of 8a since $C^I \cap D^I \cap E^I = \emptyset$ and $D^I \cup E^I = B^I$, imply $B^I \cap C^I = \emptyset$. In both cases, the implied *disjoint GS* turns the specified *overlapping* constraint redundant.

Algorithm 1 identifies implied *GS* constraints of the form $GS(C, C_1, \ldots, C_n; disjoint, overlapping)$, and removes such redundant *overlapping* constraints. It constructs an undirected graph termed *disjoint graph*, which summarizes known disjoint relations between classes. The nodes of the disjoint graph represent classes and its edges connect nodes of disjoint classes. A possible construction is described in [3], and the resulting *disjoint graph* for Figure 7a is shown in Figure 7c. Whenever the algorithm infers a *GS* with the *disjoint, overlapping* constraint, it drops the overlapping from the diagram. For Figure 7a, it removes the *overlapping* constraint on $GS(F, B, D)$. The algorithm does not add the *disjoint* constraint since this action might involve other considerations, e.g., over specification of constraints (see [3]).

Algorithm 1: Remove-Overlapping-by-disjoint

Input: A class diagram CD

Outpu: An equivalent class diagram CD'

Graph construction step: Initialize $garph_{CD}$ to be a *disjoint graph* of CD

Identification of redundant *overlapping*:

    for every $GS(C, C_1, \ldots, C_n; Const) \in CD$ where $Const = overlapping$ or *overlapping, complete* or *overlapping, incomplete*:

    If there is a clique in $garph_{CD}$ connecting the nodes of $C_1, \ldots, C_n$, *remove* the *overlapping* constraint from $Const$

End

Correctness of Algorithm 1: The algorithm removes redundant *overlapping* constraints. Therefore, it is sound since its output class diagram is equivalent to the input class diagram.

The completeness of the algorithm depends on the completeness of the disjoint graph in use. The construction of [3] is not complete, but can be strengthened by applying a preceding *propagation algorithm* that extends the input class diagram with implied disjoint constraints. For example, in Figure 8a, although $GS(A, B, C; disjoint)$ is an implied constraint, since it is not explicitly specified in the diagram, it does not appear in the disjoint graph, and therefore Algorithm 1 does not detect the redundant *overlapping* constraint. But, if the propagation algorithm is first applied to the input class diagram, implied *disjoint* constraints might be added, the disjoint graph might provide more disjointness information, and the results of the algorithm might be stronger. For the class diagram in Figure 8a, the propagation algorithm adds the $GS(A, B, C; disjoint)$ constraint, and the algorithm removes the redundant *overlapping*.

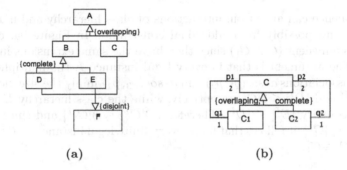

(a)   (b)

Fig. 8. Class diagrams with redundant overlapping constraints

4.2   Redundancy of *Overlapping* Due to Interaction with *Complete* Constraints

An *overlapping* constraint might be overridden by a joint *complete* constraint. In Figure 8, the multiplicity constraints on associations r_1, r_2 imply that in every legal instance I, $|C^I| = 2 \times |C_1^I|$ and $|C^I| = 2 \times |C_1^I|$, and therefore $|C^I| = |C_1^I| + |C_2^I|$. The *complete* constraint implies $|C^I| \leq |C_1^I| + |C_2^I|$. Therefore, the joint *overlapping* constraint cannot hold in any legal instance (it requires $|C^I| < |C_1^I| + |C_2^I|$), implying that it is redundant.

The **FiniteSat** algorithm of [3] can be used for detecting redundant *overlapping* constraints that appear jointly with *complete* constraints. **FiniteSat** is a detection algorithm for finite satisfiability problems in class diagrams, and it is based on the demanding semantics for existential GS constraints. This means that if an *overlapping* constraint cannot hold in any legal instance, the algorithm announces a finite satisfiability problem. The idea here is to use **FiniteSat** as a detector for redundant *overlapping* constraints: If **FiniteSat** detects a finite satisfiability problem, and the problem disappears when removing an *overlapping* constraint, it implies that the removed constraint is redundant. This approach applies only to joint *overlapping, complete* constraints since checking **Finite-Sat** on single *overlapping* constraints cannot detect redundant *overlapping* constraints. Applying this idea to the class diagram in Figure 8b indeed detects the redundancy of the *overlapping* constraint and removes it.

5   Inference Rules for Deducing Element Equivalences

Model investigation requires deep semantic analysis. Inference rules for deducing implied inter-relationships between model elements are of great help. In this section we present two inference rules for deducing class and association equivalences. These rules are representatives of a larger set of inference rules that we currently develop.

5.1   Deducing Class Equivalence

Class equivalence can arise from interactions of class hierarchy and multiplicity constraints, and possibly from additional constraints. In Figure 9a, classes C and C_1 are equivalent ($C \equiv C_1$) since they have the same extensions in all legal instances. The argument is that in every legal instance I, the multiplicity constraints on associations $assoc(p_1, p_2)$ and $assoc(p_3, p_4)$ imply the size inequalities $3|C^I| \leq |E^I|$ and $|D^I| \leq 3|C_1^I|$ receptively, while the class hierarchy $E \preceq D$ implies the inequality $|E^I| \leq |D^I|$. Therefore, $3|C^I| \leq 3|C_1^I|$ and since $C_1 \preceq C$ implies $|C_1^I| \leq |C^I|$, it follows that for in every finite legal instance I, $|C_1^I| = |C^I|$. Therefore, $C \equiv C_1$.

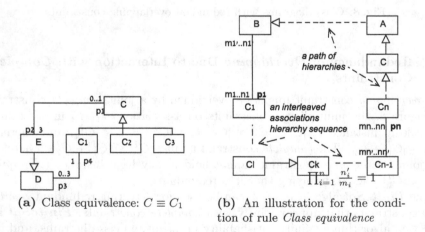

(a) Class equivalence: $C \equiv C_1$ (b) An illustration for the condition of rule *Class equivalence*

Fig. 9. Equivalence of classes and associations

Inference rule **Class equivalence** below generalizes and abstracts the last case. For this purpose we define a *property sequence* as a sequence of properties

$p_1, p_2, \ldots, p_n$, $i = 1, n - 1$, such that $target(p_i) = source(p_{i+1})$ for $i = 1, n - 1$. A sequence of properties $p_1, p_2, \ldots, p_n$ forms a *property-hierarchy sequence* if $target(p_i) \preceq^* source(p_{i+1})$ for $i = 1, n - 1$. Properties p_2, p_4 in Figure 9a form a *property-hierarchy sequence*.

Inference rule *Class equivalence*:[3]

if $C_n \preceq^* C$, $C \preceq A$, $A \preceq^* B$, and $p_1, p_2, \ldots, p_n$ is a property-hierarchy sequence such that $source(p_1) = B$ and $target(p_n) = C_n$,

then if $\prod_{i=1}^{n} \frac{max(p_i^{-1})}{min(p_i)} = 1$, then $A \equiv C$.

Soundness proof for this inference rule is sketched in the appendix.

5.2 Deducing Association Equivalence

Association equivalence can arise when two associations whose properties are constrained by inter-association constraints have the same size in every legal instance. Figure 10a, presents subsetting constraints that imply an inclusion relation between the association extensions in every legal instance, $s^I \subseteq r^I$, while the multiplicity constraints on r and s imply $|s^I| = |r^I|$. Therefore, $s^I = r^I$, implying $r \equiv s$.

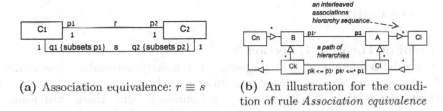

(a) Association equivalence: $r \equiv s$ (b) An illustration for the condition of rule *Association equivalence*

Fig. 10. association:equivalence

Inference rule *Association equivalence* generalizes this case: The associations form a property-hierarchy sequence whose multiplicity constraints satisfy an equality that forces the association to have the same size in every legal instance. Figure 10b illustrates the rule conditions.

Inference rule *Association equivalence*:

if $assoc(p_1), assoc(p_k)$ are associations such that $target(p_k) \preceq^* source(p_1)$, $sourcet(p_k) \preceq^* target(p_1)$, $p_k^{-1} \preceq^* p_1$ and $p_1, \ldots, p_k, \ldots, p_n$ forms a property-hierarchy sequence with $target(p_n) \preceq source(p_1)$,

then if $\prod_{i=1}^{n} \frac{max(p_i)}{min(p_i^{-1})} = 1$, then $assoc(p_1) \equiv assoc(p_k)$.

6 Related Work and Conclusions

Most works on class diagram correctness focus on *consistency* [13,14,15] and *finite satisfiability* problems [16,17,18,19,20,21,22,3,5]. There is a limited amount

---

[3] This rule generalizes the rule of Rosati [12] for finite model reasoning in *DL-Lite*, to arbitrary multiplicity constraints .

of works investigating class-diagram constraints, including their impact on correctness and quality [1,23,24,2,3,5,4,6,25,26]. The catalog in [26,27,6] presents simplification patterns for constraint interactions. Hartmann [28] presents a graph-based method for tightening multiplicity constraints with gaps in Entity-Relationship Diagrams with functional dependencies and without hierarchy constraints. Feinerer et al. [2] investigate multiplicity constraint redundancies in class diagrams with multiplicity, uniqueness and *equation* constraints.

Conclusions and future work: The paper formally defined the notion of *redundancy* using the distinction between *existential* to *universal* constraints, and introduced methods for removing redundancy and inferring element equivalence. All algorithms are now being implemented in our ***FiniteSatUSE*** tool [29].

The study of redundancy in presence of *GS* or inter-association constraints still poses major problems, due to their global nature. Another challenge involves the development of complete inference systems for fragments of the class diagram language. This research direction might be inspired from inference systems for Description Logic.

A   Appendix

I. Proof of Theorem 1, Section 3:

Let p be a boundary tight property in a finitely satisfiable class diagram CD, and assume that there exist a number k such that $min(p) < k < max(p)$ (otherwise p is already tight). Since p is boundary tight, there exist legal instances I_1, I_2 (possibly the same instance) of CD in which the boundary cardinalities of p are realized, respectively. We know that the set of legal instances of a class diagram is closed under union, and therefore $I = I_1 \cup I_2$ is also a legal instance of CD. Consequently, I is a legal instance of CD in which the boundary cardinalities of p are realized. Let o_1, o_2 be two objects such that $|p^I(o_1)| = min(p)$ and $|p^I(o_2)| = max(p)$. Denote $l = k - min(p)$. In order to realize the cardinality k of p we "move" l links from o_2 to o_1. Select $\{e_1, \ldots, e_l\} \subset p^I(o_2)$. Let I' be a new instance of CD, which is the same as I, except that $p^{I'}(o_2) = p^I(o_2) \setminus \{e_1, \ldots, e_l\}$ and $p^{I'}(o_1) = p^I(o_1) \cup \{e_1, \ldots, e_l\}$. Therefore, in I' $|p^{I'}(o_1)| = k$. I' is a legal instance of CD since: (1) $|p^{I'}(o_2)| = max(p) - (k - min(p)) > max(p) - (max(p) - min(p)) = min(p)$; and (2) Redirecting links in a legal instance of CD leaves it legal, as long as size inter-relations between association and class extensions are preserved [16,3].

II. The Tr Translation, Section 3.1

1. Initialization: $CD' := CD$.
2. For every aggregation/composition property $p^{a/c}$ in CD, remove the aggregation/composition constraint from p, but mark it as such (for example, using tagging or a stereotype).

3. For every association class $C = C^{AC}$ of an association c, with $A = class_1(C)$, $B = class_2(C)$, remove the association class constraint and add two associations $acA(aPart : A[1..1], a : C[m_2..n_2])$ and $acB(bPart : B[1..1], b : C[m_1..n_1])$. Mark C as the association class of c, and the associations acA and acB as the derived associations.

4. For every qualified association $r(p_1 : A[m_1..n_1], p_2 : B\{q : D(k)\}[m_2..n_2])^4$, remove r, add a new class Q and two new associations $rAQ(q_1 : A[1..1], q_2 : Q[k..k])$ and $rQB(qp_1 : Q[m_1..n_1], qp_2 : B[m_2..n_2])$. Mark Q as the qualifier class and qp_2 as the qualified property p_2 with $qualifier(p_2) = \langle q, D \rangle$ and $domain\_size(D) = k$.

Correctness of the Tr translation:
Tr is correct if, for $CD, CD_1, CD_2 \in \mathcal{CD}_{mul,\prec,Agg/Com,Qua,AC}$:

1. $CD_1 \equiv CD_2$ iff $Tr(CD_1) \equiv Tr(CD_2)$.
2. CD is tight iff $Tr(CD)$ is tight.

The first property is immediate since the translation has minor effects on instances of the translated class diagrams (note that the output of Tr is a *tagged* class diagram in $\mathcal{CD}_{mul,\prec}$). For showing tightness preservation we define a correspondence relation between properties of the input and output class diagrams, and show that it preserves tightness. For a property $p \in props(a)$, where a is an association/association-class in CD, the corresponding property in $Tr(CD)$ denoted by p' is defined as follows:

1. If a is an unqualified association or an association class: $p' = p$.
2. If a is a qualified association as in Figure 4a: $p'_2 = q_{p_2}$ and $p'_1 = q_{p_1}$.

Claim (Preservation of property tightness) A property p in CD is tight iff its corresponding property p' in $Tr(CD)$ is tight.
Proof (Sketch): The proof is based on constructive bijective mappings between legal instances of CD and CD', that preserve the number of links that an object has for a given property [22,3,30]. Therefore, if a property p has no redundant cardinality, so is p', and vice versa.

III. Soundness of the *Class equivalence* rule, Section 5.1: (Sketch) The constrained structure in the rule condition is illustrated in Figure 9b. From [3], it follows that in every finite legal instance I, $\frac{|A^I|}{|C^I|} \leq \prod_{i=1}^{n} \frac{max(p_i^{-1})}{min(p_i)}$. Therefore, $\frac{|A^I|}{|C^I|} \leq 1$. $C \preceq A$ implies $|C^I| \leq |A^I|$. Consequently, $|C^I| = |A^I|$, which for finite legal instance implies $A \equiv C$.

References

1. Costal, D., Gómez, C.: On the use of Association Redefinition in UML Class Diagrams. In: Embley, D.W., Olivé, A., Ram, S. (eds.) ER 2006. LNCS, vol. 4215, pp. 513–527. Springer, Heidelberg (2006)

---

4   For simplicity we refer to a single qualifier attribute.

2. Feinerer, I., Salzer, G., Sisel, T.: Reducing Multiplicities in Class Diagrams. In: Whittle, J., Clark, T., Kühne, T. (eds.) MODELS 2011. LNCS, vol. 6981, pp. 379–393. Springer, Heidelberg (2011)
3. Balaban, M., Maraee, A.: Finite Satisfiability of UML Class Diagrams with Constrained Class Hierarchy. ACM Transactions on Software Engineering and Methodology (TOSEM) 22(24), 1–24 (2013)
4. Maraee, A., Balaban, M.: Inter-association Constraints in UML2: Comparative Analysis, Usage Recommendations, and Modeling Guidelines. In: France, R.B., Kazmeier, J., Breu, R., Atkinson, C. (eds.) MODELS 2012. LNCS, vol. 7590, pp. 302–318. Springer, Heidelberg (2012)
5. Feinerer, I., Salzer, G.: Numeric Semantics of Class Diagrams with Multiplicity and Uniqueness Constraints. Software and Systems Modeling, SoSyM (2013)
6. Balaban, M., Maraee, A.: Simplification and Correctness of UML Class Diagrams – Focusing on Multiplicity and Aggregation/Composition Constraints. In: Moreira, A., Schätz, B., Gray, J., Vallecillo, A., Clarke, P. (eds.) MODELS 2013. LNCS, vol. 8107, pp. 454–470. Springer, Heidelberg (2013)
7. OMG: UML 2.4 Superstructure Specification. Specification Version 2.4.1, Object Management Group (2011)
8. Kleppe, A., Rensink, A.: On a Graph-Based Semantics for UML Class and Object Diagrams. In: Ermel, C., Lara, J.D., Heckel, R. (eds.) Graph Transformation and Visual Modelling Techniques. Electronic Communications of the EASST, vol. 10, EASST (2008)
9. OMG: OMG Object Constraint Language (OCL). Specification Version 2.3.1, Object Management Group (2012)
10. Warmer, J., Kleppe, A.: The Object Constraint Language: Getting Your Models Ready for MDA. Addison-Wesley Longman Publishing Co., Inc. (2003)
11. Balaban, M., Maraee, A.: UML Class Diagram Semantics (2014), http://www.cs.bgu.ac.il/~cd-patterns/?page_id=1695
12. Rosati, R.: Finite Model Reasoning in DL-Lite. In: Bechhofer, S., Hauswirth, M., Hoffmann, J., Koubarakis, M. (eds.) ESWC 2008. LNCS, vol. 5021, pp. 215–229. Springer, Heidelberg (2008)
13. Berardi, D., Calvanese, D., Giacomo, D.: Reasoning on UML Class Diagrams. Artificial Intelligence 168, 70–118 (2005)
14. Queralt, A., Teniente, E.: Verification and Validation of UML Conceptual Schemas with OCL Constraints. ACM Transactions on Software Engineering and Methodology (TOSEM) 21, 13:1–13:41 (2012)
15. Kaneiwa, K., Satoh, K.: On the Complexities of Consistency Checking for Restricted UML Class Diagrams. Theor. Comput. Sci. 411, 301–323 (2010)
16. Lenzerini, M., Nobili, P.: On the Satisfiability of Dependency Constraints in Entity-Relationship Schemata. Information Systems 15, 453–461 (1990)
17. Thalheim, B.: Entity Relationship Modeling, Foundation of Database Technology. Springer (2000)
18. Calvanese, D., Lenzerini, M.: On the Interaction between ISA and Cardinality Constraints. In: The 10th IEEE Int. Conf. on Data Engineering (1994)
19. Hartmann, S.: Coping with Inconsistent Constraint Specifications. In: Kunii, H.S., Jajodia, S., Sølvberg, A. (eds.) ER 2001. LNCS, vol. 2224, pp. 241–255. Springer, Heidelberg (2001)
20. Boufares, F., Bennaceur, H.: Consistency Problems in ER-schemas for Database Systems. Information Sciences, 263–274 (2004)

21. Shaikh, A., Clarisó, R., Wiil, U., Memon, N.: Verification-driven Slicing of UM-L/OCL Models. In: Proceedings of the IEEE/ACM International Conference on Automated Software Engineering, pp. 185–194. ACM (2010)
22. Maraee, A.: UML Class Diagrams–Semantics, Correctness and Quality. PhD thesis, Ben Gurion University of the Negev (2012)
23. Alanen, M., Porres, I.: A Metamodeling Language Supporting Subset and Union Properties. Software and Systems Modeling 7, 103–124 (2008)
24. Szlenk, M.: UML Static Models in Formal Approach. In: Meyer, B., Nawrocki, J.R., Walter, B. (eds.) CEE-SET 2007. LNCS, vol. 5082, pp. 129–142. Springer, Heidelberg (2008)
25. Calì, A., Gottlob, G., Orsi, G., Pieris, A.: Querying UML Class Diagrams. In: Birkedal, L. (ed.) FOSSACS 2012. LNCS, vol. 7213, pp. 1–25. Springer, Heidelberg (2012)
26. Balaban, M., Maraee, A., Sturm, A., Jelnov, P.: A Pattern-Based Approach for Improving Model Design Quality. Software and Systems Modeling (SoSyM), 1–29 (2014)
27. BGU Modeling Group: UML Class Diagram Patterns, Anti-Patterns and Inference Rules (2014), http://www.cs.bgu.ac.il/~cd-patterns/
28. Hartmann, S.: On the Implication Problem for Cardinality Constraints and Functional Dependencies. Annals of Mathematics and Artificial Intelligence 33, 253–307 (2001)
29. BGU Modeling Group: FiniteSatUSE – A Class Diagram Correctness Tool (2011), http://sourceforge.net/projects/usefsverif/
30. Maraee, A., Makarenkov, V., Balaban, B.: Efficient Recognition and Detection of Finite Satisfiability Problems in UML Class Diagrams: Handling Constrained Generalization Sets, Qualifiers and Association Class Constraints. In: MCCM 2008 (2008)

A Native Versioning Concept to Support Historized Models at Runtime

Thomas Hartmann[1], Francois Fouquet[1], Gregory Nain[1], Brice Morin[2],
Jacques Klein[1], Olivier Barais[3], and Yves Le Traon[1]

[1] Interdisciplinary Centre for Security, Reliability and Trust (SnT), University of
Luxembourg
first.last@uni.lu
http://wwwen.uni.lu/snt
[2] SINTEF ICT Norway
first.last@sintef.no
http://www.sintef.no
[3] IRISA / INRIA Centre Rennes Bretagne-Atlantique, Université de Rennes 1
last@irisa.fr
http://www.irisa.fr

Abstract. Models@run.time provides semantically rich reflection layers enabling intelligent systems to reason about themselves and their surrounding context. Most reasoning processes require not only to explore the current state, but also the past history to take sustainable decisions *e.g.* to avoid oscillating between states. Models@run.time and model-driven engineering in general lack native mechanisms to efficiently support the notion of history, and current approaches usually generate redundant data when versioning models, which reasoners need to navigate. Because of this limitation, models fail in providing suitable and sustainable abstractions to deal with domains relying on history-aware reasoning. This paper tackles this issue by considering history as a native concept for modeling foundations. Integrated, in conjunction with lazy load/storage techniques, into the Kevoree Modeling Framework, we demonstrate onto a smart grid case study, that this mechanisms enable a sustainable reasoning about massive historized models.

Keywords: Models@run.time, Model-driven engineering, Model versioning, Historized models.

1 Introduction

The paradigm of Models@run.time [8], [26] empowers intelligent systems with a model-based abstraction causally connected to their own current state. This abstract self-representation can be used by reasoning processes at runtime. For instance, this enables systems to (i) dynamically explore several adaptation options (models) in order to optimize their state, (ii) select the most appropriate one, and (iii) run a set of verifications of viability on new configurations before finally asking for an actual application. This capability enables the development of safer and more intelligent software systems. However, reasoning on the

J. Dingel et al. (Eds.): MODELS 2014, LNCS 8767, pp. 252–268, 2014.

current state of the system is sometimes not sufficient. Indeed, if the system only reacts to the current state, it may become unstable, oscillating between two configurations as conflicting events are continuously detected. To avoid this state flapping, it is necessary to consider historical information to compare past versions, detect correlations and take more sustainable and stable adaptation decisions. This scenario and the associated challenges are also illustrated in an industrial context. Creos Luxembourg S.A. is the main energy grid operator in Luxembourg. Our partnership with them is geared at making their electricity grid able to self adapt to evolving contexts (heavy wind or rain, consumption increase) to better manage energy production and consumption. This requires to make predictions on the basis of current and historical data. Here, a linear regression of the average electric load values of the meters in a region, over a certain period of time, has to be computed in order to predict the electric load for this region. This obviously requires access to the model history.

Usually, dynamic modifications operated by intelligent systems at runtime react to small changes in the state (parameter changes; unavailability of a component). These adaptations often enact only few changes to make the system fit better to its new context. Being a slight change in the execution context, or on the system's state, all these changes create successive versions. These changes have to be tracked to keep the history and help reasoners in making decisions.

Unfortunately, Models@run.time in particular and model-driven engineering in general lack native mechanisms to efficiently support the notion of model versioning. Instead, current modeling approaches consider model versioning mainly as an infrastructural topic supporting model management in the sense of version control systems commonly used for textual artefacts like source code [6], [22]. Moreover, current approaches focus more on versioning of meta-models, with a lesser emphasis on runtime/execution model instances. In contrast to this, our versioning approach regards the evolution of models from an application point of view allowing to keep track and use this evolution of domain models (at runtime) at an application level (like *e.g.* Bigtable [12] or temporal databases [25]).

The approach presented in this paper is a general concept to enable versioning of models (as runtime structures) and is not restricted to Models@run.time paradigm, although our approach is very well suited for this paradigm. An efficient support would include (1) an appropriate storage mechanism to store deltas between two model versions, and (2) methods to navigate in the modeling space (as usual), but also to navigate in history (*i.e.* in versions). To overcome this limitation, current implementations usually create their own *ad-hoc* historization solutions that usually come with at least two major drawbacks. First, *ad-hoc* mechanisms make the maintenance complicated and sometimes less efficient than native mechanisms. Secondly, the realization of the models storage is often a simple list of complete models for each change (or periodically), creating either a linear explosion of the memory needed for storage, or a strong limit in the history depth. Moreover, the combination of these two drawbacks makes the navigation in space and versions (models and history) a real nightmare for developers in terms of algorithmic complexity, performance and maintenance.

This paper tackles this issue by including versioning as a native concept directly managed within *each model element*. This inclusion comes with native mechanisms to browse the versions of model elements to enable the navigation in space (model) and history (versions). The paper is structured as follows. Section 2 describes the fundamental ideas and mechanisms of our contribution. Section 3 gives details on how we implemented this idea into the Kevoree Modeling Framework. Based on this implementation, we evaluate our approach in section 4 on a smart grid case study and compare it to classical approaches. Finally, we discuss the related work in section 5 before section 6 concludes.

2   Native Versioning for Models at Runtime

This section describes the concepts and mechanisms, which are necessary to enable (1) the versioning of model elements and (2) the navigation in space (model) and history (versions).

2.1   A *Path* to Reach Elements in the Modeling Space

There are different ways to identify an element within a model: static identity-based matching (unique identifiers), signature-based matching [30], similarity-based matching, and custom language-specific matching [10], [23]. This is needed, for example, to detect changes in a model, and to merge and compare models. To allow model elements to evolve independently and enable an efficient versioning of these elements, we rely in our approach on unique identifiers (UID). We use the *path* of a model element as its unique identifier within a model. Directly inspired by the select operator of relational databases and by XPath [14], the *path* defines a query syntax aligned with the MOF [29] concepts. The navigation through a relationship can be achieved with the following expression: **relationName[IDAttributeValue]**. The **IDAttribute** is one attribute tagged as ID in the meta-model. This expression defines the **PATH** of an element in a MOF relationship. Several expressions can be chained to recursively navigate the nested model elements. Expressions are delimited by a /. It is thus possible to build a unique path to a model element, by chaining all sub-path expressions needed to navigate to it from the root model element, via the containment relationships. For instance, let us consider a model that has a collection *vehicles* of *Vehicle*, identified by a plate number. Further, each vehicle has a collection *wheels* of *Wheels* identified by their location (FL:Front Left, etc.). In this case, the path to access the front left wheel of the vehicle "KG673JU" is: *vehicles[KG673JU]/wheels[FL]*. Our definition of UID only relies on domain elements (relationships and attributes) and thus does not require an additional technical identifier. It is important to note that the **IDAttribute** alone does not define uniqueness. Uniqueness is only defined in combination with the reference. Therefore, in the example two wheels named FL can exist but only in two different vehicles.

2.2   Reaching Elements in the Versioning Space

The mechanism of path allows to uniquely identify and efficiently access model elements in the modeling space, but does not consider the notion of version. Since elements in a model usually evolve at different paces, versions shouldn't be considered at the model level but on a model element level. For example, the rim of the front left wheel of vehicle "KG673JU" could have been changed after an accident. Therefore, we could have two versions of the front left wheel, one with the old rim and one with the new one. Using only the path *vehicles[KG673JU]/wheels[FL]* to identify the wheel is not sufficient. To address this new requirement, we introduce a version identifier (VI) in conjunction with the path. This makes it possible to retrieve a model element in a specific version and enables the base navigation in history (space of versions). A timestamp, a number, or a string are examples for valid VIs. A model element version is therefore uniquely identified by its path together with a version identifier. This is shown in figure 1. This concept allows to create an arbitrary number of ver-

Fig. 1. Model element version identifier

sions during the lifetime of an element. Figure 2 shows an exemplary lifecycle of a model element e. The first version (with version identifier v_1) of model element e is created at time t_1 and added to the model. Then e evolves over time and two additional versions (with version identifiers v_2 respectively v_3) are created at t_2 respectively t_3. Finally, at t_4 e is removed from the model and its lifecycle ends. The extension of the concept of path with a version identifier enables basic

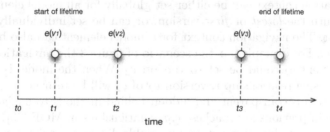

Fig. 2. Lifecycle of a model element

navigation in modeling space and versions, without any impact on the business modeling API. To support this non intrusiveness, and allow for more complex navigation in space and versions, we use the notion of *navigation context*.

2.3   Enhancing Navigation Capabilities with Navigation Context

To ease the navigation in versions, we enrich the modeling API with three basic operations to navigate in versions. These can be called on each model element:

The *shift* operation switches the modeling space to another version. The *previous* operation is a shortcut to retrieve the direct predecessor (in terms of version) of the current model element. The *next* method is similar to the *previous* operation, but retrieves the direct successor of the current model element.

These operations allow to independently select model element versions. Even if this mechanism is powerful, the navigation in such models can rapidly become very complicated. Indeed, a relationship r from an element e_1 to an element e_2 is no longer uniquely defined because of the versioning. Thus, the navigation between model elements can no more rely on relations (in space) only. Figure 3 shows two model elements, e_1 with only one version and e_2 with three versions. The version of e_2, which has to be returned when navigating the relationship r

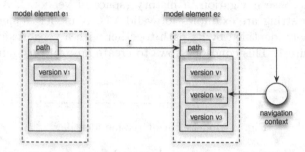

Fig. 3. Different versions of a model element and their relations

is ambiguous. Since each model element can have several versions, a selection policy has to be defined to navigate from one model element to a related. This navigation is thus along two dimensions (space and version). To cope with this problem, we define a *navigation context*.

This navigation context can be either set globally for all model elements, *e.g.* to always return the *latest* or *first* version, or can be set individually for each model element. The navigation context for a model element can also be set to a *specific version*. For example, for the scenario of figure 3 the navigation context for model element e_2 could be set to version v_2. When the model is traversed from e_1 to e_2 using relationship r, version v_2 of e_2 will be returned.

This resolution is transparent and hidden behind methods to navigate in the model. Unlike in previous approaches (*e.g.* relationships in MOF [29]), the navigation function is no longer constant but yields different results depending on the navigation context.

2.4 Leveraging Traces to Store Versions

The storage of model element versions relies on the possibility to get a serialized representation of all attributes and relationships of a model element. For this purpose we use so called *traces*. A trace defines the sequence of atomic actions necessary to construct a model element (or a complete model). Each model element can be transformed into a trace and vice versa [9]. A trace includes all attribute and relationship information of the model element. Listing 1.1 shows a trace for one model element.

Listing 1.1. Trace of a model element

```
{
"type":"SET","src":"meters[m3]","refname":"consumption","content":"100kWh"
"type":"ADD","src":"meters[m3]","refname":"reachable","content":"hubs[hub2]"
}
```

The listing shows a trace of a model element with an attribute *consumption* and a relationship *reachable*. The value *hubs[hub2]* of relation *reachable* shows how we leverage the path concept in our traces to uniquely identify a model element within a model. We use the JSON [15] format for a lightweight representation and storage of traces.

The version identifier in conjunction with the path (extended path) can be used as *key* and the trace as *value*. This is shown in figure 4. The data can then

Fig. 4. Storage concept for versioned model elements

be stored using arbitrary back ends *e.g.* key/value stores, relational databases, in RAM (as cache), or even in common version control systems like Git [2].

This section described the foundation of our contribution. To assess its suitability in real cases, we implemented this idea into the KMF project [17].

3   Implementation in KMF

This section presents the implementation of the proposed approach into the Kevoree Modeling Framework. The source is available on the project web page[1].

3.1   The Kevoree Modeling Framework

KMF [17], [18] is an alternative to EMF [11], specifically designed to support the Models@run.time paradigm in terms of memory usage and runtime performance. The code generator of KMF generates a modeling API from an Ecore metamodel and offers several features, *e.g.* (1) event-based listeners, (2) management of persistence, (3) different serialization formats (XMI [28] and JSON [15]), and more recently, (4) the option to compile for Java [19] and JavaScript [16].

3.2   Unique IDs and Model Elements Paths in KMF

As described in section 2, our contribution assumes the availability of an attribute, which is able to uniquely identify model elements within relationships. To enforce this, KMF generates a method *getID()*. If one or several attributes are

---
[1] http://kevoree.org/kmf

tagged as IDs in the meta-model, the *getID()* method returns a concatenation of the ID attributes' values, ordered alphabetically on the attributes' names. If no ID attribute is specified, KMF adds one and the generated API automatically injects a UID value at creation, though developers are strongly encouraged to provide a more readable, domain-specific value.

In addition, we also assume the uniqueness of the container for any model element. This property is actually ensured by EMF, and KMF also complies to this convention: apart from the root element that is not contained, every model element has to be present once in a containment collection within the entire model [29]. Then, the unique identifier ensures the uniqueness of model elements in the containment collection. By chaining these pieces of information from the root, KMF can create a path that uniquely identifies each model element in the scope of the model. This defines the semantics to navigate in the model along the space dimension.

As presented in the contribution section, the activation of the versioning of model elements implies an extension of this path mechanism to enable the localization of a model element in both version and modeling dimensions. If the conjunction of the version identifier (VI) to the path is a simple idea, its interpretation to resolve a real model element is more intricate. Moreover, it is important to not pollute the modeling space navigation with versioning concerns. Therefore, we introduce a navigation context that is used to precisely drive both the navigation in versions and support the resolution mechanisms of modeling elements (used by the path resolver). This navigation context is implemented by a special object given to the factory of the generated API. This object seamlessly determines which version should be resolved while the model is traversed.

3.3   Traces and Load/Save Mechanisms

Loading and saving model versions can be efficiently managed by big data-like tools, such as key-value stores. The extended path (path and version ID) of a model element is used as key, and the serialized trace of this elements as value. We provide an expandable datastore interface and several implementations of NoSQL storages. Google LevelDB [5] is used by default. It is optimized for an efficient handling of big data, can be easily embedded into applications, and most importantly, it has proved to be very fast for our purpose (see section 4). The data storage implementation itself is not part of our contribution, instead we intend to provide an efficient layer for versioning of model elements on top of already existing storage technologies. As history data can quickly become very big (millions of elements), they may no longer fit completely into memory. We thus implement a lazy loading [1] mechanism, which leverages our serialization strategy and our notion of path. Attributes and relationships are now only loaded when they are accessed (read or written). Until this happens, we use proxies [1] containing only the path and version identifier, to minimize memory usage. This has been achieved by extending KMF so that relationships are dynamically resolved when the model is traversed. It is important to note that our proxy mechanism works at the model element level rather than at the model level. It first must be determined which version of a related model element must be retrieved. This depends on the navigation context. After this, the actual model element version can be loaded from storage. Load (*get*) and save (*put*) operations are very efficient using extended paths as keys to uniquely identify model element versions. Lazy loading a model element in a specific version requires just one *get* operation from the datastore. This allows to manage models, including histories of arbitrary size, efficiently and it hides the complexity of resolving and navigating versioned data behind a modeling API.

3.4   Navigation Mechanisms

Modeling approaches use meta-model definitions to derive domain specific APIs. Following this idea, our implementation generates an extended API that in addition provides operations to manipulate and navigate the history of model elements. It is illustrated here on a simplified smart grid meta-model definition that consists of a smart meter with an attribute for electric load and a relationship to the reachable surrounding meters. The API provides functions to create, delete, store, load, and navigate model element versions. In addition the API can be used to specify the navigation context on which elements should be resolved while navigating the model. Listing 1.2 shows Java code that uses a Context **ctx** (abstraction to manipulate model element versions) demonstrating some of these operations. In the first part of the listing below, the modeling API is used to create and manipulate a version v_1 of a smart meter element e_1. In the second, the navigation context is defined so that element e_1 is resolved to version v_1 and e_2 to v_2.

Listing 1.2. Usage of the modeling API

```
// creating and manipulating model element versions
e1_1 = ctx.createSmartMeter("e1","v1");
e1_1.setElectricLoad(712.99);
e1_1.addReachables(ctx.load("e2"));
e1_2 = m1.shift("v2");
e1_2.setElectricLoad(1024.4);

// definition of the navigation context
ctx.navDef("e1","v1");
ctx.navDef("e2","v2");
r_e1 = ctx.load("e1");
assert(r_e1.getElectricLoad()==712.99);
r_e2 = r_e1.getReachables().get(0);
assert(r_e2.getVersion()=="v2")
```

4   Evaluation

The native support of versioning at the level of model elements enables the construction of domain specific models, aware of history that, for instance, can empower reasoning processes. To evaluate this claim, this section analyses the impact of using our approach on an industrial case study, which is provided by Creos Luxembourg. In a nutshell, with this case study we evaluate the performance of a model-based reasoning engine that aggregates and navigates smart grid state information to take corrective actions, like shutting down a windmill in case of overproduction. This reasoning is based on a domain model, which is periodically filled with live data from smart meters and sensors. In this context, our approach is used to store and track the history of the smart grid sate and smart-grid elements' values. A new version of a model element is created each time this model element is updated.

The validation is based on three key performance indicators (KPI): (1) evolution of time and memory required to update a value in the model, (2) gain on time for standard navigation operations in the model (*e.g.* for a reasoning process), and (3) impact on the size required for the persistence of history-aware models. For each KPI, we compare our approach with the classic model sampling strategy taking a snapshot of the entire model for each modification (or periodically). The measured memory value for KPI-1 is main memory (RAM), for KPI-2 disk space. The time measured is the time required to complete the process (depending on the KPI). All experiments are conducted on an Intel core i7 CPU with 16GB RAM and an SSD disk. The full sampling approach and our approach both use a Google LevelDB database for storage and run on the Java Virtual Machine 8. We start our evaluation with a description of the meta-model used in the case study.

4.1   Smart Grid Meta-Model

The smart grid is an emerging infrastructure leveraging modern information and communication technology (ICT) to modernize today's electricity grid. Figure 5 shows an excerpt of the smart gird meta-model that we designed together with our industrial partner Creos Luxembourg. It describes the concepts required to model and store an abstraction of the smart grid infrastructure currently deployed in Luxembourg. We use this meta-model to evaluate all KPIs. This meta-model is of central importance for the following evaluation. Smart meters, concentrators, and their topology allow to reason about communication systems and messages exchanged, while electric segments and measured consumption data are used to reason about consumption/production. Smart meters installed at customers sites continuously measure consumption information and propagate it through network communication links. Concentrators then push these data into the smart grid domain model.

4.2   KPI-1: Impact on Model Updates (CRUD)

To evaluate the impact of our approach on model update operations, we analyse modifications of two magnitudes: (1) a large update (LU) that consists in the creation of a new concentrator and a smart meter subtree (1000 units) and (2) a minor update (MU) that consists in updating the consumption value measured for a specific smart meter already present in the domain model. The size of each update is constant and we vary the size of the domain model and the history (number of versions) of measured values, by repeating the addition of model elements. We grow the domain model from 0 to 100.000 elements, which

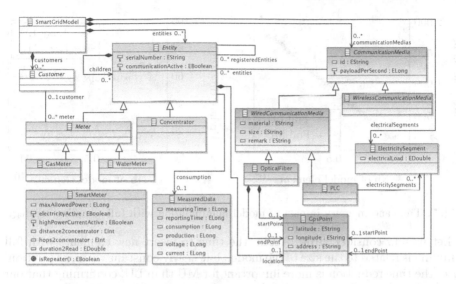

Fig. 5. Smart grid meta-model [4]

approximately corresponds to the actual size of our Luxembourg smart grid model. The results of KPI-1, in term of heap memory and time, are depicted in figure 6 and figure 7. The full sampling strategy is presented on the left, our approach on the right.

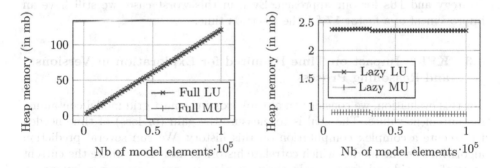

Fig. 6. Memory impact of model manipulation with full and lazy sampling strategies

Let us first consider **memory**. The full sampling strategy depends on the size of the model, as reflected by the linear progression of the heap memory size required to insert fixed size updates. In contrary, our approach results in two flat curves for LU and MU updates, showing that the memory required depends only on the size of the update, not on the model size. This is verified by the fact that minor modifications (MU) require less memory than LU and both are constant and under 2.5MB while the full sampling requires up to 100MB.

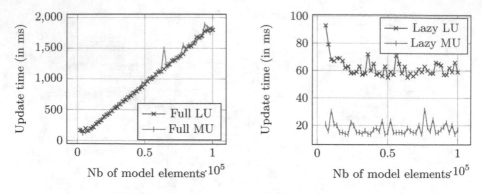

Fig. 7. Time and memory impact of model manipulation with full sampling strategy

Let us now consider **time**. Again, the time to insert new elements with full sampling is related to the size of the model, but nearly constant with our solution. Also, the time reduction is more important for MU than LU, confirming that our approach reduces the necessary time to modify elements. KPI-1 demonstrates that even in the worst case scenario, where all elements evolve at the same pace, our approach offers a major improvement for CRUD operations (factor of 33 for time and between 50 to 100 for memory).

Finally, let us consider **batch insertions**. To validate this result, we additionally performed a batch insert operation in full sampling and with our solution. This batch consists of 10.000 historical values for each meter, resulting in a model of 1 million elements. We obtain as result **267s** to insert with the full sampling strategy and **16s** for our approach. Even in this worst case, we still have an improvement of a factor **17** for the insertion time.

4.3 KPI-2: Impact on Time Required for Exploration in Versions and Reasoning Process

For this evaluation, we consider an already existing smart grid model containing measurement values. The goal is to measure the gain (or loss) of time needed to execute a complex computation on this history. We run several prediction algorithms on the model, which correlate historical data to evaluate the current state of the grid and, for example, throw an alert in case of an overconsumption.

We define two kind of predictions for the smart grid, at two different scales, resulting in 4 different reasoning strategies: (1) small deep prediction (SDP), (2) small wide prediction (SWP), (3) large deep prediction (LDP), and (4) large wide prediction (LWP). Wide prediction means that the strategy uses a correlation of data from neighbour meters, to predict the future consumption. In a deep prediction, the strategy leverages the history of the customer to predict its consumption habits. Both approaches perform a linear regression to predict the future consumption using two scales: large (100 meters) and small (10). Results and time reduction factors are presented in the table 1. The gain factor of our approach, compared to full sampling, is defined

Table 1. Reasoning time in ms for consumption predictions

Type	SDP	SWP	LDP	LWP
Full	1147.75 ms	1131.13 ms	192271.19 ms	188985.69 ms
Lazy	2.06 ms	0.85 ms	189.03 ms	160.03 ms
Factor	557	1330	1017	1180

as $Factor = (Full\ Sampling\ time\ /\ Native\ Versioning\ time)$. The gain factor is between **557** and **1330**, reducing the processing time from minutes to seconds. Although, we perform the computation for only one point of the grid, it has to be multiplied by the number of smart meters to evaluate in a district. Now, the gain highlighted here has already allowed to drop the time required to analyse the entire grid, from hours of computation to seconds. Beyond Models@run.time usage, this enables reasoning processes to react in near real-time (milliseconds to seconds), which is required for smart grid protection reactions.

4.4   KPI-3: Versioning Storage Strategy Overhead Evaluation

In this section, we study and evaluate the overhead induced by our approach, compared to the classic full model sampling strategy. Our goal is to detect the percentage of modifications of a model, in a single version, above which the full sampling approach creates less overhead. In other words, which percentage of modifications makes the overhead of our solution a disadvantage in terms of storage, despite its navigation gains are still valid.

For this evaluation, we load an existing model (containing 100 smart meters), update the consumption value of several meters, serialize it again and store the size. By varying the percentage of meters updated per version (period), we can compare the size of the storage required for the diff with our approach, and the full sampling. To ensure a fair comparison we use a compact JSON serialisation format for both strategies. Results are depicted in Figure 8. The full sampling

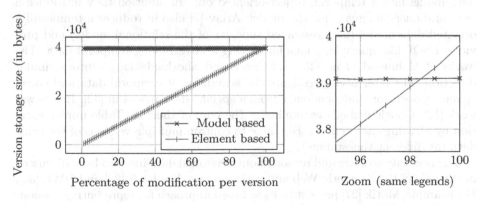

Fig. 8. Impact on the storage required to save versions

mechanism implies 39.1Kb of storage per model, regardless of the percentage of modifications. This is a serious overhead for small modifications. Our strategy requires a variable amount of memory, from 393 bytes for 1% of change to 39.8Kb for 100% (complete change of the model). Also, linear augmentation of changes in the model with our approach creates a linear augmentation of the storage. This confirms that our independent storage strategy for each model element has no hidden side effect.

Our storage offers a reduction of **99.5%** for 1% of change, but an increase of only 1.02% for 100% of modifications. This means that, up to **98.5%** of modifications of a model, our approach needs less memory than full sampling. Also, the overhead of 1.02% for full model change storage has to be related to the features enabled by this overhead (navigation, insertion time gains, comparison time gains). In this context, we consider the overhead acceptable.

Beside runtime usage improvements, this validation proves that we can offer nearly constant memory and time consumption for model-based contexts, which allows to face potentially massive history. These improvements are mainly due to lazy-load and efficient path mechanisms, which by construction reduce the floating memory window to read and write model elements. Similarly to how NoSQL databases scale, we carefully reuse the modeling hierarchy concept to fit with the datastore organization that offers the best performance, which explains this very considerable gain. Finally, this validation demonstrates that our approach is suitable for the manipulation of massive historical model.

5 Related Work

Considering versioning (or time) as a crosscutting concern of data modeling has been discussed for a long time, especially in database communities. In [13] Clifford *et al.* provide a formal semantic for historical databases and an intentional logic. Rose and Segev [31] incorporate temporal structures in the data model itself, rather than at the application level, by extending the entity-relationship data model into a temporal, object-oriented one. In addition they introduce a temporal query language for the model. Ariav [7] also introduces a temporally-oriented data model (as a restricted superset of the relational model) and provides a SQL-like query language for storing and retrieving temporal data. The works of Mahmood *et al.* [25] and Segev and Shoshani [33] go into a similar direction. The later also investigate the semantics of temporal data and corresponding operators independently from a specific data model in [32]. In a newer work [12], Google embeds versioning at the core of their BigTable implementation by allowing each cell in a BigTable to contain multiple versions of the same data (at different timestamps).

The necessity to store and reason about versioned data has also been discussed in the area of the Semantic Web and its languages, like RDF [24] and OWL [35]. For example, Motik [27] presents a logic-based approach for representing versions in RDF and OWL.

Recently, the need to efficiently version models has been explored in the domain of model-driven engineering. However, model versioning has been mainly considered so far as an infrastructural issue in the sense that models are artifacts that can evolve and must be managed in a similar manner to textual artifacts like source code. Kerstin Altmanninger *et al.* [6] analyze the challenges coming along with model merging and derive a categorization of typical changes and resulting conflicts. Building on this, they provide a set of test cases which they apply on state-of-the-art versioning systems. Koegel and Helming [22] take a similar direction with their EMFStore model repository. Their work focuses on how to commit and update changes and how to perform a merge on a model. Brosch *et al.* [10] also consider model versioning as a way to enable efficient team-based development of models. They provide an introduction to the foundations of model versioning, the underlying technologies for processing models and their evolution, as well as the state of the art. Taentzer *et al.* [34] present an approach that, in contrast to text-based versioning systems, takes model structures and their changes over time into account. In their approach, they consider models as graphs and focus on two different kinds of conflict detection, operation-based conflicts between different graph modifications and the check for state-based conflicts' on merged graph modifications. These works consider versioning at a model level rather than at a model element level. Moreover, these approaches focus on versioning of meta-models whereas our work focuses on versioning of runtime/execution models. Our approach enables not only to version a complete model, but considers versioning and history as native mechanisms for any model element. Moreover, versioning in the modeling domain is usually considered from a design / architecture / infrastructural point of view, and models are versioned as source code files would be. In contrast to this, our versioning approach regards the evolution of model elements from an application point of view (*e.g.* Bigtable [12] or temporal databases [25]). It allows to keep track of the evolution of domain model elements —their history— and use this history efficiently on an application level.

Most of the above mentioned work address storing and querying of versioned data but largely ignores the handling of versioning at an application level. However, many reasoning processes require to explore simultaneously the current state and past history to detect situations like a system state flapping. Our approach proposes to consider model versioning and history as native mechanisms for modeling foundations. We not only efficiently store historical data (what is done in other works before), but we propose a way to seamlessly use and navigate in historized models. Also, we do not extend a specific data model (*e.g.* the relational data model or object-oriented one) but use model-driven engineering techniques to integrate versioning as a crosscutting property of any model element. We aim at providing a natural and seamless navigation into the history of model element versions. Just like version control systems, *e.g.* Git [2], we only store incremental changes rather than snapshots of a complete model.

6   Conclusion

The use of models to organize and store dynamic data suffers from the lack of native mechanism to handle the history of data in modeling foundations. Meanwhile, the recent evolutions of model-driven engineering, and more precisely, the emergence of the Models@run.time paradigm spreads the use of models to support reasoning at runtime. Therefore, the need for efficient mechanisms to store and navigate the history of model element values (*a.k.a.* dynamic data) has strongly increased. The contribution presented in this paper aims at addressing this need, adding a version identifier as a first-class feature crosscutting any model element. This approach, coupled with the notion of trace and lazy load/save techniques, allows model elements to be versioned independently from each other without the need to version a complete model. Moreover, this paper describes the navigation methods introduced on each model element to enable the basic navigation in versions. Finally, we defined a navigation context to simplify and improve the performances of navigation between model elements coming from heterogeneous (different) versions.

We evaluate the added value of this work on a case study from the smart grid domain, defined with an industrial partner. The validation relies on an implementation of the approach into the Kevoree Modeling Framework. This evaluation shows the efficiency of the storage and navigation mechanisms compared to full sampling and *ad-hoc* navigation techniques. It also demonstrates that in the worst case (*i.e.* when all model elements are modified at the same pace) the storage overhead is negligible (1.02%), while our navigation mechanism still offer constant performances. Even if the evaluation has been run in use cases linked to the Models@run.time paradigm, we are convinced that this approach can also be used in any kind of applications using versioned data. For example, we use a derivation of this approach to enable what we call *time-distorted* context representations to manage a huge amount of temporal data in runtime reasoning processes [21]. This has been proven especially useful in the context of reactive security for smart grids [20].

In future work we plan to: (i) integrate a declarative query language on top of our approach to improve the selection of model element versions, instead of relying only on the three basic operations *shift*, *previous*, and *next*, (ii) use distributed data stores like HyperDex DB [3], and (iii) define reusable patterns of version navigation to tame the complexity of reasoning process development.

Acknowledgments. The research leading to this publication is supported by the National Research Fund Luxembourg (grant 6816126) and Creos Luxembourg S.A. under the SnT-Creos partnership program.

References

1. CDO eclipsedia, http://wiki.eclipse.org/CDO (accessed: February 01, 2014)
2. Git, http://git-scm.com/
3. HyperLevelDB Performance Benchmarks, http://hyperdex.org/performance/leveldb/ (accessed: February 01, 2014)
4. KMF Samples, MoDELS14, https://github.com/kevoree/kmf-samples/models14 (accessed: March 15, 2014)
5. leveldb a fast and lightweight key/value database library by google, https://code.google.com/p/leveldb/ (accessed: February 10, 2014)

6. Altmanninger, K., Kaufmann, P., Kappel, G., Langer, P., Seidl, M., Wieland, K., Wimmer, M.: Why model versioning research is needed!? An experience report. In: Proceedings of the Joint MoDSE-MC-CM 2009 Workshop (2009)
7. Ariav, G.: A temporally oriented data model. ACM Trans. Database Syst. 11(4), 499–527 (1986)
8. Blair, G., Bencomo, N., France, R.B.: Models@ run.time. Computer 42(10), 22–27 (2009)
9. Blanc, X., Mounier, I., Mougenot, A., Mens, T.: Detecting model inconsistency through operation-based model construction. In: Proceedings of the 30th International Conference on Software Engineering, ICSE 2008, pp. 511–520. ACM, New York (2008)
10. Brosch, P., Kappel, G., Langer, P., Seidl, M., Wieland, K., Wimmer, M.: An introduction to model versioning. In: Bernardo, M., Cortellessa, V., Pierantonio, A. (eds.) SFM 2012. LNCS, vol. 7320, pp. 336–398. Springer, Heidelberg (2012)
11. Budinsky, F., Steinberg, D., Ellersick, R.: Eclipse Modeling Framework: A Developer's Guide (2003)
12. Chang, F., Dean, J., Ghemawat, S., Hsieh, W.C., Wallach, D.A., Burrows, M., Chandra, T., Fikes, A., Gruber, R.E.: Bigtable: A distributed storage system for structured data. In: Proceedings of the 7th USENIX Symposium on Operating Systems Design and Implementation, OSDI 2006, vol. 7, p. 15. USENIX Association, Berkeley (2006)
13. Clifford, J., Warren, D.S.: Formal semantics for time in databases. In: XP2 Workshop on Relational Database Theory (1981)
14. World Wide Web Consortium. Xml path language (xpath) 2.0. Technical report, World Wide Web Consortium, 2nd edn. (2010)
15. Douglas Crockford. The application/json media type for javascript object notation (json). RFC 4627, IETF, 7 (2006)
16. ECMA International. Standard ECMA-262 - ECMAScript Language Specification, 5.1th edn. (June 2011)
17. Fouquet, F., Nain, G., Morin, B., Daubert, E., Barais, O., Plouzeau, N., Jézéquel, J.-M.: An eclipse modelling framework alternative to meet the models@runtime requirements. In: France, R.B., Kazmeier, J., Breu, R., Atkinson, C. (eds.) MODELS 2012. LNCS, vol. 7590, pp. 87–101. Springer, Heidelberg (2012)
18. Francois, F., Nain, G., Morin, B., Daubert, E., Barais, O., Plouzeau, N., Jézéquel, J.-M.: Kevoree Modeling Framework (KMF): Efficient modeling techniques for runtime use. Rapport de recherche TR-SnT-2014-11 (May 2014) ISBN 978-2-87971-131-7
19. Gosling, J., Joy, B., Steele, G., Bracha, G., Buckley, A.: The Java Language Specification, java se 7th edn., California, USA (February 2012)
20. Hartmann, T., Fouquet, F., Klein, J., Nain, G., Le Traon, Y.: Reactive security for smart grids using models@run.time-based simulation and reasoning. In: Cuellar, J. (ed.) SmartGridSec 2014. LNCS, vol. 8448, pp. 139–153. Springer, Heidelberg (2014)
21. Hartmann, T., Fouquet, F., Nain, G., Morin, B., Klein, J., Le Traon, Y.: Reasoning at runtime using time-distorted contexts: A models@run.time based approach. In: Proceedings of the 26th International Conference on Software Engineering and Knowledge Engineering, SEKE (2014)

22. Koegel, M., Helming, J.: Emfstore: A model repository for emf models. In: Kramer, J., Bishop, J., Devanbu, P.T., Uchitel, S. (eds.) ICSE, (2), pp. 307–308. ACM (2010)
23. Kolovos, D.S., Di Ruscio, D., Pierantonio, A., Paige, R.F.: Different models for model matching: An analysis of approaches to support model differencing. In: Proceedings of the 2009 ICSE Workshop on Comparison and Versioning of Software Models, CVSM 2009, pp. 1–6. IEEE Computer Society (2009)
24. Lassila, O., Swick, R.R.: Resource Description Framework (RDF) Model and Syntax Specification. W3C Recommendation, W3C (February 1999)
25. Mahmood, N., Burney, A., Ahsan, K.: A logical temporal relational data model. CoRR (2010)
26. Morin, B., Barais, O., Jezequel, J., Fleurey, F., Solberg, A.: Models@ run.time to support dynamic adaptation. Computer 42(10), 44–51 (2009)
27. Motik, B.: Representing and querying validity time in rdf and owl: A logic-based approac. In: Patel-Schneider, P.F., Pan, Y., Hitzler, P., Mika, P., Zhang, L., Pan, J.Z., Horrocks, I., Glimm, B. (eds.) ISWC 2010, Part I. LNCS, vol. 6496, pp. 550–565. Springer, Heidelberg (2010)
28. OMG. XML Metadata Interchange (XMI). OMG (2007)
29. OMG. OMG Meta Object Facility (MOF) Core Specification, Version 2.4.1. Technical report, Object Management Group (August 2011)
30. Reddy, R., France, R., Ghosh, S., Fleurey, F., Baudry, B.: Model composition - a signature-based approach. In: Aspect Oriented Modeling (AOM) Workshop Held in Conjunction with MODELS/UML 2005 Conference, Montego Bay, Jamaica (2005)
31. Rose, E., Segev, A.: Toodm - a temporal object-oriented data model with temporal constraints. In: Teorey, T.J. (ed.) ER (1991)
32. Segev, A., Shoshani, A.: Logical modeling of temporal data. In: Proceedings of the 1987 ACM SIGMOD International Conference on Management of Data, SIGMOD 1987, New York, NY, USA (1987)
33. Segev, A., Shoshani, A.: The representation of a temporal data model in the relational environment. In: Rafanelli, M., Svensson, P., Klensin, J.C. (eds.) SSDBM 1988. LNCS, vol. 339, pp. 39–61. Springer, Heidelberg (1989)
34. Taentzer, G., Ermel, C., Langer, P., Wimmer, M.: A fundamental approach to model versioning based on graph modifications: From theory to implementation. Software and System Modeling 13(1), 239–272 (2014)
35. World Wide Web Consortium W3C. Owl 2 web ontology language. structural specification and functional-style syntax. Technical report (2009)

Modelling Adaptation Policies
as Domain-Specific Constraints*

Hui Song[1], Xiaodong Zhang[2], Nicolas Ferry[1], Franck Chauvel[1],
Arnor Solberg[1], and Gang Huang[2]

[1] SINTEF ICT, Oslo, Norway
{first.last}@sintef.no
[2] Peking University, Beijing, China
{xdzh,hg}@pku.edu.cn

Abstract. In order to develop appropriate adaptation policies for self-adaptive systems, developers usually have to accomplish two main tasks: (i) identify the application-level constraints that regulate the desired system states for the various contexts, and (ii) figure out how to transform the system to satisfy these constraints. The second task is challenging because typically there is complex interaction among constraints, and a significant gap between application domain expertice and state transition expertice. In this paper, we present a model-driven approach that relieves developers from this second task, allowing them to directly write domain-specific constraints as adaptation policies. We provide a language to model both the domain concepts and the application-level constraints. Our runtime engine transforms the model into a Satisfiability Modulo Theory problem, optimises it by pre-processing on the current system state at runtime, and computes required modifications according to the specified constraints using constraints solving. We evaluate the approach addressing a virtual machine placement problem in cloud computing.

1 Introduction

As software systems and their interactions with the executing environments are becoming more and more complex, many systems are required to adjust themselves at runtime to harmonize with their dynamic environments. Such self-adaptations can be seen as guided transitions between system states (such as the system's structure, configuration, environments, etc.). A key challenge to build such self-adaptive systems [1] is to develop the adaptation policies that guide such transitions [2,3]. To develop appropriate policies, developers usually need to cope with the following two concerns: (i) to identify the constraints on the system states for the various contexts, which determine when the system needs to be adapted, and what are the desired states after adaptation. (ii) to

* This work is partially funded by the European Communitys Seventh Framework Programme (FP7/2007-2013) under grant agreement numbers: 318484 (MODAClouds), 600654 (DIVERSIFY) and 318392 (Broker@Cloud), and the National Natural Science Foundation of China (Grant No. 61361120097, 61222203, U1201252).

J. Dingel et al. (Eds.): MODELS 2014, LNCS 8767, pp. 269–285, 2014.

figure out the appropriate transitions between system states that satisfy these constraints. Developers specify these transitions in a policy language (e.g., in event, condition, action (ECA) rules). Figuring out the transitions is particularly challenging, because the constraints usually have complex *interactions* with each other, i.e., a transition that satisfies one constraint may violates another. Moreover, there is typically a conceptual gap between constraints in the application domain (e.g., cloud computing, health care, etc.), and transitions in a state-transition model (e.g., ECA or state machines).

In this paper, we propose a model-driven approach where developers can directly specify the constraints as adaptation policies, using concepts specific to the application domain and applying the object oriented constraint specification language, the OCL [4]. Our runtime engine then dynamically computes the required modifications on the current system to satisfy the constraints.

This approach is based on our previous work [5], which showed that SMT (Satisfiability Modulo Theory) constraint solving [6] can be used to compute adaptation decisions from constraints in First Order Logic (FOL). However, we used a simple SMT theory based on variables and operations, and therefore it only supports adaptation of numeric configurations. To support domain-specific modelling of constraints, more expressive theories to encode structural information such as objects and references between them, are needed. This implicates the challenge to transform expressive OCL constraints to SMT. Moreover, the previous work lacks a way to assist developers in specifying the constraints. To address these challenges, we present the following contributions in this paper.

- A modelling language based on MOF and OCL to specify adaptation policies as application domain concepts and constraints applying these concepts;
- A new method to encode object-oriented models and constraints to SMT instances, to enable the use of SMT constraint solving for adaptation.
- A new partial evaluation semantics on OCL, which realises the systematic transformation from OCL constraints to formulas used by SMT, and optimizes the formulas by embedding the current system states into them.

We have applied the approach on a representative self-adaptation problem, the dynamic mapping of virtual machines to physical machines in clouds. The case study shows that the approach is able to specify classical adaptation policies, and produces desired adaptation decisions. The partial evaluation significantly improves the performance of constraint solving, making it applicable at runtime.

The rest of this paper is organised as follows. Section 2 introduces a running example, and outlines the approach. Sections 3, 4 and 5 present our modelling language, the generation of SMT instances and the computation of adaptation decision using SMT solving, respectively. Section 6 shows our case study. Section 7 discusses related approaches and Section 8 concludes the paper.

2   Approach Overview

2.1   Motivating Example

Managment of the mapping of virtual machines (VM) to physical machines (PM) in private clouds can be treated as a dynamic adaptation problem. Different from renting VMs from public clouds, an organisation that sets up its own private cloud has the full control of the infrastructures (i.e., PMs) behind the VMs. As the system keeps evolving (e.g., new VMs are provisioned, applications are deployed on VMs), the infrastructure administrators need to adjust the placement and configuration of VMs, in order to optimise the overall deployment.

Figure 1 illustrates a simplified private cloud, where three VMs are placed on two PMs, each VM requires and provides different numbers of CPU cores and memory sizes (unit in GB). We assume that the adaptation engine is capable of altering the VM placement and the provided CPU cores. Early approaches on VM placement mainly consider resource limitations and consolidations (e.g., a single VM's CPU core number should not exceed its hosting PM, total VM memory should not exceed the PM's capacity, and using as few PMs as possible to save energy) [7]. These concerns implies migrating vm3 to pm1.

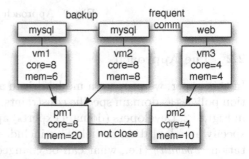

Fig. 1. A simplified VM placement problem

However, there are other concerns that impact the adaptation decisions. For example, based on the applications shown in Figure 1 we can see that vm1 and vm2 are replicated for backup purposes (we simplified the identification of backup relations between VMs: Any two VMs that host applications with the same name are backup to each other). The two VMs should be placed in different PMs so that a physical crash would not halt both VMs and makes the application data unavailable. Moreover, if vm2 and vm3 are communicating frequently, they should ideally be deployed on two PMs that are "close" in terms of latency, or even the same PM. Considering these two objectives, a potential modification is to swap vm1 and vm3, and decrease the CPU cores of vm1, even though this violates the objective of consolidation. Finally, migrating VMs is an expensive operation, depends on their memory sizes. When a to-be-migrated VM is big, a better choice may be to keep the current configuration.

As highlighted by the example, an adaptive system typically have many constraints, and an action that satisfies one constraint may violate others. Manually developing adaptation policies by exhausting all the constraints to figure out appropriate actions is not practical for complex systems.

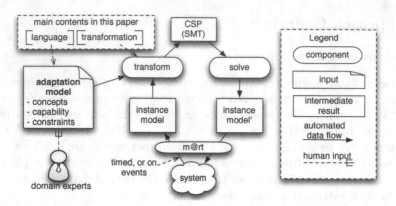

Fig. 2. Approach architecture

2.2 The Approach

In this paper, we propose a model-driven approach to enable specifying adaptation policies as domain specific constraints. The overall architecture is illustrated in Figure 2. Developers (domain experts) apply their knowledge of the domain to specify an adaptation model. This includes the base domain *concepts*, the adaptation *capability* (i.e., what can be changed by adaptation), and the *constraints* applying the domain concepts to specify what are the desired system states for various contexts. From the adaptation model, we perform an automated adaptation at runtime, using three components. The *models@runtime engine* maintains an updated instance model monitoring the system state (through a causal connection). From the current instance model and the adaptation model, the *transformation engine* interprets *what the constraints imply on the current system state*, and generates an SMT instance, which is fed to the *constraint solver* to compute the appropriate target system state, taking into account the constraints, their priorities, and the cost of system modifications. Finally, the models@runtime engine propagates the changes to the real system.

On the basis of our previous work on models@runtime engine [8] and constraint solving for adaptation [5], this paper is focused on the *front-end* of this approach, i.e., the modelling language for domain-specific constraints, and the transformation to an SMT instance. At this stage, we base our work on the *closed world assumption*, i.e., the number of objects under each type is not subjected to be changed by the adaptation. This assumption is reasonable in our VM placement example: It is the administrator's duty to provision or terminate VMs, whereas the adaptation engine optimises the deployment of them.

3 Constraint Modelling

We provide a prototype language based on MOF and OCL to assist the modelling of adaptation policies as constraints. Figure 3 is a snapshot of the model for the

```
vmplc.constraint ⊠

 9⊝ class VM{
10      id String name        Integer mem
11      config Integer core : {domain = Set{1,2,4,8} cost=20}
12      config PM plc : { cost=(mem*10) }
13⊝     VM[*] backup : {derived
14          VM.allInstances()->select(v|v<>self and v.app.name=self.app.name) }
15      ref VM[*] frqt     ref App app
16      constraint (hard) CoreLimit: self.core<=self.plc.core
17      constraint (priority = 80) BackupSplit: backup->forAll(e|e.plc<>self.plc)
18⊝     constraint (priority = 30) FrequentNear :
19          frqt->forAll(v|v.plc.near->includes(self.plc)) }
20⊝ class PM{
21      id String name
22      Integer mem    Integer core   ref PM[*] near
23      ref VM[*] hosting:{derived VM.allInstances()->select(plc=self)}
24      constraint(hard) MemLimit: hosting->collect(e|e.mem)->sum() < mem
25      constraint(priority=10) Consolidation: hosting->size()=0}
```

Fig. 3. Constraints for VM placement

VM placement problem, taken from our text-based modelling editor with syntax checking and auto-completion. The modelling process has two steps: defining the concepts in the domain, and specifying the constraints applying the concepts.

The concept modelling is to specify the *types* of elements that compose the system states (e.g., the concepts VMs, PMs at Line 9 and 20), the *attributes* of these types (such as VM.mem at Line 10, for the memory required by a VM), and the *relations* between them (e.g., VM.plc at Line 12 records on which PM a VM is placed).

A property (attribute or relation) marked by "[*]" is a multi-valued one. Derived property can be defined by an OCL query. For example, the set of backups of an VM is the subset of VM instances that host Apps with the same name. Developers also need to define *what properties can be changed by adaptation* (which are marked by keyword config, such as VM.plc at Line 12), and *the changing scope of such a property* (which is defined by an OCL expression in type of collection, such as the domain of VM.core at 11).

Constraint modelling captures the developers' concerns regarding *what are the desired system states*, such as MemoryLimit (Line 24) and BackupSplit (Line 17), with the meanings discussed above. In our language, a constraint is defined as an boolean-typed OCL expression, inside a target class. Take the MemLimit constraint as an example, the direct meaning of the OCL expression is as follows: For each PM, we get the hosted VMs on it (which in turn is derived from the configurable reference VM.plc), collect the mem of these VMs, and calculate the sum of them. Then we claim that this summary should be less than or equal to the mem of the PM. Each constraint is assigned with a priority between 0 and 100, indicating how important it is. A hard constraint is the one that must be satisfied. Each configurable property has a cost, indicating the importance to maintain the current values, e.g., the cost of changing a VM's placement (i.e., VM migration) is proportional to its memory size.

4   SMT Instance Generation

In this section, we first give an overview about SMT, illustrated by our running example. After that, we summarise the mapping from an adaptation model to the SMT instance. Finally, we present a partial evaluation approach to transform and simplify OCL constraints into formulas in SMT.

4.1   SMT Overview

In order to apply automated constraint solving for adaptation, we convert the adaptation problem into an SMT instance composed of *functions* and *constraints*, based on the theories of uninterpreted functions [9], algebraic data types [10], linear arithmetic, and first order logic (FOL). An *uninterpreted function* is a function that declares domains and a codomain, but without a definition about the concrete mapping between them. A domain or codomain can be a primitive data type (integer, real or boolean), or an enumeration. Here we define enumerations using *algebraic type theory*, which supports defining a type from limited and disjoint constructors[1]. The constraints are boolean-valued FOL formulas on these functions, connected by arithmetic and logic operators. An SMT solver searches possible interpretations for the functions, satisfying all the constraints.

Figure 4 shows a sample SMT instance. It is divided in three parts.

$$VM : \{vm_1, vm_2, vm_3\}, \; PM : \{pm_1, pm_2\}, \; \text{int, boolean}$$

$$vc : VM \to \text{int}, \; pc : PM \to \text{int}, \; vmem : VM \to \text{int}, \; pmem : PM \to \text{int}$$

$$plc : VM \to PM, \; frqt : VM \times VM \to \text{bool}, \; near : PM \times PM \to \text{bool}$$

$$\forall vm, pm. \; (plc(vm) = pm \Rightarrow vc(vm) \leq pc(pm))$$

$$\forall pm. \left(\sum_{vm \in VM} \text{ite}(plc(vm) = pm, vmem(vm), 0)) \leq pmem(pm) \right)$$

$$\forall vm, vm'. \, (frqt(vm, vm') \Rightarrow near(plc(vm), plc(vm'))) , \forall pm. \, (near(pm, pm))$$

$$vc(vm_1) = 8, vmem(vm_1) = 6, plc(vm_2) = pm_1, frqt(vm_2, vm_3)...$$

Fig. 4. VM placement in SMT

The first part defines the realm of this VM placement problem, in the form of functions and their domain types. Under a closed-world assumption, the number of objects of type VM or PM is not subject to change by the adaptation, and therefore each type is an enumeration of its current objects (Of course, administrators can still add or remove VMs and PMs, and the new VMs can

---

[1] For example, an enumeration Colour with red, green, and blue can be defined as (type C::=r|g|b), meaning that the type C has three unique constructors. Algebraic type theory is supported by SMT solvers such as Z3 [11]

be moved between PMs by our adaptation engine). The functions for virtual cores (vc), physical cores (pc), virtual memory ($vmem$) and physical memory ($pmem$) from the enumerations to primitive types represent states of objects. The functions placement (plc), frequent ($frqt$) and near ($near$) represent the relations between objects. Placement (plc) is a *functional relation*, specifying that a VM is placed on one and only one PM. By contrast, frequent ($fqrt$) is an example of *binary relation*. For two VMs vm and vm', $frqt(vm, vm') = $ **true** means they are communicating frequently.

The second part of the SMT instance defines the constraints applying FOL formulas. The first constraint specifies that the number of CPU cores required by a vm cannot exceed the one provided by its hosting pm. The second constraint specifies that the total memory size of VMs hosted on the same PM should not exceed the memory provided by this PM. The constraint computes the sum of VM's memories utilizing a predefined ite(if-then-else) function from the SMT-LIB standard [12], which returns the second or the third parameter based on if the first one is true or false, respectively. The constraint denotes to iterate over all vms, and if and only if a vm is placed on the specific pm its memory is added to the sum. The third constraint depicts that two frequently communicating vms should be deployed to pms that are *near* to each other (remark that a PM is also considered to be *near* to itself).

The third part of the SMT instance expresses the current state of the model instance as a set of equations between function calls and values. The excerpt of Figure 4 is according to the state shown in Figure 1.

Solving these SMT constraints can be very time-consuming. However, the constraints can be simplified significantly based on knowledge of the current system state (i.e., the third part), making the solving much more efficient. For example, according to Figure 1, we know that there is one and only one pair of VMs (vm2 and vm3) that are frequently communicating, and this will not be changed after the adaptation. Therefore, we can weave this known information into the constraints and rewrite the third constraint in Figure 4 simply as $near(plc(vm_2), plc(vm_3))$. In our approach, we provide to directly generate such simplified constraints.

4.2   Mapping from Adaptation Model to SMT

In order to transform the adaptation model into an SMT instance, we need systematic mappings from the elements in the adaptation model to their corresponding representations in SMT. Table 1 summarises these mapping rules. A class is mapped into an enumeration, with its objects as the enumerable items, and primitive types are transformed to the corresponding integer, real or boolean types in SMT (according to mc in Table 1). Objects and primitive data are mapped to enumeration items or primitive values (mo). A C2-typed single-valued property p defined in class C1 is mapped to an uninterpreted function with one parameter, while a multi-valued one (marked by a "*" in the table) is mapped to a function with two parameters (mp). The two functions plc and $frqt$ in Figure 4 are examples for the two categories, respectively. The OCL constraints,

Table 1. Mapping from adaptation model to SMT instance.

model	SMT	name
class C with objects o1, o2	enum C $\{o_1, o_2\}$	mc
types `int`, `real`, `boolean`	SMT types: $\mathbb{Z}$, $\mathbb{R}$, $\mathbb{B}$	
object o: C	enum item $o \in C$	mo
value v:	literal value v	
single property: `C1.p:C2`	function $p : C_1 \to C_2$	mp
multiple property: `C1.p:C2[*]`	function $p : C_1 \times C_2 \to \mathbb{B}$	
constraint, derivation, domain	FOL formula	PE
property value: o.p=d	$p(o) = d$	ms
o.p=D=$\{d_i \mid i \in 1..n\}$	$(\bigwedge_{d_i} a(o, d_i)) \wedge (\bigwedge_{d_j} \neg a(o, d_j)) d_j \in C_2 - D$	

and the derivation and domain definitions are mapped to FOL formulas (such as the ones shown in the second part of Figure 4). The transformation (named PE) will be shown in the next section. Finally, we generate constraints from the current values of properties (ms). If a single valued property p of object o has value d, we enforce $p(o) = d$. However, for a multi-valued p, the value will be a set D of data or enumeration items. The generated constraint enforces that for any $d_i \in D$, $p(o, d_i)$ is true, and for any other d_j, $p(o, d_j)$ is false.

4.3   Partial Evaluation of OCL Constraints

We use partial evaluation (PE) [13] to transform the OCL constraints into SMT predicates such as the ones shown in the second part of Figure 4, and simplify the results based on the static information in the current model instance. In particular, PE takes three inputs: an *OCL expression*, a *static model* and a *context*, and outputs FOL formulas. The following example illustrates how we notate partial evaluation in our approach.

$$[\![\texttt{self.core<self.mem-2}]\!]_{\{\texttt{self} \mapsto \texttt{vm2}\}}(m_s) = (< (\text{core vm2}) \; 6)$$

The *OCL expression* is written inside the brackets $[\![]\!]^2$. The *static model* m_s is the part of a model instance that does not change after adaptation, e.g., below is the static model corresponding to Figure 1

```
vm2:VM{mem=8, frqt=[vm3], app=[app1], core =_, plc=_}
pm2:PM{mem=10, core=4, near=[]}
```

Here we give every dynamic property (defined by `config` in Figure 3) an undefined value "_". The *context* τ is a map from variables to values or objects in m_s, and in this example, $\tau = \{\texttt{self} \mapsto \texttt{vm2}\}$, meaning that the variable `self` in the OCL expression represents `vm2`. The output of PE is a FOL formula, written

---

[2] We borrow the "$[\![]\!]$" notation from denotational semantics, which indicates that PE can be understood as another semantics to OCL language, i.e., a function from a static model to a FOL formula, depending on a context.

in the standard SMT-LIB language [12] following the style of prefix notation. This output has the same meaning of $core(vm2) < 6^3$. In this example, since vm2.mem=8 is known in m_s, we directly evaluate self.mem-2 into a value 6, whereas since vm2.core is unknown, we translate it into a function call.

The Fidelity Property PE should guarantee the *fidelity* of the transformation from OCL to SMT, which means any adaptation result that satisfies the generated SMT should also satisfy the original OCL constraints, and vice versa. Specifically, a static model m_s can be complemented with dynamic information (notated as m_d), so that $m_s + m_d$ is a complete model and therefore can be *fully* evaluated by a common OCL engine. Fidelity means that no matter what m_d we give on m_s, $(\llbracket e \rrbracket_\tau(m_s) = \llbracket e \rrbracket_\tau(m_s + m_d)) \wedge \mathsf{ms}(m_d)$ is always true. Here, $\llbracket e \rrbracket_\tau(m_s + m_d)$ degrades into normal OCL evaluation, and $\mathsf{ms}(m_d)$, as defined in Table 1, is a set of predicates encoding the dynamic information. For example, the sample above satisfies fidelity, because if we give vm2.core a value smaller than 6 (say 5), then the full evaluation results true, and $(core(vm_2) < 6 = \mathbf{true}) \wedge core(vm_2) = 5$ holds. It is the same when vm2.core > 6.

PE is executed in a recursive way, following the OCL syntax tree [4]. For example, the first step to evaluate the example above will be:
$\llbracket \texttt{self.core<self.mem-2} \rrbracket_\tau(m_s) = (< \ \llbracket \texttt{self.core} \rrbracket_\tau(m_s) \ \llbracket \texttt{self.mem-2} \rrbracket_\tau(m_s))$,
and after that $\llbracket \texttt{self.mem-2} \rrbracket_\tau(m_s) = (- \ \llbracket \texttt{self.mem} \rrbracket_\tau(m_s) \ 2) = (- \ 8 \ 2) = 6$.

In the following, we explain how we do PE by defining the transformation rules on the typical OCL syntax structures.

We start from the basic building blocks of OCL expressions. For a literal constant of primitive value, we directly transform it into the corresponding value (Equation 1). For the reference to a variable v, we obtain its value from the context τ and return it (2). The let statement (3) introduces a new variable into the main expression. We evaluate the source expression e_1 into result r, and add a new variable mapping $v \mapsto r$ into the context dictionary τ, so that the variable v in e_2 will be r in the subsequent evaluation.

$$\llbracket \texttt{literal} \rrbracket_\tau(m_s) = \mathsf{mo}(\text{literal}) \qquad (1)$$

$$\llbracket \texttt{v} \rrbracket_\tau(m_s) = r, (v \mapsto r) \in \tau \qquad (2)$$

$$\llbracket \texttt{let v=e}_1 \texttt{ in e}_2 \rrbracket_\tau(m_s) = \llbracket e_2 \rrbracket_{\tau \cup \{v \mapsto r\}}(m_s) \textbf{ where } r = \llbracket e_1 \rrbracket_\tau(m_s) \qquad (3)$$

The transformation of OCL property calls is the main point to encode object-oriented structures into FOL formulas (4). We first evaluate the source expression e into result r. If r is an object (which means that e purely depends on the static model), and $r.p$ has a value v in the static model, we directly return v. However, if $r.p$ is undefined, or if r is a formula (which means that e depends on dynamic information), we compose a new formula using the functions

---

[3] We use SMT-LIB to distinguish the transformation outputs (i.e., an SMT "program") from the calculations within the evaluation. For example (f 5) means a SMT formula that call function f with parameter 5, while $\mathsf{mo}(o)$ means that PE obtains the enumeration item for object o

and constants resolved from p and r, respectively. The composition method pc (Equation 5) creates a function call if the property is single-valued. Otherwise, it enumerates all the objects o_i in the property type, and creates an ite for each of them: if $f(s, o_i)$ is true then o_i is returned, otherwise, an empty value $\bot$ is returned. We introduce an empty value $\bot$ whose semantics is that for any binary operation $*$ and value x, $x * \bot = x$. For example, $[\![\texttt{self.plc}]\!]_{\texttt{self} \mapsto \texttt{vm2}} = \{(\texttt{ite} (= (\texttt{plc vm2}) \texttt{pm1}) \texttt{pm1} \bot), (\texttt{ite} (= (\texttt{plc vm2}) \texttt{pm2}) \texttt{pm2} \bot)\}$. This result satisfies Fidelity, because if we place vm2 to an arbitrary PM, the result will be this PM plus $\bot$, equivalent to the result of a full OCL evaluation. Equation (6) defines the derivation: the property call $\texttt{e.p}$ will be replaced by the expression ed defined for p, with self redirected to the source expression e.

$$
\begin{aligned}
&[\![\texttt{e.p}]\!]_\tau(m_s) = \begin{cases} v & \textbf{if } (r.p \mapsto v) \in m_s \\ pc(\texttt{mp}(p), \texttt{mo}(r), \texttt{mc}(p.type)) & \textbf{if } (r.p \mapsto \_) \in m_s \\ pc(\texttt{mp}(p), r, \texttt{mc}(p.type)) & \textbf{if } r \textbf{ is a formula} \end{cases} \\
&(r = [\![\texttt{e}]\!]_\tau(m_s))
\end{aligned}
\tag{4}
$$

$$
pc(f, s, c) = \begin{cases} (\texttt{f s}) & \texttt{single-valued} \\ \{(\texttt{ite (f s oi) oi } \bot) | \texttt{oi} \in c\} & \texttt{multi-valued} \end{cases}
\tag{5}
$$

$$
[\![\texttt{e.p}]\!]_\tau = [\![\texttt{let self=e in ed}]\!]_\tau, \text{if ed is the derivation expression of p}
\tag{6}
$$

PE handles and simplifies structural OCL syntax rules. For an if expression (7), we first evaluate the condition expression e_1 into r_1. If it is determined to either **true** or **false**, we return either result of the two sub expressions. Only when r_1 is a formula, we transfer the OCL branch into an ite. The second sample is the binary operation (8), such as $+$, $\times$, and etc. If both results r_1 and r_2 of the two operands are values, we calculate the result and return it. If either r_1 or r_2 is a formula, we compose a corresponding binary operation in SMT.

$$
\begin{aligned}
&[\![\texttt{if } e_1 \texttt{ then } e_2 \texttt{ else } e_3]\!]_\tau(m_s) = \begin{cases} r_2 & \textbf{if } r_1 = \textbf{true} \\ r_3 & \textbf{if } r_1 = \textbf{false} \\ (\texttt{ite } r_1\ r_2\ r_3) & \textbf{if } r_1 \in F_- \end{cases} \\
&(r_i = [\![e_i]\!]_\tau(m_s), i \in \{1, 2, 3\})
\end{aligned}
\tag{7}
$$

$$
\begin{aligned}
&[\![e_1 + e_2]\!]_\tau = \lambda m_s. \begin{cases} r_1 + r_2 & \textbf{if both } r_1 \text{ and } r_2 \text{ are values} \\ (+\ r_1\ r_2) & \textbf{if } r_1 \text{ or } r_2 \text{ is a formula} \end{cases} \\
&(r_i = [\![e_i]\!]_\tau(m_s), i \in \{1, 2\})
\end{aligned}
\tag{8}
$$

We handle composite OCL syntax rules on the basis of the primitive ones above. The **collect** operation (9) is a combination of **let** (i.e., we evaluate the main expression e_2 repeatedly, each time with a s_i from the source result). The **select** operation (10) is a combination of **if-then-else**. The resulted set will be simplified if any r_i is resolved to a $true$ or $false$: For the former case, s_i will be included into the resulted set, and for the latter case, it will be $\bot$. Similarly, **forAll** (11) is an extension of the binary **and** operation to multiple inputs. We divide the source set s into a single element s_h and the remaining set s_t. Then we evaluate s_h and s_t recursively, and combine the results by an **and**. The sum operation (12) is a similar extension to the binary operation +. We regard the size operation (13) as equivalent to first mapping each element to an integer 1, and then calculate the summary. The last important collection operations is include (14), which is often used to check if a relation holds upon two objects (e.g., Line 12 in Figure 3). We inspect the source set r_1 from e_1, and see if there is an item related to the target value r_2 evaluated from e_2. If there is an item r equal to r_2, the result is true; If there is an ite item in r_1 whose main branch equals to r_2, then whether $r_2 \in r_1$ depends on the condition r_3, and we simplify the whole operation to this condition r_3. Finally, we transform domain definition on a property into the following equivalent OCL expression (15): the value of self.p on context τ must equal to one of the values limited by e.

$$[\![e_1\text{->collect(v|e_2)}]\!](m_s) = \{[\![e_2]\!]_{\tau \cup \{v \mapsto s_i\}}(m_s) | s_i \in [\![e_1]\!]_\tau\} \tag{9}$$

$$[\![e_1\text{->select(v|e_2)}]\!]_\tau(m_s) = \lambda m_s.\{[\![\text{if } r_i \text{ then } s_i \text{ else } \bot]\!]_\tau(m_s)\}$$
$$s_i \in s = [\![e_1]\!]_\tau(m_s), r_i = [\![e_2]\!]_{\tau \cup \{v \mapsto s_i\}}(m_s) \tag{10}$$

$$[\![e_1\text{->forAll(v|e_2)}]\!]_\tau(m_s) = [\![r_h \text{ and } s_t\text{->forAll(v|e_2)}]\!]_\tau(m_s),$$
$$r_h = [\![e_1]\!]_{\tau \cup \{v \mapsto s_h\}}(m_s), \{s_h\} \cup s_t = s = [\![e_1]\!]_\tau(m_s); \tag{11}$$

$$[\![e_1\text{->sum()}]\!]_\tau = [\![r_h \text{ + } r_t\text{->sum()}]\!]_\tau; \{r_h\} \cup r_t = [\![e_1]\!]_\tau \tag{12}$$

$$[\![e\text{->size()}]\!]_\tau = [\![e\text{->collect(1)->sum()}]\!]_\tau \tag{13}$$

$$[\![e_1\text{->include(e_2)}]\!]_\tau(m_s) = \begin{cases} \text{true} & \text{if } \exists r \in r_1 : r = r_2 \\ r_3 & \text{if } \exists \text{ite}(r_3, r_2, \_) \in r_1 \\ \text{false} & \text{otherwise} \end{cases} \tag{14}$$
$$(r_i = [\![e_i]\!]_\tau(m_s), i \in \{1,2\})$$

$$[\![\text{domain e on p}]\!]_\tau = [\![e\text{->exists(x|x=self.p)}]\!]_\tau \tag{15}$$

We use the MemLimit constraint at Line 24 in Figure 3 as an example to show how PE works. The constraint is evaluated on the two PM objects, and Figure 5 shows the main steps on pm1. The PE starts from self.hosting, and is redirected to its derivation (the two OCL constraints are shown in the first two lines of Figure 5). From allInstances, the engine obtains a set of three VM objects, and the following select transforms it into a set of if-then-else. Inside it, v.plc calls a configurable property, and is therefore evaluated to a ite. After that, we push the following equation into the ite. As pm1=pm1 is always true, and ite($x, true, \bot$) = x, the set is simplifed again. Getting back to the main expression, collect substitutes the mem value for each VM object, and sum joins the three elements by "+", and replace $\bot$ by 0. Finally, we get the inequality as the final output.

5 SMT Solving

Using the generated SMT instance, we leverage an extended constraint solving approach [5] to calculate the appropriate adaptation actions. The generated SMT instance is composed of FOL formulas (SMT constraints), originating from the current context values, configuration values, and adaptation constraints. The

$$\text{self.hosting->collect(e|e.mem)->sum() <= self.mem}$$
$$\textit{derive } \text{PM.hosting: VM.allInstances()->select(v|v.plc=self)}$$
:

__allInstance__: {vm1, vm2, vm3}   __v.plc__: (ite (plc v pm1) pm1 ⊥)   __self__: pm1
__v.plc=self__: {(ite (= (ite (plc v pm1) pm1 ⊥) pm1) vm1 ⊥)... }
{(ite (ite (plc v pm1) (= pm1 pm1) ⊥) vm1 ⊥)... }
__select__: {(ite (plc vm1 pm1) vm1 ⊥), (ite (plc vm2 pm1) vm2 ⊥), (ite (plc vm3 pm1) vm3 ⊥)}
__collect__: {(ite (plc vm1 pm1) 6 ⊥), (ite (plc vm1 pm1) 8 ⊥), (ite (plc vm1 pm1) 4 ⊥)}
__sum__: (<= (+ (ite (plc vm1 pm1) 6 0) (ite (plc vm2 pm1) 8 0) (ite (plc vm3 pm1) 4 0)) 20)

Fig. 5. Sample partial evaluation steps

latter two categories are *weak constraints*, meaning that they can be violated when necessary. Each weak constraint has a weight generated from a constraint priority or a property cost. The first step is to identify a subset of constraints that we need to remove from the SMT instance in order to make the rest satisfiable. We use a weighted constraint diagnosing approach to find such a subset with the lowest total weight. The second step is to compute the system modifications to satisfy the remaining constraints. Details of this constraint solving approach can be found in our earlier publication [5].

Going back to our running example in Section 2.1, we have shown three potential adaptation solutions, i.e., migrating vm3 to pm1, switching vm2 and vm3 (and decrease pm2.core), and do nothing. They correspond to three diagnosis: {BackupSlipt, FrequentNear, mem-cost}, {mem-cost×2, core-cost, Consolidation}, {BackupSlipt, FreqentNear}, respectively, and the second one has the lowest total weight of 120 (4×10 and 8×10 for migrating two VMs, and 20 for decreasing vm2.core). The corresponding adaptation solution is vm1.plc=pm2, vm3.plc=pm1, and vm1.core=4.

6   Case Study

We apply the approach on the VM placement problem extended from the running example, and use this case study to evaluate: (i) the expressive power of the adaptation modelling language; (ii) the effect of transformation and constraint solving; (iii) the performance improvement achieved by our partial evaluation.

Implementation. We implement the adaptation modelling language on the Xtext framework and DresdenOCL toolkit [14], with a text-based syntax and a fully functioning editor (as is shown in Figure 3). We choose Z3 [6] as our constraint solver, and implement the OCL partial evaluation to generate SMT instance in Z3Py, a python-based SMT representation. The generated result is fed into the constraint solving based adaptation engine that we presented in our previous work [5]. The source code is hosted at github.com/songhui/cspadapt

Adaptation Modelling. Our adaptation model on VM placement is based on the general cloud computing concepts from CloudML [15]. We use OCL constraints to model the policies that originate from the following research approaches: 1) Deployment constraints from CloudML, such as 64 bit VM should run on 64 bit PM. 2) Resource limitation and consolidation [7]. 3) Cost of migration [16]. 4) Load balancing between PMs [17], e.g., immigrating VMs out of overloaded PMs, and scatter the VMs with synchronized peak times. 5) Run-time observed logical relations [18], such as frequently communicating VMs should be placed closely. 6) SLA matching [18], such as VMs with high stability requirement should be placed to specially protected PMs. The final adaptation model can be downloaded from `thingml.org/dist/diversify/casestudy.constraint`. The adaptation modelling shows the language's expressive power to specify different adaptation policies, and also reveals a major benefit, i.e., to ease the combination of the policies from different origins.

Adaptation Behaviour. We test the adaptation model on simulated cloud configurations. From a starting model instance, we randomly generate changes to the system, and feed the changed model to the adaptation engine. The engine outputs the suggested changes, and records the main constraints it followed and discarded when making the decision. Table 2 lists some sample traces. We choose the ones that are from the same starting state (as shown in Figure 6, where m and t stand for memory and throughput, respectively), and are only involved in 8 particular constraints. When we enlarge vm2 (see #1 in Table 2), vm1 is migrated, because it is smaller and therefore cheaper to move. However, when vm2 exceeds the capacity of pm1 (#2), itself is migrated. Their destinations are different because of the constraints we listed in the table. When we enlarge vm4 (#3), the more expensive vm5 is moved, because moving vm3 to any PMs would break more expensive constraints. When vm5 has bigger throughput (#4), vm4 is moved out to the sole valid destination pm6. But since it has synchronised peak time with vm6, the latter is moved to pm2 to avoid vm4. When vm7 has bigger throughput (#5), considering its high stability requirement, the engine moves vm9 and vm10 out of the other stable PM to make a room for vm7. However, when vm7's stability requirement is lowered down (#6), the engine will move it to a not-so-stable PM, to avoid the cost of moving two VMs. #7 illustrates how we do consolidation: when v8 is not active, the engine moves it out to free pm4, because the cost of immigration is lower than the weight of the consolidation constraint. When vm6 and vm9 are observed to be frequently communicating, the engine moves vm9 to a nearby PM, and brings vm10 as well. The numbers of constraints in *follows* and *discards* imply the complexity of making the decision.

Performance. The runtime performance of constraint-driven adaptation is acceptable for medium sized systems. We create 6 model instances from the adaptation model on VM placement. In this models, the total number of VMs and PMs are from 15 to 60, and total number of properties are from 140 to 560. For each case, we launch the standard adaptation process for 50 cycles, each started from randomly generated changes (0.5 to 8.5 changes in average), and the average adaptation durations are 0.1, 1.4, 2.2, 7.1, 7.9 and 12.3 seconds, for each model instance. The experiments are performed on a MacBook Pro with Intel i5 CPU and 4G memory. The performance is acceptable since it is still a

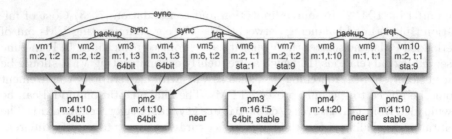

Fig. 6. Starting system status of the sample results

Table 2. Sample adaptation actions from the VM placement case study.

MC=Migration Cost, SP=Synchronized Peaktime, LB=Load Balance, ML=Memory Limit, BU=Backup, FR=Frequent Communication, ST=Stability, CS=Consolidation, B64=64 bit

# change	adaptation	follows	discards
#1 vm2.m:3	vm1->pm4	MC SP LB BU	CS
#2 vm2.m:5	vm2->pm3	ML BU	MC CS
#3 vm4.m:4	vm5->pm3	MC ML FR BU B64	MC CS
#4 vm5.t:5	vm4->pm3, vm6->p2	B64 BU ML FR LB	MC ST CS
#5 vm7.t:6	vm7->pm5, vm9vm10->pm3	FR ST LB	MC CS
#6 vm7.t:6, vm7.st:1	vm7->pm4	MC LB	ST CS
#7 vm8.t:1	vm8->pm2	CS BU	MC
#8 frqt(vm6,vmm9)	vm9->pm2, vm10->pm3	MC LB FR	MC CS

short time relative to the time it takes to modify topologies and configurations in cloud. Typically migrating one virtual machine in a cloud takes from a half to several minutes. In order to inspect the improvement caused by partial evaluation, we run another 50 cycles for each case from random changes, but with partial evaluation switched off, generating FOL formulas as shown in Figure 4. The adaptation durations are then 0.3, 8.2, 31.5, 49.3, 51.3 are 129.2 seconds, which are significantly longer than the ones with PE. Furthermore, the fraction of reduction increases with the larger models (e.g., the fraction is 3 times faster for the simplest model and about 10 times faster for the largest one)

7 Related Work

Research approaches on self-adaptive systems provide many different ways to define adaptation policies. The ECA type of rules are most widely adopted, such as the event triggering in [19] and [20], the guard-action rules in [21], etc. Kephart and Walsh [22] discussed the advantage of declarative policies over imperative ECA rules. Floch et al. [23] utilise declarative properties and utilities functions to capture adaptation policies, but they require predefined system configurations instead of calculate them at runtime. The DiVA project [24] defines a small language to capture constraints as policies, and utilises the Alloy constraint solver to obtain the result. In this work, we support the general purpose OCL language with higher expressive power, and tolerate the conflicts in constraints.

Model driven engineering is widely used to tame the complexity of developing adaptive systems. One branch is to model the system states in high-level architectures, such as in [25] and [26]. But the policies on top of their architectures are essentially ECA rules. Another branch is to support the development process of self-adaptive system. Brun et al. [27] propose a programming model for self-adaptive systems, based on control loops. Cheng et al. [28] and Baresi et al. [29] use goal-based modelling to help derive adaptation policies from requirements. Such approaches are complementary to the work in this paper, and our future plan is to utilise goal models to elicit adaptation constraints from requirements.

The transformation from constraints to SMT instances is related to the approaches that generate constraint satisfiability problems from class diagrams [30,31] or OCL constraints [32], for the purposes of design time verification. When using constraints to guide adaptation at runtime, the searching space for constraint solving is much smaller than at design time, because the context data are known and not changeable. This is the main idea behind our partial evaluation to optimise the generated SMT problem, and differentiate our approach from the existing ones. Partial evaluation [13] is a compiling technique to optimise target code by pre-processing constant values in the source code, and is widely used to support domain specific languages [33]. In our approach, we widen the concept of "constant values" to the current context in an adaptive system.

The modelling process for adaptation constraints is inspired by the construction of domain-specific modelling languages [34,35]: We support domain experts in defining the concepts in a particular application domain, and then the constraints are specified in a domain-specific way, applying these concepts.

8 Conclusion

This paper presents a model-driven approach to developing self-adaptative systems. We provide a language for modeling declarative adaptation polices, in the form of domain-specific constraints. Our runtime engine generates an SMT problem from the constraints, optimises it based on the current system state, and calculates the appropriate system reconfigurations. From our previous work, the new contributions in this paper include a modelling language, a new method to encode structural information in object oriented models into SMT, and a new partial evaluation semantics on OCL based on the encoding.

The main limitation of the current approach is the *closed world assumption*. In practice, we loosen this assumption by adding a small number of stub objects before constraint solving, and if any stub object is referred by a real object after the solving, we launch a create-object request to the system. Our future work on this is to generalise this approach and assist developers in customising where a new object is required. The approach can be also used together with an outer adaptation loop that adds or removes VMs, either a manual or an automated one. The case study in the current stage is still a proof of the idea. We will seek for bigger scale applications involving third-party developers, based on our cloud computing research projects.

References

1. de Lemos, R., et al.: Software engineering for self-adaptive systems: A research roadmap. In: de Lemos, R., Giese, H., Müller, H.A., Shaw, M., et al. (eds.) Self-Adaptive Systems. LNCS, vol. 7475, pp. 1–32. Springer, Heidelberg (2013)
2. Salehie, M., Tahvildari, L.: Self-adaptive software: Landscape and research challenges. ACM Transactions on Autonomous and Adaptive Systems (TAAS) 4(2), 14 (2009)
3. Kephart, J.: Research challenges of autonomic computing. In: ICSE, pp. 15–22. IEEE (2005)
4. Object Management Group: OMG Object Constraint Language (OCL), http://www.omg.org/spec/OCL/2.3.1/PDF/
5. Song, H., Barrett, S., Clarke, A., Clarke, S.: Self-adaptation with end-user preferences: Using run-time models and constraint solving. In: Moreira, A., Schätz, B., Gray, J., Vallecillo, A., Clarke, P. (eds.) MODELS 2013. LNCS, vol. 8107, pp. 555–571. Springer, Heidelberg (2013)
6. de Moura, L., Bjørner, N.S.: Z3: An efficient smt solver. In: Ramakrishnan, C.R., Rehof, J. (eds.) TACAS 2008. LNCS, vol. 4963, pp. 337–340. Springer, Heidelberg (2008)
7. Hermenier, F., Lorca, X., Menaud, J.M., Muller, G., Lawall, J.: Entropy: A consolidation manager for clusters. In: Proceedings of the 2009 ACM SIGPLAN/SIGOPS International Conference on Virtual Execution Environments, pp. 41–50. ACM (2009)
8. Song, H., Xiong, Y., Chauvel, F., Huang, G., Hu, Z., Mei, H.: Generating synchronization engines between running systems and their model-based views. Models in Software Engineering, 140–154 (2010)
9. Bryant, R.E., Lahiri, S.K., Seshia, S.A.: Modeling and verifying systems using a logic of counter arithmetic with lambda expressions and uninterpreted functions. In: Brinksma, E., Larsen, K.G. (eds.) CAV 2002. LNCS, vol. 2404, pp. 78–92. Springer, Heidelberg (2002)
10. Guttag, J.V., Horning, J.J.: The algebraic specification of abstract data types. Acta Informatica 10(1), 27–52 (1978)
11. Microsoft Research, http://rise4fun.com/z3/tutorial/guide
12. Barrett, C., Stump, A., Tinelli, C.: The SMT-LIB Standard: Version 2.0. Technical report, Department of Computer Science, The University of Iowa (2010), http://www.SMT-LIB.org
13. Jones, N.D., Gomard, C.K., Sestoft, P.: Partial evaluation and automatic program generation. Prentice-Hall, New York (1993)
14. Demuth, B.: The dresden ocl toolkit and its role in information systems development. In: Proc. of the 13th International Conference on Information Systems Development, ISD 2004 (2004)
15. Ferry, N., Rossini, A., Chauvel, F., Morin, B., Solberg, A.: Towards model-driven provisioning, deployment, monitoring, and adaptation of multi-cloud systems. In: CLOUD 2013: IEEE 6th International Conference on Cloud Computing, pp. 887–894 (2013)
16. Meng, X., Pappas, V., Zhang, L.: Improving the scalability of data center networks with traffic-aware virtual machine placement. In: INFOCOM, 2010 Proceedings IEEE, pp. 1–9. IEEE (2010)
17. Bobroff, N., Kochut, A., Beaty, K.: Dynamic placement of virtual machines for managing sla violations. In: 10th IFIP/IEEE International Symposium on Integrated Network Management, IM 2007, pp. 119–128. IEEE (2007)

18. Zhang, X., Zhang, Y., Chen, X., Liu, K., Huang, G., Zhan, J.: A relationship-based vm placement framework of cloud environment. In: Proceedings of the 2013 IEEE 37th Annual Computer Software and Applications Conference, pp. 124–133. IEEE Computer Society (2013)

19. Keeney, J., Cahill, V.: Chisel: A policy-driven, context-aware, dynamic adaptation framework. In: Proceedings of the IEEE 4th International Workshop on Policies for Distributed Systems and Networks, POLICY 2003, pp. 3–14. IEEE (2003)

20. Kephart, J.O., Das, R.: Achieving self-management via utility functions. IEEE Internet Computing 11(1), 40–48 (2007)

21. David, P.C., Ledoux, T., et al.: Safe dynamic reconfigurations of fractal architectures with fscript. In: Proceeding of Fractal CBSE Workshop, ECOOP, vol. 6 (2006)

22. Kephart, J., Walsh, W.: An artificial intelligence perspective on autonomic computing policies. In: IEEE International Workshop on Policies for Distributed Systems and Networks, pp. 3–12. IEEE (2004)

23. Floch, J., Hallsteinsen, S., Stav, E., Eliassen, F., Lund, K., Gjorven, E.: Using architecture models for runtime adaptability. IEEE Software 23(2), 62–70 (2006)

24. Morin, B., Barais, O., Jezequel, J., Fleurey, F., Solberg, A.: Models@ run. time to support dynamic adaptation. Computer 42(10), 44–51 (2009)

25. Garlan, D., Cheng, S., Huang, A., Schmerl, B., Steenkiste, P.: Rainbow: Architecture-based self-adaptation with reusable infrastructure. Computer 37(10), 46–54 (2004)

26. Sicard, S., Boyer, F., De Palma, N.: Using components for architecture-based management: The self-repair case. In: ICSE, pp. 101–110. ACM (2008)

27. Brun, Y., et al.: Engineering self-adaptive systems through feedback loops. In: Cheng, B.H.C., de Lemos, R., Giese, H., Inverardi, P., Magee, J. (eds.) Self-Adaptive Systems. LNCS, vol. 5525, pp. 48–70. Springer, Heidelberg (2009)

28. Cheng, B.H.C., Sawyer, P., Bencomo, N., Whittle, J.: A goal-based modeling approach to develop requirements of an adaptive system with environmental uncertainty. In: Schürr, A., Selic, B. (eds.) MODELS 2009. LNCS, vol. 5795, pp. 468–483. Springer, Heidelberg (2009)

29. Baresi, L., Pasquale, L., Spoletini, P.: Fuzzy goals for requirements-driven adaptation. In: RE, pp. 125–134. IEEE (2010)

30. Maoz, S., Ringert, J.O., Rumpe, B.: CD2Alloy: Class diagrams analysis using alloy revisited. In: Whittle, J., Clark, T., Kühne, T. (eds.) MODELS 2011. LNCS, vol. 6981, pp. 592–607. Springer, Heidelberg (2011)

31. Cabot, J., Clarisó, R., Riera, D.: Verification of UML/OCL class diagrams using constraint programming. In: Software Testing Verification and Validation Workshop, pp. 73–80. IEEE (2008)

32. Cabot, J., Clarisó, R., Riera, D.: UMLtoCSP: A tool for the formal verification of uml/ocl models using constraint programming. In: ASE, pp. 547–548. ACM (2007)

33. Mernik, M., Heering, J., Sloane, A.M.: When and how to develop domain-specific languages. ACM Computing Surveys (CSUR) 37(4), 316–344 (2005)

34. Kelly, S., Tolvanen, J.P.: Domain-specific modeling: enabling full code generation. John Wiley & Sons (2008)

35. France, R., Rumpe, B.: Model-driven development of complex software: A research roadmap. In: 2007 Future of Software Engineering, pp. 37–54. IEEE Computer Society (2007)

Scalable Armies of Model Clones
through Data Sharing

Erwan Bousse[1], Benoit Combemale[2], and Benoit Baudry[2]

[1] University of Rennes 1, France
erwan.bousse@irisa.fr
[2] Inria, France
{benoit.combemale,benoit.baudry}@inria.fr

Abstract. Cloning a model is usually done by duplicating all its runtime objects into a new model. This approach leads to memory consumption problems for operations that create and manipulate large quantities of clones (e.g., design space exploration). We propose an original approach that exploits the fact that operations rarely modify a whole model. Given a set of immutable properties, our cloning approach determines the objects and fields that can be shared between the runtime representations of a model and its clones. Our generic cloning algorithm is parameterized with three strategies that establish a trade-off between memory savings and the ease of clone manipulation. We implemented the strategies within the Eclipse Modeling Framework (EMF) and evaluated memory footprints and computation overheads with 100 randomly generated metamodels and models. Results show a positive correlation between the proportion of shareable properties and memory savings, while the worst median overhead is 9,5% when manipulating the clones.

1 Introduction

Cloning a model consists in obtaining a new and independent model identical to the original one. An implementation of this operation can be found in the EcoreUtil.Copier class of the Eclipse Modeling Framework (EMF) [11], which consists in first creating a copy of the runtime representation of a model (*i.e.* the set of Java objects that represent the model) and then resolving all the references between these objects. Such an implementation is also known as *deep cloning*. This implementation is effective to produce valid, independent clones. However it has very poor memory performances for operations that require manipulating large quantities of clones (e.g. genetic algorithms [6], design space exploration [10] or model simulation traces [8]).

We address the performance limitations of current deep cloning operations by leveraging the following observation: given a metamodel and an operation defined for this metamodel, the operation usually writes only a subset of this metamodel. That means that it is possible to identify the *footprint* of the write accesses of these operations on a metamodel. This footprint is the set of *mutable* parts of the metamodel, *i.e.* elements that can be modified by an operation. The counterpart

J. Dingel et al. (Eds.): MODELS 2014, LNCS 8767, pp. 286–301, 2014.

of these elements, the *immutable* elements, are definitively stated at the creation of objects. Our intuition is the following: knowing the immutable elements of the metamodel, data could be shared between the runtime representation of a given model and its clones, saving memory when generating the clone.

In this paper, we propose a new *model cloning algorithm*, which implements different strategies to *share immutable data between clones*. This contribution relies on a specific runtime representation of the model and its clones in order to share the data and still provide an interface that supports the manipulation of the clones independently from each other. We articulate our proposal around the following questions:

– Considering that we know which parts of a metamodel are mutable, how can we avoid duplicating immutable runtime data among cloned models?
– Can it effectively save some memory at runtime when creating a high number of clones as compared to EMF cloning implementation ?

Our goal is both to give a solution that can be implemented in various existing execution environments, and to provide concrete evidence of the efficiency of such an approach on a widely used tool set: the Eclipse Modeling Framework (EMF). Section 2 motivates our problem. We present a list of requirements for cloning operators, and give the intuition of our idea regarding existing cloning techniques. Section 3 defines what we call model cloning and what are runtime representations of models. Section 4 presents the main contribution of this paper: a new approach for efficient model cloning. The idea is to determine which parts of a metamodel can be shared, and to rely on this information to share data between runtime representations of a model and its clones. We provide a generic algorithm that can be parameterized into three cloning operators (in addition to the reference *deep cloning* one): the first one only shares objects, the second only shares fields, and the third shares as much data as possible. Section 5 describes our evaluation, which was done using a custom benchmarking tool suite that relies on random metamodel and model generation. Our dataset is made of a hundred randomly generated metamodels and models, and results show that our approach can save memory as soon as there are immutable properties in metamodels. Finally, Section 6 concludes.

2   Motivation and Position

In this section we give requirements for cloning operators, and we explain how our idea is related to existing approaches

2.1   Requirements for Cloning

New activities have emerged in the model-driven engineering community in recent years, which all rely on the automatic production of large quantities of models and variations of models. For example, several works rely on evolutionary computation to optimize a model with respect to a given objective [3, 6].

Optimization in this case, consists in generating large quantities of model variants through cloning, mutation and crossover and selecting the most fitted. In the field of executable domain specific modeling languages, modeling traces [8] (*i.e.* set of *snapshots* of the executed model) is a way to verify and validate the system through visualization or analysis of traces. Yet, a complete model trace consists in copying the state of the model at each simulation step, producing large quantities of model variants. Design space exploration [10] is the exploration of design alternatives before an implementation, which requires the generation of the complete design space (*i.e.* set of variations, which are models).

All these new MDE techniques produce *large* sets of models that originate from few models. From a model manipulation point of view, all these techniques require the ability to *clone*—possibly many times—an original model, and to query and modify the clones as models that conform to the same metamodel as the original. More precisely, we identify four requirements for model manipulation in these contexts

Req #1 scalability. Runtime representations of models must scale in memory.

Req #2 manipulation performance. It is necessary to manipulate the clones as efficiently as any model.

Req #3 model interface. The clones and the original model must be manipulated through the same interface.

Req #4 metamodel independence. Support model manipulation through a reflexive layer (the model operation is defined independently of a given metamodel).

Our work defines novel cloning operators that reduce the memory footprint of clones, while trying to comply with the aforementioned requirements. In particular, we evaluate the relevance of our solution with respect to the following four research questions:

RQ#1 Do the new operators reduce the memory footprint of clones, compared to deep cloning?

RQ#2 Can a clone be manipulated with the same efficiency as the original model?

RQ#3 Can a clone be manipulated using the same generated API as the original model?

RQ#4 Can a clone be manipulated using the reflective layer (e.g. as stated in the MOF Reflection package)?

2.2   Existing Cloning Approaches and Intuition

Object copying has existed since the beginning of object-oriented programming languages [4] with the *deep* and *shallow* copy operators. While the second operator does not ensure the independence of a clone and is thus not of interest, the first is at the basis of model deep cloning. Concerning models, the EMF provides a class named EcoreUtil.Copier with operations for deep copying sets of objects, which can trivially be used to implement a model deep cloning operator. Yet, as stated previously, this operator does not fit our needs. In [5], Karsai et al. added model cloning to the Generic Modeling Environment (GME) in order to support model *prototyping*, *i.e.* applying the concepts of object prototyping [7] to models. However, this work considers that changes made in a model are reflected in its clones, whereas by definition a clone is independent from its origin. Overall, to our knowledge, no work attempted to tackle the requirements that we identified.

In terms of memory management, *copy-on-write* (a.k.a. lazy copy) is a widespread way to reduce memory consumption. The idea is the following: when a copy is made, nothing is concretely copied in memory and a link to the original element is created. At this point, both elements are identical, and accordingly reading the copy would in fact read the origin directly. But when writing operations are made on the copy, modified elements are effectively copied so that the copy keeps its own state and appears like a regular and independent element. Applied to model cloning, the runtime object configuration of a clone obtained using this technique would eventually only contain written mutable elements of the original model, which meets our need to reduce memory footprint (Req #1). However, it adds a considerable amount of control flow at runtime in order to detect when copies must be done, and such copies can happen unpredictably depending on the manipulations; this contradict the need for efficient clones (Req #2). More importantly, depending on the programming language used, this technique can be very difficult to implement; for instance, Java is pass-by-value, making it impossible to dynamically change the value of a variable from a different context (*i.e.* updating all references to an object that was just effectively copied), which is required to dynamically copy a model progressively and transparently.

Our intuition is that while deep cloning is easy to implement but memory expensive, and copy-on-write is memory-efficient but complicated with poorly efficient clones, it is possible to provide operators *in between* these two extremes. Similarly to the way copy-on-write discovers *dynamically* which parts of a model are mutable when copying written elements, our idea is to *statically* determine which elements that have to be copied at runtime. Such elements are opposed to the ones that can be referenced by both the original runtime representation and its clone. We present an approach based on this idea in the next section.

3   On Model Cloning

The purpose of this section is to clarify what we mean by the runtime representation of a model and to precisely define what we call a clone in this work.

3.1   Modeling

Since we focus on the runtime representation of models, we consider a metamodel to be the definition of a data structure. More precisely, we rely on the Meta-Object Facility (MOF) [9] that defines a metamodel as an object-oriented structure.

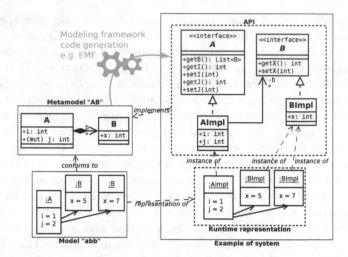

Fig. 1. Example of modeling and EMF usage with a sample metamodel AB and a sample model abb

Definition 1. *A metamodel is an object oriented model defining a particular domain. More precisely, a metamodel is composed of classes composed of properties, a property being either an attribute (typed by a datatype) or a reference to another class. In practice, we consider a MOF model.*

Since a metamodel is composed of classes, a model that conforms to this metamodel is quite intuitively a set of objects that are instances of these classes.

Definition 2. *A model is a set of objects that conforms to a metamodel. Conformity means that each object in the model is an instance of one class defined in the metamodel. An object is composed of fields, each being based on a property of the corresponding class.*

During its lifecycle, a model can change in two possible ways: by creating/deleting objects or by changing values of fields of objects. We designate as *mutable* elements both the elements of a model that may change over time and the metamodel parts that define these elements. Our approach considers a given object configuration in order to produce a clone, and is thus not influenced by the creation of deletion of objects.

Definition 3. *A property of a class of a metamodel is* mutable *if, in each object instance of this class, the value of the field corresponding to this property can change after the construction of the object. Dually, a property is said to be* immutable *if its value cannot change after construction.*

Fig. 1 shows a metamodel named AB that is composed of two classes A and B. A has two attributes i and j and one reference b. j is mutable as specified by (mut). B has a single attribute x. Below the metamodel, a model abb conforms to AB and is composed of one object instance of A and two objects instance of B.

3.2   Implementation of Metamodels and Models

Specific execution environments are necessary to use metamodels and models. The Eclipse Modeling Framework (EMF) is one of the most popular. It generates Java interfaces and classes that implement a given metamodel, providing concrete mechanisms to create *runtime representations* of models that conform to the metamodel. We define a runtime representation as follows:

Definition 4. *The* runtime representation *of a model is the set of runtime data that is sufficient to reflect the model data structure. It must be manipulated through an interface that is consistent with the corresponding metamodel.*

Top right of Fig. 1 shows the API (Java interfaces and classes) generated by the EMF generator. Interfaces A and B define services corresponding to the data structure of the original metamodel AB, while Java classes AImpl and BImpl implement these interfaces. These elements support the instantiation and manipulation of runtime representations—here, Java object configurations—of models that conform to the metamodel. The bottom right of the figure shows a runtime representation of abb.

Note that a runtime representation that is eventually obtained using the EMF is structurally very similar to the original model: each object is represented by a Java object; each reference is represented by a Java reference; and each attribute is represented by a Java field. Yet runtime representations could theoretically take any form, as long as they are manipulated through an API that reflect the metamodel. One could imagine "empty" objects that get data from a centralized data storage component, or the use of a prototype-based programming language to create consistent runtime representations without defining classes.

3.3   Cloning

In this paper, we consider *cloning*[1] to be at the intersection of two main ideas: the exact duplication of elements and the independence of the obtained clone. Applied to models, a clone is therefore an independent duplication of some existing model. We define a clone as follows:

Definition 5. *A* clone *is a model that is, when created, identical to an existing model called the origin. Both models conform to the same metamodel and are independent from one to another*

Cloning a model is a deterministic procedure that has a unique possible output (*i.e.* a model identical to the original model). However there are multiple ways to implement this procedure for a given runtime environment. We therefore introduce the idea of *cloning operator* as follows:

Definition 6. *A* cloning operator *is an operator that takes the runtime representation of a model as input and returns the runtime representation of the clone of the model.*

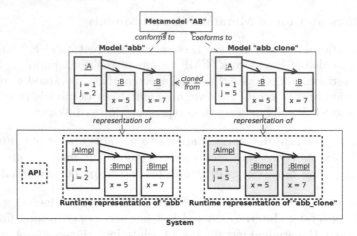

Fig. 2. Following Fig. 1, *deep cloning* of the model `abb`, which created a new model `abb_clone` along with a new runtime representation in memory. Then `abb_clone` diverged from `abb` by changing its j value.

Fig. 2 gives an example of cloning: the model `abb_clone` is a clone that was created at some point from the model `abb`. The moment the clone was created is important, since it is an independent model that can completely diverge from its origin; on this example, `abb_clone` already changed and has a different j value.

At the bottom right of Fig. 2, the runtime representation of `abb_clone` was obtained using the *deep cloning* operator. However, as stated in the previous section, runtime representations of models can virtually take any form, as long as it can be manipulated through an API consistent with the metamodel. This is what we investigate in the next section, where we present our main contribution: cloning operators that reduce the memory footprint of runtime representations of clones through data sharing.

4   Memory Efficient Cloning Operators

In this section we present our main contribution: an approach for memory efficient cloning through data sharing among runtime representations. For this work, we consider that input runtime representations were obtained using the EMF, *i.e.* each input runtime representation is identical to its model. Moreover, for our clones to be compliant with EMF, we ensure that each object of a clone is implemented by exactly one runtime object.

4.1   Data Sharing Strategies

When using the deep cloning operator, each object of a runtime representation is duplicated, which means twice as many objects and fields in memory. Our

---

[1] In terms of vocabulary, it is very similar to *copying*, and the choice of word is mostly a matter of habit. In this paper we rather *copy* objects and *clone* models.

intuition is that since we know which parts of a metamodel are immutable, it must be possible to avoid duplicating some runtime objects and fields by safely using them for both the runtime representations of a model and its clones. Given a model conforming to a metamodel, we call *shareable* both the elements that can be shared between the runtime representations of the model and its clones, and the parts of the metamodel that define these elements.

In Section 2, we defined Req #2 (efficient manipulation of clones) and Req #4 (ability to define generic operations). However, sharing objects and fields between runtime representations necessarily breaks one or both of these requirements. First, if the same runtime object is shared between two runtime representations, it is supposed to represent two distinct objects—one per model. Therefore, it is possible for each of these objects to have a different *container*, since both objects are conceptually separate. The problem is that the MOF Reflection package states that each object must provide a `container()` operation that returns the unique container of an object, which is implemented in an operation of EMF EObject called `eContainer()`. Unfortunately, when a shared EMF runtime object is used, there is no way to know in which context (*i.e.* model) this manipulation occurs, and this operation thus cannot always return a unique container as expected. Therefore, generic operations that rely on this operation cannot be used on clones, which contradicts our Req #4. Second, we rely on a *proxy* design pattern to share the fields of runtime objects: a runtime object with a shareable field can be copied into a new runtime object without this field, but with a reference pointing to the original runtime object to provide access to this field. However, there is an overhead when accessing shared data through these proxy objects, which can be an issue with respect to Req #2.

Data sharing is essential to reduce the memory footprint of clones, which is our primary objective. Consequently, we designed several strategies that establish trade-offs between memory savings and satisfaction of Req #2 and Req #4. Modelers can then decide how to tune the cloning algorithm with respect to their specific needs. We provide four strategies that implement different interpretations of shareable metamodel elements:

DeepCloning   Nothing is shareable.

ShareFieldsOnly   Only immutable attributes are shareable.

ShareAll   Shareable elements are immutable attributes, classes whose properties are all shareable, and immutable references pointing to shareable classes.

ShareObjOnly   Same shareable classes as ShareAll, while properties are not.

If implementing the *DeepCloning* and *ShareFieldsOnly* strategies is quite straightforward, *ShareAll* and *ShareObjOnly* are more complicated because of a double recursion: shareable properties depend on shareable classes, and conversely. This can be solved using a fixed-point algorithm, or using the Tarjan algorithm [12] to compute strongly connected components of a metamodel seen as a graph. We choose Tarjan in our implementation. Our approach to memory management through data sharing is quite close to the *flyweight* design pattern from Gamma et al. [2], which consists in identifying mostly immutable objects in order to share them between multiple objects. The main difference is that this pattern specifies that the mutable part of shared objects must be a parameter of all the operations of the objects, which contradicts our first requirement since the API of the clones hence differs from the one of the original model.

4.2   Generic Cloning Algorithm

Before defining our algorithms for model cloning, we introduce data structures and primitive functions on which the algorithms rely. We use pseudo-code inspired from prototype-based object-oriented programming [7], *i.e.* creating and manipulating objects without defining classes. The goal is to define the algorithms independently from any API that may be generated by a particular modeling framework. We consider the following structures and operations:

a runtime object o is created completely empty (*i.e.* no fields) using the *createEmptyObject*() operation. Fields can be added using *addField*(*name,value*), and can be retrieved using *getFields*().

a strategy is an object that implements one of the strategies given Section 4.1 with three operations:

   isFieldShareable(f) returns true if, at the metamodel level, there is a shareable property represented by f.

   isObjShareable(o)   returns true if, at the metamodel level, the class of the object that match this runtime object is shareable.

   isObjPartShareable(o)   does the same, but for *partially shareable* classes, *i.e.* non-shareable classes with shareable properties.

copyObject(o)   returns a copy of a runtime object o, i.e., a new object with the same fields and the same values. This is equivalent to the operation *copy* of EMF EcoreUtil.Copier

a runtime representation is a set of runtime objects. It can be created empty with *createEmptyRR*(), and it can be filled with objects using *addObject*(o).

a map is a data structure that contains a set of ⟨key,value⟩ pairs. It can be created with *createEmptyMap*() and be filled with *addKeyValue*(*key, value*).

resolveReferences (*map*) is an operation that, given a *map* whose keys and values are runtime objects, will create references in the values based on the references of the keys. This is equivalent to the operation *copyReferences* of EMF EcoreUtil.Copier.

The operation *copyObjectProxy*(o,*strategy*) is presented as Algorithm 1. It is parameterized by a strategy and an original object o, and it copies in a new object all the fields of o, except those considered shareable by the strategy. The last line of the operation creates a link to the original object in order to keep a way to access to the shareable data. Fig. 3 illustrates this operation with a simple object o that has two fields x and y: x is not copied in p, but can still be accessed using the reference *originObj*.

The second operation is *cloning*(*rr, strategy*), the cloning algorithm itself, presented as Algorithm 2. It takes a runtime representation rr as input and a

---

Algorithm 1. *copyObjectProxy*

Data:
o, a runtime object
strategy, the strategy used (*i.e.* what is shareable)
Result: *p*, a proxy copy of *o*

1 **begin**
2     $p \leftarrow$ *createEmptyObject*()
3   **for** $f \in$ getFields*(o)* **do**
4   **if** $\neg$ strategy.isFieldShareable*(f)* **then**
5   *p.addField(f.name, f.value)*
6   *p.addField(*"originObj"*, o)*

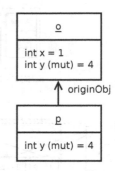

Fig. 3. Example of proxy object: *p* is a copy of *o*.

Algorithm 2. *cloning*

Data:
rr, a runtime representation of a model
strategy, the strategy used (*i.e.* what is shareable)
Result: rr_{clone}, a runtime representation of the clone

1 **begin**
2     $rr_{clone} \leftarrow$ createEmptyRR()
3   *copyMap*$\leftarrow$ createEmptyMap()
4   **for** $o \in rr$ **do**
5   **if** strategy.isObjShareable*(o)* **then**
6         $rr_{clone}.addObject(o)$
7   *copyMap.addKeyValue(o, o)*
8   **else if** strategy.isObjPartShareable*(o)* **then**
9   *copy* $\leftarrow$ copyObjectProxy*(o,strategy)*
10        $rr_{clone}.addObject(copy)$
11   *copyMap.addKeyValue(o, copy)*
12   **else**
13   *copy* $\leftarrow$ copyObject*(o)*
14        $rr_{clone}.addObject(copy)$
15   *copyMap.addKeyValue(, o, copy)*
16   resolveReferences(*copyMap*)

Table 1. Cloning operators obtained, one per strategy

	Objects not shared (RQ #4 ok)	Objects shared (RQ #4 not ok)
Fields not shared (RQ #2 ok)	*DeepCloning*	*ShareObjOnly*
Fields shared (RQ #2 not ok)	*ShareFieldsOnly*	*ShareAll*

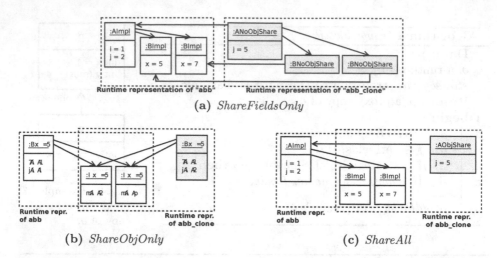

(a) *ShareFieldsOnly*

(b) *ShareObjOnly*   (c) *ShareAll*

Fig. 4. Runtime representations of models `abb` and `abb_clone` of Fig. 2 obtained with the different cloning operators.

considered strategy, and returns a runtime representation rr_{clone} of a clone of the model of rr. Depending on the strategy outputs, each object is processed differently. If the object o is shareable, it is simply added in rr_{clone}, and is thus shared between rr and rr_{clone}. If o is partially shareable (not shareable but with shareable fields), a proxy copy of o is added to rr_{clone}. Finally, if o is not shareable at all, a regular copy is put in rr_{clone}.

4.3   Family of Cloning Operators

From our single cloning algorithm, we eventually obtain four cloning operators depending on the strategy used. We sum up the possibilities in Table 1, and we illustrate them with examples in Fig. 4. *DeepCloning* clones without any form of data sharing. *ShareFieldsOnly* clones using proxy objects to share as many fields as possible; Fig. 4a shows an example where each runtime object has a reference to the runtime object from which it originates. *ShareObjOnly* clones with object sharing only; Fig. 4b shows an example where B runtime objects are referenced by both models. Finally, *ShareAll* clones with both objects and fields sharing; Fig. 4c shows an example where only j is kept by the A runtime object.

In section 4.1, we listed four research questions to evaluate our cloning operators. Without proper benchmarking, we cannot answer the memory consumption (RQ #1) question yet. Concerning the efficiency when manipulating clones (RQ #2), we do not expect *ShareFieldsOnly* and *ShareAll* to comply because of proxy objects. As they rely on of object sharing, *ShareObjOnly* and *ShareAll* are not compatible with generic operators that use the MOF `container()` reflective operation (RQ #4). However, our clones perfectly comply with the need to be manipulable by operations defined for the metamodel of the original model

(RQ #3). This is illustrated by our implementation, which allows each clone to be manipulated using the EMF Java API generated for the metamodel.

4.4 EMF-Based Implementation

We implemented our approach in Java with as much EMF compatibility as possible, which required us to face two main challenges. First, we had to extend EMF libraries—including implementations of EObject and Resource—to ensure that *containment* references are handled consistently in each model. Second, our approach relies on proxy objects, which are easy to create dynamically using a prototype-based object oriented language. However, with a class-based object oriented language such as Java, the fields of an object are determined by its class at design-time. We thus have to generate appropriate classes beforehand, which we do with a java-to-java transformation using EMF and MoDisco [1] to remove non-shareable properties of generated EMF implementations. More details about the implementation can be found in the companion web page of the paper: http://diverse.irisa.fr/software/modelcloning/.

5 Evaluation and Results

This section presents our evaluation. First we describe our dataset, then what we measure and the metrics considered for our metamodels, and finally the obtained results and how they relate to the requirements stated in Section 2.

5.1 Dataset

To evaluate this work, we need both various metamodels and models that conform to these metamodels. For the metamodels part, we developed a random Ecore model generator. We parameterized it the following way: a maximum number of 100 classes per metamodel, 250 properties per class and 50 mutable properties (which are properties with a _m suffix) per class. We use weighted randomness to create different kinds of properties, with the following weights: 30% of integers, 30% of booleans, 30% of strings, and 10% of references. For the models part, we generate for each metamodel a single model in a deterministic way that covers the whole metamodel. It starts from the roots, navigates through each composition and creates a maximum of two objects per encountered class. Then, all attributes are initialized with random values and references with random objects. We could have generated more models per metamodel, but our goal was to illustrate how our operators behave with varying *metamodels*, each with different shareable parts. For more information concerning the evaluation process you can refer to our companion web page http://diverse.irisa.fr/software/modelcloning/.

5.2 Measures

To verify that we reached our main objective, we must measure the memory consumption of the runtime representations of the clones, and more precisely

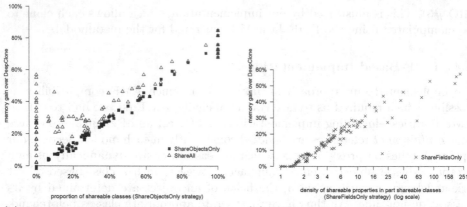

(a) Memory gain for the *ShareObjOnly* and *ShareAll* operators, with varying proportion of shareable classes

(b) Memory gain with *ShareFieldsOnly* against density of shareable properties in part. shareable classes (log scale)

Fig. 5. Memory gain results obtained for 1000 clones

the memory gain compared at the *DeepCloning* operator. For precise memory measures, we create a heap dump at the end of each evaluation run, and we analyze it using the Eclipse Memory Analyzer (MAT) [2]. The second measure we make is the read-access performance of the runtime representations of clones, compared to the one of the original model. We expect to see some performance decrease when proxy runtime objects are involved We proceed by measuring the amount of time required to navigate 10 000 times through each object of a model while accessing each of their properties.

5.3   Metrics

To embrace the variety of metamodels, we consider two metrics: the proportion of shareable classes when using either the *ShareObjOnly* or the *ShareAll* strategy, and the density of shareable properties within partially shareable classes when using the *ShareFieldsOnly* strategy. The first metric most likely correlates with the memory gain for operators that share objects, and the second for the operator that only shares fields.

5.4   Results

Each measure was done by creating the model of the metamodel, cloning it 1000 times with the chosen operator, and measuring both the memory footprint and the efficiency of one of the clones.

Fig. 5a shows the memory gain of the *ShareObjOnly* and *ShareAll* operators over the *DeepCloning* operator with varying proportion of shareable classes. We

---

[2] http://www.eclipse.org/mat/

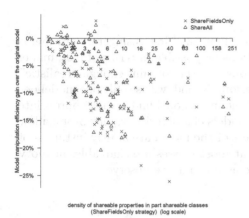

Fig. 6. Manipulation time gain for the *ShareFieldsOnly* and *ShareAll* operators, with varying density of shareable properties in part. shareable classes (log scale)

can see that the more shareable classes there are, the more memory gain there is. This relation appears linear for *ShareObjOnly*, and less regular for *ShareAll*. This is quite normal since the first operator only relies on object sharing, while the second is also influenced by the amount of shareable properties that can be shared through proxies. We also observe that *ShareAll* is always better that *ShareObjOnly*, which was expected since it shares fields in addition to objects. Some points may look surprising at position 0%, however they are simply caused by metamodels with very few classes and a high amount of shareable properties. Thus, sharing fields of such metamodels quickly gives very high gains.

Fig. 5b shows the memory gain of the *ShareFieldsOnly* operator over the *Deep-Cloning* operator with varying density of shareable properties within partially shareable classes. We observe a correlation between gain and the metric, and the gain raises up to approximately 40%. This operator gives overall worse results that the *ShareObjOnly* and *ShareAll* operators, but can give better results in some situations (e.g. metamodels with mostly partially shareable classes).

Finally, Fig. 6 presents the model manipulation efficiency gain over the run-time representation of the model originally cloned. We observe that, as expected because of the proxy design pattern, the operators *ShareFieldsOnly* and *ShareAll* both suffer from a little performance decrease. The median overhead is -9,5% for *ShareFieldsOnly* and -5.9% for *ShareAll*.

Overall, the results match our expectations. On the one hand, memory gain measures show that our operators are as good as *DeepCloning* when no parts arc shareable, and are better and better as the quantity of shareable parts raises. Therefore, all our operators satisfy the need to reduce the memory footprint of clones (RQ #1). On the other hand, manipulation efficiency measures show that there is a little overhead when manipulating clones obtained by our opera-tors *ShareFieldsOnly* and *ShareAll*. Thus, as we foresaw, these operators do not comply with the efficiency requirement (RQ #2).

5.5   Threats to Validity

We identified two main threats to our evaluation. First, using random meta-models, we hope to cover as many situations as possible in terms of metamodel design. Yet, have no way to be sure that our dataset contains enough "realistic" designs, as we have no metric for this criterion. Second, we use only one model per metamodel, which even if it covers the whole metamodel and is thus appropriate to evaluate our approach regarding metamodels characteristics, may overshadow some situations. For instance, if the objects of the model are mostly instances of non-shareable classes despite the fact that most classes are shareable, memory gain would not correlate with this metric as much as we observe.

6   Conclusion

Model cloning is an operation to duplicate an existing model that can be used in many kinds of applications. We identified four requirements for cloning operators: to be able to apply domain operators on clones, to have some memory gain over deep cloning, to be able to apply generic operators on clones, and to be able to manipulate clones as efficiently as their original model. Our goal was to provide cloning operators compliant with the first two requirements while satisfying the last two if possible. The approach we presented consists in sharing both runtime objects and fields between runtime representations of a model and its clones. We give four possible strategies to determine which parts of a metamodel are share-able, and we use these strategies to parameterize a generic cloning algorithm. We obtain four cloning operators, each being more appropriate for a specific situation. *DeepCloning* is the most basic operator with no memory footprint reduction, but that can be used in all situations where memory consumption is not an issue. *ShareFieldsOnly* shares fields of immutable attributes, which reduces the memory footprint of the clones but also introduces an overhead when manipulating them. *ShareObjOnly* shares objects to reduce significantly the memory footprint, but produced clones are not compatible with generic operations that rely on the `container()` specifiec in the MOF Reflection package. Finally, *Share-All* shares both objects and remaining shareable fields, which saves even more memory, but with the weaknesses of the two previous operators. Our evaluation was done using a hundred randomly generated metamodels, and results show both memory gain over *DeepCloning* for all three other operators, and a loss of manipulation efficiency for *ShareObjOnly* and *ShareAll* operators.

To pursue this work, a possible direction would be to automate the choice of a cloning operator. For instance, it must be possible using static analysis of operations to determine whether the reflexive layer is used or not, and more precisely to detect the use of EMF `eContainer()`. This would give the possibility to automatically disable cloning operators that forbid the use of this operation.

Acknowledgement. This work is partially supported by the ANR INS Project GEMOC (ANR-12-INSE-0011).

References

1. Bruneliere, H., Cabot, J., Jouault, F., Madiot, F.: MoDisco: A Generic and Extensible Framework for Model Driven Reverse Engineering. In: Proceedings of the IEEE/ACM International Conference on Automated Software Engineering, ASE 2010, pp. 173–174. ACM, New York (2010)
2. Gamma, E., Helm, R., Johnson, R., Vlissides, J.: Design patterns: Elements of reusable object-oriented software. Addison-Wesley (1994)
3. Goings, S., Goldsby, H., Cheng, B.H.C., Ofria, C.: An ecology-based evolutionary algorithm to evolve solutions to complex problems. In: Proc. of the Int. Conf. on the Simulation and Synthesis of Living Systems, ALIFE (2012)
4. Goldberg, A., Robson, D.: Smalltalk-80: The Language and Its Implementation. Addison-Wesley Longman Publishing Co., Inc., Boston (1983)
5. Karsai, G., Maroti, M., Ledeczi, A., Gray, J., Sztipanovits, J.: Composition and Cloning in Modeling and Meta-Modeling. IEEE Transactions on Control Systems Technology 12(2), 263–278 (2004)
6. Kessentini, M., Sahraoui, H.A., Boukadoum, M.: Model transformation as an optimization problem. In: Czarnecki, K., Ober, I., Bruel, J.-M., Uhl, A., Völter, M. (eds.) MODELS 2008. LNCS, vol. 5301, pp. 159–173. Springer, Heidelberg (2008)
7. Lieberman, H.: Using prototypical objects to implement shared behavior in object-oriented systems. In: Conference Proceedings on Object-oriented Programming Systems, Languages and Applications, OOPLSA 1986, pp. 214–223. ACM, New York (1986)
8. Maoz, S.: Model-based traces. In: Chaudron, M.R.V. (ed.) MODELS 2008 Workshops. LNCS, vol. 5421, pp. 109–119. Springer, Heidelberg (2009)
9. OMG. Meta Object Facility (MOF) Core Specification (2013)
10. Saxena, T., Karsai, G.: MDE-Based Approach for Generalizing Design Space Exploration. In: Petriu, D.C., Rouquette, N., Haugen, Ø. (eds.) MODELS 2010, Part I. LNCS, vol. 6394, pp. 46–60. Springer, Heidelberg (2010)
11. Steinberg, D., Budinsky, D., Paternostro, M., Merks, E.: EMF: Eclipse Modeling Framework, 2nd edn. Addison-Wesley (December 2008)
12. Tarjan, R.: Depth-First Search and Linear Graph Algorithms. SIAM Journal on Computing 1(2), 146–160 (1972)

Three Cases of Feature-Based Variability Modeling in Industry[*]

Thorsten Berger[1], Divya Nair[1], Ralf Rublack[3], Joanne M. Atlee[4],
Krzysztof Czarnecki[5], and Andrzej Wąsowski[5]

[1] University of Waterloo, Waterloo, Canada
[2] University of Leipzig, Leipzig, Germany
[3] IT University of Copenhagen, Copenhagen, Denmark

Abstract. Large software product lines need to manage complex variability. A common approach is variability modeling—creating and maintaining models that abstract over the variabilities inherent in such systems. While many variability modeling techniques and notations have been proposed, little is known about industrial practices and how industry values or criticizes this class of modeling. We attempt to address this gap with an exploratory case study of three companies that apply variability modeling. Among others, our study shows that variability models are valued for their capability to organize knowledge and to achieve an overview understanding of codebases. We observe centralized model governance, pragmatic versioning, and surprisingly little constraint modeling, indicating that the effort of declaring and maintaining constraints does not always pay off.

1 Introduction

Many modern systems contain an increasing amount of *variability* to tailor systems for different customers and hardware. Variability can be realized using a wide range of mechanisms including static and dynamic configuration parameters, components, frameworks, and generators. Variability-rich systems range from large industrial product lines [12,32,1] to prominent open-source software, such as the Linux kernel [7] with over 11,000 configuration options—aka *features* [26].

Variability in these systems has to be managed. Variability modeling, the discipline of describing variability in formal representations—*variability models*—is one of the key techniques to deal with complex variability. Variability models, such as feature [26,14] or decision [35,16,13] models, provide abstractions of the variabilities present in software. They allow engineers to scope systems and to plan their evolution; they can also be used for system configuration and derivation using automated tools, such as configurators and generators.

However, variability modeling, as any modeling layer, comes at a cost. Models have to be created and maintained, tools introduced, developers trained, and possibly the organization restructured. These costs may outweigh any realized

---

[*] Partially supported by ARTEMIS JU (grant n°295397)

J. Dingel et al. (Eds.): MODELS 2014, LNCS 8767, pp. 302–319, 2014.
© Springer International Publishing Switzerland 2014

benefit, such as a high degree of automation or decreased time-to-market—two benefits often emphasized in the literature. But surprisingly, although hundreds of publications target variability modeling techniques [10,22,9], little is known about actual practices in the industry. This scarcity of published empirical data impedes research progress and the improvement of methods, languages, and tools.

We attempt to address this gap with an exploratory case study of variability modeling in three companies. Our objective is to provide contextualized empirical data on practices, and to elicit perceived strengths and weaknesses of variability modeling. The analysis of each case is guided by three research questions:

- *How are variability models created and evolved (RQ1)?* We investigate modeling practices, such as strategies to identify features and to modularize, evolve and scale models. We also gather core characteristics of the models.
- *What are the benefits (RQ2) and what are the challenges (RQ3) of variability modeling?* We identify technical, organizational, and commercial values and challenges of modeling, as experienced and perceived by practitioners.

To put this empirical data into context, we also inquire organizational structures supporting the practices, and elicit scales, architectures, and technologies of the respective software product lines.

This case study is part of our ongoing effort to improve the empirical understanding of variability modeling. We previously surveyed companies in their use of variability modeling [5] and conducted semi-structured interviews with eight of them. In the present work, we select three companies and describe and analyze them in-depth. Our selection represents a broad range of development scales from very small (two developers) to ultra-large (100 development teams); comprises domains that commonly use variability modeling (automotive, industrial applications/energy, and eCommerce [5]); and covers all product-line adoption strategies (proactive, extractive, and reactive [27]). In contrast to quantitative research, our goal is not too reach any statistically significant deductions, but to describe the practices that were successful in three heterogeneous cases. We provide rich descriptions of three selected cases rather than analyzing all interviews, such as using Grounded Theory [20], which is the subject for future work.

We proceed as follows. Sect. 2 introduces variability modeling and related work. Sect. 3 describes our methodology. Sect. 4 presents results for all cases. Sect. 5 compares the cases, Sect. 6 discusses threats to validity, and Sect. 7 concludes.

2   Background and Related Work

We previously studied variability modeling in systems software [6]. That study revealed the significance of feature and decision modeling concepts in languages conceived by practitioners. It also showed that additional concepts (such as defaults, visibility conditions, derived features) are needed to scale modeling. Interestingly, the models had very different characteristics (size, shape, constraints)

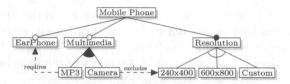

Fig. 1. Simple feature model (adapted from [18])

than models considered in research. In the present work, we strive to gain insight into how the results from the previous study relate to industrial practices. Our preceding survey [5] showed that feature models were among the most popular notations, but also that a wide range of notations and tools is used. It also confirmed the existence of large models—which have been reported before [39,38,29], but without any further characteristics, such as the use or complexity of constraints.

In the present study, all of our subjects use feature models. These are hierarchical structures of features, together with constraints that restrict valid feature combinations. Fig. 1 shows the model of a Mobile Phone. It always (solid dot) has the feature Resolution and optionally (hollow dot) has the features EarPhone or Multimedia, or both. Multimedia is an OR group (select at least one) and Resolution an XOR group (select exactly one). Further constraints reside in the hierarchy (child-parent implication) and in additional cross-tree constraints (*requires* and *excludes*). For instance, MP3 requires an Earphone. In practice, constraints may be more complex. Some languages support rich constraints (e.g., arithmetic) over features with non-Boolean values, such as numbers and strings [31,6].

Variability modeling is a core activity in software product line engineering (SPLE) [12]. Although detailed industrial experience reports on SPLE exist, only few focus variability modeling. The "Software Product Line Hall of Fame" [1], a catalog of SPLE case studies [37], and a practice-oriented book [28] contain information on adoption practices, organizational structures, and architectures, but offer little insight into the use of variability models, their sizes and contents, and the techniques used to build them. In fact, recent literature reviews on the evaluation of variability modeling lament the lack of empirical work on this topic [11,9,22,10]. Exceptions are industrial experience reports. Grünbacher et al. [21] emphasize that techniques need to be customized to the organizational context in which they are used; Reiser et al. [33] request compliance constraints for the same purpose; Riebisch et al. [34] point out the use of feature models by non-software developers; Gillan et al. [19] identify a lack of documented methodologies to create feature models. These reports are complementary to our study, but cannot provide a coherent picture. Finally, variability modeling can be seen as an instance of model-driven development (MDD). Hutchinson et al. [24,25] study MDD practices and experiences in industry. They reveal success factors for applying MDD, such as incremental adoption, organizational commitment, and integration with existing development processes. While these results are relevant to variability modeling, we strive to gain insights specific to variability modeling.

Table 1. Variability model characteristics, variable artifacts, and variability mechanisms

	consulting company	component producer	car manufacturer
notation	feature model	feature model	semi-structured feature lists
tools	CaptainFeature	pure::variants	TeamCenter (prev. Excel)
modularization	single model	single model	hierarchy of models
model sizes (features, approx.)	40	1,100	top level: 300–500, intermediate level: up to 800, low-level: up to 3000
feature types	100% Boolean	95% Boolean, 5% integers and strings	100% Boolean
feature kinds	mandatory, optional	mandatory, optional	mandatory, optional
model hierarchy depths	5–6	3–4	2–3
cross-tree constraints	none	very few	none
custom relations	none	*recommended*	marketing relevance
variable artifacts	code, help system database schema	code (requirements and test cases planned)	code, logical design blocks, components, Simulink models
variability mechanisms	custom preprocessor and code generator	C preprocessor and dynamic parameters	C preprocessor and dynamic parameters
feature-to-artifact mapping	hard-coded in generator (imperative)	pure::variants' family model, feature Makefiles	informal textual descriptions and architecture diagrams

3   Methodology

We conducted semi-structured interviews with knowledgeable representatives from eight organizations identified in our previous survey [5]. In this paper, we explore three of these cases in depth. Our selection criteria were that the cases (i) represent a wide range of organizational sizes, (ii) stem from domains that most frequently apply variability modeling according to the survey, and (iii) cover all of the three common adoption strategies: proactive, extractive, and reactive [27].

Each of the interviews lasted one hour on average. We allowed the interviewees to speak freely, but assured coverage of the following five topics: *Context* of variability modeling, including organizational structure, variability mechanisms, programming languages, and technologies; *Practices (RQ1)* used to create and evolve models, including roles and responsibilities of the actors involved; *Characteristics* of models, including size, shape, modeling elements, and richness of constraints; *Benefits (RQ2)* of variability modeling; and *Challenges (RQ3)* experienced. The interviews were recorded, transcribed, and analyzed by extracting information relevant to the research questions.

4   Results

We report the results in a structured narrative form together with interpretations. For each case, we provide the *context*; then in the first subsection the *practices (RQ1)*; in the second subsection the *benefits (RQ2)*; and in the third subsection the *challenges (RQ3)* of variability modeling. Interview quotes are prefixed with **A**, **B**, and **C** for the respective subjects, and our questions with **Q**.

Table 1 summarizes the *characteristics* of the respective models, the types of artifacts whose variability they describe, and variability mechanisms.

4.1   Consulting Company

Our first subject is a small ($\leq$ 50 employees) consulting company delivering customized web-based e-commerce and enterprise applications. The company specializes in MDD of software solutions for customers. We interviewed a department lead, acting both as a software architect and developer. Our case study focuses on a Java web-shop system that was in production for 2–3 years. Its purpose was to explore the potential of generator-based SPLE using variability management and modeling solutions originating from research—including feature models, a feature-model configurator, and a code generator framework. The latter is the main variability mechanism: it conditionally compiles source files after preprocessing them with a home-grown preprocessor. The development can be characterized as follows:

- *Research-driven*: The company followed a textbook approach to variability modeling. It adopted practices mainly originating from [14], using a feature model and a code generator for product derivation.
- *Small-scale*: The development team comprised two developers, both working on the code, the generator framework, and the feature model (40 features).
- *Prototype-based*: The company started with a prototype to experiment and to gain experience with software product lines and feature modeling. The prototype went into production and was sold to six customers.
- *Fully platform-oriented*: All artifacts are integrated into one platform. New customer requirements are always realized within the platform.
- *Re-active*: The product line and the feature model are the result of decomposing an initial product into features.

Modeling Practices (RQ1). The company developed a feature model with the goal of configuring and deriving products automatically. It used the relatively simple tool CaptainFeature [3], which had usability issues, but no better tool existed in 2002. The interviewee emphasized the preference for having a tool that supported the exact graphical notation of feature models (Fig. 1). This representation of variability could be handled sufficiently well for a small model of 40 features, using the tool's zoom capabilities. To create models, the developers performed a domain analysis of the web-shop domain, including customer requirements. The developers modeled both variability (optional features) and commonality (mandatory features) of the product line. In this manner, following advice and processes from SPLE literature, the developers scoped the product line. New features were introduced either when requested by customers or when the team saw added value for future customers:

A: *The question in our case was rather: What can we sell to the customer? What would be the added value a customer might want to have [...]? We always looked at it from the perspective of what we can sell.*

A core part of a model is the feature hierarchy, which was developed top-down, based on domain-specific ontological relationships (*part-of*):

A: *We tried to come up with logical relationships between the features [...] we had a feature that was called "Catalog System". That was the basis, since a shop* *always has a catalog. If you cannot display articles, then you just don't have a shop. Underneath, we put features such as "Shopping Cart", since only when you have a catalog, it makes sense to take the shopping cart as a feature.*

However, decomposing the initial product might have influenced the creation of the feature model, and optional features mapped to artifacts might stem from a bottom-up approach. Thus, the commonality (domain modeling) was likely created top-down, while the actual variability was created bottom-up.

The resulting feature model had around 40 Boolean features and was relatively balanced. Our interviewee estimated around 2–6 children per non-leaf feature on average, and a maximum depth of 5 or 6 levels. The model was under-constrained. Although constraints among features existed, only hierarchy constraints and feature groups (OR and XOR, Fig. 1) were modeled and could be used to support the configuration process.

The model evolved rarely and only 2–3 features were added per new customer. The overall structure of the feature model was also rarely changed and feature were never removed. Feature additions almost never affected existing functionality.

Benefits (RQ2). Our interviewee sees the main benefit of variability modeling in organizing the information needed to maintain an overview understanding of the system. He emphasizes that the tool and the model provide management facilities that are useful to summarize product capabilities, to understand relationships between features, and to see the assignment of features to customers.

The company also sees benefit in a feature-model configurator. However, shortcomings in it can negatively impact the configuration process. Yet, the company experienced no significant impact given the limited scale of the system:

A: *The tool wasn't really that optimal [...] we had no real support where we could see that feature X conflicts with feature Y [...] We might have sometimes reached a point where we didn't know what happens why, or when the nesting was too deep. But that wasn't anything dramatic.*

In the literature, a common argument for SPLE is the reduced time-to-market. When asked about this benefit, our interviewee responded:

A: *I'd answer with a clear "depends on." It reduces time-to-market when I can rely on a basis and only have to make small changes for a client. On the other hand, I cannot do it rashly or without care, because otherwise I break something in my product family, which is not planned either. Where it also helps is when the customer wants exactly what we already implemented, then the time-to-market really converges to zero.*

In summary, the company considered its prototype successful and reused most of its infrastructure in a subsequent system: a jewelry-ring configurator developed for a ring manufacturer. The company developed a DSL used to describe properties of rings, in order to generate 3D models of them. This DSL used feature-model concepts, but introduced domain-specific terminology and language elements to facilitate a fine-grained configuration of the rings. Interestingly, it also introduced feature cardinalities [15], which allow multiple instantiations (cloning) of features, since a prototyped feature model became too wide and shallow.

Challenges (RQ3). Despite rare evolution, the co-evolution of the variability model and the product-line infrastructure is considered as a major challenge:

A: *I think the biggest problem we faced at that time and also today, and which is not really solved yet, is the evolution: To exactly know how to evolve features, on which implementation components they depend, so that you don't break anything when you work in the generator. I mean, to keep the complete overview: what is there and how does it all play together?*

Interestingly, even though one of the main purposes of feature models is to allow non-experts (customers) to configure a product, this turned out to be difficult, as the customers did not have the right prerequisites:

A: *Currently, we use it just internally. When we started in 2003, the underlying idea was also to build a frontend from the feature model where the customer can freely configure—exactly like the paradigm. But we abandoned this idea relatively quickly, because it is still very difficult for the customer [...] In the end, you need a consultant who tells the customer what he needs, because that is the first problem. And then [you need] to understand what that means in our configuration.*

Another challenge lies in the organization of teams. Since the company is small, the same developers were building the platform infrastructure and target products simultaneously. Developers would get confused working in both worlds:

A: *We tried to develop the generator and target code in parallel. That was rather driven by the theory. But we noticed that it doesn't really make sense, I mean it slows us down [...] When you work in both worlds and you come to a spot in the target code where variability is addressed, you always automatically ask yourself whether it's something that you resolve in the target code or in the generator. And then you start pondering what makes most sense, and you loose time, although it's not your task to think about that as a target code developer.*

4.2   Component Producer

Our next subject is a large ($\leq$25,000 employees) vendor of electronic and mechanical components for end-user and industrial applications. The company has a large portfolio of products, many of which are derived from ad-hoc product lines, often using a clone-and-own approach. We interviewed two software architects responsible for variability management in a division that develops a product line of software controllers for power electronics. The product line has twelve products, which are fully integrated into the platform, and over 30 optional add-ons for sub-products maintained outside the platform. The product line has been in production since 2005. In 2009, variability modeling was introduced using the tool pure::variants [8], which also provides variability mechanisms: a "family model" representing the source files, and a build system. The C/C++ preprocessor handles fine-grained variations. The binding of variability is mainly static, but the shipped products include a large number of runtime parameters, which can be configured by customers in a semi-static manner (they are normally not changed during normal operation of a component, only in the configuration phase). The codebase has 1.5M lines of C++ (98%) and C code, distributed over 10,000 files with around 14,000 conditional compilation directives. The development can be characterized as follows:

- *Research-driven*: SPLE and variability modeling practices were adopted in interaction with consultants and researchers.
- *Medium-scale*: The feature model has slightly more than 1100 features. The product-line-development involves around 60 software engineers.
- *Mostly platform-oriented*: Core parts of the product line are integrated into one platform. Customer-specific artifacts (sub-products) exist outside.
- *Extractive*: The product line and the feature model are results of a migration of existing individual products originating from a clone-and-own approach.

Modeling Practices (RQ1). Variability is modeled using a single centralized feature model. Features are mapped to code using a family model. Building, maintaining, and evolving the feature model is under the control of one expert: **B:** *We have a colleague who [...] really has the domain knowledge, because he took care of all the development [...]. He consults with the other development teams. [...] So we try to have one place, or one person that is responsible. But then it's not the case that he decides all the things. So, whenever we have an issue, we try to organize a workshop or a meeting [...], it's actually his responsibility to make [sure] [...] that it's correct.*

The modelers focus on building the hierarchy (child-parent) relationship between features and try to avoid cross-tree constraints; few exist in the model. However, they begun adding custom relationships, such as "recommended". The latter often indicates bug fixes, which are actually modeled as features, since not every customer has an interest in enabling them. Some exploit the "invalid" behaviors in their applications and prefer to keep them without fixing.

The variability models are under-constrained. Dependencies among source files are not modeled in the family model, which could be used by pure::variants to verify configurations. Instead, the company finds it easier to maintain tested configurations of its twelve main products instead of exhaustively modeling all constraints. The few dependencies used are primarily binary "requires" and "excludes" relations. There are no numeric or string constraints in the feature model. Instead, complex constraints are put into the feature-to-code mapping as presence conditions of source files. This strategy is interesting, as it reduces constraints both in the variability model and the family model, which contains no dependencies at all. The team strives to keep all models simple.

The hierarchy of the feature model is reasonably well balanced. The engineers avoid deep trees and consider a maximum depth of three or four levels reasonable. Yet, problems with finding the optimal grouping of features occur in some cases: **B:** *Then actually it becomes too flat somehow. So, it's a question of how to group them. We're still working on the optimal way. But I think four, that's really the maximum. We don't have really like huge trees over there.*

The resulting model has around 1100 features. Evolution of it is mostly limited to adding features. Feature removal occurs within rare, but important, clean-up tasks. The hierarchy is also relatively stable without any major refactoring. The overall growth rate of the model is estimated at around 5–10% per year, with up to 50 new features per release, 3–4 times a year. Versioning is considered orthogonal to modeling, so models are versioned but not features (i.e., no multiple temporal versions of features in the model).

Benefits (RQ2). Our interviewees emphasize the organization of knowledge and the visualization of variability as the main benefits. Naming and organizing features makes them visible and accessible to developers, encouraging reuse:

B: *The first one is that it's visible, you see the features that you had in the code, before, and actually you see the features of the whole product line. Before, they saw features of the specific products. And then there was a process to make sure that the new features were propagated to the rest of the product.*

Q: So you know what's common?

B: *This, and actually now you can see them. I think the best is you can see relationships, to actually know what configurations are allowed and what are not allowed. That was also not so easy to express in the past [...] This is from the developer's point of view. But it's also, we can see that from the, say project development, it's also important, because before we noticed that the same functionality was implemented twice within the same project, basically they haven't realized that. They implemented the same features.*

Q: Because it was not visible?

B: *Yes, exactly. So it's not only from the development point of view; now you can somehow understand the code easily; you can see the dependencies between the features; you know actually how this code works. And there's also documentation that is attached to the modeling. So you can generate documentation automatically.*

Although our interviewees could not estimate increased productivity quantitatively, they claimed substantial quality improvements by employing SPLE and feature modeling, that it reduced the number of critical bugs significantly. They also claimed that time-to-market was significantly reduced due to automated product derivation. Interestingly, the organization presently strives for further automation by linking features to portfolio and requirements models.

Challenges (RQ3). The interviewees expressed three challenges related, respectively, to organization, modeling, and development. First, it is difficult to convince all stakeholders to invest in core assets when the organization has a matrix structure. Such an organization has two opposing forces: those who optimize for short-term revenue by resorting to clone-and-own approaches with less (short-term) development effort, and those who insist on proper SPLE activities to assure revenue and less maintenance effort in the long run, but with higher (short-term) effort:

B: *In a big, big, really big company that has this [inertia], it's easier to enforce things also, because the management can actually push the things. [Our company] is in the middle, it's not very big, it's not a small one. So there's some kind of let's say, maybe not fight, but some kind of*

Q: pushback?

B: *Yes, between the development and the management. And that's actually a challenge, because introduction of a product line requires that there's some kind of organizational structure introduced [...] So people will have to start thinking in terms of developing assets that can be reused and this can be achieved only if you have a group that takes care of [...] domain engineering. And I'd say in the really big companies, maybe they have somehow the will to invest in actually organizing the whole undertaking. Whereas in the companies that are in the middle, it's some kind of a strained situation when we have product development that is really looking at the business and economy point of view, and then we have the technology people, or the part that are developing the product, that are pushing really for doing things the right way. And then the management is somehow in between. [...] Because we have to earn money, so business tells them we have to earn money. But we cannot do it the way we do it.*

The second challenge concerns modularization of the model. It was difficult to find a good structure when trying to separate product-specific features. Both common and product-specific features exist, as well as commonalities between these two groups. It is also possible to have many different combinations between the groups. Thus, the result would have been an intricate model.

The third expressed challenge concerns the high amount of conditional compilation directives in the code and the additional variability model layer that developers need to take into account:

B: *I think the biggest problem is that the developers are used to working for a long time on the same abstraction level, basically text. Now somehow we introduce a concept, a new way of working, because they cannot just, for example, merge everything at the source code level. They also have to think about models [...] So whenever they add a feature, they have to add the feature to the model. So later whenever they merge back the integration branches, they have to merge all the artifacts. They just have to learn about the modeling part. But I think the modeling in pure::variants, I think the way they realize that is a big advantage. Because in the past, they did it all in source code. So you had a huge header file with features enabled and disabled. The dependency was hardly expressed.*

4.3   Car Manufacturer

The third subject is a very large ($\leq 150,000$ employees) car manufacturer producing over 400,000 cars per year. From three main platforms, an estimated number of three million different car models can be derived. Our interviewee is a software architect who was involved in modeling and managing variability. The product-line engineering comprises two major activities: *development* of car components and *manufacturing* of cars. Our focus is on the development, which uses features to capture variability. Features are mapped to hardware and software article numbers to facilitate the manufacturing. The software is mainly written in C, with a few exceptions, such as the infotainment system relying on C++ and Java. Variability mechanisms comprise component composition, conditional compilation with the C preprocessor, and dynamic adaptation at car startup using configuration options. The latter allow finer-grained variations, while features are generally coarser-grained. The development can be characterized as follows:

- *Practice-driven*: Software variability-management strategies are an adaptation of the mechanical manufacturing processes, which have evolved over decades.
- *Large-scale*: There are three main vehicle software platforms. 50–100 teams constantly interact with one another on individual subsystems of the platform.
- *Multi-level modeling*: Three levels of feature models are maintained in the company, each level facing different dynamics and governance.
- *Heterogeneous modeling*: The company uses diverse modeling approaches, including behavior modeling (Simulink) and structural modeling using a specific subset of UML (Sparx Systems Enterprise Architect).
- *Pro-active*: Product-line engineering was adopted from the beginning. Single-system development was infeasible due to the huge diversity. The current platforms are the result of a slow evolution over 15 years.

Modeling Practices (RQ1). Feature models are used on different organizational levels to describe the variability of the in-car software. All models are stored in a database, the TeamCenter product lifecycle management tool [2]. Before that, Excel was used. Each of the three platforms has a top-level model describing the "complete vehicle level" with around 300–500 features. Most of these are customer-visible features with a few exceptions, such as "remote diagnostics". The top-level model is built and maintained by a central group in the company. Features are refined into lower-level models to a maximum of three levels. For instance, the infotainment system has an "intermediate" level with 700–800 features and a low-level model with up to 3000 features. For other subsystems, fewer levels suffice, such as the chassis system with two levels.

Often, just a superset of the actual variability is modeled: finer-grained variability is realized by configuration options or via dynamic adaptation. Thus, the feature modeling concepts used are very simple, without any strong formalization. Structural grouping of features according to functionalities exists, such as for chassis, powertrain, or comfort features in the top-level model. Features are tagged as optional or mandatory, together with information about their relevance for marketing purposes. Only Boolean features exist; more types, such as enumerations (up to ten values) and integers, occur in the dynamic configuration options managed separately from features. Neither feature groups (OR/XOR, Fig. 1) nor cross-tree constraints are modeled. Although many exist, they are only documented informally or contained in the manufacturing database. Likewise, the mapping between features and software components or other models is only informally documented. Checking constraints does not play a role in development:

C: *We do that check in the manufacturing though, because we have a lot of constraints. I mean, two physical things can't occupy the same place physically.*

*So, for example, if you have an engine of this size, there are things that you
cannot have because it's so big. And that type of constraints we have, or checks,
we have in the manufacturing. And we also do that, the same thing to software,
for example, this software article is not compatible with that one. But, we don't
do that a lot in development, but in manufacturing.*

The different model levels face different governance and evolution. The top-
level is very stable, with updates only occurring at specific "update" events
twice a year. There, features are primarily added. Old features are removed, but
usually directly replaced with new ones. The low-level models are highly volatile.
For instance, the infotainment subsystem changes almost weekly.

Given all of these large-scale practices, the company never aimed for a
configurator-based approach to facilitate more automated derivation processes.
The latter is partly handled by a home-grown manufacturing tool, which combines
hardware and software article numbers during manufacturing, while adhering to
dependencies. Thus, the prime reason for variability modeling is the management
of variability, which does not require more formal modeling techniques.

Benefits (RQ2). Our interviewee sees the largest benefit of variability modeling at the requirements level: in scoping products, understanding configuration
spaces, maintaining development overviews, and fostering communication across
teams. Further benefit lies in marketing and coordination of new model releases:
C: *I would say the most important purpose is to agree between the R&D organization and with the product planning organization over the content of each
product. And based on that, you, what I'd say, you break down, or derive the
requirements on each subsystem to realize these features. In most cases, these
features are realized by several subsystems co-operating.*

Our interviewee expressed a neutral opinion about the value of variability
modeling in our previous survey. According to him, feature modeling in its simplest form, as practiced in the company, provides the mentioned benefits, but
provides little assistance with product configuration and derivation activities.

Challenges (RQ3). Our interviewee sees the biggest challenge in organizational
and cultural issues among heterogeneous teams. While he expressed some issues
with code, his focus as a software architect was primarily on the organizational
level, where he is concerned about interaction and efficient use of modeling:
C: *We have a lot of dependencies between subsystems and between teams, so it's
quite difficult for the teams to work autonomously [...] I think there is an inherent
complexity, because the number of interfaces is also great [...] If we look at the
present processes at [...] when it comes to modeling, it seems like we're aiming to
[...] keeping practices, which means that we're trying to align the modeling efforts
between different domains, we try to align the design artifacts that we are using,
and so on. And [we focus] on keeping the traceability between the different kinds
of artifacts that we use—the feature models, the software in itself, the different
[...] component models, AUTOSAR component models, our design model, our
architecture model, and so on. So we put a lot of effort in maintaining all these
design artifacts in a consistent way [...] My personal opinion is that I don't
think that's the right way to go, because since the complexity of our systems is*

exponentially increasing [...] we actually need to identify ways of working such that different development teams can work more autonomously, that they can use the tools they need for their specific problems [...]

In summary, our interviewee is concerned with handling the many dependencies between subsystems and establishing a harmonized collaboration between teams. While he observes that processes are heading towards textbook practices that strive to unify the current diversity in modeling approaches and introduce coherent traceability, he would prioritize autonomous teams over a unified architecture, which is increasingly complex due to a high amount of dependencies. The whole development might become even harder to manage with increasing effort spent on maintaining traceability and explicitly modeled dependencies.

5 Cross-Case Analysis

We now conduct a cross-case analysis and discuss commonalities and differences across cases. After summarizing the context in which variability modeling is performed, we compare practices (RQ1), benefits (RQ2), and challenges (RQ3).

Our cases applied variability modeling in very different contexts. The *consulting company* used feature modeling and SPLE as known from the literature, using the original graphical notation, a configurator, and a generator that resolves variability in an automated process. Although these web shops generated revenue, the project was a means to experiment and to gain expertise in variability modeling. For the *component producer*, feature modeling and SPLE was a core strategy to conquer complexity and maintenance issues stemming from a previous clone-and-own approach. Their practices originated from a close collaboration with researchers and the vendor of their modeling tool. The company was open to adopt solutions from research and saw the value of the solutions in lower time-to-market and increased code quality, but faced friction between demands for short-term revenue and the necessity of systematic variability management for long-term advantages. The *car manufacturer* applied feature modeling at a much larger scale and with simpler modeling concepts than both previous subjects. Practices originated from an engineering culture that had evolved over decades. While the other subjects strive for higher automation, unification, and integration of modeling, the reported experience suggests that textbook approaches might not work, or their effort might outweigh any potential benefit to this organization.

Practices (RQ1). *Limited constraint modeling:* Our most surprising finding is that all subjects avoid modeling constraints. This observation is in contrast to our previous observations in systems software, where detailed constraints are formally defined in rich languages. However, while configuration in our subject companies is performed by only a few knowledgeable domain experts, the systems software projects are configured by a large number of third-party users in ways that are not closely controlled by the platform developers. The latter setting requires constraint modeling, choice propagation, and conflict resolution facilities in order to guide users to correct configurations and prevent incorrect ones. These facilities do not seem to be essential in the context of our subjects.

Centralized model governance: Variability models need to be controlled centrally. While in the consulting company, the total development team was too small to draw any conclusion, the other subjects apply strict governance of either the whole model (component producer) or the top-level model (car manufacturer). Either one expert or a central team control the evolution and maintenance of the model. Interestingly, this observation confirms Hypothesis 1 in our study [4] on variability mechanisms in software ecosystems.

Furthermore, larger organizations, such as the car manufacturer, even require clear responsibilities per feature: it has to be defined, specified (e.g., by writing use cases) and developed by a dedicated entity in the organization.

Pragmatic versioning: We have not found any sophisticated support for versioning. One could, for example, imagine specific modeling elements for deprecated or experimental features, version annotations, or constraints over versions of features. Instead, the component producer uses an ordinary version control system for the whole model, and the car company applies a pragmatic solution: features have a unique identifier capturing lifecycle information. This approach, however, would lead to highly redundant constraints when modeled among features.

Domain knowledge in feature hierarchies: Our first subject built the feature hierarchy using domain knowledge. This indicates that hierarchical relations between features in fact represent domain-specific, ontological relationships. This observation supports insights from our previous work on reverse engineering feature models [36,30]. Thus, feature models contain unique ontological information, and building a feature hierarchy can hardly be automated and will have to be done by domain experts in a largely manual effort.

Top-down and bottom-up creation of models: All our subjects obviously needed some amount of top-down knowledge and analysis. The first two subjects also used the code of existing products to identify features. Thus, we believe that the creation of models that are used to configure products will be often created by a mixture of top-down and bottom-up approaches.

Benefits (RQ2). *Organization of knowledge:* The most important benefit of variability modeling, emphasized by all interviewees, is the organization of knowledge. This benefit resembles perceived benefits of MDD [24]—companies appreciate the potential of MDD to ease communication and to overview the development.

Visualization and scoping. All interviewees appreciate the visualization and product-scoping capabilities of feature models. Most of them were able to better understand product functionalities. The consulting company found it beneficial to see which customers have which features. The component producer was even able to identify duplicate implementations of certain features.

Configurator support: The insignificance of configuration in the three industrial cases is surprising, which is in contrast to our previous study of systems software (Sect. 2). We conjecture cost/benefit considerations. Configurators require formally declared constraints and, according to our previous experience, also proper usage of different constraint types (e.g., configuration constraints, visibility constraints, default constraints) to leverage a configurator. Such effort would not pay off for our subjects, and even with intelligent configurators, users can spend substantial time configuring products when intricate constraints exist [23].

Challenges (RQ3). *Mindset changes:* Introducing variability modeling requires mindset changes of all actors. As can be seen from the component producer, developers commonly think at one abstraction level and struggle with trying to maintain features (at another abstraction level). Even in the consulting company, where the developers had bought into modeling, both struggled with developing application code and infrastructure code in parallel. The situation for the car manufacturer was different, however. SPLE was an adaptation of mechanical-engineering practices that have a long tradition; thus, developers always understood that single-systems or cloning-based development is infeasible.

Short-term versus long-term benefit: SPLE requires discipline from all actors—specifically, to consistently co-evolve models and code. In a matrix organization, there is a higher risk of conflict between proponents and opponents of systematic variability management. Actors who strive for short-term revenue might fall back to clone-and-own for product derivation, leading to high maintenance in the future, as the clone requires maintenance. Establishing a culture for systematic management and modeling is a core challenge.

Evolution: All subjects primarily add features and seldom remove features or restructure the hierarchy. The consulting company mentioned that evolution was challenging as it requires understanding the feature-to-code mapping and the impact of feature changes, to avoid breaking the system. The car manufacturer expressed concerns about exploding complexity of their development, but not specifically about the (simple) models. Although the company strives for increased commonality of the software for all car models, whether this effort will affect features or only the finer-grained configuration options remains an open question.

6   Threats to Validity

External validity. Our findings originate from only three cases. However, we do not attempt to reach any statistical generalizations from the data, but describe substantial cases in their full richness. In fact, case-study research does not aim at representativeness, which is impossible to assess since the whole population of cases is usually unknown. Our selection of cases is based on theoretical sampling [17]. We chose them according to three criteria (Sect. 3) among all of our subjects. A limitation of our study is that all subjects successfully applied variability modeling. Studying failed attempts would be valuable future work.
Internal validity. Our findings rely on interview data, since no other data-sources (e.g., artifacts) were available. We interviewed actors centrally involved with variability modeling. Still, triangulating our results with data gathered using other methods, such as action research or ethnographic field studies, would

be valuable future work. Interestingly, the practices of the car manufacturer correlate with our experiences with another car manufacturer of similar size, improving our confidence in the results. Last, the interview data could be biased due to leading or misphrased questions. We did pre-tests and carefully analyzed the transcripts, omitting responses that indicated uncertainty. The consulting company interview was done in German. We carefully, almost literally, translated it.

7   Conclusion

We have provided empirical data on variability modeling in successful industrial applications. The reported experiences show that feature models are perceived as intuitive and simple notations that organize unique domain knowledge and foster understanding and collaboration among developers. Many practices are pragmatic, such as versioning, the mix of top-down and bottom-up modeling, central model governance, or the very limited constraint modeling. Interestingly, instead of declaring and maintaining constraints, our subjects prefer to manage a set of configurations or to let experts configure products. Thus, the primary benefit of variability modeling lies in variability management—organizing, visualizing, and scoping features—less in configuration and automation for our subjects. Yet, the benefits require acceptance of an additional abstraction level and discipline in maintaining models. Otherwise, long-term advantages can be compromised for quick revenue, which we found is especially a problem in matrix organizations.

References

1. Product Line Hall of Fame, http://www.splc.net/fame.html (accessed March 2014)
2. TeamCenter, http://www.plm.automation.siemens.com/en_us/products/teamcenter/ (accessed July 2014)
3. Bednasch, T.: Konzept und Implementierung eines konfigurierbaren Metamodells für die Merkmalmodellierung. Master's thesis, Fachhochschule Kaiserslautern (October 2002)
4. Berger, T., Pfeiffer, R.H., Tartler, R., Dienst, S., Czarnecki, K., Wasowski, A., She, S.: Variability mechanisms in software ecosystems. Information and Software Technology (2014)
5. Berger, T., Rublack, R., Nair, D., Atlee, J.M., Becker, M., Czarnecki, K., Wąsowski, A.: A survey of variability modeling in industrial practice. In: VaMoS (2013)
6. Berger, T., She, S., Lotufo, R., Wasowski, A., Czarnecki, K.: A study of variability models and languages in the systems software domain. IEEE Transactions on Software Engineering 39(12) (2013)
7. Berger, T., She, S., Lotufo, R., Wąsowski, A., Czarnecki, K.: Variability modeling in the real: A perspective from the operating systems domain. In: ASE 2010 (2010)
8. Beuche, D.: Pure::variants Eclipse Plugin, user Guide. pure-systems GmbH (2004), http://web.pure-systems.com/fileadmin/downloads/pv_userguide.pdf

9. Chen, L., Ali Babar, M.: A survey of scalability aspects of variability modeling approaches. In: SCALE (2009)
10. Chen, L., Ali Babar, M., Ali, N.: Variability management in software product lines: A systematic review. In: SPLC (2009)
11. Chen, L., Ali Babar, M., Cawley, C.: A status report on the evaluation of variability management approaches. In: EASE (2009)
12. Clements, P., Northrop, L.: Software Product Lines: Practices and Patterns. Addison-Wesley (2001)
13. Czarnecki, K., Grünbacher, P., Rabiser, R., Schmid, K., Wąsowski, A.: Cool features and tough decisions: A comparison of variability modeling approaches. In: VAMOS (2012)
14. Czarnecki, K., Eisenecker, U.W.: Generative Programming: Methods, Tools, and Applications. Addison-Wesley, Boston (2000)
15. Czarnecki, K., Helsen, S., Eisenecker, U.: Formalizing cardinality-based feature models and their specialization. Software Process Improvement and Practice 10(1) (2005)
16. Dhungana, D., Grünbacher, P.: Understanding decision-oriented variability modelling. In: ASPL (2008)
17. Eisenhardt, K.M., Graebner, M.E.: Theory building from cases: Opportunities and challenges. Academy of Management Journal 50(1), 25–32 (2007)
18. Gheyi, R., Massoni, T., Borba, P.: Automatically checking feature model refactorings. The Journal of Universal Computer Science 17(5), 684–711 (2011)
19. Gillan, C., Kilpatrick, P., Spence, I., Brown, T., Bashroush, R., Gawley, R., et al.: Challenges in the application of feature modelling in fixed line telecommunications. In: VaMoS (2007)
20. Glaser, B., Strauss, A.: The discovery of grounded theory: Strategies for qualitative research. Aldine de Gruyter (1967)
21. Grünbacher, P., Rabiser, R., Dhungana, D., Lehofer, M.: Model-based customization and deployment of Eclipse-based tools: Industrial experiences. In: ASE 2009 (2009)
22. Hubaux, A., Classen, A., Mendonça, M., Heymans, P.: A preliminary review on the application of feature diagrams in practice. In: VaMoS 2010 (2010)
23. Hubaux, A., Xiong, Y., Czarnecki, K.: A user survey of configuration challenges in linux and ecos. In: VaMoS (2012)
24. Hutchinson, J., Rouncefield, M., Whittle, J.: Model-driven engineering practices in industry. In: ICSE (2011)
25. Hutchinson, J., Whittle, J., Rouncefield, M., Kristoffersen, S.: Empirical assessment of mde in industry. In: ICSE (2011)
26. Kang, K., Cohen, S., Hess, J., Nowak, W., Peterson, S.: Feature-oriented domain analysis (FODA) feasibility study. Tech. Rep. CMU/SEI-90-TR-21, Software Engineering Institute, Carnegie Mellon University, Pittsburgh, PA (November 1990)
27. Krueger, C.W.: Easing the transition to software mass customization. In: van der Linden, F.J. (ed.) PFE-4 2001. LNCS, vol. 2290, pp. 282–293. Springer, Heidelberg (2002)
28. van der Linden, F.J., Schmid, K., Rommes, E.: Software Product Lines in Action: The Best Industrial Practice in Product Line Engineering. Springer (2007)
29. Loesch, F., Ploedereder, E.: Optimization of variability in software product lines. In: SPLC (2007)
30. Nadi, S., Berger, T., Kästner, C., Czarnecki, K.: Mining configuration constraints: Static analyses and empirical results. In: ICSE (2014)

31. Passos, L., Novakovic, M., Xiong, Y., Berger, T., Czarnecki, K., Wasowski, A.: A study of non-boolean constraints in variability models of an embedded operating system. In: FOSD (2011)
32. Pohl, K., Böckle, G., Van Der Linden, F.: Software product line engineering: foundations, principles, and techniques. Springer-Verlag New York Inc. (2005)
33. Reiser, M., Tavakoli, R., Weber, M.: Unified feature modeling as a basis for managing complex system families. In: VaMoS (2007)
34. Riebisch, M., Streitferdt, D., Pashov, I.: Modeling variability for object-oriented product lines. In: Buschmann, F., Buchmann, A.P., Cilia, M.A. (eds.) ECOOP 2003 Workshop Reader. LNCS, vol. 3013, pp. 165–178. Springer, Heidelberg (2004)
35. Schmid, K., Rabiser, R., Grünbacher, P.: A comparison of decision modeling approaches in product lines. In: VaMoS (2011)
36. She, S., Lotufo, R., Berger, T., Wąsowski, A., Czarnecki, K.: Reverse engineering feature models. In: ICSE (2011)
37. Software Engineering Institute: Catalog of software product lines, http://www.sei.cmu.edu/productlines/casestudies/catalog/index.cfm
38. Steger, M., Tischer, C., Boss, B., Müller, A., Pertler, O., Stolz, W., Ferber, S.: Introducing PLA at bosch gasoline systems: Experiences and practices. In: Nord, R.L. (ed.) SPLC 2004. LNCS, vol. 3154, pp. 34–50. Springer, Heidelberg (2004)
39. Sugumaran, V., Park, S., Kang, K.C.: Software product line engineering. Communications of the ACM 49(12), 29–32 (2006)

Supporting Multiplicity and Hierarchy in Model-Based Configuration: Experiences and Lessons Learned

Rick Rabiser[1], Michael Vierhauser[1], Paul Grünbacher[1],
Deepak Dhungana[2], Herwig Schreiner[2], and Martin Lehofer[3]

[1] Christian Doppler Lab MEVSS
Johannes Kepler University, Linz, Austria
`rick.rabiser@jku.at`
[2] Siemens AG Österreich
Corporate Technology, Vienna, Austria
`deepak.dhungana@siemens.com`
[3] Siemens VAI
Metals Technologies, Linz, Austria
`martin.lehofer@siemens.com`

Abstract. When developing large-scale industrial software systems engineers need to instantiate, configure, and deploy diverse reusable components. The number of component instances required depends on customer requirements only known during configuration and is typically unknown when modeling the systems' variability. Also, the hierarchy of dynamically created component instances leads to complex dependencies between configuration decisions. Dealing with component multiplicity and hierarchy thus requires an approach capable of expressing the dependencies among dynamically instantiated components and configuration decisions. Furthermore, users need tool support for navigating the complex decision space during configuration. In this experience paper we report on applying a decision-oriented modeling approach for defining component variability, multiplicity, and hierarchy. We further present a configuration tool that guides end users through the complex decision space. We report applications of the approach to industrial software systems and describe patterns and lessons learned.

Keywords: Variability models, multiplicity, hierarchy, configuration tool.

1 Introduction and Motivation

Managing the variability of industrial software systems is challenging [1,2]. Engineers of such systems frequently capture domain experts' knowledge regarding the characteristics of the reusable components and the restrictions on how they can be combined in variability models [3]. Such models define the possible system variants and provide a foundation for automating the product configuration process.

J. Dingel et al. (Eds.): MODELS 2014, LNCS 8767, pp. 320–336, 2014.

Many existing variability modeling approaches [3] assume that a product variant can be derived by selecting a subset of available features satisfying the constraints defined in the variability model. However, the assumption that the set of components for a product variant can be statically inferred based on a feature configuration often does not hold in industrial settings [4]. Our experience shows that instead complex industrial systems are built incrementally during configuration by creating multiple instances of components, wiring different component instances, and configuring their properties. The composite nature of the components implies that the containment hierarchy of the component instances also has to be taken into account. Existing approaches [3] provide capabilities for dealing with the multiplicity of reusable components and managing the hierarchy of dynamically created component instances. However, tool support is still immature, in particular end users lack support for the dynamic and complex configuration process.

This paper describes experiences we gathered while developing and applying a product line approach in the industrial automation domain. In particular, we report about two experiences: (i) we describe how component multiplicity and hierarchy can be supported by extending an existing variability modeling language [5] and (ii) we present a configuration tool, which enacts the models and supports end users in creating and configuring component instances. It also supports users to navigate in the hierarchically structured decision space.

This experience paper significantly extends an earlier workshop paper [6] in which we presented the motivation and basic modeling concepts. Here we describe industrial requirements for modeling and configuring components (Section 2). We summarize capabilities of existing modeling approaches (Section 3) and provide an overview of our approach for modeling multiplicity and hierarchy (Section 4). We describe our tools for defining and enacting the models (Section 5). We discuss the application of our approach to three industrial automation systems and present typical modeling patterns (Section 6). We discuss lessons learned (Section 7) and conclude the paper.

2   Industrial Requirements

We use an example from the industrial automation domain to motivate the requirements for variability modeling and configuration support. MULTIROLL automates and optimizes the controlled movement and cooling of molten steel in continuous casting machines (see Fig. 1). After the molten steel passes through the mold—where it is cast into the desired shape—the strand is immediately supported by closely spaced rollers which support the walls of the strand against the ferro-static pressure. The rollers must be carefully selected for use with different casting practices and different steel grades to assure highest performance even under transient casting conditions.

MULTIROLL comprises different hardware and software components that need to be instantiated and configured to meet different customer requirements and plant characteristics. A continuous casting machine has a variable number of

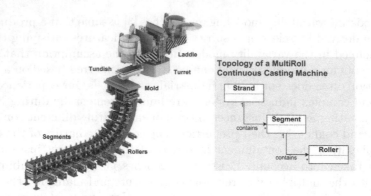

Fig. 1. Rollers in a casting machine support the walls of a metal strand after it leaves the mold. Configuring the rollers is crucial for achieving the desired steel quality.

strands and each strand can have a variable number of rollers, which vary with respect to cooling capability, steel quality requirements, and casting conditions. The final product variant thus depends on the multiplicity of different components like Roller Variants or Segments as well as Life-Cycle Steps and Service Performance Parameters of the rollers. Depending on the utilization, workload and steel grades to be produced different types of rollers need to be installed at the casting machine which vary in terms of size and diameter, initial costs, maintenance periods, and cooling mechanisms. Each machine is equipped with a variable number of segments in which the rollers are installed depending on the dimension of the plant, the target production, and the desired utilization. Different segment types are used in different positions within the casting line. For example, specific vertical segments are used within the first meters of a casting line before the strand is bent to a horizontal position. Depending on the type of rollers and their utilization, different life cycles and maintenance periods are applicable. For example rollers of type A can support a 5-iteration life cycle where a roller is skimmed and refurbished multiple times before it needs to be replaced, whereas for rollers of type B only a 3-iteration life cycle can be guaranteed under certain circumstances.

Configuring MULTIROLL involves dynamically instantiating software components to address the customer requirements. Modeling the variability of MULTIROLL requires defining its topology, i.e., the actual *hierarchy* of the caster as well as the rules and constraints for strands, segments, and rollers. The product architecture allows defining a variable number of segments and rollers for each strand. Therefore, the physical structure and characteristics of the target environment are essential for determining the different components needed for building the system meeting a customer's requirements.

The derivation of specific product variants requires the creation and administration of multiple instances of the different components contained in a strand at the various levels of the hierarchy. MULTIROLL cannot be modeled without considering *multiplicities* as the number of segments and rollers is unknowable during variability modeling. For instance, during configuration time a customer might decide that a *Strand* consists of two *Segments* with *Segment*$_1$ consisting of 20 *Rollers* and *Segment*$_2$ consisting of 30 *Rollers*. Each of these component instances has to be configured individually.

The configuration decisions needed for configuring all dynamically instantiated components are typically not known during modeling and need to be created on the fly. Furthermore, the components are composite in nature which leads to a hierarchical and dynamic structure of the configuration decisions. Modelers from industry have thus demanded an approach which supports modeling variability, hierarchy, and multiplicity of components.

Hierarchy and multiplicity have also strong implications on model-based configuration tools for end users. For instance, during configuration, the possible configuration paths and hierarchical structure of complex systems need to be presented intuitively and comprehensibly. The usability of end-user configuration tools [7] is thus an essential requirement.

3 Existing Modeling Approaches

Defining the composition of components and their interaction is a primary purpose of architecture specification [8]. Architecture description languages (ADLs) [9] model architectural elements and their relation in terms of sub-systems, components, ports, interfaces, and connectors. While some ADLs provide variability mechanisms [10,11] they provide only limited support to define the variability of the instantiated components. Also, ADLs typically do not provide abstractions for end users performing configuration.

Issues of multiplicity and hierarchy have been addressed by existing variability modeling approaches. In cardinality-based feature modeling [12] each feature has a cardinality to define how many clones of the feature can be included in a concrete configuration. Orthogonal modeling approaches document software product line variability in dedicated models independent of its realization in the various product line artifacts. An extension to the OVM notation [2] has been proposed, which introduces cardinality-range dependencies [13]. Decision-oriented approaches define a set of decisions adequate to distinguish among the members of a software product line and to guide the derivation and configuration of products. Approaches such as Synthesis [14] and FAST [15] also support modeling cardinalities of decisions. However, these approaches do not consider component hierarchies and there is no tool support for enacting variability models with cardinalities to support configuration. SimPL [16] supports modeling multiplicity and hierarchy with a UML-based variability modeling approach. However, it also lacks guidance for the derivation of products and end-user configuration support.

In addition, numerous approaches exist addressing specific related variability modeling issues: Dhungana et al. [4] presented a new technique for reasoning over cardinality-based feature models based on generative constraint satisfaction. Riebisch et al. [17] presented a new notation for feature diagrams, emphasizing the multiplicity of sets of features. Tool support for feature modeling with cardinalities is also described as part of the modeling language Clafer [18] which uses Alloy as the underlying reasoning mechanism. The feature modeling tool Forfamel [19] uses answer set programming (smodels) for reasoning over multiple instances. The approach by Gomez and Ramos [20] allows to translate cardinality-based feature models to domain variability models using model-to-model transformations to take advantage of existing generative programming tools and validation formalisms.

Although these approaches cover multiplicity and hierarchy each approach addresses only parts of the industrial requirements. In particular, an integrated approach is needed supporting both interactivity during configuration to guide end users and modeling of multiplicity and hierarchy. We thus chose a decision-oriented approach with support for guiding end users in configuration [7,5] and extended it with support for multiplicity and hierarchy.

4   Modeling Multiplicity and Hierarchy of Variable Components

We developed a modeling approach and embedded DSL supporting multiplicity and hierarchy of variable components to address our industrial requirements. We illustrate the key modeling concepts of the approach (cf. our earlier workshop paper [6]) using the MULTIROLL example.

4.1   Modeling Constructs

Our approach covers two levels as shown in Fig. 2: Component variability is defined by specifying configuration decisions and assets, i.e., abstractions of solution space building blocks. Following the idea of Configurable Units [21] the components expose to the external world a variability interface, i.e., the configuration decisions which can be configured by resolving the defined variability. Multiplicity and hierarchy are addressed by defining the types of configurable components in the system and their structure during configuration.

Component Variability. Our model addresses component variability in terms of configuration decisions and assets as defined in the DOPLER modeling approach [5].

Decisions represent problem space variability of reusable components, i.e., user visible choices leading to different component variants. Modelers need to define the decision type (Boolean, string, number, or enumeration) and its dependencies to other decisions. For instance, the required segments of MULTIROLL can be defined as a decision of type number. A decision can depend on other decisions *hierarchically* (if it needs to be made before other decisions) or *logically* (if the answer affects other decisions). For example, the decision about the number of segments becomes visible to the user during configuration only if the number of strands has already been set.

Assets represent abstractions of technical solution space elements. Meta-modeling allows adaptations to domain-specific concepts by defining concrete

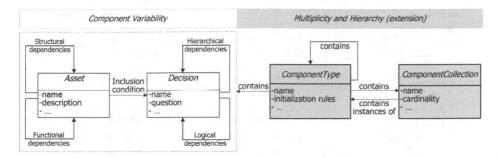

Fig. 2. Extended DOPLER meta-model with the new model elements `ComponentType` and `ComponentCollection`

types, attributes, and allowed relationships between assets. Structural dependencies are used to specify the physical organization of the assets (e.g., consists of, contributes to, is predecessor of, is successor of). Functional dependencies specify relationships stemming from the underlying implementation of a system and can be represented with relationship links like requires or excludes. Finally, *inclusion conditions* are expressions defining when an asset is present in a system variant depending on the values assigned to decisions during configuration.

Multiplicity and Hierarchy. We added two new modeling elements (cf. Fig. 2) to DOPLER's core meta-model to support component hierarchies in the model:

A `ComponentType` represents a configurable unit in a complex system and serves as a wrapper and recursive container for Decisions and Assets. The dependency `ComponentType` *contains* `ComponentType` is used to model the containment hierarchy of component types (cf. Fig. 3 (a) – Segment contains Roller). Furthermore, a `ComponentType` can contain an arbitrary number of `ComponentCollections`.

A `ComponentCollection` is a container for managing runtime instances of component types. This element is vital for defining rules and constraints over the runtime instances of components, for instance, when iterating over the instances. The dependency `ComponentType` *contains* `ComponentCollection` is required to manage the associated component instances (cf. Fig. 3 (b) – Segment contains a collection of Rollers). The dependency `ComponentCollection` *contains instances of* `ComponentType` is used to specify the type of configurable components that can be stored in a `ComponentCollection` (cf. Fig. 3 (c) – the collection of Segments contains components of type Segment). A `ComponentCollection` is always bound to a specific `ComponentType` and thus contains instances of one particular type.

4.2   Example

Fig. 3 depicts a partial variability model of the MULTIROLL system. A `Strand` consists of the component type `Segment`. Each segment maintains a collection of runtime instances of `Segment` in a container called `segments`. Configuration decisions in the strand have effects on the decisions in the segment. For instance,

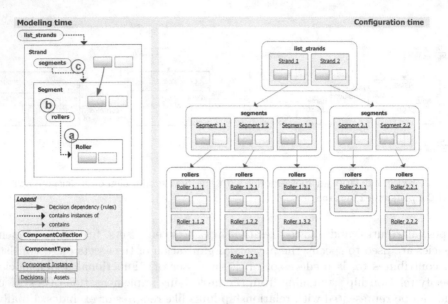

Fig. 3. A partial variability model of the MULTIROLL system supporting multiplicity of `ComponentType` elements organized in a containment hierarchy. Each node in the hierarchy consists of both decisions and assets (instances not shown in Figure).

the user configuring the strand can specify the number of segments. For each segment selected a number of assets (software components) will be included in a configured product automatically [5]. At the root of the variability model the `ComponentCollection` `list_strands` represents the collection of all strands being configured.

The hierarchical decomposition of components resembles a feature model at first sight, but in our approach each node in the hierarchy is a Configurable Unit containing the core modeling elements Decisions and Assets.

4.3   Configuration Time Behavior

The new modeling elements `ComponentType` and `ComponentCollection` require more sophisticated language constructs to specify configuration time behavior in the variability models. We use an embedded DSL with Java as a host language to define the rules for this behavior. Rules consist of firing `conditions` (Boolean expressions) and `actions`—functions affecting the configuration. Rules can be triggered when model elements are instantiated or after the user makes a configuration decision in the configuration tool.

Decision effect rules are triggered after a decision value has been changed. All rules associated with a certain decision are fired after that decision value changes (either directly by the user or as the result of other rules). For example, as soon as the user sets the value of decision `calculateWeight` a rule may be triggered to sum the weight of all component instances of a certain type (e.g., of all rollers).

Initialization rules are triggered once when a component is created. For example, every strand in the MULTIROLL system consists of at least one segment in which rollers move the solidifying steel. This can be expressed using an init rule that is executed whenever a new instance of `Strand` is created resulting in a `Default` `Segment` in each strand accessible through the collection `segments`.

4.4 Working with Component Instances

In addition to basic actions for value assignment we introduced actions for managing instances of components maintained in a `ComponentCollection` at runtime and for iterating over runtime instances of components, accessing decisions, and configuring other properties:

Creating new instances of components at runtime can be done by specifying a rule on a `ComponentCollection`, which manages the newly created instance or by specifying a decision effect rule. As a `ComponentCollection` defines the type of objects it can hold, the required type is instantiated automatically. For example, if the number of segments in the strand depends on a user decision, the modeler can add a decision `numSegments` to the `ComponentType` `Strand` and associate a decision effect rule adding the required number of Segments to the `ComponentCollection` `segments`. This rule is executed at configuration time as soon as the value of the decision `numSegments` changes due to user input or due to another rule. The newly instantiated `Segments` are now part of the configuration, so the decisions associated to the `Segments` must also be instantiated for each instance of the `Segment`. The same paradigm continues deeper in the hierarchy, where the user can decide for each `Segment` about the number of `Rollers` and so on. *Removing specific instances* of a component from the `ComponentCollection` is similar to adding the instances. *Iterating over the instances* of components in the collections is for instance required whenever the modeler needs to assert global properties of the system. For example, to calculate the total number of rollers in the caster, the modeler has to iterate over all the segments and rollers in each segment to aggregate data from all constituent components. *Specifying cross-components rules* is possibly by referring to instances by name. For example, to ensure that "the 1st roller of the 2nd segment must have the same diameter as the 3rd roller of the 4th segment", a rule can be specified.

5 Tool Support for Model-Based End-User Configuration

As DOPLER is already in use in different industrial projects [5], we realized the described modeling capabilities by extending the DOPLER tool suite for modeling and configuration.

5.1 Model Execution Engine

We developed an engine that allows executing the rules defined in the variability model. Variability models are mapped to Java classes to support enacting the models during configuration. At configuration time a class is generated and compiled on the fly. The decisions represent variables in the Java class whereas decision types are mapped to basic data types (e.g., Boolean, String, Integer). Boolean expressions describing decision and asset dependencies as well as rules are internally transformed to methods. The initialization rules are transformed to class constructor statements that are automatically executed upon class instantiation. A `ComponentType` is mapped to an inner class mirroring the hierarchy modeled in the variability model. A `ComponentCollection` is mapped to a standard Java `java.util.Collection` class. The model-to-Java transformation is performed on the fly and the resulting class is subsequently compiled by invoking the *Java Compiler* through the compiler API. Resulting compilation warnings and errors produced by the Compiler are used to provide instant feedback to the modeler regarding the validity of the defined rules and the model in the editor. As the rule engine needs to selectively fire and propagate the effects of rules, we use an off-the-shelf byte-code analyzer component [22] to work with the `class` representation of variability models. Modifications of the structure or content of a variability model during modeling result in the immediate re-generation and re-evaluation of the corresponding Java representation.

5.2　Configuration Tool

We extended the existing DOPLER *product configurator* [7] to support configuration with multiple instances of decisions and assets (cf. Fig. 4). The Runtime Elements view depicts a hierarchy of components and provides an overview of the created instances. When the user selects a component, the Decisions view displays all configuration options of this component instance. For example, in Fig. 4 the root component RollerSimulator1 is selected. Decisions in one `ComponentType` can be further categorized into several tabs (in the figure: General, Machine Definition, Life Cycle Definition) to support the user by displaying related decisions in groups. For each component instance, the user can make the decisions and thereby trigger the rule propagation and evaluation of decision dependencies in the compiled Java class.

The tree shown in the runtime elements view dynamically adapts based on the user's decisions and can become quite large over time depending on the number of created instances and the depth of the hierarchy. Our product configurator tool thus provides additional features to guide users in working with the component hierarchy. Besides basic features for *expanding and collapsing elements* the user can focus on one particular runtime element, i.e., *select a subtree* as current context in the runtime elements view. This eases working with deeper hierarchies. The user may also apply *type-based and textual filters* to further reduce the complexity of the configuration tree. A *progress bar* (cf. Fig. 4 bottom left) indicates how many of the currently existing instances have already been fully configured (all decisions part of the component instance have been made). On top of the decisions view a breadcrumb navigation bar provides further support by facilitating the quick navigation through different tree levels. The user can select a component instance in the runtime elements view and use the context

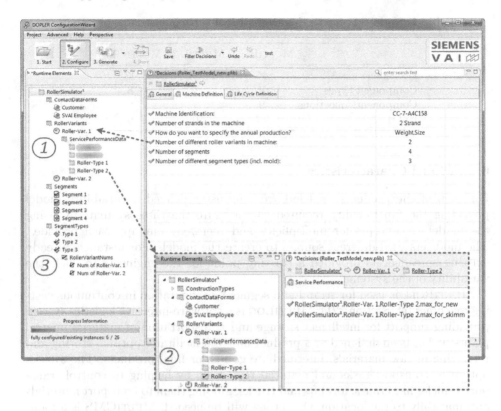

Fig. 4. Configuring MULTIROLL products with support for multiplicity and hierarchy based on DOPLER variability models. The DOPLER product configurator provides a Runtime Elements view and a Decisions view. Making decisions updates the Runtime Elements tree, selections in the Runtime Elements tree update the Decisions view. Parts of the figure are blurred due to non-disclosure agreements.

menu to *apply decision values to all instances*. This allows to quickly configure all instances by just making the decisions of one instance. Afterwards, the user can adapt decisions of different instances to configure the desired deviations among instances. The tool also supports *dynamic adaptation of decision and asset attribute names* based on placeholders which are automatically resolved for each run-time instance. This can be used, e.g., to present instance-specific questions to users. For example, instead of asking users about the number of rollers in the segment the question can be automatically adapted for each instance to allow questions such as "How many rollers are available in the 2nd segment?".

6   Modeling Patterns in Industrial Applications

We report on experiences of applying our approach to three industrial applications: MULTIROLL, MULTILOG, and MULTICMS. Each of these three applications is a real product line containing multiple hardware and software components. We report model characteristics and modeling patterns we discovered.

Table 1. Variability model characteristics of three industrial applications

	MultiRoll	MultiLog	MultiCMS
Decisions	45	102	43
ComponentTypes	9	6	8
ComponentCollections	9	7	9
Rules	12	18	6

6.1 Model Characteristics

For each of the products modelers from industry defined a variability model providing the functionality required to configure the three systems by using the modeling concepts for multiplicity and hierarchy our approach provides. The modelers used different sources to create the models. For instance, already existing spreadsheets provided a starting point for the engineers to elicit the variability of the systems.

MultiRoll is used for strand and segment configuration in continuous casting machines (cf. Section 321). MultiLog is a software-intensive logistics system providing support for intelligent storage and transportation of material in steel plants. It has been designed as a product line and facilitates optimal storing and retrieving of raw materials, intermediate goods, or final products. The system optimizes transport tasks and material relocation by helping to control transport vehicles like cranes, forklifts and trucks, guiding them to transport materials automatically to the location where they will be needed. MultiCMS is a monitoring system for metallurgical plants. Each plant contains several equipment locations where data is captured and subsequentially processed by PLCs (Programmable Logic Controller). The PLCs are in turn configured by various Data Blocks and Channels which need to be mapped to monitoring specifications. This data is used to assess the equipment status within the various plant facilities.

The resulting variability models (cf. Table 1) range from about 40 to 102 decisions (which are instantiated multiple times together with `ComponentType` elements at runtime). Decisions are part of `ComponentType` elements representing rollers, segments, bays or configuration blocks. All three models contain a similar amount of `ComponentType` elements (6 to 9) and `ComponentCollection` elements (7 to 9). A `ComponentType` is defined once at top-level and then used multiple times within in the product hierarchy. Each product contains various rules to instantiate the components, to define dependencies or to calculate attribute values by iterating over instances.

6.2 Modeling Patterns

When modeling MultiLog, MultiRoll, and MultiCMS we frequently encountered three patterns related to multiplicity and hierarchy. These patterns are of general interest for researchers as well as practitioners facing similar modeling challenges. We report these patterns and their implementation in the extended DOPLER approach. We use Gamma et. al.'s design pattern structure [23] and describe intent, motivation, example, context, and solution for each pattern.

Predefined Multiplicity. The modeler should be supported when defining a predefined number of component instances which will later be instantiated at runtime.

Motivation: If the number of component instances is already known at modeling time the number of dynamic instances can be predefined by default.

Example: Both MULTIROLL and MULTILOG need exactly two contact data forms for user data input and the `ContactDataForm` has to be instantiated twice. This is already known at modeling time and will not change during configuration. At runtime, whenever a roller or stockyard configuration model is instantiated, the two contact forms (one for the customer and one for the contact person on vendor side) and associated decisions are automatically generated for the user.

Context: This situation can be visualized using a decision table with a fixed number of rows (representing instances of a type) and a fixed number of columns (representing configuration decisions of the instance). Each cell of the table represents a decision value to be set for the component instance (rows).

		Decisions	
ComponentCollection	*ComponentTypes*	name	address
	Customer		
ContactDataForms	SVAI Employee		

Solution: A new component (e.g., `ContactDataForm`) is defined in the variability model, including the decisions related to the component (e.g, `name, address`). A `ComponentCollection` (e.g., `ContactDataForms`) is created to hold the instances of that type. A rule is added to the container of the component, to instantiate a fixed set of instances, i.e., Customer and SVAI Employee, as shown in the following example.

```
MultiRoll.init ->
        ContactDataForms.add("Customer");
        ContactDataForms.add("SVAI_Employee");
```

Single-dimensional Multiplicity. If the number of instances of components is known only at configuration time, instances have to be generated dynamically based on user input.

Motivation: In many cases the number of instances is not known at modeling time. However, the modeler should be able to define the component only once and specify the number of instances required at runtime.

Example: MULTICMS supports a flexible number of PLCs to be configured for a single project. Therefore, the user must make a decision on the number of PLCs required for his context. A `ComponentType PLC` defines the parameters to be set for a PLC (such as id, name, and type).

Context: This situation can be visualized using a decision table with multiple rows (representing instances of a component type) and a fixed number of columns (representing configuration decisions of the instance). Each cell of the table represents a decision value of the selected component instance.

		Decisions		
ComponentCollection	*ComponentTypes*	id	name	type
	PLC 1			
plcs	PLC 2			
	. . .			

Solution: To support such scenarios a decision can be defined to capture the required number of instances at configuration time (e.g., PLCs). This can either be done by directly asking the user or by inferring the required number from other decisions. The rule that is fired as a result of changing the decision adds instances of a certain component type to a collection `plcs` as shown in the listing below. Depending on the user choice the required PLCs are instantiated and added to the `ComponentCollection plcs`. Each created element is represented in the configuration tool as one item in the runtime elements tree that provides a set of decisions (i.e., the columns of the table shown above) upon selection for the selected instance.

```
decisionNumPLCS.rule ->
    plcs.add("PLC", numPLCS);
```

Multi-dimensional Multiplicity. In this case the number of instances of components and the number of decisions per instance are both known only at configuration time.

Motivation: The modeler should be able to define a variable number of decisions per component instance and a variable number of component instances.

Example: This scenario can be found when configuring the amount of rollers of a specific variant for each Segment Type (cf. Fig. 4–(3)). Depending on the user selection the required number of Segment Types have to be added to the `ComponentCollection SegmentTypes`. Each of these elements contains another `ComponentCollection RollerVariantNums` which holds the same number of elements as Roller Variants (cf. Pattern Single-dimensional multiplicity). Each instance of the `ComponentType Num of Roller-Var.` provides a configuration decision for defining the amount of rollers of this variant within the selected Segment Type.

Context: The situation in which the number of configurable components and the number of parameters for each component are unknown at modeling time can be visualized using a decision table in which both the rows and the columns depend on configuration decisions. In this case, each cell of the table corresponds to a set of configuration decisions and not just a single decision.

		ComponentCollection/-Types		
		rollerVariants		
ComponentCollection	*ComponentTypes*	RV. 1	RV. 2	...
	Type1	decisions	decisions	...
	Type2	decisions	decisions	...
segmentTypes	...	...	...	...

Solution: The decisions that must be instantiated multiple times are wrapped in a new component type (e.g., `RollerVariant`). A decision is defined to capture the required number of instances at configuration time (e.g., `decisionNumVariants`). The rule that is fired as a result of changing the decision iterates through another dynamically created instance collection and adds instances to the component (e.g., `rollerVariants`) as shown in the following listing.

```
decisionNumVariants.rule ->
segmentTypes.add("Type", numOfSegmentTypes);
for(SegmentType st: segmentTypes.getAll(){
  st.rollerVariants.add("RV.", decisionNumVariants);
}
```

7 Discussion and Lessons Learned

We discuss lessons learned for both researchers and practitioners requiring support for multiplicity and hierarchy.

Modeling precision and complexity. Existing modeling languages provide extensive support for defining the structure and topology of systems, i.e., the hierarchy of configurable components. Variability modeling approaches on the other hand allow defining the hierarchy of features and the possible system variants. We have learned that in order to be useful in practice a variability modeling approach must also allow defining the actual system structure. The expressiveness of the modeling constructs and the rule language features of our approach satisfied the requirements regarding multiplicity and hierarchy. However, our experiences in modeling industrial systems also show that these benefits come at an expense. The approach allows to represent complex industrial scenarios but at the same time modeling becomes more challenging. For instance, the mechanisms for querying and manipulating runtime instances of configurable components increase the complexity of the modeling language. We improved tool support for modelers and added capabilities for code completion, syntax highlighting, and syntax checking to address this additional complexity.

Trade-offs of using an embedded DSL. Instead of developing a new language we decided to use Java as a host language of our embedded DSL to avoid the "yet another language" syndrome. Modelers in the domain already used Java which accelerates the adoption of the tools and increases acceptance. Furthermore, the use of a general purpose language makes it easy to extend the approach, e.g., by adding new types of rules and actions to the rule engine. On the other hand the benefits of modeler acceptance and extensibility come at the expense of sacrificing analyzability as the cost of verifying formal properties of the rule base – e.g., consistency, cycle-freeness, and redundancy – ranges from polynomially decidable to undecidable. Driven by industrial requirements, in our case, testing was primarily done through test runs and simulated configuration sessions which allowed the use of Java as a host language.

Navigation support for different users. While it is comparably easy to syntactically define multiplicity and hierarchy in variability models, developing a user interface that hides the complex internal structure of the configuration space from end users while still providing guidance is challenging. Also, the different responsibilities and skills of end users in configuration need to be supported with different views and perspectives in the configuration tool. We extended the DOPLER configuration tool [7] with a runtime elements view and capabilities to work with multiple instances in a hierarchy. The existing role and user concept in DOPLER allows us the tailoring of the UI to the specific needs and skills of end users. In a hierarchical configuration process with multiple levels, this can for example be used to restrict the configurable part of the runtime elements tree depending on the currently active role leaving the rest invisible or not editable. Also, filters for certain types can be applied automatically to further restrict the configuration tree.

8   Conclusions

We described a modeling approach for dealing with multiplicity and hierarchy of configurable components. Based on an industrial example we discussed modeling requirements and described an implementation of the approach in the DOPLER tools. A new modeling layer for dealing with multiplicity was added to an existing modeling approach. Existing projects can be migrated to the extended approach easily if needed. Support for enacting variability models is provided by mapping the variability models to Java. A configuration tool supports end users in navigating through the complex decision space. We assessed the usefulness of our approach by applying it to three different industrial products. We also documented frequent modeling patterns and discussed lessons learned.

Acknowledgments. This work has been supported by the Christian Doppler Forschungsgesellschaft, Austria.

References

1. van der Linden, F., Schmid, K., Rommes, E.: Software Product Lines in Action – The Best Industrial Practice in Product Line Engineering. Springer, Heidelberg (2007)
2. Pohl, K., Böckle, G., van der Linden, F.: Software Product Line Engineering: Foundations, Principles, and Techniques. Springer (2005)

3. Czarnecki, K., Grünbacher, P., Rabiser, R., Schmid, K., Wasowski, A.: Cool features and tough decisions: A comparison of variability modeling approaches. In: 6th Int'l Workshop on Variability Modelling of Software-Intensive Systems, Leipzig, Germany, pp. 173–182. ACM (2012)
4. Dhungana, D., Falkner, A., Haselböck, A.: Configuration of cardinality-based feature models using generative constraint satisfaction. In: 37th EUROMICRO Conference on Software Engineering and Advanced Applications, Oulu, Finland, pp. 100–103. IEEE (2011)
5. Dhungana, D., Grünbacher, P., Rabiser, R.: The DOPLER meta-tool for decision-oriented variability modeling: A multiple case study. Automated Software Engineering 18(1), 77–114 (2011)
6. Dhungana, D., Schreiner, H., Lehofer, M., Vierhauser, M., Rabiser, R., Grünbacher, P.: Modeling multiplicity and hierarchy in product line architectures: Extending a decision-oriented approach. In: 3rd International Workshop on Variability in Software Architecture, Collocated with WICSA 2014. ACM, Sydney (2014)
7. Rabiser, R., Grünbacher, P., Lehofer, M.: A qualitative study on user guidance capabilities in product configuration tools. In: 27th IEEE/ACM Int'l Conference Automated Software Engineering, Essen, Germany, pp. 110–119. ACM (2012)
8. Shaw, M., Garlan, D.: Formulations and formalisms in software architecture. In: van Leeuwen, J. (ed.) Computer Science Today. LNCS, vol. 1000, pp. 307–323. Springer, Heidelberg (1995)
9. Medvidovic, N., Taylor, R.N.: A classificiation and comparison framework for software architecture description languages. IEEE Transactions on Software Engineering 26(1), 70–93 (2000)
10. Matinlassi, M.: Comparison of software product line architecture design methods: COPA, FAST, FORM, KobrA and QADA. In: 26th International Conference on Software Engineering (ICSE 2004), pp. 127–136. IEEE CS, Edinburgh (2004)
11. Dashofy, E., van der Hoek, A., Taylor, R.: A highly-extensible, XML-based architecture description language. In: Working IEEE/IFIP Conference on Software Architecture (WICSA 2001), pp. 103–112. IEEE Computer Society, Amsterdam (2001)
12. Czarnecki, K., Helsen, S., Eisenecker, U.: Formalizing cardinality-based feature models and their specialization. Software Process: Improvement and Practice 10(1), 7–29 (2005)
13. Maersk-Møller, H.M., Jørgensen, B.N.: Cardinality-dependent variability in orthogonal variability models. In: 6th Workshop on Variability Modeling of Software-Intensive Systems, Leipzig, Germany, pp. 165–172. ACM (2012)
14. Software Productivity Consortium, "Synthesis guidebook," SPC-91122-MC. Herndon, Virginia, Tech. Rep. (1991)
15. Weiss, D., Lai, C.: Software Product-Line Engineering: A Family-Based Software Development Process. Addison Wesley Professional (1999)
16. Behjati, R., Yue, T., Briand, L., Selic, B.: SimPL: A product-line modeling methodology for families of integrated control systems. Information and Software Technology 55(3), 607–629 (2013)
17. Riebisch, M., Böllert, K., Streitferdt, D., Philippow, I.: Extending feature diagrams with UML multiplicities. In: 6th World Conference on Integrated Design and Process Technology, Pasadena, California (2002)
18. Bąk, K., Czarnecki, K., Wąsowski, A.: Feature and meta-models in Clafer: Mixed, specialized, and coupled. In: Malloy, B., Staab, S., van den Brand, M. (eds.) SLE 2010. LNCS, vol. 6563, pp. 102–122. Springer, Heidelberg (2011)

19. Asikainen, T., Männistö, T., Soininen, T.: A unified conceptual foundation for feature modelling. In: 10th Int'l Conference on Software Product Lines, Baltimore, ML, USA, pp. 31–40. IEEE (2006)

20. Gómez, A., Ramos, I.: Cardinality-based feature modeling and model-driven engineering: Fitting them together. In: 4th Int'l Workshop on Variability Modelling of Software-Intensive Systems, Linz, Austria, pp. 61–68. ICB Research Report No. 37 (2010)

21. Object Management Group, Common variability language, OMG initial submission (2010), http://www.omgwiki.org/variability/

22. Bruneton, E.: ASM 4.0 - a java bytecode engineering library. Whitepaper, OW2 Consortium (2011)

23. Gamma, E., Helm, R., Johnson, R., Vlissides, J.: Design Patterns: Elements of Reusable Object-Oriented Software. Addison-Wesley (1994)

Propagating Decisions to Detect and Explain Conflicts in a Multi-step Configuration Process

Jaime Chavarriaga[1,2], Carlos Noguera[2],
Rubby Casallas[1], and Viviane Jonckers[2]

[1] Universidad de los Andes, Colombia
{ja.chavarr908,rcasalla}@uniandes.edu.co
[2] Vrije Universiteit Brussel, Belgium
{jchavarr,cnoguera,vejoncke}@vub.ac.be

Abstract. In configuration processes with multiple stakeholders, conflicts are very likely because each decision maker has a different concerns and expectations about the product. They may not be aware of features selected by others or the restrictions that these selections impose. To help solve the conflicts, this paper introduces a new approach to provide *explanations* about their causes. Our approach is based on representing features from different concerns using different Feature Models (FMs), and relating them through Feature-Solution Graphs. An FSG contains dependency relationships between two FMs: one feature from the left side forces or prohibits the selection of features in the right side feature model. The strategy to detect and explain conflicts is based on propagation of constraints over the FSGs. We claim that our approach is more expressive and efficient than when using a single FM that contains all concerns and SAT solvers to detect conflicts.

Keywords: Multi-level configuration processes, Feature Models, Feature-Solution Graphs, Conflict explanation.

1 Introduction

Feature Models (FMs) represent alternatives and restrictions to configure a product. They are widely used to analyse the commonality and variability in a set of products [1], and to support configuration processes where one or many stakeholders select which options include into a specific product [2,3].

In feature-based approaches, a *product configuration* includes a selection of features from one or several feature models. An *invalid configuration* usually means that stakeholders have different perspectives and expectations on the product and, for some reasons, their selections produce a conflict. A *configuration conflict* may arise when the stakeholders configuring a product select features that cannot be selected at the same time. To determine if a configuration is valid or without conflicts, i.e., it satisfies the constraints of a feature model, many approaches rely on Constraint Programming (CSP) [4] or/and satisfiability solvers (SAT solvers) [5].

J. Dingel et al. (Eds.): MODELS 2014, LNCS 8767, pp. 337–352, 2014.
© Springer International Publishing Switzerland 2014

The main issue with these approaches lies in their inability to explain the reasons of conflicts without further process. For instance, after a conflict is detected, CSP-based approaches may use diagnosis theory to repair the configuration [4], i.e., select and deselect automatically some features in order to transform an invalid configuration into a valid configuration, but they do not provide concrete information about the reasons of conflicts. On the other hand, SAT-based approaches may exploit strategies to isolate some constraints during evaluation on SAT solvers such as MaxSAT[5] and HUMUS[6] to obtain information about conflicts and suggest solutions, but there are some cases where all the defects are not detected or incorrect information is provided [7].

Other approaches, instead of detecting conflicts they focus on *preventing conflicts* by *feature model specialization* [2]. Once one or more features are selected, the feature models are modified, i.e., specialized, to remove those features that conflict with the already selected. However, because these approaches prevent all the conflicts, a stakeholder cannot determine why something cannot be selected, i.e., the explanation of the conflict is impossible.

The main contribution of this paper is a configuration process that can explain conflicts if they occur. The strategy relies on: (1) a process of feature model specialization that updates the model without removing features from it, instead, features are marked as not-selectable. We call this FMs, conflict-tolerant FMs. (2) modeling multiple Feature Models, one per stakeholder or concern (3) Feature-Solution Graph (FSGs) that relates features in one model to the features that must be selected or cannot be selected in other feature models when they are selected; (4) an algorithm to propagate decisions from one FMs to the others marking the features in these models as mandatory or non-selectable according to the consequence of the decisions made (5) an algorithm to explain conflicts by finding the features that cause the conflicts using the FSGs updated after propagating the decisions.

The rest of paper is organized as follow: Section 2 presents a motivating case, Section 3 presents our approach. Section 4 presents an evaluation of the approach, Section 5 summarizes the related work, and Section 7 concludes the paper.

2   Motivating Example

When developing and deploying applications in the cloud, software architects face the challenge of conciliating architectural decisions with the options and restrictions imposed by the chosen cloud provider.

In Software Architecture, an architectural decision can be seen as a two-step process: selecting architectural tactics to promote quality attributes and choosing design alternatives to implement those tactics. Available design alternatives are limited by the offer of the provider. When configuring the cloud platform and its services as directed by the chosen tactics, the architect must be mindful of conflicts among the available alternatives. These trade-offs amongst the desired quality attributes can be difficult to detect, understand and ultimately solve.

In this scenario, at least two different stakeholders are involved: on one hand, the architects that are concerned about the quality attributes and architectural tactics, and on the other hand, the technical leaders that are concerned about the technological options they can use to implement the application.

For example, to promote performance the architect may want to use a tactic called "Reduce Overhead" and to promote availability she can choose a tactic called "Active Redundancy". On the other hand, the technical leader can opt by selecting the option a Load Balancer in Jelastic and High Availability option in Glassfish. Although these choices seem valid for each stakeholder, they may lead to a conflict because the "Reduce Overhead" tactic aims to eliminate any additional processing such as the required by load balancers to process HTTP headers or by the High Availability option to replicate data for application's state and sessions.

In the context of software architecture, many of the choices are trade-off decisions. When conflicts arise, architects have to deal with those decisions and to negotiate about which options must be deselected or selected in order to solve them. Thus, it is very important to understand what quality attributes are involved and why. We want to provide, when the choices of the stakeholders are in conflict, an explanation about which features selected in other feature models are the cause.

3 Detecting and Explaining Conflicts

The main contribution of our work is the ability to explain conflicts in terms of selected features. In our strategy, we specialize feature models tolerating conflicts during the propagation process, and maintaining structures that allow us to trace the decisions and explain the reasons of conflicts. This section presents an overview of the process[1].

3.1 Conflict-Tolerant Feature Models

To tolerate conflicts, we propose feature models where features can be typed as *non-selectable*, in addition to the standard *mandatory* and *optional* types. Our feature models allow features to carry more than one type at the same time. Thus, a feature model can be well-formed even when a feature is *mandatory* and *non-selectable*. Notice that normally, a feature model would not be constructed using non-selectable features, rather the type is used to make explicit the cases in which *a feature cannot be selected* due to constraints in the model propagated during the configuration process.

In our approach, we distinguish *full mandatory* features as those that must be included in all the configurations (i.e. the mandatory features which ancestors are also mandatory features). Notice that a feature model is invalid[2] if any *full mandatory* feature is also *non-selectable*.

---

[1] A formal definition of the approach is presented in a technical report[8]

[2] If there are no valid configurations for a feature model.

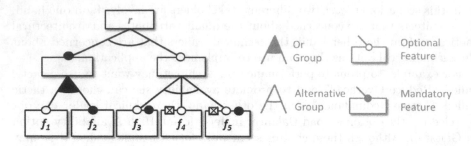

Fig. 1. Example feature model supporting multiple types. A cross-box is used to indicate *non-selectable feature*.

Figure 1 shows a feature model, result of a configuration step, supporting multiple types and non-selectable features. It includes an optional feature f_1 and a mandatory feature f_2 as traditional feature models. These features are in an *Or Group* denoting that both can be included in a valid configuration. In addition, the model includes a feature f_3 that has an optional and an additional mandatory type (i.e. effectively rendering the feature mandatory). The feature f_4 is optional and non-selectable (i.e. it is non-selectable or a dead feature) and feature f_5 is optional, mandatory and non-selectable (i.e. a conflicting feature that makes its parent non-selectable). The feature f_2 is *full mandatory* because it and all its ancestor features are mandatory. Features f_3, f_4 and f_5 are in an *Alternative Group*, i.e. only one of them can be included in a valid configuration. Notice that the presented feature model is valid because no *full mandatory* feature is also *non-mandatory* (e.g. a configuration including root, f_2 and all its ancestors is a valid configuration).

3.2   Feature-Solution Graphs (FSGs)

We specify selectable features in a configuration process using feature models and *feature solution graphs (FSGs)* that relate two feature models. Instead of using a single feature model, we define a different feature model for each concern, and a set of relationships from features of one concern to features in the next concern. When a feature in the left-side model is selected, using the relationships in the FSG, we can affect features in the right-side model. We define two types of relationships that reflect specialization operations for the defined feature models. For a given configuration c and f and f' features of the left and right hand side feature models of an FSG respectively:

Forces. A relation $f \xrightarrow{forces} f'$ denotes that the feature f' must be converted to full-mandatory when f is included in the configuration c.

Prohibits. A relation $f \xrightarrow{prohibits} f'$ denotes that the feature f' must be typed as a non selectable feature when f is included in c.

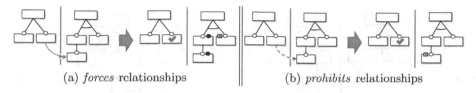

(a) forces relationships   (b) prohibits relationships

Fig. 2. Effect of *forces* and *prohibits* relationships in a feature model specialization

3.3   Configuration Process

During a configuration process, stakeholders make decisions by selecting features to include in a configuration. We propose here an algorithm to propagate those decisions by selecting and making non-selectable other features. This propagation of decisions is achieved through a *feature model specialization*, a transformation that takes a feature model and yields another feature such that the set of valid configurations of the resulting model is a subset of the valid configurations of the original feature model. Informally, an FSG holds the information to perform a feature model specialization. The specialization process takes the features of a valid configuration in the left-side feature model, obtains the relationships defined in the FSG that start on these features, and modify the types of the features in the right-side model where those relationships end.

Figure 2 shows, for each type of relationship in a *FSG*, how the right-side feature model is specialized according to the semantics that we have associated to the relationships.

Forces. Figure 2.a shows an FSG where a feature in the left-side has a *forces* relationship to a feature in the right-side. Then, if that feature is selected in the left-side, the corresponding feature in the right-side is converted into a *full-mandatory* feature, adding a *mandatory* type to that feature and all its ancestors.

Prohibits. Figure 2.b shows a *prohibits* relationship: if the feature in the right-side is selected, a *non-selectable* type is added to the corresponding feature in the left-side.

Our *propagation of decisions* makes explicit all *mandatory* and *non-selectable* features in the right-side feature model, either because: 1) they are originally marked or, 2) they are a result of the *forces* and *prohibits* relationships in the FSG, or 3) they are a result of the constraints defined in the right-side feature model.

In addition, this propagation creates new relationships in the FSG representing, for each selected feature in the left-side model, which additional features in the right-side model are converted to *mandatory* or *non-selectable* in consequence. This updated graph maintains a trace that is later used to explain conflicts.

Figure 3 shows how a propagation of decisions updates an FSG. The left side shows an FSG where a feature in the right-side model has a *forces* relationships

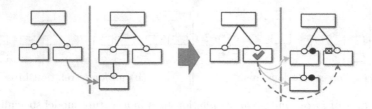

Fig. 3. Propagation of decisions into new relationships in the feature-solution graph

to a feature in the left-side model. After propagation, new relationships are added into the FSG to denote, for the original feature in the first model, which additional features are *suggested* and *prohibited*.

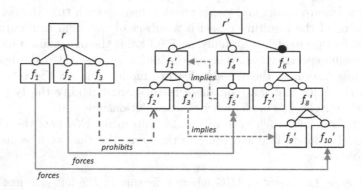

Fig. 4. Example FSG

As a more complete example, Figure 4 presents two feature models and FSG relating features of the left-side model with features of the right-side model. These relationships specify that feature f_1 in the left-side *forces* the feature f'_{10} in the right side, the feature f_2 *forces* f'_5 and f_3 *prohibits* f'_2.

According to these relationships, each time a stakeholder selects one of the features f_1, f_2 and f_3, variability in the right-side feature model is modified by adding new types to the features in that model. In addition, new relationships are added to the FSGs to represent which selection caused those new types. Figure 5 shows the updated FSGs that result from selecting each feature in the left-side model.

As we already mentioned, propagating the selection of a feature results in a set of changes on the right-side feature model. For instance, Figure 5.a shows the propagation of selecting f_1 assuming that that f_1 forces f'_{10}: First, f'_{10} must become in a *full mandatory* feature, thus the features f'_{10} and its ancestors, i.e. the feature f'_8, must be marked as *mandatory*. Then, because each of those features now marked as *mandatory* are part of *alternative groups*, other features in

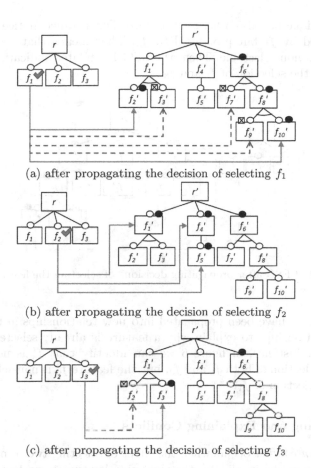

(a) after propagating the decision of selecting f_1

(b) after propagating the decision of selecting f_2

(c) after propagating the decision of selecting f_3

Fig. 5. Updated FSGs after propagating decisions of selecting each feature f_1, f_2 and f_3

that group must be typed as *non-selectable*, i.e. the features f_7' and f_9'. In addition, because f_3' *implies* f_9' (a non-selectable) feature, f_3' becomes *non-selectable* too. Finally, because f_3' is *non-selectable* and it is in an alternative group with only other feature, that feature f_2' must be typed as *mandatory*. Besides the new types in the right-side feature model, new relationships are added to the FSG to denote that f_1 suggests f_2', f_8' and f_{10}', and prohibits f_3', f_7' and f_9'.

Figure 5.b shows that propagating the decision of selecting f_2, considering that f_2 forces f_5', adds relationships to the FSG that represent that f_2 suggests f_5', f_4' and f_2'. Figure 5.c shows that propagating the decision of selecting of f_3, considering that f_3 prohibits f_2', results in that f_3 prohibits f_2' and suggests f_3'.

When a stakeholder selects two or more features, that decisions can be also propagated. Figure 6 shows the updated FSG after propagating the decision of selecting f_1 and f_3. The resulting FSG includes the relationships presented in figures 5.a and 5.c but also other relationships. For instance, notice that feature f_2' is suggested by f_1 but prohibited by f_3. That means that the feature f_1', parent of f_2' is non-selectable. Then, the FSG is updated indicating that f_1' is prohibited by the selection of f_1 and f_3.

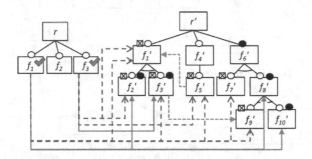

Fig. 6. Excerpt of FSG after propagating decisions of selecting the features f_1 and f_3

Once decisions have been propagated into new relationships in the FSG, we use these relationships to explain why a feature is already selected or is non-selectable. For instance, in figure 6 we can identify that f_5' is non-selectable because the selection of both f_1 and f_3, but the feature f_9' is non-selectable only because the selection of f_1.

3.4   Detecting and Explaining Conflicts

A *configuration conflict* occurs when the effect of selecting two or more features in the left-side model invalidates the right-side because some feature becomes *full mandatory* and *non-selectable*.

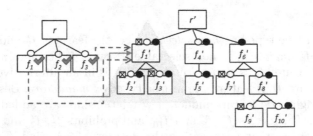

Fig. 7. Excerpt of FSG after propagating decisions of selecting all features f_1, f_2 and f_3

Using the example above, if only two of the features f_1, f_2 and f_3 are selected, the resulting feature model is valid. However, selecting all three features results in conflicting features: full mandatory features that are non-selectable. Figure 7 shows some updated relationships after propagating decisions in FSGs. It includes relationships that show that feature f_1' is suggested by f_2 but, at the same time, prohibited by f_1 and f_3. Note that, at least, f_1', f_2' and f_3' are *full mandatory* and *non-selectable* at the same time, i.e. they are *conflicting features* that invalidate the feature model.

4   Revisited Example

In this section we describe how to model alternatives in a configuration process, and how to detect and explain configuration conflicts using feature-solution graphs. In addition, this section discusses the expressiveness, efficiency and limitations of our approach.

4.1   Modeling Architectural Decisions

In Section 2, we have presented a scenario where software architects and technical leaders decide how to design and deploy applications. We model that scenario specifying decisions for each concern in a different feature model, i.e., a feature model for the concern *architectural tactics* and another feature model for *platform options*. In addition, we are using Feature-Solution Graphs (FSGs) to represent, for each architectural tactic, which options must be used to implement it.

We propose Feature-Solution Graphs (FSGs) to relate architectural tactics, as presented in [9], with their implementation, in this case, using the Jelastic cloud provider [3]. In fact, we can reuse the feature model of architectural tactics and to define a new feature model for other technological domain and to relate them with FSGs.

In Figure 8, we have an excerpt of that Feature-Solution Graph (FSG)[4][10]. This FSG includes two feature models, one representing architectural tactics and the other representing cloud platform configuration options. A set of relationships describes, for each tactic, which configuration options can be selected and which should not.

For instance, this FSG shows that the architectural tactic "Passive Redundancy" for Availability is implemented in Jelastic by configuring the *Load Balancer* option with any of the application servers. In addition, it also shows that tactic "Active Redundancy" is implemented by configuring the *Load Balancer* and the *HA (High Availability)* option in *Glassfish* Application server. Also, it shows that tactic "Reduce Overhead" for Performance is implemented by not selecting the *HTTP Load Balancer* option.

---

[3] http://www.jelastic.com

[4] Technical report and example feature models are available at http://soft.vub.ac.be/~jchavarr/jelastic-fsg/

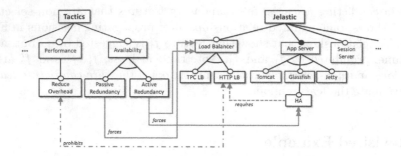

Fig. 8. Excerpt of a Feature-Solution Graph representing Architectural Tactics and the corresponding configuration options in Jelastic

4.2 Conflict Detection and Explanation

Our approach focuses on detecting and explaining configuration conflicts propagating decisions in one feature model into the other model. After a feature is selected in the left-side model, the algorithm performs a set of changes on the right-side feature model to represent the effects of that selection.

For instance, Figure 9 shows the propagation after "Active Redundancy" is selected in the left-side in two steps. First, because the tactic in the left side *forces* the *Load Balancer* and the *High availability*, these features in the right side must be marked as mandatory. In addition, because *High availability requires* the *HTTP Load Balancer*, the latter is also marked as mandatory.

Along with the marks to the features, the propagation also creates relationships to describe which feature in the left side cause the modification in the right side. Note in Figure 9 that a new set of relationships shows that "Active Redundancy" *forces* the *Load Balancer*, the *HTTP Load Balancer* and the *High Availability* option; and *prohibits* the *TCP Load Balancer*, the *Tomcat* and the *Jetty* options.

Figure 10 shows the propagation after the "Reduce Overhead" tactic is selected in the left-side. During the propagation, the process add some marks to denote that a feature is not-selectable, and a set of relationships to describe which features are *prohibiting* these non-selectable features.

When both tactics "Reduce Overhead" and "Active Redundancy" are selected, there is a conflict. Figure 11 shows the propagation after both tactics are selected. On one hand, the "Reduce Overhead" prohibits the use of the *HTTP Load Balancer*, and on the other hand, the "Active Redundancy" forces the selection of the *HA* option in Glassfish, a feature that requires the *HTTP Load Balancer*. Note that while one tactic forces the selection of a configuration option, the other tactic prohibits its selection (i.e. there is a configuration conflict). The conflict is then: *HTTP Load Balancer* is at the same time mandatory and non-selectable.

To determine why a feature in the right-side is in conflict, we can use the *forces* and *prohibits* relationships in the FSG. For instance, to explain to a software

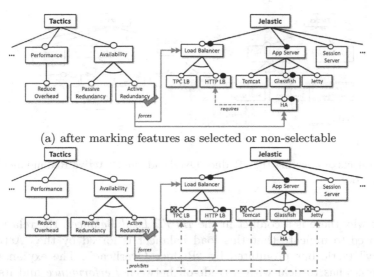

(a) after marking features as selected or non-selectable

(b) after creating new *forces* and *prohibits* relationships
to denote which features are the cause

Fig. 9. Effects of selecting the "Active Redundancy" architectural tactic in the features of Jelastic

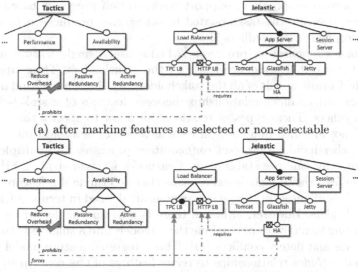

(a) after marking features as selected or non-selectable

(b) after creating new *forces* and *prohibits* relationships
to denote which features are the cause

Fig. 10. Effects of selecting the "Reduce Overhead" architectural tactic in the features of Jelastic

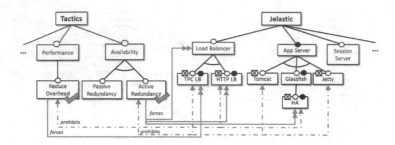

Fig. 11. Effects of selecting the "Reduce Overhead" and "Active Redundancy" architectural tactics

architect why there is a conflict in the *HTTP Load Balancer*, the relationships can be used to indicate that this load balancer is forced by the "Active Redundancy" tactic but prohibited by "Reduce Overhead". The explanation is: the architect has to deal with a trade-off between *Performance* and its tactic "Reduce Overhead" and *Availability* and its tactic "Active Redundancy".

5   Related Work

There are several proposals to support configuration processes based on Feature Models, covering the tasks related to configuring products, detecting and explaining configuration conflicts [3].

Multi-stage configuration processes [2,11,12] use a single feature model to represent the variability independently of the stakeholders. These approaches combine the feature models of all the stakeholders in a single model and introduce new *implies* and *excludes* relationships between features of a stakeholder and features of others. These types of relationships allow to specify that a feature must be or not included in a configuration as an effect of a selection.

On the other hand, *Multi-level configuration* processes use multiple feature models, normally, one per stakeholder. Czarnecki, Classen et al. [2,11] use annotations in features to include expressions that determine if a feature must be included in a configuration. These expressions are defined in terms of features of other stakeholders. However, although there is a feature model for each stakeholder, existing formalizations combine these models into a single FM to validate configurations and detect conflicts [11]. This integrated feature model includes *requires* and *excludes* relationships to relate features of one concern to features of other concerns. However, these relationships are aimed to define constraints about which features can be selected at the same time but not to describe the effect of a decision in one concern into other concerns.

In contrast to existing proposals, we use Feature-Solution Graphs [13,14] to support configuration processes with multiple concerns. These *Feature-Solution Graphs* were proposed to represent, after a selection of features, which components must be included in the application. We have extended these graphs to support processes with many concerns organized in a sequence of feature models, where decisions performed in one feature model affect decisions that must be made in the further feature models.

In any of these types of configuration processes, an *Invalid configuration* is a selection of features that does not satisfy the constraints defined in the corresponding feature models. There are many approaches to detect conflicts during configuration [15,11,5] and provide information about the conflicts [4,6] based on constraint programming (CSP) and SAT solvers. In contrast, we have defined an algorithm to propagate decisions along feature-solution graphs in order to detect and explain conflicts. Our propagation updates relationships between feature models that allow us to explain why some feature cannot be selected or which features are causing a conflict.

6 Discussion

6.1 Expressiveness

As we pointed out in the related work, the main difference between our approach and the other multi-stage configuration approaches, is the use of multiple feature models and feature-solution graphs to related them instead of a single feature model to represent the alternatives for multiple stakeholders.

From the expressiveness point of view, this means: (1) our approach uses sets of smaller and easier to process reusable feature models, where each one represents the alternatives for a single stakeholder, and (2) it uses "forces" and "prohibits" relationships with additional semantics that allow us to propagate the decisions performed by one stakeholder in a feature model into the subsequent feature models; besides, during this propagation process we can create traceability links that help us to explain why a feature is selected or not, and furthermore to explain later conflicts if they appear.

Finally, we introduce conflict-tolerant feature models that allow us to detect conflicts without removing elements in the model. In contrast to other approaches [2], these features models can be specialized without removing features and keeping traceability links to selected and non-selectable features. Thus, an automatic process can be later use these traceability links with to explain detected conflicts.

6.2 Efficiency

An advantage of our approach is that it considers a reduced number of features during the analysis. As reviewed by other authors[16], the performance of analyzing feature models depends on their size. Multi-level configuration approaches merge the feature models for each concern into a larger model in order to analyze it. This merging results in larger feature models that takes more time to process. In contrast, our approach exploits that we can organize small feature models in sequence and propagate decision made by stakeholders in one model to other feature models.

Other existing approaches perform two different processing tasks: one to detect if there is a conflict, and other to determine the conflict causes [7]. These approaches, after detecting a conflict, start to analyze again the model using subsets of the selected configuration to determine which is causing the conflict. That implies executing again the process for analyzing each combination. Instead of that, our approach uses a single propagation process to detect and explain conflicts. This process is amenable to incremental processing, that is hard or impossible to do in SAT or CSP approaches.

Regarding the algorithm complexity of our approach, it is mainly determined by the propagation across the relationships between the feature models and the feature groups and relationships in the right side. While other approaches rely on SAT solvers, that are NP complete problems, or CSP programs where the searched space of the constraint satisfaction problem may be as large as 2^{m+n}, where m is the number of features and n the number of relationships and feature groups in both left-side and right-side models, our propagation algorithm complexity is in the order $r * lm * ln$ where r is the number of prohibit and forces relationships, lm is the number of features and ln the number of relationships and feature groups in only the right side feature model.

6.3 Limitations

Our propagation algorithm works on basic feature models or models with group cardinality. In these models, we can propagate that a feature should be selected or not, and detect conflicts when the same feature should be selected and not selected at the same time. However, this algorithm is not aimed to work on feature models with instance cardinality (i.e. cloneable features) or extended models with constraints about attributes in the features. In these models, constraints and relationships may imply that, after selecting some feature, other features must be cloned or some attribute values must be modified. Although we can propagate decisions altering the model, conflicts cannot be detected only checking if the same feature should be selected and not selected at the same time. These models may have other different types of conflicts (e.g. more clones of a feature or higher values in attributes than the allowed).

In addition, our algorithm works efficiently propagating decisions in a sequence of feature models. That means that selections in one feature model have effects in the following feature models but not effects in the already selected models. There are many configuration processes that follow these patterns and can be benefited by our approach. However, there are also other configuration processes where decisions in some feature models may have effects in decisions in preceding feature models.

7 Conclusions

We have presented an approach to detect configuration conflicts, and explain the causes of conflicts using feature-solution graphs and feature models that tolerate conflicts.

Our approach is based on feature models that can be specialized without removing features, because each feature can be typed at the same time as *mandatory*, *optional* and *non-selectable*. We use FSGs to specify how features in one level affect features in other levels. These FSGs support *forces*, and *prohibits* relationships. In addition, our configuration process uses these relationships to propagate decisions from one level (left-side feature model) to the next one (right-side feature model). A conflict is detected when, at the same time a feature becomes mandatory and non-selectable. Thanks to the relationships between the two feature models we can trace the reasons of the conflict and to give an explanation that can help solve it.

We can make equivalent our work to the SAT solvers approach to detect configuration conflicts. Thus, we can transform our *forces*, and *prohibits* relationships for *includes*, and *excludes* relationships and use the SAT solvers to find conflicts. Our advantage, in this case, is that we use *forces*, and *prohibits* semantics not only to constrain features but to propagate decisions and to find the causes of the conflicts. In addition, because our algorithm does not need to process all the features of all the concerns, it performs better than others using CSP and SAT solvers.

In recent approaches, once they detect conflicts, they use CSP or SAT solvers to find fixes to the configuration. We are planning further work on providing fixes in addition to the explanations, and to overcome the other limitations explained above.

Acknowledgements. Carlos Noguera is funded by the AIRCO project of the Fonds Wetenschappelijk Onderzoek. Jaime Chavarriaga is a recipient of a COLCIENCIAS fellowship.

References

1. Kang, K.C., Cohen, S.G., Hess, J.A., Novak, W.E., Peterson, A.S.: Feature-Oriented Domain Analysis (FODA) feasibility study (CMU/SEI-90-TR-021). Technical report, Software Engineering Institute, Carnegie Mellon University (1990)
2. Czarnecki, K., Helsen, S., Eisenecker, U.: Staged Configuration through Specialization and Multilevel Configuration of Feature Models. Software Process: Improvement and Practice 10(2), 143–169 (2005)
3. Hubaux, A., Tun, T.T., Heymans, P.: Separation of Concerns in Feature Diagram languages: A Systematic Survey. ACM Computing Surveys 45(4), 1–23 (2013)
4. White, J., Schmidt, D., Benavides, D., Trinidad, P., Ruiz-Cortes, A.: Automated Diagnosis of Product-Line Configuration Errors in Feature Models. In: 12th International Software Product Line Conference (SPLC 2008), pp. 225–234 (2008)
5. Janota, M.: SAT Solving in Interactive Configuration. PhD thesis, University College of Dublin (2010)
6. Nöhrer, A., Biere, A., Egyed, A.: Managing SAT inconsistencies with HUMUS. In: Proceedings of the Sixth International Workshop on Variability Modelling of Software-Intensive Systems, Leipzig, Germany, January 25-27, pp. 83–91. ACM (2012)
7. Nöhrer, A., Biere, A., Egyed, A.: A Comparison of Strategies for Tolerating Inconsistencies during Decision-Making. In: 16th International Software Product Line Conference (SPLC 2012), pp. 11–20. ACM (2012)

8. Chavarriaga, J., Noguera, C., Casallas, R., Jonckers, V.: Supporting Multi-Level Configuration with Feature-Solution Graphs: Formal Semantics and Alloy implementation. Technical report, Vrije Universiteit Brussel (2013)
9. Bass, L., Clements, P., Kazman, R.: Software Architecture in Practice. Addison-Wesley Professional (2012)
10. Chavarriaga, J., Noguera, C., Casallas, R., Jonckers, V.: Architectural Tactics support in Cloud Computing Providers: the Jelastic case. In: Proceedings of the International ACM Sigsoft Conference on the Quality of Software Architectures, QoSA 2014 (2014)
11. Classen, A., Hubaux, A., Heymans, P.: A Formal Semantics for Multi-Level Staged Configuration. In: Benavides, D., Metzger, A., Eisenecker, U.W. (eds.) Third International Workshop on Variability Modelling of Software-Intensive Systems (VaMoS 2009). ICB Research Report, vol. 29, pp. 51–60. Universität Duisburg-Essen (2009)
12. Hubaux, A., Heymans, P., Schobbens, P.Y., Deridder, D., Abbasi, E.: Supporting Multiple Perspectives in Feature-Based Configuration. Software and Systems Modeling (SoSyM), 1–23 (2011)
13. de Bruijn, H., van Vliet, H.: Scenario-based Generation and Evaluation of Software Architectures. In: Dannenberg, R.B. (ed.) GCSE 2001. LNCS, vol. 2186, pp. 128–139. Springer, Heidelberg (2001)
14. Janota, M., Botterweck, G.: Formal Approach to integrating Feature and Architecture Models. In: Fiadeiro, J.L., Inverardi, P. (eds.) FASE 2008. LNCS, vol. 4961, pp. 31–45. Springer, Heidelberg (2008)
15. Benavides, D., Segura, S., Trinidad, P., Ruiz-Cortés, A.: FAMA: Tooling a framework for the automated analysis of Feature Models. In: First International Workshop on Variability Modelling of Software-intensive Systems, VAMOS (2007)
16. Pohl, R., Lauenroth, K., Pohl, K.: A Performance Comparison of Contemporary Algorithmic Approaches for Automated Analysis Operations on Feature Models. In: Proceeedings of the 26th IEEE/ACM International Conference on Automated Software Engineering (ASE 2011), pp. 313–322. IEEE (2011)

An MDA Approach for the Generation of Communication Adapters Integrating SW and FW Components from Simulink

Marco Di Natale[2], Francesco Chirico[1], Andrea Sindico[1],
and Alberto Sangiovanni-Vincentelli[3]

[1] Elettronica SpA, Roma, Italy
{Sindico.Andrea,Francesco.Chirico}@elt.it
[2] TECIP Institute, Scuola Superiore S. Anna, Pisa, Italy
marco.dinatale@sssup.it
[3] EECS Dept, University of California at Berkeley
alberto@eecs.berkeley.edu

Abstract. We present the tools, metamodels and code generation techniques in use at Elettronica SpA for the development of communication adapters for software and firmware systems from heterogeneous models. The process start from a SysML system model, developed according to the platform-based design (PBD) paradigm, in which a functional model of the system is paired to a model of the execution platform. Subsystems are refined as Simulink models or hand coded in C++. In turn, Simulink models are implemented as software code or firmware on FPGA, and an automatic generation of the implementation is obtained. Based on the SysML system architecture specification, our framework drives the generation of Simulink models with consistent interfaces, allows the automatic generation of the communication code among all subsystems (including the HW-FW interface code).

Keywords: System Engineering, Model-Driven Architecture, Model-Based Design, Platform-Based Design, Automatic Code Generation.

1 Introduction

In our previous work [1] we described the methodology and the process in use at Elettronica SpA for the development of complex distributed systems. The process benefits from the complementary strengths of different Model-driven approaches such as domain-specific modeling languages, Model-Driven Architecture (MDA) [4] and Model-Based Development (MBD) [5]. Starting from requirement capture, our approach follows the tenets of Platform-Based Design (PBD)[2], in which a functional model of the system is paired to a model of the execution platform. In this work, we focus on the tools and techniques used for the automatic generation of communication adapters between components generated from Simulink models and implemented in software or firmware. The target application is a high speed radar processing system, in which a stream of PDMs (Pulse Descriptor Messages), obtained by sampling RF signals are processed to

J. Dingel et al. (Eds.): MODELS 2014, LNCS 8767, pp. 353–369, 2014.
© Springer International Publishing Switzerland 2014

discover and classify of emitters. PDM sequences arrive at a rate of 10^6 messages per second and to produce the results within the time constraints, the processing is partitioned in an FPGA front processor data is controlled and feeds data to a SW classifier.

The starting point is an architecture-level SysML model of the system and its component subsystems, defined according to PBD, which separates the functional model from the model of the execution platform, and the physical architecture. A third model represents the deployment of the functional subsystems onto the computation and communication infrastructure and the HW devices. Some of the functional subsystems are refined, simulated and prototyped using the Simulink environment [10]. These subsystems must adhere to the Simulink (synchronous reactive) execution semantics. In addition, domain-specific SysML [6] extensions define the execution platform and the mapping relationships between the functions and the platform (which defines the model of the software tasks and the FPGA implementation, among others), the mapping of ports into the programmable HW registers, and the mapping of functional code (including the code generated from Simulink) onto a model of threads and processes.

We define model-to-text transformations for the subsystems refined in Simulink to generate an interface specification (ports and port types) consistent with the SysML subsystem definition. The subsystem is then refined as a Simulink model and validated by simulation and an implementation for it is generated. For functionality deployed onto a SW thread, a SW implementation is generated (a dedicated C++ class, with an interface defined by the Simulink Coder/Embedded Coder [10] standards). An FPGA implementation is automatically generated for components mapped onto programmable HW.

Our framework provides the generation of the communication code that sends and receives data to and from the automatically generated subsystems and those subsystems for which a manual implementation is required. This is done by creating an abstraction layer around each component, with a standard interface that is defined and implemented leveraging the SysML DataFlow port definitions. The (internal) connections between the standard wrapper abstractions and the internal implementations are defined using:

- A standard interface for reading and writing ports for handwritten code.
- A layer that remaps to the standard interface defined by the Mathworks software code generator (for subsystems implemented in Simulink and automatically refined in software).
- A translation to a standard driver interface for reading/writing from/to FPGA registers in the case of an (automatic) firmware implementation.

The (external) connections among the wrapper code abstractions are realized in a different way according to where the component functions (and the wrappers) are allocated for execution.

In summary, the main contributions of our work are the following:

- The definition of a SysML profiles that extends MARTE to express the realization of embedded functionality as software or firmware components.
- An environment for the generation of communication wrappers towards the automatic generation of implementations from the Simulink environment

with deployment onto FPGA (in this case also a driver layer is generated) or in SW. This avoids the need to program code that is mostly tedious, consisting of data marshalling, and automatically selects the mechanisms for data consistency when needed.
- An implementation that is entirely based on open source tools and standard languages (except, of course, for the integrated Simulink models and the code generated from those).

The organization of the paper is the following. Section 2 provides an outline to our methods, tools and models for the generation of the adapters , including an outline of the structure of the generated code. Section 3 outlines the relationships (and provides a comparison) with previous work in this context. Section 4 defines all the stereotypes and metamodels used in our flow to represent the design of the system components and the generation of the driver code towards the programmable HW. Section 6 provides the details of methods and tools for the integration of Simulink components and Section 7 discusses the generation of the communication code. Finally, Section 8 provides the conclusions.

2   Outline of The Process, Models and Code Generation

The main objective of the models and tools presented in this paper is to enforce the consistency of the developed components with respect to a SysML system description and introduce automation in the generation of the code that performs data communication and synchronization among the functional subsystems.

The starting point for our methodology is a SysML model as in the left side of Figure 1. The model is organized according to a layered structure (each layer in a separate package [1]). The *Functional description* consists of a set of SysML blocks communicating through standard and flow ports (top part of the figure). Some of these blocks are identified as subsystems executing according to a synchronous reactive semantics, refined and validated in Simulink.

A separate package in the SysML system model identifies the execution platform for the system, including a model of the execution HW, with computing nodes, boards, cores and FPGAs (bottom-left part of the figure). Each core is associated with the operating system managing the execution of the software processes and threads residing on it. Finally, a third package defines the allocation of the functional subsystems onto the execution platform. This layer defines the model of the software threads and processes, of the communication messages and the allocation of functionality onto threads (for software implementations) or programmable HW.

Following the system-level architecture description in SysML, components are designed, refined, and implemented using different methods and technologies. Components that define complex algorithms or control laws are modeled, simulated, and verified as Simulink models. For these components, an implementation path making use of automatic generation tools is used. Other components are designed in UML and then refined as manually written C++ code.

Two software layers, generated automatically from the SysML model description provide for the interaction between the subsystem functionality and the FPGA implementations (access to the HW platform, as described in Section

5) and for the communication and interactions among functional components.
The communication among the data ports of all functional subsystems is realized through code automatically generated from the SysML Mapping layer and
consisting of a number of software wrappers that provide an API for accessing
the data ports specified in SysML with the correct type information (shown in
light blue, in Figure 1). These wrappers translate from a standard interface for
the access to ports (directly used by hand-written components) to the standard
interface to the SW functions automatically generated by Simulink and/or the
driver functions automatically generated for the access to FPGA functionality
in the case of functionality mapped onto programmable HW.

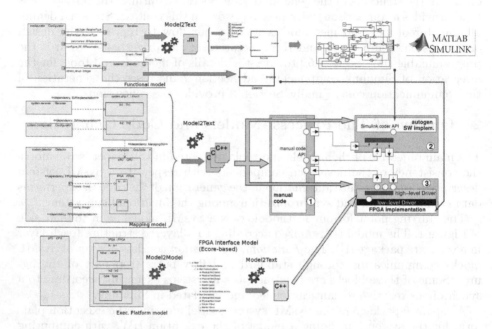

Fig. 1. The generated wrappers provide for the communication among subsystems

3   Related Work

The match of a functional and execution architecture is advocated by many in
the academic community (examples are the Y-cycle [12] and the Platform-Based
Design PBD [2]) and in the industry (the AUTOSAR automotive standard is
probably the most relevant recent example) as a way of obtaining modularity
and separation of concerns between functional specifications and their implementation on a target platform. The OMG [3] and the MDE similarly propose
a staged development in which a PIM is transformed into a Platform Specific
Model (PSM) by means of a Platform Definition Model (PDM) [13].

The development of a platform model for (possibly large and distributed) embedded systems and the modeling of concurrent systems with resource managers
(schedulers) requires domain-specific concepts. The OMG MARTE [7] standard
is very general, rooted on UML/SysML and supported by several tools. MARTE

has been applied to several use cases, most recently on automotive projects [15]. However, because of the complexity and the variety of modeling concepts it has to support, MARTE can still be considered as work in progress, being constantly evaluated [14] and subject to future extensions. Several other domain-specific languages and architecture description languages of course exist, such as, for example EAST-AADL and the DoD Architectural Framework.

Several other authors [18] acknowledge that future trends in model engineering will encompass the definition of integrated design flows exploiting complementarities between UML or SysML and Matlab/Simulink, although the combination of the two models is affected by the fact that Simulink lacks a publicly accessible meta-model [18]. Work on the integration of UML and synchronous reactive languages [19] has been performed in the context of the Esterel language (supported by the commercial SCADE tool), for which transformation rules and specialized profiles have been proposed to ease integration with UML models [20]. With respect to the general subject of model-to-model transformations and heterogeneous models integration, several approaches, methods, tools and case studies have been proposed. Some proposed methods, such as the GME framework [21] and Metropolis [22]) consist of the use of a general meta-model as an intermediate target for the model integration.

A large number of works deal with the general subject of integration of heterogeneous models. Examples are the CyPhy/META Toolchain at Vanderbilt [17] and the work on multiparadigm modeling (a general discussion in [16]). In both cases, emphasis is placed on the role of domain-specific languages and model trasformations in the general context of large and distributed Cyber-Physical systems. Other groups and projects [23] have developed the concept of studying the conditions for the interface compatibility between heterogeneous models. Examples of formalisms developed to study compatibility conditions between different Models of Computation are the Interface Automata [24] and the Tagged Signal Language [25].

4   SysML Profiles for PBD

We defined SysML profiles to express concepts that are required for our scope (and of general use to specify resources and complex embedded systems designs). Overall, the stereotype definitions contained in these profiles follow the general organization of *Functional*, *Platform* and *Mapping* models.

4.1   Functional Modeling

The functional model contains the definition of the subsystems, at some level of refinement of the system functional architecture. Each subsystem processes input signals and produces outputs, according to a port-based interface. The profiles that apply to the functional model must support the code generation stage allowing the identification of the subsystems with a synchronous execution semantics. The profile *FunctionalModels* defines the stereotypes.
<<FunctionalSystem>> applies to Block, and identifies the root block (or system) in the functional model.

<<SRSubsystem>> applies to Block and defines a subsystem that processes signals according to a synchronous reactive semantics, that is where the functional behavior consists of a single processing stage or activity (typically activated on a periodic time base), which synchronously samples all inputs, reads the internal state and updates the subsystem state and its output.

<<SimulinkSubsystem>> specializes SRSubsystem and defines a subsystem that is modelled and defined according to the Simulink semantics.

4.2 Platform Modeling

The execution platform and the mapping models define the structure of the HW and SW architecture that supports the execution of the functional model.

The execution platform is defined in a package called *PlatformModels*. Blocks represent hardware components at different levels of granularity, but also classes of basic software, including device drivers, middleware classes and operating system modules.

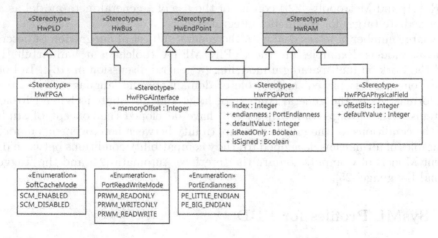

Fig. 2. A SysML profile for the description of Interfaces to programmable HW

The MARTE profile provides several concepts that can be leveraged for the definition of the hardware and software platform. For our code generation, we need to identify what subsystems are implemented in SW, running on a core and using services provided by a given operating system, and what subsystems are implemented on programmable HW (FPGA). Also, we need a model describing the register interface of the FPGA, offering not only the register abstraction but also a higher level description of a hardware "port".

For the definition of processors, MARTE offers the stereotype definition of «HwProcessor» and the stereotype «HwPLD» for the definition of FPGAs and FPGA interface registers. The modeling elements to specify the register interface of an FPGA, however, are not easily found. For this reason, we defined our taxonomy of stereotypes for FPGA components and interfaces. Programmable hardware components are derived as a refinement of the MARTE «HwPLD»

(Figure 2). The hardware interface is represented by a stereotype «HwFPGAInterface». The registers in the addressing space can be grouped in contiguous sets intended to be accessed for a homogeneous set of data/information and called «HwFPGAPort». The stereotyped definition of FPGA Port objects is obtained from the SysML Block (not the SysML port, because it is itself the composition of other objects and the Port entity in SysML cannot be a composite of other ports). A Hardware interface block typically consists of a number of FPGA Ports, in turn composed by atomic data items denominated FPGA Physical Field. The main stereotypes with their properties (Figure 2) are:

<<HwFPGA>> refines «HwFPGA» and defines an FPGA component.

<<HwFPGAInterface>> refines the MARTE stereotypes «HwBus» (to define address and data bus widths), «HwEndPoint» and «HwRAM» (for addressing modes, memory size), which in turn apply to Block. It is used for the description of the Interface to a programmable HW component (the component itself is identified by its interface). It uses the MARTE properties

addressWidth (from «HwBus», representing the address bus width).

wordWidth (from «HwBus», representing the data bus width). In both cases, legal values are 8, 16, 32, and 64.

and defines the additional property

memoryOffset a long representing the physical address of the first word in the programmable HW address space.

<<HwFPGAPort>> refines «HwEndPoint» and «HwRAM» (which apply to Block), from which the property memorySize defining the port size (the number of bits required for storing the information carried by the entire Port) is inherited. It is used to identify structured information that the programmable hardware will read or write as a whole (the description of its properties is omitted for space reasons).

<<HwFPGAPhysicalField>> refines «HwRAM». It defines a hardware register representing a field of information in a Port.

For the software part of the platform, we are interested in defining the Operating system running on a given Processor. In this case, MARTE states that "Operating systems may be represented through properties of the execution platform or, requiring significantly more detail, modeled as software components". For the second option, however, no stereotypes are offered. Therefore, we defined our own stereotype <<SwOperatingSystem>>, which only has an enumerated property with the OS name. In our code generation (described in the next section) the operating system information is only used to check whether a communication implementation using the boost library is possible.

4.3 Mapping Model

The profile *Mapping* defines the stereotypes of general use for the mapping of functions onto a platform, including the stereotypes for the mapping of functions onto a SW architecture of processes and threads and the messaging.

For our code generation, we are interested in knowing whether the communication between two functional subsystems is implemented as intrathread, interthread, interprocess or remote. Therefore, we need to identify *Processes* and

Threads in the software implementation model. MARTE provides the stereotype *SwConcurrentResource*, which is cumbersome and possibly confusing. The
<<SwSchedulableResource>> stereotype is recommended for the well-known
concepts of *Process* (which should also inherit from <<MemoryPartition>>),
Thread, or *Task* and comes with 39(!) stereotype attributes defining each and
every aspect related to its management.

Our mapping profile contains the definition of the following stereotypes:

<<MappedSystem>>, applies to Block, and identifies the root block of the mapping
model. The Mapping model includes a functional model, a platform model, a
process model and a message model.

<<ProcessModel>> applies to Block, and identifies the root block of the model
of all the processes in the system. A ProcessModel can recursively contain a
ProcessModel or a set of Processes

<<Process>> applies to Block and identifies a Process or a SW application. A
Process may (should) contain Threads.

<<Thread>> applies to Block and identifies a concurrent unit of execution.

In addition, we had to define deployment relations. We built on the MARTE
«Allocation» stereotype to define an implementation mapping between the functional layer subsystems and the platform. The provided stereotypes are:

<<SWdeployment>> refines Allocation to specify an implementation of a func-
tional subsystem (all the operations and actions in it) by a thread.

<<FPGAdeployment>> refines Allocation to specify an Implementation of a func-
tional subsystem (all operations and actions in it) by an FPGA.

<<AutoGenerated>> defines a deployment (an implementation) for which auto-
matic generation is supported.

<<ManagingOS>> refines Allocation to specify a mapping relationship between a
process and the real-time operating system managing it.

4.4 An Example

Figure shows the BDD and IBD views (Block Definition Diagram and Internal Block Diagram, standard SysML views) of a very simple example of functional model, with three subsystems communicating through SysML flow ports:
a *Configurator*, a *Detector* and a *Receiver*. The functional model is defined in
the package *FunctionalModels*. The types that apply to the flow ports are defined in the package *InterfaceDataTypes*. The model is only meant to provide an
example of communication scenarios and is void of any functional content (not
representative of the real industrial application)

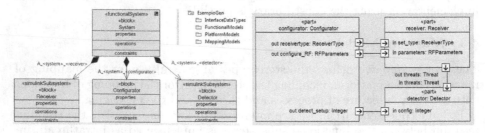

Fig. 3. The ibd showing the port connections for the a sample model

The corresponding platform model is shown in Figure 4, with a single node containing a CPU and an FPGA, which has in turn one interface with three ports. For one of the ports, the details of its physical fields are provided. Finally, the mapping model defines how the functional model is realized on the execution platform. This mapping information is in the package MappingModels to allow full independence and reusability of the functional and platform parts.

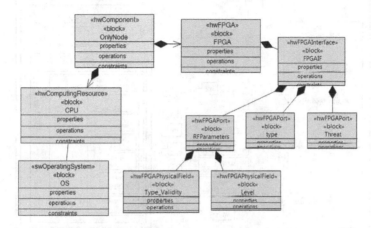

Fig. 4. The platform model for the example

The mapping model information for our example is represented in an ibd diagram as in Figure 5. The Detector and Configurator subsystem instances in the functional system model are deployed as software implementations onto two threads (Thread1, and Thread2, defined in a Process model package, which is part of the mapping model), which are in turn part of a Process Process1, executing on the CPU of our node. The Receiver part is mapped as an FPGA deployment onto the node FPGA. The interface ports of this block are implemented on an FPGA interface. The mapping between ports with primitive types on the functional side and implemented by a single register (no physical field) on the hardware side can be defined directly. For ports with structured types, each single field of the port type must be mapped onto a register (physical field) of the FPGA. This is performed by exposing the internal properties of the structured type (the imported reference to the port type) and building mapping relationships between each type property and a physical field. All mapping relationships (except those originating from the process/thread model) are defined through a stereotyped constraint, which is itself part of the mapping model. This allow to keep the functional and platform models completely independent, while at the same time, providing the necessary information for the code generation stage.

5   Generation of The FPGA Driver Code

The communication with a functionality implemented by programmable HW is structured in layers. The firmware function is accessed through a set of control

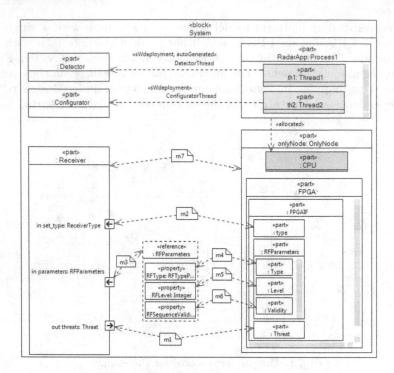

Fig. 5. The mapping model for the example

and data registers implemented on the FPGA and mapped in the memory space. Access to the FPGA registers is provided by a low-level driver, which is manually developed and provides basic read and write functions, according to an interface defined as *IBusAccess* and used by the upper layers. Read and write operations are overloaded according to the width of the data bus. For example, for a 64-bit data bus the functions are simply:

```
Read(char*address, unsigned long &in)
Write(char*address, unsigned long &in)
```

On top of this driver, an upper layer with set of higher-level operations is automatically generated. This layer maps application objects with structured data types onto elementary (bus-width) data registers and provides for caching, fragmentation and reassembly, notification of events and endianness conversions.

This higher-level layer is automatically generated from the SysML model of the FPGA Interface with a model-to-text transformation, from the Platform model into a set of C++ classes.

The generated code has the following structure. Two classes (in a pair of .ccp and .h files) are generated for the device.

A class called *NAME_HW_INTERFACE*Cacheddriver implementing a cache for all FPGA registers. The purpose of the cache class is to save time upon reading and writing into the HW only when values change (commands are requested).

A class *NAME_HW_INTERFACE*driver providing port-level access functions for reads and writes. for each port the following operations are generated:

Get(&t*NOME_PORT_x* values), to read values from the Port (registers).
Set(&t*NOME_PORT_x* values), to write value into all the HW registers associated with the port.
Reset*NOME_PORT_x* () to reset the values of all the registers associated with the port to their default values.

In addition, a class constructor is generated, with a reference to the low-level driver functions implementing the reads and writes on the physical registers.

6 Refinement of Simulink Subsystems

A top-down development flow makes use of transformations from the SysML <<SRSubsystem>> block into the specification of a Simulink Subsystem, complete with its ports and datatype specification as *Bus Objects* (the tool-specific type/class declarations). An Acceleo [9] module transforms the SysML block and generates a Matlab script that creates in the Matlab environment a set of Bus Object specifications mirroring the definitions of the data types in the SysML model; one file for each enumerated type in the SysML type specifications that apply to the subsystem ports; and a script that generates the boundary of the subsystem with its ports (as described in [11]). The subsystem is then defined internally and simulated, until its behavior is defined in a satisfactory way. When the Simulink model is completed, the automatic generation of its FPGA (if firmware) or C++ code implementation (if software) implementation is performed using Simulink Coder.

The generated FPGA implementation communicates with the other subsystems using a set of memory-mapped registers, accessed using the drivers described in the previous section. The C++ generated code follows the conventions of the code generator: for each subsystem, a class is generated with name *SubsystemName*ModelClass. The class has operations for the subsystem initialization and (if required) termination, and a **step** operation for the runtime evaluation of the block outputs given the inputs and the state. The Simulink Coder conventions defines how the interface ports translate into arguments of the **step** and allows to define the data types in an external (user provided) file. Listing 1.1 shows the code generated for the Receiver subsystem in our example.

Listing 1.1. Code generated for the Receiver subsystem

```
class ReceiverModelClass {
 public:
  void initialize();              /* model initialize function */
  /* model step function */
  void step(const ReceiverType &arg_In1,
            const RFParameters &arg_In2,
            Threat *arg_Out1);
  ReceiverModelClass();           /* Constructor */
  ~ReceiverModelClass();          /* Destructor */
}
```

7   Subsystem Deployment and Communication Code Generation

Some of the subsystems defined in the SysML functional model are refined in Simulink and an implementation is automatically generated for them. Other subsystems are developed as hand-written code or implemented by purposely designed HW or firmware. The software infrastructure that provides communication and synchronization among blocks, and realized as port and subsystem wrappers is automatically generated from the SysML model using Acceleo transformations that create application-specific classes (and objects) refining library classes.

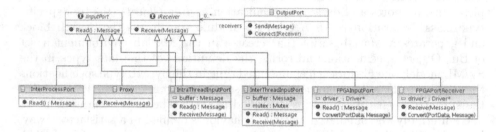

Fig. 6. Hierarchy of classes for subsystems ports

The class hierarchy defining the subsystem wrappers is simple. A virtual base class *SubsystemWrapper* is at the root of the hierarchy. Two classes are derived from it: *SubsystemSimulinkWrapper*, the base class for subsystems modelled by Simulink, and *SubsystemCppWrapper*, the base class for subsystems developed in C++ by hand (FPGA-implemented components do not have a wrapper). These classes are statically defined in a library. The Acceleo scripts define subsystem-specific classes derived from them. The communication between subsystems takes place through instances of port classes, whose hierarchy is depicted in Figure 6. The following template classes are defined:

OutputPort<Message> (base class for output ports): a concrete class implementing the following methods:

> Send(Message), to send data (at runtime) to the connected blocks,
> Connect(IReceiver), invoked at initialization time to connect the port to an instance of the *IReceiver* class in a corresponding input port or stub (for interprocess communication).

IInputPort<Message> (base class for input ports): an abstract class defining the method:

> Read(Message), to read the data received on the port from the subsystem methods.

IReceiver<Message>: an abstract class defining the method:

> Receive(Message), to receive data from an OutputPort.

Listing 1.2 shows the code of the `OutputPort` class. The Send method forwards the data to all connected IReceiver(s) that provide the data buffers. Concrete instances of input ports inherit from *IInputPort*. They also inherit from *IReceiver* when connected to output ports in the same process. *IntraThreadInputPort* and *InterThreadInputPort* inherit from the abstract interfaces *IInputPort* and *IReceiver*, allowing direct transmission of the Message data between different subsystems in the same process. Both store the Message data in an instance variable upon reception. The class *InterThreadInputPort* provides thread-safe access to its internal buffer using the protection method provided by the OS on the CPU hosting the process (currently only *boost mutexes* are supported).

Listing 1.2. Code of the Output port class

```
template < typename Message >
class OutputPort
{
public:
  OutputPort () {}
  virtual ~OutputPort () {}
  virtual void Send (const Message &message) {
    for (typename ReceiversVector :: const_iterator
        i=receivers_ . begin ();
        i != receivers_ . end (); ++i)
        (*i)->Receive (message);   }
  virtual void Connect (IReceiver <Message > *receiver) {
    receivers_ . push_back (receiver);   }
protected :
  typedef std :: vector < IReceiver <Message >*> ReceiversVector ;
  ReceiversVector receivers_ ;
};
```

The separation between *IReceiver* and *IInputPort* is necessary when the output port and the connected input port belong to components mapped into different processes.

In this case, the *OutputPort* instance will be connected to a proxy object derived from *IReceiver* (living in the same process), which will then implement a (currently socket-based) inter-process communication to send data to the matching *IInputPort* instance on the other process. In Figure 6, this is represented by the classes *InterProcessInputPort*, derived from *IInputPort*, and *Proxy*, derived from *IReceiver*. This allows the users to ignore the details of specific implementations and only rely on the Send/Received methods with maximum portability.

The classes generated for the communication of **C++ hand-written** subsystems inherit from *SubsystemCppWrapper* and provide only the concrete definition of the communication ports and read/write operations for accessing them. The behavior of the subsystem is then manually coded (the listing of the generated code is quite straightforward and omitted for space reasons).

The **Simulink wrapper** instantiates the ports to communicate with the other subsystems and provides two methods **Init** and **Step**, that encapsulate the corresponding automatically generated methods.

Listing 1.3. Code generated for the Receiver subsystem (of Simulink type)

```
class SubsystemReceiver : public SubsystemSimulinkWrapper {
public:
    SubsystemReceiver();
    virtual void Init();
    virtual void Step();
    InterThreadInputPort<ReceiverType> *getSet_type();
    InterThreadInputPort<RFParameters> *getParameters();
    OutputPort<Threat> *getThreats();
private:
    InterThreadInputPort<ReceiverType> set_type_;
    InterThreadInputPort<RFParameters> parameters_;
    OutputPort<Threat> threats_;
    ReceiverModelClass simulink_receiver_;
};
...
void SubsystemReceiver::Init(){
    simulink_receiver_.initialize();
}
void SubsystemReceiver::Step() {
    ReceiverType input1 = set_type_.Read();
    RFParameters input2 = parameters_.Read();
    Threat output1;
    simulink_receiver_.step(input1, input2, &output1);
    threats_.Send(output1);
}
```

The SubsystemReceiver class generates for our example (shown in listing 1.3) defines the **parameters** and **set_type** ports. These ports receive input from the Configurator subsystem, which is mapped to another thread. Hence, their implementation is thread-safe. The user has the responsibility of writing the periodic thread that invokes the **Step** method of the generated subsystem wrapper class after the **Send** methods are called for all the output ports connected to the input ports of the subsystem block.

The **FPGA communication code** consists of port and receiver wrappers that encapsulate the high level driver functions and connect to the input and output ports of the components communicating with an FPGA subsystem (listing 1.4). The library code consists of a base class *FPGAInputPort* used to derive the Acceleo-generated classes implementing the input ports of a SW component connected to an FPGA subsystem output port.

When reading, the **Read** operation forwards the request to a **Get** operation from the FPGA driver port. For FPGA input ports, a dedicated Receiver is provided. A Send to a port connected to an FPGA input results in a **Set** on the FPGA driver. In both cases, the Acceleo-generated code mainly consists in overriding the definition of the **Convert** operation, translating the fields of the data port type into the PhysicalFields of the FPGA physical port, according to the mapping specified in the SysML model.

Listing 1.4. library classes for FPGA ports and receivers

```
template<typename Message, class Driver, typename PortData>
class FPGAInputPort : public IInputPort<Message> {
public:
  FPGAInputPort(Driver *driver) : driver_(driver) {}
  virtual Message Read() {
    PortData data; Message message; driver_->Get(data);
    Convert(data, message);
    return message;
  }
protected:
  virtual void Convert(const PortData &data, Message &msg)=0;
private:
  Driver *driver_;
};
...
template<typename Message, class Driver, typename PortData>
class FPGAPortReceiver : public IReceiver<Message> {
public:
  explicit FPGAPortReceiver(Driver *driver):driver_(driver){}
  void Receive(const Message &message) {
    PortData data; Convert(message, data);
    driver_->Set(data);
  }
... };
```

Finally, an additional code section is generated for each process to perform the **initialization** of all the components in the threads/processes and connecting their ports. A reference to the FPGA driver managing the FPGA registers accessed by the subsystems in the process is passed to the reading components and a receiver class is defined for each input FPGA port.

8   Conclusions and Future Work

We presented the flow and related tools (mostly open source, the backbone is provided by the open source Eclipse Modeling Framework (EMF) [8] and its metamodeling, model-to-model and model-to-code transformation capabilities) used for the automatic generation of communication adapters to automatically generated software and firmware components (from Simulink) and hand-coded classes. The generates adapters guarantee conformance with a SysML specification and adherence to the Simulink execution semantics and conformance with a generic model of an FPGA driver interface, which alleviates the tedious programming of selecting and coding the appropriate data passing pattern. Future work includes the full extension to adapters for networked (distributed) communication on heterogeneous stacks.

References

1. Sindico, A., Di Natale, M., Sangiovanni-Vincentelli, A.: An Industrial Application of a System Engineering Process Integrating Model-Driven Architecture and Model Based Design. In: ACM/IEEE 15th MODELS Conference, Innsbruck, Austria
2. Sangiovanni-Vincentelli, A.: Quo Vadis, SLD? Reasoning About the Trends and Challenges of System Level Design. Proceedings of the IEEE 95(3), 467–506 (2007)
3. The Object Management Group, http://www.omg.org
4. Mukerji, J., Miller, J.: Overview and Guide to OMG's Architecture, http://www.omg.org/cgi-bin/doc?omg/03-06-01
5. Paterno, F.: Model-Based Design and Evaluation of Interactive Applications. Springer, London (1999)
6. The System Modeling Language, http://www.sysml.org/docs/specs/OMGSysML-v1.1-08-11-01.pdf
7. Modeling Analysis of Real Time Embedded Systems (MARTE) profile, http://www.omg.org/spec/MARTE/1.0/PDF/
8. The Eclipse Modeling Framework, http://www.eclipse.org/modeling/emf/
9. Acceleo, http://www.acceleo.org/pages/home/en
10. SIMULINK, http://www.mathworks.it/products/simulink/
11. Sindico, A., Di Natale, M., Panci, G.: Integrating SysML With SIMULINK Using Open Source Model Transformations. In: SIMULTECH, pp. 45–56 (2011)
12. Kienhuis, B., Deprettere, E.F., van der Wolf, P., Vissers, K.: A methodology to design programmable embedded systems - the y-chart approach. In: Deprettere, F., Teich, J., Vassiliadis, S. (eds.) SAMOS 2001. LNCS, vol. 2268, pp. 18–37. Springer, Heidelberg (2002)
13. Mellor, S.J., Kendall, S., Uhl, A., Weise, D.: MDA Distilled. Addison Wesley Longman Publishing Co. Inc., Redwood City (2004)
14. Koudri, A., Cuccuru, A., Gerard, S., Terrier, F.: Designing Heterogeneous Component Based Systems: Evaluation of MARTE Standard and Enhancement Proposal. In: Whittle, J., Clark, T., Kühne, T. (eds.) MODELS 2011. LNCS, vol. 6981, pp. 243–257. Springer, Heidelberg (2011)
15. Wozniak, E., Mraidha, C., Gerard, S., Terrier, F.: A Guidance Framework for the Generation of Implementation Models in the Automotive Domain. In: EUROMICRO-SEAA, pp. 468–476 (2011)
16. Mosterman, P.J., Vangheluwe, H.: Computer Automated Multi-Paradigm Modeling: An Introduction. Simulation. Transactions of the Society for Modeling and Simulation International 80(9), 433–450 (2004), Special Issue: Grand Challenges for Modeling and Simulation
17. Sztipanovits, J., Koutsoukos, X., Karsai, G., Kottenstette, N., Antsaklis, P., Gupta, V., Goodwine, B., Baras, J., Wang, S.: Towards a Science of Cyber-Physical System Integration. Proceedings of the IEEE, Special Issue on Cyber-Physical Systems 100(1), 29–44 (2012)
18. Vanderperren, Y., Dehaene, W.: From uml/sysml to matlab/simulink: Current state and future perspectives. In: Proceedings of the Conference on Design, Automation and Test in Europe, DATE 2006, Leuven, Belgium (2006)
19. Benveniste, A., Caspi, P., Edwards, S., Halbwachs, N., Le Guernic, P., de Simone, R.: The synchronous languages 12 years later. Proceedings of the IEEE 91(1) (January 2003)

20. Berry, G., Gonthier, G.: The synchronous programming language ESTEREL: Design, semantics, implementation. Science of Computer Programming 19(2) (1992)
21. Karsai, G., Maroti, M., Ledeczi, A., Gray, J., Sztipanovits, J.: Composition and cloning in modeling and meta-modeling. IEEE Transactions on Control System Technology (special issue on Computer Automated Multi-Paradigm Modeling) 12, 263–278 (2004)
22. Balarin, F., Lavagno, L., Passerone, C., Watanabe, Y.: Processes, interfaces and platforms. embedded software modeling in metropolis. In: Sangiovanni-Vincentelli, A.L., Sifakis, J. (eds.) EMSOFT 2002. LNCS, vol. 2491, pp. 407–416. Springer, Heidelberg (2002)
23. Eker, J., Janneck, J.W., Lee, E.A., Liu, J., Liu, X., Ludvig, J., Neuendorffer, S., Sachs, S., Xiong, Y.: Taming Heterogeneity—the Ptolemy Approach. Proceedings of the IEEE 91(2) (January 2003)
24. de Alfaro, L., Henzinger, T.: Interface automata. In: Proc. of the 8th European Software Engineering Conference Held Jointly with 9th ACM SIGSOFT International Symposium on Foundations of Software Engineering, Vienna, Austria (2001)
25. Lee, E., Sangiovanni-Vincentelli, A.: A Unified Framework for Comparing Models of Computation. IEEE Trans. on Computer Aided Design of Integrated Circuits and Systems 17(12), 1217–1229 (1998)

A UML Model-Driven Approach to Efficiently Allocate Complex Communication Schemes

Andrea Enrici, Ludovic Apvrille, and Renaud Pacalet

Institut Mines-Telecom, Telecom ParisTech, CNRS/LTCI, Biot, France
{andrea.enrici,ludovic.apvrille,renaud.pacalet}@telecom-paristech.fr

Abstract. To increase the performance of embedded devices, the current trend is to shift from serial to parallel and distributed computing with simultaneous instructions execution. The performance increase of parallel computing wouldn't be possible without efficient transfers of data and control information via complex communication architectures. In UML/SysML/MARTE, different solutions exist to describe and map computations onto parallel and distributed systems. However, these languages lack expressiveness to clearly separate computation models from communication ones, thus strongly impacting models' portability, especially when performing Design Space Exploration. As a solution to this issue, we present Communication Patterns, a novel UML modeling artifact and model-driven approach to assist system engineers in efficiently modeling and mapping communications for parallel and distributed system architectures. We illustrate the effectiveness of our approach with the design of a parallel signal processing algorithm mapped to a multiprocessor platform with a hierarchical bus-based interconnect.

Keywords: Model Driven Engineering, Hardware-Software Co-Design, Design Space Exploration, Parallel Computing, Embedded Systems.

1 Introduction

Today's embedded systems are more and more realized as parallel systems where the processing and the control are distributed over a network of interconnected subsystems. Such systems are typically deployed to perform parallel computing for data-dominated applications where performance is driven by both data processing and data transfers. Currently, we find these parallel and distributed systems both at the chip level (e.g., Multi-Processors Systems on Chip) or in domains where the electronics components are physically distributed over the structure of the whole system (e.g., automotive and avionics systems). In this context, an important challenge is to efficiently program these complex architectures where interactions between computations and transfers, from both hardware and software points of view, significantly impact the software development (e.g., time-to-market of new products, development time and costs).

Among the possible approaches that can be taken to alleviate application software development, there is raising the level of abstraction at which these systems

J. Dingel et al. (Eds.): MODELS 2014, LNCS 8767, pp. 370–385, 2014.

are programmed, e.g., with the aid of Model Driven Engineering [1]. Thus, instead of manually programming a parallel and distributed system, a developer can separately model both the application(s) - i.e., the functional part of the system - and the candidate resources - i.e., the hardware architecture - therefore abstracting out low-level details (e.g., memory addressing modes) with the guidance of Electronic Design Automation tools. Then he/she selects the architecture units for executing the function's workload (*mapping*) and once a solution compliant with the predefined performance requirements is reached, the application code can be generated via automated model transformations. Finding a mapping solution compliant to some performance requirements (i.e., Design Space Exploration, DSE) is typically an iterative process: performance numbers are first extracted from mapping models. Then, according to these numbers, pre-mapping models are improved and the process starts over until performance numbers converge to the desired performance requirements.

The performance of a data-dominated application executed on a parallel and distributed system is driven both by computations (i.e., processing) and by communications (e.g., data transfers). However, UML/SysML models intertwine both computation entities (i.e., classes/blocks) and communication entities (i.e., relationships/ports) aspects within the same diagrams. This lack of separation of concerns causes serious issues when models are to be modified due to DSE. As communications cannot be described separately from computations, input models must be re-designed from scratch each time a mapping alternative does not match the desired performance requirements. Thus, models mix information about the functionality of an application (i.e., the computations to be carried out) with information that is specific to a given architecture (i.e., how data can be transferred). This dramatically limits models' portability, transformations and impacts the time, costs and quality of a model-driven design.

In response to the above issues, this paper presents a novel approach and the corresponding artifacts to separately describe and map communications and computations, independently of the pair application-architecture. We apply our modeling approach to DiplodocusDF, a UML Model-Driven Engineering methodology for the rapid prototyping of data-dominated applications onto heterogeneous Multi-Processor System-on-Chip (MPSoC) architectures. In the scope of DiplodocusDF, we make use of its UML/SysML modeling facilities that are supported by the open source toolkit TTool [2]. Last, we show the benefits of our TTool/DiplodocusDF via the Design Space Exploration of a complete system composed of a signal processing application mapped onto an MPSoC architecture.

The rest of this paper is organized as follows. In Section 2 we describe in greater detail the problem statement accompanied by a clarifying example. Section 3 presents our systematic approach to separate computations and communications in the input specification models. Section 4 applies these principles to the modeling assets available in UML/SysML and demonstrates how we are able to solve the example problem of Section 2. The case study of Section 5 presents the implementation of our approach in TTool/DiplodocusDF, in the context of a complete pair application-architecture. Section 6 discusses our contributions with respect to related works and Section 7 concludes the paper.

2   Problem Statement

In this section we will describe the problem statement in greater detail. We start with a discussion related to the application of the Y-chart approach [3] to map UML/SysML application models onto parallel and distributed architectures. Next, we extend the discussion with a practical example and state the problems that we aim at solving in this article.

2.1   Design Space Exploration with the Y-chart in UML/SysML

The problem that system engineers face when working with parallel and distributed architectures is the many design alternatives involved. The Y-chart approach (see Fig. 1) has been proposed as a methodology to help designers "to explore the design space of an architecture template in a systematic way, to design programmable embedded systems that are programmable and satisfy the design constraints" [3]. It has become a de facto standard approach underlying many Electronic Design Automation (EDA) tools and methodologies.
It is our belief, however, that applying the Y-chart of Fig. 1 to map applications modeled in UML/SysML, onto parallel and distributed architectures, is inefficient. This is due to a lack of separation of concerns in the application models between operations (i.e., processing and control operations), represented in UML diagrams as classes, and their dependencies, represented in UML diagrams as relationships. Indeed, the semantics associated by UML/SysML diagrams to relationships works well for applications mapped to architectures where operations are sequentially executed onto centralized units. Typically in these contexts, communications[1] have a small impact on performance and are executed on simple point-to-point paths (e.g., memory-bus-memory). On the other hand, relationships in UML/SysML diagrams are not suited to describe dependencies among operations when the latter are executed by parallel and distributed units that require intensive communications on complex paths, affecting performance.

2.2   A UML/SysML Producer-Consumer Example in TTool

Fig. 2 depicts the scenario of our example modeled in TTool. Fig. 2a shows a sample application made up of a pair of producer-consumer operations, interconnected by a relationship $ch1$ which represents the exchange of data from the producer to the consumer. Fig. 2b illustrates a sample architecture where the producer-consumer application is mapped. The producer operation is mapped to

---

[1] In this article we loosely use the word communications to refer to any transfer of data or control items.

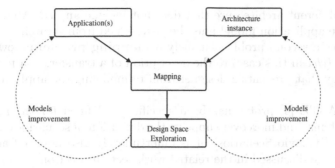

Fig. 1. The Y-chart approach for the design of programmable embedded systems

the Digital Signal Processor (DSP) DSP1, the consumer operation to the Central Processing Unit (CPU) CPU1. Due to the capabilities of DSP1 and CPU1, we can imagine that DSP1 is able to directly store its output data only to Memory1 and CPU1 is able to directly retrieve its input data only from Memory2. Thus, in order to execute the consumer operation, a transfer is needed to move the producer's data from Memory1 to Memory2. Moreover, such a transfer can either be issued with a bus transaction or with a Direct Memory Access (DMA) transaction. So how to describe it in UML/SysML?

We encounter here a first problem, namely **a modeling problem**: a lack of expressiveness to describe at the same time (1) a specific transfer, (2) the architecture units involved and (3) the way the transfer is performed. Typically what a system designer would do is to create a second instance of the application model of Fig. 2a, as depicted in Fig. 2c. In the latter an additional operation is injected between the producer and the consumer to imitate how data can be transferred with a DMA transaction. However, such an arrangement does not

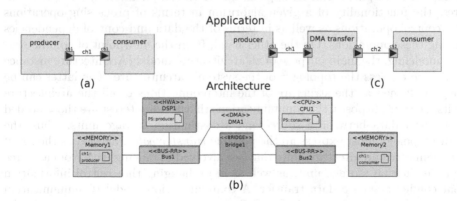

Fig. 2. A sample producer-consumer application mapped over an architecture in UML/SysML with TTool

prevent us from running into another issue if, for instance, it turns out that the DMA transaction is not efficient enough or if we want to map the application model to a different architecture that does not include any DMA engine. In either case the application model must be re-designed from scratch.

Thus, we face a second problem, namely **a mapping problem**: how to map a relationship ($ch1$ in this case) to the description of a transfer, in a portable way (i.e., in a way that prevents a designer from re-modeling the application)?

If the MARTE [4] profile has been specifically defined for the modeling of complex systems, and moreover supports the definition of scenarios for the usage of resources (BehaviorScenarios), it is unfortunately also not well adapted for reasons that are discussed in the related work section (Section 6).

3   The Approach

Fig. 3 shows a global view of the approach we propose in response to the modeling and mapping problems introduced in Section 2. The overall goal of our approach is to assist the system designer with a systematic methodology to separately define the modeling assets that are needed to describe a **triplet application-architecture-communications**. This separation of concerns aims at minimizing the intersection between modeling concepts that would otherwise be mixed in the application and the architecture descriptions. We believe that this lack of separation of concerns is at the root of the modeling and mapping problems of Section 2. In this section, we describe how the Y-chart approach of Fig. 1 is extended to accommodate for separate models for the application, the architecture and communications. At the same time we define the vocabulary of some key concepts that will be used throughout the paper.

In our vision, a **communication model** (Communication modeling box) acts as a an interface between the application and the architecture models. On one hand, the main purpose of an application model (Application(s) box), is to express the functionality of a given algorithm in terms of processing operations and control operations as well as in terms of the data and control dependencies among these operations. On the other hand, from the viewpoint of communication modeling, the main purpose of an architecture model (Architecture instance box) is to express the topology[2] of the system's architecture. The latter can be roughly defined as the structure of the interconnections of all the architecture units. For our purposes, the communications that are of interest are those needed to transfer data between a source and a destination storage units. Thus, the above topology must express all the possible *transfer paths*, defined as the set of interconnected architecture units that are involved in moving data from a source to a destination storage unit, as well as in exchanging the control information that configure such a data transfer. A communication model (Communication modeling box) aims to match the needs expressed by data dependencies in the application, to the capacity of an architecture to serve such needs. In order to capture these concepts, we need a communication model to elegantly express the architecture units that participate in a data transfer, the *transfer components*,

---

[2] The topology includes performance parameters.

and to allow a system designer to describe the *transfer algorithm* that must be put in place to move data according to the dependencies of the application. More specifically, we define a *transfer algorithm* as the set of activities that must be executed by the *components* to move data in a *transfer path*. Also the mapping phase (Mapping box) must be defined to accommodate for our separation of concerns and it is composed of two stages. First, the workload of the application algorithm in terms of processing and control operations is projected over the specific architecture instance. In this stage, the designer selects the architecture units that will execute the processing and control operations. Next, the workload expressed by the control and data dependencies of the application is projected onto the *transfer paths* of the specific architecture instance through the communication models (*components* and *algorithm*). When exploring different mapping alternatives in the design space, we now dispose of separate modeling assets - i.e., application, communication and architecture models - that can be individually modified without impacting on each other.

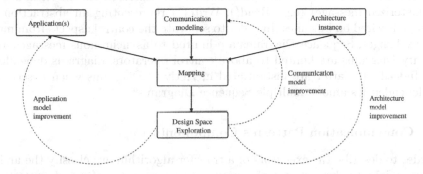

Fig. 3. The Y-chart approach extended with the separation of concerns between the application and the architecture models

4 Communication Modeling and Mapping in UML/SysML: Communication Patterns

In this section we put into effect the principles described in our extended Y-chart approach with the modeling assets available in UML/SysML. Next, we practically show how these assets can be used to solve the producer-consumer issues illustrated in Section 2. We regroup the UML/SysML modeling assets under the name of Communication Pattern, that defines a single modeling artifact used to model one or more transfers.

4.1 Models for the Communication Pattern's Transfer Algorithm

In order to model a transfer algorithm, we first need to abstract out the *activities* that take place in the communication protocols or standards of the architecture instance. Further, we need to compose these *activities* and express their dependencies by means of some sort of structure or hierarchy. In the scope of

UML/SysML, the diagrams that we estimated to be suitable for these purposes are Behavior Diagrams, and more specifically both Activity and Sequence Diagrams. The Activity Diagrams of a Communication Pattern capture the structure and dependencies of the simple and repeatable *activities* that are part of a transfer algorithm (e.g., program a DMA, execute a bus transaction). Each of these simple and repeatable *activities* is then described either directly by Sequence Diagrams or recursively via other Activity Diagrams. Within an Activity Diagram, *activities* are composed by operators to describe concurrency, sequencing, choice and iteration. The latter two are governed by control variables that are global to a given Activity Diagram and to all the diagrams that it references. An Activity Diagram is associated to a set of components which is global to all the diagrams it references.

The Sequence Diagrams of a Communication Pattern describe the way components interact in order to execute an activity, a well as the order in which these *interactions* are executed. The lifelines of Sequence Diagrams are associated to instances of components. *Interactions* are described via the exchange of parameterized messages (e.g., Read(), Write()) representing an abstraction of the signals wired on bus lines. In order to separate the control aspects from message exchanges, Sequence Diagrams are limited to asynchronous messages and Activity Diagrams are limited to above control operators, diagrams dependencies. Indeed, the latter are instantiated in Activity Diagrams when describing the dependencies among multiple Sequence Diagrams[3].

4.2 Communication Pattern's Components

In order to describe the executors of a transfer algorithm, we classify the architecture units into three classes of components: *storage*, *transfer* and *controller*.

- A *storage component* is an architecture unit whose main functionality is to store input/output data produced or consumed by a processing operation, e.g., a RAM memory, a buffer.
- A *transfer component* is an architecture unit whose main functionality is to physically move data items between components, e.g., a AMBA bus, a CAN bus, a DMA.
- A *controller component* is an architecture unit whose main functionality is to coordinate a data transfer by configuring a *transfer component*, e.g., a Central Processing Unit, a microcontroller, a Digital Signal Processor.

When modeling a communication (Communication modeling box in Fig. 3) we use these three classes of components to describe a generic transfer algorithm independently of the architecture units of a given instance. This abstraction allows the transfer algorithm to be portable with respect to the system's architecture.

---

[3] In analogy with a computer program, we can see the messages exchanged in Sequence Diagrams as the low-level instructions of a given *transfer algorithm*. These instructions are grouped into the *activities* captured by both Activity and Sequence Diagrams. Activities can be thought of as routines in programming languages.

Finally, when projecting the application workload expressed by data dependencies onto the architecture, (Mapping box in Fig. 3) these abstract components are mapped to the specific units of the architecture instance.

4.3 Modeling the Consumer-Producer Problem with Communication Patterns

In this subsection we illustrate how a Communication Pattern can solve the modeling and mapping problems for the producer-consumer example of Section 2.

In the architecture model of Fig. 2b, according to our classification of components, we dispose of: two storage objects (i.e., Memory1 and Memory2), four transfer objects (i.e., Bus1, Bus2, Bridge1 and DMA1) and two controller objects (i.e., DSP1 and CPU1). In the application of Fig. 2a, we have two processing operations (i.e., producer and consumer) and one data dependency (i.e., channel ch1). The mapping of the application workload in terms of processing operations has already assigned the producer to DSP1 and the consumer to CPU1. The access capabilities of DSP1 and CPU1 force the producer output data to reside in Memory1 and the consumer input data to be accessible from Memory2. This scenario thus defines the need to have one transfer from Memory1 to Memory2. Such a transfer can be executed in two ways either via a bus transaction or a DMA transaction. When modeling we know nothing about the performance numbers of the two transfer options, so we have to model the communication in the most generic possible way; thus, in terms of components we need two storage, one controller and three transfer components. The transfer algorithm is fairly simple given we only have one data dependency; it is illustrated in Fig. 4a: first the transfer component is programmed by the controller (ProgramTransfer box), then data is moved iteratively from the source to the destination storage by the transfer component (ExecuteTransfer box, loop operator) until an integer counter reaches the value zero. At this point the controller is informed of the completion (AcknowledgeTransfer box). Fig. 4b illustrates the Sequence Diagram corresponding to the activity ExecuteTransfer of the algorithm, Fig. 4a. Data is moved from the source storage to the destination storage via the transfer components.

4.4 Mapping the Producer-Consumer Problem with Communication Patterns

During mapping phase, the behavior diagrams of a Communication Pattern are arranged to match the capacity of the architecture instance. Since in our consumer-producer example we deal with only one data transfer we dispose of the full architecture capacity and we do not need to arrange the algorithm modeled in the Activity Diagram of Fig. 4a. However, in case the producer-consumer application required an algorithm to model multiple transfers, the algorithm would have been arranged to match the limited parallelism available in Fig. 2b.

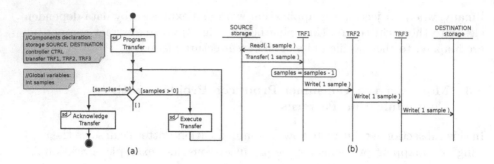

Fig. 4. The transfer algorithm for the consumer-producer example (a). The interactions among components corresponding to the ExecuteTransfer activity of the algorithm (b).

In the latter, there are two transfer paths from Memory1 to Memory2: (1) Bus1-Bridge1-Bus2 if a bus transaction is to be issued or (2) Bus1-DMA1-Bus2 in case a DMA transaction is to be issued. The choice between which of the two paths performs best is a matter of performance analysis and will not be treated in this paper as we are concerned with the pure modeling aspects. At this point, all we need to do is to map the Communication Pattern's components to the architecture units and individually arrange the algorithm's activities (Sequence Diagrams) accordingly. The ExecuteTransfer activity of the algorithm of Fig. 4a is shown in Fig. 5a for the transfer path corresponding to the DMA transaction and in Fig. 5b for the bus transaction. In Fig. 5a the three transfer components are mapped to units Bus1, DMA1 and Bus2, whereas in Fig. 5b they are mapped to units Bus1, Bridge1 and Bus2. In both cases the message exchanged within the activity ExecuteTransfer must be adapted to describe the exact operating mode of the architecture units, e.g., data passes through Bridge1 one sample per time, while 2 samples are stored in DMA1's internal buffer before they can be forwarded to Memory2.

5   Case Study

So far, we have showed to the reader the effectiveness of our works to the sample producer-consumer example of Section 2, demonstrating how our approach and Communication Patterns technically solve what we called the modeling and mapping problems for complex communication schemes. In this section, we demonstrate the effectiveness of our approach and of Communication Patterns in the context of a complete system application-architecture, when Design Space Exploration comes into play.

5.1   TTool/DiplodocusDF

As part of our works, we integrated the approach presented in this article in DiplodocusDF [5], a UML Model-Driven Engineering methodology for the design and rapid prototyping of data-dominated applications on heterogeneous

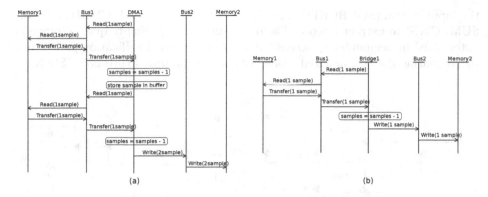

Fig. 5. The Sequence Diagram for the ExecuteTransfer activity of Fig. 4 mapped onto the transfer path Bus1-DMA1-Bus2 (a) and onto the transfer path Bus1-Bridge1-Bus2 (b)

real-time embedded systems. To support this extension of DiplodocusDF, we implemented the diagrams needed by Communication Patterns into TTool [2], a toolkit for the edition, simulation and formal verification of UML/SysML diagrams supporting DiplodocusDF. An application model in TTool/DiplodocusDF is implemented as a composition of SysML Block Definition and Block Instance diagrams, where the behavior of each block is described by a SysML State Machine. An application model describes an algorithm from a functional view, with processing and control tasks interconnected by data and control dependencies. On the other hand, an architecture instance in TTool/DiplodocusDF is described by a UML Deployment Diagram made up of a set of generic interconnected units (e.g., bus, CPU, DMA) decorated with performance parameters. At mapping level an application is projected onto an architecture by respectively associating SysML blocks to nodes in the Deployment Diagram, via UML artifacts.

So far, we have integrated the mapping of the Communication Pattern diagrams and components onto a transfer path in the architecture Deployment Diagram as well as the association of a data dependency in the application to a Communication Pattern. Such a mapping has been implemented with a UML artifact within the architecture Deployment Diagram.

5.2   A Parallel Application: High Order Cumulants

The application for this case study is a classification algorithm, High Order Cumulants (HOC) as implemented in [6], that is used in cognitive radio by a transmitter to sense the spectrum and detect if another user is currently transmitting in the same frequency range. The SysML diagram for the application algorithm, as modeled in DiplodocusDF with TTool, is illustrated in Fig. 6. For the sake of simplicity, in Fig. 6 the control operations and control dependencies are omitted and only the dataflow view (processing operations and data dependencies) of the model is displayed. The HOC algorithm operates on segments of the input stream (SOURCE) that are independently processed (CWM1, CWM2, SUM, CWS) to extract a score. The occupancy of a specific frequency range is determined by accumulating scores (ACC) over a given classification period and by comparing the accumulated scores with a pre-computed threshold (SINK).

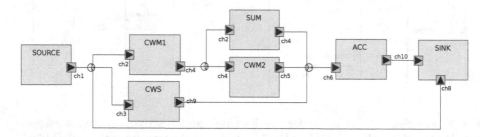

Fig. 6. Dataflow view of the SysML diagram for the HOC application, as modeled in DiplodocusDF with TTool

5.3   A Parallel and Distributed Hardware Architecture: Embb

The target hardware architecture for HOC is Embb [7]. Embb is a generic baseband architecture dedicated to signal processing applications. Fig. 7a shows the architecture Deployment Diagram of the overall topology, as modeled in DiplodocusDF with TTool. Embb is composed of a processing subsystem and a control subsystem. In the former, left-hand side of Fig. 7a, samples coming from the air are processed in parallel by a distributed set of Digital Signal Processors (DSP1 through DSPn) interconnected by a crossbar (Crossbar). The control subsystem, right-hand side of Fig. 7a, is where the control operations of the HOC application are executed. The latter run on a Control Processing Unit (MAINcpu) in charge of configuring and controlling both processing operations performed by the DSPs and the data transfers. The CPU of the control subsystem disposes of a memory unit (MAINmemory) and a bus interconnect (MAINbus). The latter is linked to the processing subsystem via a bridge (Bridge1). Fig. 7b illustrates the internal architecture of a DSP: each unit is equipped with a local control unit (DSPcpu), a processing core (DSP) and a Direct Memory Access unit (DSPdma) to transfer data in and out of the local memory (DSPmemory).

5.4   Design Space Exploration with Communication Patterns

In the application graph of Fig. 6, we apply Communication Patterns to describe the transfers associated to channels ch1, ch2, ch3 and ch8 as the parallelism between CWM1 and CWS allows to describe two mapping scenarios. As a first scenario, we map SINK to the MAINcpu, SOURCE to DSP1 and the pair CWM1,2 to DSP2. Given the topology of the architecture, SINK, SOURCE and CWM1,2 store data respectively in MAINmemory, DSP1memory and DSP2memory. Thus, to move data produced by SOURCE we need a Communication Pattern to model

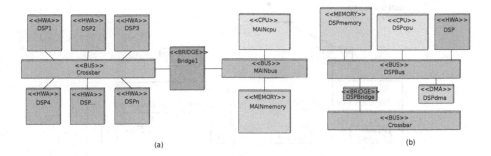

Fig. 7. The Deployment Diagrams of an architecture instance of Embb, a MPSoC platform dedicated to signal processing applications. Part (a) displays a global architecture of Embb with its processing subsystem (left-hand side) and control subsystem (right-hand side). Part (b) depicts the internal architecture of each Digital Signal Processor within the processing subsystem.

one transfer that serves CWM1,2 (ch2, ch3) and a second transfer that serves SINK (ch8). To do so, the ease of use of Communication Patterns allows us to extend the structure of the Activity Diagram of Fig. 4a with a second transfer as showed in Fig. 8. The latter illustrates one possible transfer algorithm where data is transferred to SINK (Transfer1) and to CWM1,2 (Transfer2), simultaneously. As a second mapping scenario, we associate CWM1,2 to two different DSP units, namely DSP2 and DSP3 in Fig. 7. Again we can re-use the Communication Pattern of Fig. 8, adapting it to model three transfers that each serve CWM1, CWM2 and SINK. Fig. 9 displays one of the possible transfer algorithms where data is delivered in parallel to SINK (Transfer1), CWM1 (Transfer2) and CWM2 (Transfer3).

Discussion Due to limits of space in this paper, we do not provide the Sequence Diagrams for the transfer algorithms of Fig. 8 and Fig. 9, nor the post-mapping Activity Diagrams. Thanks to the separation of concerns between control aspects (Activity Diagrams) and message exchanges (Sequence Diagrams), different mapping alternatives are investigated by re-adapting only Activity Diagrams. This reduces considerably the efforts spent during Design Space Exploration as well as design time and costs. At the beginning of a design, it is inevitable to build from scratch the transfer algorithm, choose the components and arrange both of them according to specific transfer paths selected at mapping phase. However, when different mapping alternatives come out, diagrams can be re-used with little changes: only the transfer algorithm in the Activity Diagrams has to be modified. Sequence Diagrams that are specific to transfer paths that have already been explored, are re-used without further modifications.

6   Related Work

In the literature, the problem of modeling and mapping complex communication schemes is tackled within the larger context of a complete system design. With

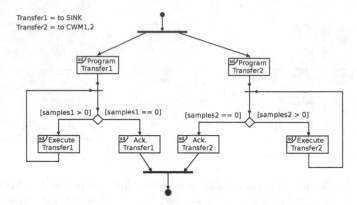

Fig. 8. The Activity Diagram for an algorithm modeling two parallel transfers

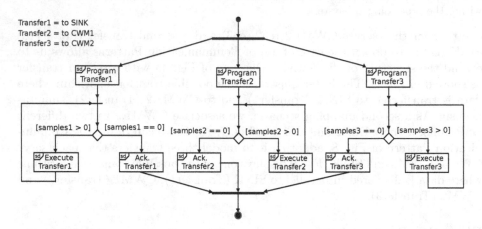

Fig. 9. The Activity Diagram for an algorithm modeling three parallel transfers

respect to our contributions we roughly divide existing approaches in two categories: *manual* and *automatic*, based on the way Design Space Exploration is performed. We label as *automatic* an approach where Design Space Exploration is performed by Computer Aided Design (CAD) tools which automatically find a mapping solution and evaluate its performance numbers, from input specifications of a pair application-architecture. In this case, no separation of concerns between application and architecture is needed in input specifications, as most of the DSE efforts are charged to CAD tools. Consequently, input specifications are based on formalisms that can be easily handled by a computer, e.g., dataflow models, process networks. Examples of what we define automatic approaches are Daedalus [8], [9], Metropolis [10], Ptolemy [11], PeaCE/HoPES [12], SCE [13], SystemCoDesigner[14], DOL [15].

We call *manual* those approaches where it is up to the user to manually define a mapping solution whose performance numbers are then analyzed by CAD tools. Within this category we find works based on UML/MARTE such as GAS-PARD [16], MOPCOM [17], Koski [18] and [19], [20] dedicated to both hardware and software synthesis. These approaches rely on a refinement process that progressively lowers the level of abstraction of input models. However, such a refinement does not completely separate the application (software synthesis) or the architecture (hardware synthesis) models from the communications, as we defined in Fig. 3. MARTE [4] shares many commonalities with our approach, in terms of the capacity to separately model communications from the pair application-architecture. For such a purpose, MARTE proposes Behavior Scenarios and Steps (Communication Steps). However, these assets are designed for performance and timing analysis, rather than DSE. Consequently, they intrinsically lack a separation between control aspects and message exchanges as we proposed in Activity and Sequence Diagrams. MARTE does not integrate a systematic methodology for DSE and does not define the necessary abstraction levels, proposing only a distinction between logical and physical level. In the context of our Communication Patterns, these levels of abstraction have been the subject of a previous publication [21].

With respect to the above classification, we can place TTool/DiplodocusDF in the category of the manual approaches as it is up to the user to find a suitable mapping for the input models. Performance analysis can be automated in TTool/DiplodocusDF by means of scripting facilities but it is not comparable to the solutions proposed by the above *automatic* approaches.

Independently of the works we presented, in the past edition of MODELS Arkin et al. [22] proposed a model-driven approach and tool, to automate the mapping of parallel algorithms onto parallel platforms. Interestingly enough, the authors introduce their definition of a Communication Pattern to describe the dynamic behavior of the nodes of a parallel platform via communication paths made up of a pair source-destination nodes and a route between the two. Their Communication Patterns target larger systems and are presented in the frame of an approach where separate steps define the architecture, communication and application similarly to Fig. 3. From the description available in [22] the aim and context of their Communication Patterns is clear and similar to ours. However, with respect to our works, it is not clear what the effective expressive power of such Communication Patterns is, what can be exactly represented in terms of architecture units, transfer algorithm and how they are employed during DSE.

7 Conclusion

In this paper we have provided a systematic approach and its implementation to separately model and map communications from a pair application-architecture, in the frame of the Y-chart approach. In response to the modeling problem, we introduced Communication Patterns and their implementation with UML/SysML modeling diagrams. In the latter, we further introduced an additional separation of concerns between control aspects (Activity Diagrams) and message exchanges (Sequence Diagrams). In response to the second problem, we defined the mapping of data dependencies in the application onto transfer paths in the architecture. We illustrated our solution, first, by means of a simple producer-consumer example and secondly, within the context of a complete application (HOC) and architecture (Embb). Moreover, we provided an implementation of the overall approach we propose in TTool.

Although we have applied Communication Patterns to a MPSoC architecture and a signal processing application, we believe that our contribution is general. We believe it can be applied to other data-dominated applications (e.g., video and image processing) and to other types of distributed architectures (e.g., automotive). In the approach we presented, we have proposed that input specification are manually modeled and mapped. Such a manual approach may constraint the applicability of our solution to systems with a limited number of components. Nevertheless, it is our intuition that our Communication Patterns may scale well also for larger systems (i.e., hundreds of components) via the creation of libraries of communication models.

In our future works we will focus on generating application code from automatic transformation of models that result from the approach we proposed in this paper. Additionally, we will complete the implementation of our approach by extending the simulator of TTool/DiplodocusDF with the support for performance analysis with Communication Patterns.

Acknowledgements. The research leading to these results has been conducted in the framework of the Celtic-Plus project SPECTRA (CP07-013) which has been partially funded by the French "Direction générale de la compétitivité, de l'industrie et des services (DGCIS)", the "Ministry of Finance and Economy / Business Development Agency" of the Monaco Principality and the "AVANZA2" framework of Spanish Industry, Tourism and Commerce Ministry (Ministerio de Industria, Turismo y Comercio).

References

1. Schmidt, D.C.: Model-Driven Engineering. IEEE Computer 39(2) (2006)
2. TTool, http://ttool.telecom-paristech.fr
3. Kienhuis, B., Deprettere, E.F., van der Wolf, P., Vissers, K.: A Methodology to Design Programmable Embedded Systems - The Y-chart Approach. In: Embedded Processor Design Challenges: Systems, Architectures, Modeling, and Simulation, SAMOS, pp. 18–37 (2002)
4. Object Management Group. A UML profile for MARTE (2014), http://www.omgmarte.org
5. Gonzalez-Pina, J.M.: Application Modeling and Software Architectures for the Software Defined Radio. PhD Dissertation, Telecom ParisTech (2013)
6. SACRA, Spectrum and Energy efficiency through multi-band Cognitive Radio: D6.3, Report on the Implementation of selected algorithms, http://www.ict-sacra.eu/public_deliverables/
7. Muhammad, N.-U.-I., Rasheed, R., Pacalet, R., Knopp, R., Khalfallah, K.: Flexible Baseband Architectures for Future Wireless Systems. In: EUROMICRO Digital System Design, pp. 39–46 (2008)

8. Thompson, M., Nikolov, H., Stefanov, T., Pimentel, A.D., Erbas, C., Polstra, S., Deprettere, E.F.: A Framework for rapid system-level exploration, synthesis and programming for multimedia MP-SoCs. In: CODES-ISSS, pp. 9–14 (2007)
9. Nikolov, H., Thompson, M., Stefanov, T., Pimentel, A.D., Polstra, S., Bose, R., Zissulescu, C., Deprettere, E.F.: Daedalus: Toward composable multimedia MP-SoC design. In: Design Automation Conference (DAC), pp. 574–579 (2008)
10. Balarin, F., Watanabe, Y., Hsieh, H., Lavagno, L., Passerone, C., Sangiovanni-Vincentelli, A.: Metropolis: An integrated electronic system design environment. IEEE Computer 36(4), 45–52 (2003)
11. The Ptolemy Project (2014), http://ptolemy.eecs.berkeley.edu
12. Ha, S., Kim, S., Lee, C., Yi, Y., Kwon, S., Joo, Y.-P.: PeaCE: A hardware-software codesign environment for multimedia embedded systems. ACM Transactions on Design Automation of Electronic Systems 12(3), 1–25 (2007)
13. Dömer, R., Gerstlauer, A., Peng, J., Shin, D., Cai, L., Yu, H., Abdi, S., Gajski, D.: System-on-chip environment: A SpecC-based framework for heterogeneous MPSoC design. EURASIP Journal on Embedded Systems 2008(3), 1–13 (2008)
14. Keinert, K., Streubühobar, M., Schlichter, T., Falk, T., Gladigau, J., Haubelt, C., Teich, J., Meredith, M.: SystemCoDesigner - An automatic ESL synthesis approach by design space exploration and behavioral synthesis for streaming applications. ACM Transactions on Design Automation of Electronic Systems 14(1), 1–23 (2009)
15. Thiele, L., Bacivarov, I., Haid, W., Huang, K.: Mapping Applications to Tiled Multiprocessor Embedded Systems. In: 7th International Conference on Application of Concurrency to System Design (ACSD), pp. 29–40 (2007)
16. Gamatie, A., Le Beux, S., Piel, E., Ben Atitallah, R., Etien, A., Marquet, P., Dekeyser, J.L.: A Model-Driven Design Framework for Massively Parallel Embedded Systems. ACM Transactions on Embedded Computing Systems 10(4), 1–36 (2011)
17. Lecomte, S., Guillouard, S., Moy, C., Leray, P., Soulard, P.: A co-design methodology based on model driven architecture for real time embedded systems. Mathematical and Computer Modelling 53(3-4), 471–484 (2011)
18. Kangas, T., Kukkala, P., Orsila, H., Salminen, E., Hännikäinen, M., Hämäläinen, T.D.: UML-based multiprocessor SoC design framework. ACM Transactions on Embededded Computing Systems 5(2), 281–320 (2006)
19. Vidal, J., de Lamotte, F., Gogniat, G., Soulard, P., Diguet, J.-P.: A co-design approach for embedded system modeling and code generation with UML and MARTE. In: Design and Automation Test in Europe (DATE), pp. 226–231 (2009)
20. Vidal, J., de Lamotte, F., Gogniat, G., Diguet, J.-P., Soulard, P.: UML design for dynamically reconfigurable multiprocessor embedded systems. In: Design and Automation Test in Europe (DATE), pp. 1195–1200 (2010)
21. Enrici, A., Apvrille, L., Pacalet, R.: Communication Patterns: A Novel Modeling Approach for Software Defined Radio Systems. In: 4th International Conference on Advances in Cognitive Radio (COCORA), pp. 35–40 (2014)
22. Arkın, E., Tekinerdogan, B., İmre, K.M.: Model-Driven Approach for Supporting the Mapping of Parallel Algorithms to Parallel Computing Platforms. In: Moreira, A., Schätz, B., Gray, J., Vallecillo, A., Clarke, P. (eds.) MODELS 2013. LNCS, vol. 8107, pp. 757–773. Springer, Heidelberg (2013)

Model-Integrating Software Components

Mahdi Derakhshanmanesh[1], Jürgen Ebert[1], Thomas Iguchi[1],
and Gregor Engels[2]

[1] University of Koblenz-Landau, Institute for Software Technology, Germany
{manesh,ebert,tiguchi}@uni-koblenz.de
[2] University of Paderborn, Department of Computer Science, Germany
engels@uni-paderborn.de

Abstract. In order to handle complexity of software systems, component-based as well as model-driven approaches have become popular in the past. In a model-driven development process the problem arises that over time model and code may be not aligned. Thus, in order to avoid this steadily increasing distance between models and code, we propose the integration of (executable) models and code at the component level. Redundancy – the source of inconsistencies – is reduced by interpreting models directly. Moreover, variability and adaptivity can be achieved by querying and transforming the embedded models. As the basis for such Model-Integrating Components (MoCos), we introduce a component realization concept that is compatible with existing component technologies. We provide a reference implementation using Java, OSGi and TGraphs and apply it successfully in a feasibility study on Android[TM].

Keywords: Model-integrating component, model execution, flexibility.

1 Introduction

In *Model-Driven Development* (MDD) [9], [22] models are used to describe a system. At some point in the development process, code is generated from these models. Despite all efforts (e.g., round-trip engineering), this generation step is often a source of inconsistencies between model and code artifacts as they evolve.

Currently, models and code artifacts are kept separately and are – at most – connected by links, e.g., to maintain traceability or a "causal connection" at runtime. In that setup, the model and source code parts that comprise a *logical unit of functionality* are not always kept together. Thus, understanding and reusing associated parts of models and code may become tedious.

Modularization concepts proposed in *Component-Based Development* (CBD) are well-established to manage the development of complex software and to achieve reuse [23]. Yet, component concepts for realizing software architectures have been traditionally targeted at the programming language level. To the best of our knowledge, carrying executable models as first-class constituents of components has not been in their focus. Even if models are executed, they are usually not software components. A modular approach is required to construct complex software systems, though.

J. Dingel et al. (Eds.): MODELS 2014, LNCS 8767, pp. 386–402, 2014.

In this paper, a realization concept for the combination of models and code in the form of *Model-Integrating Components* (MoCos) is introduced. MoCos are the basis for a novel *Model-Integrating Development* (MID) approach for software systems. A MoCo is a non-redundant, reusable and executable combination of logically related models and code in an integrated form where both parts are stored together in one component. MoCos enable the interplay of code with (i) design-time models of software (e.g., feature models, documentation), (ii) reflective models@run.time [8] as well as (iii) stand-alone, non-reflective and possibly executable models. A sketch of the core idea is given in Figure 1.

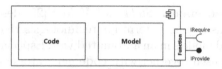

Fig. 1. High level sketch of a MoCo

The *code part* of a MoCo allows better performance than model execution for performance-critical functionality. Moreover, it supports the use of existing software libraries and enables the connection to third-party middleware.

The *model part* of a MoCo supports flexibility and comprehensibility of the component as all models can be queried and transformed (using dedicated languages) and may be interpreted to achieve *direct model execution* [12]. This supports software engineers with evolving components and system administrators with observing and managing a running system. We discussed the feasibility of this *query/transform/interpret* (QTI) approach in our previous work on engineering Self-Adaptive Software (SAS) [5].

Code and models are both *first-class entities* in MID with equal rights. The *component realization concept* proposed in this paper supports the modular development of software systems where users of components cannot differentiate between MoCos or other, more traditional, components. This component realization concept is independent of a specific component model, and we present it in the form of an abstract template that is compatible with existing technologies.

Fundamental research is required to tackle the associated challenges. The *contributions* of this paper are as follows:

(C1) *Defining a generic and modular realization concept for model-integrating software:* The practicability and usability of the MID approach depends significantly on design decisions that govern the structure and behavior of the model-integrating components. Based on the vision introduced earlier, a component realization concept for MoCos is developed.

(C2) *Providing a reference implementation for the realization concept:* Based on the design of the component realization concept, a reference implementation for MoCos is constructed. It is the technical basis for the conducted feasibility study. The concrete implementation is done in *Java*, because the Java Virtual Machine (JVM) is a portable execution platform. The

component technology chosen is *OSGi* [24] due to its dynamic capabilities
and the modeling *technological space* [19] is provided by *TGraphs* [13] .

(C3) *Evaluating the approach's potential for success:* The feasibility of the presented work is evaluated in the form of a *feasibility study*. The main concern
of this study is to examine the component realization concept's applicability on a mobile platform (limited resources) with different modeling languages. We explore how the concept can be realized with state-of-the-art
component technology and discuss the results and threats to validity.

2   Related Work

Model-Driven Development. *Stahl and Völter* [22] describe *Model-Driven
Development* (MDD) as a generic term for technologies that derive executable
source code from formal models in an automated way. Especially Domain-Specific
Languages (DSLs) are used together with code generators and interpreters.

A special variant of MDD can be found in OMG's *Model-Driven Architecture*
(MDA) that focuses on the separation of (domain) functionality and implementation technology. *Kleppe et al.* [18] describe the core concepts of MDA such
as the multi-staged transformations from source to target models. *Herrmann et
al.* [15] describe an interesting list of *MDA problems* as a motivation for their
compositional modeling approach.

There are also efforts to integrate models and code. For instance, *Tolvanen* [25]
describes why, in practice, models are usually dropped after the first code generation phase. He recommends the adequate application of DSLs with mature
modeling tools to move models to an adequate abstraction level for avoiding
redundancy between models and code.

Blair et al. [8] shaped the notion of "models@run.time" which has become
a mature field of research [7]. Adequately abstract models reflect the behavior
and structure of the programmed system and are causally connected to it. That
way, software can be monitored by querying its models and it can be adapted
by transforming them.

In a white paper on direct model execution by *E2E technologies* [12], it is described how the company successfully develops flexible business applications by
encoding a significant part of the logic in executable models. Results from extensive benchmarking of interpreting behavioral models are presented by *Höfig* [16].
He concludes that even though model interpretation is slower than compiled
code, the enhanced flexibility can pay off.

Existing MDD approaches specifically focus on transforming models to code.
Hence, knowledge is kept redundantly in code and models. Dependencies between
models and generated code may get lost during multiple stages of transformation,
though. To reduce redundancy, we propose to keep (some) design-time models
as an inherent part of software at runtime and to replace programmed behavior
with additional executable models where appropriate.

Component-Based Development. Components support reuse and the modular development of complex software systems. *Szyperski et al.* [23] give a comprehensive introduction to software components and cover the fundamental concepts, properties and methods of *Component-Based Development* (CBD).

Crnkovic et al. [10] identify and discuss the basic principles of component models and provide a *classification framework* for them. A wide range of existing component models is classified and discussed in-depth. The authors also clarify that existing modeling languages derived from the Unified Modeling Language (UML), like xUML [20], may be translated to executable components, but "...do not operate with components as first-class citizens...".

On the technical side, modern dynamic component models such as *OSGi* [24] support the loading, unloading and updating of components at runtime. This enables flexible systems that can be adapted at the granularity of components (architectural reconfiguration).

Usually, the topics of models and software components have not been mixed. The work of *Ballagny et al.* [6] is an exception to this where a state-based component model for self-adaptation is introduced that is based on components that carry models at runtime. In contrast to our generic approach, these models are always UML state machines.

Existing CBD approaches aim at reuse, exchangeability or performance at the implementation level and support the development of large software systems. Yet, their symbiosis with arbitrary modeling languages and especially with executable models has not been inspected well. The Model-Integrating Components (MoCos) presented in this work are an attempt towards closing this gap.

3 Component Realization Concept

In this section, we describe the *component realization concept* for MoCos in the form of a template that describes a *pattern* for developing software components. The template does not rely on any specific capabilities of an existing component model. Rather, it is meant to be implementable by using an existing component technology of choice.

In the broader sense, every existing component (e.g., a Java EE bean or an OSGi bundle) can be seen as a simple MoCo that does not carry a model. The intention behind this perspective is to stress the *compatibility* of the presented approach with any available component technology.

The main goal of this section is to define the conceptual foundation for flexible, model-integrating software components that – when instantiated for a specific application context – tackle the challenges described earlier in Section 1.

Subsequently, we use the term "MoCo" for referring to (i) the *template* for software components that can be realized in various technologies as well as to (ii) the concrete *instances* of this template for a given application area.

All MoCos communicate with each other via specific ports. There is an arbitrary number of *functionality ports* encapsulating core functionality. There is also an arbitrary number of *management ports* that provide access to the internals of a component for administration purposes.

The key characteristic that distinguishes components in our concept from existing ones is that each MoCo may consist of a *code* module and a *model*

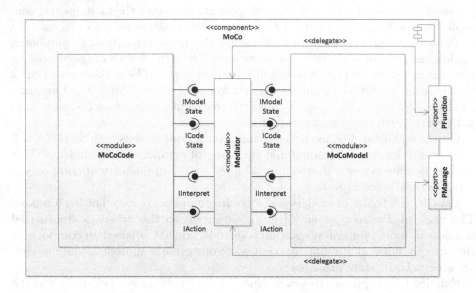

Fig. 2. Structural view on the MoCo template and its constituents

module. Both parts are first-class entities of the component realization concept and each one can be executable. Hence, behavior and data can be represented as models or as code – the full *spectrum of MoCos* [11] from (i) *code-only* to (ii) a *mixture of code and models* to (iii) *model-only* is supported.

Assuming that a comprehensive technological modeling space exists, the model part of a MoCo can be accessed and modified systematically by queries and transformations during development but also at runtime. Variants of a MoCo can be derived during development by extracting only the needed functionality for a specific product (*tailoring*), and deployed MoCos can be evolved at runtime to face changes in the operating environment, too (*adapting*).

The *MoCo template* exposes the main parts of any component to be created according to our approach. It is a *specification* of the possible constituent concepts of concrete MoCo instances. This template must be implemented and instantiated for a specific context of use. Next, we describe the structure of the MoCo template along its illustration given in Figure 2.

3.1   External View

Judging from the outside, all MoCos show a similar structure to their users. This *external view* on the structure is described in the following.

MoCos can have two kinds of ports: (i) the `PFunction` port and (ii) the `PManage` port. While `PFunction` groups the conventional set of interfaces of a component, `PManage` groups interfaces for systematically accessing and manipulating the internals of a MoCo. Both are the major contact-points between a component and its environment such as other components or software engineering tools. The important aspect is that pure *functional* application logic can be clearly distinguished from the services that are required or provided to *manage* the MoCo during its life-cycle.

PFunction. The PFunction port represents a logical grouping of all *core functionality* that is either required or provided by the component. There are no special restrictions for the design of this port and, because the set of required and provided interfaces depends on the concrete application domain, no detailed interfaces can be illustrated here. Functionality can be implemented by code or by models, internally. This is hidden from the MoCo's users.

The PFunction port is *optional* for all MoCos. Components that automatically start their task without further dependencies do not require it.

PManage. The PManage port represents a logical grouping of all *management functionality* that is either required or provided by the component. To manage a MoCo, we rely heavily on applying techniques from *model-driven development* (MDD) [22,9] such as querying and transforming models using languages designed specifically for these tasks. This is an essential prerequisite for realizing MoCo-specific functionality to support tailoring and adapting processes.

The PManage port is *optional* for all MoCos. Components that do not need to be observed or manipulated, e.g., from a software engineering tool or an *adaptation manager* [21], do not require it.

3.2 Internal View

The encapsulated details are not so much of interest for the users of MoCos, but component developers need to be familiar with guidelines for the internal design of MoCos. The *internal view* on the structure is described in the following.

From a coarse-grained perspective, the MoCo template comprises three modules[1]:(i) MoCoCode, (ii) Mediator and (iii) MoCoModel. Note, that the code and the model are not illustrated on top of each other in Figure 2 but reside side-by-side to hint at their equally important roles.

MoCoCode. The MoCoCode is a module that holds stable, efficient and well-tested core functionality. Parts of the provided services of the MoCo can be implemented in code like in all traditional ways of building software components. Not every MoCo needs to implement its application behavior in plain code, though. Models can be used to realize similar functionality, as well.

The realization concept does not require the code to be structured in a predefined way. In cases where the MoCoCode shall cooperate and interact with the MoCoModel module, standardized ways of implementation for single program elements (e.g., classes, interfaces) are proposed, though.

---

[1] Here, a *module* is a structured and logically coherent group of software elements.

These *prepared program elements* support interfacing with the `Mediator` module and/or the MoCo's ports. For example, some of the data fields may need to be exposed for read/write access and methods may need to be marked as replaceable by modeled behavior. Hence, it may be required to prepare some of the code – for instance by applying a sequence of refactorings [4] – to allow communication with other modules within the MoCo.

MoCoModel. The `MoCoModel` module primarily contains and manages the set of *models* that contribute to the functionality of the component. It is up to the designer of a MoCo to plan and decide what kinds of modeling languages to use in the specific application domain.

Each model conforms to a *meta-model* that describes its abstract syntax. Moreover, *constraints* may be defined and stored with the meta-model as needed.

Model semantics is described via *model interpreters* that traverse the abstract syntax graph of a model. There may be an arbitrary number of such interpreters for a given meta-model (i) to achieve the same task in multiple technologies, e.g., a GUI interpreter for Android user interfaces and another one for web-based interfaces, (ii) or to perform different tasks, e.g., execute a model's behavior or visualize it for human inspection.

Mediator. The `Mediator` module provides the technical means for connecting the `MoCoCode` and the `MoCoModel` so they can cooperate, i.e., exchange data as well as mutually trigger the invocation of behavior.

Regarding its position between `MoCoCode` and `MoCoModel`, the `Mediator` module plays the role of (i) a potentially bidirectional *data synchronizer* (propagation of state information from code to models and vice-versa) and (ii) a *behavior provider* (provision of executable models for code and programmed methods for models). This is reflected by the internals of the `Mediator` and especially by its associated interfaces.

Moreover, the `Mediator` forwards any call to the exposed interfaces at the MoCo's ports to an implementation available in the `MoCoCode` or in the `MoCoModel`.

Interfaces. The connection between model and code within a MoCo is a critical part of the design w.r.t. performance and genericity. We propose an *extendable base set* of interfaces as a part of the MoCo template. In Table 1, each interface is listed and its purpose is described.

These internal interfaces are not visible to users of the component, but they need to be well-understood by software engineers that implement new MoCos or migrate existing code. They shall be seen as *types of interfaces*, so there may be multiple instances of each. We do not claim that this is a complete set (for any task or domain of applications), but we have gained a high level of confidence that these interfaces are truly useful during component design and at runtime, based on previous work and our conducted as well as ongoing feasibility studies.

Table 1. Overview of internal interfaces of the MoCo template

Interface	Description
IModelState	provides functionality for accessing the model in MoCoModel via an API or a dedicated model query/transformation language.
ICodeState	provides functionality for extracting information on the state of elements in MoCoCode as well as for editing it.
IInterpret	provides functionality to execute parts of a model in MoCoModel by traversing its abstract syntax representation.
IAction	provides handles to arbitrary (atomic) actions realized in MoCoCode.

4   Reference Implementation

Besides the required choice of (i) a *programming language*, the realization of MoCos requires (ii) a concrete *component model* and (iii) a solid *technological space* [19] for handling models.

For programming, we chose *Java* because it is widely known and provides a virtual machine for many different hardware and software environments. Additionally, Java supports multi-language development, i.e., different programming languages can be executed by its virtual machine. Well-known JVM languages are Closure, Groovy, Scala, JRuby and Jython as well as JavaScript. In fact, the modeling languages used in MoCos can be seen as a part of a multi-language approach, too, since model interpreters are also executed by the JVM.

For components, we chose *OSGi*'s [24] dynamic component model as it is the technological basis for mature plug-in environments such as the Eclipse IDE. It supports changes to components, i.e., bundles or (declarative) services, at runtime so MoCos can be loaded or replaced during operation, too. There are various implementations of the OSGi specification. We use *Apache Felix* [1].

For modeling, we chose our versatile modeling library *JGraLab* [3]. It provides a mature and efficient implementation of *TGraphs* [13], powerful query and transformation languages as well as many additional utilities in the form of a Java library. Models can be accessed and changed via an API that can be generated from their meta-models. Meta-models are expressed as UML class diagrams in the *IBM Rational Software Architect* [2] tool.

4.1   MoCo Core API

In this section, we give an overview of our current implementation of the *MoCo Core API* that supports developing components according to the MoCo template. In the following, we describe the structure and the rationale behind its internal architecture.

The *external structure* of a MoCo depends on the chosen component model. Hence, a clear mapping of a MoCo's wrapping and ports to the component model's elements is required. In our case, each MoCo is represented by an OSGi bundle. Ports are represented by packages that contain plain old Java interfaces, i.e., OSGi service declarations.

The *internal structure* of a MoCo is less dependent on the chosen component model and, thus, can be supported by our reusable implementation to maintain a similar structure across all MoCos. While modules are represented by packages, there is a set of basic types to realize their internals. An excerpt of these types is illustrated in Figure 3.

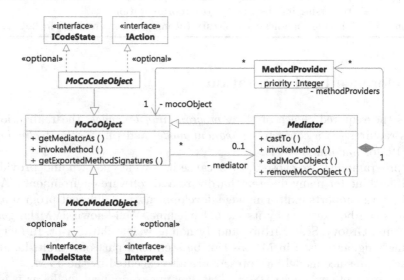

Fig. 3. Overview of the essential MoCo Core library classes

This implementation is centered around a base type called `MoCoObject`, in analogy to the `Object` base type in Java. This abstract class is the elementary type for representing *entry points* to constituents of all three modules of the MoCo template. More specifically, there is: (i) the `MoCoCodeObject` for representing parts of the `MoCoCode`, (ii) the `MoCoModelObject` for representing parts of the `MoCoModel` and (iii) the `Mediator` for representing the similarly named module. Additionally, the internal interfaces introduced in the MoCo template are available as a mix of Java interfaces and annotation types.

At its heart, the internals of each MoCo consist of a *network* of `MoCoObject` instances. `MoCoModelObjects` as well as `MoCoCodeObjects` register a defined subset of their methods with the central `Mediator`. This *component-specific mediator* can be fully generated from the set of interfaces available at a MoCo's ports by using a utility class offered by MoCo Core. It acts like a *proxy* to the actual realization of the component's interfaces that may be either programmed in code or by a mix of query/transform/interpret operations on a model. Each `MoCoModelObject` can access the actual model (here: the TGraph).

Users of the MoCo can consume a Java interface that is implemented by a mix of pure code and (executable) models without noticing any difference. A form of dynamic dispatching performed by the `Mediator` enables this *partial interface implementation* as follows:

When a MoCo's service – offered via a `PFunction` or `PManage` interface – is consumed, the call is delegated from the port to the `Mediator`. Based on the signature of the called interface method and an internal *resolution strategy* (e.g., based on priority, accuracy or expected performance), the `Mediator` identifies a suitable registered `MethodProvider` that encapsulates a handle to the actual realization provided by a `MoCoCodeObject` or `MoCoModelObject`. Finally, method invocation is done via Java reflection.

For communication between a `MoCoModelObject` and a `MoCoCodeObject`, the `Mediator` can be asked for a handle to an implementation of the required type.

5   Feasibility Study: Insurance Sales App

In order to *study the feasibility* of the introduced MoCo template and its reference implementation, we developed a fictional scenario of an insurance company that equips its field staff with an assistive *Insurance Sales App* (ISA) for the Android™ mobile platform. Although fictional, our selected scenarios are based on information collected in interviews at a German insurance company.

Fig. 4. Screenshot of ISA's insurance form on Android

We found this context to be suitable for the study, because it requires a flexible software solution. In the insurance domain, parts of the application logic such as the fee computations depend on frequently changing laws and other impact factors so the software needs to be *permanently evolved*. Moreover, different user roles (e.g., car or home insurance specialist) require *different variants* of ISA. In addition, parts of the fee calculations may even depend on geo-locations so the app needs to *adapt itself automatically* to support its users.

The primary goals to be achieved with this feasibility study were (i) to explore the feasibility of building software with MoCos (*practicality*), (ii) to gain realistic hands-on experience with the development workflow and design of MoCos (*implementation*) and (iii) to experience how to embed different (executable) modeling languages in MoCos (*genericity*).

5.1   ISA User Workflow

The typical *workflow* of an ISA user consists of the following steps:
1. The user starts ISA and is presented with a simple log-in screen, that is more of a user role picker consisting of two buttons for car and home insurance specialists respectively.

2. After picking a role, ISA shows a menu with a selection of three different insurance product calculation forms for the chosen domain.
3. Clicking an insurance product menu item opens a form with input fields for entering data such as customer age, yearly income, amount of children and a calculate button. The screenshot in Figure 4 shows this form.
4. Upon button click ISA calculates a monthly insurance product fee based on the entered data and displays it at the bottom of the form.

At any time, the user can log out again using an application menu entry. That function resets the state of the app and the log-in screen shows up again.

5.2   ISA Architecture

ISA has been implemented in a completely component-based manner. The *ISA architecture* is illustrated with a UML component diagram in Figure 5. Components can *provide* and *use* interfaces. A provided interface is illustrated as a "ball" with a direct connection to the realizing component. Usage of these interfaces is illustrated by dashed lines with an open arrow head. Stereotypes are used to mark simple components (<<component>>), conventional Android components (<<app>>) and MoCos (<<moco>>). Port interfaces of MoCos are marked with the <<pFunction>> or the <<pManage>> stereotype.

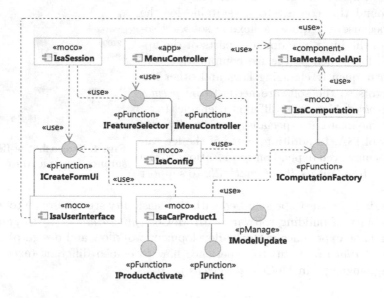

Fig. 5. Logical view of the ISA architecture with one active insurance product

The `IsaMetaModelApi` component provides an API for creating and editing models from the three modeling languages used throughout the app. This API is fully generated by JGraLab tools based on the meta-model diagram. One language represents *features* and trace links to implementing components, a second language encodes *graphical user interfaces* and a third one represents *insurance fee computation formulas*.

The host Android app starts the `IsaSession` MoCo which uses the `ICreate-FormUi` interface to display the role picker. This interface is realized by the `IsaUserInterface` MoCo which receives a GUI model as input. GUI models are encapsulated by product-specific MoCos such as `IsaCarProduct1`. `IsaUserInterface` traverses the GUI model and builds a corresponding Android view hierarchy that is immediately visible. The view hierarchy is kept in sync with the GUI model using an event system.

Upon user role selection, `IsaSession` selects the corresponding role feature through `IFeatureSelector`. This interface allows access to the feature configuration of ISA which is managed by the `IsaConfig` MoCo. Here, a feature configuration is a feature model [17] with a valid feature selection.

`IsaConfig` contains a model interpreter that can execute feature configurations to achieve architectural reconfiguration.[2] If the selected user role was changed, then `IsaConfig` updates the application's main menu by using the `IMenuController` interface to display a list of available insurance products for the selected role. The `MenuController` implements this functionality.

Otherwise, if an insurance product feature has been selected, `IsaConfig` determines the corresponding OSGi bundle that implements the product feature and activates it.[3] Deactivation of features and the stopping of associated OSGi bundles is done analogously. In this example, `IsaCarProduct1` is activated.

Example MoCo: IsaCarProduct1. To give a concrete example, the implementation structure of `IsaCarProduct1` MoCo is described subsequently.

- *Ports:* In the logical architecture shown in Figure 5, `IsaCarProduct1` uses the `ICreateFormUi` and `IComputationFactory`. In this specific Java-based implementation, the use of interfaces is realized by passing references to an `activate` method offered by `IProductActivate`. This interface belongs to the MoCo's `PFunction` port. `IReport` is another functionality-related interface that enables the printing of details about this specific product's insurance fee. In terms of management capabilities, this particular MoCo supports adapting its contained application model via the `IUpdateModel` interface.
- *Mediator Module:* In this example, the mediator simply receives calls to the MoCo's ports and delegates them to the registered internal `MoCoObject` instances that are located either in the `MoCoModel` or in the `MoCoCode` module.
- *MoCoCode Module:* The `EmailReportGenerator` is a `MoCoCodeObject` that can generate an email with details on the selected insurance product offer based on data stored in the MoCo's product model. This functionality is offered to users via `IPrint`. The `EmailReportGenerator` can use the mediator to access the embedded product model's state.

---

[2] ISA can be seen as a *Dynamic Software Product Line* (DSPL) [14].

[3] The details of OSGi bundle handling via Apache Felix are not visualized in Figure 5.

- *MoCoModel Module:* The `ProductActivator` is a `MoCoModelObject` that implements the `activate()` method offered by the MoCo's `IProductActivate` port interface. References to two model interpreters are passed to this initialization procedure: a computation model interpreter and a GUI model interpreter. References to both are stored and used internally.

This MoCo carries the `ProductModel`, which consists of two parts as illustrated in Figure 6: the `CarProduct1ComputationModel`[4] and the `CarProduct1-GuiModel`. Internally, both parts are represented by a single TGraph. This is possible, because both sub-models conform to the same *integrated meta-model*. There are links between GUI elements and computation variables in order to read user input from input fields (`loadInto`) or to output a computed result to a text view (`storeIn`). These links are used by the two model interpreters.

The embedded `ProductModelManager` controls access to the product model. Moreover, it facilitates adapting of the product's business logic and corresponding GUI representation with model transformations via `IModelUpdate`.

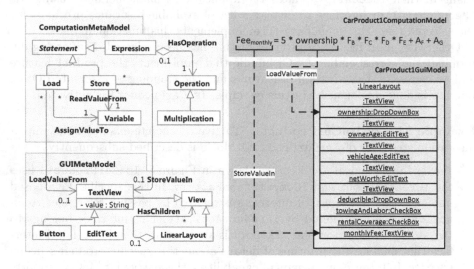

Fig. 6. Excerpt of integrated ISA meta-model and the compound product model in IsaCarProduct1 consisting of a fee formula and a GUI (here shown in concrete syntax)

5.3 Discussion

We are convinced that integrating models and code in the broader context of component technology is feasible and interesting. Choosing an adequate language and the fraction of the component to be modeled is a *creative task*. Based on

---

[4] Insurance fee calculations are simplified.

the expected need for adaptation at runtime or for technology independent representation of knowledge, component developers have the opportunity to embed their own *Domain-Specific Modeling Languages* (DSMLs).

MoCos can be consumed as usual but additional management functionality may be available at the PManage port to enable runtime adaptation via queries and transformations. Changes to a model in a MoCo have an immediate impact at runtime. In ISA for example, corrections to the insurance fee formula in IsaCarProduct1 can be made via the IModelUpdate interface.

In case that software is already being developed in a model-driven manner, some of these design-time models can be also used at runtime. For example, the IsaConfig MoCo introduced in Figure 5 carries a feature model that was developed to describe possible configurations of ISA at design time. This model can be used to determine the components needed for a certain ISA variant (tailoring), but it can be also used at runtime for architectural reconfiguration.

By designing the meta-models for each individual modeling language, software engineers are forced to introduce concepts and their relationships (also across meta-models) explicitly. The visual models enhance communication, too. In addition, a similar effect as in MDA can be observed. While models include the domain-specific knowledge (e.g., the basic GUI elements), a model interpreter encodes the technology-specific knowledge (e.g., about Android GUIs). When migrating a "model-only" MoCo to another platform, model interpreters may need to be replaced but the modeled application logic can be fully reused.

In the following, we revisit the initially stated issues.

- *Reducing redundancy:* At the artifact level, the MoCo concept reduces redundancy in the sense that it systematically embeds executable models into software components. For this subset of models, no code is generated. The models are directly executed by model interpreters. There is no redundancy unless it is introduced willfully. At runtime, patterns like architectural reflection and models@run.time are based on propagating values from code objects to a reification layer. Thereby, redundancy is introduced deliberately which requires a thorough construction of the "causal connection" between models and code. This is supported by the Mediator.

- *Achieving variability and adaptivity:* Since models are integrated parts of MoCos, runtime querying and transformation of models is supported. Thereby, self-adaptation is possible (e.g., using event-condition action rules) using the services of the technological modeling space. Tailoring of components is supported by similar operations: Models in MoCos can be edited within an editor and model transformations can be applied as a part of build scripts. That way, variants of a MoCo can be derived based on a variability model, for instance, to support software product line engineering. Adapting and tailoring are based on the same operations of the modeling technological space.

- *Avoiding inconsistencies between model and code:* MID builds on the ideas of MDD. Especially, when keeping the domain-logic in models and the platform-specific technical logic in code, the core ideas of MDD may still be used. Furthermore, the MoCoCode may be developed in a model-driven manner.

In this case, the handling of consistency between the models and the code derived from them (*vertical consistency*) does also not differ from MDD. Consistency between code and models inside a MoCo (*horizontal consistency*) must be handled by the development technique like in conventional consistency assurance between several code parts. But, consistency between several models inside one MoCo may potentially also be described explicitly using the technological modeling space's constraint description language.

In principle, the models of a MoCo may be also used to generate its Mo-CoCode. Here, the model may either be deleted after code generation (which we call *freezing* of the model) or it may be kept (which would be another example of the deliberate use of redundancy inside the MoCo). In the latter case, the demand for consistency of model and code is an instance of horizontal consistency, since both do coexist inside one component.

6   Conclusions and Future Work

In this paper, we motivate our perspective on why we believe that *Model-Integrating Development* (MID) based on *Model-Integrating Components* (Mo-Cos) is a desirable long-term goal. Based on a feasibility study, we conclude that – although no silver bullet – the envisioned direction is a reasonable *alternative way* to developing flexible software that provides promising opportunities.

There are some *threats to validity* related to our presented work. First, our impression that the presented approach is feasible is based on a *single study* with only a single component technology. Hence, we have not inspected all kinds of constellations of MoCos possible in the spectrum from code-only to model-only, yet. Experiences from our previous works with runtime models [5] hint at the validity of our assumption, though.

While not small, the *size of the study* is not "industrial scale". Especially the writing of queries, transformations and model interpreters will be more challenging, the more concepts and relationships a meta-model consists of. Therefore, software engineers need a check list that supports them with making the decision on what parts to model and what parts to program. We plan to establish such best practices in the context of software engineering processes.

An integrated development environment for MoCos is desirable to support software engineers. In addition, topics such as component hierarchies and ways to support software engineers with implementing model interpreters need to be discussed. Further case studies and a mature technological modeling space can prepare the MoCo concept for use in practice. During the two-years project "MoSAiC", we will cover these and further aspects comprehensively.

Acknowledgements. This ongoing work is supported by the Deutsche Forschungsgemeinschaft (DFG) under grants EB 119/11-1 and EN 184/6-1.

References

1. Apache Felix Homepage, `https://felix.apache.org/` (accessed May 3, 2014)
2. IBM Rational Software Architect Homepage, `http://www-03.ibm.com/software/products/en/ratisoftarch` (accessed July 8, 2014)
3. JGraLab Hompage, `http://jgralab.uni-koblenz.de` (accessed February 28, 2014)
4. Amoui, M.: Evolving Software Systems for Self-Adaptation. Ph.D. thesis, University of Waterloo, `http://uwspace.uwaterloo.ca/bitstream/10012/6643/1/AmouiKalareh_Mehdi.pdf` (accessed July 8, 2012)
5. Amoui, M., Derakhshanmanesh, M., Ebert, J., Tahvildari, L.: Achieving Dynamic Adaptation via Management and Interpretation of Runtime Models. Journal of Systems and Software 85(12), 2720–2737 (2012), `http://www.sciencedirect.com/science/article/pii/S0164121212001458`
6. Ballagny, C., Hameurlain, N., Barbier, F.: MOCAS: A State-Based Component Model for Self-Adaptation. In: 2009 Third IEEE International Conference on Self-Adaptive and Self-Organizing Systems, pp. 206–215 (September 2009)
7. Bencomo, N., France, R.B., Götz, S., Rumpe, B.: Summary of the 8th International Workshop on Models @ Run.time. In: MoDELS@Run.time (2013), `http://ceur-ws.org/Vol-1079/summary.pdf` (accessed July 8, 2014)
8. Blair, G., Bencomo, N., France, R.B.: Models@run.time. Computer 42(10), 22 27 (2009)
9. Brambilla, M., Cabot, J., Wimmer, M.: Model-Driven Software Engineering in Practice. Morgan & Claypool (2012), `http://www.mdse-book.com/`
10. Crnkovic, I., Sentilles, S., Vulgarakis, A., Chaudron, M.R.V.: A Classification Framework for Software Component Models. IEEE Transactions on Software Engineering 37(5), 593–615 (2011)
11. Derakhshanmanesh, M., Ebert, J., Engels, G.: Why Models and Code Should be Treated as Friends. Softwaretechnik-Trends (2014) Presented at MMSM – a satellite event of Modellierung 2014 (to appear, 2014), `http://akmda.ipd.kit.edu/fileadmin/user_upload/akmda/mmsm/MMSM2014-Proceedings.pdf`
12. E2E Technologies: White Paper: Direct Model Execution – The key to IT productivity and improving business performance (April 2008), `http://www.omg.org/news/whitepapers/2008-05-05_E2E_White_Paper_on_Direct_Model_Execution.pdf` (accessed July 9th, 2014)
13. Ebert, J., Riediger, V., Winter, A.: Graph Technology in Reverse Engineering, The TGraph Approach. In: Gimnich, R., Kaiser, U., Quante, J.,, W. (eds.) 10th Workshop Software Reengineering (WSR 2008), vol. 126, pp. 67–81. GI, Bonn (2008)
14. Hallsteinsen, S., Hinchey, M., Park, S., Schmid, K.: Dynamic Software Product Lines. Computer 41(4), 93–95 (2008)
15. Herrmann, C., Krahn, H., Rumpe, B., Schindler, M., Völkel, S.: Scaling-Up Model-Based-Development for Large Heterogeneous Systems with Compositional Modeling. In: Software Engineering Research and Practice, pp. 172–176 (2009)
16. Höfig, E.: Interpretation of Behaviour Models at Runtime - Performance Benchmark and Case Studies. Ph.D. thesis, Technical University of Berlin (2011), `http://opus.kobv.de/tuberlin/volltexte/2011/3065/pdf/hoefig_edzard.pdf` (accessed July 8, 2014)

17. Kang, K.C., Cohen, S.G., Hess, J.A., Novak, W.E., Peterson, A.S.: Feature-Oriented Domain Analysis (FODA) Feasibility Study. Tech. Rep. Software Engineering Institute, Carnegie Mellon University (November 1990), http://www.sei.cmu.edu/reports/90tr021.pdf (accessed July 8, 2014)
18. Kleppe, A., Bast, W., Warmer, J.B.: MDA Explained: The Model Driven Architecture: Practice and Promise. Addison-Wesley (2003)
19. Kurtev, I., Bézivin, J., Aksit, M.: Technological spaces: An initial appraisal. In: CoopIS, DOA'2002 Federated Conferences. Industrial track (2002)
20. Mellor, S.J., Balcer, M.: Executable UML: A Foundation for Model-Driven Architectures. Addison-Wesley Longman Publishing Co., Inc., Boston (2002)
21. Salehie, M., Tahvildari, L.: Self-Adaptive Software: Landscape and Research Challenges. ACM Trans. Auton. Adapt. Syst. 4(2), 14:1–14:42 (2009)
22. Stahl, T., Völter, M.: Model-Driven Software Development. Wiley (2006)
23. Szyperski, C., Gruntz, D., Murer, S.: Component Software - Beyond Object-Oriented Programming, 2nd edn. Addison-Wesley (2002)
24. The OSGi Alliance: OSGi Core Release 5. Tech. Rep. March, The OSGi Alliance (2012), http://www.osgi.org/Download/File?url=/download/r5/osgi.core-5.0.0.pdf (accessed July 8, 2014)
25. Tolvanen, J.P.: How to Integrate Models and Code (2012), http://www.infoq.com/articles/combining-model-and-code (accessed February 28, 2014)

Experiences in Applying Model Driven Engineering to the Telescope and Instrument Control System Domain

Luigi Andolfato, Robert Karban, Marcus Schilling, Heiko Sommer,
Michele Zamparelli, and Gianluca Chiozzi

European Southern Observatory, Karl-Schwarzschild-Str. 2, Garching bei München, Germany
{landolfa,rkarban,mschilli,hsommer,mzampare,gchiozzi}@eso.org

Abstract. The development of control systems for large telescopes is frequently challenged by the combination of research and industrial development processes, the bridging of astronomical and engineering domains, the long development and maintenance time-line, and the need to support multiple hardware and software platforms. This paper illustrates the application of a model driven engineering approach to mitigate some of these recurring issues. It describes the lessons learned from introducing a modeling language and creating model transformations for analysis, documentation, simulation, validation, and code generation.

Keywords: model driven engineering, telescope control systems, model transformation, model validation, code generation.

1 Introduction

1.1 The European Southern Observatory Programmes

The European Southern Observatory (ESO) is an intergovernmental astronomy organization that carries out ambitious programmes focused on the design, construction and operation of observing facilities. ESO has its headquarters in Garching bei München (Germany) and operates three observing sites in Chile: La Silla, Paranal, and Chajnantor. The two major programmes of ESO during the last 20 years were the Very Large Telescope (VLT) and the Atacama Large Millimeter Array (ALMA).

The VLT [16] is an optical-light astronomical observatory and consists of an array of four telescopes, each with a main mirror of 8.2m diameter, that can observe together or individually and four smaller (1.8m) telescopes dedicated to interferometry, making it the largest facility of its kind. The construction of the VLT started in 1988 and it has been fully operational at the Paranal Observatory since the year 1999.

ALMA [17] is a global partnership between the scientific communities of East Asia, Europe and North America with Chile. It comprises an array of 66 12-metre and 7-metre diameter antennas observing at millimeter and sub-millimeter wavelengths. Its construction started in 1998 and in early 2013 it was handed over to the science operations at the Chajnantor site.

J. Dingel et al. (Eds.): MODELS 2014, LNCS 8767, pp. 403–419, 2014.
© Springer International Publishing Switzerland 2014

1.2   Telescope and Instrument Control Systems

An astronomical observation consists of collecting electromagnetic radiation (such as visible light) emitted or reflected from a distant celestial target. Optical telescopes collect the light. Instruments create images analyzed for intensity, size, morphology, or spectral content. Telescope and instruments form a tightly coupled system [19].

Control systems for astronomical observing facilities execute observing blocks, defining celestial targets, necessary boundary conditions (e.g. required atmospheric conditions), and observing modes (e.g. quality of the wave front) to produce scientifically-relevant data. The Telescope Control System (TCS) main goal is to maintain wave front or radio signal quality throughout the duration of the observation. The Instrument Control System (ICS) is responsible for acquiring the scientific data using the TCS to receive the wave front. The TCS includes all hardware, software, and communication infrastructure required to control the telescope and the dome. It provides access to the opto-mechanical components, manages and coordinates system resources, and performs fault detection and recovery. Large observing facilities involve the control and coordination of distributed actuators and sensors, the real-time compensation of atmospheric turbulences, and the coordination of the safety functions to protect humans and the system itself from hazardous situations.

When building control systems for large science facilities, like telescopes, a number of challenges have to be faced. Telescopes and their instruments are interdisciplinary and software intensive systems with long operational life-times between 10 and 50 years. While two generations of telescopes are typically 15 years apart, introducing major technological changes, new instruments are introduced every year and are bound to the telescope's technology.

Although they are one-of-a-kind experimental machines with many components that had never been built before (e.g. nanometer accuracy position actuators, very low noise CCDs), they have to guarantee high dependability. For example the VLT requires maximum technical downtime of 3% during the observation time.

Most of the time, it is not possible to perform complete system tests before the deployment in the operational environment. This is due to different ambient and observing condition constraints and to the cost of integrating the full system which can be afforded only once. Therefore the architecture needs to build in the capability to cope with last minute changes such as modifications in the control system hierarchy, different combination of actuator and sensors, different interaction of distributed control loops.

Despite the fact that those systems are at some point handed over to science operations, they are never frozen but evolve over their lifetime. New scientific objectives may require additional functionalities, or hardware and software can become obsolete. The result is a telescope with subsystems and instruments running on different control SW releases or even different versions of hardware and software infrastructure. A key element of the software infrastructure is the software platform which is used to develop the control applications and includes operating systems, programming languages, communication middleware, IDEs, application frameworks, real-time database, logging, alarms, configuration and error handling services. The overview of the software platforms used for various ESO programmes is given in Table 1.

Table 1. Software platforms at ESO

Software Platform	Programme	OS	RTOS	Languages	Middle-ware
VLTSW	Very Large Telescope	Linux	VxWorks	C, C++, TCL/TK	Proprietary messaging system
ACS	Atacama Large Millimeter Array	Linux	Linux RT	C++, Java, Python	CORBA, DDS
SPARTA [34]	Very Large Telescope	Linux	VxWorks	C, C++, Java, TCL/TK	CORBA, DDS
Rapid Prototype	Any	JVM	N/A	Java	RabbitMQ [31]

2   Modeling Environment

2.1   Evolution of Modeling Environment

The first successful attempt[1] to apply model transformation to the development of telescope control software was the Local control unit Server Framework (LSF) tool. LSF was created in 2000 to help building the applications running on the real-time local control units providing access to HW. In order to build an LSF application, a configuration file containing information on the number and type of devices to control is processed by a Tcl script which produces the skeleton code of an application with call-backs for custom code to be completed by the developer. In addition, LSF provides a predefined state machine implementation where the developer can hook in code for predefined actions. An LSF application can be extended by adding more device definitions in the configuration files and reapplying the transformation. LSF has been extensively used for the development of the Auxiliary Telescopes Control Software (ATCS), Phase Reference Image and Micro-arcsecond Astrometry (PRIMA) control software, and the Active Phase Experiment (APE).

In 2004, inspired by LSF, a tool suite called Workstation Software Framework (WSF) was developed to generate soft real time supervisory applications [1]. WSF was initially created to build the supervisory applications of the PRIMA control software and later successfully adopted for the development of applications for many other projects of the Very Large Telescope program such as the Interferometric Supervisor Software configuration process, the Delay Lines rail-alignment tool, the APE project, and the New Generation CCD (NGC). In the beginning WSF applications were generated from a configuration file containing the textual description of their behavior in the form of a state machine. Later on, tools were developed to transform Rational ROSE and MagicDraw UML State Machine models into the text configuration file.

---

[1] Earlier, the use of Rhapsody code generation capabilities was investigated and considered too constraining because of the dependency on proprietary run-time libraries.

The modeling tools acted as a front end to facilitate the creation of Statecharts [10] since, with increasing complexity the maintenance of the text description became significantly more time-consuming. The applications generated by WSF were based on the State design pattern [11].

A development parallel to WSF was started in 2004 for the ALMA programme. The ALMA Project Data Model generator (APDMGen) generates, at the beginning only from XML schema and later also from UML class diagrams, the data classes representing the data model: complex data structures to describe science targets, calibrations, data quality requirements, or hardware configurations.

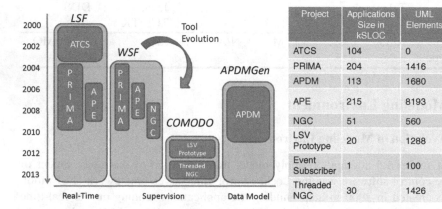

Project	Applications Size in kSLOC	UML Elements	FTE
ATCS	104	0	14
PRIMA	204	1416	14.4
APDM	113	1680	6
APE	215	8193	17.3 5
NGC	51	560	3
LSV Prototype	20	1288	0.4
Event Subscriber	1	100	0.1
Threaded NGC	30	1426	0.2

Fig. 1. The left panel shows the projects (blue boxes) developed using code generation tools (brown boxes) in the last 13 years (Y axis). The type of applications built is also reported (X axis). The right panel lists the projects and some information on size and cost: the second column provides the application size in kSLOC; the third column is the size of the input model in terms of UML Elements and their subclasses with the exception of profiles and libraries; the last column is the effort expressed as Full Time Equivalents (FTE), including application specific (meta-) modeling.

In 2009, based on the experience gained with WSF, a new project was started to create a platform independent transformation tool to develop state machine driven applications. Two new main requirements were introduced: the possibility to support multiple software platforms[2] like the control software for the Very Large Telescope (VLTSW) and the Alma Common Software (ACS), and the ability to interpret state machines. The first requirement focused on enabling model reusability across different platforms allowing the developers to create applications regardless of the target development and execution environment. The second requirement aimed at reducing the size of the generated applications by decoupling the application from the state machine execution engine and to provide the capability of changing the state machine logic at runtime allowing for fast last minute changes. The project delivered a toolkit, called COMODO [2], which has been used to develop the Telescope Control Local

---

[2]   Note that LSF and WSF tools are specific to the VLT platform and APDMGen works only for the ACS platform.

Supervisor (LSV) prototype running on a rapid prototyping software platform based on Java and RabbitMQ [31], to redevelop a new multi-threaded version of the NGC for the VLTSW platform, and to create the Event Subscriber application for the ACS platform. **Fig. 1** summarizes the evolution of the code generation tools at ESO and provides an idea on the size and cost of the projects.

In order to maximize the return on investment of modeling, more applications of model transformations were explored in addition to the ones targeted on the final production code. For example model simulation was used to get an early feedback on the logical correctness of the model especially in the context of collaborating state machines. Initially simulation was applied in order to understand some principles of State Analysis methodology [15] and later on to verify the behavior of telescope control architecture. However, it became quickly clear that proper model validation could be better achieved using a model checking approach. Therefore COMODO was extended to support a transformation to the Java Pathfinder model checker to be able to formally validate state machine models [6]. This transformation was applied to validate the control software design of the PRIMA Variable Curvature Mirror and, in collaboration with NASA/JPL, to verify part of the Soil Moisture Active Passive fault protections system [21].

To guarantee consistency between models and documentation some effort was spent in 1999 to implement a "one document" approach [36] where HTML and Word documents were produced using Telelogic DocExpress from Rational ROSE models. Unfortunately the transformation framework offered insufficient control over the generated artifacts and therefore this approach was used only in the ATCS project. Ten years later a plug-in for MagicDraw, the Model Based Document Generator [18][24], was developed in-house with ownership over the transformation allowing full compliance with ESO documentation templates.

Finally, the recent Conceptual Modeling Framework (CMF) initiative aims at enforcing model correctness using ontologies to capture more formally business rules.

2.2   Current Status

The modeling environment currently in use is based on the following elements.

UML™ / SysML™ modeling languages and MagicDraw®. MagicDraw [29] is a commercially available software and system modeling tool with teamwork support. It supports UML 2 [27] and, via plug-in mechanism, SysML [28]. The Cameo Simulation Toolkit® [30] is a plug-in for MagicDraw which provides an extendable model execution framework based on OMG fUML [35] and W3C SCXML [4] standards.

Conceptual Modeling Ontology. The Conceptual Modeling Ontology (CMO) is an ontology language similar to OWL2 [33] introduced, in form of UML Profile, to permit the expression of business specific concepts and relationships recurring across all our models. It has been developed by ESO based on work done by NASA/JPL [23] and some experiences in defining DSLs using SysML [24]. CMO is also used to express the mapping between the ontology and the UML meta-model elements. Various layers of interdependent ontologies are supported.

Conceptual Modeling Framework. The Conceptual Modeling Framework (CMF) is an approach, under development at ESO, for turning UML into a domain specific modeling language. It transforms ontologies written in CMO into UML profiles, the associated validation rules and custom diagram editors. The generated validation rules are used by MagicDraw's validation engine which can run on-demand or can constantly check the model in the background while it is being edited. MagicDraw customization features are used to adjust the diagram editor to only offer certain element types to the modelers according to the specified ontology.

Model Based Document Generator. The Model Based Document Generator (MBDG [18][24]) is a profile and a plug-in for MagicDraw developed by ESO to be able to write documents as SysML models and to transform them into DocBook [25] XML files. Since documents and system models coexist within the same modeling environment, duplication of information is avoided and consistency is automatically maintained. The generated DocBook files can be converted into different document formats such as PDF.

APDMGen. The ALMA Project Data Model generator is a toolkit, developed by ALMA and based on openArchitectureWare [22], to transform UML class diagrams into XML schemas and Java data classes.

Java Pathfinder model checker. Java Pathfinder (JPF) [32] is a system to verify executable Java byte code programs. JPF was developed at the NASA Ames Research Center and open sourced in 2005. It provides an extension, called jpf-statechart [6], used to execute and systematically verify Statecharts models.

SCXML Engine. The SCXML engine is required to interpret the SCXML documents that describe applications behavior. For Java applications, the Apache Commons SCXML [5] is used, while for C++ the scxml4cpp library has been developed by ESO. The Apache Commons SCXML is also used by Cameo Simulation Toolkit.

COMODO Ontology and Profile. The COMODO ontology, based on CMO, captures the concepts and relations required to describe the structure and behavior of component based distributed systems. The COMODO profile is the UML representation of the COMODO ontology [3]. COMODO ontology and profile have been developed by ESO to be used by the COMODO Toolkit.

COMODO Toolkit. COMODO Toolkit transforms UML models, based on the COMODO profile, into different artifacts depending on the target platform.

In addition to the VLTSW, ACS, and Rapid Prototype software platforms, it supports plain Java, and Java Pathfinder model checker by generating Java code compliant with jpf-statechart[3]. A summary of the artifacts and activities involved in a COMODO transformation is given in **Fig. 2**. For all target platforms, the input model, together with some configuration information such as the part of the model to transform and the target platform itself, is transformed by COMODO into:

- One or more application skeletons.
- One SCXML document compliant with the StateChartsXML notation defined by the W3C [4] for each UML State Machine[4]. The mapping between UML and SCXML has been defined in [2].
- Test code.
- Build files (ant or makefile).

The generated artifacts together with the developer's implementation of the actions and do-activities are compiled and linked with platform specific libraries such as the SCXML engine (Apache Commons SCXML library [5] or scxml4cpp library).

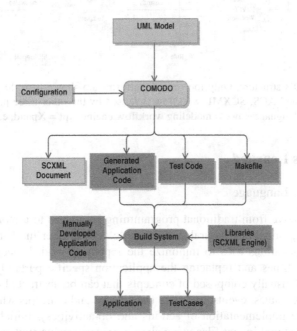

Fig. 2. COMODO data flow: in dark gray the platform dependent artifacts and activities; in light gray the platform independent ones

---

[3] By inserting manually assertions in entry/exit/transition actions it is possible to verify properties of the system.

[4] For the Java Pathfinder Statecharts platform the SCXML document is not used.

COMODO is composed of a java front-end processing the input parameters and triggering the execution of the modeling workflow (EMF MWE [12]) specific to the target platform, a set of Check model validation rules applied to the UML model, a set of Xpand [13] templates organized by target platform (VLTSW, ACS, etc.) and target language (C++, Java, XML, text, etc.), and a library of Xtend functions to navigate the model (**Fig. 3**)[5].

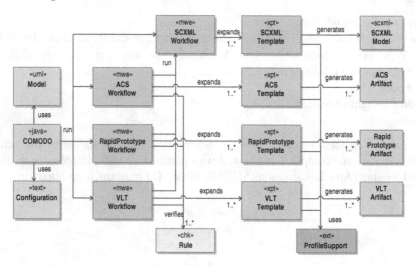

Fig. 3. COMODO's structure. Only four target platforms are shown here: SCXML, VLTSW, Rapid-Prototype, and ACS. SCXML workflow is reused by the other three platforms. Stereotypes indicate the language: mwe = modeling workflow engine, xpt = Xpand, ext = Xtend.

3   Lessons Learned

3.1   Modeling Language

The process to move from traditional programming languages to a more abstract language has been gradual and natural. For example, a developer in charge of building ten or more applications tries to minimize the repetitive work by copying the first application nine times and replacing the application specific parts. The application specific parts are usually composed of concepts that can be abstracted using a modeling language (like states, events, and state transitions) and concepts which are hard to abstract (like the implementation of actions and do-activities). Initially the abstract information was stored in text files using simple property-value syntax or using XML schemas. However for large models we quickly felt the need to use a graphical notation to group parts of the model and emphasize certain view points. In addition, models based on topological concepts (e.g. Statecharts) are easier to appreciate using

---

5   MWE, Check, Xpand, and Xtend were part openArchitectureWare toolkit [22] and are now included in the Eclipse Modeling project [14].

visual formalism than text [20][7]. Therefore WSF, APDMGen, and COMODO tools provide the ability to process models created with graphical UML modeling tools. Unfortunately UML and related tools are not as simple and fast to make small changes as a text language and a text editor. They require some skills which can be easily forgotten if the tools are used only once or twice per year (as it may be the case during the software maintenance phase). Two opposite needs have been observed:

- During development, when models have to be frequently changed, reviewed and discussed, the graphical representation of models containing topological information is very important since it is easier to understand and more compact.
- During maintenance, the software has to be modified few times per year. The maintenance engineers are infrequent users of our graphical tooling. They feel they can apply small changes to the model much more quickly in a text editor.

At the moment, we support both textual (SCXML, XML schemas) and graphical representation (UML Class diagrams and State Machine models) as successfully adopted in WSF in the past. In order to avoid diverging of the two representations, changes to the textual one must be recorded and ported back to the graphical one. The lesson learned is that we need to restrict and customize the user interface of the modelling tool to provide only a subset of UML specialized on Statecharts and composite structures.

3.2   Obsolescence Management of Tool Chain

Due to the long development and operational life time, the obsolescence of a third-party tool chain and the associated competence is a major concern. A number of risks have been identified, in particular for modeling and model transformations activities. They are related to the unavailability and/or change of:

- UML/SysML modeling tool (MagicDraw and plug-ins)
- UML profile and meta-model (EMF UML2)
- transformation languages (Xpand, Xtend) and modeling frameworks (EMF)
- competent people

The first UML tool integrated with WSF has been RationalROSE by Rational (now IBM). Later on MagicDraw became our standard UML tool. The porting of the models from RationalROSE to MagicDraw was done manually since the automatic export/import procedures to XMI did not work, since UML meta-models were different. Despite the Model Interchange Working Group effort [37][6], still today it is a challenge to port models between different UML commercial tools. This is definitely a problem since large telescopes have more than 20 years life time and we cannot afford to rely only on a single tool vendor or to manually port large models. At the

---

[6]   The test case examples proposed are trivial and cover only a subset of UML. For example, in the State Machine examples history states, internal transitions, nested orthogonal regions, and different types of triggers and behaviors are not covered.

moment, in order to avoid vendor lock in, COMODO supports UML models in the EMF UML2 XMI format.

Changes in the meta-model bear the risk of corrupting existing models because sometimes the migration path from one version to another is not well defined. In particular when meta-model elements disappear, as it happened from UML 2.3 to 2.4 where the ExecutionEvent event type became obsolete causing potential data loss (avoided by developing an ad-hoc M2M transformation).

An intermediate vendor independent representation of the model (e.g. EMF XMI and SCXML) is used to mitigate the risks associated to the modeling tools and UML. Transformation languages and modeling frameworks were selected among the ones with larger user base, open source, and most compliant with standards. Concerning the competences, a small team with modeling and model transformation know how was established. The team is in charge of providing modeling support to the projects and customizes the transformations.

3.3   Transformation Ownership

A key point in the successful adoption of MDE is the ability to customize the transformations to have full control over the generated artifacts [8]. This allows:

- generating code conforming to project standards, guidelines and platforms
- producing documentation using the organization's templates
- supporting changes to the meta-model
- managing problems downstream the tool chain such as new versions (or deficiencies) of libraries and compilers

3.4   Platform Independent Modeling

During the creation of COMODO, the definition of the ontology has been the most time-consuming activity. We believe that this is a general issue since the ontology definition is an iterative process involving domain specialists capturing the necessary semantics to enable an efficient and correct transformation. The ontology had to be adapted many times before a stable compromise between formality and practicability could be found. The UML profile resulting from the ontology is platform independent and is designed to be used for all ESO target platforms[7]. Platform specific information, when needed, is provided directly to the model-to-text transformation tool via command line arguments or a configuration file. This approach intentionally avoids the Platform Independent Model (PIM) to Platform Specific Model (PSM) model-to-model transformation, suggested in [26], since this introduces not negligible development and maintenance costs, especially when dealing with UML as target meta-model. For example, the type of target platform is given as a configuration parameter to the tool and does not appear in the model.

---

[7] Features appearing in the meta-model and semantically irrelevant for a specific target platform are ignored by the transformation tool.

3.5   Modeling vs. Coding

An important lesson learned from WSF development relates to the amount of generated code. Even though model-to-text transformations take usually an insignificant amount of time, the compilation of the generated code can be time-consuming. Therefore it is important to be able to transform only part of the model: in this way we avoid rebuilding the whole system at each modification. Moreover, preference should be given to the usage of configurable libraries instead of code generation. For example, control applications created with WSF are based on the State Design pattern which requires the generation of one C++ class per state while applications created by COMODO use a state machine engine library able to execute SCXML documents. In the latter case only the SCXML description of the state machine has to be generated. In general our transformations are targeted for "rich" software platforms: platforms which include all common services required by the applications (such as logging, messaging, error and alarm handling, configuration management, etc) and do not need to be generated.

3.6   Semantic Consistency

There are different flavors of Statecharts semantic [9] and to avoid inconsistency it is important to stick to one across the tool chain. For example, UML does not specify any language construct to query at run-time the current Statechart configuration ("inState()" or "In()" as defined in [10]). In SCXML the active Statechart configuration is updated after invoking the exit actions and before invoking the entry actions. We chose SCXML's over alternative implementations for the following reasons:

- It provides well defined syntax and operational semantic as pseudo-code
- The relevant features of UML State Machines can be easily mapped to SCXML
- The same engine is used for model simulation, production code, and prototyping

Unfortunately the validation step, currently based on jpf-statecharts, is not following the SCXML semantics.

3.7   Archive Generated Artifacts

Despite the risk of using outdated artifacts, we keep under version control generated code in addition to the models for the following reasons:

- To have quick access to the generated artifacts (e.g. for urgent modifications in an operational environment) and speed-up the build process.
- To verify that models are equivalent by comparing the generated artifacts.

The second point is very important since it avoids having to repeat system tests when models have to be ported to new tools or to evaluate the impact of changes in the meta-model.

We also learned that, when using commercial tools, any floating license server application should be subject to the same version control procedures as the rest of the tool chain. Failing to do so prevented us from running legacy versions of the tool.

3.8   Model Correctness

Due to complexity, sometimes weak semantics and general purpose of UML/SysML it is necessary to customize it and guide the modeler with standardized patterns and conventions. The compliance of the user model with the defined rules can be verified in various ways (e.g. offline analysis). However, we have observed that one effective way is giving the modeler immediate feedback during the modeling activity to create upfront a model which is correct by construction. This can be achieved by reducing the number of choices that modelers can make, prescribe certain modeling patterns, and come up with concise semantics. CMO and CMF are conceived for this purpose. CMO, following the recommendations given in [23], focuses on conveying in UML syntax the logical organization of a conceptual ontology whose essential constituents are unary concepts and reified binary relationships. This approach has the advantage that the ontology and the user model can be modeled with a single tool and the same language (UML/SysML). It has been used to define a number of reusable ontologies: foundational ontologies (Interface Ontology, Structural Ontology), engineering oriented ontologies (Protocol Ontology, Connector Ontology), telescope oriented ontologies (Telescope Instrument Ontology).

3.9   Roundtrip and Annotated Code

From the beginning we avoided round-trip transformations since transforming back the code and merging it into the model is considered too expensive to implement and maintain. Instead, a clear separation of generated code from manually crafted code is preferred. Generated code is stored in dedicated files which can be referenced using delegation or inheritance mechanisms.

Moreover, we observed that is not efficient to model the behavior of actions and activities because it requires the same time (in the best case, since code editing capabilities within the modeling tool cannot compete with a conventional IDE) as writing the target code and introduces additional transformation from UML or platform independent action languages (e.g. ALF) to the target code. If the model is annotated with target code then the model-to-text transformation has to be executed every time the model or the annotated code is modified. In addition the model is not platform independent anymore[8].

---

[8]   In the executable models or model simulation scenario the annotated code is usually a simplification of the final production code. A mapping of simulation code to final production code can be quite challenging.

3.10   Reusable Modeling

Solutions to recurring problems of control application can be extracted in the form of a set of modeling patterns documented and collected in a catalog similarly to Design Patterns. Some examples of state machine modeling patterns are described in [1].

For particular domain specific classes of applications, the whole model is used as a template to be copied and pasted. Certain elements of the model are parameters (e.g. events or actions in state machines) that can be replaced with concrete arguments.

3.11   Cost / Benefit Analysis of Model Transformations

ESO's primary goal is the delivery of telescopes and instruments and not the development of modeling tools. It is therefore important to constantly compare the effort of abstracting information and transforming it into specialized artifacts with the cost of creating the specialized artifacts manually.

Given a generic SW application, it is always possible to find an abstraction of the application, called model, and define its source code as composed of two parts: one that is model dependent (MD) and one that is model independent (MI). A very simple abstraction is, for example, a function name: the model is simply the name of the function. Using this abstraction the function's source code can be separated into two parts: the name of the function (model dependent because it is generated) and the body of the function (model independent because it is hand crafted) without the name of the function.

If TAPPL is the total effort, measured for example in Full Time Equivalent (FTE), spent to develop an application, then:

$$TAPPL = TMI + TMD \tag{1}$$

where:

- TMI = is the average effort spent to develop by hand the model independent part of an application
- TMD = is the average effort spent to develop by hand the model dependent part of an application

A model-to-text transformation requires:

- the definition of a source meta-model (TMMDEF)
- the ability to navigate models based on the source meta-model (TMMNAV)
- the creation of the templates required to generate the target artifacts (TTPL)[9]
- the creation of the model to transform (TM)

Therefore the effort[10] to build N applications using model to text transformation is:

$$TAPPL = TMMDEF + TMMNAV + TTPL + N * (TMI + TM) \tag{2}$$

---

[9] TTPL includes also the development of libraries used by the templates.
[10] The effort to apply the transformation is considered to be negligible.

The efficiency of developing an application using model to text transformation with respect to developing the application by hand requires the comparison the cost of the two approaches:

$$TMMDEF + TMMNAV + TTPL + N * (TMI + TM) \leq N * (TMI + TMD)$$

$$(TMMDEF + TMMNAV + TTPL) + N * TM \leq N * TMD \qquad (3)$$

The model transformation approach is more efficient if:

$$(TM \leq TMD) \text{ and } (N \text{ is big enough})$$

N has to be big enough so that the fixed cost for the creation of the meta-model (TMMDEF), the development of the tool to navigate the meta-model (TMMNAV) and the templates (TTPL) is absorbed by the difference between writing by hand the model dependent code and creating the model. The model transformation approach tends to be more efficient with simple meta-models easy to navigate and that allow the creation of compact models. Note that, for projects within the same organization, ambiguities in the effort measurement can affect in the same way both terms of eq. 3.

For example, the NGC project, composed of five applications based on WSF, required about 3 FTEs to implement the same functionalities of a similar project (FIERA) which took about 6.9 FTEs. Both projects were done by roughly the same team. The average effort for the NGC model independent part of an application (TMI) equals the total effort minus the effort to build its model; i.e. $(3 - 0.1*5) / 5 = 0.5$. The average effort for the NGC model dependent part of an application (TMD) equals the effort to build FIERA minus the model dependent part; i.e. $(6.9/5 - 0.5) = 0.88$. WSF development required for the definition of the meta-model (TMMDEF) about 0.02 FTE and for the development of the parser (TMMNAV) 0.76 FTE. The definition of the templates (TTPL) took 1.76 FTE. Using the simple linear model the breakeven point is reached at $N=3.3$ so that for every further application we save 0.78 FTEs.

In case of K transformations (3) becomes:

$$(TMMDEF + TMMNAV + \sum TTPL_i) + N * TM \leq N * \sum TMD_i, i = [1 .. K]$$

And therefore:

$$(TM \leq \sum TMD_i) \text{ and } (N \text{ is big enough})$$

This is similar to (3) except that the sum of the effort to develop the templates for various transformations has to be taken into account.

Note that with modern transformation languages like Xpand, writing templates is, in our opinion, very similar to writing normal code. However the assumption TTPL = TMD cannot be made since TTPL includes some of the effort of generalizing MD.

The maintenance activities like adding new features, fixing bugs, or porting to a newer (version of the) SW platform, can affect the model independent part of the application or the model dependent part. In the former case the cost is the same for both approaches. In the latter case the modification may have to be applied to the meta-model, the templates, or the models. Changes to the meta-model are the most expensive since they can imply modifications of the models, templates and/or the tool to navigate the model. Changes to the templates are more efficient by a factor N-1 (where N is number of applications) with respect to the traditional approach. Changes to the models are in general more efficient since the level of abstraction is higher and dependencies (i.e. side-effects introduced by the change) are more evident.

4   Conclusions

In this paper we have presented our experiences in moving from document and code centric development to a process driven by models. The main focus is on behavioral models because they have turned out to be most beneficial for the telescope and instrument software. The model as a single source of information allows having consistency across different transformed artifacts such as code, documentation, simulation, and analysis. Automatic transformations simplify for a wider audience of engineers the usage of specialized tools without requiring expert skills. In addition models are easier to analyze by model checkers than the final target code, thanks to the higher level of abstraction and reduced computational complexity. However we observed that not everything is worth modeling. Therefore we defined a key performance indicator (as a function of the model dependent and the model independent code) to constantly measure the effort introduced by abstracting information and compare it with the effort required by the traditional development practices.

Large Telescope Control Systems have long operational life-time and are evolving continuously. New scientific instruments are constantly introduced and the obsolete components of HW and SW platforms have to be replaced. The ability of transforming domain specific models into new or upgraded target SW platforms by simply updating templates introduces significant advantages. In contrast to the traditional SW development approach, changes can be propagated across a number of existing applications in a systematic and well defined way. The same type of flexibility is also beneficial when dealing with the last minute changes required during the on-site integration and deployment.

Two major problems have been encountered when applying a model driven development process: the possible lack of semantic integrity and consistency among the produced artifacts, and the shortage of modeling competences during the maintenance activities. The former applies to domain specific ontologies that are mapped to standard modeling languages, and to the structural and behavioral models that are used as a source for simulation, validation and code generation. The latter concerns the ability to maintain generated code in a highly dependable system like a telescope without modeling skills.

Acknowledgments. The authors would like to thank N. Rouquette, S. Jenkins, A. Kerzhner from NASA/JPL for the discussions on the ontological modeling, N. Jankevicius from NoMagic for the collaboration on the Simulation Toolkit, and C. Cumani and A. Balestra for providing the effort measurements on NGC and FIERA projects.

References

1. Andolfato, L., Karban, R.: Workstation Software Framework. In: Proceedings of the Society of Photo-Optical Instrumentation Engineers, vol. 7019, pp. 70191X-1 (2008)
2. Andolfato, L., Chiozzi, G., Migliorini, N., Morales, C.: A platform independent framework for statecharts code generation. In: Proceedings of the 13th International Conference on Accelerator and Large Experimental Physics Control Systems (2011)
3. Chiozzi, G., Andolfato, L., Karban, R., Tejeda, A.: A UML profile for code generation of component based distributed systems. In: Proceedings of the 13th International Conference on Accelerator and Large Experimental Physics Control Systems (2011)
4. World Wide Web Consortium: State Chart XML (SCXML) Working Draft Published (December 6, 2012)
5. Apache Commons SCXML, http://commons.apache.org/proper/commons-scxml
6. Mehlitz, P.: Trust Your Model - Verifying Aerospace System Models with Java Pathfinder. In: Proc. IEEE Aerospace Conf. 2008, Big Sky, MT, March 1-8 (2008)
7. Harel, D.: Statecharts in the Making: A Personal Account. Communications of the ACM 52(03), 6 (2009)
8. Wagstaff, K.L., Benowitz, E., Byrne, D.J., Peters, K., Watney, G.: Automatic code generation for instrument flight software. In: Proceedings of the 9th International Symposium on Artificial Intelligence, Robotics, and Automation in Space (2008)
9. Crane, M.L., Dingel, J.: UML vs. Classical vs. Rhapsody statecharts: Not all models are created equal. Software and Systems Modelling 6(4) (2007)
10. Harel, D.: Statecharts: A visual formalism for complex systems. Science of Computer Programming 8(3), 231–274 (1987)
11. Gamma, E., Helm, R., Johnson, R., Vlissides, J.: Design Patterns: Elements of Reusable Object-Oriented Software, pp. 305–313. Addison-Wesley (2002)
12. Eclipse Modeling Framework: Modeling Workflow Engine, https://projects.eclipse.org/projects/modeling.emf.mwe
13. Klatt, B.: Xpand: A Closer Look at the model2text Transformation Language. In: 12th European Conference on Software Maintenance and Reengineering (2008)
14. Eclipse Modeling Project, http://www.eclipse.org/modeling
15. Ingham, M.D., Rasmussen, R.D., Bennett, M.B., Moncada, A.C.: Engineering Complex Embedded Systems with State Analysis and the Mission Data System. AIAA Journal of Areospace Computing Information and Communication 2(12) (2005)
16. Wirenstrand, K.: VLT telescope control software: status, development, and lessons learned. In: Proc. SPIE 2003, vol. 4837, p. 965 (2003)
17. Casasola, V., Brand, J.: The exciting future of (sub-)millimeter interferometry: ALMA. In: Proceedings of the 54th National Meeting of the Italian Astronomical Society (2010)
18. Model Based Document Generator, http://sourceforge.net/projects/mbse4md/?source=directory
19. Bely, P.Y.: The design and construction of large optical telescopes. Springer (2003)
20. Harel, D.: On visual formalism. Communications of the ACM 31(5) (1988)
21. Gibson, C., Karban, R., Andolfato, L., Day, J.: Formal Validation of Fault Management Design Solutions. Presented at the Java Pathfinder Workshop 2013 (2013)
22. Haase, A., Voelter, M., Efftinge, S., Kolb, B.: Introduction to openArchitectureWare 4.1.2. In: Model-Driven Development Tool Implementers Forum (MDD-TIF 2007) (co-located with TOOLS 2007) (2007)

23. Jenkins, J., Rouquette, N.: Semantically Rigorous Systems Engineering Using SysML and OWL. In: 5th International Workshop on Systems & Concurrent Engineering for Space Applications (2012)
24. Karban, R., Zamparelli, M., Bauvier, B., Chiozzi, G.: Three years of MBSE for a large scientific programme: Report from the Trenches of Telescope Modelling. In: Proceeding 22nd Annual INCOSE International Symposium (2012)
25. Walsh, N.: DocBook 5: The Definitive Guide. O'Reilly Media (April 2010)
26. Frankel, D.: Model Driven Architecture – Applying MDA to Enterprise Computing, p. 191. OMG Press (2003)
27. Unified Modeling Language (UML), http://www.omg.org/spec/UML
28. System Modeling Language (SysML), http://www.omgsysml.org
29. MagicDraw, http://www.nomagic.com/products/magicdraw.html
30. Cameo Simulation Toolkit, http://www.nomagic.com/products/magicdraw-addons/cameo-simulation-toolkit.html
31. RabbitMQ, http://www.rabbitmq.com
32. Java Pathfinder, http://babelfish.arc.nasa.gov/trac/jpf
33. OWL 2 Web Ontology Language, http://www.w3.org/TR/owl2-overview
34. Fedrigo, E., Donaldson, R.: SPARTA: The ESO standard platform for adaptive optics real time applications. In: Proc. SPIE, vol. 6272 (2006)
35. Semantics of A Foundational Subset for Executable UML models (FUML), http://www.omg.org/spec/FUML
36. Chiozzi, G., Duhoux, P., Karban, R.: VLTI Auxiliary telescopes: A full Object Oriented approach. In: Proc. SPIE 2000, vol. 4009-03, p. 5 (2000)
37. Model Interchange Working Group (MIWG), http://www.omgwiki.org/model-interchange/doku.php

Model Driven Grant Proposal Engineering

Dimitrios S. Kolovos, Nicholas Matragkas,
James R. Williams, and Richard F. Paige

Department of Computer Science, University of York,
Deramore Lane, York, YO10 5GH, UK
{dimitris.kolovos,nicholas.matragkas,
james.r.williams,richard.paige}@york.ac.uk

Abstract. We demonstrate the application of Model Driven Engineering techniques to support the development of research grant proposals. In particular, we report on using model-to-text transformation and model validation to enhance productivity and consistency in research proposal writing, and present unanticipated opportunities that were revealed after establishing an MDE infrastructure. We discuss the types of models and the technologies used, reflect on our experiences, and assess the productivity benefits of our MDE solution through automated analysis of data extracted from the version control repository of a successful grant proposal; our evaluation indicates that the use of MDE techniques improved productivity by at least 58%.

1   Introduction

The majority of experience reports in the field of Model Driven Engineering come from adopters in the software development industry and typically involve modelling and generating software. Here, we report on the use of Model Driven Engineering techniques in the context of research grant proposal development. Proposing and running collaborative research projects is one of the main activities undertaken by academics, and in our experience, existing tooling and processes for supporting some steps of this activity are sub-optimal. In this paper, we describe how we used MDE techniques to automate some of the laborious and error-prone steps of this activity, and report on the delivered productivity benefits, which we have measured through automated analysis of data from the version control repository of a successful proposal.

The rest of the paper is organised as follows. In Section 2, we outline the process of developing grant proposals and highlight its laborious and error-prone steps. In Section 3 we present how we applied Model Driven Engineering techniques to automate these steps, and discuss some key decisions we had to make along the way, and in Section 4 we present some measurements that demonstrate the obtained productivity improvements, and reflect on our experiences. In Section 5 we discuss related work and in Section 6 we conclude the paper.

J. Dingel et al. (Eds.): MODELS 2014, LNCS 8767, pp. 420–432, 2014.

2   Background

Often, a research project commences with the formation of a consortium comprising several academic and industrial partners, and is followed by the collaborative development of a grant proposal that outlines the objectives, technical organisation, and management of the project. In particular, the technical work needs to be decomposed into a number of work packages consisting of specific tasks and deliverables. Multiple partners can contribute to each work package and each partner can lead on the preparation and production of multiple deliverables.

Typically, proposal documents need to adhere to a template provided by the funding body, which prescribes their structure and formatting. Often, such templates require different views of the same information that appears in multiple places in the proposal (e.g. effort per work package, effort per partner, deliverables per work package, project deliverables ordered by delivery date). As a result, consistency of the proposal is an issue: if, for example, the effort associated with producing all of the deliverables in a project does not match the effort allocated to all partners in the project, there is a consistency problem (and such problems may be reflected in the proposal's review scores). To make matters worse, the information that could lead to inconsistencies in the proposal may change frequently during the core stages of development (e.g. the effort allocated to a partner for a particular work package may change several times during negotiations, or the deadline for a deliverable may be modified several times). Changes to this kind of information may require some substantial effort to implement in the proposal. For example, updating the due date of a deliverable in a proposal under the European Commission's 7th Framework Programme[1] template, requires updates in two separate tables (deliverables by chronological order, project Gantt chart), and in the section of the proposal that describes the deliverable itself. Similarly, modifying the effort of a partner in a work package requires updates in two different tables (effort per partner, effort for work package). In our experience, this information will change many times during the life-cycle of the proposal, and maintaining these views in a consistent state manually is both tedious and error-prone.

3   Model Driven Grant Proposal Engineering

In the spirit of MDE – that is, in the spirit of automating repetitive and error-prone tasks through the use of models and automated model processing – and in order to reduce the accidental complexity involved in developing grant proposals, we decided to use MDE techniques to automatically generate different views (tables, graphs, Gantt charts) of core proposal information. The generation process would be based on an abstract model of important information, and as a result the different views would be guaranteed to be consistent by construction.

---

[1] http://cordis.europa.eu/fp7/home_en.html

In this section we discuss our operating context, the approach we followed, and the challenges and opportunities we encountered along the way.

3.1 Context

We focus on the process of developing proposals for EC-funded, ICT[2]-focused, collaborative, targeted research projects (STREP), however, developing proposals for other types of collaborative projects and research funding bodies should not be too dissimilar. Such proposals typically take between 3-6 months to prepare and involve 6-9 partner organisations from academia and industry, each participating with at least one representative in the proposal development phase. Proposals themselves range from 70-120 pages in length, and include technical, management and financial sections; technical and financial sections are most likely to change frequently during proposal development, whereas management sections tend to be reasonably stable. Partner representatives involved in the preparation of such projects typically have a computer science background or at least above-average computing skills. Our typical setup for collaborative development of such proposals involves a Subversion version control repository to which all partner representatives have read/write access, and which hosts the proposal document, distributed across many smaller LATEX files in order to minimise merge conflicts.

3.2 Approach

Modelling To improve the internal consistency of the proposal and automate the repetitive steps of the proposal development process, we followed a bottom-up iterative approach in which we used an XML document to model the proposal we were working on at the time. We chose plain XML instead of a rigorous modelling framework, such as the Eclipse Modelling Framework [1], primarily due to XML's agility; using XML, we would be able to engage in exploratory modelling without being constrained by a rigid *metamodel*, and we would also not need to engage in metamodel-model co-evolution activities. On the other hand, by choosing XML we would miss strong typing and built-in support for cross-references between model elements – which we considered to be a fair trade-off in the context. Another agile option would have been to use an annotated general-purpose diagram [2] however, we considered XML to be more suitable as we anticipated that the information we would need to capture in the proposal model would have a predominantly hierarchical (as opposed to graph-based) structure. After a few iterations, we converged to a first version of the XML document that captured the work packages, tasks, deliverables, and milestones of the project (see Figure 1 for a *conceptual* metamodel to which project models conform to, and Listing 1.1 for a sanitised excerpt from a successful[3] proposal).

---

[2] Information & Communication Technology.
[3] http://www.ossmeter.org

```
1   <?xml version="1.0"?>
2   <project name="OSSMETER" duration="30"
3      title="Automated Measurement and Analysis of Open-Source
           Software" >
4
5      <wp title="Requirements & Use Cases" leader="TOG" type="RTD">
6         <effort partner="TOG" months="6"/>
7         <effort partner="York" months="6"/>
8
9         <task title="Use Case Analysis"
10           start="1" end="6" partners="TOG, York, ..."/>
11        <deliverable title="Project Requirements"
12           due="6" nature="R" dissemination="PU" partner="TOG"/>
13     </wp>
14
15     <milestone title="Requirements and case studies completion"
           month="6"/>
16     <milestone title="Project completion" month="30"/>
17
18     <partner id="York" name="University of York"
19        country="United Kingdom"/>
20  </project>
```

Listing 1.1. Sanitised excerpt of the model of the OSSMETER project

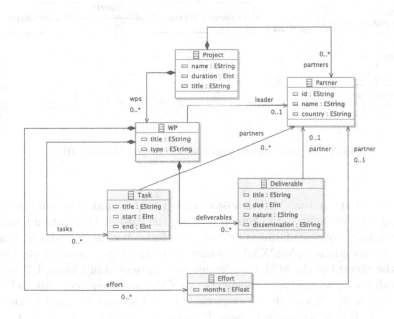

Fig. 1. Conceptual metamodel for project models

Model-to-text Transformation Our next activity was to decide how to best integrate any LaTeX content that we would generate from the constructed proposal model, with the hand-crafted parts of the proposal. We considered two options. The first option was to mix generated and hand-crafted content and rely on the M2T transformation engine's capabilities to preserve hand-crafted content upon re-generation. The second option was to keep generated and hand-crafted content separate, by producing a single file that would contain a number of auto-generated LaTeX commands which we could then reference from the hand-crafted LaTeX files. The main advantage of the first option was that contributors would not need to memorise any generated LaTeX commands; the main advantage of the second option was that we would enable contributors to use the generated LaTeX-commands in arbitrary locations in the proposal, without needing to adapt the generator every time. Automated content assistance and previewing facilities in modern LaTeX editors partially compensate for the shortcomings of the second approach, so as illustrated in Figure 2, we chose to produce a single LaTeX file containing a set of generated commands, which could then be imported by the main proposal file.

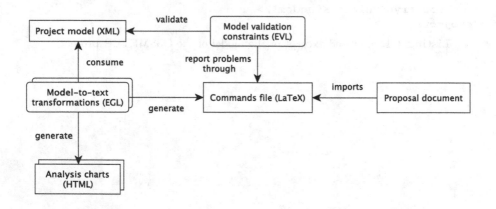

Fig. 2. Overview of the organisation of our MDE solution

In terms of the actual M2T transformation that would generate the LaTeX commands file, we chose to implement it using the Epsilon Generation Language [3], both because of prior familiarity with it but also because it provides built-in support for consuming plain XML documents in an elegant manner [4]. For example, the excerpt of the M2T transformation[4] presented in Listing 1.2, iterates through all work package (*wp*) elements in the XML document presented in Listing 1.1 (*t_wp.all* in line 2) and then through their *task* children (*wp.c_task* in line 5) to generate a LaTeX command (*workPackageAndTaskList* in line 1) that

---

[4] The complete M2T transformation is 529 lines long.

presents the project's work packages and tasks[5]. The executable content of an EGL template is contained within the [% %] tags (e.g. lines 3, 5, 7, 8), text-emitting instructions are contained within the [%= %] tags (e.g. [%=wp.a_title%] in line 4), and everything outside these tags is treated as static text.

```
1  \newcommand{\workPackageAndTaskList} {
2      \begin{itemize}
3      [%for (wp in t_wp.all) { %]
4          \item \textbf{ [%=wp.getId()%]   [%=wp.a_title%] }
5          [%for (task in wp.c_task) { %]
6              \subitem Task [%=task.getId()%]   [%=task.a_title%]
7          [%}%]
8      [%}%]
9      \end{itemize}
10 }
```

Listing 1.2. Excerpt of the proposal model to LaTeX M2T transformation

Having generated a consistent set of commands, we could now import them from the main proposal LaTeX document and use them in arbitrary places. Listing 1.3 illustrates an excerpt of the main proposal document that uses generated LaTeX commands (i.e. *projectDuration*, *projectName*, *workPackageAndTaskList*, *numberOfMilestonesAsWord*).

```
1  \subsubsection{Project Planning - Timeline and Effort
       Distribution}
2  \label{sec:projectPlanning}
3
4  The project duration will be \projectDuration months.
5
6  The \projectName project will be articulated in the following
       work packages:
7
8  \workPackageAndTaskList
9
10 We foresee \textbf{\numberOfMilestonesAsWord milestones} ...
```

Listing 1.3. Excerpt of the main proposal document that uses generated LaTeX commands

Model Validation Our next step was to define validation constraints for project models. We chose to express these constraints using the Epsilon Validation Language [5], for similar reasons to the ones discussed above. In Listing 1.4 we demonstrate two of the defined constraints that are evaluated for all *task*

---

[5] Naming conventions such as the use of *t_* and *c_* prefixes in Epsilon's XML integration driver are discussed in detail in [4].

elements (*context t_task* in line 1) of the proposal model. The first constraint (*EndAfterStart* in line 3), checks that the start date of a task always precedes its end date (line 4), and produces an appropriate error message if this condition is not met (line 5). Similarly, the second constraint (*constraint WithinTheProject* in line 8) checks that the end date of the task does not extend beyond the project completion date (line 9). To present any identified problems to the contributors of the proposal, unsatisfied constraints produce a new LATEX command (*generatedWarnings*), which is then imported from the main proposal document.

```
1   context t_task {
2
3       constraint EndAfterStart {
4           check : self.i_end > self.i_start
5           message : "Task " + self.getId() + " ends before it
                starts"
6       }
7
8       constraint WithinTheProject {
9           check : self.i_end <= t_project.all.first().i_duration
10          message : "Task " + self.getId() + " ends after the end
                of the project"
11      }
12  }
```

Listing 1.4. Validation constraints for PropoGen models

Deployment To enable other contributors to invoke our MDE solution locally, we had to develop and distribute a standalone runnable application. In the interest of simplicity, we developed a self-contained executable Java bundle (JAR) on which users could drag-and-drop their project model to invoke the validation constraints and M2T transformation discussed above. The JAR had to include a complete copy of the EGL/EVL execution engines as well as the actual transformation and validation constraints.

On a side-note, attempting to bundle the Epsilon execution engines into a self-contained JAR file was as useful exercise in itself as collecting and packaging all required dependencies turned out to be quite challenging. As a result of this exercise, Epsilon now provides pre-bundled standalone JAR files[6] that developers can use in their standalone (i.e. non-Eclipse-based) Java or Android applications with minimal effort.

3.3   Unexpected Opportunities

As discussed above, our initial motivation for modelling project proposals was so that we could eventually generate LATEX content that was tedious and error-prone to maintain manually. However, after developing the LATEX M2T transformation discussed above, we realised that we could now also produce interesting

---

[6] http://www.eclipse.org/epsilon/download/

visualisations for quality assessment purposes from the same model. For example, we developed an additional M2T transformation that generates tree-map charts such as the one displayed in Figure 3, which visualises the distribution of effort across different work packages of the project, and Sankey charts, such as the one illustrated in Figure 4 which visualises the contributions of different work packages to the milestones of the project – both of which we have found to be extremely useful for establishing confidence in the balance of the project: one aspect that evaluators tend to study is whether the work/effort/contribution balance is well distributed across partners, themes and work packages (and hence both risk and workload are suitably mitigated and managed).

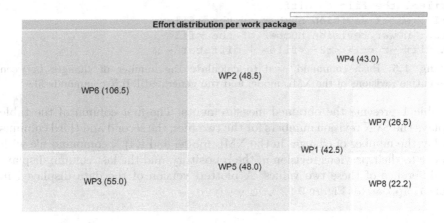

Fig. 3. Tree map visualising the distribution of effort per work package

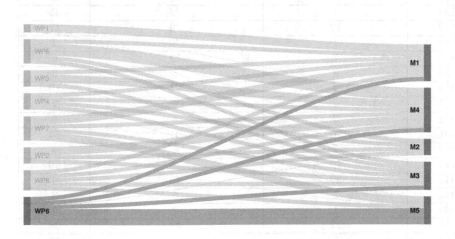

Fig. 4. Sankey diagram visualising how work packages contribute to project milestones

4   Evaluation

In this section we assess the productivity benefits delivered by the XML to LaTeX M2T transformation by analysing data from a recent project proposal that was developed between August 2012 - January 2013. In particular, we measure the number of added, removed and deleted lines of text across consecutive versions of the model and the generated LaTeX commands file, using the *svn diff* and *diffstat* tools as displayed in Listing 1.5. The rationale for doing this is that in the absence of the M2T transformation, we would have needed to perform the same changes to the LaTeX commands file manually.

```
#<file>: the file to diff
#<r1>: older revision number of the <file>
#<r2>: newer revision number of the <file>
svn diff -r <r1>:<r2> <file> | diffstat - m
```

Listing 1.5. Bash command used to calculate the number of changes between consecutive revisions of the XML model and the generated LaTeX commands file

Table 1 presents the obtained measurements. The first column of the table displays the SVN revision numbers for the two files, the second and third columns display the number of changes in the XML model and LaTeX command file with respect to their previous revision in the repository, and the last column displays the difference of these two values. A plotted version of the data displayed in Table 1, appears in Figure 5.

Table 1. Changes in the XML model and generated LaTeX command file by revision

Revision	Changes (XML model)	Changes (generated LaTeX)	Difference
3558	30	38	8
3595	1	46	45
3645	12	29	17
3646	1	3	2
3649	7	13	6
3675	2	5	3
3913	2	21	19
3914	2	9	7
3922	2	8	6
3991	16	31	15
3992	2	6	4
4019	16	75	59
4044	39	43	4
4045	2	5	3
4065	1	2	1
4075	11	39	28
4088	5	15	10
4091	28	42	14
Total	**179**	**430**	**251**

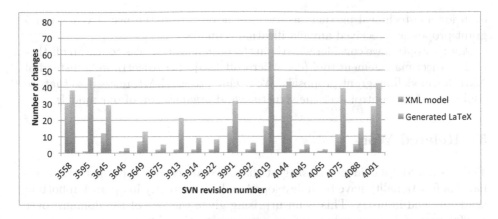

Fig. 5. Plotted data from Table 1

The obtained measurements demonstrate that the M2T transformation delivered a productivity improvement of ∼58% over the lifecycle of the proposal. The latest version of the model for that proposal comprised 256 lines of XML (13,194 bytes) while the generated LaTeX command file comprised 676 lines of dense text (56,694 bytes). Although we do not have hard supporting evidence, it is reasonable to assume that it is also significantly easier and faster to locate and update information in the XML document instead of the LaTeX command file, which has a potential to further amplify the productivity improvement figure obtained above.

4.1 Reflection

Compared to 3-layer metamodelling architectures such as EMF, plain XML is clearly sub-optimal from a technical point of view for capturing interconnected models as it lacks features such as support for cross-references and types. In a non-collaborative environment, we would have most likely used EMF to capture grant proposal models, as this would have also simplified the subsequent model-to-LaTeX transformation.

However, if we were to use EMF in a collaborative environment, we would have needed to implement and distribute standalone language-specific editors (i.e. Eclipse RCP applications) to all partners involved. As RCP applications are platform-specific, we would have needed to export and distribute several permutations of the editor for different operating systems. Moreover, with every change of the metamodel, we would have needed to distribute a new version of the editor application (and most likely deal with the confusion that multiple versions of the same editor can cause).

By choosing to model projects using plain XML, we eliminated the need for developing, maintaining and distributing specialised editors. Despite having some initial concerns about requiring partners to edit XML directly, providing a comprehensive first version of the XML document appears to have been sufficient even for non-technical partners as we have never – over the last 3 years and 5 grant proposals – received any clarification requests.

Another option we considered early in the design process was to use an off-the-shelf project management tool (e.g. Microsoft Project, ProjectLibre[7]) instead of XML for modelling grant proposals. We decided to use XML instead so that we could have finer control over the structure and organisation of our models.

5   Related Work

There is anecdotal evidence to suggest that several bespoke solutions with comparable functionality have been developed and are currently in operation both in academia and industry. This is unsurprising given the size of the domain (over 16,000 proposals were submitted in response to the European Commission's Horizon 2020 calls in April 2014 alone[8]). However, to the best of our knowledge, there is no published work that reports on the organisation, architecture and evaluation of such systems, nor of the specific use cases that such systems aim to support.

In a wider context, several approaches have been proposed for automatically generating system reports, documents and manuals from models in different domains. Hyperdoc [6], is a toolkit that provides support for automated generation of manuals for interactive systems (e.g. VCR players) from state-machine models. Hyperdoc applies graph analysis techniques in order to identify the shortest path between pairs of states and provide efficient instructions to the end-user of the product. In [7], the authors present an approach for generating manuals for families (product lines) of industrial automation systems, using the DOPLER variability modelling tool, DocBook as the target document format, and XSLT for model transformation. In [8], the authors demonstrate how system documents and reports can be generated using a model-based approach from SysML viewpoints and views. In a different domain, in [9], the authors demonstrate how multimedia presentations can be specified at a high level of abstraction using XML, and then compiled using XSLT transformations into concrete artefacts targeting different delivery platforms. XSLT and XML are also used to support processing of highly structured documents with *signing requirements* (e.g., to comply with security policies and governance requirements) in [10], though no explicit metamodel is used in this work.

In [11], the authors provide a systematic review of 34 approaches for generating requirements documents from software engineering models such as UML, user-interface, and goal models and identify a number of best practices including support for 1) bidirectional traceability, 2) structural correspondence between the models and the generated documents, 3) generation of documents in a modifiable format, 4) incremental synchronisation when models change and 5) tailoring the generated document according to its target readership. The approach

---

[7] http://www.projectlibre.org

[8] http://www.sciencebusiness.net/news/76612/Record-numbers-apply -for-Horizon-2020-first-round-funding (Last accessed: July 1, 2014)

proposed in this paper is consistent with best practices 2-5 and provides some support for traceability – mainly from the document back to the project model through the generation of LaTeX commands with human-readable identifiers (e.g. \workPackageOneTitle).

6 Conclusions

In this paper we have presented how we have applied MDE techniques to automate repetitive and error-prone tasks in the context of the collaborative development of grant proposals. We have demonstrated how grant proposals can be modelled and validated at a high level of abstraction and how model-to-text transformation can then be used to produce correct-by-construction LaTeX macros automating the most tedious and error-prone parts of the process. We regard this application as highly successful and an essential asset for our work on collaborative research projects. Indeed, we have shared this MDE application with partners and colleagues elsewhere, who now use it as part of their proposal development activities.

Acknowledgements. This research was part supported by the EPSRC, through the Large-Scale Complex IT Systems project (EP/F001096/1) and by the EU, through the OSSMETER FP7 STREP project (#318736) and the MONDO FP7 STREP project (#611125).

References

1. Steinberg, D., Budinsky, F., Paternostro, M., Merks, E.: EMF: Eclipse Modeling Framework. Addison-Wesley (2008)
2. Kolovos, D.S., Matragkas, N.D., Rodriguez, H.H., Paige, R.F.: Programmatic muddle management. In: XM@MoDELS, pp. 2–10 (2013)
3. Rose, L.M., Paige, R.F., Kolovos, D.S., Polack, F.A.C.: The Epsilon Generation Language (EGL). In: Schieferdecker, I., Hartman, A. (eds.) ECMDA-FA 2008. LNCS, vol. 5095, pp. 1–16. Springer, Heidelberg (2008)
4. Kolovos, D.S., Rose, L.M., Matragkas, N., Williams, J., Paige, R.F.: A Lightweight Approach for Managing XML Documents with MDE Languages. In: Proc. 8th European Conference on Modeling Foundations and Applications, Copenhagen, Denmark (July 2012)
5. Kolovos, D.S., Paige, R.F., Polack, F.A.C.: On the Evolution of OCL for Capturing Structural Constraints in Modelling Languages. In: Abrial, J.-R., Glässer, U. (eds.) Büorger Festschrift. LNCS, vol. 5115, pp. 204–218. Springer, Heidelberg (2009)
6. Thimbleby, H.: Combining systems and manuals. In: Proc. Human-Computer Interaction, HCI 1993, vol. VIII, pp. 479–488. University Press, BCS (1993)
7. Rabiser, R., Heider, W., Elsner, C., Lehofer, M., Grünbacher, P., Schwanninger, C.: A flexible approach for generating product-specific documents in product lines. In: Bosch, J., Lee, J. (eds.) SPLC 2010. LNCS, vol. 6287, pp. 47–61. Springer, Heidelberg (2010)

8. Delp, C., Lam, D., Fosse, E., Lee, C.-Y.: Model based document and report generation for systems engineering. In: 2013 IEEE Aerospace Conference, pp. 1–11 (March 2013)
9. Villard, L., Roisin, C., Layaïda, N.: An xml-based multimedia document processing model for content adaptation. In: King, P., Munson, E.V. (eds.) DDEP-PODDP 2000. LNCS, vol. 2023, pp. 104–119. Springer, Heidelberg (2004)
10. Brooke, P.J., Paige, R.F., Power, C.: Document-centric xml workflows with fragment digital signatures. Softw., Pract. Exper. 40(8), 655–672 (2010)
11. Nicolás, J., Toval, A.: On the generation of requirements specifications from software engineering models: A systematic literature review. Inf. Softw. Technol. 51(9), 1291–1307 (2009)

Agile Model-Driven Engineering in Mechatronic Systems - An Industrial Case Study

Ulf Eliasson[1], Rogardt Heldal[2], Jonn Lantz[1], and Christian Berger[3]

[1] Volvo Car Group, Sweden
ulf.eliasson@volvocars.com jonn.lantz@volvocars.com
[2] Chalmers University of Technology, Sweden
heldal@chalmers.se
[3] University of Gothenburg, Sweden
christian.berger@gu.se

Abstract. Model-driven engineering focuses on structuring systems as well as permitting domain experts to be directly involved in the software development. Agile methods aim for fast feedback and providing crucial knowledge early in the project. In our study, we have seen a successful combination of MDE and agile methods to support the development of complex, software-driven mechatronic systems. We have investigated how combining MDE and agile methods can reduce the number of issues caused by erroneous assumptions in the software of these mechatronic systems. Our results show that plant models to simulate mechanical systems are needed to enable agile MDE during the mechatronic development. They enable developers to run, verify, and validate models before the mechanical systems are delivered from suppliers. While two case studies conducted at Volvo Car Group confirm that combining MDE and agile works, there are still challenges e.g. how to optimize the development of plant models.

Keywords: Model Driven Engineering, Agile, Mechatronic Software Development, Virtual Testing, Assumptions, Plant Models.

1 Introduction

Developers working on complex embedded systems are consciously and unconsciously making assumptions early in the project about properties and behavior of other components in the system [1, 17, 21]. For example, a developer might make the implicit assumption that the velocity signal from one component is supposed to be in km/h, but it is in fact provided as m/s. These assumptions are often difficult to verify until later phases in a project, such as subsystem integration, because it is common that development is distributed within and between companies. When assumptions lead to unexpected behavior, the costs for fixing these issues increase rapidly the longer they go undetected [19]. Therefore, there is a clear need to address the negative impact of assumptions already early during the development.

J. Dingel et al. (Eds.): MODELS 2014, LNCS 8767, pp. 433–449, 2014.

Today's automotive industry undergoes a rapid transformation from a mainly mechanical industry into a computerized electromechanical industry where cars are composed of several mechatronic systems, which interact with their surroundings, e.g. autonomous emergency braking. Already twelve years ago it was estimated that 80% of the automotive innovation stems from electronics [13], mainly driven by software, and the size and complexity of software in cars have continued to grow exponential [7]. For example, a modern hybrid electric car has more than 100 electronic control units (ECU), collaborating in a complex in-vehicle network and executing several gigabytes of software.

Sequential development processes that are traditionally used during vehicle development have shown to be insufficient for handling such an exponential growth of software [5,7]. Furthermore, car manufacturers consider vehicle functions powered by software as a competitive advantage and hence, they tend to develop an increasing amount of this software in-house. Thus, innovation cycles can be shortened as well.

We conducted a case study at the Volvo Car Group (VCG) in Sweden at the Department of Electric Development to better understand challenges originating from combining MDE with agile methods. The main findings from this study are:

- It is possible to combine MDE and agile methods during the development of complex mechatronic systems at automotive original equipment manufacturers (OEM) to gain more knowledge earlier in the projects and decrease the number assumptions.
- Virtual test environments to validate software components are a flexible instrument to support MDE and agile to improve the quality of software regarding wrong assumptions.

Overview: In Sec. 2, we present the development process at VCG to provide the background on how software development is usually carried out at automotive OEMs and Sec. 3 outlines the problem domain and motivation. In Sec. 4, we present our research questions and the methods we used to address them. Sec. 5 reports about the design and results from an exploratory study that was conducted as a pre-study to address RQ-1 and to derive RQ-2 and RQ-3. To address these derived research questions, we did two case studies at VCG, which are reported in Sec. 6. The findings from the investigated cases are analyzed and discussed in Sec. 7. Related work is described in Sec. 8 before a summary and conclusion is provided.

2   Background

Mechatronic development, such as for a modern car, involves software, hardware and mechanical development. The widely adopted model for this distributed development is the V-model, see Fig. 1. The V-shape represents the journey for each component in the car, from the high level requirement and design, via

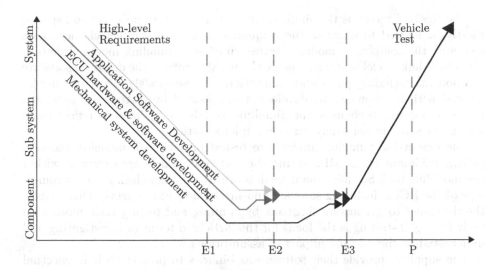

Fig. 1. The V-model as it is implemented at VCG for a car development project. Software, hardware and mechanical development happens in parallel and is integrated at certain points during the project.

the detailed component development and up to verification of the integrated component in the product.

As shown in Fig. 1, the overall system development process at VCG is a sequential process with a number of points in time where artifacts are to be delivered. There are three tracks of parallel development: (a) the software components (SWC), (b) the hardware like ECU, and (c) mechanical parts. E1-E3 are electronic integration points and P is where the software should be production ready. The OEM has an overall system responsibility but purchases mechanical systems, hardware and software from suppliers. The suppliers then deliver their components for integration in later phases of the project. VCG has traditionally ordered all the software from suppliers, except for the engines. Recently, an initiative for developing more software in-house has been initiated to keep domain knowledge as a competitive advantage within the company and to improve the speed of innovation.

To meet deadlines in the project, the in-house software development needs to be started before suppliers deliver their components. This is a major challenge for the development teams because they do not have the components available to validate that their assumptions on the behavior of the component are correct.

At the beginning, all requirements and the system design for the next iteration is captured as a model inside a custom-made tool, referred to as SysTool. This model contains, among other things, software components, the requirements they should realize, their deployment on ECUs within the car, and the communication between them. At a certain point in time, this model is frozen and no new changes are allowed until the next iteration starts. These freezes usually last for 20 weeks.

The SysTool model is the single point of truth with respect to two aspects: Firstly, it is used to schedule the communication on the in-vehicle networks; secondly, the component model is transformed into Simulink model skeletons. Each Simulink model represents an ECU with skeletons of the deployed software components including ports and connections. These models are then complemented with functionality by developers as specified by textual requirements. If the system model changes, the Simulink models are updated to reflect these adaptations and preserve any existing implementation.

The executable Simulink models are tested in a virtual, model-in-the-loop (MIL), environment. In MIL-testing the software models are executed within the modeling tool. So-called plant models are used for simulating the surroundings of the ECUs, including software and mechanical components. This enables the developer to get instant feedback by running and testing their models on their PCs. MIL-testing is the focus for this article in terms of investigating and understanding the role and impact of assumptions.

The suppliers provide their software as binaries to protect their intellectual property (IP). Code is generated from in-house models, compiled to a binary and linked with the supplier modules. The resulting software is transferred to the hardware and tested in hardware-in-the-loop (HIL) test rigs. HIL testing means that the code is executed on the intended ECU-hardware and uses real network buses but the rest of the environment surrounding the ECU is simulated. Due to the fact that suppliers provide binaries, this is the first time that both, in-house and supplier developed software, can be integrated and validated together.

The final phase of testing is when software and hardware is integrated with the mechanical systems in a complete prototype vehicle and tested. In these prototypical cars, the whole system is tested altogether.

3   Motivation and Problem Domain

Many systems in today's vehicles are so-called cyber-physical systems (CPS), which use sensors and mechatronic parts to realize their functionality. These systems include assistant systems like adaptive cruise control, safety-critical systems like autonomous emergency braking, but also mechatronic systems like electronically supported steering. While some of the software development for a car is conducted in-house, other parts of the software as well as a majority of the hardware and mechanical components are developed and provided by suppliers. When the software development takes place in-house, mechatronic components, which are used to obtain data from the surroundings or to interact via actuators with the surroundings, are not available yet and hence, the software development would be partially based on assumptions about the behavior and data to be expected from such hardware and mechatronic components. The in-house development cannot be delayed until suppliers have delivered their finished systems as this would make it impossible to meet project deadlines.

Additionally, a standardization of hardware and software platforms like AUTOSAR [9] would have the potential of facilitating the integration and lower the number of platform-related assumptions. However, the automotive industry has a long tradition of optimizing on component price, since the hardware cost is still believed to dominate the total production costs and thus, packing and weight are valuable. Therefore, there is no breakthrough of component standardization yet, which could help to reduce the potential risk of relying on assumptions.

In order to achieve faster feedback as well as better utilizing the expertize of domain experts in-house VCG has decided to use the executable software modeling language Simulink. This permits one to simulate and test the code continuously and translates it automatically into C code whenever necessary. It also enables in-house engineers with domain expertise to implement solutions themselves.

Having the above in mind we wanted to improve on the way of developing mechatronic systems by combining elements from MDE with agile development methods. There are different methods and techniques called agile but they share a number of concepts, such as having working software early, rapid feedback reducing the time between decisions and seeing the consequences, taking advantage of faster and less formal communication and focusing on how to best utilize the skills and talents of the people in the organization [6, 10]. The focus in this study has been on having working systems early in contrast to writing specifications and requirement documents up front, faster feedback by short iterations and more direct communication with stakeholders.

We are only looking at agile MDE within single ECUs. The input and output to the ECUs are exported from the SysTool and the design process on this level follows the overall system process common for the whole car project. However, even when being constrained to one ECU it is complicated to achieve agile development for mechatronic systems, since the connected physical systems are not always available and therefore require plant models as part of the virtual test environment. Without these plant models of mechanical parts one will not have an executable system early.

4 Research Questions and Methods

With the said-to-be standard tooling of Matlab Simulink in the automotive industry, the OEMs and their suppliers are successful adopters of model-driven engineering (MDE). Considering the aforementioned problem domain, the goal of this study is to investigate the challenges for MDE at an automotive OEM, when (un-)consciously depending on assumptions during in-house software development.

RQ-1: What are the causes that lead to assumptions in distributed mechatronic development and what are the consequences?

RQ-2: Does the combination of MDE and agile methods increase the knowledge in earlier phases of the project compared to a plan driven process?

RQ-3: What impact does faulty assumptions within the test environment have on the product and process?

Our study incorporates an exploratory study as a pre-study and two case studies. The exploratory study was conducted to address RQ-1, investigating the challenges regarding software, hardware, and mechanical assumptions by conducting interviews with developers, requirement engineers, testers, and architects. The design of the interview was semi-structured with open-ended questions, which allowed the interviewees to focus on topics as they arose during the discussion. The design and results for the exploratory study are described in Sec. 5.

The results from the semi-structured interviews were used to cluster topics to identify main challenges. From these topics, the research questions RQ-2 and RQ-3 were derived and two case studies were designed to follow upon on these topics. In the case studies, data was collected by observation and complementary semi-structured interviews. The results were validated by discussions with involved participants in the projects. The design and results for the case studies are described in Sec. 6.

The findings from the application of both methods are analyzed and discussed in Sec. 7.

5   Exploratory Study to Prepare the Case Studies

To address RQ-1, we conducted an exploratory study as a series of semi-structured expert interviews with open-ended topics. In this section, we report about the design and results of this exploratory study according to the guidelines of Shull et al. [19].

5.1   Design of the Semi-structured Interviews

The exploratory study consisted of eight semi-structured interviews with eight engineers. In general the interviewees had a background in electronics, physics, automation or mechanical engineering and a long-term experience in mechatronic and automotive development. The interviewees were sampled from different roles and working on different levels in the development project covering engineers working with software development and writing detailed requirements, testers on different levels, as well as developers working on the electronic architecture for the complete vehicle.

The following topics were open-ended discussed and recorded for post-processing:

- Background of the interviewee including role and responsibilities
- Type of involvement during the development process
- Experiences with assumptions:
  - Concrete examples for assumptions during the development
  - How wrong assumptions were identified and corrected
  - How corrected assumptions were documented afterwards

The interviews took on average 45 minutes and were very informative in terms of initiating reflection processes while discussing with the interviewees.

5.2   Results from the Semi-structured Interviews

Motivational factors for challenges stated from interviewees could be boiled down to having their roots in the sequential development process used on system level at VCG. To pass the project stage gates, decisions have to be taken before having the complete knowledge for deriving well-informed decisions. Thus, this gap of missing knowledge is filled in by assumptions as depicted by Fig. 2.

The earlier an engineer has to make a decision the higher is the risk of faulty assumptions that lead to unwanted side-effects of defects, which need to be fixed later. Furthermore, these assumptions can only be verified at the integration points when the different parts of the system are delivered. Since the integration often happens late in the development project, any serious issues that are discovered at this time are obviously costly and time-consuming to fix.

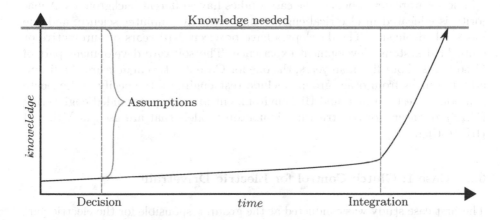

Fig. 2. A process that require early decisions regarding requirements, design or implementation details, before having any activities on building the knowledge needed will inevitably force its participants to make assumptions. These assumptions can be faulty, consequences of which will be visible first after the first real integration, usually leading to a huge increase in needed activities at the final stages of the project.

The main finding, confirmed with the involved interviewees, was that there is a clear need for earlier and faster feedback to the developers and designers of systems. This clearly shows that there is a need for agile methods to support delivering and integrating in increments early to build knowledge for making more informed decisions and getting early feedback on if their solution is heading in the right direction.

From the feedback of the interviewees in this exploratory study, we derived the research questions RQ-2 and RQ-3, which shall be followed up on with two subsequent case studies.

6   Case Studies

From our exploratory study, we derived the research questions RQ-2 and RQ-3, which are addressed by two case studies conducted at VCG. Here, we report about the case studies according to the guidelines from Runeson and Höst [18].

6.1   Case Study Design

The two cases are from different units in electric development department at VCG. The first case (Case 1) is from Electrical Propulsion Systems (EPS). EPS is the unit at VCG that develops the components for electrical and hybrid vehicles. The second case (Case 2) is from Central Electronic Module (CEM). CEM is responsible for an ECU within the car, which holds a collection of functionality that is central, such as locking and headlight control.

The software developers in the case studies have different backgrounds. A majority is educated in electrical engineering, some in computer science, and one has studied physics. The developers have between 2-10 years of automotive or embedded systems development experience. The software development part of Case 1 was about five man years, the one for Case 2 is two man years. Additionally, resources from other groups include test engineers to specify and execute component tests in MIL and HIL environment and computer aided engineering (CAE) engineers for constructing simulation models that are used in MIL and HIL testing.

6.2   Case 1: Clutch Control for Electric Drivetrain

The first case study was conducted at the group responsible for the electric part of the drivetrain in the hybrid car under development. Between the traditional and electrical drive train there is a clutch that is required to safely engage when the electric engine should be used. The study investigated the development of the software that controls the clutch.

Way of Working. The team used MDE techniques to develop their software. The wrappers for the behavior models were automatically generated from a system model and then complemented by the actual behavior implementation. A virtual environment was built to quickly iterate, test, and get feedback on their implementation. This virtual environment contains a number of models that simulate mechanical and software systems (plant models) for those components that have not been delivered from suppliers yet. The models needed for the simulation were developed by an in-house team specializing in CAE and verification. The basic functionality was implemented and tested against the plant models to avoid waiting for the first prototype vehicle with the real hardware and mechanical systems.

Results. In relation to research question RQ-2, we saw that there was a strong development of the plant models, e.g. of the clutch, from a simple model to a more detailed and realistically parameterized model. The work bench utilizing the plant models was used to continuously test the software models during the development work. Although the early executable models were not completely matching the final mechanics, they allowed flexible testing of the early controller software in a way which would have been very difficult or impossible without the virtual environment.

The test bench that was designed to run the controller software and plant models was optimized in collaboration between all involved parties, spanning over three groups. The methods were very different e.g. from Case 2, which demonstrates the importance of agility. Later in the project, when faulty assumptions were discovered, both controller code and plant model could be corrected locally with continuous testing on the developers PCs. One should note that both CAE team and control system developers were at that time used to the model design and had the understanding required to adjust it rapidly.

Considering RQ-3, in early car tests when the controller software was combined with a real clutch, there were indeed problems. The clutch did not behave as the CAE team had thought, since assumptions on the behavior of the clutch's teeth was proved wrong. This prevented the clutch from engaging properly. It took about one month of calendar time for identifying what the problem was, implementing a fix and get it deployed on the prototype vehicle. However, as soon as the problem was identified the resulting changes to fix the controller code were small and mainly parameter-related and the overall design was not affected.

6.3   Case 2: Active High Beam Headlight

The second case study investigated the way how the software for the active high beam headlights (AHBH) was developed. AHBH are used to let the headlight use the high beam but still not blind fellow motorists. This is done by identifying other vehicles using the cameras in the car and then mechanically obstruct the light to put the other vehicles in shade. This helps to keep the visibility at the sides of the road high at the same time as not blinding other road users.

Way of Working. This project was in the beginning a requirement engineering project following a classical waterfall process. The functional hardware, camera and image analysis system was developed, with well defined APIs and reasonably good specifications. Hence, detailed specifications existed of the sensor and actuator systems. The function was specified at high level, mainly using PowerPoint presentations describing customer use cases, but the control system, intended to be developed in a VCG ECU, was undefined. The solution was to engage an external expert in MDE to be part of the development team for a few months, creating a simulation environment, a demonstration/visualization environment and a first version of the control software, which was based on the supplied API and high level requirements. Later on the project was taken over by the original team, strengthened with a software modeling engineer. The second half of the project was carried out mainly in the laboratory, switching between software modeling and test in HIL rigs and on a real vehicle in a garage. Hence, plant models were used to little extent. The modeling environment was used for software modeling and visualization, and for simulations running with videos and recorded data from the supplier device and camera as input.

Results. With respect to RQ-2, much was learned using the available demonstration model by quickly trying out different solutions and algorithms. Before the simulation and demonstration environment was available the team struggled with getting approval from management to go ahead. The project was literally stuck. When the test environment with the demonstrator, including also the first version of the control software, was built it did not only help to start up the project work but also to communicate the ideas and to obtain approval.

Regarding RQ-3, the lack of a real, closed loop, plant model created assumptions of ideal actuators and sensors in the system. As a direct consequence, the early versions of the controller software was over-engineered in terms of implemented algorithms and code that the mechanical system could not support. This also resulted in an unnecessary complex architecture, judging from the design of the final version. The accuracy of the system actuators especially, regarding reaction speed, finally led to a significant simplification of the controller algorithm. The architecture and design of the first and more advanced controller software influenced also later versions, still showing signs of over-engineering.

Another assumption was caused by the visualization, which was created using simple light shape overlay on a 2D video with no 3D compensation or more advanced light rendering. Moreover, the edges of the overlay were unrealistically sharp, as the calculated image represented a plane only about five meters in front of the car. When the developers finally got into a car with the essential equipment installed, it was obvious that the spread of the light was higher than they had assumed by basing it on their visualization and the solution had to be rethought. Regarding this assumption one should also note that it was not unveiled during laboratory tests, although the real equipment was present, since the beam was projected on a screen inside the laboratory.

6.4   Interpretation of Results

In both of the case studies we found that the use of virtual test environments significantly improved the knowledge in early stages of the projects. The test environments enabled reliable tests of prototypes and assumptions about externally developed technology.

We found that the development team in Case 2 had little progress at all before gaining access to a virtual environment for testing. Looking at Case 1 one could see that having virtual testing available from the start enabled the software models to grow faster and more organically than if they had followed the overall system process where decisions had to be made upfront, such as in the start of Case 2. The software model in Case 1 also showed less signs of over-engineering compared to Case 2. Furthermore, in Case 1, more effort was spent on a realistic plant model, compared to Case 2 where the visualization was prioritized. Observing the progress, we note more late issues caused by faulty assumptions related to hardware and mechanics in Case 2, which were also reworked in longer time. Finally, Case 2 suffered from late issues, found in traffic situations, which theoretically could have been discovered much earlier using more advanced simulation environments.

By integrating and executing the software models in a virtual environment the developers were forced to address holes in their knowledge. Hence correct knowledge was gained although models or virtual environments included assumptions. This gain of knowledge is visualized in Fig. 3. Faulty assumptions were indeed discovered in vehicle tests in both use cases. Nevertheless, the time to fix these issues was shortened by a realistic simulation environment in Case 1.

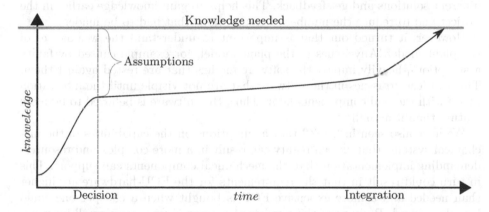

Fig. 3. By being able to integrate and execute tests more frequently using plant models and virtual environments the developers can build and validate knowledge also early in the project. Although numerous assumptions still have to be made, since the mechanical system or other parts of the mechatronic system are unknown to the developers, the ability to conduct simulations will increase the knowledge. At the first real integration there will obviously still be a risk for faulty assumptions, but the knowledge gap is significantly reduced.

The plant models in Case 1 was constructed from specifications, intended for the external supplier developing the equipment, and suffered both from smaller inconsistencies and incompleteness. Some simplifications were also made, forced by limited understanding of the mechanical behavior of the clutch. Furthermore, the plant model developer and the function developers worked in separate groups. Hence, the team developing plant models lacked some contextual background for the intended use case of the plant models as well as direct contact with the supplier. However, the benefit of having software tested with plant models before deploying in real vehicles greatly outweighed losses due to an incomplete process or problems with communication.

Finally one should note that some architecture decisions, e.g. regarding communication between ECUs, still had to be done upfront. The teams expressed frustration over this but a solution would require changing the overall systems process as we reported on in our previous work [8].

7   Analysis and Discussion

The case studies unveiled that applying MDE in combination with agile helped to address the challenge of shortened development cycles. Together with a virtual test environment, it was possible to relax the dependency on mechanical components provided by suppliers later during the development. This would not be possible in mechatronic development otherwise.

Furthermore, this environment enabled short iterations to experiment with different solutions and get feedback. This helps to gain knowledge earlier in the project and to reduce the number of assumptions that had to be made.

However, it turned out that is important to understand the weaknesses of the plant model. Any issues in the plant model, for example caused by faulty assumptions, heavily impact the software models that are tested against them. This can lead to issues in the software that are not visible until the integration phase with the real components later. Thus, the software is believed to be more mature than it actually is.

We have also seen in Case 2 that assumptions on the capabilities of the mechanical systems that exceed reality can result in a more complex and resource-demanding implementation than the mechanical components can support. This in turn could result in that the requirements for the ECU-hardware are higher than needed and a more expensive ECU is bought when a cheaper one could have been used. Because of the number of cars produced, even small increases in cost for a component have an impact in the profits of the OEM. E.g. if an ECU costs 10 USD more than a less expensive one that would suffice, and 100 000 cars are produced, the profit shrinks with 1 000 000 USD just caused by one component.

Delaying software development until the mechanical systems are delivered is not an option, as that would delay the whole project. But there are some potential methods that could possibly decrease the number of assumptions in the virtual testing environment.

One solution is that the suppliers deliver plant models of their mechanical systems. This should in theory give the OEM more accurate plant models to base their development on. However, for a number of reasons not all suppliers are willing to share their models. This could often be traced back to a way of protecting their IP. The other one is that, in the cases where suppliers do deliver plant models, they only provide them as black boxes. This makes it impossible for the OEM to verify that the model is actually working correctly. There have been cases where a model delivered from a manufacturer of a mechanical system was shown to be incorrect when compared to the real component and without insight into a model it is hard for the OEM to investigate where the issue lies, in the software model or the plant model. It also prevents the OEM to see if the plant model is fit for the testing. E.g. if the plant model provided does not simulate the teeth within the clutch it would not be possible to verify that the algorithm within the software model could calculate the correct offset needed for successfully engaging the clutch.

Alternatively, plant models could be built in-house but verified by the supplier. Most suppliers of mechanical systems have environments where they could execute such models. This would have the potential of avoiding structural and fundamental mistakes in the plant models.

Even though using plant models and MIL-testing for rapid prototyping seems to be promising, there are also aspects that need to be considered. It is time-consuming to construct and maintain the plant models and integrate them in the MIL environment; furthermore, developers or testers need to develop the test cases for the MIL-testing. Here, the task seems to be rather less attractive because the implementation will be tested on the prototypical real vehicle later anyway; however, the gains of having an early validation in a virtual test environment needs to be underlined properly. This is also confirmed by the participants in our studies who see otherwise the risk of not meeting deadlines in the demand of shorter development cycles.

As the groups studied in the case studies have not had in-house software development before, there was no previous software development process that needed to be adjusted to allow for MDE and agile. Furthermore, the toolchain could also be built from the ground up to support agility.

To address threats to validity in our studies, we follow the guidelines from Wohlin et al. and Runeson and Höst [18, 22, 23].

Construct Validity: The subjects in our exploratory study were experts in how to build embedded software for automotive systems. We validated our result by discussing our findings with the interviewees. The case studies were conducted on two projects where the resulting artifacts of the projects were components that will be used in cars delivered to customers at VCG. By having two studies, effects, which might be present only in one case could be reduced.

Internal Validity: The main objective for the studied cases was primarily on delivering a running system with high quality in the end. Effects that would favor MDE or agile methods could be reduced.

External Validity: There are a lot of companies where hardware, mechanical parts, and software need to interplay well like trucks, radars, and pumps etc. For many of these companies our findings can be of interest and stimulate similar studies.

Reliability: The analysis was conducted by the authors. Our findings and conclusions were confirmed with the participants of the studies in feedback and discussion rounds to reduce the risk of dependency on the conducting researchers.

8   Related Work

Matinnejad [16] has done a review on the existing agile model-driven development (AMDD) processes. They think that an intelligent compromise can be done to gain the advantages from the two different approaches to software development. We have seen that there might not be such a big contradiction between MDE and agile. Instead they two complement each other well, especially in a distributed mechatronic domain where it enables to develop and test against yet to be delivered components. However, we agree that there are benefits from combining the two and that it is an area that needs more interest and research.

Zhang et al. [24] applied agile MDD on a development project for real-time telecommunication. The project was considered successful and was delivered on time. MDD was only applied to two of five components, the other three components were "hand-coded". They saw a threefold increase in productivity in terms of lines of code compared to hand-coding and that the defect density was lower in code generated from models. They also saw that there was a steep learning curve for the organization to adopt to MDD and agile methods. Therefore they thought that short-term benefits were not likely but the long-term benefits still made it worthwhile. We however observed that the engineers at VCG instead could get started faster with software development due to the fact that they were allowed to work in a tool that was close to their domain and that was familiar from their engineering education.

Kulkarni et al. [11] reported on their experience with agile MDD in their development projects of business systems. They found that some activities were not suitable to be conducted in short sprints and that code generation and transformations can be a bottleneck. They solved this by introducing meta-sprints that do not necessarily have to deliver working software but can comprise for example design documents or an evaluation of a set of design strategies. In our studies and experience from VCG a major point in the success of MDE is that they use a product for their software modeling that is mature and where the C-code generation is already tested and stable.

Auweraer et al. [2] have also identified the need for virtual testing to enable concurrent development of mechanical components and the software for controlling it. However, their motivation is to accelerate the design process and not to enable software development at the OEM while the mechanical component is developed somewhere else. Therefore they do not discuss the problem of the OEM having a gap of knowledge of the mechanical system, or software processes.

Virtual test environments are proved to be successful especially for highly complex cyber-physical systems like self-driving cars as outlined by Berger, 2010 [3] and Berger and Rumpe 2012 [4]. These systems will play an increasingly important role in the future with more and more diverse product families and shorter development cycles. Faster and precise feedback of the quality for implementation models when using these simulation-based virtual test environments will be the competitive advantage for automotive OEMs.

Research has been done on different ways of modeling assumptions to verify them [12, 14, 20]. These approaches can be divided into two classes, formal or semi-formal [15]. Formal approaches, such as Tirumala 2006 [20] try to capture assumptions in a model and formalize their attributes, so that these can be verified automatically. Semi-formal approaches, such as Lewis 2004 [14] and Lago 2005 [12] capture the assumptions in a model but their attributes is free text and could therefore not be checked by a machine. Such approaches were initially considered, however we found them not feasible. Firstly, without having the properties of the real system such a model will in itself contain assumptions and the result of a verification could not be trusted. Secondly, it would add a new tool and language for the engineers to not only use but also to learn. With them already being on a tight schedule it was deemed impossible to introduce such tools. It could be a good exercise to make the developers more aware of the assumptions they are making, but the ones that will cause problems are the ones that are not explicitly thought about. Experience from practice shows that assumptions will always be made and capturing them all seems impossible.

9   Conclusion and Future Work

In our case studies we have seen that MDE and agile methods can successfully be combined to develop software for complex mechatronic systems. Together with virtual test environments, it enables an organization to start developing and test their software before they receive deliveries of mechanical and software components from their suppliers. We saw that it was possible for the developers to quickly iterate their implementation and get feedback. This made the developers aware of holes in their knowledge that needed to be addressed, and it allowed for exploring solutions and build knowledge before writing the final requirements and committing to a design.

It was obvious that assumptions made when constructing the models for the simulated environment had great impact on the software models constructed. Faulty assumptions in the simulation of yet to be delivered components caused issues in the software. These issues were discovered at integration but feedback from involved engineers let us conclude that the advantages with fast feedback, building knowledge, and a more mature solution earlier outweigh the fact that not all issues are caught in the virtual test environment.

For the future, we aim for automating further parts of the testing and reach continuous integration and deployment. Both in a model based virtual test environment but also for hardware-in-the-loop testing and finally to deploy the new software to prototypical vehicles.

For the problems caused by faulty plant models there are two directions to further explore with better collaboration between suppliers and OEMs. One would be to get access to their white box models of their mechanical components as part of the business agreement. The other potential way is to keep the construction of plant models in-house but have the supplier on-site to verify them.

References

1. Albayrak, O., Kurtoglu, H., Biaki, M.: Incomplete software requirements and assumptions made by software engineers. In: Asia-Pacific Software Engineering Conference, APSEC 2009, pp. 333–339. IEEE (December 2009)
2. Van der Auweraer, H., Anthonis, J., Bruyne, S.D., Leuridan, J.: Virtual engineering at work: The challenges for designing mechatronic products. Engineering with Computers 29(3), 389–408 (2013)
3. Berger, C.: Automating Acceptance Tests for Sensor-and Actuator-based Systems on the Example of Autonomous Vehicles. Citeseer (2010)
4. Berger, C., Rumpe, B.: Engineering autonomous driving software. In: Experience from the DARPA Urban Challenge, pp. 243–271. Springer (2012)
5. Broy, M.: Challenges in automotive software engineering. In: Proceedings of the 28th International Conference on Software Engineering, ICSE 2006, pp. 33–42. ACM, New York (2006)
6. Cockburn, A., Highsmith, J.: Agile software development, the people factor. Computer 34(11), 131–133 (2001)
7. Ebert, C., Jones, C.: Embedded software: Facts, figures, and future. IEEE Computer 42(4), 42–52 (2009)
8. Eliasson, U., Burden, H.: Extending agile practices in automotive MDE. In: XM 2013 Extreme Modeling Workshop, p. 11 (2013)
9. Fürst, S., Mössinger, J., Bunzel, S., Weber, T., Kirschke-Biller, F., Heitkämper, P., Kinkelin, G., Nishikawa, K., Lange, K.: AUTOSARA worldwide standard is on the road. In: 14th International VDI Congress Electronic Systems for Vehicles, Baden-Baden (2009)
10. Highsmith, J., Cockburn, A.: Agile software development: the business of innovation. Computer 34(9), 120–127 (2001)
11. Kulkarni, V., Barat, S., Ramteerthkar, U.: Early experience with agile methodology in a model-driven approach. In: Whittle, J., Clark, T., Kühne, T. (eds.) MODELS 2011. LNCS, vol. 6981, pp. 578–590. Springer, Heidelberg (2011)
12. Lago, P., van Vliet, H.: Explicit assumptions enrich architectural models. In: Proceedings of the 27th International Conference on Software Engineering, ICSE 2005, pp. 206–214. ACM, New York (2005)
13. Leen, G., Heffernan, D.: Expanding automotive electronic systems. Computer 35(1), 88–93 (2002)
14. Lewis, G., Mahatham, T., Wrage, L.: Assumptions management in software development. Software Engineering Institute (August 2004)
15. Mamun, M.A.A., Hansson, J.: Review and challenges of assumptions in software development. In: The Second Analytic Virtual Integration of Cyber-Physical Systems Workshop (2011)
16. Matinnejad, R.: Agile model driven development: An intelligent compromise. In: 2011 9th International Conference on Software Engineering Research, Management and Applications (SERA), pp. 197–202 (August 2011)
17. Miranskyy, A., Madhavji, N., Davison, M., Reesor, M.: Modelling assumptions and requirements in the context of project risk. In: Proceedings of the 13th IEEE International Conference on Requirements Engineering, pp. 471–472. IEEE (September 2005)
18. Runeson, P., Höst, M.: Guidelines for conducting and reporting case study research in software engineering. Empirical Software Engineering 14, 131–164 (2008)

19. Shull, F., Singer, J., Sjøberg, D.I.: Guide to advanced empirical software engineering. Springer (2008)
20. Tirumala, A.S.: An Assumptions Management Framework for Systems Software. Ph.D., University of Illinois at Urbana-Champaign, United States – Illinois (2006)
21. Uchitel, S., Yankelevich, D.: Enhancing architectural mismatch detection with assumptions. In: Seventh IEEE International Conference and Workshop on the Proceedings of the Engineering of Computer Based Systems, ECBS 2000, pp. 138–146. IEEE (2000)
22. Wohlin, C., Runeson, P., Höst, M., Ohlsson, M.C., Regnell, B., Wesslén, A.: Experimentation in software engineering. Springer (2012)
23. Yin, R.K.: Case study research: Design and methods, vol. 5. Sage (2009)
24. Zhang, Y., Patel, S.: Agile model-driven development in practice. IEEE Software 28(2), 84–91 (2011)

Using UML for Modeling Procedural Legal Rules: Approach and a Study of Luxembourg's Tax Law

Ghanem Soltana, Elizabeta Fourneret, Morayo Adedjouma,
Mehrdad Sabetzadeh, and Lionel Briand

SnT Centre for Security, Reliability and Trust, University of Luxembourg,
Luxembourg, Luxembourg
{firstname.lastname}@uni.lu

Abstract. Many laws, e.g., those concerning taxes and social benefits, need to be operationalized and implemented into public administration procedures and eGovernment applications. Where such operationalization is warranted, the legal frameworks that interpret the underlying laws are typically *prescriptive*, providing *procedural rules* for ensuring legal compliance. We propose a UML-based approach for modeling procedural legal rules. With help from legal experts, we investigate actual legal texts, identifying both the information needs and sources of complexity in the formalization of procedural legal rules. Building on this study, we develop a UML profile that enables more precise modeling of such legal rules. To be able to use logic-based tools for compliance analysis, we automatically transform models of procedural legal rules into the Object Constraint Language (OCL). We report on an application of our approach to Luxembourg's Income Tax Law providing initial evidence for the feasibility and usefulness of our approach.

1 Introduction

Legal compliance is a major concern for governments. In domains such as taxation and social benefits, laws need to be operationalized so that they can be implemented into administrative procedures and software systems. Such operationalization is typically performed by putting in place a legal framework, comprised of legislation, regulations, and circulars, aimed at providing a detailed interpretation of the underlying laws. These frameworks are often *prescriptive*: they provide step-by-step guidance in the form of *procedural rules* as to what needs to be done for compliance. Procedural legal rules are closely linked to the behavior of eGovernment applications. To illustrate, consider Article 2 from Luxembourg's Income Tax Law [14], describing how taxpayers are classified as resident and non-resident:

Article 2.[1] *Individuals are considered resident taxpayers if they have their address in the Grand Duchy. Individuals are considered non-resident taxpayers if they do not reside in the Grand Duchy but have a local income within the definition of Article 156.*

To be able to analyze whether a software system complies with the taxpayer classification described in the law, one could develop a UML model like the one

---

[1] The article has been translated from the original French text and simplified.

J. Dingel et al. (Eds.): MODELS 2014, LNCS 8767, pp. 450–466, 2014.

in Fig. 1: The domain model in Fig. 1(a) captures the main concepts and associations in Article 2 of the Income Tax Law; and the OCL expression in Fig. 1(b), written in the context of `TaxPayer`, provides a procedural rule for distinguishing between resident and non-resident taxpayers (L. 2-5 and 7-13, respectively).

To be a resident taxpayer, one must have a Luxembourgish address (L. 2-3). If such an address exists (L. 4), the taxpayer is deemed resident (L. 5). To be a non-resident taxpayer, one must have a local income (L. 7-8) but no local address. If these requirements are met (L. 9), the taxpayer is deemed non-resident (L. 10). A model like that in Fig. 1 makes the underlying legal article amenable to automated analysis. In particular, one can use such a model to check whether the outcome produced by a software system

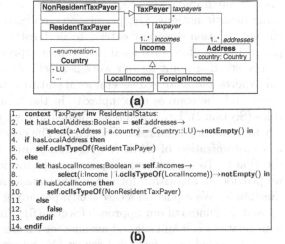

Fig. 1. (a) domain model for a legal article, (b) procedural rule for the article (expressed as OCL)

is consistent with the law. For example, using existing OCL evaluators such as Eclipse OCL [11], one can verify if a system correctly classifies taxpayers (instances of the model in Fig. 1(a)) into resident and non-resident.

Before a model such as the one in Fig. 1 can be used for automated analysis, it needs to be reviewed and validated by legal experts. To aid with validation, it is helpful to express procedural rules such as that in Fig. 1(b) in a visual manner.

This paper develops a visual and at the same time semantically-precise way to model procedural legal rules. Our approach follows the Domain-Specific Modeling (DSM) paradigm; but rather than building a new language, we use UML's built-in customization mechanism, namely *profiles* [22], to adapt UML for use in our context. Using UML is motivated by its widespread use, commercial tool support, and the availability of standard extension mechanisms in the language.

Our work addresses a real need observed during our collaboration with our public service partner, CTIE (Centre des Technologies de l'Information de l'Etat). CTIE is Luxembourg's national center for information technologies and responsible for developing eGovernment services for the state. CTIE already applies Model Driven Engineering (MDE), including UML and its extensions, for system development and is interested in enhancing its development methods with means for modeling legal rules. An important consideration for CTIE is for the models to be palatable to governmental stakeholders without IT background, but who have familiarity with simple conceptual models and business process models from earlier exposure and training.

The approach we propose in this paper is not meant as a general solution for modeling all types of legal rules. In particular, we focus on prescriptive legal frameworks where legal rules are procedural. This situation is typical of highly-regulated domains such as taxation and social benefits. In general, however, many legal frameworks, e.g. privacy laws, are declarative, with rules defined using deontic notions, i.e., permissions, obligations, and prohibitions [24]. Our current solution does not extend to declarative legal rules. In the rest of this paper, we therefore take legal rule to mean "procedural" legal rule.

The starting point for our work is a field study, where we interacted with legal experts and analyzed several legal statutes, to identify both the information needs and the sources of complexity in the formalization of (procedural) legal rules (Section 2). Drawing on our field study, we define a UML-based methodology for modeling legal rules (Section 3). The core component of the methodology is a customization of UML Activity Diagrams, defined through a UML profile (Section 4). To use for analysis purposes the models resulting from our approach, we provide an algorithm for automatic transformation of the models into OCL (Section 5). We report on a case study, providing initial evidence for the feasibility and usefulness of our approach (Section 6). Finally, we compare our approach with related work and suggest avenues for future work (Sections 7–8). The paper is accompanied by a technical report [26] where we provides additional details about our UML profile and automated transformation to OCL.

2   Field Study of Legal Rules

Our field study applies a Grounded Theory (GT) process [8], whereby observations and analysis of collected data are used for defining the problems to be addressed. In our context, we apply GT to define (1) what needs to be expressed in models of legal rules, i.e., the information requirements that such models should meet; and (2) factors that lead to complexity in models of legal rules and thus need special consideration in an approach targeted at building such models.

We began our field study with a series of meetings with legal experts, totaling ≈ 15 hours. The purpose of these meetings was (a) for the researchers to develop familiarity with legal concepts; (b) to define a suitable scope for the laws to consider; and (c) to identify representative legal rules for further investigation. Taxation was selected as the scope for the study, partly because of the priorities of the legal experts in our study, and partly because of the tax law's large societal impact. Our field study resulted in several observations, outlined below.

Information Requirements. To identify the information needs in the specification of legal rules, we analyzed selected legal texts concerned with personal income taxes. While personal income taxes are only one facet of the tax law, the experts deemed the scope to be largely representative within the tax domain and the closely related domain of social benefits delivery. With help from legal experts, we identified, read, and interpreted the legal provisions relevant to personal income taxes. Our analysis covered a summary of direct taxes levied by the Government of Luxembourg, 16 articles from Luxembourg's Income Tax

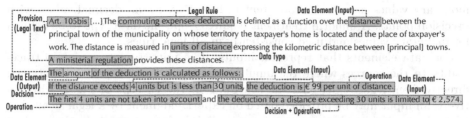

Fig. 2. Excerpt of Article 105bis from *LITL* (translated from French)

Law (for brevity, referred to as *LITL* in the remainder of this paper), three regulations, one tax scale, and several official web pages and circular letters.

While reading the above material, we applied a standard technique from qualitative data analysis [8,21,9] for analyzing text, and classifying, describing, and connecting the information presented in it. We annotated each important concept with a label denoting the nature of the concept, i.e., a meta-concept. Each time that a new meta-concept was encountered, we defined it in a glossary. As we proceeded through the text, we either created new labels or reused previous ones based on the definitions we had. We illustrate our analysis over an excerpt, shown in Fig. 2, of Art. 105bis of *LITL*. The excerpt, a simplified translation of the original French text, covers many of the information requirements identified by our study. The meta-concepts gleaned from the excerpt are shaded and labeled.

The **(Legal) Rule** the excerpt is concerned with is calculating the deduction a taxpayer is eligible for in relation to their commuting expenses. A rule may depend on several **Provisions**. It is important to maintain traceability from rules to the provisions they depend on. This is necessary both for reasoning about compliance and also for managing change in a predictable way. For the commuting expenses deduction, these provisions are: Art. 105bis of *LITL*, and an abstract reference to a ministerial regulation. *LITL* does not cite any regulation explicitly, as regulations may vary from year to year. The regulation that was in effect for commuting distances at the time our study was conducted is the ministerial regulation of February 6, 2012 ("règlement ministériel du 6 février 2012").

Each rule is made up of a set of **Decisions** and **Operations**, describing the (procedural) flow of the rule. An example decision from the excerpt is: *"If the distance exceeds 4 units but is less than 30 units"*; an example operation is setting *"the deduction [amount to be] €99 per unit of distance"*.

There are several **Data Elements** in the excerpt, denoting inputs to, outputs from, or intermediate values computed within the rule. For example, *distance* is an input to and *amount* is the output from the rule. The constants in the text, e.g., €2,574, are marked as input. This choice is motivated by the fact that constants may change over time and thus need to be treated explicitly.

Data elements are typed. The types are sometimes specified in the text, e.g., the excerpt states that *distance* is measured in certain units; but most often, the types are implicit, e.g., for monetary values and dates. One of the goals of our analysis was to identify and restrict the data types associated with the inputs and outputs of legal rules. Doing so is important for improving consistency. For example, all mathematical operations, e.g., summation and multiplication, over monetary values have to be consistent in how they round decimal values with precision points. A uniform treatment requires a specific data type to be defined for monetary values and used consistently in all legal rules.

For data elements that represent inputs, it is important to maintain traceability to the sources where the inputs come from. Some inputs are obtained directly from legal texts, e.g., the constants in the excerpt of Fig. 2. Alternatively, an input may be provided based on expert judgment by a legal agent. For example, to decide whether a company is eligible for certain deductions, a tax officer may need to determine whether the accounting performed by the company is adequate. Finally, an input may be derived from a physical or electronic data record, e.g., the *distance* input mentioned in the excerpt.

We distinguish different sources for inputs. The distinctions are important for better elaboration and validation of legal rules. For example, elaborating the inputs derived from electronic records often requires consultation with both legal experts and IT staff; whereas, inputs based on expert judgment or legal texts typically only concern legal experts.

Based on our analysis above, we have developed an abstract information model, shown in Fig. 3, for legal rules. The model is organized into three packages, in line with the three main observations from the analysis, namely: (1) capturing legal rules as decisions and operations, (2) maintaining traceability, (3) restricting data types to what is essential.

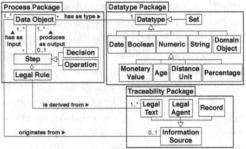

Fig. 3. Information model for legal rules

The `Process` package in Fig. 3 defines the concepts related to the flow of a rule. Each `Legal Rule` is made up of a set of `Steps`, which can be either `Decisions` or `Operations`. Each step has `Data Objects` as input and output. The `Traceability` package groups the information sources to which traceability needs to be maintained from the elements in the `Process` package. Rules need to be traceable to `Legal Texts`. Inputs need to be linked to the `Legal Text`, `Legal Agent`, or `Record` where they originate from. The `Datatype` package contains a partial list of data types identified in our study. There is a special data type, named `Domain Object`, to enable handling instances of domain concepts, e.g., `TaxPayer` (see Fig. 1(a)). In addition, the data types include a composite type, `Set`, to enable handling sets of objects. Note that the data types in Fig. 3 are specific to the tax law and may require tailoring if the approach is applied to other laws and regulations.

Complexity Factors. We considered nine legal rules from *LITL* in our analysis of complexity factors. Six of these concern requirements on taxpayers' records (e.g, the taxpayer classification in Fig. 1). The rest concern the calculation of income tax credits. We captured these rules in OCL (total of 108 OCL lines, excluding comments and blanks). Our investigation of the resulting OCL constraints alongside our interactions with legal experts led to the following observations:

– *Navigation*: Navigation expressions in OCL tend to be lengthy for legal rules. For example, Art. 127 of *LITL* sets a cap on the costs a taxpayer can claim for the care of dependents. Calculating this cap requires identifying the dependents who live in the same household as the taxpayer but are not taxpayers themselves, and for whom the taxpayer receives some allowance. The corresponding OCL navigation expression (the OCL context being `TaxPayer`) is as follows:

```
self.taxPayerDependents→select(dependent:Person| not dependent.oclIsTypeOf(TaxPayer) and
    dependent.addresses→intersection(self.addresses)→notEmpty() and
    dependent.allowances.amount→sum()>0)
```

The complexity of navigation expressions is caused in part by the expressive (and thus long) labels of domain model elements in legal contexts, and in part by the richness of legal rules and the need for multiple navigation levels.

– *Branching*: Legal rules often have numerous decision branches, capturing the different cases where they apply and the corresponding actions to take. To illustrate, we recall the example of Fig. 1. Even for the simple task of classifying taxpayers into resident and non-resident, we need two if-then-else statements (or similarly complex propositional logic equivalents of if-then-else). This number rises to six or seven for more complex rules. Feedback from legal experts indicate that branching statements negatively impact comprehension.

– *Iteration*: OCL iterator operations (e.g., `select`, `exists`, `forAll`, `iterate`) are often inevitable in legal rules. For instance, in the navigation expression given earlier for identifying eligible dependents, one has to iterate over the dependents to determine which ones satisfy the desired criteria. Our interaction with legal experts suggests that iterations, specially nested ones, reduce comprehensibility.

Our approach, described next, take steps to address the observed information requirements and complexity factors.

3   Modeling Methodology

An overview of our modeling methodology is shown in Fig. 4. The legal texts and the specific provisions within them that are relevant to the legal rules of interest are provided as input by legal experts. The modeling step in the methodology includes two parallel but interrelated tasks: (1) modeling the domain and (2) modeling the legal rules. Both tasks require close interaction with legal experts to ensure a sound understanding of the underlying legal notions. The first task results in a domain model, providing a precise

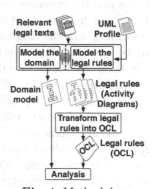

Fig. 4. Methodology

representation of the concepts and relationships in the input legal texts. As is common in object-oriented analysis, we use UML class diagrams for representing domain models [18]. A domain model excerpt for Article 2 of *LITL* was shown in Fig. 1(a). We follow standard practices for domain modeling and thus do not elaborate this task further. For guidelines, see [18].

The second modeling task, i.e., modeling of the legal rules, is performed using a customization of UML Activity Diagrams (ADs). ADs have long been used for modeling procedural aspects of systems and organizations [17]. The procedural nature of legal rules makes ADs a good match for our needs. Our customization of AD's is based on UML profiles [22].

The domain model in our methodology is an instrument for elaborating the information that legal rules use as input. It is thus best to conduct tasks (1) and (2) *in tandem* and not sequentially. Doing these tasks in parallel ensures that the domain model is aligned with the legal rules in terms of data needs, and further narrows the scope of domain modeling to what is necessary for supporting the legal rules of interest. Once the legal rules have been modeled using our tailored AD notation, the models are automatically translated into OCL. The resulting OCL expressions along with the domain model can then be used for automated analysis using OCL evaluators [11] and OCL solvers [7,1].

Our main technical goal in this paper is to present the profile we have developed to customize ADs for expressing legal rules, and to describe how ADs built using our profile are transformed into OCL. The profile and the OCL transformation are respectively tackled in Sections 4 and 5.

4   UML Profile for Legal Rules

Our profile's stereotypes are shown in the first column of Table 1, followed by a description in the second column. The third column shows the UML meta-class(es) that each stereotype extends. We distinguish two kinds of stereotypes: (1) those that directly represent concepts from the information model of Fig. 3, and (2) those that are auxiliary, providing additional information about model elements. The fourth column in Table 1 shows the mapping between the stereotypes and the concepts and packages of our information model. Auxiliary stereotypes are marked as *Auxiliary* in the column. The *Datatype* package of the information model is not represented through stereotypes. Instead, typing information is attached directly to the input and output nodes of ADs. The profile diagram, the relevant fragment of the UML metamodel, and our datatype library are provided in the supplementary material [26].

We illustrate our profile over the Commuting Expenses Deduction rule from the excerpt of Article 105bis given in Fig. 2. The French term for this deduction is "Frais de Déplacement". We refer to this deduction as *FD*. In Fig. 5, we show how the FD rule is modeled using an AD. The «rule» stereotype applied to the AD in this figure indicates that the AD is a legal rule. The AD is further annotated with a «context» stereotype denoting the OCL context in which the AD is being specified. The context is always an instance of a class from the underlying domain model. For the AD in Fig. 5, the context is an instance of the TaxPayer class from the domain model.

The core of the AD in Fig. 5 is a calculation procedure. The procedure yields a value of 0 (zero) when a taxpayer is deemed not eligible for FD, i.e., when distance > minimal_distance is false. For an eligible taxpayer, the procedure yields the result of multiplying three quantities: (1) a flat rate (constant) from the law, denoted flat_rate, (2) the distance between a taxpayer's work and home

Table 1. UML profile stereotypes

Stereotype	Description	UML Metaclass(es)	Concept & Package	
«rule»	Defines an activity as a legal rule	`Activity`	Legal Rule	
«iterative»	Defines an iterative region	`ExpansionRegion`		
«context»	Defines the OCL context in which a legal rule is being specified	`Activity`	*Auxiliary*	
«decision»	Defines a decision step	`DecisionNode`	Operation	
«calculate»	Defines an operation that calculates a value	`OpaqueAction`		
«assert»	Defines an operation that checks an assertion	`OpaqueAction`	*Auxiliary*	*Process*
«in»	Defines an input to a legal rule	`ActivityParameterNode,` `InputPin`	Data Object	
«out»	Defines an output from a region	`OutputPin`		
«intermediate»	Defines an intermediate value resulting from a calculation	`CentralBufferNode`	*Auxiliary*	
«formula»	Defines the formula for a calculation	`Constraint`	*Auxiliary*	
«statement»	Defines the logical expression for an assertion	`Constraint`	*Auxiliary*	
«fromlaw»	Declares a (constant) input as originating from a legal text	`ActivityParameterNode,` `InputPin`	Legal Text	
«fromagent»	Declares an input as being provided by a legal expert	`ActivityParameterNode,` `InputPin`	Legal Agent	*Traceability*
«fromrecord»	Declares an input as being retrieved from a record (e.g., a database)	`ActivityParameterNode,` `InputPin`	Record	
«query»	Defines the query for obtaining an input from its respective source	`Comment`	*Auxiliary*	

addresses, denoted `distance`, and (3) a prorated ratio representing the full-time equivalent period during which the taxpayer has been employed over the course of the tax year, denoted `prorata_period`. The formula applies up to a maximum home-to-work distance threshold, denoted `maximal_distance` and specified in the law. Beyond this threshold, a nominal rate, denoted `maximal_flat_rate`, is applied irrespective of distance but prorated as discussed above.

As illustrated in Fig. 5, the decisions and calculations are marked respectively with the «decision» and «calculate» stereotypes. Each calculation has a «formula» constraint attached, providing the formula for the calculation. The result of a calculation is always stored in a (typed) intermediate variable marked by the «intermediate» stereotype, e.g., `expected_amount` in Fig. 5.

Each legal rule concludes with an assertion: an operation marked by the «assert» stereotype and providing an implicit Boolean output for the rule. Specifically, an assertion is used to ascertain that the outcome produced by a system or a human agent matches the outcome envisaged by the legal rule. Associated with an assertion is a constraint with the «statement» stereotype, defining the Boolean claim that needs to be checked. For example, the assertion in Fig. 5 checks whether the value of FD on a taxpayer's file, denoted `actual_amount`, matches the value computed by the rule, denoted `expected_amount`.

Inputs to decisions and operations are represented by small rectangles with a gray shade and an «in» stereotype. The origin of each input is captured through one of the following stereotypes: «fromlaw», «fromrecord» or «fromagent». Each input has a query attached to it, represented as a comment with a «query» stereotype. A query provides details on how an input is obtained from its source. The «fromlaw» stereotype is used for inputs that are constants and specified in a legal text, e.g., `flat_rate`. For these inputs, the query provides a traceability link

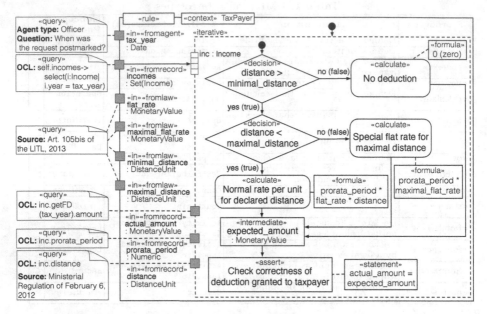

Fig. 5. Activity Diagram for Commuting Expenses Deduction (FD)

to the legal provision where the constant is defined. The «fromrecord» stereotype is used for inputs derived from a record, e.g., incomes. For these, the query is an OCL expression over the underlying domain model. Additional information may be provided along the OCL expression such as the legal text that describes the input, e.g., distance. Finally, «fromagent» stereotype is applied to inputs that originate from a legal agent, e.g., tax_year. For these, the query provides information about the agent type (role) authorized to provide the input as well as the question that the agent needs to answer.

The legal rule in Fig. 5 takes into account the fact that a taxpayer may have multiple (simultaneous or sequential) employment activities, and thus multiple incomes and work addresses. To correctly compute the FD for a taxpayer, one needs to iterate over *all* incomes gained by the taxpayer and ensure that the computation of the FD portion for each income is consistent with the law. To capture this iterative behavior, we use expansion regions from the AD notation. An expansion region is an activity region that executes multiple times over the elements of an input collection [22]. The legal rule of Fig. 5 has one expansion region with incomes as its input collection. UML provides three execution modes for expansion regions: *iterative, parallel,* and *stream* [22]. Of these, our profile uses only the iterative mode, marked by the «iterative» stereotype. In this mode, executions are performed sequentially and according to the order of elements in the input collection. The name of the region's expansion node, inc in our example, serves as an alias for the iterator element in an individual execution. This alias can be used in the OCL expressions associated with the inputs of the expansion region, e.g., the OCL expression in the query attached to prorata_period.

The expansion region in the legal rule of Fig. 5 does not require an explicit output because the assert operation occurs within the expansion region. Our profile allows expansion regions to have an explicit output. This is useful for capturing complex iterative calculations, e.g., computing the total amount of benefits received by the dependents of a taxpayer. We use the «out» stereotype to denote the (explicit) output of an expansion region, if one exists.

Consistency Constraints. To apply our profile in a sound manner, a number of consistency constraints need to hold. We provide a complete list of these constraints in the supplementary material [26]. The consistency constraints are aimed at enforcing the following: (1) Completeness of the information in models of legal rules, e.g., to ensure that the source for each input has been specified through the application of an appropriate stereotype and a query; (2) Mutually exclusive application of certain stereotypes, e.g., to ensure that each input has one and only one source stereotype («fromlaw», «fromrecord» or «fromagent») applied to it; and (3) Restrictions on the structure of ADs. Most notably, these structural restrictions ensure that the flows do not give rise to cyclic paths, and further that only the notational elements allowed by our methodology are being used. All consistency constraints can be enforced as the models are being built.

We next describe how ADs built using our profile are transformed into OCL.

5   Transforming Legal Rules into OCL

In this section, we provide an algorithm to automatically transform ADs to OCL, and illustrate this model-to-text transformation over the Commuting Expenses Deduction (FD) rule discussed in Section 4. The choice of OCL as the target language for the transformation is motivated by OCL being part of the UML and further to benefit from existing testing and simulation frameworks, e.g., [1], that are built around OCL. This section does not cover all the implementation details of our transformation. See the supplementary material for full details [26].

The algorithm for the transformation, named **ADToOCL** and shown in Alg. 1, takes as input an Activity Diagram, $\mathcal{AD}$, and an element $\in \mathcal{AD}$. Specifically, $\mathcal{AD}$ is an instantiation of the UML metamodel fragment for activity modeling, and element is an object within this instantiation. We assume that $\mathcal{AD}$ satisfies the consistency constraints of our profile (Section 4). To ensure consistency between the semantics of activity diagrams and that of the OCL constraints generated from them, we further assume that $\mathcal{AD}$ uses only deterministic decisions.

Initially, the algorithm is called over $\mathcal{AD}$ with element pointing to the root Activity instance in $\mathcal{AD}$. In Fig. 6, we show the OCL constraint resulting from the application of Alg. 1 to the FD rule of Fig. 5. Note that when our approach is applied, analysts work over the ADs and are not exposed to such complex OCL constraints. The generated constraints are meant for use by OCL engines.

The transformation is based on a set of predefined patterns. These patterns are detailed in the supplementary material [26]. Each pattern is defined as a graph P. If P is matched to a subgraph of $\mathcal{AD}$ rooted at element, the appropriate OCL fragment for P is generated. For example, consider the intermediate value

---

Alg. 1: ADToOCL

Inputs : (1) An Activity Diagram, $\mathcal{AD}$. (2) An element $\in \mathcal{AD}$.
Output: An OCL string, result.

```
1  if (element is NULL) then
2  │    return ' ' /* Return empty string */
3  end if
4  Let P be the transformation pattern applicable to element.
5  Let input_1, ..., input_n be the non-declared inputs required by P.
6  foreach input_i do
7  │    result ← result+ADToOCL(AD, input_i)
8  end foreach
9  if (element is not a DecisionNode) then
10 │    Let st_1, st_2 respectively be the opening and closing OCL fragments obtained from applying P.
11 │    Let next be the next element to visit. /* ... chosen based on P and its outgoing flow */
12 │    result ← result+st_1+ADToOCL(AD, next)+st_2
13 │    if (element is an ExpansionRegion with an output) then
14 │    │    Let out denote the output element.
15 │    │    result ← result+ADToOCL(AD, out)
16 │    end if
17 else
18 │    Let f_1, ..., f_m be the outgoing flows from element. /* m ≥ 1 */
19 │    foreach f_i do
20 │    │    if (i = 1) then
21 │    │    │    result←result+'if('+element.name+')='+f_i.name+'then'+ADToOCL(AD, f_i.target)
22 │    │    else
23 │    │    │    result←result+'else if('+element.name+')='+f_i.name+'then'+ADToOCL(AD, f_i.target)
24 │    │    end if
25 │    end foreach
26 │    result ← result+'else false'+'endif'+...+'endif'     [m times]
27 end if
28 return result
```

(Left margin brackets: Input declarations — lines 4–8; Transforming non-decisions — lines 9–16; Transforming decisions — lines 17–26)

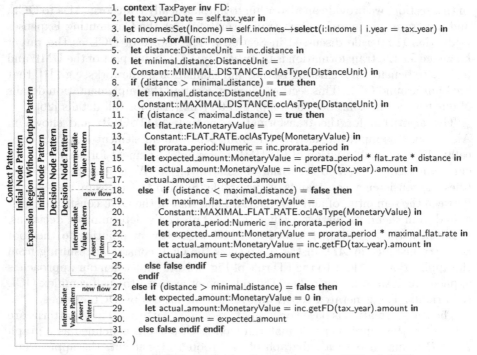

1. **context** TaxPayer **inv** FD:
2. **let** tax_year:Date = self.tax_year **in**
3. **let** incomes:Set(Income) = self.incomes→**select**(i:Income | i.year = tax_year) **in**
4. incomes→**forAll**(inc:Income |
5.   **let** distance:DistanceUnit = inc.distance **in**
6.   **let** minimal_distance:DistanceUnit =
7.   Constant::MINIMAL_DISTANCE.oclAsType(DistanceUnit) **in**
8.   **if** (distance > minimal_distance) = **true then**
9.   **let** maximal_distance:DistanceUnit =
10.   Constant::MAXIMAL_DISTANCE.oclAsType(DistanceUnit) **in**
11.   **if** (distance < maximal_distance) = **true then**
12.   **let** flat_rate:MonetaryValue =
13.   Constant::FLAT_RATE.oclAsType(MonetaryValue) **in**
14.   **let** prorata_period:Numeric = inc.prorata_period **in**
15.   **let** expected_amount:MonetaryValue = prorata_period * flat_rate * distance **in**
16.   **let** actual_amount:MonetaryValue = inc.getFD(tax_year).amount **in**
17.   actual_amount = expected_amount
18.   **else   if** (distance < maximal_distance) = **false then**
19.   **let** maximal_flat_rate:MonetaryValue =
20.   Constant::MAXIMAL_FLAT_RATE.oclAsType(MonetaryValue) **in**
21.   **let** prorata_period:Numeric = inc.prorata_period **in**
22.   **let** expected_amount:MonetaryValue = prorata_period * maximal_flat_rate **in**
23.   **let** actual_amount:MonetaryValue = inc.getFD(tax_year).amount **in**
24.   actual_amount = expected_amount
25.   **else false endif**
26.   **endif**
27. **else if** (distance > minimal_distance) = **false then**
28.   **let** expected_amount:MonetaryValue = 0 **in**
29.   **let** actual_amount:MonetaryValue = inc.getFD(tax_year).amount **in**
30.   actual_amount = expected_amount
31. **else false endif endif**
32.)

(Left margin labels for brackets: Context Pattern; Initial Node Pattern; Expansion Region Without Output Pattern; Initial Node Pattern; Decision Node Pattern; Decision Node Pattern; Intermediate Value Pattern; Assert Pattern; Intermediate Value Pattern; Assert Pattern — new flow; Intermediate Value Pattern; Assert Pattern — new flow)

Fig. 6. Generated OCL expression for the example of Fig. 5 (FD)

expected_amount in FD. There is a pattern, *Intermediate Value Pattern*, that deals with such values. This pattern has the following shape: an action with the «calculate» stereotype connected by a flow to an intermediate value with the «intermediate» stereotype. The application of this pattern generates a **let** expression which defines an intermediate value based on a given calculation. This pattern is applied three times during the transformation of FD for the three calculations that lead to expected_amount. The OCL fragments for these three applications are shown on L. 15, 22, and 28 of the constraint in Fig. 6.

The transformation process is recursive and mimics a depth-first traversal of the underlying graph of $\mathcal{AD}$. There are three main parts to this process: (1) input declarations (Alg. 1, L. 4-8); (2) transformation of all elements other than decisions (Alg. 1, L. 10-16). Within this class of elements, additional processing is necessary for expansion regions to propagate their output if they have one (Alg. 1, L. 13-16); and (3) transformation of decision nodes (Alg. 1, L. 18-26).

The first part of the transformation process concerns identifying all inputs to be declared before transforming a given element (Alg. 1, L. 5). Each such input is transformed into a **let** expression (Alg. 1, L. 6-8). To illustrate, consider the decision distance > minimal_distance in FD. The inputs to this decision are transformed into L. 5-7 of the constraint in Fig. 6. This is performed before the transformation of the decision itself (Fig. 6, L. 8). An input may have dependencies to other inputs, e.g., incomes (Fig. 6, L. 3) depends on tax_year (Fig. 6, L. 2). Such dependencies are handled through the recursive call of L. 7 in Alg. 1.

The second part of the process handles non-decisions. This is where the initial call to Alg. 1 begins to unwind. The initial call is handled by the *Context Pattern*, which transforms the context information attached to an Activity instance via the «context» stereotype. There are no inputs associated with the *Context Pattern*. Handling the pattern thus reduces to executing L. 10-12 of Alg. 1. The opening OCL fragment (st_1) resulting from the application of this pattern is L. 1 of Fig. 6; the closing fragment (st_2) is empty. Then, on L. 12 of Alg. 1 a recursive call is made with *next* set to the initial node of FD. The unwinding of this recursive call generates the remainder of the OCL constraint (Fig. 6, L. 2-32). On the left side of Fig. 6, we mark the scope of each recursive call and the respective pattern. To avoid clutter, calls that handle input declarations are not marked.

The third and final part of the process transforms decisions into if-then-else statements. This part is analogous to what we previously described.

We have implemented our transformation using Acceleo [10] – a model-to-text transformation tool for Eclipse. Our Acceleo implementation is closely aligned with the way we present the transformation in Alg. 1. While we currently support only OCL as the target language for the transformation, it is possible to modify our text generation rules to support other languages, e.g., Alloy [16].

6   Evaluation

We report on an industrial case study where we apply our approach to *LITL*. The case study is an initial step towards answering the following Research Questions

(RQs): **RQ1.** *Is the approach expressive enough to model complex legal rules?* **RQ2.** *Is the level of effort required by our approach reasonable?* And, **RQ3.** *Are the ADs built using our approach structurally less complex than OCL constraints written directly?* In the longer term, we plan to perform more extensive user studies to evaluate the approach in a more thorough manner.

Our case study builds on an initiative by the Government of Luxembourg to improve its eGovernment services in the area of taxation. One of the main objectives of the initiative is to ensure that these services remain *verifiably compliant* with the tax law as the law evolves. A key prerequisite for verification of compliance is to have analyzable models of the tax law. Our case study develops such models for a substantial fragment of the income tax law. The case study was conducted in collaboration with our public service partner, CTIE.

Study selection and execution. Our study concerns a set of legal rules from *LITL*. Luxembourg has two complementary schemes for income taxes: (1) withholding taxes from salaries, and (2) assessing taxes based on a declaration. Our study focuses on the former scheme. The basis for withholding is a *tax card*, detailing the tax deductions and credits that apply to an income. Deductions are expense items subtracted from the gross income before taxes. Credits are items applied either against the taxes due or paid to the taxpayer in cash. A tax card provides information about five deductions and three credits. The deductions are for commuting expenses (FD), miscellaneous expenses (FO), spousal expenses (AC), extraordinary expenses (CE), and special expenses (DS). CE is decomposed into three sub-categories and DS into six. The credits are for salaried workers (CIS), pensioners (CIP), and single parents (CIM).

The above deductions and credits give rise to 15 legal rules. We applied our methodology described in Section 3 for expressing these rules. This resulted in a domain model and 15 ADs built using our profile. The domain model has 7 packages, 61 classes, 15 enumerations, 106 attributes, and 24 operations. The distribution for the number of elements in the ADs is given in the box plot of Fig. 7. The element

Fig. 7. # of AD elements (distribution)

count for each AD is the sum of the number of inputs, outputs, decisions, actions, flows, intermediate variables, expansion regions, and constraint/comment boxes.

Discussion. We next discuss the RQs that motivated our study. The three tax credits in our study (CIS, CIP, and CIM) were used previously in our investigation of OCL complexity factors (Section 2) along with six other rules that are unrelated to the case study. Since we had a priori knowledge about the tax credits, the AD models for the tax credits are uninteresting for RQ1. To mitigate learning effects, we further exclude these three models when discussing RQ2.

RQ1. Our profile provided enough expressiveness to conveniently capture the legal rules in our study. One of the factors we considered in our models was to avoid nested structures, particularly nested expansion regions. Although our profile and OCL transformation can handle nesting, models containing nested

Table 2. Comparison of complexity: direct use of OCL vs. OCL fragments in ADs

		FD		FO		AC		CE1		CE2		CE3		DS1		DS2		DS3		DS4		DS5		DS6		CIS		CIP		CIM	
		M	A	M	A	M	A	M	A	M	A	M	A	M	A	M	A	M	A	M	A	M	A	M	A	M	A	M	A	M	A
Complexity metrics	C_1 (# navigations)	1	5	12	5	11	10	10	5	6	2	12	6	6	6	8	3	17	11	9	3	4	3	9	6	6	2	6	3	13	7
	C_2 (# if statements)	3	0	5	0	6	0	7	0	4	0	4	0	4	0	3	0	6	0	4	0	3	0	3	0	2	0	2	0	3	0
	C_3 (# collection_op's)	3	0	6	0	3	3	17	2	8	0	10	1	8	3	4	1	12	3	8	0	3	1	5	1	6	4	6	4	5	1
	C_4 (# iterative_op's)	3	1	5	1	8	6	9	2	5	1	7	1	6	4	4	2	7	6	5	1	3	2	4	2	2	1	2	1	5	4

structures can be hard to comprehend. In our study, we could avoid nesting in all models by choosing a suitable OCL context for each of the legal rules.

RQ2. We are interested in measuring the level of effort as an indicator for whether the approach has a realistic chance of adoption in practice. The ADs were built by the first author, who has 6 years of formal training in computer science and 3 years of experience in MDE. The models were built following a half-day tutorial on personal income taxes by legal experts. The domain model was developed simultaneously with the ADs, as suggested in Section 3. Developing the 12 ADs for tax deductions took ≈ 40 person-hours (ph) including the effort spent on the domain model. This is an average of 3.3 ph per AD. The 3 ADs for tax credits took ≈ 7 ph to build, i.e., an average of 2.3 ph per AD. Only the tax deductions are representative in terms of effort, due to reasons discussed earlier. Once built, the ADs were presented to a group of six legal experts in a half-day training and walkthrough session. We received positive feedback from the legal experts involved in our study; however, we have not yet conducted a detailed user study to thoroughly assess our approach. We consider the overall effort to be worthwhile as the resulting models provide a complete characterization of the tax card, which applies to a large majority of the taxpayers.

RQ3. Our profile limits the use of OCL to the inputs, formulas, and statements of ADs. In this way, the profile to a large extent shields users from OCL and the structural complexity of OCL expressions. Reynoso et al. [23] argue that reductions in OCL structural complexity bring about reductions in cognitive complexity and improvements in understandability. The aim of RQ3 is to measure the value of our profile in terms of structural complexity reduction when compared to the situation where legal rules are directly written in OCL. This comparison provides preliminary insights as to whether our profile can result in more intuitive and understandable specifications of legal rules.

To answer RQ3, the second author manually wrote constraints for the tax deductions, in a similar manner to the tax credits (Section 2). We then compared these constraints to the OCL expressions used in the ADs, i.e., the OCL expressions to which the users of our profile are exposed. For the comparison, we selected a subset of the OCL structural complexity metrics proposed by Reynoso et al. [23]. Our selection was driven by what we deemed relevant to the complexity factors observed in our field study (Section 2). Specifically, we consider the following metrics: number of navigations (C_1), number of if-then-else statements (C_2), number of operations on collections, e.g., any, sum, excludes (C_3), and number of iterative operations, e.g., select, forAll (C_4). C_1 and C_2 respectively reflect the *navigation* and *branching* complexity factors; C_3 and C_4 both relate to the *iteration* complexity factor.

Table 2 shows the metrics, across all the deductions and credits, for manually-written OCL constraints (denoted, **M**) vs. the OCL fragments used in the ADs (denoted, **A**). As the table suggests, the ADs built using our approach lead to reductions in structural complexity. In particular, the AD's reduce on average: C_1 by 45%, C_2 by 100%[2], C_3 by 72%, and C_4 53%. The structural complexity that carries over to the ADs is primarily caused by the OCL expressions that define the inputs to the ADs. To validate the ADs with non-software engineers, one can replace these expressions with intuitive descriptions without any impact on the ADs. Finally, we need to emphasize that the complexity reductions seen are only suggestive of benefits, but not definitive evidence for them. Further empirical validation remains essential to determine whether the complexity reductions indeed translate into improved understandability.

7   Related Work

In this section, we compare our approach with several areas of related work.

Legal Rules. van Engers et al. [28] express legal rules via OCL; however, they use OCL directly in their specifications. Our approach provides a model-based solution for expressing legal rules. Breaux et al. [5] describe a rule-based framework for legal requirements. Nevertheless, they do not operationalize these requirements. The legal rules in our approach are in contrast executable.

Verification of Legal Compliance. Compliance verification has long been studied for *business processes* in domains such as healthcare [12,13] and finance [15]. Few strands however address compliance for *software systems*. Notable among these is work by Maxwell et al. [19], where they derive system compliance rules from legal texts, and by Breaux [4] where he extracts finite state machines from legal texts to guide system compliance checking. These earlier strands focus on capturing the functional requirements of software systems. Our approach instead focuses on modeling software systems in terms of inputs and expected outputs (as envisaged by the law), and irrespectively of specific system functions.

Visualization of Logical Languages. Bottoni et al. [3] and Stein et al. [27] propose visualizations for OCL, and Amàlio et al. [2] – for the Z language [25]. These approaches are not tailored to legal rules and lack means for addressing the information requirements and complexity factors discussed in Section 2.

Model-to-OCL Transformation. Cabot et al. [6] construct OCL transformations of domain-specific language rules, and Milanović et al. [20] derive OCL constraints from integrity rule models. These approaches neither address legal rules nor tackle the transformation of activity diagrams, as done in our approach.

---

[2] The 100% reduction is due to the fact that the ADs in our study do not contain if-then-else statements, as all branching behaviors are captured using decision nodes.

8   Conclusion

We proposed a UML-based approach for modeling procedural legal rules. The key component of the approach is a profile for activity diagrams. To enable automated compliance analysis, we defined a transformation that produces OCL specifications from activity diagrams built using our profile. We presented a preliminary evaluation of our approach.

Our approach focuses on prescriptive legal frameworks. In the future, we would like to investigate how and to what extent our approach can accommodate declarative frameworks and notions such as permissions and obligations. Another topic for future work is to conduct more field studies and generalize our UML profile to a larger set of legal domains. Further, a more thorough evaluation of our approach is essential. In particular, the legal experts in our study underwent training before they were able to understand our models. Legal experts trained in other approaches, e.g., mathematical logic, may have done equally well. User studies are necessary to determine what advantages and disadvantages our approach offers compared to the direct use of logic. Finally, we plan to study how our models can support automated analysis tasks such as simulation.

Acknowledgement. Financial support was provided by CTIE and FNR under grant number FNR/P10/03. We are grateful to members of Luxembourg Inland Revenue Office and CTIE for sharing their valuable insights with us.

References

1. Ali, S., Zohaib Iqbal, M., Arcuri, A., Briand, L.: Generating test data from OCL constraints with search techniques. IEEE Transactions on Software Engineering 39(10), 1376–1402 (2013)
2. Amàlio, N., Kelsen, P., Ma, Q., Glodt, C.: Using VCL as an Aspect-Oriented Approach to Requirements Modelling. Transactions on Aspect-Oriented Software Development 7, 151–199 (2010)
3. Bottoni, P., Koch, M., Parisi-Presicce, F., Taentzer, G.: Consistency checking and visualization of OCL constraints. In: Evans, A., Caskurlu, B., Selic, B. (eds.) UML 2000. LNCS, vol. 1939, pp. 294–308. Springer, Heidelberg (2000)
4. Breaux, T.: A method to acquire compliance monitors from regulations. In: Proc. of 3rd Intl. Wrkshp. on RE and Law (RELAW 2010), pp. 17–26 (2010)
5. Breaux, T.: Exercising due diligence in legal requirements acquisition: A tool-supported, frame-based approach. In: Proc. of 17th IEEE Intl. Requirements Engineering Conf. (RE 2009), pp. 225–230 (2009)
6. Cabot, J., Clarisó, R., Guerra, E., Lara, J.: A UML/OCL framework for the analysis of graph transformation rules. Software and Systems Modeling 9(3), 335–357 (2010)
7. Cabot, J., Clariso, R., Riera, D.: Verification of UML/OCL class diagrams using constraint programming. In: Proc. of 2008 IEEE Conf. on Software Testing Verification and Validation Wrkshp. (ICST 2008), pp. 73–80 (2008)
8. Corbin, J., Strauss, A.: Basics of Qualitative Research: Techniques and Procedures for Developing Grounded Theory, 3rd edn. SAGE Publications (2008)

9. Dey, I.: Qualitative data analysis - A user-friendly guide for social scientists. Routledge (1993)
10. Eclipse Foundation: Acceleo - transforming models into code, http://www.eclipse.org/acceleo/ (last accessed: March 2014)
11. Eclipse Foundation: Ecore tools, http://www.eclipse.org/ecoretools/ (last accessed: March 2014)
12. Ghanavati, S., Amyot, D., Peyton, L.: Towards a framework for tracking legal compliance in healthcare. In: Krogstie, J., Opdahl, A.L., Sindre, G. (eds.) CAiSE 2007. LNCS, vol. 4495, pp. 218–232. Springer, Heidelberg (2007)
13. Goedertier, S., Vanthienen, J.: Designing compliant business processes with obligations and permissions. In: Eder, J., Dustdar, S. (eds.) BPM Workshops 2006. LNCS, vol. 4103, pp. 5–14. Springer, Heidelberg (2006)
14. Gov. of Luxembourg: Modified income tax law of December 4, 1967 (2013)
15. Hassan, W., Logrippo, L.: Requirements and compliance in legal systems: A logic approach. In: Proc. of 1st Intl. Wrkshp. on RE and Law (RELAW 2008), pp. 40–44 (2008)
16. Jackson, D.: Software Abstractions Logic, Language, and Analysis. The MIT Press (2006)
17. Korherr, B., List, B.: Extending the UML 2 activity diagram with business process goals and performance measures and the mapping to BPEL. In: Proc. of 2nd Intl. Wrkshp. on Best Practices of UML (ER BP-UML 2006), pp. 7–18 (2006)
18. Larman, C.: Applying UML and Patterns: An Introduction to Object-Oriented Analysis and Design and Iterative Development, 3rd edn. Prentice Hall (2004)
19. Maxwell, J., Anton, A.: Checking existing requirements for compliance with law using a production rule model. In: Proc. of 2nd Intl. Wrkshp. on RE and Law (RELAW 2009), pp. 1–6 (2009)
20. Milanovic, M., Gasevic, D., Giurca, A., Gerd, W., Devedzic, V.: Towards sharing rules between OWL/SWRL and UML/OCL. Electronic Communications of European Association of Software Science and Technology 5, 2–19 (2007)
21. Miles, M., Huberman, A.: Qualitative data analysis: An expanded sourcebook. SAGE (1994)
22. Object Management Group: UML 2.2 superstructure specification (2009)
23. Reynoso, L., Genero, M., Piattini, M.: Towards a metric suite for OCL expressions expressed within UML/OCL models. Journal of Computer Science and Technology 4(1), 38–44 (2004)
24. Ruiter, D.: Institutional Legal Facts: Legal Powers and their Effects. Kluwer Academic Publishers (1993)
25. Smith, G.: The Object-Z specification language. Kluwer (2000)
26. Soltana, G., Fourneret, E., Adedjouma, M., Sabetzadeh, M., Briand, L.: Using UML for modeling legal rules. Tech. Rep. TR-SnT-2014-3, Interdisciplinary Centre for Security, Reliability and Trust (SnT) (March 2014), http://people.svv.lu/soltana/Models14.pdf
27. Stein, D., Hanenberg, S., Unland, R.: A graphical notation to specify model queries for MDA transformations on UML models. In: Aßmann, U., Akşit, M., Rensink, A. (eds.) MDAFA 2003/2004. LNCS, vol. 3599, pp. 77–92. Springer, Heidelberg (2005)
28. van Engers, T., Gerrits, R., Boekenoogen, M., Glassée, E., Kordelaar, P.: POWER: using UML/OCL for modeling legislation - an application report. In: Proc. of 8th Intl. Conf. on Artificial Intelligence and Law (ICAIL 2008), pp. 157–167 (2001)

Resolution of Interfering Product Fragments in Software Product Line Engineering

Anatoly Vasilevskiy and Øystein Haugen

SINTEF, Pb. 124 Blindern, 0314 Oslo, Norway
{anatoly.vasilevskiy,oystein.haugen}@sintef.no

Abstract. The Common Variability Language (CVL) allows deriving new products in a software product line by substituting fragments (placement) in the base model. Relations between elements of different placement fragments are an issue. Substitutions involving interfering placements may give unexpected and unintended results. However, there is a pragmatic need to define and execute fragments with interference. The need emerges when several diagrams are views of a single model, such as a placement in one diagram and a placement in another diagram reference the same model elements. We handle the issue by 1) classifying interfering fragments, 2) finding criteria to detect them, and 3) suggesting solutions via transformations. We implement our findings in the tooling available for downloading.

Keywords: Graph transformations, software product lines, fragment substitutions, adjacent, interference, cvl, conflict resolution.

1 Introduction

Software Product Line Engineering (SPLE) [1] has proved itself as a valuable approach to produce configurable and customizable systems. CVL is a domain-specific language [2,3] for variability modeling [4] which enables defining software product lines. The variability model is typically organized in a tree of features. A resolution of the tree structure constitutes a particular product. Defining the features [5] comprises a variability modeling (VM) process. There are several approaches to variability modeling which make use of the feature concept, e.g. the cardinality-based feature modeling approach by Czarnecki et al. [6]. Pohl et al. [1]

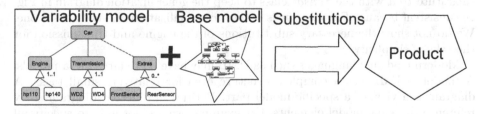

Fig. 1. CVL product derivation workflow

J. Dingel et al. (Eds.): MODELS 2014, LNCS 8767, pp. 467–483, 2014.

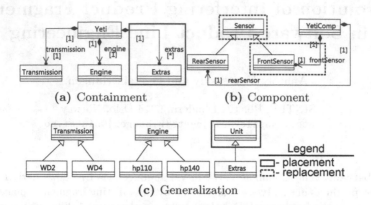

(a) Containment   (b) Component

(c) Generalization

Fig. 2. Containment, component and generalization (with placement and replacement fragments)

describe the Orthogonal Variability Model (OVM) methodology that prevents cluttering of a base language with variability concepts. The Common Variability Language (CVL) [7] exploits the feature term, defines variability orthogonally and specifies how to derive a concrete product [8, 9]. Fig. 1 sketches how CVL derives a product. The feature tree defines all possible configurations of a car, i.e. a car comprises an engine with two possible options (hp110, hp140), transmission (WD2, WD4) and some extra equipment (FrontSensor, RearSensor). We would like to have an engine with one hundred ten horsepower (hp110), two wheel drive transmission (WD2) and front sensor (FrontSensor) for our car; therefore, we need to choose the corresponding features. An engineer selects desired features defining the Resolution tree in CVL. We illustrate this definition by gray shading in the Feature tree, see Fig. 1.

To derive a product we specify how these abstract features are related to their concrete representations in a base model. In Fig. 2, there are three UML [10] class diagrams modeling the base model of a car. The derivation process is a set of substitutions which remove elements of a placement fragment and inject elements of a replacement. We have also defined two substitutions on our base model in Fig. 2. We replace the *Extras* class and corresponding containment (placement fragment, the diagram in Fig. 2a) with the *FrontSensor* class and associated containment relation (replacement fragment, the diagram in Fig. 2b). We also substitute *Unit* with the *Sensor* class to keep the generalization diagram in Fig. 2c consistent because *FrontSensor* is a *Sensor* specialization and not a *Unit* one. We do not show the necessary substitutions of the engine and transmission for the sake of simplicity.

Modern modeling languages such as UML may have quite large meta-models. A model in UML has a complex structure even for relatively small tasks. A diagram is a view of a specific model part. Entities in different diagrams may reference the same model elements. For example, we are not able to specify all modifying elements for the car base model as a single selection in one diagram

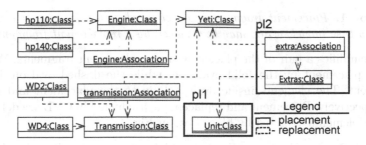

Fig. 3. Simplified instance diagram

since the involved classes and associations are present in different diagrams. A modeling practice shows that an engineer works only with one diagram at a time focusing on a specific part of a model.

In the instance diagram (see Fig. 3) of the UML meta-model [10], we show all components presented in Fig. 2. We use arrows to show links between objects. The UML meta-model specifies even more objects and links than shown in the figure. Fig. 3 outlines that even though the selections are made in different diagrams (containment and generalization) and may look completely independent, there are direct references from one placement to the other. We call such relations between fragments *adjacent*. In the given example, the result of the substitutions is well understood, i.e. we want a car with the front sensor which is a specialization of the *Sensor* class. However, if the substitutions are carried out independently as in MoSiS CVL [11, 12], the adjacent relation leads to an incorrect final product.

In the paper we explain our approach to the adjacent relation using an ABC example, present formal criteria and sketch algorithm to resolve this relation. Further, we apply the suggested approach on the presented motivation example to demonstrate the adjacent resolution technique. In addition, we categorize other problematic inter-placement relations and propose solutions to tackle them. We show that the graph rewriting techniques and tools [13–16] do not give us a necessary vehicle for conquering the presented challenges.

We organize the rest of the paper as follows. Section 2 covers background and related works. Section 4 gives a classification of the placement interferences using the ABC example for simplicity. In Section 5, we discuss the adjacent relation between placements while Section 6 elaborates all crossing cases. We walk through the introduced approach against the motivation example in Section 7. Finally, Section 8 concludes our work.

2 Background

2.1 Variability Realization in CVL

The basic concepts for a variability realization in CVL are placement fragment, replacement fragment and substitution combining them.

Definition 1. *Placement fragment is a set of elements forming a conceptual 'hole' in a base model, which may be replaced by a replacement fragment.*

Fig. 4 exemplifies a pair of the placement and replacement fragments. We highlight the placement by the solid oval line, while the dashed oval outlines the replacement. The elements inside ovals belong to the placement and replacement respectively. Placement and replacement fragments in CVL are defined via boundary elements depicted by black dots in Fig. 4.

Definition 2. *Boundaries are elements which represent the edges of a placement or replacement fragment.*

Definition 3. *ToBoundary is a boundary that represents a reference going from the outside to the inside of a placement or replacement fragment.*

Definition 4. *FromBoundary is a boundary that represents a reference going from the inside to the outside of a placement or replacement fragment.*

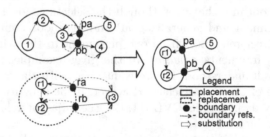

Fig. 4. Basic CVL concepts

A variability expert defines a placement or replacement using our tool through a simple selection procedure on a model. These elements inside placement or replacement may reference entities outside the given selection. Boundaries cut these references. Fig. 4 shows four boundary elements, i.e. two for the placement fragment (*pa* - toBoundary, *pb* - fromBoundary) and two for the replacement fragment (*ra* - toBoundary, *rb* - fromBoundary).

A subsequent execution of substitutions fragments modifies a base model deriving a new product in CVL.

Definition 5. *Fragment substitution is an operation that substitutes model fragment (placement fragment) for another (replacement fragment).*

The result of one fragment substitution is found in the rightmost of Fig. 4. The operation removes the placement elements and copy the contents of the replacement onto the recently cleared placement fragment.

Definition 6. *A binding is a map between a placement and replacement boundary elements.*

We specify that the element *5* should reference element *r1* and *r2* should point to *4* in the derived product via the binding of *pa* to *ra* and *pb* to *rb* respectively. Thus, bindings control substitutions instructing how replacement elements glue into existing structures.

3 Related Works

3.1 Conflicts in CVL

Oldevik et al. [17] analyze conflicts and confluence between substitution fragments in CVL. The paper states that transformations in CVL can be mapped to graph transformations in general case and checked using the critical pair analyzes. In our work we give more elaborated classification of interferences, check their confluence using graph transformation based tools, define solutions, formalize them and implement in the substitution engine [1].

Svendsen et al. [18] analyze conflicts in CVL on a Train Control Language (TCL) [19] example. They discuss two kinds of conflicts: border inconsistency and element inconsistency. The authors propose an algorithm to deal with inconsistencies in the base model by recording evaluation of the CVL model. Further, they use the original and evolution CVL models to derive a product. To perform the product derivation they analyze contextual information. Absence or shortage of the context may prevent an automatic product derivation. In our approach, we suggest evolving one CVL model and claim that the necessary information to derive a product automatically is always in the model. In addition, we illuminate other conflicts and propose solutions.

3.2 Confluence of Graph Transformations

Confluence of conflicting graph transformations plays a major role in the graph rewriting theory. Conflicts between transformations occur if transformations share common elements, the graph rewriting theory calls such transformation non-parallel independent. Heckel, Küster and Taentzer [16] give theoretical bases for identifying the parallel independence between transformations in terms of the rewriting theory. If two transformations are parallel independent then the local Church-Rosser theorem states that the transformations can be performed in any order yielding the same result [20]. Thus, we can speak of confluence in the parallel independent transformations. We do not consider confluence of placement fragments without any relations between each other in this paper rather address cases where fragments are non-parallel independent (in terms of the graph rewriting theory). Confluence is also feasible for non-parallel independent transformations when all their critical pairs are confluent. A critical pair analysis of our motivation example reveals a non-confluent graph transformation system [21]. Therefore, the desired product is not possible to derive in the given settings. The basic graph approach is not capable of resolving the adjacent relation in general since the critical pair analysis reveals a non-confluent system.

---

[1] One can find instructions to set up experiments at http://goo.gl/9WD8Gx

3.3 Feature-Oriented and Delta-Oriented Programming

Feature-oriented programming (FOP) [22] is a step-wise refinement approach by Batory et al. [23] to the development of complex systems. A core idea of the step-wise refinement approach is that a product may emerge by adding features incrementally to a simple base model. Hence, we can avoid conflicts during a product derivation, which is different with respect to the CVL methodology of defining fragments. Batory et al. show that the approach can be applied to both code and non-code artifacts given that one defines the composition operation for each kind of artifacts.

Delta-oriented programming (DOP) [24] is an extension of the FOP paradigm and a novel programming language approach which operates with deltas to derive a product. Deltas allow removing elements from a product which is not generally allowed in the feature modeling. One may define a SPL on any language using the DOP paradigm. The approach proposes to resolve all conflicts between deltas by specifying the order of their resolution. The notion of deltas is somehow similar to fragments in CVL. However, one may define several fragments modifying the same elements in a model, which is a core distinction. Moreover, we consider substitutions as independent operations which the CVL engine may apply potentially in the arbitrary order. Therefore, the ordering is not a solution to conflicting fragments at least within the current CVL semantics. In addition, any specific resolution order of the adjacent fragments does not solve the problem with dangling references.

3.4 Aspect-Oriented Programming

Aspect-oriented Programming (AOP) is an approach to weave cross-cutting concerns into a program. Aspects are developed as separate units which can be applied independently. Lauret et al. [25] state that AOP suffers from a well-known composition issue i.e. several concerns are applied to the same join point. The problem is known as the aspect interference issue. Lauret et al. suggest inserting *executable assertions* to detect different kind of interference between aspects. As a solution to avoid undesirable interferences, the authors suggest ordering of conflicting advises. The notion of aspects is highly relevant to fragments in CVL which can be applied to the same model elements. However, the ordering of fragments to resolve conflicts is somewhat different with respect to CVL where substitution operations do not have any particular order. In addition, ordering of substitutions does not help with adjacent fragments.

4   Placement Interference

4.1 Definitions and Concepts

A placement fragment forms a conceptual 'hole' in a base model according to Definition 1. The fragment substitution operation removes all elements of the placement creating a 'hole' in the model. Subsequently, the substitutions fills this 'hole' out with a copy of the replacement fragment. Any placement fragment is defined by means of boundary elements in CVL. Boundary elements reference objects outside and inside placement/replacement fragments (see Fig. 4) defining gluing points and elements to remove. Outside boundary references point to elements beyond a placement fragment. Boundary references outline also a set of affected elements (neighboring elements or gluing points), which we do not remove during a resolution process. We do not explicitly select these elements. Hence, we can conclude that a placement affects a set of objects which is wider than the set of the explicitly outlined objects by an engineer.

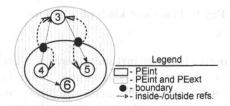

Fig. 5. Internal and external placement elements (PEint, PEext)

Definition 7. *Placement Element internal (PEint) is a set of all elements referred by inside boundary references and all elements in the transitive closure of all references from the elements in the set, but cut off at elements found through outside boundary references.*

Definition 8. *Placement Element external (PEext) is a set of all elements referred by outside boundary references.*

In Fig. 5 PEint = {4, 5, 6} and PEext = {3}. Thus, we define two sets of elements (PEint, PEext), which are affected by a selection. The dashed arrows pointing to *3* are *outside boundary* references, while the dashed arrows pointing to *4* and *5* are *inside boundary* references. The oval in Fig. 5 with the solid black border outlines PEint while the solid gray line highlights the union of PEint and PEext. Finally, we can conclude that PEint is a placement fragment in the CVL terminology, while PEext is a set of elements which relations are affected.

4.2   Kinds of Interference

A variability engineer defines a set of elements to substitute via a selection in a base model. This selection is a set of objects which defines a placement fragment. This selection defines PEint that is a placement fragment and set of the affected elements, i.e. PEext. Thus, we can discuss relations between placements in terms of set relations. To find all possible relations between two different fragments we consider PEext ⋃ PEint for each fragment and look for intersections between these unions. If the unions do not intersect then the substitution process goes

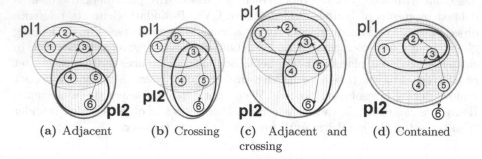

(a) Adjacent   (b) Crossing   (c) Adjacent and   (d) Contained
crossing

Fig. 6. Placement kinds of interference

smoothly. We do not discuss this case further. There are three unique intersection cases considering other combinations and simple 2x2 table. An overlap only between two PEext does not cause malformed configurations during resolution in MoSiS CVL [11]. Thus, we are left with two basic overlapping kinds. There is also a special case for an intersection between PEints, namely when one placement is fully contained by another placement. The given interference kinds are not mutually exclusive. Fig. 6 depicts four overlapping relations between placements which we will elaborate in the subsequent sections.

Definition 9. *Adjacent placements are placements, where $PEint_1$ intersects $PEext_2$.*

Definition 10. *Adjacent relation is a reference between two elements in different adjacent placements.*

Definition 11. *Crossing placements are placements, where $PEint_1$ intersects $PEint_2$.*

Definition 12. *Crossing relation is a reference between two elements in different crossing placements.*

Fig. 6 shows three cases, where two placements conform to the definition of crossing placements.

Definition 13. *Contained placements are placements, where $PEint_1 \subseteq PEint_2$.*

Definition 14. *Contained relation is a reference between two elements in different contained placements.*

5   Adjacent Placements

Independent substitutions of interfering placements cause dangling references in a variability model. Fig. 7 demonstrates a derivation process in MoSiS CVL [11]. There are two adjacent placements and corresponding replacements in Fig. 7a.

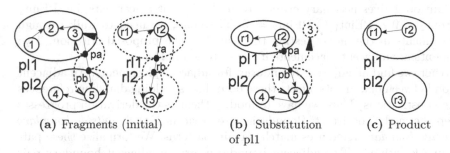

(a) Fragments (initial)   (b) Substitution   (c) Product
                                      of pl1

Fig. 7. Product (invalid) derivation without adjacent resolution

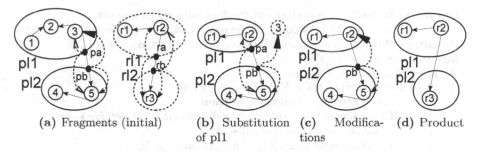

(a) Fragments (initial)   (b) Substitution (c)   Modifica- (d) Product
                                  of pl1   tions

Fig. 8. Product (valid) derivation with adjacent resolution

We bind *pa* to *ra* and *pb* to *rb* to specify substitutions. A substitution of the adjacent fragment *pl1* results in a dangling *outside boundary* reference going from *pb* to the object *3* (an arrow with the filled large head) in Fig. 7b. Note, the object *3* is not in the model any more. A subsequent substitution of the second adjacent fragment *pl2* in MoSiS CVL yields an invalid product due to this reference, i.e. the product in Fig. 7c misses a link between *r2* and *r3*. Graph transformation tools (Henshin [26], EMorF [27]) consider the given transformations as non-confluent since the first substitution disables the second one. Thus, the desired substitutions are not feasible applying the graph techniques either. Fig. 8 sketches the derivation process with a necessary adjustment (see Fig. 8c) of the dangling reference to obtain the expected product in Fig. 8d.

The case shows that we cannot consider substitutions with adjacent placements as independent. We need to see these transformations together. A solution for the problem is to modify the variability model during an execution. In our example, if the *outside boundary* reference of *pb* (see Fig. 8b) pointed to the object *r2*, then the resolution would yield the proper model. Fig. 8c exemplifies the required adjustment of the *outside boundary* reference. Thus, an essence of our approach to adjacent placements is to find and correct dangling references in such a way that they point to correct objects all the way through a derivation process. Summarizing, the adjacent resolution is a threefold process: 1) find adjacent placements, 2) find adjacent boundaries, 3) fix references of the adjacent boundaries during a product derivation.

Definition 9 gives necessary criteria to find adjacent placements, i.e. $PEint_1$ $\bigcap PEext_2 \neq \emptyset \wedge PEint_1 \bigcap PEint_2 = \emptyset$. Therefore, we need to walk through all placements in the model testing them against the proposed criterion. Two placements are adjacent placements if the criterion holds.

Further, we find all adjacent boundaries for adjacent placements. An adjacent relation between placements affects these boundaries yielding dangling references during substitutions. Thus, we have to modify them as the derivation progresses to keep the model consistent. Boundaries are adjacent if their *outside boundary* and *inside boundary* references match certain patterns. We formalize these patterns in Algorithm 1. Two adjacent boundaries are an adjacent boundary pair if these boundaries conform to the same match pattern. In Fig. 8a, the bound-

---

Data: *boundariesPlc1* - boundaries of the first adjacent placement,
　　　　 boundariesPlc2 - boundaries of the second adjacent placement
Result: *adjBoundaryCurrent, adjBoundaryStale* - boundary maps
for $b1 \in boundariesPlc1$ **do**
  for $b2 \in boundariesPlc2$ **do**
    if $IsInstanceOf(b1) = FromBoundary$ **and**
    $IsInstanceOf(b2) = ToBoundary$ **then**
      if $b1.inside \triangle b2.outside = \varnothing$ **and** $b2.inside \subseteq b1.outside$ **then**
        $adjBoundaryCurrent[b1] \leftarrow b2$;
        $adjBoundaryStale[b1] \leftarrow copyBoundary(b2)$;
      end
    end
    if $IsInstanceOf(b1) = ToBoundary$ **and**
    $IsInstanceOf(b2) = FromBoundary$ **then**
      if $b1.outside \triangle b2.inside = \varnothing$ **and** $b1.inside \subseteq b2.outside$ **then**
        $adjBoundaryCurrent[b1] \leftarrow b2$;
        $adjBoundaryStale[b1] \leftarrow copyBoundary(b2)$;
      end
    end
  end
end

Algorithm 1. Procedure to find adjacent boundaries

---

aries *pa* and *pb* constitute an adjacent boundary pair. Informally, an adjacent boundary pair is a pair of adjacent boundaries which cut the same adjacent relation.

Fig. 8c shows a modification we have to execute once we substitute *pl1*. We need to modify an adjacent boundary of the adjacent pair. The modification is a twofold process, i.e. 1) walk through adjacent boundaries of a not yet substituted placement removing pointers to invalid objects, e.g. the object *3* 2) correct boundary references to point to just replaced elements, e.g. object *r2* (see Fig. 8c). Algorithm 2 presents formally the outlined procedure. This procedure eliminates the dangling reference from the boundary *pb* to an element in the placement *pl1*.

Data: *boundaries* - boundaries of a not yet substituted adjacent placement;
      adjBoundaryCurrent - a map that stores adjacent boundary pairs and
      their current references; *adjBoundaryStale* - map that stores adjacent
      boundary pairs and their stale references (before substitution)

Result: fixed outside and inside boundary references

for $b \in boundaries$ **do**
    if $IsInstanceOf(b) = ToBoundary$ **then**
        $b.outside \leftarrow adjBoundaryCurrent[b].inside$;
    end
    if $IsInstanceOf(b) = FromBoundary$ **then**
        $b.outside \leftarrow b.outside \setminus$
        $adjBoundaryStale[b].inside \bigcup adjBoundaryCurrent[b].inside$;
    end
end

Algorithm 2. Fixing boundary references for adjacent placements

6   Kinds of Crossing Placements

6.1   Approach Overview

Fig. 6b, Fig. 6c and Fig. 6d outline all possible crossing kinds between placements. An engineer may define placement fragments in different diagrams that leads to crossing placements in the base model. An attempt to substitute these two placements one by one, results in dangling references and malformed products. In addition, two substitutions may replace elements of the crossing twice. This may cause different final products depending on the substitution order.

We argue that crossing placements should be considered as a single placement as well as their replacement fragments. Thus, we introduce a unionization procedure as a solution for this case. The crossing may originate from either a pragmatic need or an error in a variability definition. Therefore, we must be able to distinguish the cases. Required information for the decision is already in a variability model. By checking for unionizing crossing fragments we 1) spot erroneous variability definitions, tackle cases where the unionization operation is possible, 2) reduce the overall amount of substitutions facilitating the derivation process and 3) widen the semantics of the fragment definition which may enhance the variability specification process.

6.2   Crossing Placements

Two substitutions with crossing placements should be resolved as a single substitution, i.e. we should attempt to unionize the given placements and corresponding replacements. Boundary elements in CVL fully define placement and replacement fragments; therefore, we can alter boundaries in order to adjust fragments. The unionization of crossing fragments removes boundary elements which are internal to the unionized fragment. Boundary elements are removed when their *outside boundary* references point to elements inside the unionized

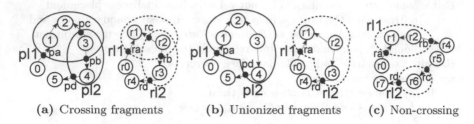

(a) Crossing fragments   (b) Unionized fragments   (c) Non-crossing

Fig. 9. Crossing fragments

placement since this contradicts the definition [7]. In Fig. 9a, we bind pa to ra, pb to rb, pc to rc and pd to rd. The boundary elements pb and pc are internal w.r.t. the unionized placement as well as rb and rc. Thus, we remove these boundaries to unionize the placement and corresponding replacement fragments. The unionization result is in Fig. 9b.

Let us now consider the same placement fragments from Fig. 9a and replacements in Fig. 9c. We bind the boundaries as in the previous case. The unionization approach suggests removing the placement boundary elements pb, pc and corresponding boundaries rb, rc. This unionizes the placement fragments. On the contrary, the replacement fragments become inconsistent and the remaining boundaries do not define a unionized replacement. In addition, the unionization of the non-crossing fragments does no make any sense. We consider an error in a variability definition when placement fragments overlap, but their replacements do not intersect or the replacement overlap of a different kind.

6.3 Crossing and Adjacent Placements

Fig. 10a shows an example of two placements and replacements that are both adjacent and crossing. We cannot apply to such fragments the adjacent technique since it does not handle the crossing relation. While the unionization procedure should eliminate the adjacent relation between two crossing placements. The boundary elements pc and pb define the overlap of the kind crossing placements, and pe and pf constitute the adjacent case. As in the crossing case, the boundary elements pc, pb and rc, rb have to be removed when we unionize two placements. These boundaries are internal w.r.t. the newly unionized placement and replacement. The reference in Fig. 10b (which creates the adjacent relation between $pl1$ and $pl2$), is an internal link now. Hence, the adjacent relation is eliminated and there is no any interference . The pure crossing case is a special case of the crossing placements with the adjacent relation. Thus, developed criteria should be capable to handle both cases. The suggested unionization approach can tackle pure adjacent placements. However, unionization needs to consider relations between corresponding replacements. Thus, it reduces the amount of valid fragment definitions. The adjacent resolution method does not count on relations between replacement fragments. Therefore, the adjacent resolution method is

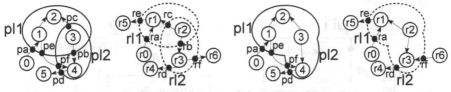

(a) Placements and replacements   (b) Unionization of placements and re-
                                        placements

Fig. 10. Adjacent and crossing fragments

more applicable to adjacent placements and can handle more cases than the
unionization technique.

6.4 Contained Placements

An example of the contained placements in Fig. 6d. If we execute a containing
placement, then the corresponding contained placement is never substituted.
This resolution order never brings problems to the derivation process. On the
contrary, a subsequent execution of the contained fragment and containing placement results in dangling references. We consider the contained placements as a
potential problem in variability definition due to this ambiguity. The unionization procedure is also feasible for contained placements. We cannot find examples
where such configuration is practically useful. Thus, we suggest unionizing for
crossing fragments and reporting every time the substitution engine discovers
contained placements.

7   Example Walkthrough

Let us finally walk through our motivation example from the introduction section. Fig. 11a and Fig. 11b depict two placement and replacement fragments
which specify the desired transformation, i.e. we want to derive a car with a
front sensor. In order to substitute *pl1* onto *rl1*, we bind *pa* to *ra*, *pb* to *rb*, while
pl2 substitution is achieved via binding of *pc* to *rc*, and *rd* is bound to *null* (we
do not need this relation in the final model). We do not show inside-/outside
boundary references just for the sake of neatness in the figures. The given placements in Fig. 11a are adjacent. Two adjacent boundaries *pb* and *pc* constitute
the adjacent pair, i.e the *outside boundary* references of *pl1* and *pl2* point to
the elements of the opposite placements. Hence, the outside references of these
boundaries have to be modified during a transformation process.

Let us first substitute *pl1*, the outside boundary reference of *pc* points to
Extras:Class which does not exist in the model; therefore, it is a broken reference.
We know that *pc* is an adjacent boundary and should be modified to reference
FrontSensor:Class. This reference is taken from *inside boundary* reference of

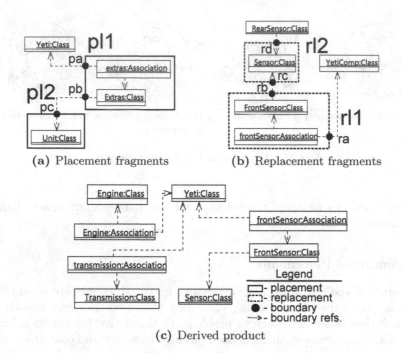

(a) Placement fragments   (b) Replacement fragments

(c) Derived product

Fig. 11. Simplified instance diagram - walk through

rc which is bound to *pc*. Therefore, we are able to perform a substitution of *pl2*, where the substitution engine restores the link down to *Sensor:Class* from *FrontSensor:Class*. Two subsequent substitutions yield the product in Fig. 11c, which conforms to our expectations and definitions. We achieve the same result even if we perform substitutions in a different order.

We implemented the suggested approach in the CVL tool [1]. The procedure does not require any human interaction and completely automated as a derivation progresses.

8   Conclusion

CVL is a language to define software product lines. The language has the notion of fragments to specify elements to substitute in a model. Modern modeling languages may have complex meta-models; therefore, the tools, which implement the corresponding meta-models, may use different diagrams to represent a model and facilitate the development process. Fragments defined in different diagrams may interfere in a model causing unintended results during a product derivation. A variability engineer can define interference intentionally, reflecting a pragmatic need to specify substitution fragments in different diagrams, or by accident where overlaps indicate a failure in a variability model. In this article, we classify the fragment interferences, i.e. adjacent, crossing, adjacent and crossing, contained placements. For each kind we define the detection criteria and how to handle them properly.

We have implemented the findings in the substitution engine developed at SINTEF [1] as well as demonstrated the proposed method to the adjacent relation on the motivation example. The engine performs substitutions, has functionality to detect and solve the adjacent relation. The resolution process of the adjacent relation includes the following steps: 1) detect adjacent relations, 2) find adjacent boundaries, 3) modify the adjacent boundaries. The engine executes the adjacent resolution procedure after a single substitution step to keep a variability model consistent all the way through a derivation process. The adjacent detection between placement fragments is a costly procedure. There are C_n^2 possible combinations, where n is the number of placement fragments and order is not important. Thus, we require to suggest optimizations to speed up this step. It is a part of our future work.

We have introduced the unionization approach to fragments with the crossing relation. There are three kinds of the crossing relation, i.e. crossing fragments, adjacent and crossing fragments, contained fragments. We demonstrate that the unionization approach is feasible only when placements and corresponding replacements have similar crossing kinds. Otherwise, a variability model is not consistent; thus, we assert an error. We argue that a case with contained placements indicates a potential problem in variability definition. The crossing resolution technique requires further elaboration and is not implemented in the engine yet which is a part of the future work.

Acknowledgment. The work has been carried out within the VARIES project [28]. We would like to thank our colleague at SINTEF for their valuable insights, as well as, anonymous reviewers and Maria Vasilevskaya at the Linköping University, Sweden for their helpful comments.

References

1. Pohl, K., Böckle, G., van der Linden, F.J.: Software Product Line Engineering: Foundations, Principles and Techniques, 1st edn. Springer Publishing Company, Incorporated (2010)
2. Van Deursen, A., Klint, P., Visser, J.: Domain-specific languages. Centrum voor Wiskunde en Informatika (2000)
3. Tolvanen, J.P., Kelly, S.: Integrating models with domain-specific modeling languages. In: Proceedings of the 10th Workshop on Domain-Specific Modeling, DSM 2010, pp. 10:1–10:6. ACM, New York (2010)
4. Bayer, J., Gerard, S., Haugen, Ø., Mansell, J., Møller-Pedersen, B., Oldevik, J., Tessier, P., Thibault, J.P., Widen, T.: Consolidated Product Line Variability Modelling. In: Käköla, T., Duenas, J.C. (eds.) Software Product Lines, pp. 195–241. Springer, Heidelberg (2006)
5. Kang, K.C., Cohen, S.G., Hess, J.A., Novak, W.E., Peterson, A.S.: Feature-Oriented Domain Analysis (FODA) Feasibility Study. Technical Report CMU/SEI-90-TR-21 ESD-90-TR-222, Carnegie Mellon University, Pittsburgh, Pennsylvania 15213 (1990)

6. Czarnecki, K., Wasowski, A.: Feature Diagrams and Logics: There and Back Again. In: IEEE 11th International Software Product Line Conference (SPLC 2007), pp. 23–34 (September 2007)

7. OMG: Common Variability Language (CVL). OMG, OMG document: ad/2012-08-05 (2012)

8. Haugen, Ø., Møller-Pedersen, B., Oldevik, J., Olsen, G.K., Svendsen, A.: Adding Standardized Variability to Domain Specific Languages. In: 12th International Software Product Line Conference, SPLC 2008, pp. 139–148 (2008)

9. Haugen, Ø., Wasowski, A., Czarnecki, K.: CVL: common variability language. In: Proceedings of the 16th International Software Product Line Conference, SPLC 2012, vol. 2, pp. 266–267. ACM, New York (2012)

10. OMG: Unified modeling language: Superstructure version 2.0, formal/05-07-04 (2005)

11. Haugen, Ø.: CVL Tool from SINTEF (2010), Also available as http://www.omgwiki.org/variability/doku.php?id=cvl_tool_from_sintef

12. Haugen, Ø., Wasowski, A., Czarnecki, K.: Cvl: common variability language. In: Kishi, T., Jarzabek, S., Gnesi, S. (eds.) SPLC, p. 277. ACM (2013)

13. Heckel, R.: Graph Transformation in a Nutshell. Electronic Notes in Theoretical Computer Science 148(1), 187–198 (2006)

14. Pfaltz, J.L., Rosenfeld, A.: Web grammars. In: Proceedings of the 1st International Joint Conference on Artificial Intelligence, IJCAI 1969, pp. 609–619. Morgan Kaufmann Publishers Inc., San Francisco (1969)

15. Pratt, T.W.: Pair grammars, graph languages and string-to-graph translations. J. Comput. Syst. Sci. 5(6), 560–595 (1971)

16. Heckel, R., Kster, J., Taentzer, G.: Confluence of typed attributed graph transformation systems. In: Corradini, A., Ehrig, H., Kreowski, H.-J., Rozenberg, G. (eds.) ICGT 2002. LNCS, vol. 2505, pp. 161–176. Springer, Heidelberg (2002)

17. Oldevik, J., Haugen, Ø., Møller-Pedersen, B.: Confluence in Domain-Independent Product Line Transformations. In: Chechik, M., Wirsing, M. (eds.) FASE 2009. LNCS, vol. 5503, pp. 34–48. Springer, Heidelberg (2009)

18. Svendsen, A., Zhang, X., Haugen, Ø., Møller-Pedersen, B.: Towards evolution of generic variability models. In: Kienzle, J. (ed.) MODELS 2011 Workshops. LNCS, vol. 7167, pp. 53–67. Springer, Heidelberg (2012)

19. Svendsen, A., Olsen, G.K., Endresen, J., Moen, T., Carlson, E.J., Alme, K.-J., Haugen, Ø.: The future of train signaling. In: Czarnecki, K., Ober, I., Bruel, J.-M., Uhl, A., Völter, M. (eds.) MODELS 2008. LNCS, vol. 5301, pp. 128–142. Springer, Heidelberg (2008)

20. Ehrig, H.: Introduction to the algebraic theory of graph grammars (a survey). In: Claus, V., Ehrig, H., Rozenberg, G. (eds.) Graph Grammars 1978. LNCS, vol. 73, pp. 1–69. Springer, Heidelberg (1979)

21. Vasilevskiy, A.: Conquering overlapping fragments in CVL. Master's thesis, University of Oslo (UiO), pp. 42–58 (2013)

22. Batory, D.: Feature-oriented programming and the ahead tool suite. In: Proceedings of the 26th International Conference on Software Engineering, ICSE 2004, pp. 702–703. IEEE Computer Society, Washington, DC (2004)

23. Batory, D., Sarvela, J., Rauschmayer, A.: Scaling step-wise refinement. IEEE Transactions on Software Engineering 30(6), 355–371

24. Schaefer, I., Bettini, L., Bono, V., Damiani, F., Tanzarella, N.: Delta-oriented programming of software product lines. In: Bosch, J., Lee, J. (eds.) SPLC 2010. LNCS, vol. 6287, pp. 77–91. Springer, Heidelberg (2010)

25. Lauret, J., Waeselynck, H., Fabre, J.C.: Detection of interferences in aspect-oriented programs using executable assertions. In: 2012 IEEE 23rd International Symposium on Software Reliability Engineering Workshops (ISSREW), pp. 165–170 (November 2012)
26. Arendt, T., Biermann, E., Jurack, S., Krause, C., Taentzer, G.: Henshin: Advanced concepts and tools for in-place emf model transformations. In: Petriu, D.C., Rouquette, N., Haugen, Ø. (eds.) MODELS 2010, Part I. LNCS, vol. 6394, pp. 121–135. Springer, Heidelberg (2010)
27. Klassen, L., Wagner, R.: Emorf-a tool for model transformations. Electronic Communications of the EASST 54 (2012)
28. ARTEMIS 2011, Project Number: 295397, VARIES: VARiability In safety critical Embedded Systems (2012-2015)

Ontology-Based Modeling
of Context-Aware Systems

Daniel Lüddecke[1], Nina Bergmann[1], and Ina Schaefer[2]

[1] Volkswagen AG, Group Research, 38440 Wolfsburg, Germany
{daniel.lueddecke,nina.bergmann}@volkswagen.de
[2] Technische Universität Braunschweig, 38106 Braunschweig, Germany
i.schaefer@tu-braunschweig.de

Abstract. Context-aware systems aim to improve the interaction between a computer and a human being by using contextual information about the system itself, the user, and their environment. The number of relevant contextual information is expected to grow rapidly within the next years which tends to result in a complex, error-prone and hence, expensive task of programming context-aware systems. Model-based development can overcome these issues. Current approaches do not allow to model calculation of reliabilities and do not offer options to handle multiple sources of contextual information.

In this paper, we present an approach of modeling contextual information of a context-aware system using the example of a context-aware in-car infotainment system. In particular, we show how developers of context-aware in-car infotainment systems can model reliability calculations of contextual information and handling of multiple sources of contextual information by using a hybrid, ontology-based modeling technique.

Keywords: Context-aware, ontology, infotainment, modeling.

1 Introduction

A context-aware computer system *observes* its user and his or her environment to get an understanding of the situation the user is in: The user's *context*. Having this understanding, the system is able to react to the user's context in terms of system behaviour or parametrization. This concept seems to be beneficial in the automotive domain and in particular in the domain of in-car infotainment systems.

Whereas in the 1980s in-car infotainment systems mainly featured radio functionality, today's in-car infotainment systems offer many extended features, including enhanced media playback from different sources like smartphones or brought-in flash storages, navigation functionality, or traffic announcements. The number of features that users and drivers will demand from future infotainment

J. Dingel et al. (Eds.): MODELS 2014, LNCS 8767, pp. 484–500, 2014.

systems is expected to grow rapidly[1]. Hence, it is important to explore interaction concepts which allow using feature-rich infotainment systems without distracting the driver from his or her primary task: Driving the car. It may become necessary to e.g. adapt the user interface of the in-car infotainment system to the speed of the car or the age of the user.

Along those concepts, it is inevitable to study software architectures and methods which allow developers to design and implement such in-car infotainment systems. Feature-rich infotainment systems are likely to have a perception of what the user wants to do and what the situation around the car is about. In order to understand the car's situation, it becomes necessary to build a *context-aware* in-car infotainment system. However, people developing context-aware in-car infotainment systems will not necessarily be computer scientists and may not have an expertise in building complex software systems. They will rather be people with an understanding of how users (drivers) interact with the in-car infotainment system. Among others, this is why this paper aims for a model-based approach of developing context-aware in-car infotainment systems.

The modeling technique we present in this paper offers solutions to the following problems:

– modeling contextual information and their relations
– modeling reliability calculations of contextual relations
– modeling handling of multiple sources of contextual information

Corollary, the focus of our proposed technique is not on the actual context-aware system, but rather on the retrieval and processing of contextual information. The contextual processing takes place in subsequent software systems, e.g. in a component trying to identify a user's intention. Therefore these subsequent systems need high level context data and information about the current situation. The techniques presented in this paper allow creating systems which are able to deliver such high level context data.

This paper is structured as follows: The next section provides background information on context-aware systems and context modeling. Afterwards, we define requirements for our model in Section 3 and present our approach in Section 4. We will validate the requirements in a use case-based evaluation in Section 5, before we conclude with an overview of related work and an outlook on future work in Section 6 and 7.

2   Background

In this section, we give some background information on context-aware systems in general and in an automotive environment. We also show techniques for modeling contextual information and for dealing with uncertain and unreliable data, which form the base for our approach.

---

[1] Connect with your car, Consumer Reports magazine, April 2013,
   last accessed July 2014
   http://www.consumerreports.org/cro/magazine/2013/04/connect-with-your-car

2.1   Context-Aware Systems and Context Modeling

In an automotive environment, especially in in-car infotainment systems, contextual information can be separated into three main categories: Driver, car and their environment [24,20]. Data regarding the driver may contain the driver's stress level, appointments, communication behavior and the destination or motivation of the current route. Data about the car may contain its type, power and fuel capacity or current status including warning messages and available fuel amount. Also sensor data and data from driver assistance systems belong to the car category, e.g. current speed and position according to GPS. The environment category contains everything from outside the car, e.g. the weather, traffic, date and time of day, and the presence of important places (POIs) near the route.

Context-aware systems read low level context data, e.g. from sensors, process the data to high level context data or even whole situations, and react or change their parameters according to the context [5]. Context data include everything which may have an impact on the system. In a system for automatic volume control, a high level context may be the in-cabin acoustic level. This is depending on the speed of the vehicle and the RPM of the vehicle's engine, which are low level contexts in this case, since the high level context can be determined based on them.

To work with context in a computer system, a model to store and process context data is needed. A special model for working with contextual information brings some benefits: The model helps to specify relationships and a hierarchy of context data. It also allows to create rules for a reasoning process that supports the workflow of extracting high level context data and situations from low level context data. Several different types of context models can be found in literature. An overview on them is given in the survey paper by Strang and Linnhoff-Popien [21] and the survey paper by Bettini et al. [5].

State of the art in context modeling are ontology-based models [5,21]. An ontology contains knowledge of a certain domain and can model hierarchies and dependencies between context data. It is possible to infer new facts based on the knowledge in the ontology using a reasoner. A common language for ontologies is OWL [15] which will be used as the base of our approach in union with its rule-based extension SWRL [11].

To model uncertainty in context-aware systems, common methods are e.g. Bayesian networks or fuzzy logic [5]. The presented context models lack a standardized support for processing uncertainty, unreliability or incomplete information as they may appear in an automotive environment. Thus, we will create an object-oriented model extension based on fuzzy logic which is used to represent the reliability of context sources and contextual information. Hence, we create an ontology-based hybrid context model.

2.2   OWL and SWRL

OWL [15] is a language to define the structure of an ontology, based on first order logic. It structures data using *classes* and *properties*. OWL classes can be seen as categories of data and behave similar to mathematical sets, but can also be compared to classes of the object-oriented paradigm. Actual data is added in form of *individuals*. An individual can be compared to *objects* of the object-oriented paradigm which are instances of classes. An example of an ontology is shown in Figure 1.

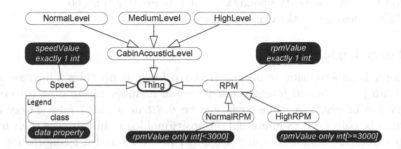

Fig. 1. Example of an OWL ontology for classifying a cabin acoustic level

This sample ontology is composed of eight classes. The class RPM represents information about the current revolutions per minute of a vehicle's engine. Speed covers a vehicle's speed. CabinAcousticLevel represents an acoustic level of a vehicle's cabin which can be either a NormalLevel, a MediumLevel or a HighLevel. Ontologies are able to define hierarchies between classes. The superclass of all OWL classes is called Thing (cf. Object in Java). NormalRPM and HighRPM are subclasses of RPM, indicating that they are a more specific RPM.

Properties attached to a class can either be *data properties*, which resemble attributes of defined data types (e.g. integer, string, etc.), or *object properties*, which resemble relations to other classes. Since the revolutions per minute are measured as an integer value, RPM has a data property called rpmValue of data type int with the restriction that there has to be *exactly one value* for this property. Properties are inherited from classes to their subclasses. Hence, NormalRPM and HighRPM inherit RPM's data property rpmValue. However, there are data property restrictions made to NormalRPM and HighRPM, which are used to classify a RPM as NormalRPM if the rpmValue is below 3,000 or as a HighRPM if rpmValue is greater or equal than 3,000.

The main benefit of the ontology shown in Figure 1 is to classify an acoustic level of the passenger cabin to *normal, medium* or *high*. For our example, we assume that this classification is dependent on the speed of the vehicle and the revolutions per minute of the engine. *SWRL rules* help to define which *speed-rpm combination* will lead to which cabin acoustic level. SWRL enhances OWL with rule-based decisions and simple calculations as well as comparisons which cannot be modeled in standard OWL. SWRL rules are composed of a conjunction of preconditions and a result that is performed if all preconditions are fulfilled [11]. In order to classify a cabin acoustic level as HighLevel, we define that we need a `HighRPM` and a `Speed` with a `speedValue` above 60mph. Hence, we need the following SWRL rule to classify an individual of `CabinAcousticLevel` as `HighLevel`:

> IF there is an individual of the class `CabinAcousticLevel` (named `c`)
> AND there is an individual of the class `HighRPM` (named `r`)
> AND there is an individual of the class `Speed` (named `s`)
> AND the data property `speedValue` of `s` is greater than 60
> THEN `c` belongs to the class `HighLevel`.

2.3 Fuzzy Logic

Fuzzy logic is an extension to normal Boolean logic. It provides a finer segmentation than just *true* and *false* since a degree of membership $m \in [0,1]$ to every category can be given. A value could e.g. be *0.3 true* and *0.7 false*. Fuzzy logic values can be combined as in normal propositional logic. In this case their membership values are combined using a t-norm for AND and a t-conorm for OR. There exist several possible calculation norms, e.g. the product norm or the min-max norm [13]. The product norm states that the membership $m(A \wedge B = true)$ is equal to $m(A = true) \cdot m(B = true)$. The membership $m(A \vee B = true)$ is equal to $m(A = true) + m(B = true) - m(A = true) \cdot m(B = true)$. This theory will be used to model a reliability value for our approach. It fits well for handling the reliability of sources since calculation results behave similar to reliability assumptions in reality. A value which is combined from several sources which are all necessary (AND connection) is less or equal reliable than the single values from the sources since different, maybe unrealiable values are combined. A value with several redundant sources (OR connection) gets more reliable than the single values from the sources since the sources support each other and thus the result can be trusted.

3 Requirements

In this section, we identify requirements for a model-based approach of processing contextual information in a context-aware in-car infotainment system. The requirements raised in this section are based on our experiences in developing in-car infotainment systems. Nevertheless, we will use our running example of classifying a cabin acoustic level (cf. Figure 1) to explain the requirements.

R1: Aggregation and Abstraction. In our running example we aggregate a vehicle's speed and the revolutions per minute of the car's engine to a cabin acoustic level. Hence, one of the basic requirements an approach for context modeling has to meet is the ability to aggregate single, simple contextual information (most-likely measured by a sensor) to more complex values or even entire situations a car and its driver are in. Furthermore, the modeler needs a possibility to express how this aggregation works and which contextual information is aggregated to *new* contextual information.

R2: Hierarchy of Contextual Information. To aggregate contextual data more easily, the modeler has to be able to classify contextual information to subclasses (e.g. a RPM may be *normal* or *high*). Hence, it is necessary to map such hierarchical compositions to the context model which describes the context of the driver, the vehicle and their environment.

R3: Diversity of Contextual Information. Contextual information differs a lot with regard to its characteristics. Some data do not change during the whole lifetime of a car (e.g. type of the car), some data may change during a drive (e.g. the country the car is in), and some data changes in milliseconds (e.g. speed of the car, or an engine's RPM). In addition to this, contextual information differ in their data types. Most likely, there will be data types like Boolean values, numeric values, textual values, and complex combinations of such simple data types. With respect to our running example, it may happen that a cabin acoustic level is also influenced by the type of the car which may be represented as a String. Hence, a model describing relations of contextual information must be able to support different data types of contextual information as well as different rates of them.

R4: Data from Multiple, Unreliable Sources. When modeling the classification of a cabin acoustic level by using speed and RPM of the car and its engine respectively, the modeler does not have any knowledge of the reliability of the speed and the RPM. A speed may be measured by different sources (e.g., incremental rotary encoder and GPS) with different reliabilities. Whereas the incremental rotary encoder (which is typically used to visualize the speed of the car to the driver) has a high reliability, the reliability of a speed calculated via GPS will be much lower. The modeling approach has to allow multiples sources which deliver the same kind of data (e.g., speed) and express how to deal with different reliabilities of these multiple sources.

R5: Comprehensibility. Model-based development enables people who are not used to implement software systems by using a programming language like C, C++, or Java by offering them a solution of abstractly modeling the software system. In order to support such people by creating context-aware in-car infotainment systems, modeling contextual information and their relations has to be easy and comprehensible. This may require sufficient tool support for creating context models.

R6: Extensibility. Designing and developing a context-aware in-car infotainment system has to be future-proof in terms of new contextual information becoming relevant for a context-aware in-car infotainment system. It should be possible to add new sources of contextual information to the context model without changing the way the context model and the software-architecture evaluating the context model perform. In case of our running example, it may happen that a sensor measuring the cabin acoustic level will be included in future cars. Hence, an approach with a defined set of inputs and outputs is not appropriate for modeling contextual information and their relations.

4   Ontology-Based Modeling of Contextual Information

In this section, we present our approach of modeling contextual information for a context-aware in-car infotainment system.

We choose ontologies as the basis of our modeling technique, because they meet almost all of the requirements presented in Section 3: OWL ontologies support hierarchies and logical reasoning (cf. requirement R1). SWRL rules offer extended possibilities to design rules with calculations and comparisons (cf. R2) of different data types (cf. R3). OWL allows to add new sources of contextual information by adding them to the ontology and make use of them in further calculations (cf. R6). OWL and SWRL are standardized by the W3C and there are mature APIs like the OWL API[2] for Java, reasoners like Pellet[3] and editors like Protégé[4]. OWL ontologies can be seen as state of the art and are used in various context-aware systems [5,6,9].

However, OWL lacks support for handling unreliability and multiple data sources (cf. R4). Since OWL and SWRL are not domain-specific to modeling a context-aware (in-car infotainment) system, the comprehensibility is expected to be low when using OWL and SWRL without any domain-specific adaption (cf. R5). Hence, we extend OWL by adding an object-oriented part to handle multiple data sources with different reliabilities. In addition, a possibility to handle the link between OWL data and real data sources in the car is devised.

4.1   Handle Multiple Sources of Contextual Information

The central idea of the proposed system is that a modeler does not have to think about programming details. If he wants to use a source, he just has to know a few facts to link an OWL class to it. This OWL class has to be defined as an input class. The system automatically tries to find corresponding sources for *input* classes at runtime, reads data from the sources and transforms the data into OWL individuals of OWL classes to which the source definition belongs to. These individuals are used as input for data processing via OWL and SWRL rules. Classes, whose individuals are results of the processing and should be given to other systems later, can be defined as *output classes*. A definition as both, input and output, is possible, too. This may be useful if a value provided by an input source should be changed with respect to other values. Hence, this value would be input at output at the same time.

To link an OWL class to a source, an identifier is needed to state which source should be used. A source which provides the expected content understands the identifier, so that the system can automatically use it as a source for content of this OWL class at runtime. OWL offers the possibility to link a class to attributes in the form of data properties (concrete values) and object properties (relations between individuals). To read them from the source, the modeler has to be able to give the source a property identifier and the name of the OWL property, which has to be filled with data belonging to this identifier. There are two different types of sources. For some sources, the system can add itself as a listener and wait for data. This is called a push source. For other sources, the

---

[2] http://owlapi.sourceforge.net
[3] http://clarkparsia.com/pellet
[4] http://protege.stanford.edu

system has to read data on its own with a certain frequency, which is called a pull source. This depends on the type of source and has to be stated by the modeler, too.

The definition of source information is done using OWL annotations. Annotations for classes defined in OWL can be interpreted as a kind of comments to these classes. The annotations have to be made for an OWL class to describe its task (in- or output) and its source understandable to the system. We provide a base ontology containing a set of annotations to specify the additional information about sources as described above.

As stated by requirement R4, a modeling technique of contextual information has to allow modeling of how an aggregation of contextual information should behave if there are multiple sources. We propose to achieve this by annotations which can be added to an OWL class. For example, using the annotation sourceName, will connect an OWL class with a source of real data of the car. Figure 2 shows our running example supplemented by several annotations. Annotations made to OWL classes are evaluated during runtime of the context-aware in-car infotainment system. The OWL class Speed is annotated with the following: exchangeType = Exchange_In states that an individual of the class Speed has to be created for every source which delivers information about the vehicle's speed. Sources which provide such information can be identified by a *source name*. This link between the ontology and the data source is guaranteed by the annotation sourceName = SpeedSource (sourceType = Source_Push indicates that a speed source automatically sends updates without any need for polling). If there are multiple sources providing information about the current speed of the vehicle, the question comes up which speed information should be chosen. Our approach allows to model which source should be used. However, we do not need to know the exact sources during modeling time. Our approach offers various possibilities of selecting sources. For the RPM of the vehicle's engine, we modeled to merge different values of all sources (sourceSelection = Select_MergeAll). In this case we defined to calculate the average of the data property rpmValue by using the annotation valueCombination = Calculation_Average. Using the annotation sourceSelection = Select_HighestConf, allows to choose the source with the highest confidence, for example. Every source defines its confidence. Hence, we have to trust sources about their confidence.

4.2 Combination of Unreliable Information

With respect to our beforehand deduced requirements, a strategy to represent the reliability of sources of contextual information is needed. This can be used to express that a source from the car is more reliable than a source on the internet or to differentiate the reliability of different sensor types. The reliability is supposed to have an impact on the calculation results, so a result is only as reliable as the data used for its calculation.

As a concept to support all theses ideas, we propose the *confidence* value. The confidence is a value $conf \in [0, 1]$. It is interpreted as a fuzzy Boolean value for reliability, so $conf(X) = 0.8$ means *fact X is reliable* $= (0.8 \ true, 0.2 \ false)$.

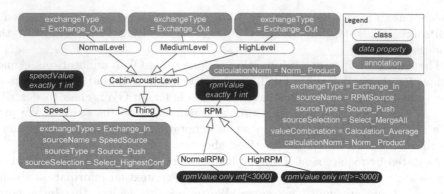

Fig. 2. Running example of classifying a cabin acoustic level supplemented by annotations to enable handling of multiple sources with different reliabilities

The confidence is calculated for every assertion of an individual to a class. For new data, the confidence from the source is used. For calculated data, the confidence can be calculated according to the rules that lead to the new facts. Therefore, fuzzy logic calculation norms can be used. Which norm the system should use during runtime can again be defined by an annotation (e.g., `calculationNorm = Norm_Product`) Using this concept, the right source out of multiple sources could be selected by using the highest confidence. For cases, in which the source with the highest confidence is not necessarily the best one, a $weight \in \mathbb{N}$ for the sources is added, so that the source with the highest weight can be selected. In other cases even data from all sources in parallel could be desired. If it is necessary to combine the values from various sources, the system also has to know how to calculate combinations for numeric values. Besides it has to be chosen whether it is sufficient that only one source provides data or whether all available sources have to provide data before the merged data is added to the system. All theses selections depend on the context data and its use. So the modeler has to make these decisions.

Figure 3 shows an exemplary calculation of the confidence: s is an individual of Speed and r is an individual of RPM are created from sources S and R and get the confidence of their sources. c is a predefined individual of CabinAcousticLevel and is used to be put into one of the subclasses of CabinAcousticLevel during reasoning. Since it is predefined it has the confidence 1.0. We assume that s has a speedValue of 120 and r has an rpmValue of 3500. So r is identified as an individual of HighRPM, the confidence for this fact is 0.8, too. The assertion to class HighLevel is calculated using a SWRL rule. All preconditions of the rule, "there exists an individual of class CabinAcousticLevel", "there exists an individual of class Speed with speedValue greater than 60" and "there exists an individual of class HighRPM", are met by c, s and r. So the rule is processed and c is asserted to class HighLevel. This is an AND condition, so the product norm has been chosen to calculate the confidence of this result. So $conf(c\ individual\ of\ HighLevel) = 1.0 \cdot 0.9 \cdot 0.8 = 0.72$.

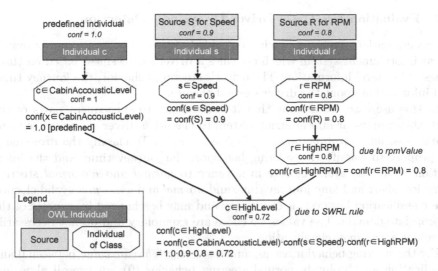

Fig. 3. Example for confidence calculation

5   Implementation and Evaluation

In this section, we evaluate our approach of modeling contextual information by modeling an extensive part of a context-aware in-car infotainment system. Therefore, we first present our implementation before introducing our evaluation use case. Finally, we check which of the requirements (cf. Section 3) we met and which remain open.

5.1   Implementation

For our evaluation use case we used a setup composed of a CAN bus simulation and an OSGi-based software architecture, which is connected to the CAN bus simulation. Every source which is specified in our context model needs an OSGi-Service which propagates the data (e.g., a vehicle speed coming from the simulated CAN bus) so that our system is able to use such data as input for reasoning the context model.

After creating this *evaluation base*, we are able to create our context model for processing contextual information. We used the open-source ontology editor *Protégé*[5] for creating this model. This model can be read by our system and is evaluated in real time whenever source data do change. However, for reading and reasoning the context model no model-specific implementation is necessary. To visualize results, we implement a software component which listens to ontology classes which are modeled as output of the ontology reasoning.

---

[5] http://protege.stanford.edu/

5.2   Evaluation Use Case: Driver Drowsiness Detection

For an evaluation of our approach, we decided to build a part of a context-aware in-car infotainment system which classifies a driver's drowsiness based on three types of low level information: The driver's steering behavior, the journey time, and information about the driver's eyelid closure.

In this use case, we assume that it is necessary to subsequent parts of the context-aware in-car infotainment system to classify a driver's drowsiness to *no drowsiness*, *medium drowsiness*, or *high drowsiness*. To classify the drowsiness, we propose to classify the steering behavior, the journey time, and the information about the eyelid closure in advance to *normal* and *abnormal* steering behavior, *short* and *long* journey time, and *normal* and *abnormal* eyelid closure. The classification however, is exemplary and may be changed by experts of the appropriate domain. The values we chose are exemplary and do not necessarily represent an *optimal* classification.

For the steering behavior, we assume a *steering behavior value* between 0 and 1 indicating an absolutely normal steering behavior (0), an overall abnormal steering behavior (1) or something in between. We assume that this value is calculated by a preceding controller connected to the steering column. We propose to classify the steering behavior to normal if the steering behavior value is less than 0.8 and abnormal otherwise.

For the journey time, we assume that we do have access to a value which indicates how long the car is steered without interruption. Hence, we assume that the journey time is basically characterized by a *duration* in minutes. We further propose, to classify a journey time as short if the duration is less than 120 minutes, and as long otherwise.

For the information about the eyelid closure, we assume two values: An average duration of eyelid closures over the last minutes and an eyelid closure frequency. We exemplary propose to classify an eyelid closure to *normal* if the average duration of an eyelid closure is less than 400 milliseconds and the time between two eyelid closures is more than 5 seconds, otherwise we assume the eyelid closure of the driver as *abnormal* and classify it as such.

Figure 4 summarizes the beforehand mentioned relations as an OWL ontology. The driver's steering behavior and the the journey time can be classified by an OWL reasoner because we modeled data property restrictions to them which allow classification similar to the classification of an engine's RPM in our running example (cf. Figure 1). To classify an eyelid closure however, we have to add the following SWRL rules to this ontology:

i) $e \in EyelidClosure \land e.avg\_duration < 400$
   $\land e.frequency > 5 \Rightarrow e \in NormalEyelidClosure$
ii) $e \in EyelidClosure \land$
   $(e.avg\_duration \geq 400 \lor e.frequency \leq 5) \Rightarrow e \in AbnormalEyelidClosure$

For finally classifying the driver's drowsiness, we make the following assumptions: If steering behavior and eyelid closure are normal and the journey time is short, we classify the drowsiness as *no drowsiness*. If one of these three contextual

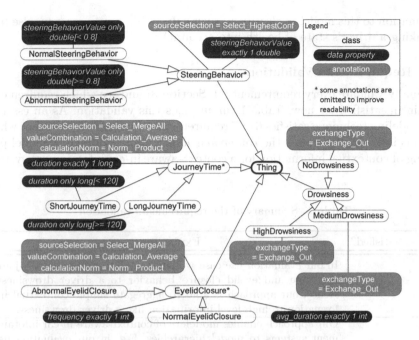

Fig. 4. Ontology model of an exemplary driver drowsiness detection using a driver's steering and eyelid closure behavior and a journey time to classify a driver's drowsiness to *no*, *medium*, or *high* drowsiness

information (steering behavior, eyelid closure and journey time) is abnormal or long respectively, we classify the driver's drowsiness as medium. If two or more of these contextual information are abnormal or long respectively, we classify the driver's drowsiness as high. This classification again is just exemplary. To achieve this classification, we add the following SWRL rules to the ontology:

iii) $d \in Drowsiness \land s \in NormalSteeringBehavior \land$
$j \in ShortJourneyTime \land e \in NormalEyelidClosure$
$\Rightarrow d \in NoDrowsiness$

iv) $d \in Drowsiness \land ((s \in AbnormalSteeringBehavior \oplus$
$j \in LongJourneyTime) \oplus e \in AbnormalEyelidClosure)$
$\Rightarrow d \in MediumDrowsiness$

v) $d \in Drowsiness \land ((s \in NormalSteeringBehavior \oplus$
$j \in ShortJourneyTime) \oplus e \in NormalEyelidClosure)$
$\Rightarrow d \in HighDrowsiness$

With this context model, composed of an ontology including custom annotations, and a set of SWRL rules, we are now able to classify a driver's drowsiness by taking the driver's journey time, steering and eyelid closure behavior into account.

Journey time, steering and eyelid closure behavior are the contextual information in this exemplary use case. However, it is possible to add further contextual information to this model to classify a driver's drowsiness even more precise (e.g. by taking a driver's state of health into account).

5.3 Requirements Validation

We finally validate every requirement (cf. Section 3) and see which requirements remain unsatisfied for now. Table 1 summarizes this validation. As an essence, our modeling technique satisfies 6 of 7 requirements. The only requirement which remains unknown for now is the *comprehensibility* of our apprach to model processing of contextual information for a context-aware in-car infotainment system.

Table 1. Summary of the requirements validation

Req.	Satisfied?	Explanation
R1	yes	In our evaluation use case we aggregate steering behavior, journey time and eyelid closure behavior to a driver drowsiness. Hence, our approach is able to aggregate simple contextual information to high level information like a driver drowsiness.
R2	yes	Our approach enables modelers of context-aware in-car infotainment systems to model hierarchies. E.g. in our evaluation use case we modeled a normal steering behavior as a sub-classes of steering behavior.
R3	yes	Our evaluation use case contains data properties of the types long, double and int. Hence, it is possible to use diverse data types.
R4	yes	By the use of annotations we added the possibility to model how the system should behave if multiple sources delivering the same contextual information are present during runtime. We also added possibilities to model how reliability values of different sources of contextual information are combined. Hence, our approach is able to handle information from multiple, unreliable sources.
R5	unknown	The comprehensibility of our approach remains unknown for now because we designed our evaluation ontology by ourselves and did not yet ask in-car infotainment modelers to design a context-aware system. We expect difficulties especially when creating SWRL rules without any further, domain-specific support.
R6	yes	If a modeler wants to add more parameters to a drowsiness detection, he or she could easily add these to the ontology and add rules using these values.

6   Related Work

There are several approaches to add context-awareness to automotive systems. Many driver assistance systems may be regarded as context-aware, but they only regard data from a certain limited domain for the special processing they need for their task [24]. As shown in the following paragraphs, there are also attempts to use context-awareness in the domains of infotainment, navigation and to create context-aware architectures for the combination of data from various driver assistance systems.

Several systems try to help the driver in handling the car. Zhang et al. use an ontology-based system with a layered architecture to improve safety and comfort with a telematics system [26]. Also, Madkour et al. propose a system with this ability based on context-awareness using ontologies [14]. Ablaßmeier et al. [1] and Bader [3] created systems that shall only provide neccessary information to the driver. Both use Bayesian networks to support decisions. Wu et al. use OWL and see the car as a special case of an intelligent room [25]. Rodriguez et al. [18] want to show information about local shops based on the context and the users behavior in the past.

Driver assistance systems improved by context-awareness are presented by Fuchs et al. [7]. Also, Tönnis et al. [23] show such a system in which they want to detect the driving situation based on contextual information. Hoch has created a system to provide driver assistance systems with context [10]. His example is a context-aware lane departure detection based on video observation of the driver. Sun et al. [22] and Kannan et al. [12] try to realize critical situations based on context and want to show appropriate warning messages.

Context-awareness may also be used for entertainment purposes. Park et al. [17] and Baltrunas et al. [4] want to select music based on the context and a driver's preferences. Alt et al. [2] aim to use short stops e.g. at a traffic light, to provide the right bits of entertainment for this situation.

Münter et al. [16] describe use cases for a context-aware navigation system that fits its grade of support for the driver to the driving situation. Context could also be used to detect the drivers motivation for a tour, so that additional information about the tour's goal may be displayed, as proposed by Rodzina et al. [19].

Gringoleit [8] aims to use a context-aware system to reduce the energy consumption in the car. Since not all systems have to work at the same time, context information can be used to deactivate systems which are unnecessary in the current situation.

It can be concluded that ontology-based models are state of the art when modeling context-aware systems. Handling of uncertain and unreliable data is only part of a few systems. The techniques are mostly used to make suggestions, not to process context data. Most systems are created specifically for their field of application. Ontologies and processing rules are predefined and included in the systems.

The approach proposed in this paper has a different focus than the related work presented in this section. It is a generic system with respect to context information processing. There are no predefined ontology or rules, also the kind and number of data sources is not given in advance. The modeler is able to define and model everything he or she needs, so many different parts of the infotainment system can be improved using data from our approach. Another advantage of our system is the mechanism to deal with uncertain and unreliable data and data from more than one source.

7   Conclusion and Future Work

Current in-car infotainment system are created during a model-based development. Adding contextual information to them necessarily leads to the problem of how to model contextual information and their relations. The approach presented in this paper shows how processing of contextual information can be modeled. We used an ontology-based model to describe the *real world* and added possibilities to model uncertainty and unreliability of data within this ontology. We also developed techniques to model handling of multiple sources of contextual information.

To evaluate our approach, we defined requirements a modeling technique for processing contextual information has to meet, modeled an extensive automotive use case using our proposed modeling techniques, and finally validated the requirements.

We will extend these evaluation in a future work by e.g. comparing our approach to standard OWL/SWRL or completely different techniques of modeling contextual information. Furthermore, we will consider high-level contextual information. In particular, we will look into modeling a user's intention using high-level contextual information and how we can create an integrated modeling process for an entire context-aware in-car infotainment system. We also aim for a domain-specific editor for creating context-aware in-car infotainment systems and an appropriate evaluation of this editor by comparing it to other techniques of creating context-aware in-car infotainment systems.

After creating and evaluating the entire development process of context-aware in-car infotainment systems, we aim to check and if needed improve the performance of our approach to enable it to run on target hardware (e.g. a *real* in-car infotainment system).

References

1. Ablassmeier, M., Poitschke, T., Reifinger, S., Rigoll, G.: Context-Aware Information Agents for the Automotive Domain Using Bayesian Networks. In: Smith, M.J., Salvendy, G. (eds.) HCII 2007. LNCS, vol. 4557, pp. 561–570. Springer, Heidelberg (2007)
2. Alt, F., Kern, D., Schulte, F., Pfleging, B., Shirazi, A.S., Schmidt, A.: Enabling Micro-Entertainment in Vehicles Based on Context Information. In: AutomotiveUI 2010: Proceedings of the 2nd International Conference on Automotive User Interfaces and Interactive Vehicular Applications, pp. 117–124. ACM (2010)
3. Bader, R.: Proactive Recommender Systems in Automotive Scenarios. PhD thesis, Technische Universität München (2013)

4. Baltrunas, L., Kaminskas, M., Ludwig, B., Moling, O., Ricci, F., Aydin, A., Lüke, K.-H., Schwaiger, R.: InCarMusic: Context-Aware Music Recommendations in a Car. In: Huemer, C., Setzer, T. (eds.) EC-Web 2011. LNBIP, vol. 85, pp. 89–100. Springer, Heidelberg (2011)
5. Bettini, C., Brdiczka, O., Henricksen, K., Indulska, J., Nicklas, D., Ranganathan, A., Riboni, D.: A survey of context modelling and reasoning techniques. Pervasive and Mobile Computing 6(2), 161–180 (2010)
6. Chen, H., Finin, T., Joshi, A.: An Ontology for Context-aware Pervasive Computing Environments. The Knowledge Engineering Review 18(03), 197–207 (2003)
7. Fuchs, S., Rass, S., Lamprecht, B., Kyamakya, K.: A Model for Ontology-based Scene Description for Context-aware Driver Assistance Systems. In: Ambi-Sys 2008: Proceedings of the 1st International Conference on Ambient Media and Systems. ICST (Institute for Computer Sciences, Social-Informatics and Telecommunications Engineering) (2008)
8. Gringoleit, F.: Context Modeling for Dynamic Configuration of Automotive Functions. Master thesis, Technische Universität München (2012)
9. Gu, T., Wang, X.H., Pung, H.K., Zhang, D.Q.: An Ontology-based Context Model in Intelligent Environments. In: Proceedings of the Communication Networks and Distributed Systems Modeling and Simulation Conference (CNDS 2004), pp. 270–254 (2004)
10. Hoch, S.: Kontextmanagement und Wissensanalyse im kognitiven Automobil der Zukunft. PhD thesis, Technische Universität München (2009)
11. Horrocks, I., Patel-Schneider, P.F., Boley, H., Tabet, S., Grosof, B., Dean, M.: SWRL: A Semantic Web Rule Language Combining OWL and RuleML, http://www.w3.org/Submission/SWRL
12. Kannan, S., Thangavelu, A., Kalivaradhan., R.: An Intelligent Driver Assistance System (I-DAS) for Vehicle Safety Modelling using Ontology Approach. International Journal of UbiComp. 1(3), 15–29 (2010)
13. Kruse, R., Gebhardt, J., Klawonn, F.: Fuzzy-Systeme. Teubner, Stuttgart (1995)
14. Madkour, M., Maach, A.: Ontology-based Context Modeling for Vehicle Context-aware Services. Journal of Theoretical and Applied Information Technology 34(2), 158–166 (2011)
15. Motik, B., Patel-Schneider, P.F., Parsia, B.: OWL 2 Web Ontology Language: Structural Specification and Functional-Style Syntax, 2nd edn., http://www.w3.org/TR/owl-syntax
16. Münter, D., Kötteritzsch, A., Linder, T., Hofmann, J., Hussein, T., Ziegler, J.: Einflussfaktoren für eine situationsgerechte Navigationsunterstützung im Fahrzeug. In: Reiterer, H., Deussen, O. (eds.) Mensch & Computer 2012, pp. 163–172. Oldenbourg (2012)
17. Park, H.-S., Yoo, J.-O., Cho, S.-B.: A Context-Aware Music Recommendation System Using Fuzzy Bayesian Networks with Utility Theory. In: Wang, L., Jiao, L., Shi, G., Li, X., Liu, J. (eds.) FSKD 2006. LNCS (LNAI), vol. 4223, pp. 970–979. Springer, Heidelberg (2006)
18. Rodriguez Garzon, S., Poguntke, M.: The Personal Adaptive In-Car HMI: Integration of External Applications for Personalized Use. In: Ardissono, L., Kuflik, T. (eds.) UMAP Workshops 2011. LNCS, vol. 7138, pp. 35–46. Springer, Heidelberg (2012)
19. Rodzina, L., Kristoffersen, S.: Context-Dependent Car Navigation as Kind of Human-Machine Collaborative Interaction. In: CTS 2013: International Conference on Collaboration Technologies and Systems, pp. 253–259. IEEE (2013)

20. Schäuffele, J., Zurawka, T.: Automotive Software Engineering, 5th edn. Springer Vieweg (2013)
21. Strang, T., Linnhoff-Popien, C.: A Context Modeling Survey. In: UbiComp 2004: 6th International Conference on Ubiquitous Computing. Workshop on Advanced Context Modelling, Reasoning and Management. LNCS, vol. 3205. Springer, Heidelberg (2004)
22. Sun, J., Wu, Z., Pan, G.: Context-aware smart car: from model to prototype. Journal of Zhejiang University Science A 10(7), 1049–1059 (2009)
23. Tönnis, M., Fischer, J.G., Klinker, G.: From Sensors to Assisted Driving - Bridging the Gap. Journal of Software 3(3), 71–82 (2008)
24. Winner, H., Hakuli, S., Wolf, G.: Handbuch Fahrerassistenzsysteme: Grundlagen, Komponenten und Systeme für aktive Sicherheit und Komfort, 1st edn. Vieweg+Teubner (2009)
25. Wu, Z., Wu, Q., Cheng, H., Pan, G., Zhao, M., Sun, J.: ScudWare: A Semantic and Adaptive Middleware Platform for Smart Vehicle Space. IEEE Transactions on Intelligent Transportation Systems 8(1), 121–132 (2007)
26. Zhang, D.Q., Wang, X.H., Hackbarth, K.: OSGi Based Service Infrastructure for Context Aware Automotive Telematics. In: VTC 2004: 59th IEEE Vehicular Technology Conference, vol. 5, pp. 2957–2961. IEEE (2004)

Comprehending Feature Models Expressed in CVL

Iris Reinhartz-Berger[1], Kathrin Figl[2], and Øystein Haugen[3]

[1] Department of Information Systems, University of Haifa, Israel
iris@is.haifa.ac.il
[2] Institute for Information Systems & New Media, Vienna, Austria
kathrin.figl@wu.ac.at
[3] SINTEF and Department of Informatics, University of Oslo, Norway
oystein.haugen@sintef.no

Abstract. Feature modeling is a common way to present and manage variability of software and systems. As a prerequisite for effective variability management is comprehensible representation, the main aim of this paper is to investigate difficulties in understanding feature models. In particular, we focus on the comprehensibility of feature models as expressed in Common Variability Language (CVL), which was recommended for adoption as a standard by the Architectural Board of the Object Management Group. Using an experimental approach with participants familiar and unfamiliar with feature modeling, we analyzed comprehensibility in terms of comprehension score, time spent to complete tasks, and perceived difficulty of different feature modeling constructs. The results showed that familiarity with feature modeling did not influence the comprehension of mandatory, optional, and alternative features, although unfamiliar modelers perceived these elements more difficult than familiar modelers. OR relations were perceived as difficult regardless of the familiarity level, while constraints were significantly better understood by familiar modelers. The time spent to complete tasks was higher for familiar modelers.

Keywords: Variability analysis, Software Product Line Engineering, Model Comprehension.

1 Introduction

With the proliferation of software systems as an essential part of almost any business, their requirements increased and became more complex. Against this background, the variety of software artifacts has also heightened and a fundamental challenge is figuring out how to manage this variety. One way to tackle these challenges is analyzing and representing variability. Variability is extensively studied in the field of Software Product Line Engineering [1, 2] which aims at supporting the development and maintenance of families of software products, termed software product lines.

A systematic review published in 2011 [3] shows that variability management in software product lines is primarily done utilizing feature-oriented modeling. A *feature diagram* is a tree or graph that describes the end-user visible characteristics (features)

J. Dingel et al. (Eds.): MODELS 2014, LNCS 8767, pp. 501–517, 2014.
© Springer International Publishing Switzerland 2014

of systems in a software product line and the relationships and constraints (dependencies) between them. Different feature-oriented languages have been proposed over the years. However, no standard feature-oriented modeling language has emerged yet. Recently, some initiatives in this direction started in the Object Management Group (OMG), yielding the submission of the Common Variability Language (CVL) proposal [4]. CVL is a domain-independent language for specifying and resolving variability. It facilitates the specification and resolution of variability over any instance of a Meta-Object Facility (MOF)-based language (such an instance is termed a base model). Lately, CVL was recommended for adoption as a standard by the Architectural Board of OMG.

A prerequisite for effective variability management is comprehensible representation of variability. However, there are few empirical studies that analyze difficulties in understanding variability representations in general and feature diagrams in particular. To fill this gap, the main aim of this study was to examine the cognitive difficulty of understanding variability in feature modeling. In order to address this challenge we conducted an exploratory study using CVL models, perceiving CVL as an emerging standard that uses feature-oriented principles for specifying and representing variability. We concentrate on the variability abstraction part of CVL, which provides constructs for specifying variability without defining the concrete consequences on the base model. We further seek to answer in this study how modeler's familiarity with feature modeling influences comprehension difficulties. Differences between novices and experts can point on specific problems in comprehension. In addition, it is of specific interest how the target user group of CVL, modelers who are familiar with feature modeling, comprehend CVL and can easily switch from feature models to CVL models, as comprehensibility of a new modeling language is an important basis for its acceptance in practice.

The rest of the paper is structured as follows. Section 2 reviews the related work and provides the required background on CVL. Section 3 elaborates on the experiment design and procedure, while Section 4 presents the analysis procedure and the results. Section 5 discusses the results and the threats to validity. Finally, Section 6 summarizes and points on future research directions.

2   Related Work and Background

2.1   Comparison of Feature Modeling Languages

Comparison of feature modeling languages is mainly done using classification frameworks or according to lists of characteristics. Istoan et al. [5], for example, suggest a metamodel-based classification of variability modeling approaches: methods may use a single (unique) model to represent both commonality and variability or distinguish and keep separate the variability model from the base model. Methods that use a single model may annotate the base model by means of extensions or combine a general, reusable variability meta-model with different domain metamodels. Methods that use separate models specify the variability model using notations such as feature diagrams, decision models, or CVL [4]. Istoan et al. further compared the artifacts of these methods in the metamodel and model levels.

Czarnecki et al. [6] compared feature modeling and decision modeling along ten dimensions: applications, unit of variability (features vs. decisions), orthogonality, data types, hierarchy, dependencies and constraints, mapping to artifacts, binding time and mode, modularity, and tool aspects. They further showed how the main properties of feature modeling and decision modeling are reflected in three specific methods including an initial version of CVL.

Schobbens et al. [7] surveyed and compared seven feature diagram notations. These notations differ in their graph types (trees vs. directed acyclic graphs – DAG), the supported node types (e.g., cardinality support), the supported graphical constraint types (namely, "requires", "excludes", none, or both), and the supported textual constraint types (i.e., textual composition rules support). In a later work, Heymans et al. [8] evaluated the formal properties of feature diagram languages using Krogstie et al.'s semiotic quality framework [9] and Harel and Rumpe's guidelines for defining formal visual languages [10]. The list of evaluation criteria included: (1) expressiveness: what can the language express? (2) embeddability: can the structure of a diagram be kept when translated to another language? and (3) succinctness: how big are the expressions of one and the same semantic object?

Djebbi and Salinesi [11] provided a comparative survey on four feature diagram languages for requirements variability modeling. The languages are compared according to a list of criteria that includes readability, simplicity and expressiveness, type distinction, documentation, dependencies, evolution, adaptability, scalability, support, unification, and standardizeability.

Haugen et al. [12] proposed a reference model for comparing feature modeling approaches. This model makes distinction between the generic sphere, which includes feature models and product line models, and the specific sphere, which includes feature selection and product models. Standard languages, annotations, and special domain-specific languages are compared based on this reference model.

Comparing product line architecture design methods, Matinlassi [13] suggested an evaluation framework that is based on Normative Information Model-based Systems Analysis and Design (NIMSAD) [14]. According to this framework, there are four essential categories of elements for method evaluation: (1) context, including specific goals, product line aspects, application domains, and methods inputs/outputs; (2) user, including target groups, motivation, needed skills, and guidance; (3) contents, including method structure, artifacts, architectural viewpoints, language, variability, and tool support; and (4) validation, including method maturity and architecture quality.

All the above studies concentrate on the expressiveness of the compared languages, while usability-related issues follow a "feature comparison" approach. The drawback of such an approach is the subjectivity in developing both the comparison checklist and its interpretation. In addition, the above studies neglect comprehensibility, which is an important issue in modeling, as the abstract goal of modeling is to formally describe some aspects of the physical and social world around us for the purpose of understanding and communication [15].

Recent research has started to examine comprehensibility aspects of variability modeling languages. The work in [8] looks into comprehensibility appropriateness, namely whether or not language users understand all possible statements of the language. Comprehensibility appropriateness is, however, handled subjectively through embeddability and succinctness.

Conducting two experiments, Reinhartz-Berger and Tsoury [16, 17] compared the comprehensibility of Cardinality-Based Feature Modeling (CBFM) [18] and Application-based DOmain Modeling (ADOM) [19]. The comparison is based on comprehensibility of commonality- and variability-related concepts, including mandatory and optional elements, dependencies, variation points and variants. The experiments were conducted with small numbers of participants with similar background and experience. Accordingly, the conclusions were limited and concentrated on the differences between the methods: the feature-oriented CBFM and the UML-based ADOM.

To summarize, comprehensibility of feature modeling languages still needs to be assessed empirically. To fill this gap, we concentrate in this study on identifying difficulties in understanding feature models expressed in CVL. Next, we briefly present CVL.

2.2   Common Variability Lanaguge (CVL)

As noted, CVL facilitates the specification and resolution of variability over any base model defined by a metamodel. Its architecture consists of variability abstraction and variability realization. *Variability abstraction* supports modeling and resolving variability without referring to the exact nature of the variability with respect to the base model. *Variability realization*, on the other hand, supports modifying the base model during the process of transforming the base model into a product model.

In this study, which concentrates on the variability abstraction part of CVL, the main examined concepts are VSpecs (variability specifications), their relationships, and constraints. *VSpecs* are technically similar to features in feature modeling and can be divided into four subclasses: (1) choices – require yes/no decisions, (2) variables – require providing values of specified types, (3) VClassifier (variability classifiers) – require creating instances and resolving their variability, and (4) CVSpec – composite VSpecs. The VSpecs are organized in trees that represent logical constraints on their resolutions (configurations). VSpec children are related to their parents higher in the tree in two different ways: (1) Mandatory or optional: The positive resolution of a child may be determined by the resolution of the parent (mandatory) or can be independently determined (optional). (2) Group multiplicity: A range is given to specify how many total positive resolutions must be found among the children: XOR/alternative – exactly one, OR – at least one.

Finally, constraints express dependencies between elements of the variability model that go beyond what is captured in the tree structure. Two types of constraints are primarily supported in CVL: (1) A implies B – if A is selected, then B should be selected too (this constraint is known as "requires" in feature modeling), and (2) Not (A and B) – if A is selected, then B should not be selected and vice versa (this constraint is known as "excludes" in feature modeling).

As an example, consider Fig. 4(a) in the appendix. This figure describes the allowed variability in Skoda Yeti cars, a sport utility vehicle model of Skoda: the fuel of these cars is either diesel or benzin; the gear is either manual or automatic; the drive is either 2-weel-drive or 4x4; and the gadget level is either active or adventure. These configurations are further restricted by the constraints, e.g., a Skoda Yeti car whose gadget level is active and its fuel is diesel must have a manual gear (i.e., it cannot have an automatic gear). Fig. 4(b) further elaborates on the possible configurations of extra features in Skoda Yeti cars: such a car may have heated front pane, sunset, or panorama roof; it may have parking heater; and it may have styling package (and if so it may also have offroad styling).

3   Experiment Design and Procedure

3.1   Research Goal

Following Wohlin et al.'s guidelines [20], the goal of our exploratory study was to:
Analyze the effect of feature modeling familiarity on the comprehension difficulties of CVL, an emerging common variability language;
For the purpose of evaluation;
With respect to comprehension score in terms of percentage of correct solution, time spent to complete tasks, and participants' perception of difficulty;
From the point of view of modelers;
In the context of students of information systems, informatics and business.

3.2   Research Planning and Design

We derived from the above goal the following research questions and settings:

RQ1: Are there differences in the difficulty to comprehend CVL models for modelers who are familiar with feature modeling in general, in comparison to those who are unfamiliar with it?

To answer this research question we followed a quasi-experimental between-subject design. We classified participants into two distinct groups: participants familiar/unfamiliar with feature modeling. The exact classification procedure is explained in Section 3.6. The *independent variable* in this case was familiarity with feature modeling, while the *dependent variables* were comprehension scores (measured using the percentage of correct solution), time spent to complete tasks, and difficulty perception using self-rated difficulty of specific element types.

There is a long tradition of researching domain familiarity in terms of expert-novice differences in the area of system development. Petre [21] has argued that "experts 'see' differently and use different strategies than novice graphical programmers". Prior research has revealed that experts develop language-independent, abstract problem representations, so-called schemas, which make similar tasks for them easier. In light of these theoretical considerations we conjecture that comprehending

CVL models should be easier for modelers who are familiar with feature modeling. We hypothesize that as follows:

H1a. Familiarity with feature modeling will be positively associated with the comprehension score.

H1b. Familiarity with feature modeling will be positively associated with the time spent to complete tasks.

H1c. Familiarity with feature modeling will be negatively associated with the perceived difficulty of specific feature modeling constructs.

The second research question is divided into the following two parts:

> **RQ2a**: Which feature modeling constructs are difficult to understand?
> **RQ2b**: Are there specific difficulties in comprehending CVL models for modelers who are familiar with feature modeling, in comparison to those who are unfamiliar with it?

To answer the second research question we used a within-subjects design. The selected *independent variable* was element type, namely mandatory, optional, and alternative (XOR) features, as well as OR relations and feature constraints (dependencies). The *dependent variables* were comprehension score, time spent, and self-rated difficulty of the specific feature modeling elements. As it is not possible to construct comprehension tasks that only demand the understanding of "basic" elements, namely, mandatory, optional, and alternative features, we could only assess their subjective, but not their objective, difficulty. However, it was possible to objectively determine comprehension score and time to complete tasks related to OR relations and constraints.

We refrain from hypothesis development for the second research question, as it would not be helpful in such an exploratory setting [22]. While a considerable amount of literature has been published on expert-novice difference in general (RQ1), no research has been conducted on the comprehension of specific feature modeling constructs (RQ2) up to now. To our knowledge this is the first study evaluating comprehension of CVL, thus there is neither an adequate empirical nor a theoretical basis available to formulate a priori hypotheses.

3.3   Experimental Material

The *objects* of the experiment were two CVL models describing different sets of features of Skoda Yeti cars. The CVL models for the experiment were built by Prof. Haugen, who is the founder of CVL and is familiar with the possible Skoda Yeti configurations from the Norwegian Skoda public web pages. The first model (see Fig. 4a in the appendix), named "basic", describes basic features of Skoda Yeti. It includes mandatory and alternative features (using XOR relations), as well as four "implies" ("requires") constraints. The number of valid configurations is 6. The second model (see Fig. 4b in the appendix), named "expanded", describes advanced (extra) features. It includes optional features and an OR relationship, as well as two "excludes" constraints (phrased as "not (A and B)"). The number of valid configurations in this case is much higher.

3.4   Tasks

The tasks were embedded within an online questionnaire. On each model ten questions were asked, examining whether specific configurations of Skoda Yeti are allowed according to the model. These questions can be described as surface-level tasks which measure comprehension of models more directly than deep-level tasks, which require participants to work with the models in a usage context [23]. For our research goal of checking the comprehensibility of a relatively new language, surface-level model comprehension tasks are most appropriate.

The participants were presented with the model and one question at a time. They had to choose between the following answers: Correct, Wrong, Cannot be answered from model, I don't know. After answering a question, the participant proceeded to the next question, but could not return to previous questions. This way we could measure the time needed to answer an individual question. The questions used in the experiment appear in the appendix.

3.5   Procedure

The participants were requested to open the online questionnaire. There, they had to fill first a pre-questionnaire that was composed of two parts. The purpose of the first part of the pre-questionnaire was to obtain general information about the participants and their background, including age, gender, degree and subject of studies, and familiarity with feature modeling. To measure self-rated familiarity with feature modeling, which was one of the independent variables, we adopted the three-item modeling grammar familiarity scale of Recker [24]: (1) Overall, I am very familiar with feature diagrams; (2) I feel very confident in understanding feature diagrams; (3) I feel very competent in modeling feature diagrams.

The second part of the pre-questionnaire aimed to objectively examine the prior knowledge of the participants in modeling. This part included three models in three languages: ER, BPMN, and feature diagrams. The participants had to state in which language each model was specified and answer three comprehension questions about the models. Each question presented a statement and four possible answers: Correct, Wrong, Cannot be answered from model, I don't know.

After filling the pre-questionnaire, the participants were presented with slides explaining and exemplifying the variability abstraction part of CVL (the participants also got hard-copies of these slides which they could consult while answering the questions). The participants had to study CVL variability abstraction part on their own from the slides and proceed to the main questionnaire. The main questionnaire included two CVL models of Skoda Yeti cars and two sets of questions, each of which referred to a different model (basic vs. expanded). To avoid any order effects due to fading attention, we used two different samplings of the main questionnaire, in which models were arranged in a different sequence. As noted, the models and questions of the main questionnaire appear in the appendix.

The time spent on each question was recorded by the online questionnaire. No rigid time constraints were imposed on the participants.

After completing the questions on each model, the participants had to fill a post-part questionnaire that collected feedback on the tasks and the difficulty to understand different model elements (mandatory and optional features, XOR and OR relations). The answering options ranged from 1=very easy to 7=very difficult. In addition, the participants could report on difficulties they experienced in open text fields.

3.6   Participants

Participants were recruited from three different classes from information systems, informatics and business curricula with prior training in modeling. Indeed, it can be argued that using students to evaluate a language that aimed at software professionals is problematic, but it has been shown in [25] that students have a good understanding of the way industry behaves, and may work well as subjects in empirical studies in specific areas, such as requirements engineering. Additionally, students are a relatively homogenous group concerning knowledge about and experience with conceptual modeling [26].

The executions of the experiment took place in the spring semester of 2013 in three courses that deal with modeling in the University of Haifa, the Vienna University of Economics and Business, and the University of Oslo. To assure sufficient motivation, the experiment was defined as an obligatory exercise or participants received approximately 5% course credit for participating. A total of 38 students participated in the study.

We now turn to the categorization of participants as familiar/unfamiliar with feature modeling. Since CVL is a relatively new language there are so far no "experts", however familiarity with feature modeling can serve as an adequate proxy. We use an extreme group selection approach to define two clearly distinct groups on the continuous variable familiarity in order to heighten power of statistical tests [27]. 15 participants were categorized as not familiar with feature modeling. They had answered the question "are you familiar with feature diagrams?" negatively. Regarding those who had answered this question affirmatively, we crosschecked the mean score of the scale familiarity with feature diagrams (3 items). We also assessed the reliability of this scale, which was adequate (Cronbach's alpha = 0.96). According to Nunnally and Bernstein [28] Cronbach's alpha should be higher than 0.8 to combine items in a mean value. The answering options for this scale ranged from 1=strongly disagree to 7=strongly agree. We concluded that only participants with a mean threshold value of 3.5 for this scale could be regarded as "familiar". Based on this criterion, 6 participants were excluded. In addition we checked whether all of these "familiar" participants also had correctly identified the figure of the feature diagram in the pre-questionnaire. This objective test led to further exclusion of one participant. Overall 7 participants were excluded as they were neither unfamiliar nor sufficiently familiar with feature modeling, resulting in 16 participants who were categorized as familiar with feature modeling. The final sample consisted of 31 participants: 22 males (58%) and 16 females (42%) with a mean age of 28 years.

Table 1. Differences in participants' skills

	Unfamiliar with feature modeling (n=15)		Familiar with feature modeling (n=16)		Statistical Test
	Mean	SD	Mean	SD	
Feature modeling test score (3 points possible)	1.20	0.77	2.13	0.89	$T_{df=29}=-3.09$ $p=0.00$
Modeling score test (8 points possible)	4.00	1.25	4.19	0.91	$T_{df=29}=-0.48$ $p=0.64$

We performed t-tests to demonstrate differences between the groups (see Table 1 for detailed results). As expected, participants of the familiar group scored better in the feature modeling test, while no significant differences in the modeling pre-test were found. This means that the students in the unfamiliar group were familiar with modeling in general, but unfamiliar with feature modeling and these differences may affect their difficulties in comprehending CVL models.

4   Analysis Procedure and Experiment Results

Data analysis was performed using SPSS 19. We first present the effects of familiarity with feature modeling on comprehension. We then refer to difficulties to comprehend specific model elements. Finally, we present results on comprehension difficulties as perceived and reported by the participants.

4.1   Comprehension and Familiarity with Feature Modeling

To answer the first research question (RQ1: Are there differences in the difficulty to comprehend CVL models for modelers who are familiar with feature modeling in general, in comparison to those who are unfamiliar with it?), we performed an analysis of covariance (ANCOVA) for repeated measures (basic and expanded models) for each dependent variable (comprehension score and time spent). The independent variable was familiarity with feature modeling (familiar vs. unfamiliar). Familiarity had a significant influence on the comprehension score (F=2.60, p=0.01). Participants familiar with feature modeling achieved a comprehension score of 85% on average, while unfamiliar participants achieved only 69%, lending support to H1a, which had predicted a positive association between familiarity and comprehension score. In addition, the interaction effect of familiarity and model (basic vs. expanded) was significant (F=9.68, p=0.00). As can be seen in Fig. 1 there was almost no performance difference between familiar and unfamiliar modelers in the expanded model, but a clear difference in the basic model. As noted, the basic model included only XOR relations and mandatory features, as well as "implies" ("requires") constraints, while the expanded model included an OR relation and "excludes" con-straints. H1a can only be partially supported in case of the basic model.

There was also a significant influence of familiarity on time (F=5.39, p=0.03). Contrary to our expectations, however, participants familiar with feature modeling took more time to complete tasks (418 seconds vs. 298 seconds). Thus, H1b could not be supported, i.e., familiarity is negatively associated with time spent.

To control for possible order effects, we had included a second independent variable in the analyses – model order – which represents the order in which models were presented to the participants. Model order had two values: 'basic first' – the basic model was presented first and 'basic later' – the expanded model was presented first. We found that the model order did not have any significant effect on the comprehension score, but it influenced the time spent; there was a significant interaction effect of model (basic vs. expanded) and model order (F=9.00, p=0.01). Participants spent more time on answering questions on the first model they were presented with than for the second model.

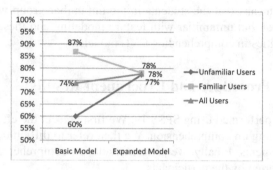

Fig. 1. Familiarity and Comprehension of Basic and Expanded Models

4.2   Difficulties to Comprehend Specific Model Elements

In order to answer the second research question (Which feature modeling constructs are difficult to understand? Are there specific difficulties in comprehending CVL for modelers who are familiar with feature modeling, in comparison to those who are unfamiliar with it?), we identified two model elements which could be addressed in seperation from other elements via comprehension tasks and whose comprehension deserve special attention: constraints and OR relations.

To check whether comprehension tasks which demand understanding of constraints in general are more difficult to understand than tasks without constraints, we performed again ANCOVAS. Overall, there was no difference between the comprehension of questions which involved constraints (79% correctness) and questions which did not involve constraints (81%). However, participants spent more time to solve questions without constraints (43 seconds) than with constraints (25 seconds; F=26.20, p=0.00). Familiarity has a significant influence on comprehension score (F=5.29, p=0.03) and time spent (F=4.74, p=0.04) as already reported in the prior analysis. We further observed that there is a significant interaction effect of familiarity and the existence of constraints (F=4.76, p=0.04) on comprehension score. As can be seen in Fig. 2 below, there is a larger performance difference of comprehension for questions involving constraints. While participants familiar with feature modeling achieved an average comprehension score of 90% on questions involving constraints, unfamiliar participants achieved only 67%. The difference in questions not involving constraints is smaller (84% vs. 78%, respectively). These results strengthen support for H1a (familiarity is positively associated with the comprehension score) in case constraints are involved.

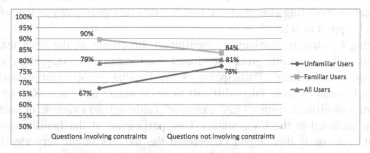

Fig. 2. Familiarity and Comprehension of Constraints

Another worth-mentioning result refers to OR relations, which were only included in the expanded model. We grouped questions according to the semantics of the OR relation: none – no option appears in the question, one – exactly one option appears, and many – two or more options appear. Comparisons between the three groups were analyzed with ANCOVAS. We found significant main effects of OR relations on comprehension score ($F=3.18$, $p=0.05$) and time spent ($F=8.53$, $p=0.00$). As can be seen in Fig. 3, questions including no option ('none') were the easiest for both groups. Questions including no option ('none') took on average most time (40 seconds), followed by one option selection ('one', 48 seconds) and multiple selections ('many', 26 seconds). The analysis further showed that for those tasks from the expanded model familiarity had no effect on the comprehension score, but on time, as discussed in the previous section. There were no significant interaction effects with familiarity.

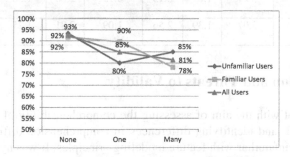

Fig. 3. Familiarity and Comprehension of OR Relations

4.3   Perceived Comprehension Difficulties

To find out whether familiarity with feature modeling changed the difficulties participants experienced, we performed a series of t-tests. Table 2 gives descriptive statistics and the details of the analyses. Note, we used 7-point scale for these items, with

1=very easy and 7=very difficult. Basic elements, namely, mandatory, optional, and alternative (XOR) features, were rated significantly more difficult by participants having no prior experience with feature models. There was no difference between the groups for the difficulty rating of OR relations, which were only included in the expanded model. As familiarity was associated negatively with perceived difficulty of specific feature modeling constructs in 4 of 5 cases (the gray rows in the table), the results lend support to H1c.

Regarding constraints, participants mentioned difficulties in the open text fields. Participants of the unfamiliar group mentioned that "learning and mapping constraints were a little [bit] difficult". Participants of the familiar group mentioned that "the 'implies' relationships were fairly difficult to understand" and "the NOT (A and B) [constraint] was difficult without [an] example" (although an example of such a constraint was included in the CVL slides). One participant of the familiar group also stated that "the constraints helped understand the model's intent very clearly". The participants further mentioned difficulties that we had not explicitly asked for, including the unclear meaning of parent-child relations in the feature tree ("It's hard to understand if feature can be used without his parent") and the lack of explicitness of all feature combinations ("Many combinations were not specified directly in the model").

Table 2. Comprehension difficulties as reported by the participants

	Unfamiliar with feature modeling		Familiar with feature modeling		Total		t	p
	M	SD	M	SD	M	SD		
mandatory features (basic model)	3.40	1.55	2.13	0.72	2.74	1.34	2.91	0.01
optional features (basic model)	3.67	1.63	2.19	0.83	2.90	1.47	3.14	0.00
optional features (expanded model)	3.33	1.35	2.31	1.01	2.81	1.28	2.40	0.02
XOR relations (basic model)	3.27	1.67	2.13	0.72	2.68	1.38	2.45	0.02
OR relations (expanded model)	3.07	1.39	2.56	1.09	2.81	1.25	1.13	0.27

5   Discussion and Threats to Validity

This study set out with the aim of assessing the comprehensibility of feature models expressed in CVL and identifying differences in comprehension difficulty for modelers familiar or unfamiliar with feature modeling principles. It was hypothesized that participants familiar with feature modeling would comprehend CVL models better and faster and experience less difficulties. And indeed, the results showed that comprehension score was higher and perceived difficulty lower for familiar modelers. This result is in line with findings of [29] who showed that familiarity with models in a specific domain also enables modelers to understand a new modeling language in that domain faster and with less effort.

It is interesting to note that the performance difference for familiar modelers was higher for the model which mainly included XOR relations than the second CVL model which included an OR relation. A possible explanation for this result is that OR relations in general are difficult to understand and that familiarity with feature modeling not necessarily trains modelers in understanding OR relations nor enables a cognitive advantage for understanding this construct. Further findings support this interpretation, because familiar and unfamiliar modelers subjectively rated the difficulty of OR relations similarly and while multiple selections ('many') were more difficult than 'one' or 'none' OR selections, familiarity did not interact with the comprehension of OR relations. Research findings on deductive reasoning with natural language connectives provide a theoretical explanation for the high cognitive difficulty of inclusive ORs. "OR" is likely to be misinterpreted in its exclusive form, not as an inclusive OR-operator [30]. Based on empirically detected comprehension difficulties, other model domains as process modeling have advised in modeling guidelines to avoid inclusive OR gateways altogether [31]. While this option is not feasibility for the area of feature modeling, still our results can be used to adopt training material and to inform modeling practitioners to be cautious in case of OR relations.

In addition, familiar modelers had a clear advantage in understanding textual constraints in CVL models in comparison to unfamiliar modelers. The observed difference could be attributed to the familiarity of the modelers with feature modeling. An implication of this result for modeling practice includes the need to put a specific emphasis on making constraints easier to understand for novice modelers. A possibility to achieve this goal might be to place textual constraints spatially close to respective features in the model, thus following the spatial contiguity rule [32] if possible. Indeed, the currently developed CVL tool supports associating constraints closely to the relevant features.

Unexpectedly, familiarity with feature modeling was negatively related to time. This result might sound counterintuitive at first sight, however there are possible interpretations. Knowing the notation may increase the doubts, requiring more time and not necessarily improving the performance. Participants might also be more motivated to solve the comprehension tasks correctly and work harder and longer to solve them if they already have prior experience in that modeling domain. Furthermore, unfamiliar modelers have lower comprehension of OR relations and constraints than familiar modelers, but familiar modelers spent long time to achieve their better comprehension. This may be due to the perception of familiar modelers that OR relations and constraints are more difficult – a perception that made them spend more time on those questions. This is similar to experienced drivers who slow down properly in curves.

As with all studies, the reader should bear in mind that a number of limitations associated with laboratory experiments need to be acknowledged [20]. One source of weakness regarding external validity includes the use of student subjects. However, the participants had received training in modeling and, therefore, we do believe that they serve as an adequate proxy for future modelers of CVL. In addition, we assured that random influences to the experimental setting were low to improve conclusion validity. First, participants were committed to the experiment by making the experiment an obligatory exercise or giving course credit (of about 5%) for participation. Second, the students self-studied CVL, so no influence of the lecturers' capabilities, knowledge, and opinions were introduced to the CVL training.

Despite the clear support for the hypothesized associations, the generalizability of findings reported here should be undertaken with caution, because we could only include two different CVL models in the study and we selected a specific feature modeling language – the variability abstraction part of CVL. As the two models included in the questionnaire were typical representatives we argue that they provided a reasonable test of comprehensibility, thus, assuring construct validity. The selection of the language was done perceiving CVL as an emerging standard which systematically includes the main feature modeling concepts. However, only further experiments with other feature modeling languages and models can confirm or disconfirm the generalizability of our results.

6   Conclusions and Future Work

The purpose of the current study was to determine comprehensibility of feature models as expressed in CVL and possible difficulties for different user groups. We found that familiarity with feature modeling did not influence the comprehension of basic elements, namely mandatory, optional, and alternative features, although unfamiliar modelers perceived these elements more difficult than familiar modelers. OR relations were perceived as difficult regardless of the familiarity level, while constraints were significantly better understood by familiar modelers. The time spent to complete tasks was higher for familiar modelers. The findings from this study add to the current body of knowledge on feature modeling by investigating comprehension and have relevant implications for practice and research. The results further add to a growing body of literature on novice-expert differences in modeling research. Our results also offer important suggestions for training in feature modeling. While understanding of mandatory and optional features, constraints and XOR relations is important in the training of users new to feature modeling, understanding of OR relations remains difficult even for experienced modelers. In addition, results can be used to guide feature modeling language developers in their design efforts and help in ongoing revision of CVL. Our initial results provide evidence that CVL is comprehensible for novice and expert modelers and that they can read such models after a short training.

Several opportunities for future research emerge from our study. For instance, further experimental investigations with a larger variety of models would be required to estimate comprehension difficulty of specific modeling elements. Future studies could also extend this work and examine difficulties in modeling (and not just understanding) variability using CVL. Finally, comprehension difficulties can be researched in additional feature modeling languages, as well as in the variability realization part of CVL.

References

1. Pohl, K., Böckle, G., van der Linden, F.: Software Product Line Engineering: Foundations, Principles, and Techniques. Springer (2005)
2. Clements, P., Northrop, L.: Software Product Lines: Practices and Patterns. Addison-Wesley, Boston (2001)
3. Chen, L., Ali Babar, M.: A systematic review of evaluation of variability management approaches in software product lines. Information and Software Technology 53, 344–362 (2011)
4. Haugen, Ø.: Common Variability Language (CVL) – OMG Revised Submission. OMG document ad/2012-08-05 (2012)
5. Istoan, P., Klein, J., Perouin, G., Jezequel, J.-M.: A Metamodel-based Classification of Variability Modeling Approaches. In: VARiability for You Workshop, pp. 23–32 (2011)
6. Czarnecki, K., Grünbacher, P., Rabiser, R., Schmid, K., Wąsowski, A.: Cool features and tough decisions: A comparison of variability modeling approaches. In: Proceedings of the Sixth International Workshop on Variability Modeling of Software-Intensive Systems, pp. 173–182. ACM, Leipzig (2012)
7. Schobbens, P.-Y., Heymans, P., Trigaux, J.-C.: Feature Diagrams: A Survey and a Formal Semantics. In: Proceedings of the 14th IEEE International Requirements Engineering Conference, pp. 136-145. IEEE Computer Society (2006)
8. Heymans, P., Schobbens, P.Y., Trigaux, J.C., Bontemps, Y., Matulevicius, R., Classen, A.: Evaluating formal properties of feature diagram languages. IET Software 2, 281–302 (2008)
9. Krogstie, J., Sindre, G., Jørgensen, H.D.: Process Models Representing Knowledge for Action: A Revised Quality Framework. European Journal of Information Systems 15, 91–102 (2006)
10. Harel, D., Rumpe, B.: Meaningful Modeling: What's the Semantics of "Semantics"? Computer 37, 64–72 (2004)
11. Djebbi, O., Salinesi, C.: Criteria for Comparing Requirements Variability Modeling Notations for Product Lines. In: Workshops on Comparative Evaluation in Requirements Engineering, pp. 20–35 (2006)
12. Haugen, Ø., Møller-Pedersen, B., Oldevik, J.: Comparison of System Family Modeling Approaches. In: Obbink, H., Pohl, K. (eds.) SPLC 2005. LNCS, vol. 3714, pp. 102–112. Springer, Heidelberg (2005)
13. Matinlassi, M.: Comparison of software product line architecture design methods: COPA, FAST, FORM, KobrA and QADA. In: Proceedings of the 26th International Conference on Software Engineering, ICSE 2004, pp. 127–136 (2004)
14. Jayaratna, N.: Understanding and Evaluating Methodologies: NIMSAD, a Systematic Framework. McGraw-Hill, Inc. (1994)
15. Mylopoulos, J.: Conceptual Modeling and Telos. In: Loucopoulos, P., Zicari, R. (eds.) Conceptual Modeling, pp. 49–68. John Wiley and Sons, New York (1992)
16. Reinhartz-Berger, I., Tsoury, A.: Experimenting with the Comprehension of Feature-Oriented and UML-Based Core Assets. In: Halpin, T., Nurcan, S., Krogstie, J., Soffer, P., Proper, E., Schmidt, R., Bider, I. (eds.) BPMDS 2011 and EMMSAD 2011. LNBIP, vol. 81, pp. 468–482. Springer, Heidelberg (2011)
17. Reinhartz-Berger, I., Tsoury, A.: Specification and Utilization of Core Assets: Feature-Oriented vs. UML-Based Methods. In: De Troyer, O., Bauzer Medeiros, C., Billen, R., Hallot, P., Simitsis, A., Van Mingroot, H. (eds.) ER Workshops 2011. LNCS, vol. 6999, pp. 302–311. Springer, Heidelberg (2011)

18. Czarnecki, K., Kim, C.H.P.: Cardinality-based feature modeling and constraints: a progress report. In: International Workshop on Software Factories at OOPSLA. ACM (2005)
19. Reinhartz-Berger, I., Sturm, A.: Utilizing domain models for application design and validation. Inf. Softw. Technol. 51, 1275–1289 (2009)
20. Wohlin, C., Runeson, P., Höst, M., Ohlsson, M., Regnell, B., Wesslén, A.: Experimentation in Software Engineering – An Introduction. Kluwer Academic Publishers (2000)
21. Petre, M.: Why looking isn't always seeing: readership skills and graphical programming. Commun. ACM 38, 33–44 (1995)
22. Kumar, S., Karoli, V.: Handbook of Business Research Methods. Thakur Publishers (2011)
23. Parsons, J., Cole, L.: What do the Pictures mean? Guidelines for Experimental Evaluation of Representation Fidelity in Diagrammatical Conceptual Modeling Techniques. Data and Knowledge Engineering 55 (2005)
24. Recker, J.: Continued Use of Process Modeling Grammars: The Impact of Individual Difference Factors. European Journal of Information Systems 19, 76–92 (2010)
25. Svahnberg, M., Aurum, A., Wohlin, C.: Using students as subjects - an empirical evaluation. In: Proceedings of the Second ACM-IEEE International Symposium on Empirical Software Engineering and Measurement, pp. 288–290. ACM, Kaiserslautern (2008)
26. Siau, K., Loo, P.-P.: Identifying Difficulties in Learning UML. Information Systems Management 23, 43–51 (2006)
27. Preacher, K., Rucker, D., MacCallum, R., Nicewander, W.: Use of the Extreme Groups Approach: A Critical Reexamination and New Recommendations. Psychol Methods 10, 178–192 (2005)
28. Nunnally, J.C., Bernstein, I.H.: Psychometric Theory. McGraw-Hill, New York (1994)
29. Recker, J., Dreiling, A.: The Effects of Content Presentation Format and User Characteristics on Novice Developers' Understanding of Process Models. Communications of the Association for Information Systems 22 (2011)
30. Naess, A.: A Study of 'Or'. Synthese 13, 49–60 (1961)
31. Mendling, J., Reijers, H., van der Aalst, W.M.P.: Seven process modeling guidelines (7PMG). Information and Software Technology 52 (2010)
32. Moody, D.L.: The "Physics" of Notations: Towards a Scientific Basis for Constructing Visual Notations in Software Engineering. IEEE Transactions on Software Engineering 35, 756–779 (2009)

Appendix: Experiment's Models and Questions

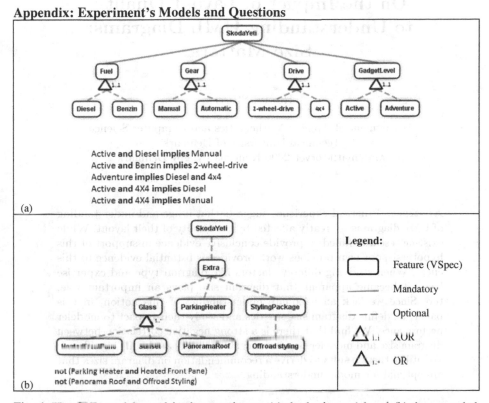

Fig. 4. The CVL models used in the experiment: (a) the basic model and (b) the expanded model

Basic Model Questions	Expanded Model Questions
A Skoda Yeti car can have the following combination of features:	
1. Manual and Diesel	1. Parking-Heater and Styling-Package
2. Adventure and Benzin	2. Panorama-Roof and Offroad-Styling
3. Automatic and 4x4	3. Parking-Heater and Offroad-Styling
4. Adventure and 2-wheel-drive	4. Parking-Heater and Heated-Front-Pane
5. Active and Diesel and Automatic	5. Parking-Heater and Styling-Package and Offroad-Styling
6. Diesel and Automatic and 4x4	6. Sunset and Parking-Heater and Styling-Package
7. Active and Benzin and 4x4	7. Heated-Front-Pane and Sunset and Panorama-Roof
8. Adventure and Manual and 4x4	8. Sunset and Panorama-Roof and Parking-Heater and Offroad-Styling
9. Active and Benzin and Manual and 2-wheel-drive	9. Heated-Front-Pane and Sunset and Styling-Package and Offroad-Styling
10. Automatic and Adventure and Benzin and 2-wheel-drive	10. Heated-Front-Pane and Sunset and Panorama-Roof and Styling-Package

On the Impact of Layout Quality
to Understanding UML Diagrams:
Size Matters

Harald Störrle

Department of Applied Mathematics and Computer Science
Technical University of Denmark
Matematiktorvet 2800 Kongens Lyngby Denmark

Abstract. Practical experience suggests that usage and understanding of UML diagrams is greatly affected by the quality of their layout. While existing research failed to provide conclusive evidence in support of this hypothesis, our own previous work provided substantial evidence to this effect. When studying different factors like diagram type and expertise level, it became apparent that diagram size plays an important role, too. Since we lack an adequate understanding of this notion, in this paper, we define diagram size metrics and study their impact to modeler performance. We find that there is a strong negative correlation between diagram size and modeler performance. Our results are highly significant. We utilize these results to derive a recommendation on diagram sizes that are optimal for model understanding.

1 Introduction

The Unified Modeling Language (UML) has been the *"lingua franca of software engineering"* for over a decade now. It is a generally held belief that visual languages are superior to textual languages in that they support human perceptual and thought processes, and that this is also true for the UML, in fact, that this is a major reason for the success of UML. However, there are actually few research results to support this belief. There *is* a large body of experimental results on the layout of UML class diagrams and how it affects human understanding and problem solving, but the findings are ambiguous, and sometimes unintuitive. In particular, only very small effects have been found in vitro. For instance, Eichelberger and Schmid note that *"We could not identify [...] a significant impact [by diagram quality]."* (cf. [9, p. 1696]).

On the other hand, practical experience in industrial software projects suggests a much higher impact of good or bad layout, and previous work by the author strongly supports this hypothesis (see [28,29]). Inspection of our data and a qualitative study with our study participants suggested, however, that the size of the models portrayed in the diagrams might be a relevant factor. In order to study this question, we define a precise notion of diagram size and re-examine existing data sets of substantial size (78 participants, well over 1200

J. Dingel et al. (Eds.): MODELS 2014, LNCS 8767, pp. 518–534, 2014.

measurements). Our working hypothesis is that modeler performance correlates negatively with diagram size. We also hypothesize, that layout quality[1] matters more with increasing diagram size: small diagrams are easy to use irrespective of the layout quality simply because they are small; modelers simply cope with bad layout. With increasing diagram size, however, the visual and/or mental capacity of a modeler is stretched, so that the layout quality impacts modeler performance. In other words, layout quality matters more, and is more apparent for larger diagrams. We analyze the diagram size metrics and various modeler performance indicators, including errors, preference/assessment, and cognitive load (cf. [13]).

If we can indeed correlate diagram size with modeler performance, however, we can exploit this relationship conversely to determine limits to the size of diagrams that afford being understood easily and correctly by modelers. Such limits might be helpful as guidelines to inexperienced modelers, such as students.

2   Related Work

The layout of graphs (in the mathematical sense) has been a longstanding research challenge, both with respect to automatic layout and to various aspects of usability, e.g., diagram comprehension, user preferences, and diagrammatic inference. Based on the rich knowledge on general graphs, research on the layout of UML has started with those of UML's notations that are closest to graphs, namely, class diagrams (cf. [23,7,10,33,18]), and, to a lesser extent, communication diagrams (see e.g. [17,20] who use UML 1 terminology). Other types of UML diagrams, in contrast, have only attracted little interest so far (e.g. use case diagrams [8], or sequence diagrams, cf. [2,32]). There is only little work on the Business Process Model and Notation (see [5]), and even less on UML activity diagrams [21].

Research on aspects of UML class diagrams has mostly focused on the impact of isolated low-level layout criteria such as line bends, crossings, and length. Unsurprisingly, each of these properties has little impact by themselves and are hard to prioritize. The more elusive higher levels like layout patterns, diagram flow, and the correspondence between a diagram and its intended message seem to have not yet been studied empirically at all. The influence of the expertise level, on the other hand, has been studied [1,22].

The main focus of previous work on UML diagram types and their layout has been with one of four aspects: diagram comprehension (cf. [25,26,15,20] and/or user preference (cf. [18,31]), automatic layout (cf. [7,10,16,8,4]), or one of a variety of diagram inference tasks, e.g., program understanding based on visualizations (cf. [32]), or the role of design patterns in understanding (cf. [26,27]).

Most research uses controlled experiments and evaluate user performance using paper questionnaires, or online surveys. Only a few contributions have used other methods, most notably eye tracking (see [3,33,26]). After using both methods for essentially the same experiment, Sharif et al. have concluded that these

---

[1] We will elaborate on the notion of layout quality in Section 3 below.

two methods are mostly complementary wrt. comprehension tasks (cf. [24]). Thus, eye tracking is only favorable for a tightly restricted set of research questions, in particular when taking into account the considerable cost and effort involved. Having said that, most questionnaire-based approaches employ only very few participants in their experiments, typically in the range of 15 to 30, with the notable exceptions of [25], [19] and [2] involving 45, 55 and 78 participants, respectively. The research done for the current paper involved 78 participants.

3   "Good" Layout of UML Diagrams

In this section, we will briefly review the knowledge on aesthetic criteria for the layout of UML diagrams and its effects on model understanding. A detailed discussion of aesthetic criteria for class diagrams is found in [7, p. 54–65], a recent survey of empirical results on layout criteria is found in [9]. Wong and Sun [32] provide an overview of these criteria from a cognitive psychology point of view, along with an evaluation of how well these principles are realized in several UML CASE tools. Purchase et al. discuss aesthetic criteria with a view to the layout of UML class and communication diagrams (cf. [18,17]) and also provide sources to justify and explain these criteria (cf. [15]). Eichelberger [6] also discusses these criteria at length, and shows how they can be used in the automatic layout of UML class diagrams.

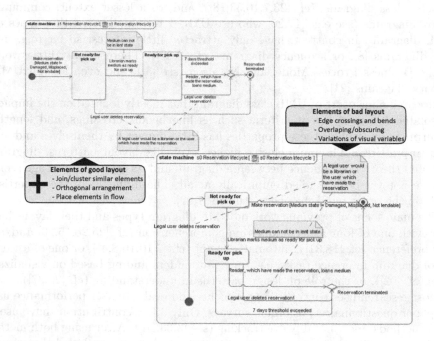

Fig. 1. Examples of good/bad layouts of a diagram as used in the study

The layout of UML diagrams is governed by four levels of design principles. First, there are the general principles of graphical design and visualization that apply to all kinds of diagrams, and probably any kind of visualization. For instance, in a good layout, elements should not obscure each other, the Gestalt principles should be respected [12], text should be shown in a readable size, elements should be aligned (e.g., on a grid), and there should be sparing and careful use of colors, and different fonts or styles.

Second, there are layout principles applying to all structures that can be considered as a graph, mathematically speaking. Thus, good layouts should avoid or minimize crossings, bends, and length of lines. Most of the empirical research on UML diagrams focuses on principles from this level, e.g., [23,7,10,33,18].

Third, there are layout principles that apply mostly only to notations like those found in UML. For instance, diagrams with some inherent ordering of elements should maintain and highlight that ordering as visual flow. Visual clutter should be reduced by introducing symmetry when possible. For instance, similar edges should be joined, similar elements should be aligned and grouped, and so on. In UML, this means that if a class has several subclasses, it might be helpful to group and align the subclasses and join the arcs indicating the inheritance-relationship. Another application is found in activity diagrams, where several consequences of a decision could be aligned and grouped.

Fourth, there is the level of pragmatics, that is, support for underlining the purpose of a diagram in order to better address the audience. Items may be highlighted by color, size, or position to guide and direct the attention of readers. On this level, rules and guidelines from lower levels may be put aside to better serve the paramount purpose of conveying the message and telling whatever story the diagram designer intends to tell.

In order to develop algorithms for creating automatic layouts that are perceived as being helpful (or "good") by human modelers, detailed knowledge about the individual criteria, their relative and absolute impact, and their formalization is needed. So, it is not surprising that most of the empirical research on UML diagrams has so far focused on studying individual principles, with an emphasis on the second group (cf. [23,7,10,33,18]). For instance, work by Purchase et al. has shown that there are many such criteria with varying degrees of impact (see e.g. [18]), though all of them seem to have a rather small impact with findings that are not highly or not at all statistically significant. Also, the ranking and contribution of these criteria may vary across different diagram types. Even between class and communication diagrams, which are rather close relatives as far as concrete syntax is concerned, [18, pp. 246] shows notable differences in the ordering and impact of layout criteria. Thus, other notations that share even less commonalities with class diagrams (e.g., activity, use case, or sequence diagrams) may need a completely different set of criteria.

For humans creating diagram layouts, on the other hand, a set of comparatively vague guidelines together with some instruction is often good enough for practical purposes. Humans may (and will) mix and match criteria from all four levels as appropriate and create what they *and their peers* perceive as high quality UML diagrams. Of course, there is still a large degree of subjectivity in this definition, but it does capture the intuition (see [28,29] for detailed evidence). Therefore, in the remainder of this paper, we will call a diagram (layout) *good*, if it mostly adheres to the criteria from all these levels, and *bad* if it mostly violates them. Generally speaking, in terms of the four levels of layout rules described above, if a diagram layout does not (significantly) violate any of the rules on the first two levels but (more or less) adopts the rules described in the latter two levels we call it a "good" layout. Conversely, we call a diagram layout "bad" if it consistently violates these rules.

4   Size of UML Diagrams

Surprisingly, there seems to be no metric for the size of UML diagrams that we can use as a basis in our correlation. So, we have to define such a metric. We will visit three of them to find the most appropriate, starting with the simplest conceivable approach of simply counting the number of diagram elements (not to be confused with the number of model elements presented or implied in the diagram). This metric has the advantage of being straightforward to compute, but does not take into account differences among the potential elements of a diagram.

Arguably, this metric is not just simple, but too simple, as it implies that all diagram elements contribute the same amount of complexity and information to the diagram. If this assumption does not hold true, we could introduce a weight factor for the individual types of elements to compensate for differences between different element types. It is not quite clear, however, what the "right" weights should be, and how to obtain them.

As a pragmatic approach to defining weights uniformly, we use the approach pursued in [30], and provide a simple classification of the elements of UML diagrams into lines, shapes, and labels, and assign one of three complexity levels to each of them (simple, medium, and large), according to the amount of cognitive load we may expect involved in processing them based on the laws of Gestalt psychology (cf. [12]). For instance, a plain association might be considered a simple line, an association with an adornment on one side (such as a composition or a directed association) might be considered a line of medium complexity, and an association with adornments on both sides might be considered a line with large complexity. Lines with several legs could be understood as sets of lines, e.g., an association with two adornments and two corners decomposes into one simple line and two medium lines (one adornment each).

- Lines include all kinds of straight or curved lines. Lines made up of n different segments are considered as n different lines. Decorations at the beginning or end of a line or line segment (such as arrow heads) are considered to be an integral part of the line but increase its complexity.
- Shapes include the basic geometric shapes like circles, rectangles, and ellipses as simple elements. Shapes that occupy a large area of a diagram and contain

other shapes are considered to be of medium complexity, while the more complex iconic shapes like a stick-person or a lightning-arrow are considered complex shapes.
- Labels are strings of text that are attached to or positioned relative to other elements. Labels are restricted to single lines. Single characters or short names are considered simple, long names are considered as medium complex, and structured expressions like sentences or operation declarations are considered to be highly complex.

With these conventions, we define diagram size as the number of elements in a diagram, weighted by their complexity (e.g., one might define the weights S: 1, M: 1.5, L: 2). This metric is substantially more difficult to compute than our first proposal above, but it reflects the intuition more accurately, and could thus be expected to be more realistic, and provide higher validity.

Still, one might argue that the second approach is too simplistic, as the influence of diagram types is not considered. After all, every UML diagram establishes a context that restricts the admissible vocabulary in this diagram to a small subset that is available for the given diagram type. For instance, there are many more notational elements in the UML sub-language of Activity Diagrams than there are in the sub-language of Use Case Diagrams. Thus, according to classic information theory, the weight of any element in an Activity Diagram ought to be higher than the weight of the elements in Use Case Diagrams.

In analogy with classic information theory, the number of choices should determine the information content (i.e., the weight) of a diagram element. We compute the information content of diagram elements as the binary logarithm of the set of similar elements a modeler may chose from, per diagram type. So, for every diagram element e from a class E of diagram elements in a given diagram type, we compute $weight(e) = log_2(|E|)$. Using this as a weight factor provides a third metric of diagram size.

Note that we disregard topological information (i.e., containment). Thus, our metric is not necessarily a measure of diagram complexity or information content. Clearly, we will need to validate these diagram size metrics. So, we computed the sizes according to each measure with some (sensible) variations for the weights of the second metric for the same 38 diagrams that have been used in [28,29]. We compared the outcomes using Pearson's product-moment correlation. Surprisingly, we found that all three measures show a very high level of correlation (between 0.967 and 0.992) with very high confidence ($p < 10^{-15}$). That is to say: the measures do not yield significantly different results. In other words, it does not matter which metric we use. So, we decide for the one that offers the practical advantage of being simple to compute, that is, in the remainder we simply count the number of diagram elements as a metric for diagram size.

5   Experimental Setup

We used [14] as a guideline for our experimental setup. We presented the participants with paper questionnaires showing one UML diagram and ten questions on the diagram, recording four categories of answers (right, wrong, "don't know", and no answer), time used, subjective assessment of the task difficulty (three questions in experiment D, and four questions in experiments E and F). The questionnaires also contained a separate sheet where we asked for personal preference, and subjective assessment of layout quality. The dependent variables are accuracy and speed of comprehension, and preference. The independent variables are the experience level of the participants (beginner/advanced/elite), the diagram type (class, sequence, state machine), the diagram size (small/large), and, of course, the layout quality (good/bad). Altogether, we ran three experiments with together 78 participants, and a completion rate of 80%. Minor adjustments and corrections were made as compared to the experimental setup reported in [28]. In the remainder, we will focus on the setup of the second and third experiment. The details of the setup are discussed below; a summary of the experimental setup and study design is shown in Fig. 2.

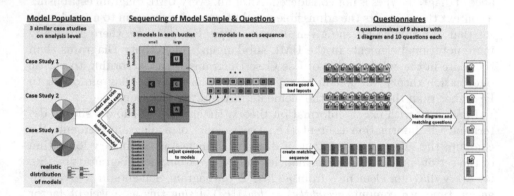

Fig. 2. The experimental setup and study design

5.1   Model Population

The models used in the experiments have been created by students as part of their coursework in a requirements engineering course taught by the author. These models belonged to one of three case studies and have been prepared by teams of 4-7 students over a period of twelve weeks with an approximate effort of 600-800 working hours for each model. For each case study, two or three teams worked in parallel; for each case study, the model of the team achieving the highest grade was selected. This procedure ensured several desirable properties.

Firstly, by using models created by students undergoing the same course and being awarded the same grade, very similar levels of modeler capability and model quality may be assumed. Furthermore, the models used exhibit a large degree of methodological homogeneity in that they are very similar in terms of model structure and size, model and diagram usage, and frequency distribution of diagram types. Also, in the models used in our experiments, model elements had their original, semantic-bearing names, whereas in some previous experiments this vital aspect seems to have been deliberately eliminated by giving meaningless synthetic names to model elements (cf. [9, p. 1697]). Secondly, due to the project oriented nature of the course, we can assert that the models underlying our experiment are realistic in the sense that their size, quality, and purpose are very close to industrial reality. Finally, all of these models used exist at the same stage of the software life cycle, namely requirements analysis.

In contrast, all earlier works seem to have used only a single case study and model, and most work has been carried out on models at the design or implementation level. Also, there is no indication in previous work as to how close to the reality of practical software development the underlying models are.

5.2   Diagram Samples and Questions

From each of the three model types selected from the model population, we chose one large and one small example of class, state machine, and interaction diagrams with particularly good or bad layout. The quality of layout is measured by the adherence or non-adherence to a number of layout rules discussed in the related work (see Section 3). This step yielded three models (one from each case study) for each of the six buckets, that is, the categories of small/large diagrams of types class/activity/use case. So we arrived at 18 models altogether which were then trimmed to fit onto a questionnaire page. We then derived two variants from each diagram exhibiting good and bad layout (i.e., two different treatments), respectively, yielding 36 different diagrams (see Fig. 1 above for good/bad layouts of a diagram; a sample questionnaire can be found at www2.compute.dtu.dk/~hsto/downloads/q2.pdf).

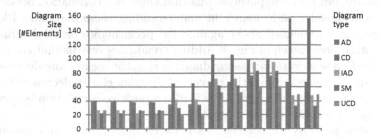

Fig. 3. Distribution of sizes and types of the diagrams used in the experiments

5.3   Participants and Completion Rates

The participants for experiments 1 and 2 were recruited among students from different computer science classes at the Danish Technical University in Lyn-

Table 1. Demographic data on the participants of all experiments, "completion" refers to the completion rate on core questions

Experiment	male	female	all	completion
1 (BEng)	29	3	33	75.1%
2 (MSc)	29	5	34	82.6%
3 (Elite)	10	1	11	90.1%
all	68	9	78	82.6%

gby. The participants for experiment 3 were recruited among elite graduate students and staff from the University of Augsburg.[2] All participants took part voluntarily with no reward or threat and under complete anonymity, i.e., it was clear to students that their performance had no influence whatsoever on their grades, for instance. Immediately before the experiment, all participants received a ten-minute introduction to those parts of the UML that were covered in the experiment.

The participants showed a wide spread in UML knowledge. In all experiments, in the core parts of the questionnaire, nine diagrams were presented and ten questions were asked per diagram. We saw an overall completion rate of these core questions of over 80%. See Table 1 for more details on the population.

6   Results

6.1   Correlations between Diagram Size and Modeler Performance

As outlined above, our initial hypothesis was that there is a correlation between diagram size and modeler performance in understanding these diagrams. Plotting the diagram size as defined above against the performance on all diagrams yielded the scatter plots shown in Fig. 4. Adding trend-lines reveals that the correlation is indeed present: with increasing diagram size, the mean score decreases while the variance increases. Similarly, perceived diagram clarity decreases with increasing diagram size. Surprisingly, there is also a positive correlation between diagram size and perception of layout quality.

We then tested properly for correlations between diagram size and modeler performance. We used the simple diagram size metric, as discussed above, and correlated it with all measures of modeler performance observed in our experiments. We calculated the correlations between diagram size and modeler performance using Pearson's product-moment correlation (`cor.test` in R). We assess the effect size of a correlation of up to 0.3 to as small (S), as large (L) for values over 0.4, and as medium (M) for values in between, see Table 2.

---

[2] These experiments correspond to the experiments D, E, and F reported before in [29].

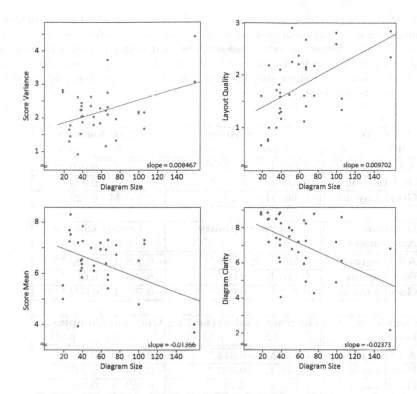

Fig. 4. Plots of various measures of modeler performance against diagram size (clockwise from left bottom): score mean, score variance, subjective assessment of layout quality and diagram clarity. The trend-lines are created from linear models.

It is quite clear that there is indeed a large correlation between increasing diagram size and decreasing mean scores. This is in line with the observation that the variance increases with diagram size: increased difficulty will provoke a greater spread of results. We have seen a similar effect in our previous studies, where the natural variance in capability of the population becomes more visible when testing poor layouts because these help less with diagram understanding. For the good layouts, individual performance differences matter less, as they are, partially, leveled by the helpful layout. This objective measure is further confirmed by the subjective measure of asking the participants to assess the clarity of the diagrams: uniformly large correlations are found between increasing diagram size and decreasing clarity. Yet more confirmation is found when considering the subjective assessment of cognitive load: with increasing size, cognitive load as expressed by subjective assessment of task complexity increases, too. Observe that subjective assessment has been found to be highly correlated with objective measures of cognitive load [11], and that both questions asked to measure cognitive load exhibit similar patterns. The negative correlation between diagram

Table 2. Pearson's product-moment correlation between diagram size and modeler performance, measured as mean and variance of objective performance (correct answers, i.e., score), different subjective assessments, and cognitive load measures. In each cell, the first number is Pearsons's r indicating the size of the correlation, the letter S/M/L classifies the effect size, the next number is the p-value, and the stars indicate its significance level.

Objective Performance	Score Mean		Score Variance	
	r ES	p SIG	r ES	p SIG
All Diagrams	−0.423 L	0.010 **	0.424 L	0.010 **
Bad Layout	−0.491 L	0.039 *	0.534 L	0.023 *
Good Layout	−0.396 M	0.104 *	0.303 M	0.222

Diagram Assessment	Layout Quality		Layout Clarity	
	r ES	p SIG	r ES	p SIG
All Diagrams	0.538 L	< 0.001 ***	−0.508 L	0.002 **
Bad Layout	0.521 L	0.027 *	−0.563 L	0.015 *
Good Layout	0.573 L	0.013 *	−0.766 L	0.0002 ***

Cognitive Load	Diagram Understanding		Diagram Complexity	
	r ES	p SIG	r ES	p SIG
All Diagrams	−0.338 M	0.044 **	−0.081 S	0.640
Bad Layout	−0.452 L	0.060 *	−0.313 M	0.207
Good Layout	−0.197 S	0.434	0.152 S	0.548

size and perceived diagram complexity might be an experimental artifact since it has no statistic significance and relatively small effect sizes.

We also see a positive correlation between diagram size and layout quality, which seems to contradict our hypothesis. We explain this by observing that it is literally obvious to most modelers that a diagram has high quality when presented with one. Answering this question for a poor diagram, on the other hand, is much harder, as it requires knowledge about what makes a poor diagram, too. In particular novice modelers have yet to appreciate the negative impact of line crossings, bends, obscuring elements and so forth.

All of these effects are substantially stronger for poor layouts than for good layouts. This is in support of our initial hypothesis that layout quality matters more with increasing diagram size. In other words: small diagrams are easy to use anyway, so bad layout can be easily compensated. For larger diagrams, however, when the visual and/or mental capacity of a modeler is reached or exceeded, the impact of layout quality becomes visible: layout quality matters more, and is more apparent for larger diagrams.

The results for objective measures and subjective assessments seem to provide stronger results than the results for cognitive load measures, although this might be attributable to factors outside of the experimental control.

Table 3. Pearson's product-moment correlation between diagram size and modeler performance, controlled for expertise level

Objective Performance	Score Mean (low/high expertise)					
	r ES		p SIG	r ES		p SIG
All Diagrams	−0.494	L	0.002 **	0.018	S	0.917
Bad Layout	−0.397	M	0.103 .	−0.173	S	0.493
Good Layout	−0.615	L	0.007 **	0.243	M	0.331

Objective Score	Score Variance (low/high expertise)					
	r ES		p SIG	r ES		p SIG
All Diagrams	0.290	M	0.086 .	0.053	S	0.764
Bad Layout	0.254	M	0.309	0.204	M	0.432
Good Layout	0.343	M	0.163	−0.085	S	0.736

Diagram Assessment	Layout Quality (low/high expertise)					
	r ES		p SIG	r ES		p SIG
All Diagrams	0.569	L	0.0003 ***	0.484	L	0.003 **
Bad Layout	0.534	L	0.023 *	0.516	L	0.028 *
Good Layout	0.615	L	0.007 **	0.536	L	0.022 *

Diagram Assessment	Layout Clarity (low/high expertise)					
	r ES		p SIG	r ES		p SIG
All Diagrams	−0.525	L	0.001 ***	−0.440	L	0.007 **
Bad Layout	−0.742	L	0.0004 ***	−0.698	L	0.001 **
Good Layout	−0.554	L	0.017 *	−0.570	L	0.014 *

Cognitive Load	Diagram Understanding (low/high expertise)					
	r ES		p SIG	r ES		p SIG
All Diagrams	−0.313	M	0.063 .	−0.199	S	0.245
Bad Layout	−0.184	S	0.465	−0.064	S	0.800
Good Layout	−0.421	L	0.082 .	−0.306	M	0.218

Cognitive Load	Diagram Complexity (low/high expertise)					
	r ES		p SIG	r ES		p SIG
All Diagrams	−0.082	S	0.634	0.042	S	0.808
Bad Layout	0.133	S	0.600	0.251	M	0.315
Good Layout	−0.349	M	0.156	−0.134	S	0.595

6.2   Correlations Differentiated by Expertise Level

Previous work by Abraho, Ricca and others [1,22] suggests that the expertise level is important in diagram understanding, and when controlling for expertise levels, more interesting phenomena become visible (see Table 3). In this table, we have used the same arrangement of values in cells as in Table 2, but have split the data between modelers with lower and higher levels of expertise (left and right, respectively). First of all, let us establish that there is indeed a performance difference in expertise level in our sub-populations. Using a one-sided Wilcoxon-test to compare the average score on good layouts for the two sub-populations, we can reject the hypothesis that the sub-populations exhibit the same performance with very high significance ($p = 0.00013$). When comparing the scores, score variances, and the cognitive load measures, participants with high expertise level are much less affected by increasing diagram size than participants with lower expertise levels. This holds irrespective of layout quality, but is even stronger for poor layouts. Some of these findings are not statistically significant, however, since analyzing the sub-populations separately drastically decreases the number of data points. Still, all correlation show the same pattern and tendencies which does add evidence to our earlier observations.

Even with the reduced population size we find significant or highly significant correlations between increasing diagram size and reduced layout clarity, particularly for poor layout where correlation exceeds -0.7 ($p < 10^{-3}$). Again, the effect is larger for poor layouts than for good ones, and again, the same pattern is found in the cognitive load measures ("Understanding" and "Complexity"), though the latter findings are not statistically significant.

6.3   Optimal Diagram Size

Based on our data, we can compute trend-lines of the correlations, as shown in Fig. 4 (bottom right). Computing a linear model yields coefficients of a linear equation (*intercept* $= 7.21$, *slope* $= -0.014$). This allows us to compute the diagram sizes at which the study participants answered a given number of questions about the diagrams correctly. It seems natural to use the boundaries of the second and third quartile as lower bound, optimum, and upper bound of expected performance. The values for these boundaries and a geometric interpretation of the relationship between quantiles of score and optimal size is given in Fig. 5.

In practice, the quality of diagrams and modelers will vary widely. When disregarding these factors, we conclude that diagrams with approximately 20 to 60 diagram elements should allow average modelers to answer approximately half of the questions about the model represented by the diagram correctly. Thus, an objective recommendation for boundaries of diagram size would be in this range, too. It would be trivial to implement such a function in a modeling tool, which could provide guidance to modelers.

7   Threats to Validity

Internal Validity. Great care has been taken to provide systematic permutations of diagrams, questions, and sequences thereof to avoid bias by carry-over effects ("learning"). Any such effects would occur similarly for all treatments and, thus, would cancel each other out. Participants have been assigned to tasks randomly. We can also safely exclude bias through the experimenter himself, since there were only written instructions that apply to all conditions identically. We correlated it with different measures, each of which was measured in

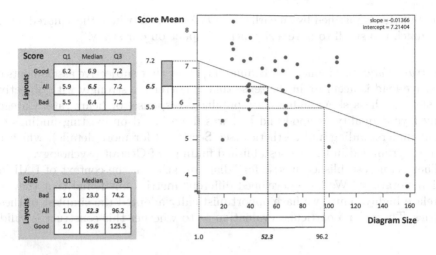

Fig. 5. The red trend-line visualizes the correlation between scores and diagram sizes. Geometrically speaking, this means to mirror the distribution of scores at the **size score** trend-line. Observe that high scores correlate to small diagram sizes.

multiple different ways to reduce the danger of introducing bias through the experimental procedure.

External Validity. The selection of the models and diagrams may be a source of bias. However, we applied objective and rational criteria to the selection, and compared to previous similar studies, we used three different diagram types (rather than just one or two), a competitively large number of models, and very realistic models. The layouts for the models were, to a large degree, used-as-found, that is, they were created under realistic conditions by people unconnected to these experiments. On top of that, our study is based on a comparatively large number of participants. So, the present study is certainly among the best validated among studies of its kind and we expect our results to be valid for UML models *in general*, i.e., we expect a markedly higher degree of external validity than previous contributions can claim.

Conclusion Validity. We have used non-parametric tests, where applicable, to compensate for skewed distributions in our data. We have consistently provided statistical significance level and the effect size with our inferences. Due to the (relatively) high number of study participants, most of the inferences we present are equipped with high or very high levels of statistic significance and large effect sizes, using Cohn's thresholds for the effect size levels for want of any better guideline. When controlling for sub-populations, the significance levels decrease, but keep showing the same patterns which is sufficient for the claims we make based on these data. We do assume a linear correlation between variables prima facie, but this is justified by an earlier ANOVA-analysis where the squared terms were much too small to have a significant impact on our study.

Construct Validity. Gopher and Braune [11] show that subjective assessments of cognitive load is accurate in the sense that it correlates strongly with objective measures such as skin conductivity, pupillary response, or heart rate. Categorizing layout quality as good and bad was done based on existing findings on layout understanding and aesthetics (see Section 2 for more details), which in turn are grounded in the well-established findings of Gestalt psychology.

There is no established metric for "diagram size" in the context of UML or similar notations. We have developed different metrics but found that they all correlate highly. Thus, we have opportunistically adopted the simplest of these metrics. There is no particular evaluation as to whether this construct is valid.

8   Conclusion

In earlier work, we established that layout quality does impact the understanding of UML diagrams [28], and that this applies irrespective of diagram type, but dependent on modeler expertise [29]. We could so far not answer the question whether diagram size had an influence, and, if so, what its magnitude would be. Thus, in this paper, we developed measures for the size of UML diagrams. Since they correlate almost perfectly on a population of 38 diagrams, we concluded that it is irrelevant which of these diagram size metrics is used. Thus we chose the pragmatically simplest metric.

Using this diagram size metric, we re-analyzed existing data sets and find strong evidence in support of our hypothesis. We conclude that high layout quality is particularly helpful for large diagrams, and that it is particularly helpful for modelers with low expertise. Based on these findings, we derive pragmatic guidelines on the optimal size of diagrams that are very easy to apply in tools, based on objective findings, and promise to be beneficial to many modelers.

The experimental procedure has been designed carefully to exclude bias of any kind, learning effects, and distortion. We have included a relatively large number of participants ($n = 78$) in our experiments, as a further contribution to validity. Most of the tests and correlations we have computed are equipped with high or very high levels of statistical significance. We consistently report completion rates, effect sizes, and similar data to allow scrutinizing our results, and allow other scientists to conduct secondary research based on our work. Thus we conclude, that our findings have a high level of validity.

Consistent with previous findings reported in [28,29], a stronger effect is seen in subjective measures (cognitive load, assessment) than in objective measures (score), pointing to cognitive mechanisms to cope with diagram complexity. We hypothesize that increasing extrinsic cognitive load will lead to stronger effects in the objective measures. One way of doing this is through dual-stimulus experiments.

References

1. Abrahão, S., Gravino, C., Insfrn, E., Scanniello, G., Tortora, G.: Assessing the Effectiveness of Sequence Diagrams in the Comprehension of Functional Requirements: Results from a Family of Five Experiments. IEEE Txn. SE 39(3), 327–342 (2013)
2. Britton, C., Kutar, M., Anthony, S., Barker, T., Beecham, S., Wilkinson, V.: An empirical study of user preference and performance with UML diagrams. In: Proc. IEEE 2002 Symp. Human Centric Computing Languages and Environments (HCC/LE), pp. 31–33. IEEE (2002)
3. Dawoodi, S.Y.P.: Assessing the Comprehension of UML Class Diagrams via Eye Tracking. PhD thesis, Kent State University (2007)
4. Dwyer, T., Lee, B., Fisher, D., Quinn, K.I., Isenberg, P., Robertson, G., North, C.: A Comparison of User-Generated and Automatic Graph Layouts. IEEE Txn. Visualization and Computer Graphics 15(6), 961–968 (2009)
5. Effinger, P., Jogsch, N., Seiz, S.: On a Study of Layout Aesthetics for Business Process Models Using BPMN. In: Mendling, J., Weidlich, M., Weske, M. (eds.) BPMN 2010. LNBIP, vol. 67, pp. 31–45. Springer, Heidelberg (2010)
6. Eichelberger, H.: Aesthetics of class diagrams. In: Proc. 1st Intl. Ws. Visualizing Software for Understanding and Analysis (VISSOFT), pp. 23–31. IEEE (2002)
7. Eichelberger, H.: Aesthetics and automatic layout of UML class diagrams. PhD thesis, University of Würzburg (2005)
8. Eichelberger, H.: Automatic layout of UML use case diagrams. In: Proc. 4th ACM Symp. Software Visualization (SOFTVIS), pp. 105–114. ACM (2008)
9. Eichelberger, H., Schmid, K.: Guidelines on the aesthetic quality of UML class diagrams. Information and Software Technology 51(12), 1686–1698 (2009)
10. Eiglsperger, M.: Automatic layout of UML class diagrams: A topology-shape-metrics approach. PhD thesis, Universität Tübingen (2003)
11. Gopher, D., Braune, R.: On the Psychophysics of Workload: Why Bother with Subjective Measures? Human Factors 26(5), 519–532 (1984)
12. Koffka, K.: Principles of Gestalt Psychology. Routledge & Kegan Paul (1935)
13. Paas, F., Tuovinen, J.E., Tabbers, H., Van Gerven, P.W.M.: Cognitive Load Measurement as a Means to Advance Cognitive Load Theory. Educational Psychologist 38(1), 63–71 (2003)
14. Pfleeger, S.L.: Experimental design and analysis in software engineering. Annals of Software Engineering 1(1), 219–253 (1995)
15. Purchase, H.C., Colpoys, L., Carrington, D.A., McGill, M.: UML Class Diagrams: An Emprical Study of Comprehension, pp. 149–178. Kluwer (2003)
16. Purchase, H.C.: Metrics for Graph Drawing Aesthtetics. J. Visual Languages and Computing 13(5), 501–516 (2002)
17. Purchase, H.C., Allder, J.-A., Carrington, D.A.: Graph layout aesthetics in UML diagrams: user preferences. J. Graph Algorithms Applications 6(3), 255–279 (2002)
18. Purchase, H.C., Carrington, D., Allder, J.-A.: Empirical Evaluation of Aesthetics-based Graph Layout. J. Empirical Software Engineering 7(3), 233–255 (2002)
19. Purchase, H.C., Carrington, D., Allder, J.-A.: Experimenting with aesthetics-based graph layout. In: Anderson, M., Cheng, P., Haarslev, V. (eds.) Diagrams 2000. LNCS (LNAI), vol. 1889, pp. 498–501. Springer, Heidelberg (2000)
20. Purchase, H.C., Colpoys, L., McGill, M., Carrington, D.: UML Collaboration Diagram Syntax: An Empirical Study of Comprehension. In: Proc. 1st Intl. Ws. Visualizing Software for Understanding and Analysis (VISSOFT), pp. 13–22. IEEE Computer Society (2002)

21. Reggio, G., Ricca, F., Scanniello, G., Di Cerbo, F., Dodero, G.: On the comprehension of workflows modeled with a precise style: results from a family of controlled experiments. Software & Systems Modeling, 1–24 (2013)
22. Ricca, F., Penta, M.D., Torchiano, M., Tonella, P., Ceccato, M.: How Developers' Experience and Ability Influence Web Application Comprehension Tasks Supported by UML Stereotypes: A Series of Four Experiments. IEEE Txn. SE 36(1), 96–118 (2010)
23. Seemann, J.: Extending the Sugiyama algorithm for drawing UML class diagrams: Towards automatic layout of object-oriented software diagrams. In: DiBattista, G. (ed.) GD 1997. LNCS, vol. 1353, pp. 415–424. Springer, Heidelberg (1997)
24. Sharif, B., Maletic, J.I.: An empirical study on the comprehension of stereotyped UML class diagram layouts. In: Proc. 17th IEEE Intl. Conf. Program Comprehension (ICPC), pp. 268–272. IEEE (2009)
25. Sharif, B., Maletic, J.I.: The effect of layout on the comprehension of UML class diagrams: A controlled experiment. In: Proc. 5th IEEE Intl. Ws. Visualizing Software for Understanding and Analysis (VISSOFT), pp. 11–18. IEEE (2009)
26. Sharif, B., Maletic, J.I.: An eye tracking study on the effects of layout in understanding the role of design patterns. In: Proc. 2010 IEEE Intl. Conf. Software Maintenance (ICSM), pp. 41–48. IEEE (2010)
27. Sharif, B., Maletic, J.I.: The Effects of Layout on Detecting the Role of Design Patterns. In: Proc. 23rd IEEE Conf. Software Engineering Education and Training (CSEE&T), pp. 41–48. IEEE (2010)
28. Störrle, H.: On the Impact of Layout Quality to Unterstanding UML Diagrams. In: Proc. IEEE Symp. Visual Languages and Human-Centric Computing (VL/HCC 2011), pp. 135–142. IEEE Computer Society (2011)
29. Störrle, H.: On the Impact of Layout Quality to Unterstanding UML Diagrams: Diagram Type and Expertise. In: Costagliola, G., Ko, A., Cypher, A., Nichols, J., Scaffidi, C., Kelleher, C., Myers, B. (eds.) Proc. IEEE Symp. Visual Languages and Human-Centric Computing (VL/HCC 2012), pp. 195–202. IEEE Computer Society (2012)
30. Störrle, H., Fish, A.: Towards an Operationalization of the "Physics of Notations" for the Analysis of Visual Languages. In: Moreira, A., Schätz, B., Gray, J., Vallecillo, A., Clarke, P. (eds.) MODELS 2013. LNCS, vol. 8107, pp. 104–120. Springer, Heidelberg (2013)
31. Swan, J., Kutar, M., Barker, T., Britton, C.: User Preference and Performance with UML Interaction Diagrams. In: Proc. 2004 IEEE Symp. Visual Languages and Human Centric Computing (VL/HCC), pp. 243–250. IEEE (2004)
32. Wong, K., Sun, D.: On evaluating the layout of UML diagrams for program comprehension. Software Quality Journal 14(3), 233–259 (2006)
33. Yusuf, S., Kagdi, H., Maletic, J.I.: Assessing the Comprehension of UML Class Diagrams via Eye Tracking. In: 15th IEEE Intl. Conf. Program Comprehension (ICPC 2007), pp. 113–122. IEEE Computer Society (2007)

Enabling the Development of Cognitive Effective Visual DSLs

David Granada, Juan M. Vara, Veronica A. Bollati, and Esperanza Marcos

Kybele Research Group, Rey Juan Carlos University,
Calle Tulipán S/N, 28933 Móstoles, Madrid, Spain
{david.granada,juanmanuel.vara,veronica.bollati,esperanza.marcos}@urjc.es
http://www.kybele.es

Abstract. The development of graphical editors for visual DSLs is far from being a trivial task. There are consequently several tools that provide technical support for this task. However, this paper shows that the analysis of the main characteristics of such tools leaves some space for improvement as regard the cognitive effectiveness of the visual notations produced with them. To deal with this issue, this work introduces CEViNEdit, a GMF-based framework for the development of visual DSLs which takes into account Moody's principles for the development and evaluation of graphical notations. To that end, CEViNEdit eases the selection of values for the visual variables of which the notation is composed, computes a set of metrics to assess the appropriateness of these values and then automates the generation of the graphical editor.

Keywords: Model Driven Engineering (MDE), Domain Specific Language (DSL), Visual Notation, Cognitive Effectiveness.

1 Introduction

Domain Specific Languages (DSLs) [1] play a cornerstone role in almost any proposal which applies the principles of the Model-Driven Engineering (MDE) [2]. The fact that they are targeted to a particular domain contributes to ease of use and greater expressiveness and allows the distance between business users and developers to be shortened [3].

Given that the two main principles of the MDE paradigm are to enhance the role of models and to increase the level of automation throughout the development process, not only modelling languages but also tool support to automate every model-processing task are needed. In particular, owing to the drastic change undergone by the role of models, modelling has probably become into the most relevant task. Tool support for this activity is therefore mandatory: just as IDEs assist developers when programming, editors have to be provided to help modellers when modelling.

The advent of the MDE has led to the emergence of a number of tools for the development of DSLs. Most of these tools implement a metamodel-based approach in which the abstract syntax of the language is first defined and then

J. Dingel et al. (Eds.): MODELS 2014, LNCS 8767, pp. 535–551, 2014.

used as the basis to produce its concrete syntax, editors and the other related artefacts (mainly transformations, model-checkers, etc.) until a DSL toolkit has been formed [4,5]. Note that only visual (modelling) DSLs are considered here: although a number of textual language workbenches already exist, such as XText or TEF, the use of textual DSLs was until recently limited to internal DSLs and programming tasks [6]. Moreover, visual DSLs are probably more appealing if the use of model-based approaches is to be extended to non-IT users [7].

Unfortunately, the aforementioned metamodel-based approach for the development of DSLs adopted by most of the existing tools, reinforces one of the main issues of existing MDE tools: Human Computer Interaction (HCI) principles and methods have been almost completely dismissed to date [8]. In particular, the definition of concrete (visual) syntaxes so far have until now consisted basically of the arbitrary assignment of graphical symbols to the concepts defined of which the abstract syntax of the language is composed. This scenario is, in some respects, related to the fact that, as occurs with any emerging paradigm, MDE-practitioners have dismissed quality aspects in favour of showing that MDE can be effectively used, i.e. proving that the new paradigm deserved attention and recognition has prevailed over the adoption of systematic and rigorous approaches, the classical trade-off between time-to-market and quality. Nevertheless, since MDE has reached certain levels of maturity, the time has come to start considering quality aspects in the development of model-based tools and proposals [9].

To contribute in this line, this work introduces CEViNEdit, an EMF-based tool that leans on Moody's principles [10] to support the model-driven development of DSLs' graphical editors, which takes into account the speed, ease and accuracy with which visual notations can be processed by the human mind (also known as *cognitive efficiency* [11]). To that end, CEViNEdit respects the metamodel-based approach but helps developers in the process of assigning graphical representations to the elements of the abstract syntax by leaning on Moody's Physics of Notations theory [10]. The underlying idea is that the design of visual notations and the choice of graphical conventions should therefore be based on theoretical principles and empirical evidence of cognitive effectiveness rather than on best practices, common sense or social opinion [12]

The reminder of this paper is structured as follows: Section 2 presents the motivation of this work; Section 3 introduces CEViNEdit, a tool that allows the evaluation and consideration of some aspects related to the cognitive effectiveness during the generation process of the graphical editors that support the DSLs; and finally, Section 4 summarizes the main conclusions derived from this work.

2 Motivation

This section present the motivation of this work. To that end, instead of the classical review of related works, the main features of existing tools for the model-driven development of graphical editors are summarized. This review serves to show that despite having achieved a certain level of maturity, existing tools have not been concerned with the quality of the visual notations supported by the editors produced.

Theoretical proposals that could be used to address this issue are then reviewed in order to back the selection of the Physics of Notations as a scientific basis that can be used to provide a new tool for the development of graphical editors for visual DSLs which takes into account cognitive effectiveness.

2.1 Tool Support for the Development of Graphical Editors

Recently, and under the assumption that MDE is getting closer to the slope of enlightenment of the technology hype cycle [4], we have undertaken certain works oriented towards the adoption of more rigorous and systematic approaches for the development of MDE tools. They were first focused on identifying best practices for the development of DSL toolkits [13] while the focus later shifted to the development of model transformations [14], provided that they are widely acknowledged to be the main assets as regards automating MDE proposals.

As well, our attempts to take advantage of the use of MDE technologies in other fields have also served to demonstrate that one of their most appealing MDE features is their ability to abstract their problems in terms of visual models (see for instance [13]) tailored to their needs. This implies the need for new DSLs that are tailored to their domains in which the development of the corresponding editors gains significance.

Therefore, in order to obtain a clear understanding of the state-of-the-art on tools for the development of graphical editors for DSLs, we therefore performed a literature review according to the guidelines proposed by Biolchini et al. [15] for the development of Systematic Literature Reviews in SE. This way, instead of the classical review of Related Works, a brief overview of the main highlights of this review follows.

The aim of the review was to identify the current state of MDE tools that support the production of graphical editors from a domain model. The following research questions were therefore posed:

- **RQ1**: Are there tools to generate editors that apply the principles of MDE?
- **RQ2**: What are the main features and functionalities of these tools?

The review of meta-modeling frameworks previously introduced in [13] were therefore taken as a starting point, and the tools listed in Table 1 were field reviewed according to the following criteria. Note that this is indeed a never-ending task since new tools appear everyday. For instance, the recent Eclipse Sirius, which is an Open Source version of Obeo Designer, has yet to be included.

Scope. Whether the tool is commercial or open source. The type of license is also stated.

Abstract Syntax. Language or notation used for the specification of the abstract syntax.

Concrete Syntax. Means used to assign a graphical notation to each concept of the abstract syntax.

Distinction between Abstract and Concrete Syntax. Whether the tool treats the abstract and concrete syntax separately.

Editing Capabilities. Subjective assessment of the ability to modify generated editors.

Use of Models. The extent to which models are used for the production of graphical editors.

Automation. The level of automation in the production of editors.

Usability. This criterion collapses different usability related issues, such as ease of use or available documentation.

Framework. Whether it is an isolated tool or runs over an existing framework.

Scientific Basis. Whether the tool follows or applies any kind of scientific theory or method to guide, derive or define visual notations. This criteria is somehow subsumed under Usability but it has been considered apart to clearly illustrate the issue addressed in this paper.

Table 1. Metatools analized

Tool	Website
Concrete	http://github.com/mthiede/concrete
DiaGen	http://www.unibw.de/inf2/DiaGen/
Eugenia	http://www.eclipse.org/epsilon/doc/eugenia/
GenGED	http://user.cs.tu-berlin.de/~genged/
GMF	http://www.eclipse.org/modeling/gmf/
Graphiti	http://www.eclipse.org/graphiti/
MetaEdit+	http://www.metacase.com/mep/
Obeo Designer	http://www.obeodesigner.com/
Poseidon	http://www.gentleware.com/poseidon-for-dsls.html
Pounamu	http://www.cs.auckland.ac.nz/pounamu/index.htm
TEF	http://www2.informatik.hu-berlin.de/tef/tool.html
Tiger	http://user.cs.tu-berlin.de/~tigerprj/
Topcased	http://www.topcased.org/

For reasons of space, Table 2 summarizes the results of the study for some of the tools analyzed[1]. In particular, Obeo Designer and MetaEdit+ (commercial tools) and EuGENia and GMF (open-source tools) were found to be those best aligned with the criteria introduced. Likewise, DiaGen results are shown to contrast the features of the aforementioned tools with those of tools which do not adopt a model-based approach.

The review showed that most of the tools analyzed properly addressed the conceptual separation between the DSL's domain model (abstract syntax) and its visual notation (concrete syntax), thus preventing the former from being polluted with unnecessary information. What is more, some tools do support

---

[1] The complete table can be found in "A Systematic Review of the Current Features of Metaeditors", p. 37, http://www.kybele.es/cevinedit/?page_id=30

Table 2. Overview of tools for development of graphical editors

Features	DiaGen	Eugenia	GMF	MetaEdit+	Obeo
Scope	OS(GPL)	OS(EPL)	OS(EPL)	Com	Com
Abstract syntax	Ecore/UML	Ecore	Ecore	GOPPRR	Ecore
Concrete syntax	DiaMetaDesign	EOL	Draw2D	Internal API	Odesign
Syntax distinction	No	Yes	Yes	Yes	Yes
Editing	✔✔	✔✔	✔✔✔	✔✔✔	✔✔✔
Models	✔✔	✔✔✔	✔✔✔	✔✔	✔✔✔
Automation	✔✔	✔✔✔	✔✔	✔✔✔	✔✔✔
Usability	✔✔✔	✔✔✔	✔✔	✔✔✔	✔✔✔
Framework	Eclipse	Eclipse	Eclipse	None	Eclipse
Cognitive eff.	No	No	No	No	No

Legend (for weightable fields): *Poor* (✔), *Good* (✔✔), *Excellent* (✔✔✔)

the automation of many of the intermediate steps involved in the generation of the editor but most of them require some manual refinements for which not very intuitive mechanisms are provided. Only some of the tools reviewed lean on the use of models while most of them were built atop of Eclipse, ensuring certain levels of interoperability with existing MDE tools. All in all, the most remarkable conclusion from the point of view of this work is that, although mature and stable model-based tools for the development of graphical (editors for) DSLs exist, none of them considers usability issues related to their visual notations.

The following section therefore provides a wide overview of existing proposals for the analysis of visual notations and introduces the one adopted to sustain a proposal with which to improve the current state of the art.

2.2 Proposals for Notation Analysis

Software Engineering currently has a number of established methods that are used to evaluate the semantics of the concepts used in different languages, but it lacks equivalent methods with which to evaluate their visual syntax, whose relevance has historically been undervalued, probably because visual notations have traditionally been considered as an informal concept, contrary to that which occurs with semantics.

Among the few works in this line that can be found in the literature, it is worth mentioning the one of Krogstie et al. on Semiotic Quality (SEQUAL) [16] and the one of Green et al. on Cognitive Dimensions (CDs) [17].

SEQUAL is based on semiotic theory and provides a list of properties with which to evaluate the quality of models and modelling languages, defining an extensive ontology of modelling language quality concepts such as: physical, empirical, syntactical, semantic, perceived semantic, pragmatic, social, knowledge, language and organizational quality.

In its current form it is far from being focused on visual notations. It was therefore discarded as a scientific basis for this work. However, some of the concepts that have to be considered in order to assess the quality of a given language according to the authors of SEQUAL, are related to the adequacy of notations. For instance, the authors argue that the *Comprehensibility Appropriateness* of a language depends on some principles directly related to visual representations, such as the ease of symbol discrimination, symbols uniformness, symbols simplicity or graphic economy [18].

The CDs proposal, which was first introduced by Green in [17] as a set of features that provide a language with which to compare the form and structure of programming languages, has been the approach regarding the usability of visual languages most frequently referenced by researchers. In short, the proposal provides a vocabulary of terms (or dimensions) that can be used to specify the details of the structure of cognitive artefacts.

Existing literature states that the CDs framework has some flaws from the point of view of this work, some of which are acknowledged by the authors:

- It was devised to be used in any type of domain [19], from spreadsheets to programming languages. In particular, it was not particularly intended to work for visual modelling languages.
- The blurred definitions of dimensions (main basis of the proposal), along with the lack of a well-defined procedure, causes confusion and hampers understanding at the time of using them [20].
- The number of dimensions has grown since the appearance of the framework, resulting in an unmanageable set of dimensions requiring simplification to target non-skilled potential users.

In contrast, the Physics of Notations (PoN) theory [10], which is briefly described in the next section, is a framework that is exclusively to the design, evaluation, comparison and improvement of visual notations.

With the advent of MDE, in which visual modelling languages have become even more relevant, Moody's proposal has gained a lot of attention as an evaluation technique since it fits perfectly with the nature of these languages while preserving complexity of application at certain admissible levels.

As a matter of fact, these principles have already been used in several works to evaluate other visual languages such as UML [21], BPMN [22] or i*[23].

2.3   The Physics of Notations

Moody's Physics of Notations theory [10] establishes nine principles with which to design, evaluate, compare and improve visual notations. These principles were defined from theory and empirical evidence brought from different disciplines such as: cognitive and perceptual psychology, graphic design, cartography, etc.

Each principle contains design strategies which may contribute towards improving visual notations, an assessment procedure that can be used to compare different notations and samples of notations that satisfy or violate the principle.

The nine principles are summarized as follows:

1. Principle of **Semiotic Clarity**: there should be a one-to-one correspondence between elements of the language and graphical symbols.
2. Principle of **Perceptual Discriminability**: different symbols should be clearly distinguishable from each other.
3. Principle of **Visual Expressiveness**: the full range and capacities of visual variables should be used.
4. Principle of **Semantic Transparency**: the appearance of visual representations should suggest their meaning.
5. Principle of **Complexity Management**: explicit mechanisms to deal with complexity should be provided.
6. Principle of **Cognitive Integration**: explicit mechanisms to support the integration of information from different diagrams should be provided.
7. Principle of **Dual Coding**: text must be used to complement graphics.
8. Principle of **Graphic Economy**: the number of different graphical symbols should be cognitively manageable.
9. Principle of **Cognitive Fit**: different visual dialects for different tasks and audiences should be used when needed.

Since it is exclusively focused on the best way to represent visually a set of constructs, the Physics of Notations also has some limitations. In particular, it does not propose any principle with which to assess the effectiveness of the composition rules of the language, which may result in cognitively inefficient diagrams. Note, however, that these composition rules are mainly inherited from the definition of the abstract syntax of the language which typically precedes the development of the concrete syntax. Solving any issue related to the assessment of composition rules would imply refining the metamodel of the language, with the consequent impact on the ecosystem of related models and transformations.

As a matter of fact, some initiatives towards moving the focus of DSL development to its notation instead of its metamodel have recently emerged in response to this scenario [24]. A notation-driven approach fits with the application of the Cognitive Dimensions framework since it eases the task of rethinking the composition rules of the language.

In contrast, the Physics of Notations theory fits better with the metamodel-driven approach adopted by most of the existing DSLs. Adopting Moody's proposal does not ensure a cognitively efficient language but provides certain levels of confidence without compromising the balance between effort and reward.

To confirm this assumption we have applied Moody's proposal to conduct a detailed analysis of the visual notation used by WebRatio [25,26], an Eclipse-based IDE for the model-driven development of Web and mobile applications [27] that implements WebML and could be considered to be one of the most successful model-based tools [28].

The data obtained allowed us to detect various problems and provide certain recommendations on how to improve the visual notation of the language, but more importantly, the analysis provided us with a number of lessons learned. One of the most relevant conclusions was that, even though the analysis of the cognitive effectiveness of any given (visual) DSL is feasible while keeping a reasonable balance in terms of effort and time, solving the problems revealed by the analysis is either impossible or at best requires too much effort. These aspects should be therefore considered from the early stages of the development of new DSLs, so that good decisions related to cognitive effectiveness are translated throughout the different stages of the development until the working implementation. These issues are dealt with in the following section. This section presents our proposal to support the development of visual DSLs graphical editors which takes into account cognitive efficiency, i.e. the speed, ease and accuracy with which visual notations can be processed by the human mind [11].

2.4   Visual Variables

Before presenting CEViNEdit, another theoretical concept must be introduced. Visual Variables are a set of elementary building blocks that can be used to graphically encode information, which are often used and referenced in each of the principles proposed by Moody's framework [10], and therefore, in our proposal.

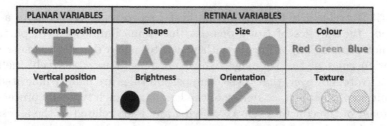

Fig. 1. Visual variables used to construct visual notations (adapted from [29])

Studies conducted on the nature of graphical symbols have identified eight different visual variables (see Figure 1) that can be used to encode information. These variables can be defined in two subsets: planar and retinal. The most important work in this regard is the seminal work of Bertin [29], which is considered to be to graphic design what the periodic table is to chemistry. Each of these visual variables has a set of properties that are used to encode certain types of information and these properties must therefore be known if effective choices are to be made.

3   CEViNEdit: Improving the Development of DSLs Visual Notations

This section introduces CEViNEdit (enabling Cognitive Effectiveness in the Visual Notation of graphic Editors)[2], a tool that supports the model-driven development of graphical editors for visual DSLs that fosters the production of cognitively effective visual notations.

---

[2] The Eclipse plug-in can be download from: http://kybele.es/cevinedit

To that end, CEViNEdit depends on the capabilities of EMF and GMF for the production of DSL toolkits [5] and the enhancement in automation that EuGENia [30] brings to the model-driven development process of GMF-based editors.

GMF is a generative component for the development of graphical editors. GMF uses a domain model (defined in terms of Ecore, the metamodeling language of EMF) and a set of additional models that establishes the relationship between elements of the domain model and their visual representations to generate the code that implements the graphical editor as an Eclipse plug-in. EuGENia is able to generate the intermediate models automatically if the domain model is previously annotated using a set of GMF-specific annotations defined in [30].

CEViNEdit therefore conforms to the metamodel-based approach adopted by GMF by improving the information with which EuGENia is fed before it is run to produce the interim models used by GMF. To that end, the user is provided with user-friendly panels that can be used to establish relationships between the elements of the domain model and its graphical representations in terms of GMF graphic abstractions as well as to set the values for the visual variables of such graphic elements. In order to drive design decisions towards the production of a cognitively effective visual notation, the user is provided with contextual help as regards the impact of selected variables on cognitive effectiveness. Furthermore, informal assessments of the current results according to some of Moody's principles can be invoked on demand. Finally, a fully functional GMF-based editor can be generated with a single click, without having to modify any of the intermediate GMF models.

The reminder of this section is structured as follows: subsection 3.1 presents the CEViNEdit metamodel, which abstracts is the basis for creating models in which the customized elements and their graphical properties are stored; subsection 3.2 provides a detailed description of the process used to develop a GMF editor with CEViNEdit; subsection 3.3 presents the possible assessment and metrics that can be obtained with the tool, according to some of the principles established in the PoN theory; finally, we present the limitations of the current version of CEViNEdit.

3.1   CEViNEdit Metamodel

In order to persist the information gathered about the graphical representation of each element of the domain model, a small DSL, whose metamodel is shown in Figure 2, has been defined. In essence, it abstracts the graphic elements that can be used as building blocks when designing GMF editors (NodeEClass, LinkEReference, etc.) and the visual variables defined by Bertin [29].

In order to bridge the specification of the abstract and the concrete syntax, every CEViNEdit model contains a Root object that stores the path to the file containing the domain model. Next, a unique Diagram object contains the rest of objects used to model which will be the GMF elements used to represent each concept, whereas a number of enumerations are provided to support the customization of each graphic element since each type of element admits different values for the visual variables.

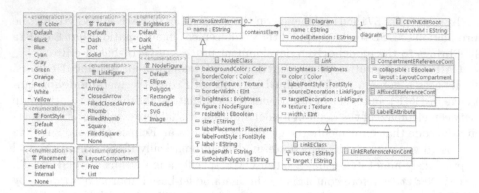

Fig. 2. CEViNEdit metamodel

3.2   CEViNEdit Development Process

This section briefly describes the user interface of CEViNEdit and the development process for the production of GMF-based editors supported by the tool. To that end, the simple yet intuitive filesystem example used by EuGENia[3] is used as case study.

Figure 3 shows some excerpts of screen-captures taken from the development of the case study with CEViNEdit . The UI is basically composed of four panels and a toolbar. The first panel (A) shows the domain model whereas the second one (B) depicts the CEViNEdit model that gathers the information about the relationships between the elements of the abstract and concrete syntax needed for the production of the GMF-based editor. The third panel (C) provides controls to set the values for the visual variables of the graphic elements comprising the notation of the DSL and thus refine these relationships, and the last panel (D) provides contextual information about the influence of the visual variable selected on cognitive effectiveness. This panel can be enabled or disabled by the user at any time. Finally, the toolbar at the top (E) allows reports to be produced, which provide information regarding the extent to which the visual notation produced with the information gathered at that time would be aligned with some of Moody's principles. Controls for the generation of the GMF-based editor are also provided.

The development process supported by CEViNEdit is depicted in Figure 4. Note that graphical abstractions are used to illustrate each step of the process according to Moody's principles.

The first step is to create an empty CEViNEdit model. The wizard then requests the location of the domain model, which can be loaded in the corresponding panel from either the Eclipse workspace or the underlying file system. The user next states which of the GMF graphic elements have been selected to represent each element of the domain model using the contextual menus shown when

---

[3] EuGENia   GMF   Tutorial: http://www.eclipse.org/epsilon/doc/articles/
eugenia-gmf-tutorial/

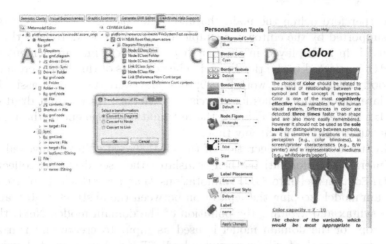

Fig. 3. CEViNedit Metaeditor

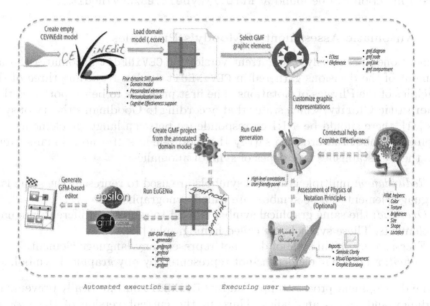

Fig. 4. Overview of the CEViNEdit development process

each element is clicked. These decisions are then collected in the second panel which depicts the CEViNEdit model. To return to the case study, the filesystem ECLass will be represented as a gmfdiagram; the File, Drive, Folder and Shortcut ECLasses are represented as gmfnodes and finally the Shortcut.target EReference and the Sync ECLass will be visualized as gmflinks.

With regard to the element selected in the CEViNEdit model (Node, Link or Compartment), the third panel shows a list of visual variables (as Color, Texture, Size, Location, Shape or Brightness) and their possible values. The user can therefore define the main characteristics of the concrete syntax that will be supported by the editor in a simple and intuitive way. To ease this task, contextual help is displayed in the fourth panel every time an element of the CEViNEdit is selected in the third panel. The contents of this help were adapted from Moody's and Bertin's work [10,29] and they were devised to assist in the appropriate selection of values for the visual variables. After a first draft of the CEViNEdit model has been defined, the automatic assessment of the resultant visual notation can be run at any time.

Finally, the automatic generation of the GMF-based editor is invoked. A series of internal transformations then translates the user decisions collected in the CEViNEdit model into GMF annotations that are attached to a copy of the domain model, keeping the separation between the abstract syntax and the concrete syntax and avoiding the pollution of the domain model. Next, the annotated copy of the domain model is used as input to create and run a new GMF project using the facilities provided by EuGENia. A screencast showing the process in action can be found at http://kybele.es/cevinedit.

3.3   Automatic Assessment of Moody's Principles

As mentioned previously, the current version of CEViNEdit automates the assessment of the decisions gathered in CEViNEdit models regarding three of the principles of the Physics of Notations. The first principle to be supported is that of **Semiotic Clarity**, which states that according to Goodman's theory of symbols [31], there should be a 1:1 correspondence between language elements and graphical symbols, in order to satisfy the requirements of a notational system. This theory establishes four types of symbol anomalies:

- *Redundancy*: multiple graphical symbols are used to represent the same language element. These symbols are called synographs [32].
- *Overload*: the same graphical symbol is used to represent different language elements. These symbols are called homographs [32].
- *Excess*: a graphical symbol does not represent any language element.
- *Deficit*: a language element is not represented by any graphical symbol.

The development process supported by CEViNEdit automatically prevents redundancy and excess anomalies. Thus, in the current version of the tool we show only those anomalies that are related to overloads and deficits. However, although the redundancy may have a negative impact on cognitive effectiveness, we consider that this option should be left open for the designer in case s/he wishes to show a given model element using different representations. We consequently plan to implement this behavior in the next version of the tool.

Figure 5 shows the **Semiotic Clarity** report for the filesystem example when the decisions related to the representation of the two Links defined result in a homograph being produced. The report also shows those elements from the domain model for which no representation has been set.

CEViNEdit also supports the assessment of the principle of **Visual Expressiveness**, which is defined as the number of variables efficiently used in a visual notation. Software Engineering notations tend to use a limited range of visual variables, each of which permits only a limited range of values, i.e., they do not favour Visual Expressiveness.

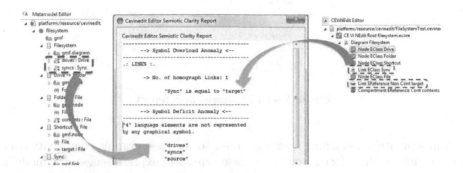

Fig. 5. Semiotic Clarity report

For instance, of the possible values for the Shape variable, the rectangle (and its possible variants) is that most frequently adopted by SE modelling languages like the UML. Nevertheless, rectangles are the least effective Shapes for human visual processing. In order to facilitate this processing, it might be preferable to use curves, 3D or icons instead [33].

The range of values used for the Colour variable deserves the same consideration, since it is one of the most cognitively effective [34]. Indeed, differences between Colours are detected even faster than those between Shapes [35].

What is more, according to research in psychophysics, each of the eight visual variables has a capacity, i.e., a number of different steps that can be perceived by human mind [10]. Given all of the above, the choice of the visual variables used (and their ranges of values) should not be arbitrary, but should depend on the type of information that one wishes to encode.

In this context, the **Visual Expressiveness** report produced by CEViNEdit provides information regarding the number of values used for each visual variable, its capacity and its saturation, i.e. the ratio between the number of values used and the capacity of each variable. This ratio illustrates to what extent the visual variable is efficiently used in the visual notation in order to avoid, among other things, a psychedelically colorful diagram. Figure 6 therefore shows a report for the filesystem editor, including the metrics computed for some visual variables.

Although it is not introduced here for the sake of space, CEViNEdit also automates the assessment of the **Graphic Economy** principle, which states that the strategy of providing graphical symbols for a language is effective until the cognitive recognition process becomes too complex.

The underlying idea is that each new symbol introduced reduces cognitive effectiveness since the number of different objects that an average human can hold in working memory is around six categories [36]. This number is therefore the upper limit for the graphic complexity.

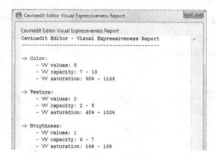

Fig. 6. Visual Expressiveness report

Unfortunately, modelling languages tend to increase graphic complexity over time owing to the effort made to increase semantic expressiveness, i.e. model's efficiency as regards reflecting the underlying reality represented by that model.

In order to help alleviate this issue, CEViNEdit informs the user about the graphic complexity of the visual notation that s/he is currently designing.

3.4   Current Limitations and Further Work

Since CEViNEdit is on-going work, the following main limitations and possible threats to validity are briefly introduced. Pointers for improvement are provided when appropriate.

In order to validate the proposal, an empirical study is needed and has consequently been planned with MSs students who will use CEViNEdit to develop a graphical editor for a set of DSLs with different grades of complexity. This signifies that not only will the feasibility and the usability of the proposal will be evaluated, but that feedback will also be gathered from end-users to address future improvements.

More work is also needed to automate the assessment of the theoretical principles which are not yet supported. Note, however, that not every principle is subject to automation. For instance, the Cognitive Integration principle, which only applies when multiple diagrams are used to represent a system. This type of problem is beyond the scope of our application, since this principle evaluates the cognitive effectiveness of systems in which different types of heterogeneous diagrams are used as occurs for example in software development with WebRatio, in which E/R, UML, BPMN and WebML diagrams are involved in the same project. However, with our proposal it is possible to generate more than one visual notation for each language, but creating different projects. It would be useful and interesting to provide the possibility to generate more than one visual notation for a single project, so that the designer could compare which one is more suited to his/her needs in real time. As well, the current version of the tool supports a limited set of GMF annotations. So, more customization options for graphical are being implemented to cover the whole spectrum of GMF annotations.

Finally, there are two more lines for further work which do not represent current limitations but are rather ambitious and potential open fields of application. On the one hand, we believe that once we are able to compute some indicators on the cognitive effectiveness of an editor's visual notation, we are in a good position to address the development of mechanisms to support automatic refinements in order to improve the indicators obtained for certain principles. It would eventually be a case of finding the appropriate algorithm and implementing it in terms of model management operators.

On the other hand, CEViNEdit is currently oriented towards fostering the interest on cognitive effectiveness for new editors but it would also be feasible to apply the idea to the assessment of existing editors which have been developed with EuGENia and/or GMF. An assessment of this nature would be performed by analyzing either the GMF annotations collected in the domain model or even the interim models used by GMF (namely gmfgraph, gmftool and gmfmap).

4   Conclusions

This paper has introduced CEViNEdit, a tool to support the model-driven development of graphical editors which enables the definition of cognitively effective visual notations according to the principles of the Physics of Notations [10].

To the best of our knowledge, CEViNEdit is the first tool to consider quality aspects in the model-driven development of graphical editors. Note, however, that this is a line in which much work needs to be done, since MDE proposals have, to date, tend to be authored by developers with a technical background but without in-depth experience of HCI or cognitive issues [8].

It is also worth noting that the use of CEViNEdit is by no means sufficient to assert that the visual notation of the graphical editor produced has no problems but it does provide certain levels of confidence. In some respects, the idea is similar to that guiding software testing: 100% code coverage is either not feasible or requires too much effort.

Beyond the functionality provided by the tool itself, this work aims to foster interest in using a scientific basis to design, evaluate, improve and compare visual notations as part of a more generic movement that MDE practitioners have started towards the inclusion of quality features in the development of modelling languages [37].

In this respect, this work serves to show that it is not only feasible to partially automate this type of quality considerations in the development of MDE tools, but also that it is feasible to do so while keeping a reasonable balance in terms of effort and time. This is particularly relevant when bearing in mind that MDE practitioners have to date focused on showing that their proposals could be efficiently applied while quality aspects have been dismissed. If we wish MDE practitioners to be concerned about quality issues, then it will allow this occur without too much extra effort. In other words, automation is key to avoiding the accidental increase in complexity brought about by dealing with quality concerns.

Acknowledgments. This research is partially funded by the MASAI project, financed by the Spanish Ministry of Science and Technology (Ref. TIN2011-22617). The authors wish to thank Angel Moreno for his valuable contributions during the implementation tasks.

References

1. Mernik, M., Heering, J., Sloane, A.M.: When and how to develop domain-specific languages. ACM Comput. Surv. 37(4), 316–344 (2005)
2. Schmidt, D.C.: Guest editor's introduction: Model-driven engineering. IEEE Computer 39(2), 25–31 (2006)
3. Ghosh, D.: Dsl for the uninitiated. Queue 9(6), 10:10–10:21 (2011)
4. Brambilla, M., Cabot, J., Wimmer, M.: Model-driven Software Engineering in Practice. Synthesis digital library of engineering and computer science. Morgan & Claypool Publishers (2012)
5. Gronback, R.: Eclipse Modeling Project: A Domain-Specific Language (DSL) Toolkit. Eclipse Series. Pearson Education (2009)
6. Volter, M.: From programming to modeling-and back again. IEEE Software 28(6), 20–25 (2011)
7. Breu, R., Kuntzmann-Combelles, A., Felderer, M.: New perspectives on software quality. IEEE Software 31(1), 32–38 (2014)
8. Whittle, J., Hutchinson, J., Rouncefield, M., Burden, H., Heldal, R.: Industrial adoption of model-driven engineering: Are the tools really the problem? In: Moreira, A., Schätz, B., Gray, J., Vallecillo, A., Clarke, P. (eds.) MODELS 2013. LNCS, vol. 8107, pp. 1–17. Springer, Heidelberg (2013)
9. Selic, B.: What will it take? a view on adoption of model-based methods in practice. Software and System Modeling 11(4), 513–526 (2012)
10. Moody, D.L.: The "physics" of notations: a scientific approach to designing visual notations in software engineering. In: ICSE (2), pp. 485–486 (2010)
11. Zhang, J., Norman, D.A.: Representations in distributed cognitive tasks. Cognitive Science 18(1), 87–122 (1994)
12. Wheildon, C., Ogilvy, D., Heard, G.: Type and Layout: Are You Communicating Or Just Making Pretty Shapes? Worsley Press (2005)
13. Vara, J.M., Marcos, E.: A framework for model-driven development of information systems: Technical decisions and lessons learned. Journal of Systems and Software 85(10), 2368–2384 (2012)
14. Bollati, V.A., Vara, J.M., Jiménez, A., Marcos, E.: Applying MDE to the (semi-) automatic development of model transformations. Information and Software Technology 55(4), 699–718 (2013)
15. Biolchini, J., Gomes, P., Cruz, A., Horta, G.: Systematic review in software engineering. Technical Report ES 679/05 (2005)
16. Krogstie, J., Sindre, G., Jørgensen, H.D.: Process models representing knowledge for action: A revised quality framework. EJIS 15(1), 91–102 (2006)
17. Green, T.R.G.: Cognitive dimensions of notations. In: Sutcliffe, A., Macaulay, L. (eds.) People and Computers, pp. 443–460. Cambridge University Press (1989)
18. Krogstie, J., Sølvberg, A.: Information systems engineering: Conceptual modeling in a quality perspective. Kompendiumforlaget, Trondheim, Norway (2003)
19. Green, T.R., Blandford, A.E., Church, L., Roast, C.R., Clarke, S.: Cognitive dimensions: Achievements, new directions, and open questions. Journal of Visual Languages & Computing 17(4), 328–365 (2006)

20. Dagit, J., Lawrance, J., Neumann, C., Burnett, M., Metoyer, R., Adams, S.: Using cognitive dimensions: Advice from the trenches. Journal of Visual Languages & Computing 17(4), 302–327 (2006)
21. Moody, D., van Hillegersberg, J.: Evaluating the visual syntax of UML: An analysis of the cognitive effectiveness of the UML family of diagrams. In: Gašević, D., Lämmel, R., Van Wyk, E. (eds.) SLE 2008. LNCS, vol. 5452, pp. 16–34. Springer, Heidelberg (2009)
22. Genon, N., Heymans, P., Amyot, D.: Analysing the cognitive effectiveness of notation 2.0 visual notation. In: Malloy, B., Staab, S., van den Brand, M. (eds.) SLE 2010. LNCS, vol. 6563, pp. 377–396. Springer, Heidelberg (2011)
23. Moody, D.L., Heymans, P., Matulevicius, R.: Improving the effectiveness of visual representations in requirements engineering: An evaluation of i* visual syntax. In: RE, pp. 171–180 (2009)
24. Wouters, L.: Towards the Notation-Driven Development of DSMLs. In: Moreira, A., Schätz, B., Gray, J., Vallecillo, A., Clarke, P. (eds.) MODELS 2013. LNCS, vol. 8107, pp. 522–537. Springer, Heidelberg (2013)
25. Granada, D., Vara, J.M., Brambilla, M., Bollati, V., Marcos, E.: Analysing the cognitive effectiveness of the webml visual notation. Technical report, School of Computer Science, Rey Juan Carlos University (2013)
26. Granada, D., Vara, J.M., Brambilla, M., Bollati, V., Marcos, E.: Analysing the cognitive effectiveness of the webml visual notation. Software and Systems Modelling (Revised and Resubmitted)
27. Acerbis, R., Bongio, A., Brambilla, M., Butti, S.: Webratio 5: An eclipse-based case tool for engineering web applications. In: Baresi, L., Fraternali, P., Houben, G.-J. (eds.) ICWE 2007. LNCS, vol. 4607, pp. 501–505. Springer, Heidelberg (2007)
28. Brambilla, M., Fraternali, P.: Large-scale model-driven engineering of web user interaction: The webml and webratio experience. Science of Computer Programming (2013) (in press)
29. Bertin, J.: Semiology of Graphics - Diagrams, Networks, Maps. ESRI (2010)
30. Kolovos, D.S., Rose, L.M., Abid, S.B., Paige, R.F., Polack, F.A.C., Botterweck, G.: Taming EMF and GMF using model transformation. In: Petriu, D.C., Rouquette, N., Haugen, Ø. (eds.) MODELS 2010, Part I. LNCS, vol. 6394, pp. 211–225. Springer, Heidelberg (2010)
31. Goodman, N.: Languages of Art: An Approach to a Theory of Symbols. Bobbs-Merrill Co. (1968)
32. Nordbotten, J.C., Crosby, M.E.: The effect of graphic style on data model interpretation. Inf. Syst. J. 9(2), 139–156 (1999)
33. Irani, P., Ware, C.: Diagramming information structures using 3d perceptual primitives. ACM Trans. Comput.-Hum. Interact. 10(1), 1–19 (2003)
34. Mackinlay, J.D.: Automating the design of graphical presentations of relational information. ACM Trans. Graph. 5(2), 110–141 (1986)
35. Lohse, G.L.: A cognitive model for understanding graphical perception. Human-Computer Interaction 8(4), 353–388 (1993)
36. Miller, G.: The magical number seven, plus or minus two: Some limits on our capacity for processing information. The Psychological Rev. 63, 81–97 (1956)
37. Solheim, I., Neple, T.: Model quality in the context of model-driven development. In: MDEIS, pp. 27–35 (2006)

JUMP—From Java Annotations to UML Profiles*

Alexander Bergmayr[1], Michael Grossniklaus[2], Manuel Wimmer[1], and Gerti Kappel[1]

[1] Vienna University of Technology, Austria
lastname@big.tuwien.ac.at
[2] University of Konstanz, Germany
michael.grossniklaus@uni-konstanz.de

Abstract. The capability of UML profiles to serve as annotation mechanism has been recognized in both industry and research. Today's modeling tools offer profiles specific to platforms, such as Java, as they facilitate model-based engineering approaches. However, the set of available profiles is considerably smaller compared to the number of existing Java libraries using annotations. This is because an effective mapping between Java and UML to generate profiles from annotation-based libraries is missing. In this paper, we present *JUMP* to overcome this limitation, thereby continuing existing mapping efforts by emphasizing on annotations and profiles. We demonstrate the practical value of *JUMP* by contributing profiles that facilitate reverse-engineering and forward-engineering scenarios for the Java platform. The evaluation of *JUMP* shows that profiles can be automatically generated from Java libraries exhibiting equal or even improved quality compared to profiles currently used in practice.

Keywords: Java Annotations·UML Profiles·Model-Based Engineering·Forward Engineering·Reverse Engineering.

1 Introduction

Since the introduction of the UML profile mechanism, numerous profiles have been developed [38], many of which are available by the OMG standardization body [36]. Even in industry, the practical value of profiles has been recognized as today's modeling tools offer already predefined stereotypes covered by such profiles. They are considered as a major ingredient for current model-based software engineering approaches [6] by providing features supplementary to the UML standard metamodel. This powerful capability of profiles can also be exploited in terms of an annotation mechanism [42], where defined stereotypes show similar capabilities as annotations in Java. Hence, deriving stereotypes from established programming libraries to produce corresponding profiles at the modeling level is desirable. For instance, IBM's Rational Software Architect provides profiles for certain Java libraries. By applying such profiles, high-level platform-independent models (PIMs) are refined into models specific to a platform (PSMs), where the platform refers to the library from which the profile was derived. Turning this forward-engineering (FE) perspective into a reverse-engineering (RE) one, existing

---

* This work is co-funded by the European Commission under the ICT Policy Support Programme, grant no. 317859.

J. Dingel et al. (Eds.): MODELS 2014, LNCS 8767, pp. 552–568, 2014.

programs can be represented as UML models that capture annotations by applying the corresponding profiles. Therefore, platform-specific profiles and their application are beneficial from both perspectives. In a reverse-engineering step, model analyzers can exploit captured stereotypes to facilitate comprehension [10], whereas profiled UML models, i.e., models to which profiles are applied, pave the way for model transformers to generate richer program code in a forward-engineering step [42].

Problem. However, to date, an effective conceptual mapping between UML and Java as a basis for an automated process to generate profiles from libraries that use annotations is still missing. As a result, profiles need to be manually developed, which is only achievable by a huge effort when considering the large number of possible annotations in Java. In the ARTIST project [4], we are confronted with this problem, as we work towards a model-based engineering approach for modernizing applications by novel cloud offerings, which involves representing PSMs that refer to the platform of existing applications, e.g., the Java Persistence API (JPA), when considering persistence, and the platform of "cloudified" applications, e.g., the Objectify library[1], when considering cloud datastores. For instance, JPA annotations at the modeling level facilitate distinguishing between plain association and composition relationships and precisely deciding on multiplicities, which is in general not easily to grasp [7]. UML models profiled by Objectify annotations enable generating method bodies even from a structural viewpoint. These examples highlight the practical value of platform-specific reverse-engineering and forward-engineering tools, which are developed in the ARTIST project.

Contribution. In this paper, we present a fully automatic transformation chain for generating UML profiles from Java libraries that use annotations. For that reason, we propose an effective conceptual mapping between the two technical spaces [25, 30]. Thereby, we continue the long tradition of investigating mappings between Java and UML [15,23,28,33]. Though, in this work, we also consider Java annotations and UML profiles in the mapping process. This necessitates overcoming existing heterogeneities that, e.g., refer to the target specification of Java annotations and other peculiarities of how Java annotation types are declared. To operationalize the conceptual mapping, we employ model transformation techniques [12] as a basis for our approach *JUMP*, which allows developers to "jump" from annotation-based Java libraries to UML profiles. We collect all the automatically generated profiles and make them publicly available in terms what we call the *UML-Profile-Store* [43], thereby complementing OMG's collection of standardized profiles with supplementary profiles for the Java platform.

Structure. In Section 2, we motivate the practical value of platform-specific profiles by a typical *JUMP* use-case and we give the background for *UML Profiles* and *Java Annotations* in terms of metamodels. We present *JUMP* in Section 3 by providing insights into our proposed conceptual mapping and elaborating effective solutions to overcome existing heterogeneities of the two languages. In Section 4, we discuss our prototypical implementation based on the Eclipse ecosystem, while in Section 5, we evaluate *JUMP*. In particular, we (i) compare our methodology how to represent annotations and annotation types in UML with methodologies used in current modeling tools and (ii) evaluate the quality of automatically generated profiles compared to profiles used in practice. Finally, in Section 6, we discuss related work and conclude in Section 7.

---

[1] https://code.google.com/p/objectify-appengine

2   Motivation and Background

To motivate the practical value of platform-specific profiles, we introduce a typical *JUMP* use-case. Then, we discuss the concepts of Java's annotation mechanism and briefly introduce UML's profile mechanism to establish the basis for our approach.

2.1   Application of Platform-Specific UML Profiles

A typical *JUMP* use-case is directed to scenarios in the context of reverse-engineering (RE) and forward-engineering (FE). They are of particular relevance for migration projects, which aim at reinterpreting existing reengineering processes [26] in the light of advanced model-based engineering approaches [17]. In this respect, UML profiles play an important role as they enable models annotated with platform-specific information [39]. To demonstrate a concrete use-case, we selected the JPA and Objectify profile from the area of data modeling. The idea is to replace the former profile by the latter one, thereby realizing a change of the data access platform as typically required by "moving-to-the-cloud" scenarios. Figure 1 depicts an excerpt of the PSMs of a typical eCommerce web application, where the platform refers to the selected profiles. From the JPA-based PSM, a sliced PIM is generated that sets the focus solely on the domain classes, i.e., annotated with JPA stereotypes, which are intended to be modified. Even better, this generated PIM interprets JPA stereotypes in terms of native UML concepts. As a result, the accuracy of the PIM is improved because it explicitly captures *identifiers*, *compositions*, and more precise *multiplicities*. These improvements of the PIM demonstrate the practical value of considering platform-specific information in the context of a model-based RE scenario. Furthermore, they leverage the refinement

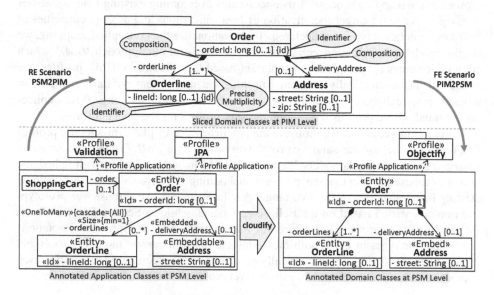

Fig. 1. Typical *JUMP* Use-Case

of the PIM towards an Objectify-based PSM without the need to identify mappings between the pertinent platforms. From the produced Objectify-based PSM, program code can be generated by also interpreting applied stereotypes in the context of a FE scenario. For instance, method bodies for CRUD operations can be generated for domain classes as they are indicated by the respective stereotypes and generated code elements can be automatically annotated. Clearly, *JUMP* acts as an enabler for both RE and FE scenarios by providing the required platform-specific profiles.

2.2 Mechanisms for Annotations in Java and Profiles in UML

Before annotations can be applied on code elements, they need to be declared in terms of annotation types. A rough overview of the main concepts behind annotations in Java is given in the metamodel depicted in Figure 2a. We extracted this metamodel from the JLS7 [37]. `AnnotationTypes` declare the possible annotations for code elements and may have, similar to Java interface declarations, optional `modifiers`. They are identified by a `name`. `AnnotationTypes` may themselves be subject for annotations. Most importantly for the context of this work is the target annotation that is represented in the metamodel as an attribute for simplicity reasons. It indicates the code elements that are valid bases for an application of an `AnnotationType`. The body of an annotation type declaration consists of zero or more `AnnotationType-Elements` for holding information of `AnnotationType` applications. They are declared in terms of method signatures with optional `modifiers`, a mandatory `type` and `name`, and an optional `default` value that is returned if no custom value is set.

With the introduction of UML 2, the profile mechanism has been significantly improved compared to the beginnings of UML [18]. In particular, a profile modeling language has been incorporated in the UML language family to precisely define how profiles are applied on UML models. Figure 2b depicts the core elements of UML's `Profiles` package and relates them to the `Classes` package of UML. As the `Stereotype` metaclass specializes the `Class` metaclass, it inherits modeling capabil-

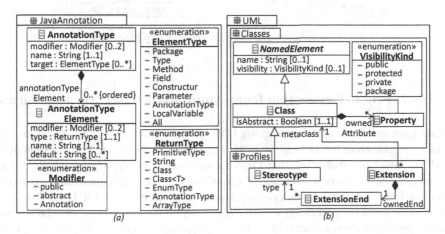

Fig. 2. Metamodel of Java Annotations and UML Profiles

ities such as properties. Defined stereotypes reference the metaclasses that are extended by the Extension relationships. The ExtensionEnd realizes the reference from the extended metaclass back to the Stereotype. Similar to Annotation-Types, Stereotypes are identified by a name property, and modified by an optional visibility and the mandatory isAbstract property.

To demonstrate the relationship between annotations and stereotypes, we set the focus on the Order class of the JPA-based PSM in Figure 1. Listing 1.1 shows the *application* of the Entity annotation type to the Order class whereas Listing 1.2 depicts the respective *declaration* at the programming level.

Listing 1.1. Application of Entity

```
package ...;
import javax.persistence.Entity;

@Entity(name = "Order")
public class Order {
    ...
}
```

Listing 1.2. Declaration of Entity

```
package javax.persistence;
import java.lang.annotation.*;

@Target(ElementType.TYPE)
public @interface Entity {
    String name() default "";
}
```

The corresponding UML-based representation is presented in Figure 3, which demonstrates the stereotype application to the Order class and the Entity declaration by a Stereotype. Similarly, at the package-level, the UML profile, which covers the Entity stereotype needs to be applied to the Order's package as a prerequisite for the stereotype application. To ensure that the Entity stereotype provides at least similar capabilities as the corresponding annotation type, the extension relationship references the UML metaclass Type. Furthermore, the stereotype comprises a property corresponding to the annotation type element name of the Entity.

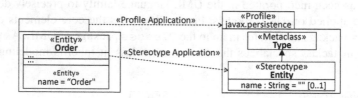

Fig. 3. Application and Definition of Entity Stereotype

3   UML Profile Generation from Annotation-Based Java Libraries

We start our investigation for generating UML profiles from annotation-based Java libraries by presenting the process of *JUMP*, as shown in Figure 4. The entry-point to *JUMP* is *Java Code* that is translated into a corresponding *Code Model*, which is considered as a one-to-one representation of *Java Code*, i.e., the transition from a text-based to a model-based representation expressed in terms of MOF [35]/EMF [14]. The *Code Model* is the basis for generating a *UML Profile*, which facilitates to capture Java annotation type declarations in terms of UML stereotypes (cf. middle of Figure 4). In turn, they serve as foundation to apply profiles as an annotation mechanism [42]. In case of

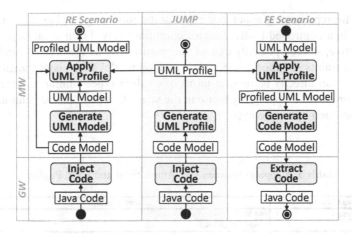

Fig. 4. Process for UML Profile Generation and their Application

reverse-engineering *Java Code* (cf. left hand side of Figure 4), the *Profiled UML Model* results from applying profiles to the generated *UML Model*, where the *Code Model* covers the annotated elements that indicate to which elements of the *UML Model* the corresponding stereotypes are applied. Similarly, in case of forward-engineering *Java Code* (cf. right hand side of Figure 4), profiles are applied to the *UML Model* even though, in this case, the *Profiled UML Model* serves as input for generating the *Code Model* from which *Java Code* is extracted. Bridging the two technical spaces [25] we are confronted with, i.e., GrammarWare (GW) [27] and ModelWare (MW) [30], is required for the two scenarios as well as *JUMP*.

3.1 Bridging Technical Spaces

Transforming plain Java code into a UML-based representation requires overcoming the different encoding and resolving language heterogeneities. Concerning the first aspect, the Java code needs to be encoded according to the format imposed by the modeling environment [5]. Concerning the second aspect, a bridge between Java and UML based on translations requires a conceptual mapping between the two languages. Instead of directly translating plain Java code into a UML-based representation, the use of a two-step approach is preferable [24], which is also applied by *JUMP*. In a first step, *Java Code* is translated into a *Code Model* that uses Java terminology and structures conforming to the Java metamodel provided by MoDisco [9]. This *Code Model* is the basis for generating UML profiles and input for the second step that is dedicated to resolving language heterogeneities by relying on the correspondences between the Java and UML metamodels.

3.2 Generating UML Profiles

To facilitate the generation of UML profiles, we present a conceptual mapping between Java's annotation concept and the concept of profiles in UML. Thereby, stereotypes play a vital role for representing annotation types at the modeling level as they enable their application in a controlled UML standard-compliant way. From a language engineering perspective, stereotypes only extend the required UML metaclasses and facilitate defining constraints and model operations, such as model analysis or transformations, because they can directly be used in terms of explicit types similar to a metaclass in UML. Our proposed mapping is generic in the sense that any declared annotation type can be represented by a stereotype.

Table 1. Mappings between Java Annotations and UML Profiles

Java Concept	UML Concept
AnnotationType a	**add** Stereotype s
a.name	s.name = a.name
a.annotationTypeElement	**add** Property p **for each** AnnotationTypeElement **in** a.annotationTypeElement
switch(a.modifier)	
case : public	s.visibility = public
case : abstract	s.isAbstract = false
case : annotation an **and** not an.type = Target	**apply** Stereotype for an.type **to** s
case : annotation an **and** an.type = Target	**add** Property p **for each** ElementType **in** a.target p.name = "base_".concat(p.type) **add** Extension e **for each** ElementType **in** a.target e.metaClass = p.type **add** ExtensionEnd f f.type = s
switch(a.target)	
case : AnnotationType	p.type = Stereotype
case : Constructor	p.type = Operation **add** Constraint {self.base_Operation.oclIsDefined() **implies** self.base_Operation.name = self.base_Operation.oclContainer().oclAsType(uml::Classifier).name}
case : Field	p.type = {EnumerationLiteral, Property}
case : LocaleVariable	p.type = Property
case : Method	p.type = {Operation, Property} **add** Constraint {self.base_Property.oclIsDefined() **implies** self.base_Property.oclContainer().oclIsTypeOf(uml::Stereotype)}
case : Package	p.type = Package
case : Parameter	p.type = Parameter
case : Type	p.type = Type **add** Constraint {self.base_Type.oclIsDefined() **implies** Set{uml::Stereotype,uml::Class,uml::Enumeration,uml::Interface} -> includes(self.base_Type.oclType())}
case : none	-- no Property p needed
case : all	p.type = {Class, Enumeration, Interface, Operation, Package, Parameter, Property, Stereotype}
AnnotationElementType a	**add** Property p
a.name	p.name = a.name
a.default	p.default = a.default
switch(a.modifier)	
case : public	p.visibility = public
case : abstract	-- no corresponding feature
case : annotation an	**apply** Stereotype for an.type **to** p
switch(a.type)	
case : PrimitiveType	p.type = uml::PrimitiveType **for** a.type
case : Class	p.type = uml::Class
case : Class<T>	p.type = uml::Class **apply** javaProfile::JGenericType Stereotype **to** p
case : EnumType	p.type = uml::Enumeration
case : AnnotationType	p.type = uml::Stereotype
case : ArrayType	-- infer lower and upper bound multiplicities

AnnotationType → Stereotype. The mapping presented in the upper part of Table 1 serves as a basis to generate a `Stereotype` from an `AnnotationType`. Thereby, not only its signature needs to be considered but also Java's `Target` meta-annotation. It determines the set of code elements an annotation type is applicable to. The `name` and, with two exceptions, the defined `modifiers` of an `AnnotationType` can straightforwardly be mapped to UML. First, the `abstract` modifier would lead to `Stereotypes` that cannot be instantiated if directly mapped. The problem is caused by Java's language definition. Although the `abstract` modifier is supported to facilitate one common type declaration production rule, it does not restrict the application of `AnnotationTypes`. To ensure the same behavior on the UML level, we never declare a `Stereotype` to be abstract. Second, because annotations are considered as modifiers, it needs to be ensured that the `Target` annotation is properly treated. In fact, the defined set of Java `ElementTypes` determines the required set of `Extensions` to UML meta-classes that specify the application context of the stereotypes.

Generally, most Java `ElementTypes` correspond well to one or more UML meta-classes. Still, constraints are required for some `ElementTypes` to precisely restrict the application scope of the generated `Stereotype` according to their intention. UML does not explicitly support a constructor meta-class. The workaround is to map the `Constructor` to `Operation` and introduce a constraint that emulates the naming convention for constructors in Java. Note that annotation types can have several target types. Thus, before validating the OCL constraint, we have to check which target is actually used in the application. Similarly, the mapping of Java methods to UML requires a constraint as a declared method of an `AnnotationType`, i.e., `Annotation-TypeElement`, is mapped to a `Property` rather than an `Operation` in UML. This is because such methods do not provide a custom realization but merely return their assigned value when they get called. `Properties` in UML provide exactly this behavior. Hence, the constraint ensures that stereotypes generated from annotation types that target Java methods are applicable also to `Property` if they are contained by a Stereotype. Finally, we use a constraint to overcome the heterogeneity of Java's and UML's scope of `Type`. Consequently, stereotypes that extend `Type` are constrained to those elements that correspond to the set of elements generalized by Java's `Type`: `AnnotationType`, `Class`, `Enumeration` and `Interface`. The clear benefit of this approach is a smaller number of generated extension relationships between stereotypes and meta-classes in the profile.

AnnotationTypeElement → Property. `AnnotationTypeElements` are mapped to `Properties` as depicted in the lower part of Table 1. Except for the fact that UML properties cannot be defined as abstract, `AnnotationTypeElements` straightforwardly correspond to `Properties`. As `AnnotationTypes` in Java cannot explicitly inherit from super-annotations, the abstract modifier is rarely used in practice. To fully support all return types of `AnnotationTypeElements`, we introduce a `Stereotype` to properly address the fact that `java.lang.Class` provides generic capabilities, which is not the case for UML's meta-class `Class`. Hence, we apply our custom `JGenericType` stereotype to properties with return type `Class<T>`.

4   Implementation and Collected Profiles

To show the feasibility of *JUMP*, we implemented a prototype based on the Eclipse ecosystem. We developed three transformation chains— *JavaCode2UMLProfile*, *Java-Code2ProfiledUML*, and *ProfiledUML2JavaCode*—to realize *JUMP* and the RE and FE scenarios introduced in Figure 1. For injecting *Java Code*, we employed MoDisco [9]. Hence, *JUMP* can be considered as a model discoverer to extract UML profiles from Java libraries. To realize the FE scenario, we extended the Java-based transformer provided by Obeo Network[2]. The prototype and the collection of profiles that we have generated for the evaluation of *JUMP* is available at the *UML-Profile-Store* [43]. It covers 20 profiles, comprising in total over 700 stereotypes. To share these profiles with existing community portals, we submitted them also to ReMoDD [16].

5   Evaluation

The evaluation of *JUMP* is twofold. First, we compare it with existing modeling tools regarding their representational capabilities for dealing with the declaration and application of Java annotation types. Second, we compare UML profiles automatically generated by *JUMP* with UML profiles delivered by IBM's Rational Software Architect. Thereby, our focus is on estimating the quality of the generated UML profiles.

5.1   Methodological Evaluation

As several commercial and open-source modeling tools provide modeling capabilities for UML and the Java platform, the aim of this study is to investigate on their methods for dealing with the application and declaration of annotations. For that reason, we set the focus on a Java-based reverse-engineering example that includes annotations and their declarations. We aim to answer the following research question ($RQ1$).

RQ1: What are the methods of current modeling tools to represent Java annotation types and their applications in UML and what are the practical implications?

To answer $RQ1$, we define a set of comparison criteria that mainly address (i) how the conceptual mapping between Java and UML for annotations is achieved by current modeling tools and (ii) the generative capabilities of these tools regarding profiles. Based on the defined criteria, we evaluate six representative modeling tools and JUMP.

Comparison Criteria. As there are different approaches on how annotation types and their applications are represented at the modeling level, the first and the second comparison criteria ($CC1$ and $CC2$) refer exactly to these extensional capabilities. The third criterion ($CC3$) refers to the support of generative capabilities regarding profiles.

−$CC1$: How are Java annotations applied to UML models?

−$CC2$: How are Java annotation type declarations represented in UML?

−$CC3$: Is the generation of UML profiles from Java code supported?

Selected Tools. We selected six major industrial modeling tools that claim to support reverse engineering capabilities for Java and UML, as summarized in Table 2.

Evaluation Procedure. We defined a simple reference application [43] that declares

---

[2] http://marketplace.eclipse.org/content/uml-java-generator

a Java class to which we applied an annotation type from an external library. For the purpose of importing the application, we activated the offered functionality of the modeling tools required for a reverse-engineering scenario from Java to UML. While some of the modeling tools are delivered with standard configurations, other modeling tools allow configurations to change the reverse-engineering capabilities by using specific wizards. Moreover, some modeling tools go one step further and allow modifications on the transformation scripts used for the import of Java code. We evaluated the capabilities of the modeling tools offered in the standard settings and explored the different wizard configurations if supported, but we restrained from modifying transformation scripts.

Results. The results of our comparison are summarized in Table 2. Regarding the mapping between Java annotations and UML, we identified that the investigated modeling tools apply one of three significantly different approaches: (i) annotations are considered as a *built-in* feature of the modeling tool, (ii) a *generic* profile for Java is provided, which enables capturing annotations and their type declarations, and (iii) profiles are offered, which are *specific* to a Java library or even an application with custom annotation type declarations. Modeling tools with built-in support for annotations allow their application to arbitrary elements and so to UML elements. Clearly, such an approach facilitates to capture Java annotations, though the type declaration of the annotation in terms of a UML element and its application are not connected. The genericity of this approach, which goes beyond UML models, is clearly one reason for such a behavior. Providing a generic profile for Java means that the modeling tool emulates the representational capabilities of Java, which includes annotations. Although with this approach, the connection of annotation type declarations and their applications can be ensured, the native support of UML for annotating elements with stereotypes is still neglected. However, explicitly defined stereotypes for declared annotation types facilitate their reuse in a UML standard-compliant way and allow model operations to directly exploit them. With specific profiles for Java annotation types, these drawbacks can be overcome. While all evaluated modeling tools provide support for generating profiled UML class diagrams, none of them is capable of generating profiles from Java code.

Table 2. Comparison Results

Modeling Tool			Mapping (Java -> UML)		UML Profile Generation
Name	Version	Availability	Annotation Application	Annotation Declaration	
Visual Paradigm www.visual-paradigm.com	10.2	commercial free community edition	Built-in Tool Feature	Class	-
Rational Software Architect www.ibm.com/developerworks/rational/products/rsa	8.5.1	commerical free for academice use	Specific Profiles	Stereotype	-
Magic Draw www.nomagic.com	17.0.4	commerical free trial version	Generic Java Profile	Interface	-
Enterprise Architect www.sparxsystems.com	9.3	commerical free for academice use	Built-in Tool Feature	Interface	-
Altova UML www.altova.com/umodel.html	2013	commerical free for academice use	Generic Java Profile	Interface	-
ArgoUML argouml.tigris.org	0.34	open-source	Generic Java Profile	Interface	-
JUMP	1.0.0	open-source	Specific Profiles	Stereotype	+

5.2 Quality Evaluation

As UML profiles are already offered by current modeling tools, the aim of this study is to investigate their quality in comparison with profiles automatically generated by *JUMP*. For that reason, we conducted a positivist case study [32] based on real-world Java libraries to evaluate the commonalities and differences between generated profiles and profiles used in practice by following the guidelines of Roneson and Hörst [41]. In this study, we aim to answer the following research question ($RQ2$).

$RQ2$: *How is the quality of UML profiles automatically generated from annotation-based Java libraries compared to UML profiles used in practice?*

To answer $RQ2$, we define the requirements of the case study, briefly mention the used Java libraries, and specify the measures based on which the comparison is conducted. Then, we discuss the results of our study not only from a syntactic perspective, but also from a semantic one. The rationale behind this two-step approach is that even though a syntactical matching process for comparing the profiles provides already valuable results, some interesting correspondences may still be uncovered because of potential syntactical and structural heterogeneities [46] between the compared profiles and the conservative matching strategy applied for the syntactical comparison.

Case-Study Design. To conduct this study, the source code of Java libraries that exploit annotations is required. Furthermore, we require existing profiles that claim to support the selected Java libraries at the modeling level. To accomplish an appropriate coverage of different scenarios, the selected Java libraries ideally comprise different intrinsic properties with respect to the design complexity and exploited language elements. Unfortunately, profiles specific to Java libraries in reasonable quality are rarely available. Consequently, in the process of selecting the Java libraries for this study, we were also confronted with the actual offering of modeling tools. IBM's Rational Software Architect (RSA) is obviously close to *JUMP* and offers several profiles of well-known Java libraries mainly for code generation purposes. Thus, we conducted this study by relying on profiles of RSA in version 8.5.1. We selected four established Java libraries for which the source code is available and a corresponding RSA profile in the same major version is offered: Java Persistence API (JPA), Enterprise Java Beans (EJB), Struts and Hibernate. RSA offers them in a UML standard-compliant way. Consequently, we could directly compare them without an intermediate conversion step. All the case-study data including the Java libraries and the profiles are available at our project web site [43].

Case-Study Measures. The measures used in the case study are based on model comparison techniques [29]. Thus, we are interested in equivalent elements that reside in our generated profiles and in the RSA profiles, elements that reside in both solutions but still show differences in their features, and elements that are only available in one of the compared solutions. The measures for estimating the quality of the generated profiles are collected in a two-step matching process. While the first step automatically collects measures based on syntactic model comparison, the second step relies on manually processing differences produced in the first step to deal with semantic aspects.

In the syntactic model comparison, we compute the following measures for certain model elements. To determine element correspondences, we employ as matching heuristic name equivalence, i.e., only if two elements have completely the same name, they are considered to be corresponding. If an element has no name, such as the `Extension` relationship, it is considered that the elements are corresponding if their source and target elements correspond. Finally, fine grained comparison of the feature values for the given elements is performed. Regarding model elements, we set the focus on (i) `Stereotypes` that are common to both and unique either to *JUMP* or RSA, (ii) differences regarding the `Extensions` of common `Stereotypes`, and (iii) differences regarding the `Properties` such `Stereotypes` cover.

In the semantic model comparison, we take the syntactical differences as input and aim at finding additional correspondences between elements which are hardly explored by a pure syntactic comparison due to the conservative matching strategy. We investigate unmatched elements, especially stereotypes, in our generated profiles and in the RSA profiles, and reason about possible element correspondences beyond String equivalences. Finally, in the semantic processing, we further evaluate the correspondences found in the first phase due to the potential syntactical and structural heterogeneities.

Results. We now present the results of applying *JUMP* to the four selected Java libraries and compare them to the profiles offered by RSA. The full results are also available at our project web site [43]. The absolute number of generated stereotypes by *JUMP* and the provided ones by RSA are depicted in Figure 5a. Figure 5b summarizes (i) the number of stereotypes generated by *JUMP* but not covered by the RSA profiles, (ii) the number of stereotypes that are exclusively covered by the RSA profiles, and (iii) the number of stereotypes that are common to both. These results include correspondences between stereotypes detected throughout the syntactic and semantic comparison. For instance, the EJB profile of RSA covers stereotypes that refer to the `@Local` and `@Remote` annotations of the EJB library, though their signature

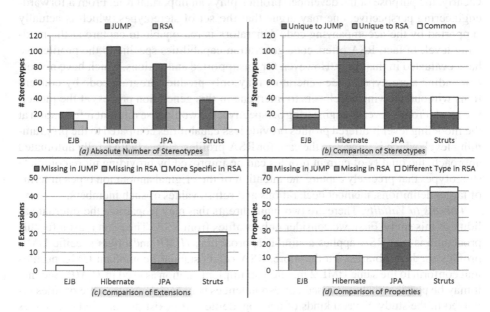

Fig. 5. Results of Quality Evaluation

additionally contains the substring "`Interface`". Another example refers to the class `QueryHint` in the JPA profile of RSA, which is in fact an annotation type in the JPA library. In our solution, the `QueryHint` is represented by a stereotype even though it is also valid to use a class instead, because the `QueryHint` can not actually be applied, but can rather only be used inside of another annotation. Although some stereotypes in the set of common ones show differences regarding the meta-classes they extend, we granted them to be equal if the extended meta-classes are related by a generalization relationship. We encountered this case in the EJB and the JPA library with respect to extensions of the meta-classes `Type` and `Class`. Stereotypes generated by *JUMP* extend the more general meta-class `Type` because the scope of Java's element type `Type` also covers `Enumeration`, `Interface` and `AnnotationType` in addition to `Class`.

The comparison regarding extensions of stereotypes common to both *JUMP* and RSA is summarized in Figure 5c. In a few cases, the RSA profiles comprise extensions to the UML meta-class `Association` to allow stereotypes on associations between elements rather than on properties contained by associations. Although both modeling variants are valid, we adhere to the second one as it is more accurate w.r.t. the target specifications of the original annotation type declarations.

Finally, in Figure 5d, the differences regarding the properties of common stereotypes are presented. Except for the JPA profile, we cover all stereotype properties of the RSA profiles. Consequently, our profiles are more complete. The main reason for missing properties in our JPA profile seems to be that RSA provides additional properties for code generation purposes, but these properties are not covered by the JPA library.

Discussion. In this study, we have demonstrated that automatically generated UML profiles from Java libraries comprise a more comprehensive set of stereotypes and features compared to profiles used in practice for the purpose of supporting such libraries. Clearly, the purpose of the developed profiles plays an important role. From a forward-engineering perspective, one may argue that the set of stereotypes, which is actually supported by the accompanying code generators is reasonable to capture at the modeling level. In fact, RSA offers code generation capabilities specific to the profiles we have evaluated in this study. However, for unsupported annotations, which have no corresponding stereotypes, code generators may only produce program code by conventions without allowing developers to intervene in this generation process at the modeling level. From a reverse-engineering perspective, we would lose relevant information at the modeling level if offered profiles provide less capabilities compared to the programming level, which is, however, the case for RSA profiles. Hence, with a fully automated approach, the quality of current profiles can be improved by providing more complete stereotypes that precisely capture the intention of the original annotation types in terms of target definitions, member declarations and return values of such members.

Threats to Validity. There are two main threats that may jeopardize the internal validity of this study. First, we consider only profiles from RSA. The main reason for this procedure is that RSA applies a similar approach as *JUMP* and offers specific UML profiles for Java libraries. Furthermore, RSA offers standard-compliant UML profiles that conform to the same UML 2 metamodel implementation as used in *JUMP*. Second, it may be possible that we missed correspondences between elements of the profiles involved in the study. Several kinds of heterogeneities [46] exist that are real challenges for model matching algorithms and, thus, may affect the results of our study. However, by applying a two-step matching process which includes a syntactic as well as semantic comparison phase, we tried to minimize the possibility of missing correspondences as a result of different naming conventions and modeling styles. While in the first phase we used a quite conservative matching strategy to avoid false positives, we applied a rather liberal strategy in the second phase to avoid losing potential correspondences.

Concerning external validity, *JUMP* sets the focus on Java annotations. Many libraries embrace them and real-world cases provide validity for annotated Java code [39]. However, we cannot claim any results outside of Java.

6   Related Work

We investigated three lines of research: (i) mappings between Java and UML, (ii) generation of UML profiles and (iii) metamodel generation from programming libraries.

Mapping Java and UML. The elaboration on the mapping between Java and UML has a long tradition in software engineering research [15, 23, 28, 33]. Round-trip engineering for UML and Java has been extensively studied in the context of the development of FUJABA [33]. One particular concept of UML that received much attention in the context of Java code generation is the association concept [2, 20, 21]. However, none of these mentioned approaches consider the transformation of annotation types and their applications from Java to UML. The only exception is the mTurnpike approach [44] that considers Java annotations at the modeling level. Thereby, round-trip transformations between UML models and Java code are realized by considering stereotypes and annotations in the transformations. In contrast, *JUMP* sets the focus on the automated generation of UML profiles that facilitate round-trip transformations or transformations in general. Besides academic efforts, today's modeling tools support the transformation of Java code to UML models, and vice versa. Their current capabilities and limitations w.r.t. *JUMP* are discussed in Section 5.1.

Generating UML Profiles. The only area we are aware of approaches that deal with the automated generation of profiles, is concerned with bridging the gap between MOF-based metamodels and UML's profile mechanism, which is also related to the discussion of an external DSMLs vs. internal DSMLs in UML. Several papers discuss the pros and cons of these approaches(e.g., [42]) and their combination (e.g., [45]). The visualization of domain-specific models in UML with profiles is discussed in [22]. Abouzahra *et al.* [1] present an approach for interoperability of UML models and DSML models based on mappings between the DSML metamodel and the UML profile. Brucker and Doser [8] go one step further and propose an approach for extending a DSML metamodel for deriving model transformations able to transform DSML models into UML models that are automatically annotated with stereotypes. A related approach is presented in [47], where mappings between the UML metamodel and a DSML metamodel are defined and processed to generate UML profiles for the given DSMLs.

Generating Metamodels. To the best of our knowledge, there is only one automated approach for generating modeling languages from programming libraries—all other automated approaches that deal with exploring libraries, such as [9], set their focus on the generation of domain models rather than a language. API2MoL [11] deals with generating metamodels based on Ecore [14] from Java APIs as well as models conforming to the generated metamodels for Java objects instantiated from the Java APIs, and vice versa. As a result, an external Domain-Specific Modeling Language (DSML) is generated from a Java API. While the general idea and motivation of the API2MoL approach is comparable to *JUMP*, there is a significant difference on how the DSML is realized. *JUMP* targets UML modelers that are familiar with UML class diagrams and generates internal DSMLs by exploiting the language-inherent extension mechanism of UML, i.e., *UML Profiles*. Furthermore, annotations are not explicitly considered in the metamodel generation process of API2MoL. One possible reason for neglecting them is that standard versions of current meta-modeling languages, such as Ecore, do not support language-inherent extension mechanisms out-of-the-box [31]. Antkiewicz *et al.* [3] present a methodology for creating framework-specific modeling languages. While we aim for an automated approach, Antkiewicz *et al.* use a manual one to create the metamodel and the transformations between model instances and instantiated objects of the frameworks. Again, annotations are not captured by the created languages. When considering the term modeling language in a broader scope, research of related fields consider ontologies as a kind of (meta-)model [19]. In particular, research on ontology extraction from different artifacts is commonly subsumed under the term *ontology learning* [13]. We are aware of only one approach for extracting ontologies from APIs [40], which neglects, however, also annotations.

To summarize, *JUMP* is—to the best of our knowledge—the first approach to generate standard-compliant UML profiles from Java libraries that exploit annotations.

7   Conclusion

With *JUMP*, we proposed an approach to close the gap between programming and modeling concerning annotation mechanisms. Thereby, we set the focus on the "Java2UML" case and demonstrated the feasibility of *JUMP* by generating high-quality UML profiles for numerous Java libraries and applied them in practical reverse-engineering and forward-engineering scenarios. The results gained by our evaluation seem promising. Still, a number of future challenges remain to further integrate programming and modeling. Some interesting differences between Java annotations and UML profiles remain to be explored. On the UML side, inheritance between stereotypes is possible, a concept that is not supported by Java for annotation types. Thus, the design quality of automatically generated UML profiles can be enhanced by exploiting inheritance. On the Java side, retention policies determine at which stages annotations are accessible. UML stereotypes are considered only at design-time. Therefore, an interesting line of future work is to support stereotype applications also during run-time, which becomes especially interesting for executable models, a research area that is currently experiencing its renaissance by the emergence of the FUML standard [34]. Furthermore, we plan to study the support of annotations in other programming languages, e.g., by investigating attributes in C# and decorators in Python, and how these concepts corresponds to UML profiles. Finally, as we set the focus in this work to platform-specific profiles, we plan to extend this scope to profiles that capture annotations independent of platforms, thereby shifting their application to a more conceptual level.

References

1. Abouzahra, A., Bézivin, J., Fabro, M.D.D., Jouault, F.: A Practical Approach to Bridging Domain Specific Languages with UML profiles. In: Proc. Workshop on Best Practices for Model Driven Software Development, pp. 1–8 (2005)
2. Akehurst, D.H., Howells, W.G.J., McDonald-Maier, K.D.: Implementing Associations: UML 2.0 to Java 5. SoSyM 6(1), 3–35 (2007)
3. Antkiewicz, M., Czarnecki, K., Stephan, M.: Engineering of Framework-Specific Modeling Languages. TSE 35(6), 795–824 (2009)
4. Bergmayr, A., Bruneliere, H., Cánovas, J., Gorroñogoitia, J., Kousiouris, G., Kyriazis, D., Langer, P., Menychtas, A., Orue-Echevarria, L., Pezuela, C., Wimmer, M.: Migrating Legacy Software to the Cloud with ARTIST. In: Proc. CSMR, pp. 465–468 (2013)
5. Bergmayr, A., Wimmer, M.: Generating Metamodels from Grammars by Chaining Translational and By-Example Techniques. In: Proc. MDEBE, pp. 22–31 (2013)
6. Brambilla, M., Cabot, J., Wimmer, M.: Model-Driven Software Engineering in Practice. Morgan & Claypool Publishers (2012)
7. Briand, L.C., Labiche, Y., Leduc, J.: Toward the Reverse Engineering of UML Sequence Diagrams for Distributed Java Software. TSE 32(9), 642–663 (2006)
8. Brucker, A.D., Doser, J.: Metamodel-based UML Notations for Domain-specific Languages. In: Proc. ATEM, pp. 1–15 (2007)
9. Bruneliere, H., Cabot, J., Jouault, F., Madiot, F.: MoDisco: A Generic and Extensible Framework for Model Driven Reverse Engineering. In: Proc. ASE, pp. 173–174 (2010)
10. Canfora, G., Di Penta, M., Cerulo, L.: Achievements and Challenges in Software Reverse Engineering. CACM 54(4), 142–151 (2011)
11. Cánovas, J., Jouault, F., Cabot, J., Molina, J.G.: API2MoL: Automating the Building of Bridges between APIs and Model-Driven Engineering. Information & Software Technology 54(3), 257–273 (2012)
12. Czarnecki, K., Helsen, S.: Feature-based Survey of Model Transformation Approaches. IBM Systems Journal 45(3), 621–646 (2006)
13. Drumond, L., Girardi, R.: A Survey of Ontology Learning Procedures. In: Proc. WONTO, pp. 1–12 (2008)
14. Eclipse Foundation: Eclipse Modeling Framework, EMF (2014), https://www.eclipse.org/modeling/emf
15. Engels, G., Hücking, R., Sauer, S., Wagner, A.: UML Collaboration Diagrams and their Transformation to Java. In: France, R.B. (ed.) UML 1999. LNCS, vol. 1723, pp. 473–488. Springer, Heidelberg (1999)
16. France, R.B., Bieman, J., Cheng, B.H.C.: Repository for Model Driven Development (ReMoDD). In: Kühne, T. (ed.) MoDELS 2006 Workshops. LNCS, vol. 4364, pp. 311–317. Springer, Heidelberg (2007)
17. France, R.B., Rumpe, B.: The Evolution of Modeling Research Challenges. SoSyM 12(2), 223–225 (2013)
18. Fuentes-Fernández, L., Vallecillo, A.: An Introduction to UML Profiles. Europ. Journal for the Informatics Professional 5(2), 5–13 (2004)
19. Gasevic, D., Djuric, D., Devedzic, V.: Model Driven Engineering and Ontology Development, 2nd edn. Springer (2009)
20. Génova, G., del Castillo, C.R., Lloréns, J.: Mapping UML Associations into Java Code. JOT 2(5), 135–162 (2003)
21. Gessenharter, D.: Mapping the UML2 Semantics of Associations to a Java Code Generation Model. In: Czarnecki, K., Ober, I., Bruel, J.-M., Uhl, A., Völter, M. (eds.) MODELS 2008. LNCS, vol. 5301, pp. 813–827. Springer, Heidelberg (2008)
22. Graaf, B., van Deursen, A.: Visualisation of Domain-Specific Modelling Languages Using UML. In: Proc. ECBS, pp. 586–595 (2007)

23. Harrison, W., Barton, C., Raghavachari, M.: Mapping UML Designs to Java. In: Proc. OOP-SLA, pp. 178–187 (2000)

24. Heidenreich, F., Johannes, J., Seifert, M., Wende, C.: Closing the Gap between Modelling and Java. In: van den Brand, M., Gašević, D., Gray, J. (eds.) SLE 2009. LNCS, vol. 5969, pp. 374–383. Springer, Heidelberg (2010)

25. Jézéquel, J.M., Combemale, B., Derrien, S., Guy, C., Rajopadhye, S.: Bridging the Chasm between MDE and the World of Compilation. SoSym 11(4), 581–597 (2012)

26. Kazman, R., Woods, S.G., Carrière, S.J.: Requirements for Integrating Software Architecture and Reengineering Models: CORUM II. In: Proc. WCRE, pp. 154–163 (1998)

27. Klint, P., Lämmel, R., Verhoef, C.: Toward an Engineering Discipline for Grammarware. ACM Trans. Softw. Eng. Methodol. 14(3), 331–380 (2005)

28. Kollman, R., Selonen, P., Stroulia, E., Systä, T., Zündorf, A.: A Study on the Current State of the Art in Tool-Supported UML-Based Static Reverse Engineering. In: Proc. WCRE, pp. 22–32 (2002)

29. Kolovos, D., Di Ruscio, D., Pierantonio, A., Paige, R.: Different Models for Model Matching: An Analysis of Approaches to Support Model Differencing. In: Proc. CVSM, pp. 1–6 (2009)

30. Kurtev, I., Bézivin, J., Akşit, M.: Technological Spaces: An Initial Appraisal. In: Proc. CoopIS, pp. 1–6 (2002)

31. Langer, P., Wieland, K., Wimmer, M., Cabot, J.: EMF Profiles: A Lightweight Extension Approach for EMF Models. JOT 11(1), 1–29 (2012)

32. Lee, A.: A Scientific Methodology for MIS Case Studies. MIS Quarterly pp. 33–50 (1989)

33. Nickel, U., Niere, J., Zündorf, A.: The FUJABA Environment. In: Proc. ICSE, pp. 742–745 (2000)

34. OMG: FUML (2011), http://www.omg.org/spec/FUML/1.0

35. OMG: MOF (2011), http://www.omg.org/spec/MOF

36. OMG: Catalog of UML Profile Specifications (2014), http://www.omg.org/spec

37. Oracle: JLS7 (2013), http://docs.oracle.com/javase/specs

38. Pardillo, J.: A Systematic Review on the Definition of UML Profiles. In: Petriu, D.C., Rouquette, N., Haugen, Ø. (eds.) MODELS 2010, Part I. LNCS, vol. 6394, pp. 407–422. Springer, Heidelberg (2010)

39. Parnin, C., Bird, C., Murphy-Hill, E.: Adoption and Use of Java Generics. Empirical Software Engineering 18(6), 1–43 (2012)

40. Ratiu, D., Feilkas, M., Jurjens, J.: Extracting Domain Ontologies from Domain Specific APIs. In: Proc. CSMR, pp. 203–212 (2008)

41. Runeson, P., Höst, M.: Guidelines for Conducting and Reporting Case Study Research in Software Engineering. Empirical Software Engineering 14(2), 131–164 (2009)

42. Selic, B.: The Less Well Known UML: A Short User Guide. In: Proc. SFM, pp. 1–20 (2012)

43. UML-Profile-Store: Project Web Site (2014),
http://code.google.com/a/eclipselabs.org/p/uml-profile-store

44. Wada, H., Suzuki, J.: Modeling Turnpike Frontend System: A Model-Driven Development Framework Leveraging UML Metamodeling and Attribute-Oriented Programming. In: Briand, L.C., Williams, C. (eds.) MoDELS 2005. LNCS, vol. 3713, pp. 584–600. Springer, Heidelberg (2005)

45. Weisemöller, I., Schürr, A.: A Comparison of Standard Compliant Ways to Define Domain Specific Languages. In: Giese, H. (ed.) MODELS 2008 Workshops. LNCS, vol. 5002, pp. 47–58. Springer, Heidelberg (2008)

46. Wimmer, M., Kappel, G., Kusel, A., Retschitzegger, W., Schoenboeck, J., Schwinger, W.: Towards an Expressivity Benchmark for Mappings based on a Systematic Classification of Heterogeneities. In: Proc. MDI, pp. 32–41 (2010)

47. Wimmer, M.: A Semi-Automatic Approach for Bridging DSMLs with UML. IJWIS 5(3), 372–404 (2009)

SIGMA: Scala Internal Domain-Specific Languages for Model Manipulations

Filip Křikava[1], Philippe Collet[2], and Robert B. France[3]

[1] University Lille 1 / LIFL Inria Lille,
Nord Europe, France
filip.krikava@inria.fr
[2] Université Nice Sophia Antipolis / I3S - CNRS UMR 7271,
06903 Sophia Antipolis, France
philippe.collet@unice.fr
[3] Colorado State University - Computer Science Department,
Fort Collins, CO 80523, USA
france@cs.colostate.edu

Abstract. Model manipulation environments automate model operations such as model consistency checking and model transformation. A number of external model manipulation *Domain-Specific Languages* (DSL) have been proposed, in particular for the *Eclipse Modeling Framework* (EMF). While their higher levels of abstraction result in gains in expressiveness over general-purpose languages, their limitations in versatility, performance, and tool support together with the need to learn new languages may significantly contribute to accidental complexities.

In this paper, we present SIGMA, a family of internal DSLs embedded in Scala for EMF model consistency checking, model-to-model and model-to-text transformations. It combines the benefits of external model manipulation DSLs with general-purpose programming taking full advantage of Scala versatility, performance and tool support. The DSLs are compared to the state-of-the-art Epsilon languages in non-trivial model manipulation tasks that resulted in 20% to 70% reduction in code size and significantly better performance.

1 Introduction

Model manipulation languages and tools provide support for automating model operations such as model consistency checking, and *model-to-model* (M2M) and *model-to-text* (M2T) transformations [41]. A number of different model manipulation technologies have been proposed, particularly within the *Eclipse Modeling Framework* (EMF) [43]. The EMF models can be manipulated directly in Java, however, a *General Purpose Programming Language* (GPL) such as Java does not conveniently express model manipulation concepts and the loss of abstraction can give rise to accidental complexities [40]. Therefore, a number of external *Domain-Specific Languages* (DSLs) for EMF model manipulation have been proposed, *e.g.*, the OMG standards including OCL [34] for navigating and expressing constraints on models, QVT [33] and MOFM2T [32] for model transformation; the Epsilon project [36] with an extensive family of model manipulation DSLs; Kermeta [31], a single, but more general imperative language for

J. Dingel et al. (Eds.): MODELS 2014, LNCS 8767, pp. 569–585, 2014.

all model manipulation tasks; and ATL [20], a M2M transformation language. External model manipulation DSLs provide language constructs that allow developers to manipulate models using higher-level abstractions. This should result in higher expressiveness and ease of use in comparison to GPLs [29].

However, there are several impediments to such approaches. Even for a simple model manipulation task users have to learn one or more new languages and tools, which may require considerable effort [11]. Users might feel limited by the more specific, but less versatile language constructs, by the language execution performance or by the provided support tools [18]. In most cases the languages build on a subset of OCL concepts for model navigation and model consistency checking. Despite that, there are well known inconsistencies, interoperability and reusability issues among these languages [22,23]. Finally, the large dependency stacks associated with these languages can make their integration into existing software projects rather challenging.

A notable exception is the Epsilon project, which alleviates some of these issues. Epsilon provides an extensive family of model management languages and tools such as *Epsilon Validation Language* (EVL) [24], *Epsilon Transformation Language* (ETL) [22], and *Epsilon Generation Language* (EGL) [38]. These task-specific languages are based on a common OCL-like expression language called EOL [23]. While this currently makes it one of the most complete language workbenches for model manipulations, we identify several shortcomings. EOL is a dynamically typed language, providing little compile time checking. Consequently, IDE features such as content assists, static checking or refactoring are rather basic in comparison to what is provided by the other approaches that use static typing. EOL lacks certain programming constructs that makes the code unnecessary lengthy in particular in the case of non-trivial model manipulations. Moreover, Epsilon DSLs are interpreted and their performance is an order of magnitude slower than the compiled languages, but they are also slower than the Eclipse implementation of the OMG stack [25]. As a result, these shortcomings also give rise to some accidental complexities, albeit of a different nature than those associated with GPLs.

These issues are not easy to alleviate. The need to provide a lot of GPL-like constructs together with the necessity of some level of Java interoperability make the external DSLs large and complex. Evolving and maintaining complex DSLs is known to be hard since it not only requires domain knowledge and language development expertise, but also involves significant language and tool engineering effort [29,13]. In this paper we propose an alternative internal DSL approach whereby model manipulation constructs are embedded into a GPL. The intent is to provide an approach that developers can use to implement many of the practical EMF model manipulations within a familiar environment with reduced learning overhead and improved usability.

An internal DSL leverages the constructs and tools of its host language. For this approach to be effective, the host GPL must be flexible enough to allow definition of domain-specific constructs. We thus use Scala [35], a statically typed object-oriented and functional programming language, to implement a family of internal DSLs, called SIGMA [28], for model consistency checking and model transformations. In this paper, our contribution is to evaluate the resulting DSLs, comparing their expressiveness and features to corresponding Epsilon DSLs in several non-trivial model manipulation tasks. We observe this results in 20% to 70% reduction in code size and significantly better performance.

The remainder of the paper is organized as follows. In Section 2 we give a quick overview of the SIGMA languages family. Section 3 develops the common infrastructure for model navigation and modification. This is used for model consistency checking described in Section 4, M2M transformations described in Section 5 and M2T transformations described in Section 6. In Section 7, we overview the current implementation and provide an evaluation of SIGMA. Finally Section 8 discusses related work and Section 9 concludes the paper.

2   SIGMA Overview

SIGMA is a family of internal DSLs for model manipulation that were created with the aim to alleviate some of the main limitations of the currently proposed approaches. It is thus not proposing new concepts in model manipulation languages, but instead providing the existing concepts with the following main requirements: (1) *Epsilon-like features and expressiveness*, (2) *competitive performance*, (3) *usable tool support*, (4) *simple testability with existing unit frameworks*, and (5) *simple integration into existing EMF projects*. We chose Epsilon since it represents the state-of-the-art model manipulation languages with proven features essential for usable model manipulation. Furthermore, it is also presented as an approach that addresses most of the shortcomings of the other external model manipulation DSLs (details in Kolovos et al. [22,24,23] and Rose et al. [38]).

SIGMA DSLs are embedded in Scala [35], a statically typed production-ready GPL that supports both object-oriented and functional style of programming. It uses type inference to combine static type safety with a *"look and feel"* close to dynamically typed languages. It is interoperable with Java and it has been designed to host internal DSLs [13]. Furthermore, it is supported by the major integrated development environments.

A typical way of embedding a shallow DSL into Scala is by designing a library that allows one to write fragments of code with domain-specific syntax. These fragments are woven within Scala own syntax so that it appears different [16]. Next to Scala flexible syntax (*e.g.* omitting semicolons and dots in method invocations, infix operator syntax for method calls, etc.), it has a number of features simplifying DSL embedding such as implicit type conversions allowing one to extend existing types with new methods, mixin-class composition (*i.e.* reusing a partial class definition in a new class) [35], and lifting static source information with implicit resolutions to customize error messages in terms of the domain-specific extensions using annotations [30]. Furthermore, Scala supports compile-time meta-programming allowing for code self-optimization and to reduce boilerplate code generation.

Figure 1 depicts the general organization of the SIGMA DSLs. The use of EMF models in SIGMA is facilitated by a dedicated support layer that underneath uses the default EMF generated Java classes and the EMF API (implementation details are given in Section 7.1). This layer provides a convenient model

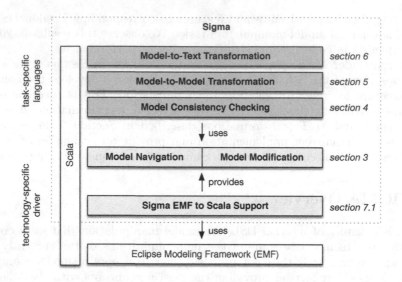

Fig. 1. Sigma EMF to Scala Support

navigation and modification support forming a common infrastructure for the task-specific internal DSLs. While currently SIGMA targets the EMF platform, other meta-modeling platforms could be used since the task-specific languages are technology agnostic (*cf.* Section 7.1).

In the following sections we detail the common infrastructure and the different task-specific DSLs. We deliberately skip some technical details about how certain DSL constructs are implemented. The complete examples with further documentation are available at the project web site [8]. For illustration purposes, in the following sections we consider a simplified *Object-Oriented* (OO) model (*cf.* companion web page [4]).

3   Common Infrastructure

Essentially, any model manipulation technique is based on a set of basic operations for model *navigation* (*e.g.* projecting information from models) and *modification* (*e.g.* changing model properties or elements) [23]. In this section we show their realization in SIGMA for EMF based models. Implementation details are discussed in Section 7.1.

Model Navigation. The model navigation support provides OCL-like expressions for convenient model querying. For example, retrieving names of all OO package elements stereotyped as singletons can be expressed using the following OCL query:

```
let singletons = pkg.ownedElements
  ->select(e | e.stereotypes->exists(s | s.name = 'singleton'))->collect(e | e.name)
```

In SIGMA, the very same query can be expressed almost identically to OCL:

```
val singletons = pkg.ownedElements
  .filter(e => e.stereotypes exists (s => s.name == "singleton")).map(e => e.name)
```

In both versions the `singletons` type is inferred from the expression.

While navigating models, one often need to filter the types of the objects to be kept during navigation. For example, selecting the operations of a package abstract classes corresponds to the following OCL expression:

```
pkg.ownedElements
  ->select(e | e.oclIsKindOf(Class) and e.oclAsType(Class).abstract = true)
  ->collect(e.oclAsType(Class).operations)
```

This is rather verbose with the recurring pattern of `oclIsKindOf`/`oclAsType`, which makes longer queries hard to read. Scala, on the other hand, provides support for pattern matching that can be used in combination with partial functions to obtain the following SIGMA code[1]:

```
pkg.ownedElements collect { case c: Class if c.abstract_ => c.operations }
```

In addition SIGMA can also prevent null pointer exceptions when navigating over potentially unset references and attributes (0..1 multiplicity). It wraps them into Scala `Option` type, a container explicitly representing an optional value, which consequently forces one to always check for the presence of the value.

Model Modification. The model modification support provides facilities for seamless creation, updates and removal of model elements. By design, the OCL does not have model modification capabilities, but in Epsilon for example, an OO singleton class can be created using the code in Listing 1.1. Using SIGMA the same model instance is created in Listing 1.2.

```
var cls = new Class;
cls.name = "MyClass";

var singleton = new Stereotype;
singleton.name = "singleton";
cls.stereotypes.add(singleton);

var op = new Operation;
op.name = "getInstance";
op.returnType = cls;
cls.operations.add(author);
```

Listing 1.1. EOL

```
val cls = Class(name = "MyClass")
val singleton = Stereotype(name = "singleton")
cls.stereotypes += singleton

val op = Operation(name = "getInstance",
    returnType = cls)
cls.features += op
```

Listing 1.2. SIGMA

These methods provide a convenient way to author complete EMF models directly in Scala. Additionally, SIGMA provides support for delayed initialization in the cases an element initialization should only happen after its containment, and for lazy resolution of contained references[2].

4 Model Consistency Checking

Model consistency checking provides facilities to capture structural constraints as state invariants and to check model instances against these constraints. In OCL or EVL, a structural constraint is a boolean query that determines whether a model element or a relation between model elements satisfies certain restrictions.

---

[1] The _ suffix to `abstract` is automatically added by the SIGMA EMF support since it is a Scala keyword.

[2] Technical details at `http://bit.ly/18javEY`

For example, in the OO model, an invariant may represent a restriction that within one package, there cannot be two classes having the same name. In SIGMA, such an invariant can be expressed as:

```
1  class ClassInvs extends ValidationContext with OOPackageSupport {
2    type Self = Class // context type
3
4    def invUniqueNamesWithinPackage =
5      self.pkg.ownedElements forall (e => e != self implies e.name != self.name)
6  }
```

Invariants are represented as regular Scala methods (line 4). They are organized into a validation context class (line 1) that specifies a context type (line 2), *i.e.*, the type of instances the invariants can be applied to. As in OCL, self represents the current instance that is being checked. The OOPackageSupport trait (*cf.* Section 7.1) mixes-in the Sigma EMF to Scala support for model navigation and modification (line 1). By organizing invariants as methods in classes we can simply reuse them through inheritance. Furthermore, it allows one to easily test invariants using any of the Java unit testing frameworks.

Listing 1.3 shows an extended OO class validation with additional features. A validation context class can narrow its applicability by providing a context guard (line 4). Invariant violation can distinguish different severity levels such as errors and warnings (line 10). In order to prevent meaningless evaluation of constraints whose dependencies are not satisfied, invariants can also have guards (line 7). Finally, a user can be provided with a feedback including a meaningful message (line 10), as well as means to repair the inconsistency with change suggestions over the affected model elements (line 11).

```
1  class ClassInvs extends ValidationContext with OOPackageSupport {
2    type Self = Class // context type
3
4    override def guard = self.annotations exists (_.name == "ignore") // context guard
5
6    def invUniqueNamesWithinPackage = guardedBy {
7      self satisfies invHasValidName // invariant guard
8    } check { // invariant body
9      self.pkg.ownedElements find (e => e != self && e.name == self.name) match {
10       case Some(c) => Error(s"Class $c has the name")
11         .quickFix("Rename '${self.name}' to '${self.name}_2'") { self.name += "_2" }
12       case None => Passed
13     }
14   }
15
16   def invHasValidName = // ...
17 }
```

Listing 1.3. Example of model consistency checking

5   Model-to-Model Transformations

M2M transformations provide necessary support for translating models into other models, essentially by mapping source model elements into corresponding target model elements. An imperative style of M2M transformation [15] is already supported thanks to the common infrastructure layer described in Section 3. On the other hand, the lower level of abstraction of the imperative transformation style leaves users to manually address issues such as orchestrating the transformation execution and resolving target elements against their source counterparts [22]. Therefore, inspired by ETL and ATL, we provide a dedicated internal DSL that combines the imperative features with declarative rule-based execution scheme into a hybrid M2M transformation language.

Transformation rules constitute the abstract syntax of the M2M transformation DSL. Similarly to ETL or ATL, a rule defines a source and a target element to which it transforms the source. It may optionally define additional targets, but there is always one primary source to the target relation. A rule can also be declared as *lazy* or *abstract*. Each non-lazy and non-abstract rule is executed for all the source elements it is applicable. Lazy rules have to be called explicitly. When a rule is executed, the transformation engine initially creates all the explicitly defined target elements and passes them to the rule that populates their content using arbitrary Scala code. Similarly to consistency checking constraints, transformation rules can optionally limit their applicability by defining a guard.

```scala
 1  class OO2DB extends M2M with OOPackageSupport with DBPackageSupport {
 2
 3    def ruleClass2Table(cls: Class, tab: Table, pk: Column) {
 4      // standard Scala
 5      tab.name = cls.name
 6      tab.columns += pk
 7      pk.name = "Id"
 8      pk.type_ = "Int"
 9
10      // SIGMA specific: target elements resolution
11      tab.columns ++= cls.properties.sTarget[Column]
12    }
13
14    def ruleProperty2Column(prop: Property, col: Column) = guardedBy {
15      !prop.multi // prevent transformation of multi-valued properties
16    } transform {
17      col.name = prop.name.toUpperCase
18      col.type_ = prop.type_.name
19    }
20  }
```

Listing 1.4. Example of M2M transformation

Listings 1.4 illustrates the internal DSL using the traditional example of OO model to database schema transformation[3]. A M2M transformation is a Scala class that extends the M2M base class with the generated package support traits for model navigation and modification (line 1). Transformation rules are represented by methods. For example, the ruleClass2Table denotes a rule that, for a given class, produces a table and a column (line 3). Additional target elements can be constructed within the rule body, but in such a case a developer is responsible for their proper containment.

During the M2M transformation, there is often the need to relate the target elements that have been already (or can be) transformed from source elements. For this purpose, SIGMA provides a set of operations. An example is shown on the line 6 where sTarget[Column] transforms class properties into columns. It does that by looking up a rule with *property-to-column* mapping, which in this case is the ruleProperty2Column rule. This operation can be applied both to

---

[3] While it is a worn example, it enables one to easily compare to similar examples provided by ETL and ATL *cf.* companion web page [4].

a single instance as well as to a collection of model elements. Similarly, SIGMA includes support for resolving source elements from their corresponding targets.

6   Model-to-Text Transformations

M2T transformations translate models into text by mapping source model elements into corresponding textual fragments. We focus on template-based approach whereby string patterns are extended with executable logic for code selection and iterative expansion [15]. This approach is used by all the major M2T transformation languages including EGL and MOFM2T. In model-driven software development, the aim is to synthesize a running system implementation and therefore our primary focus is on generating source code artifacts.

Unlike EGL and Acceleo, our internal DSL for M2T transformation is using the code-explicit form, *i.e.*, it is the output text instead of the transformation code that is escaped. This is one of the syntax limitations that cannot be easily overcome. On the other hand, from our experience, in non-trivial code generations, the quantity of text producing logic usually outweighs the text being produced. For the parts where there is more text than logic we rely on Scala multi-line string literals and string interpolations allowing one to embed variable references and expressions directly into strings.

```scala
1  class OO2Java extends M2T with OOPackageSupport {
2    type M2TSource = Class // input type for transformation
3
4    def execute = !s"public class ${root.name}" curlyIndent {
5      for (o <- root.operations) {
6        genOperation(o) // call to another template
7        !endl // extra new line
8      }
9    }
10
11   def genOperation(o: Operation) =
12     !s"public ${o.retType.name} ${o.name}()" curlyIndent {
13       !s"""
14       // TODO: should be implemented
15       throw new UnsupportedOperationException("${o.name}");
16       """
17     }
18 }
```

Listing 1.5. Example of M2T transformation

Listing 1.5 shows an example of OO class to Java transformation[4]. Following the same pattern, a M2T transformation is a Scala class extending from the M2T base class (line 1). Line 2 defines the type of model element, *i.e.*, the transformation source. A M2T transformation consists in a set of templates that are represented as methods (lines 4 and 11). The execute method is the entry point, which will be invoked when the transformation is executed. Usually, from there, a transformation is split and logically organized into smaller templates in order to increase modularity and readability.

The most common operation in a M2T transformation is a text output. A convenient way to output text in our DSL is through a unary ! (bang) operator

---

[4] Similar examples are provided for both EGL and Acceleo *cf.* companion web page [4].

that is provided on strings (*e.g.* line 4). The prefix s right before the string double quote denotes an interpolated string, which can include Scala expressions in a type-safe way.

An important aspect of any M2T transformation language is the template readability, *e.g.*, layout and indentation. The internal DSL maintains it through dedicated support for decorators, smart whitespace handling and relaxed new-lines. Decorators are nestable string operations that reformat a given block. For example, on line 4 we use curlyIndent decorator, that wraps its body into a pair of curly brackets and indent each line. Smart whitespace handler removes extra whitespace from multi-line strings that are there only for the template readability. For example the whitespaces prefixing the text on lines 14 and 15 will be discarded. Relaxed newlines loosen the necessity to output new line characters by doing it automatically after every text output. Both smart whitespace and newlines handlers are enabled by default, but can be turned off.

Finally, the DSL also allows one to fork new text sections. This makes it possible to output text into different locations at the same time. All sections are appropriately merged in the final text at the end of the transformation. This is useful for example for handling imports while generating Java code, as they can be resolved one-by-one during the model traversal.

7 Evaluation

Our aim is to propose an approach that improves the overall usability of model manipulations through DSLs. However, defining usability of a DSLs and associated tool support tend to be subjective, since it largely depends on the preferences and background of its users [41] and its improvement cannot be measured directly. Therefore, we structure the evaluation as follows. First we give details about the implementation and current applications. Next, we compare SIGMA DSLs to their corresponding Epsilon counterparts with regard to implementation effort measured in terms of code size, performance and features. Finally, we discuss the limitations of the approach and threats to validity.

7.1 Implementation

SIGMA is implemented as a Scala library which is available from the project website [8]. Its task-specific languages are all relying on a common infrastructure.

Common infrastructure. The common infrastructure aligns EMF generated Java classes with Scala to enable use of model navigation and modification notation similar to OCL and EOL. This involves (1) model navigation without *"get noise"* (*e.g.* getSuperPackage.getName becomes superPackage.name), and (2) promoting EMF collections to corresponding Scala collections to benefit from convenient first-order logic operations (*e.g.*, map, filter, collect) similar to OCL. Both issues are addressed by generating extension traits[5] that make EMF model elements interoperable with Scala. These traits implicitly extend all model classes with property accessors without the get prefix and convert

---

[5] Technical details at http://bit.ly/18javEY

EMF collections into the corresponding Scala ones. The conversion only happens at the interface level leaving the underlying data storage unchanged. In the same way, existing Scala types are extended with missing OCL operations (*e.g.* `implies`). These traits are either generated by provided SIGMA M2T transformation executed explicitly by a user or implicitly using the experimental Scala macro annotations [12].

Task-Specific Languages. The model consistency checking and M2M transformation have similar abstract syntax (*i.e.* constraints and rules) to EVL and ETL respectively, and their execution semantics is the same as defined in Epsilon. The M2T transformation is a purely imperative DSL and as such it does not contain any particular execution engine. All DSLs are implemented following the same pattern, *i.e.* organizing task-specific concerns into Scala classes that extend from a task-specific base class. The main constructs such as invariants, rules and templates are expressed as methods in order to foster reuse and extensibility.

7.2   Applications

SIGMA has been used in the SALTY project [7] to develop a modeling environment for developing self-adaptive software systems [27]. The main motivations were the shortcomings of OCL used for the initial implementation [26]. SIGMA has been also adopted by the Yourcast project [10] for M2T transformations replacing Velocity [1] and plain Java templates, gaining 20% reduction in code size, mainly thanks to more expressive model navigation and more compact text outputting constructs.

7.3   Code Comparison

In order to evaluate the overall usability of our approach we re-implemented larger Epsilon model manipulation tasks for each of the SIGMA DSLs. As suggested by the Epsilon community[6], we chose Eugenia [3] GMF Ecore constraints for model consistency checking, Unicaneer2sql [9] (an ER to relational model transformation) for M2M transformation, and Egldoc [2] (an Epsilon tool for generating Ecore documentation in HTML including Graphviz diagram) for M2T transformation. The Eugenia and Egldoc comes directly from Epsilon, which should guarantee certain quality of the source code. The complete implementation is available from the paper companion web page [4].

Table 1 summarizes the implementation effort in terms of *Source Lines of Code* (SLOC) for the three scenarios, for both Epsilon and SIGMA. Interpreting SLOC metrics is always problematic. The issue of what is the right level of *"verbosity"* in a language is complex and should not be reduced naively to just counting SLOC. Our assumption, however, is that usability is not achieved by having fewer lines of code, but instead, by having more expressive and concise code, which is beneficial to writers as well as to readers. On the other hand, code bloat resulting from code duplication and from lack of constructs that enable the building of more concise but expressive statements, is not desirable.

---

[6] http://www.eclipse.org/forums/index.php?t=rview&goto=1235103

Table 1. SLOC comparison

Scenario	Epsilon	SIGMA	difference
Model consistency checking	364 EVL	286	22%
M2M transformation	733 ETL	389	47%
M2T transformation	1400 EGL	412	70%

Most of the code reduction comes from the fact that Scala contains more general programming constructs than EOL. In particular, pattern matching and inheritance helped to reduce many of the code duplications. In the case of model consistency checking, the code reduction is the least significant one since SIGMA contains the same constraints constructs as EVL and the invariant expressions were mostly simple first-order logic queries. The EVL code is therefore almost identical to the SIGMA one and the only reduction was in the EOL helper methods. They can be expressed more concisely in Scala primarily thanks to pattern matching.

The case of M2M transformation led to a similar situation. SIGMA supports the same M2M transformation rules and thus the ETL code is very close to the SIGMA one. However, the M2M transformation involved a lot of imperative EOL code which could be reduced by using more expressive Scala statements. Furthermore, about 15% of the transformation generates text for which we could use SIGMA M2T constructs reducing the code even further.

The M2T transformation scenario involved generating both HTML code and Graphviz code. Generally, code-explicit forms of M2T transformation are not particularly suitable for generating HTML code since in this case the quantity of text outweighs the text producing logic. However, despite this, the code has been reduced by 70%. The main reason is that, by the use of inheritance, a lot of code duplication present in the EGL templates was avoided.

We do not provide a comparison of the coding time. First we do not have the measures of the Epsilon versions. Second it is always easier to port an existing code to a new language than to write it from scratch. However, we expect some strong points of the SIGMA DSLs to reduce coding time. Static type safety prevents runtime typing errors. The highly usable tool support provided by the Scala IDE [5] with a code completion and a debugger and the ability to easily run and test the transformations should facilitate development.

7.4   Performance Comparison

The performance of SIGMA is determined by the host language one and the overhead of the SIGMA API. SIGMA compiles directly into Java byte-code and thus it significantly outperforms Epsilon and other interpreted DSLs. For example, generating QVT meta-model (159 classifiers) documentation using Egldoc takes on average 8 times more time than using the SIGMA version.

However one of the concerns is related to the extensive use of implicit type conversions and other Scala constructs that might have negative performance impact. Therefore, as a part of the performance evaluation, we have implemented the same M2T transformation in SIGMA and the related M2T languages[7]. In addition, we have also implemented it in pure Java and Scala with no additional libraries. The Java version is used as a performance baseline. The Scala version is used to measure the overhead of Scala in comparison to Java and the performance penalty caused by SIGMA. The implementation in the other languages aims at evaluating our requirement of competitive performance. The M2T transformation has been chosen because (1) it uses many Scala constructs that might cause performance issues (*e.g.*, implicit conversions, string interpolation), (2) M2T transformation is one of the most often used model manipulation tasks [21], and (3) the implementation in the other languages was straightforward, limiting the possibility of misusing some features. As a concrete transformation we chose our simple OO model to Java transformation, since nearly all the listed languages provide an example that is based on it. Table 2 shows the median of 20 consecutive runs for two different model sizes, (A) corresponds to 250 classes with 50 methods and properties each, while (B) is 500 classes with 100 methods and properties each.

Table 2. Performance of different M2T languages normalized to Java version

Scenario	Java	SIGMA	EGL	Acceleo	Xtend	Kermeta	Scala
A	1.0	1.0	18.6	11.9	0.9	1.0	0.9
B	1.0	1.8	48.1	16.4	1.0	1.0	1.0

As expected, the performance of SIGMA together with the other compiled languages is close to Java, while the interpreted ones are an order of magnitude higher (also their memory footprint is double). The decrease in SIGMA performance in the case of the larger model is caused by the whitespace handling decorator. Every appended string is checked for whitespaces to be removed, and its complexity increases with the indent level. Without this decorator, the performance is again close to Java (A: 0.9, B: 1.0).

7.5   Evaluation of Requirements

In the previous section we evaluated the competitive performance requirement. The following is the evaluation of the other requirements identified in Section 2:
(1) *Epsilon-like features and expressiveness.* In Table 3, we evaluate the requirement stating that our DSL should contain similar features as in Epsilon languages, *i.e.* EOL, EVL, ETL and EGL. The listed Epsilon features are taken from the Epsilon website [6].
(2) *Usable tool support.* One of the advantages of an internal DSL is that it can directly reuse the tool support provided for the host language. As mentioned above, the recent versions of the Scala IDE [5] provide solid tools facilitating Scala development. Moreover, additional tools operating on the JVM class level such as profilers can be directly used.

---

[7] Kermeta version was put together by Didier Vojtisek, a Kermeta committer. All the source code is available from the companion web page [4].

(3) *Simple testability with existing unit frameworks.* The method-based styles of all the three languages allows to cherry-pick the fragments of model manipulation to be tested by any Java-based unit testing framework, which is especially useful for larger model transformations.
(4) *Simple integration into existing EMF projects.* Executing a model manipulation task in SIGMA is no different from executing a regular JVM-based application and therefore it can be included in many building tools.

With the basic set of Scala skills necessary to use SIGMA, we consider that the DSLs are rather small and thus less learning effort is likely to be required in comparison to language such as OCL or EOL. Finally, being an internal DSL is notably reflected in the code size of the implementation. SIGMA is currently implemented in 3500 lines of Scala code, which is an order of magnitude less than just EOL, which is an order of magnitude less than Eclipse OCL.

7.6   Limitations

Apart from the syntax limitations, an internal DSL is in general a leaky abstraction [42]. For example an implementation of guards and structural constraints can contain arbitrary code and by default. There is no simple way to make sure they are side-effect free without employing an external checker such as IGJ [45], which brings additional overhead. Traditionally, the support for domain-specific analysis, error checking and optimization has been difficult to realize in internal DSLs. However, Scala offers some more advanced methods for DSL embedding, using language virtualization and lightweight modular staging [37,13].

Depending on the target audience, the use of Scala can be seen as a drawback rather than a merit. It is a new language that has not yet reached the popularity of some of the mainstream programming languages. It might be hard to justify learning a language such as Scala solely for the purpose of model manipulation. Finally, there is a small compile-time overhead of generating the common infrastructure.

7.7   Threats to Validity

There are few potential threats to validity of the evaluation presented in Sections 7.3 and 7.4. First, the implemented model manipulation tasks represent only a small subset of possible scenarios. To the best of our knowledge, we do not know about other publicly available larger model manipulations implemented in Epsilon. In some parts, the Epsilon code itself could be improved which, would result in more concise solutions, nevertheless, we believe that this would not make a major difference.

As for the performance evaluation, it is a form micro benchmark and as such it should be considered with all the validity threats micro benchmarking brings. We have implemented only a small model manipulation task, yet, we already see the trends of the different approaches whose performance will likely remain in the same order of magnitude even for other model manipulations.

Table 3. Supported Epsilon features. (+) supported, (-) unsupported, (0) partially supported

DSL	Feature		Sigma support
EOL	Simultaneously accessing/modifying many models of (potentially) different metamodels	+	Accessing a model in SIGMA is the same as accessing a Scala/Java class
	All the usual programming constructs	+	SIGMA is based on Scala GPL
	First-order logic OCL operations	+	All OCL collection operations are supported
	Create and call methods of Java objects	+	Scala is interoperable with Java
	Dynamically attaching operations to existing meta-classes and types	+	Supported through Scala implicit conversions
	Cached operations	+	Supported using Scala implicit conversions and lazy values
	Extended properties	+	Supported using Scala implicit conversions
	User interaction	+	Supported through Scala and Java libraries
	Create reusable libraries of operations	+	Scala has notions of packages and imports that goes beyond the one in Epsilon
EVL	Distinguish between errors and warnings during validation	+	Both errors and warnings are supported
	Guarded constraints	+	Constraints can have guards (line 5-7 in Listing 1.3)
	Specify constraint dependencies	+	Constraint dependency can be specified in a guard condition (line 6 in Listing 1.3)
	Break down complex constraints to sequences of simpler statements	+	SIGMA constraints can contain arbitrary Scala code (*cf.* Section 7.6)
	Automated constraint evaluation	+	SIGMA execution semantics is the same as in Epsilon
	Out-of-the-box integration with the EMF validation framework and GMF	+	SIGMA provides an EValidator implementation
ETL	Ability to query/navigate/modify both source and target models	+	Accessing a model in SIGMA is the same as accessing a Scala/Java class
	Declarative rules with imperative bodies	+	Method signature declares a rule and the method body can contain any Scala code
	Automated rule execution	+	SIGMA execution semantics is the same as in Epsilon
	Lazy and greedy rules	+	Both rule types are supported using annotations
	Multiple rule inheritance	0	Currently, inherited rules must be called explicitly
	Guarded rules	+	Rules can have guards (lines 12-14 in Listing 1.3)
EGL	Decouple content from destination	+	The result of M2T transformation is a string that can be outputted to any destination
	Call templates (with parameters) from other templates	+	An M2T template is just a Scala class that can be used from any Scala code
	Define and call sub-templates	+	A sub-template is a Scala method that can be used from any Scala code
	Mix generated with hand-written code	-	There are several problems with mixing generated and non-generated code (*e.g.*, complicated merge, non-generated code is lost among the generated one, generated code has to be put under version control) and therefore SIGMA promotes the generation gap pattern [17] instead

8   Related Work

Cuadrado *et al.* [14] developed RubyTL, a Ruby internal DSL for ATL-like M2M transformations. Later, they used it for a comparison on the effort of building an internal DSL and an external one. They concluded that the success of an internal DSL highly depends on the selection of the host language, its support for DSL embedding, execution performance, tool support, and popularity [39]. The main difference with SIGMA is that using a dynamic language prevents any compile type checking. Also RubyTL relies on its own EMF model parser facilities and is not directly interchangeable with the mainstream EMF.

George *et al.* [18] used Scala to build a M2M transformation DSL for the EMF platform that resembles ATL. Since we use the same host language, their DSL is fully interoperable with ours, *e.g.* the common infrastructure (Section 3) can be directly used in the transformation rules. However their internal DSL is not completely type safe and they represent transformation rules directly as anonymous classes, which limits their modularity and reusability. Wider [44] presents an interesting approach to bidirectional model transformations by embedding lenses (a combinator-based approach to bidirectional term-transformations) into Scala and showed how they can be used in an MDE context. Akehurst *et al.* [11] developed a Java library for simple imperative M2M transformations. Being based on Java gives it performance and tool support advantages, as well as a wider audience. On the other hand, there is no particular support for improving the expressiveness of model navigation and modification, resulting in rather verbose and complicated code.

9 Conclusion

In this paper we have presented an alternative internal DSL approach for model manipulation whereby the supporting constructs are embedded into a GPL. We used Scala as the host language to design and fully implement SIGMA, a family of type-safe internal DSLs for EMF model consistency checking, M2M and M2T transformations. We have shown that the resulting DSLs have similar expressiveness and features found in external model manipulation DSLs, while providing competitive performance, compact implementation, and the ability to take advantage of the advanced Scala tool support.

Non-trivial model manipulation tasks often involve a lot of general purpose programming. By using a GPL such as Scala with rich general purpose programming constructs, we were able to significantly reduce the code size of the model manipulation tasks implemented in our evaluation process, without jeopardizing their readability.

Current work in progress around SIGMA consists in carrying out more evaluations to further assess the usability of the proposed DSLs. SIGMA has notably participated in the 2014 edition of the Transformation Tools contest [19]. For the future we first want to apply the Scala advanced DSL embedding techniques to address identified limitations such as the problem of *leaky abstraction*. We also plan to tackle DSL composition issues by exploring appropriate ways to couple SIGMA with other DSLs in different case studies.

Acknowledgments. This work is partially supported by the Datalyse project www.datalyse.fr.

References

1. Apache Velocity, http://velocity.apache.org/
2. Epsilon Egldoc, https://wiki.eclipse.org/EDT:EGLDoc
3. Epsilon Eugenia, http://www.eclipse.org/epsilon/doc/eugenia/

4. Paper Companion Web Page
5. Scala IDE, http://scala-ide.org/
6. The Epsilon Project Documentation, http://eclipse.org/epsilon/doc/
7. The SALTY Project, https://salty.unice.fr
8. The SIGMA Project, https://github.com/fikovnik/Sigma
9. The Unicaneer2sql Project, https://code.google.com/p/unicaneer2sql/
10. The YourCast Project, http://yourcast.fr/
11. Akehurst, D.H., Bordbar, B., Evans, M.J., Howells, W.G.J., McDonald-Maier, K.D.: SiTra: Simple Transformations in Java. In: Wang, J., Whittle, J., Harel, D., Reggio, G. (eds.) MoDELS 2006. LNCS, vol. 4199, pp. 351–364. Springer, Heidelberg (2006)
12. Burmako, E.: Scala macros: let our powers combine? In: Proceedings of the 4th Workshop on Scala (2013)
13. Chafi, H., DeVito, Z., Moors, A., Rompf, T., Sujeeth, A.K., Hanrahan, P., Odersky, M., Olukotun, K.: Language virtualization for heterogeneous parallel computing. In: Proceedings of the ACM International Conference on Object Oriented Programming Systems Languages and Applications (2010)
14. Cuadrado, J.S., Molina, J.G., Tortosa, M.M.: RubyTL: A Practical, Extensible Transformation Language. In: Rensink, A., Warmer, J. (eds.) ECMDA-FA 2006. LNCS, vol. 4066, pp. 158–172. Springer, Heidelberg (2006)
15. Czarnecki, K., Helsen, S.: Feature-based survey of model transformation approaches. IBM Systems Journal 45(3) (2006)
16. Dubochet, G.: Embedded Domain-Specific Languages using Libraries and Dynamic Metaprogramming. Ph.D. thesis, Ecole Polytechnique Fédérale de Lausanne (2011)
17. Fowler, M.: Domain Specific Languages, 1st edn. Addison-Wesley (2010)
18. George, L., Wider, A., Scheidgen, M.: Type-Safe Model Transformation Languages as Internal DSLs in Scala. In: Hu, Z., de Lara, J. (eds.) ICMT 2012. LNCS, vol. 7307, pp. 160–175. Springer, Heidelberg (2012)
19. Horn, T., Krause, C., Rose, L.: 7th Transformation Tools Contest (2014)
20. Jouault, F., Kurtev, I.: Transforming Models with ATL. In: Bruel, J.-M. (ed.) MoDELS 2005 Workshops. LNCS, vol. 3844, pp. 128–138. Springer, Heidelberg (2006)
21. Kelly, S., Tolvanen, J.P.: Domain-Specific Modeling: Enabling Full Code Generation. Wiley-IEEE Computer Society Press (2008)
22. Kolovos, D.S., Paige, R.F., Polack, F.A.C.: The Epsilon Transformation Language. In: Vallecillo, A., Gray, J., Pierantonio, A. (eds.) ICMT 2008. LNCS, vol. 5063, pp. 46–60. Springer, Heidelberg (2008)
23. Kolovos, D.S., Paige, R.F., Polack, F.A.C.: The Epsilon Object Language (EOL). In: Rensink, A., Warmer, J. (eds.) ECMDA-FA 2006. LNCS, vol. 4066, pp. 128–142. Springer, Heidelberg (2006)
24. Kolovos, D.S., Paige, R.F., Polack, F.A.C.: On the Evolution of OCL for Capturing Structural Constraints in Modelling Languages. In: Abrial, J.-R., Glässer, U. (eds.) Büorger Festschrift. LNCS, vol. 5115, pp. 204–218. Springer, Heidelberg (2009)
25. Krikava, F.: Domain-Specific Modeling Language for Self-Adaptive Software System Architectures. Ph.D. thesis, University of Nice Sophia-Antipolis (2013)
26. Krikava, F., Collet, P.: On the Use of an Internal DSL for Enriching EMF Models. In: Proceedings of the 2012 International Workshop on OCL and Textual Modelling (2012)
27. Krikava, F., Collet, P., France, R.: ACTRESS: Domain-Specific Modeling of Self-Adaptive Software Architectures. In: Symposium on Applied Computing (SAC), track on Dependable and Adaptive Distributed Systems, DADS (2014)

28. Krikava, F., Collet, P., France, R.B.: Manipulating Models Using Internal Domain-Specific Languages. In: Symposium on Applied Computing (SAC), track on Programming Languages, PL (2014)
29. Mernik, M., Heering, J., Sloane, A.M.: When and how to develop domain-specific languages. ACM Comput. Surv. 37(4), 316–344 (2005)
30. Moors, A., Rompf, T., Haller, P., Odersky, M.: Scala-virtualized. In: Proceedings of the ACM SIGPLAN 2012 Workshop on Partial Evaluation and Program Manipulation (2012)
31. Muller, P.-A., Fleurey, F., Jézéquel, J.-M.: Weaving executability into object-oriented meta-languages. In: Briand, L.C., Williams, C. (eds.) MoDELS 2005. LNCS, vol. 3713, pp. 264–278. Springer, Heidelberg (2005)
32. Object Management Group: MOF Model to Text Transformation Language (MOFM2T). Tech. rep., Object Management Group (2008)
33. Object Management Group: MOF^{TM} Query / View / Transformation (QVT). Tech. rep., Object Management Group (2011)
34. Object Management Group: OMG Object Constraint Language (OCL). Tech. rep., Object Management Group (2012)
35. Odersky, M., Altherr, P., Cremet, V., Emir, B., Maneth, S., Micheloud, S., Mihaylov, N., Schinz, M., Stenman, E., Zenger, M.: An Overview of the Scala Programming Language. Tech. rep., École Polytechnique Fédérale de Lausanne (2014)
36. Paige, R.F., Kolovos, D.S., Rose, L.M., Drivalos, N., Polack, F.A.C.: The Design of a Conceptual Framework and Technical Infrastructure for Model Management Language Engineering. In: 2009 14th IEEE International Conference on Engineering of Complex Computer Systems (2009)
37. Rompf, T., Odersky, M.: Lightweight modular staging: A pragmatic approach to runtime code generation and compiled DSLs. In: Proceedings of the Ninth International Conference on Generative Programming and Component Engineering (2010)
38. Rose, L.M., Paige, R.F., Kolovos, D.S., Polack, F.A.C.: The Epsilon Generation Language. In: Schieferdecker, I., Hartman, A. (eds.) ECMDA-FA 2008. LNCS, vol. 5095, pp. 1–16. Springer, Heidelberg (2008)
39. Sánchez Cuadrado, J., Canovas, J., Garcia Molina, J.: Comparison between internal and external DSLs via RubyTL and Gra2MoL. In: Mernik, M. (ed.) Formal and Practical Aspects of Domain-Specific Languages: Recent Developments. IGI Global (2012)
40. Schmidt, D.C.: Guest Editor's Introduction: Model-Driven Engineering. Computer 39(2) (2006)
41. Sendall, S., Kozaczynski, W.: Model transformation: The heart and soul of model-driven software development. IEEE Software 20(5), 3 (2000)
42. Siek, J.G.: General purpose languages should be metalanguages. In: Proceedings of the 2010 ACM SIGPLAN Workshop on Partial Evaluation and Program Manipulation (2010)
43. Steinberg, D., Budinsky, F., Paternostro, M., Merks, E.: EMF: Eclipse Modeling Framework, 2nd edn. Addison-Wesley Professional (2008)
44. Wider, A.: Towards combinators for bidirectional model transformations in scala. Software Language Engineering (2011)
45. Zibin, Y., Potanin, A., Ali, M., Artzi, S., Kieżun, A., Ernst, M.D.: Object and reference immutability using java generics. In: Proceedings of the the 6th Joint Meeting of the European Software Engineering Conference and the ACM SIGSOFT Symposium on The Foundations of Software Engineering (2007)

A Framework to Benchmark NoSQL Data Stores for Large-Scale Model Persistence

Seyyed M. Shah, Ran Wei, Dimitrios S. Kolovos,
Louis M. Rose, Richard F. Paige, and Konstantinos Barmpis

Department of Computer Science, University of York, UK
{s.shah,ran.wei,dimitris.kolovos,louis.rose,richard.paige,kb}@york.ac.uk

Abstract. We present a framework and methodology to benchmark NoSQL stores for large scale model persistence. NoSQL technologies potentially improve performance of some applications and provide schemaless data-structures, so are particularly suited to persisting large and heterogeneous models. Recent studies consider only a narrow set of NoSQL stores for large scale modelling. Benchmarking many technologies requires substantial effort due to the disparate interface each store provides. Our experiments compare a broad range of NoSQL stores in terms of processor time and disc space used. The framework and methodology is evaluated through a case study that involves persisting large reverse-engineered models of open source projects. The results give tool engineers and practitioners a basis for selecting a store to persist large models.

1 Introduction

Model Driven Engineering (MDE) is being applied to larger and more complex systems. The current generation of modelling and model management technologies (such as EMF [1]) are being stressed in terms of capacity to accommodate collaborative development and persistence of models larger than a few hundreds of megabytes in size. Recent research has focused on different dimensions of scalability in MDE [2], including being able to construct large models and languages in a systematic manner; enabling large teams of modellers to construct and refine large models in a collaborative manner; enhancing model querying and transformations tools so that they can cope with large models; and providing infrastructure for efficient storage, indexing and retrieval of such models.

The current standard model storage format is the XML Metadata Interchange (XMI). As XMI is based on XML, in order to access any model elements using, e.g., EMF, the complete model file needs to be parsed and loaded in memory. This implies that the larger the model file, the more time and memory needed to load it. Also, XMI inherits the verbosity of XML which means that XMI-encoded model files are much larger in size than needed in order to store the information they do. As a result, recent research has explored alternatives to XMI, particularly *NoSQL* stores, e.g., [3,4]. NoSQL stores eliminate the traditional relational structures of classical databases (see Section 2) and as such are claimed to be more appropriate for very large and heterogeneous datasets, and

J. Dingel et al. (Eds.): MODELS 2014, LNCS 8767, pp. 586–601, 2014.

arguably persisting very large models. However, numerous NoSQL datastores exist while providing different features. A clear conceptual model and method for comparing them – for large-scale model persistence – is currently missing.

Increasingly, NoSQL technologies reflect the needs of particular classes of applications; new NoSQL implementations are being introduced and existing stores adapted for new applications. As a result, NoSQL implementations can be difficult to compare, as each NoSQL implementation is suited to a specific set of applications and workloads. Furthermore, small improvements to each data store can have a large impact on performance. As development in the area is rapid, the performance profile of each implementation is subject to change. Systematic ways to compare NoSQL implementations for large-scale model persistence are also challenging to provide.

This paper aims to directly address these challenges, by proposing a framework and methodology for benchmarking NoSQL stores for large-scale model persistence. The benchmarking experiments consider a broad range of NoSQL stores, compared in terms of processor time usage and disk space usage. Our experiments consider a substantial number of NoSQL datastores, and the framework and methodology can be directly applied to further stores not considered here. We evaluate the framework and methodology via a realistic case study that involves persisting large models reverse engineered from open source projects.

2   Background

2.1   Categories of NoSQL Data Stores

This section presents a categorisation of NoSQL data stores with features common to each category. NoSQL stores tend to organise data without the table-based schemas of traditional relational databases. The broad categories of NoSQL stores considered here are key-value, document, column-oriented, graph and triple stores. A brief introduction is given below with example implementations and general characteristics of each category.

Key-value stores allow data to be dereferenced based on a key. All data is held in documents retrieved only via a primary key and not any other document value, making this the simplest data model. Although in-memory key-value stores have been available for some time [5], the release of Dynamo by Amazon [6] has led to several distributed and persistent key-value implementations. One clear advantage of key-value stores is the speed at which data can be accessed, with some implementations claiming ~100k reads and writes per second [7]. The values are stored without any schema, in a uniform document format such as JSON. As a simple data model, direct, traversable references within documents are not supported – requiring work-arounds at the application level. Examples include Amazon Dynamo [6], Apache Accummulo [8], Project Voldemort [9] and Riak [7].

Document stores are somewhat similar to key-value stores with two important differences. Multiple document types can be stored in the same system, so for example it is possible to mix JSON and XML documents. Also, indexes are created for all attributes of the stored documents, allowing documents to be dereferenced by potentially any value, sacrificing write speed for more flexibility in data access. However, document stores also have the disadvantage that traversable references are not supported, and as such, workarounds at the application level are required to support inter-document links. Similar to key-value stores, documents may have any schema and JSON is typically used as a document interchange format. Examples include MongoDB [10], CouchDB [11] and ArangoDB [12].

Distributed tabular data stores (sometimes called column-oriented or 'BigTable' [13] stores) have some of the features of document and key-value stores, yet have others in common with traditional relational databases. Data is referenced by a primary key (used to retrieve a row, or group columns) and columns in a row can be clustered on separate servers to increase retrieval performance. There is no fixed schema, and any two rows may have different columns. Direct references between rows are supported and any column can be used as a key via indexing, separately from the primary key. These stores have emerged based on the Google BigTable [13] design. A common feature in tabular stores is support for distributed data processing facilities, such as MapReduce [13]. This allows user-written data management programs; results are automatically executed and gathered in parallel across the nodes of the store. Examples of tabular stores include Apache Cassandra [14] and Apache HBase [15].

Property graph databases have some of the features of each of the above. Firstly, in common with all NoSQL stores, the graph has no fixed schema; data is stored in a graph of vertices and edges. Like document stores, a vertex can store documents, as properties and the documents are not restricted by any schema. Similar to key-value stores, vertices may be dereferenced based on a primary key and further, like tabular data stores, secondary indexes allow vertices to be accessed based on any property. Graph databases are distinct from other NoSQL stores as relationships between data (edges) provide a direct reference to vertices, so traversal of edges is instant. This makes graph databases particular suited to analysis of data where links are traversed often, such as network analysis. Examples include Neo4J [16], OrientDB [17] and TitanDB [18].

Closely related to property graph databases are triple stores, which work on the same principle but graphs are flattened into pairs of vertices with an edge between them. Vertices do not store documents; properties of a vertex are stored as additional triples. Triples may optionally conform to a schema set out in a namespace and duplicate triples are not supported.

2.2 Related Work

There has been some past research on benchmarks and benchmarking for MDE technologies, including evaluations of constraint languages [19], high-performance query languages [20], as well as transformation languages [21]. Many of the studies have considered EMF models. One conclusion that can be drawn is that substantial tuning needs to be carried out (e.g., to EMF or operations on EMF models) to achieve good performance with large EMF models. None of this past benchmarking work has considered performance of non-XMI datastores.

A comparative analysis of a small set of technologies used to store EMF models was performed, including benchmarks of prototypes based on the NoSQL databases Neo4J and OrientDB [22]. The benchmarking suggested that there is a significant benefit in using Graph-based NoSQL databases to store model data. Further analyses [3] considering Connected Data Objects (CDO[23]) as well as integration with model management tools [24] showed that use of model management is not detrimental to the performance of NoSQL databases for storing models. This work however, did not present a systematic framework or methodology for comparing individual NoSQL stores.

Various tools attempting to provide a scalable approach to storing EMF models have been proposed, such as Morsa [4], which aims to support scalable model persistence using MongoDB to store EMF models as sets of documents. MongoEMF [25] is an extension of the persistence API of EMF that stores EMF models using MongoDB. It supports basic create, read, update and delete operations as well as queries (including native MongoDB queries via inline JSON). Neo4EMF [26] supports lazy loading, storage, and unloading of large EMF models. It provides a NoSQL database persistence framework based on Neo4J. All of these tools focus on a single back-end driver and attempt to optimise their functionality with that in mind.

Other related work proposes extensible frameworks that persist large models in various back-end stores. The Connected Data Objects repository (CDO[23]) permits the storage and access of models in repositories supported by a range of back-end stores (both relational stores like MySQL[27] and NoSQL/Object stores such as MongoDB and Objectivity/DB[28]). EMF fragments [29] is a persistence layer for distributed data stores; this includes both NoSQL databases (like MongoDB or Hadoop) but also distributed file systems. EMF fragments map model fragments to URIs, which permits storing models on a wide range of distributed datastores. It supports background fragmentation of models, based on client specifications of fragmentation points. Hawk [30] creates model indexes that are used to efficiently query large sets of XMI models by providing a framework for NoSQL (such as Neo4J) or other stores as back-ends. All of these tools tend to focus on providing an application-specific platform for persisting models.

3 A Framework to Benchmark NoSQL Stores

3.1 Benchmarking Methodology

This section outlines the methodology framework used to evaluate NoSQL stores for storing and querying large-scale models. The framework presented takes inspiration from the Yahoo Cloud Service Benchmark (YCSB) framework [31], for On-Line Transaction Processing, an extensible and generic framework used to evaluate NoSQL key-value stores using synthetic data and workloads. Similar to YCSB, the current work provides drivers for several NoSQL stores, but proposes several essential improvements towards benchmarking for large-scale modelling.

Section 3.2, describes an architecture for benchmarking a broad range of model serialisation formats and NoSQL stores. Section 3.4 discusses how different types of stores can be used to persist large-scale models. Our approach also provides several ready-made driver implementations, which are benchmarked in Section 4.

Rather than the synthetic, generated data sets used in [31], we used reverse-engineered software models from real projects as benchmarking data; we argue that this is preferable in cases where real-world large models are not readily available. The GRABATs 2009 data set[1] is a set of readily available large-scale models and is used Section 4. Alternatively, the MoDisco framework [32] can be used to create further data sets from Java code projects.

For the framework we use a multi-phase run-off, to narrow down candidates and avoid benchmarking unsuitable stores. Section 3.3 sets out general and application specific requirements for large-scale model persistence. These requirements are used to select the initial candidates suitable for the application, in the first phase. The following phases involve defining the critical benchmarking tasks and minimum expected performance in each task for the intended application. After benchmarking has been carried out in each phase, stores that do not meet the minimum expected performance or do not have the required features should be eliminated. In Section 4, model persistence and model traversal performance are set as critical benchmarking tasks.

3.2   Framework Implementation

The framework is designed to be modelling technology agnostic. Although at the current stage this framework interacts with EMF [1] models only, it can be extended to support other modelling technologies such as Express [33]. The benchmark framework is made available online[2]. The framework avalaible online, so it may be downloaded and applied to commercially sensitive tools, queries and datasets.

The TinkerPop Blueprints [34] interface provides third-party drivers and an API to several NoSQL stores. Blueprints is a property graph model interface with several concrete implementations. Databases that implement the Blueprints interfaces automatically support Blueprints-enabled applications. Blueprints is open source; implemented in Java; and currently has drivers for databases such as Neo4J [16], Sail [35], Sparksee [36], Accumulo [37], ArangoDB [12], FoundationDB [38], MongoDB [10], Oracle NoSQL [39], OrientDB [17]and TitanDB [18]. Theoretically, Blueprints drivers can be developed for any database technology; the minimum requirement is that the database provides either a Java interface or a REST API.

The structure of the proposed benchmarking framework is shown in Figure 1. The framework supports a number of database technologies by implementing new or reusing existing Blueprints drivers. The persistence layer is responsible to load models defined in different modelling technologies then persist them into

---

[1] http://www.emn.fr/z-info/atlanmod/index.php/GraBaTs_2009_Case_Study
[2] https://bitbucket.org/yorkmde/benchmarks/

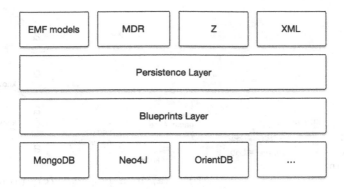

Fig. 1. Structure of the framework

the designated database. The persistence layer contains definitions of different configurations of modelling and database technologies.

3.3 Benchmark Candidate Selection and Model Persistence Requirements

This section outlines the functional and non-functional properties of NoSQL stores taken into account when selecting technologies for benchmarking. NoSQL store performance can vary widely depending on the work load; experiments and benchmarks in this paper focus on large-scale modelling, where the ability to persist models into the store, and model traversal performance are critical. Other requirements are specific to the intended application, so the guidelines here should be adapted depending on the application.

There are several application specific properties to consider for large scale modelling when using NoSQL stores:

- **CAP [40] Trade-Off**: NoSQL stores can trade-off consistency or availability, to provide partition tolerance. Partition tolerant stores can perform better on a cluster of dedicated servers at the cost of temporary inconsistency (eventual consistency) or possible unavailability of model data.
- **Native Referencing Support**: NoSQL stores may not support referencing between entities, which will require adaptation to model access clients and create an impact on performance.
- **Disk-Resident vs. in Memory Storage**: To improve performance, NoSQL stores may adopt an in-memory-only model and provide no on-disc persistence support. This is prevalent in highly available multi-node stores where replicant servers handle failure but may not be appropriate for modelling applications with single-node, client side stores or where memory is limited.
- **Data Interchange Protocol**: The protocol or API used by a store can be a significant consideration. As there is no common interface between stores,

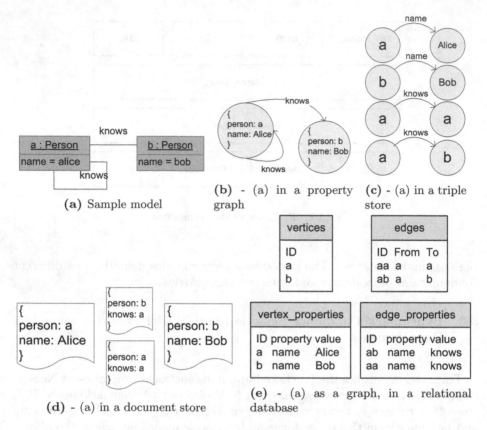

(a) Sample model

(b) - (a) in a property graph

(c) - (a) in a triple store

(d) - (a) in a document store

(e) - (a) as a graph, in a relational database

Fig. 2. Model Persistence Formats in NoSQL Stores

each provides a different set of APIs and language drivers. Stores may use HTTP-REST APIs only, which can mean significant performance overhead, or provide language specific drivers.

- **Client-Server vs. Embedded Architecture**: Several stores proved an embedded file-based architecture to increase performance, as well as the traditional client server-mode. Embedded databases are more suited to for single client applications or offline use, where high performance batch operations are used but not for distributed applications where multiple clients access models.

- **Querying Support**: Stores may provide dedicated high-level querying languages, which must be interfaced to support modelling queries, or only simple data access APIs which require implementing modelling query logic directly in the client.

3.4   Model Persistence Formats for NoSQL

The BluePrints API exposes the underlying NoSQL store as a property graph which we exploit to persist models in our benchmarking framework. The property graph model of NoSQL graph databases, such as Neo4J and OrientDB, employs a similar structure to models, making model representation straight-forward. In order to map from EMF to the BluePrints API, objects are represented as graph vertices and object-attributes are represented as properties of these vertices. Multi-valued attributes are stored as lists, which are sub-documents in the vertex properties. Relationships between objects are represented as edges in the property graph. Similar to object-attributes, reference features such as name, directionality, ends' names and containment are kept in the properties of the edge. Figure 2a shows a model that is represented as a property graph in Figure 2b.

The BluePrints drivers for each store control how property graphs are represented using the primitives provided by each type of stores. For example, in triple stores, the basic data entities are triples, that do not differentiate between object-instances and object-attributes. Triples are in the form subject-predicate-object, where subject and object are uniquely identifiable entities. To store models, triples are used for relations between objects and to store attributes, in effect flattening models to relationships, this is shown is Figure 2c. A notable aspect of this structure is that entities are only stored in triples, so can appear as the subject of several triples, and also cannot be retrieved independently of triples.

The BluePrints API may be used with any kind of data store. For example, although PostgreSQL is a relational database, it can replicate the schema-less design of a property graph store via an appropriate BluePrints driver. The four relational tables needed are Vertices, Edges, Vertex-Properties and Edge-Properties- linked by traditional relational foreign keys. An example of model persistence using this structure is shown in Figure 2e.

Several document stores and key-value stores do not support references between entities, which precludes those stores from our study because, traversing between documents has high performance over-head. Both types of stores have entities that can be used to store object instances and object attributes, as documents. In order to support key-value stores and document stores in the BluePrints property-graph model, special considerations must be made for edges. In some cases, the model persistence layer can include work-arounds to support edges with properties, for example in the case of the MongoDB BluePrints driver a dedicated document is created that links documents together, as shown in Figure 2d.

4   Case Study: Benchmarking Persistence and Traversal of GRABATS Models

To demonstrate the proposed framework, this section presents the results of benchmarking for a realistic case study that involves persisting large models reverse engineered from open source projects.

Table 1. Grabats dataset characteristics

	set0	set1	set2	set3	set4
XMI file size	9.2m	27.9m	283.2m	626.7M	676.9M
# of objects	69,680	197,699	2,082,841	4,594,899	4,961,779
# number of relations	69,806	197,965	2,083,272	4,595,522	4,962,567
# total elements	139,486	395,664	4,166,113	9,190,421	9,924,346

4.1 Dataset Characteristics

To obtain meaningful benchmarking results, there is a need for representative large models. As mentioned earlier, instead of using synthetic models, we used models reverse-engineered from open source Java projects. The JDTAST meta-model used in Java Legacy Reverse-Engineering use case, presented in the GRA-BATS 2009 contest, is used, as well as the five models provided in the contest. The JDTAST metamodel has similar concepts to the Java programming language and allows representation of Java programs as models. Five large models have been extracted from existing Java code that conform to the JDTAST meta-model. These are EMF models serialised in XMI format and they range from 69680 model elements and 69680 relationships in a 9.2MB XMI file (set0), to 4961779 model elements and 4962567 relationships in a 676.9MB XMI file (set4). Detailed characteristics of all five models are displayed in Table 1.

4.2 Experimental Setup

For most of the experiments, we used a single commercial class computer with Intel Core i7 2.3GHz CPU, 8GB of DDR3 memory and a 256GB Solid State Disk running OSX 10.9.1 and JDK 1.7.0. To run the experiments, we gave the JVM 6GB of maximum heap memory.

Table 2. Model persistence performance - time taken in seconds and disc space used, per dataset

Store	set0	set1	set2	set3	set4
Baseline	6s	15s	54s	218s	303s
Neo4J 1.x	9s (44MB)	29s (129MB)	-	-	-
Neo4J 2.x	21s (44MB)	40s (129MB)	-	-	-
Neo4J Batch 1.x	9s (14MB)	18s (44MB)	118s (334MB)	431s (744MB)	852s (805MB)
Neo4J Batch 2.x	6s (15MB)	19s (45MB)	256s (334MB)	756s (767MB)	940s (830MB)
OrientDB	16s (35MB)	39s (98MB)	438s (955MB)	1031s (2.11GB)	1127s (2.28GB)
TitanDB (BerkeleyDB)	11s (48MB)	25s (147MB)	196s (1.29GB)	814s (3.01GB)	997s (3.32GB)
TitanDB (Cassandra)	38s (75MB)	90s (165MB)	876s(1.06GB)	1967s(1.75GB)	2419s(1.81GB)
MongoDB	33s (807MB)	100s (1.28GB)	983s (4.77GB)	2537s (6.67GB)	2839s (6.98GB)
Sesame	87s (33MB)	265s (97MB)	3140s (734MB)	-	-
PostgreSQL	460s (206MB)	1216s	-	-	-
ArangoDB	420s (71MB)	1620s (194MB)	-	-	-
ArangoDB Batch	8s (71MB)	18s (104MB)	174s (641MB)	-	-

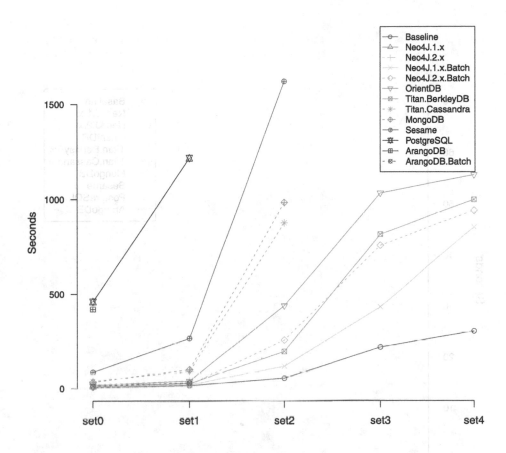

Fig. 3. Model persistence performance - time taken in seconds, per dataset

Table 3. Model traversal performance - time taken in seconds, per data set

Store	set0	set1	set2	set3	set4
Baseline	1s	1s	1s	1s	1s
Neo4J 1.x	4s	6s	12s	24s	28s
Neo4J 2.x	6s	7s	16s	27s	37s
OrientDB	3s	6s	53s	192s	870s
TitanDB (BerkeleyDB)	6s	14s	186s	2414s	-
TitanDB (Cassandra)	14s	53s	400s	1212s	1263s
MongoDB	2s	2s	16s	40s	44s
Sesame	2s	3s	17s	-	-
PostgreSQL	2s	2s	-	-	-
ArangoDB	60s	180s	-	-	-

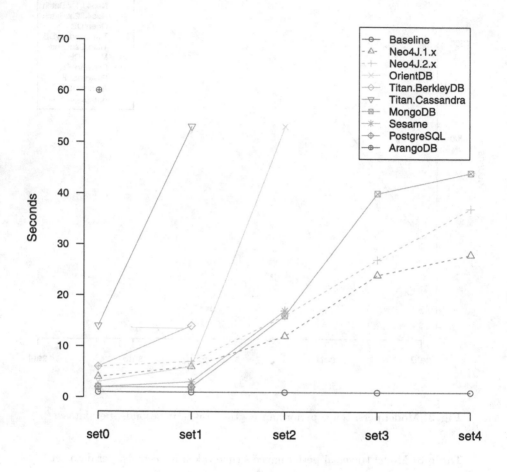

Fig. 4. Model traversal performance - time taken in seconds, per data set

4.3   Results

This section discusses the results when the benchmarking framework is applied
to the GRABATS datasets and the selected NoSQL stores. Table 2 and Figure 3
outline the results for persisting large models to each store. When persisting
models, the 'Baseline' is the time taken to load, traverse and unload each model,
without any interaction with the data store. This represents the overhead of the
framework. In traversing the data store the baseline is the overhead of starting
and executing the framework, without connecting to a data store. In Table 2, a

dash (-) indicates a data store that could not complete the benchmark, within the time or memory given. Some results shown in Table 2 and Table 3 may not appear in Figure 3 and Figure 4 to ease readability. Several interesting observations can be made about relative performance of the stores and the architecture of BluePrints drivers.

The categories outlined in Section 2 do not have any effect on performance in model persistence or model traversal. The Neo4J (versions 1.x and 2.x) and ArangoDB stores were unable to complete the benchmark for data sets set3 and set4. This is due to the architecture of the BluePrints drivers; ArangoDB, uses a client-server mechanism, so must create a separate HTTP request per insertion. Both standard Neo4j and ArangoDB drivers store a cache of each insertion (i.e. the whole graph) in memory, causing model insertion processes to run out of memory. The Neo4j store can only persist set4 and set3 when using a special 'batch' insertion driver and protocol. In Neo4J the batch driver includes the logic to modify the underlying database files directly, without a client server architecture. Also in both batch and standard from, Neo4j 1.x performs better than Neo4J 2.x, possibly due to the stability and enhanced optimisation of the older version. ArangoDB uses a client server architecture so instead uses a dedicated REST API on the server for batch insertion requests. In both 'batch' drivers, the graph is not cached and in Neo4J it is in a read-only state during model insertion and in ArangoDB the model can not be read until after insertion completes. This makes stores with bulk-insertion drivers clearly more suitable for persisting large models, where model insertion time is critical but the model will not be modified or accessed during insertion.

The TitanDB/Cassandra and TitanDB/BerkeleyDB drivers are able to insert all data sets, without using a batch insertion, because the graph is not cached by the driver in memory. However, this impacts the performance, making the store take longer to insert large models. However, the drivers highlight the difference in using an embedded database as a back-end and using client-server back-end for the store. In TitanDB/Cassandra, the textual CQL language and protocol are used to store graph data, whereas TitanDB/BerkeleyDB uses an embedded file based store to persist graphs. The difference is apparent in the benchmark results for set3 and set4, where TitanDB/BerkeleyDB takes half the insertion time of TitanDB/Cassandra. TitanDB/BerkeleyDB provides the fastest insertion time without using batch insertion, however, the driver is less stable than TitanDB/Cassandra and can run out of memory unexpectedly.

The OrientDB and MongoDB Blueprints drivers use a binary protocol to communicate with the server and do not keep a cache of the graph in memory, so they are able to insert the larger data sets without a batch driver. The insertion performance for set3 and set4 is lower than Neo4J or ArangoDB for two main reasons. During insertion the graph is read-write which means extra integrity checks are needed during insertion; and when inserting edges, the vertices must be read from the server, adding significant overhead to model reference insertion. The OrientDB and MongoDB stores are suited to workloads where model elements may be accessed or modified during insertion and model insertion time is critical.

The Sesame store driver has a similar architecture to the Neo4J driver, directly accessing the data store in embedded mode[3] to create or modify a file-based store that may later be served by a triple store. The PostgreSQL driver uses the text-based JDBC protocol to create a simple schema for storing graphs on a database server. However, Sesame and PostgreSQL were unable to complete insertion benchmarks for set3 and set4, as both cache the graphs in memory during insertion and do not support bulk insertion. These drivers are not suited to large scale model persistence.

Table 3 and Figure 4 outline the results for traversing all stored elements. In Table 3, a dash (-) indicates those data stores which could not be benchmarked as the model was not persisted in the previous benchmarking phase. Both Sesame and PostgreSQL have better relative model traversal performance than many of the others stores for set0 and set1. Sesame, performs better than Neo4J in smaller sets but not in set2, which indicates that its traversal capabilities may not scale, even if the larger stores can be persisted. These stores are not suitable for large scale model persistence in the current form, however, they may be suitable where traversal performance is important in data sets similar to set0 and set1, and insertion time is not critical.

As with model insertion, Neo4J 1.x performs better than Neo4J 2.x for model traversal, which suggests the newer version is less optimised than the older, stable release. MongoDB suffers at model insertion-time due to the indexes automatically created to address each element stored documents, which also negatively impacts on disc space used for each dataset. The indexing is beneficial, as MongoDB has similar relative performance for the larger set3 and set4 sets (within ~10 seconds) and better performance than Neo4J in the set0, set1 and set2 datasets. OrientDB also has better model traversal performance than Neo4J in set0 and set1, which seems to indicate that Neo4J does not scale down to smaller datasets as well as MongoDB or OrientDB. However, OrientDB does not perform as well as either MongoDB or Neo4J on set2, set3 or set4, indicating issues with scaling OrientDB up to larger models.

TitanDB with the relational BerkeleyDB back-end and ArangoDB were the only two store where a model was persisted but could not later be traversed, for the model in set4 and set2 respectivly, where the driver ran out of memory. This seems to indicate the limits of TitanDB when using BerkeleyDB. When using Cassandra with TitanDB, traversal performance is lower than with BerkeleyDB. The worst traversal performance is found in ArangoDB, where separate HTTP REST requests are used to retrieve individual model elements, creating a significant overhead.

---

[3] A SPARQL (REST-like) client-server architecture is available, with more overhead than the embedded triple store used in our experiments.

4.4   Threats to Validity

Standard desktop specification machines have been used to perform benchmarking, so the results are representative of a desktop environment. In future work, the NoSQL systems will be benchmarked using servers with greater resources available and the results compared with desktop-type performance.

In these experiments, the Blueprints API has been used to create a common interface to load data into and to query the stores. This allows us to treat the stores as 'black-box' and benchmark a broad range of them. This approach relies on the availability of high-quality, optimised Blueprints drivers for each data store. In the case of ArangoDB and Neo4J, batch insertion drivers are available, and Neo4J also has targeting different versions of the underlying store. However, most drivers do not support batch insertion, even where the underlying store does, which has a negative impact on performance. Similarly, the underlying data stores have various parameters that could be modified to improve performance but the configuration parameters are not always exposed by the drivers. In future work, each driver and data store will be investigated for possible optimisations, based on the obtained benchmark results.

Large models conforming to the JDT meta model have been used to benchmark a wide range of data stores. The JDT meta model stores Java source code in a model based format and the models are created from reverse engineering large Java code-bases. The largest model has 5 million class-instance elements with around 5 million references between class-instances and other models in the data set are similarly connected. The models used in benchmarking were selected based on the size and availability, so the results presented here may not be representative of other metamodels. Researchers and practitioners are invited to make available large models for benchmarking in this framework.

5   Conclusions and Future Work

We have presented a framework and methodology for benchmarking NoSQL datastores in the context of large-scale modelling applications. The framework builds on the Blueprints property graph model interface and provides a layered architecture to avoid repetition and to allow future support of non-EMF modelling technologies. The framework advocates the selection of candidate stores via a multi-stage process, which involves drawing from the literature and existing benchmarks.

There are several interesting possible extensions to the framework. The current framework can be downloaded and executed on user-specified models or queries. Applying the framework to a wide range of queries and models would help identify classes of models and queries that affect performance. Another area for further investigation is that of tuning the workloads and parameters of datastores, and recording the results in an online corpus, so developers have a range of benchmarks results for comparison.

Our experiments have investigated the persistence and traversal performance of models of different sizes, for a realistic case study that involves persisting large models reverse engineered from open source projects. The experimentation revealed that OrientDB, Neo4J (both v1.x and v2.x) and TitanDB (using BerkeleyDB) scale up well in terms of persisting large models, while Neo4J (both v1.x and v2.x) and MongoDB scale up well for querying such models. Also, unexpectedly many of the evaluated stores were unable to persist/traverse models larger than set2 in time and under the provided resources.

References

1. Steinberg, D., Budinsky, F., Merks, E., Paternostro, M.: EMF: Eclipse modeling framework. Pearson Education (2008)
2. Kolovos, D.S., Rose, L.M., Matragkas, N., Paige, R.F., Guerra, E., Cuadrado, J.S., De Lara, J., Ráth, I., Varró, D., Tisi, M., Cabot, J.: A Research Roadmap Towards Achieving Scalability in Model Driven Engineering. In: Proceedings of the Workshop on Scalability in Model Driven Engineering, BigMDE 2013, pp. 2:1–2:10. ACM, New York (2013)
3. Barmpis, K., Kolovos, D.S.: Evaluation of Contemporary Graph Databases for Efficient Persistence of Large-Scale Models. Journal of Object Technology (to appear, 2014)
4. Espinazo Pagán, J., Sánchez Cuadrado, J., García Molina, J.: Morsa: A Scalable Approach for Persisting and Accessing Large Models. In: Whittle, J., Clark, T., Kühne, T. (eds.) MODELS 2011. LNCS, vol. 6981, pp. 77–92. Springer, Heidelberg (2011)
5. Fitzpatrick, B.: Distributed caching with memcached. Linux Journal 2004(124), 5 (2004)
6. DeCandia, G., Hastorun, D., Jampani, M., Kakulapati, G., Lakshman, A., Pilchin, A., Sivasubramanian, S., Vosshall, P., Vogels, W.: Dynamo: Amazon's highly available key-value store. SIGOPS Oper. Syst. Rev. 41(6), 205–220 (2007)
7. Fink, B.: Distributed computation on dynamo-style distributed storage: Riak pipe. In: Hoffman, T., Hughes, J. (eds.) Erlang Workshop, pp. 43–50. ACM (2012)
8. Fuchs, A.: Accumulo–Extensions to Google's Bigtable Design (2012)
9. Auradkar, A., Botev, C., Das, S., De Maagd, D., Feinberg, A., Ganti, P., Gao, L., Ghosh, B., Gopalakrishna, K., Harris, B., Koshy, J., Krawez, K., Kreps, J., Lu, S., Nagaraj, S., Narkhede, N., Pachev, S., Perisic, I., Qiao, L., Quiggle, T., Rao, J., Schulman, B., Sebastian, A., Seeliger, O., Silberstein, A., Shkolnik, B., Soman, C., Sumbaly, R., Surlaker, K., Topiwala, S., Tran, C., Varadarajan, B., Westerman, J., White, Z., Zhang, D., Zhang, J.: Data Infrastructure at LinkedIn. In: 2012 IEEE 28th International Conference on Data Engineering (ICDE), pp. 1370–1381 (April 2012)
10. Chodorow, K., Dirolf, M.: MongoDB - The Definitive Guide: Powerful and Scalable Data Storage. O'Reilly (2010)
11. Brown, M.C.: Getting Started with CouchDB - Extreme Scalability at Your Fingertips. O'Reilly (2012)
12. ArangoDB, https://www.arangodb.org
13. Chang, F., Dean, J., Ghemawat, S., Hsieh, W.C., Wallach, D.A., Burrows, M., Chandra, T., Fikes, A., Gruber, R.E.: Bigtable: A distributed storage system for structured data. In: Proceedings of the 7th USENIX Symposium on Operating Systems Design and Implementation, OSDI 2006 (2006)
14. Lakshman, A., Malik, P.: Cassandra: A decentralized structured storage system. Operating Systems Review 44(2), 35–40 (2010)
15. George, L.: HBase: The Definitive Guide, 1st edn. O'Reilly Media (2011)

16. Webber, J.: A programmatic introduction to Neo4j. In: Leavens, G.T. (ed.) SPLASH, pp. 217–218. ACM (2012)
17. OrientDB, http://www.orientechnologies.com/orientdb.
18. TitanDB, http://thinkaurelius.github.io/titan
19. Kuhlmann, M., Hamann, L., Gogolla, M., Büttner, F.: A benchmark for OCL engine accuracy, determinateness, and efficiency. Software and System Modeling 11(2), 165–182 (2012)
20. Bergmann, G., Ujhelyi, Z., Ráth, I., Varró, D.: A Graph Query Language for EMF Models. In: Cabot, J., Visser, E. (eds.) ICMT 2011. LNCS, vol. 6707, pp. 167–182. Springer, Heidelberg (2011)
21. Varró, G., Schürr, A., Varró, D.: Benchmarking for Graph Transformation. In: VL/HCC, pp. 79–88 (2005)
22. Barmpis, K., Kolovos, D.S.: Comparative Analysis of Data Persistence Technologies for Large-Scale Models. In: XM@MoDELS (2012)
23. (CDO): Connected Data Objects, http://www.eclipse.org/cdo/documentation/index.php
24. Paige, R.F., Kolovos, D.S., Rose, L.M., Drivalos, N., Polack, F.A.C.: The Design of a Conceptual Framework and Technical Infrastructure for Model Management Language Engineering. In: Proc. 14th IEEE International Conference on Engineering of Complex Computer Systems, Potsdam, Germany (2009)
25. MongoEMF, https://github.com/BryanHunt/mongo-emf
26. Neo4EMF, http://neo4emf.com
27. MySQL: http://www.mysql.com/
28. ObjectivityDB, http://www.objectivity.com/products/objectivitydb
29. Scheidgen, M., Zubow, A., Fischer, J., Kolbe, T.H.: Automated and transparent model fragmentation for persisting large models. In: France, R.B., Kazmeier, J., Breu, R., Atkinson, C. (eds.) MODELS 2012. LNCS, vol. 7590, pp. 102–118. Springer, Heidelberg (2012)
30. Barmpis, K., Kolovos, D.: Hawk: Towards a scalable model indexing architecture. In: Proceedings of the Workshop on Scalability in Model Driven Engineering, BigMDE 2013, pp. 6:1–6:9. ACM, New York (2013)
31. Cooper, B.F., Silberstein, A., Tam, E., Ramakrishnan, R., Sears, R.: Benchmarking cloud serving systems with YCSB. In: Proceedings of the 1st ACM Symposium on Cloud Computing, pp. 143–154. ACM (2010)
32. Bruneliere, H., Cabot, J., Jouault, F., Madiot, F.: MoDisco: A generic and extensible framework for model driven reverse engineering. In: Proceedings of the IEEE/ACM International Conference on Automated Software Engineering, pp. 173–174. ACM (2010)
33. Ait-Ameur, Y., Besnard, F., Girard, P., Pierra, G., Potier, J.C.: Formal specification and metaprogramming in the EXPRESS language. In: Intern. Conference on Software Engineering and Knowledge Engineering SEKE, vol. 95, pp. 181–189 (1995)
34. TinkerPop: Blueprints, https://github.com/tinkerpop/blueprints/wiki
35. Broekstra, J., Kampman, A., van Harmelen, F.: Sesame: A generic architecture for storing and querying rdf and rdf schema. In: Horrocks, I., Hendler, J. (eds.) ISWC 2002. LNCS, vol. 2342, pp. 54–68. Springer, Heidelberg (2002)
36. SparkSee, http://www.sparsity-technologies.com/#sparksee
37. AccumuloDB, https://accumulo.apache.org/
38. FoundationDB, https://foundationdb.com/
39. Seltzer, M.: Oracle nosql database. Oracle White Paper (2011)
40. Brewer, E.A.: Towards robust distributed systems. In: PODC (2000)

Automated Chaining of Model Transformations with Incompatible Metamodels

Francesco Basciani, Davide Di Ruscio, Ludovico Iovino, and Alfonso Pierantonio

Department of Information Engineering Computer Science and Mathematics
University of L'Aquila, Italy
`name.surname@univaq.it`

Abstract. In Model-Driven Engineering (MDE) models are first-class entities that are manipulated by means of model transformations. The development of complex and large transformations can benefit from the reuse of smaller ones that can be composed according to user requirements. Composing transformations is a complex problem: typically smaller transformations are discovered and selected by developers from different and heterogeneous sources. Then the identified transformations are chained by means of manual and error-prone composition processes.

In this paper we propose an approach to automatically discover and compose transformations: developers provide the system with the source models and specify the target metamodel. By relying on a repository of model transformations, all the possible transformation chains are calculated. Importantly, in case of incompatible intermediate target and source metamodels, proper adapters are automatically generated in order to chain also transformations that otherwise would be discarded by limiting the reuse possibilities of available transformations.

1 Introduction

Model-driven engineering (MDE) is a software discipline that employs models for describing problems in an application domain by means of metamodels. Different abstraction levels are bridged together by automated transformations which permit source models to be mapped to target models. In MDE, model transformations play a key role and in order to enable their reusability, maintainability, and modularity, the development of complex transformations should be done by composing smaller ones [1].

The common way to compose transformations is to chain them [2,1,3,4,5], i.e., by passing models from one transformation to another. In order to chain transformations it is necessary to ensure the pre- and post-conditions of the considered transformations and to verify the *metamodels compatibility* condition, i.e., that the output metamodel of the first transformation is immersed in the input metamodel of the second one. However, in case of similar output and input metamodels (e.g., subsequent versions of the same metamodel), the metamodels compatibility condition can be too strong and would discard transformations that potentially might be chained.

In this paper, we propose an approach that under certain conditions permits to chain model transformations defined on incompatible metamodels. This is done by means of an *adapter* transformation that can be automatically synthesized from a delta model

J. Dingel et al. (Eds.): MODELS 2014, LNCS 8767, pp. 602–618, 2014.

representing the differences between the output and input metamodels of the transformations to be chained. By relying on a repository of model transformations, the system is able to automatically retrieve the model transformations that can be chained to satisfy the user request. To this end some of our results on model differencing, and metamodel/model coupled evolution [6,7] are combined.

This paper is organized as follows: In Section 2 we overview the problem of transformation composition and we motivate the needs for chaining transformations defined on metamodels that are not compatible. Section 3 describes the proposed approach. An overview of the prototypical implementation of the proposed technique is given in Section 4. After a summarizing discussion given in Section 5, related work is described in Section 6. Conclusions and research perspectives are given in Section 7.

2   Background and Motivation

Composing model transformations is a difficult problem that can be approached in two different ways [5]: by chaining separate model transformations and passing models from one transformation to another (*external composition*), or by composing two model transformation definitions into a new model transformation (*internal composition*). Even though both methods for composing transformations are important and complement each other, in this paper we focus on external composition[1].

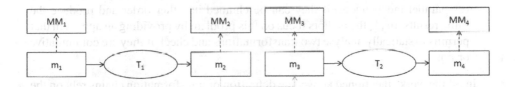

Fig. 1. Model transformation chain example with incompatible metamodels

Figure 1 shows an explanatory model transformation chain. In particular, T_1 is a model transformation that generates models conforming to the target metamodel MM_2 from models conforming to MM_1. Additionally, T_2 is a model transformation that generates models conforming to MM_4 from models conforming to the source metamodel MM_3. In general, if the input metamodel of T_2 would be also the output metamodel of T_1, then these two transformations could be chained. However, under certain conditions, two transformations can be chained even though the output metamodel of the first transformation does not correspond to the input metamodel of the second transformation as discussed later in the paper.

Over the last years, different approaches have been proposed to support the composition of model transformations (e.g., see [2,3,4,5]). The main activities that are typically performed when chaining model transformations are summarized in the following:

---

[1] For readability reasons, hereafter with the term *composition* we refer to *external composition*. Moreover, the terms *composition* and *chaining* are used interchangeably.

(1) *Specification of model transformation chains:* in this activity by considering the lo-cally available model transformations, chains are specified by means of dedicated languages. For instance, in [8] the authors propose Wires*, a domain-specific lan-guage for the specification and orchestration of ATL transformations only. Another common way to chain model transformations is to use ANT scripts [2,3,4]. In [9] the authors propose the adoption of feature models to support the design of model transformation chains. In such a work, transformations are considered as features that are properly composed as specified in the considered feature models.

(2) *Execution of the specified model transformations chains:* in this phase the chains previously specified are executed on the source models given by the user. The exe-cution environments of the adopted transformation languages are employed.

Activity (1) is the most complex one and over the last years a number of works have been proposed to support it and mainly focusing on the following aspects:

- *pre-* and *post-conditions* of transformations: when chaining transformations the conditions of applicability of a transformation (pre-conditions) and the conditions of validity of the resulting transformation (post-conditions) have to be satisfied. In [10] the authors propose an approach able to discover hidden chaining con-straints between endogenous transformations by statically analysing the transfor-mation rules. The approach is based on the adoption of Higher-Order Transforma-tions (HOT) and it is specific for ATL transformations.
- *commutativity/transformation order:* two model transformations are commutative (or parallel independent) if they can be chained in either order and produce the same results. In [1] the authors focus on this problem by providing an approach that permits to statically analyse two transformations and check if they are commutative or not.

In all the works mentioned above, the definition of transformation chains rely on the concept of *compatible metamodels* [2] as defined below.

Definition 1 (metamodels compatibility). *Let MM_1 and MM_2 be two metamodels, then MM_1 is* compatible *with MM_2 if $MM_1 \subseteq MM_2$.*

Definition 2 (transformation composability). *Let $T_1 : MM_1 \rightarrow MM_2$ be a model transformation from the metamodel MM_1 to the metamodel MM_2, and let $T_2 : MM_3 \rightarrow MM_4$ be a model transformation from the metamodel MM_3 to the metamodel MM_4. Then, T_1 and T_2 are* composable *as the sequential application $T_1 ; T_2$ if $MM_2 \subseteq MM_3$.*

Unfortunately, restricting the definition of transformation chains only for the cases of compatible metamodels can reduce the number of chains that might be potentially ob-tained. For instance, let us consider the following ATL [11] model transformations[5]:

---

[2] Apache Ant: http://ant.apache.org/

[3] Epsilon Workflow: http://www.eclipse.org/epsilon/doc/workflow/

[4] ATL-specific launch configurations and ANT tasks: http://wiki.eclipse.org/ATL/Howtos

[5] http://www.eclipse.org/atl/atlTransformations/Grafcet2PetriNet/Grafcet2PetriNet.zip

- *Grafcet_to_PetriNet*$_{1.0}$: *Grafcet* → *PetriNet*$_{1.0}$ - It generates PetriNet models conforming to the metamodel in Fig. 2.c starting from source Grafcet models (Fig. 2.a).
- *PetriNet*$_{2.0}$*_to_PNML* : *PetriNet*$_{2.0}$ → *PNML* - It generates PNML models conforming to the metamodel Fig. 2.b from PetriNet models conforming to the metamodel in Fig. 2.d.

Because of the metamodels compatibility concept previously defined, the transformations *Grafcet_to_PetriNet*$_{1.0}$ and *PetriNet*$_{2.0}$*_to_PNML* are not composable since *PetriNet*$_{1.0}$ $\not\sqsubseteq$ *PetriNet*$_{2.0}$ and *PNML* $\not\sqsubseteq$ *Grafcet*. However, by analyzing the two versions of the PetriNet metamodel in Fig. 2 it is possible to notice that there are many commonalities that might be exploited to increase the possible transformation chains. In particular, depending on the cases, it can be possible to adapt transformations like in the case of *PetriNet*$_{2.0}$*_to_PNML* in order to enable their application on some of the models produced by transformations like *Grafcet_to_PetriNet*$_{1.0}$.

In the next section, we present an approach that permit to fully automatize the activities of the chain process, and to enable the composition of transformations that could not be chained according to Def. 2. In particular, we introduce the concept of *adapter* that under certain conditions can be automatically synthesized and executed between two transformations that otherwise could not be chained.

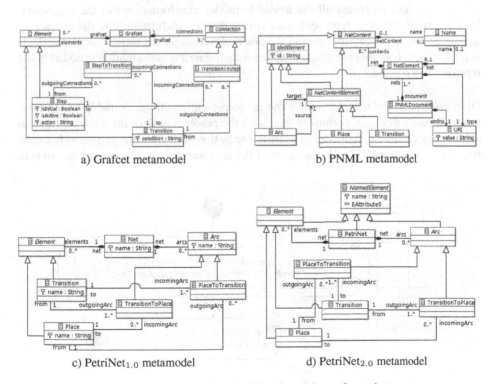

a) Grafcet metamodel   b) PNML metamodel

c) PetriNet$_{1.0}$ metamodel   d) PetriNet$_{2.0}$ metamodel

Fig. 2. Metamodels of the considered model transformations

3 Automatizing Model Transformations Chaining

As previously mentioned, several approaches have been already proposed to support the specification and execution of model transformation chains. The main focus of such works is about checking if two given transformations can be chained or not with respect to Def. 2 [1]. Then, compatibility can be exploited to manually defining chains and singularly selecting the required transformations [9,8,3].

In this section, we present an approach that exploits and complement existing works by advancing the state-of-the-art in two different directions: *(i)* the user gives as input only the source model and the target metamodel, and the system automatically derives the possible chains that can satisfy the user request, *(ii)* under certain conditions the proposed approach is able to generate chains that include non-compatible transformations through synthetised metamodel adapters.

The proposed chaining process is shown in Fig. 3. In particular, the previous activity ❶, presented in the previous section, has been enriched in order to automatize the discovery of the required transformations and their chaining with respect to the *user request*. The sub-activities of ❶ are discussed in the following.

Discovery of the required model transformations The whole activity ❶ in Fig. 3 is enabled by a novel repository of model transformations, which are stored in a directed graph-based structure as shown in Fig. 4. The nodes in the figure represent metamodels, whereas the arcs represent all the available model transformations in the repository. In other words an edge represents an existing direct transformation in the repository having as source (target) metamodel the one represented by the source (target) node. It is important to note that the graph is updated each time a transformation is added in the repository or deleted.

Derivation of model transformation chains Representing all the available transformations as shown in Fig. 4 permits to deal with the problem of deriving a transformation chain from a source metamodel to a target one as the problem of finding paths between two nodes of a graph [12]. For instance, if the user wants a transformation able to take

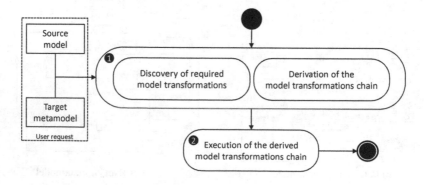

Fig. 3. Proposed model transformations chaining process

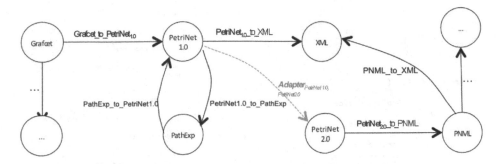

Fig. 4. Graph-based structure of a simple model transformations repository

a *Grafcet* model as input and generate a target *XML* model, then according to the transformations available in the repository shown in Fig. 4 the solution would be the chain *Grafcet_to_PetriNet*$_{1.0}$;*PetriNet*$_{1.0}$*_to_XML*.

In the next sections, we give details about the sub-activities of ❶ in Fig. 3. In particular, we focus on the management of incompatible metamodels (Section 3.1). Moreover, an initial solution to the problem of managing multiple chains that satisfy the same user request is discussed in Section 3.2.

3.1 Managing Transformations with Incompatible Metamodels

In this section, we describe the approach to support the chaining of transformations with incompatible metamodels. For instance, let us consider the repository shown in Fig. 4. In that case, it is not possible to satisfy the user who wants a chain from *Grafcet* to *PNML*. In fact, as discussed in the previous section, PetriNet$_{1.0}$ and PetriNet$_{2.0}$ are not compatible, and *Grafcet_to_PetriNet*$_{1.0}$ and *PetriNet*$_{2.0}$*_to_PNML* cannot be chained. However, it is possible to add a new transformation (see the dashed arrow labeled *Adapter*$_{PetriNet1.0,PetriNet2.0}$) that is able to adapt models conforming to PetriNet$_{1.0}$ so to enable their manipulation and transformation from *PetriNet*$_{2.0}$*_to_PNML* .

In order to discuss how to obtain the adapter transformation let us consider the explanatory transformation rules of *Grafcet_to_PetriNet*$_{1.0}$ and *PetriNet*$_{2.0}$*_to_PNML* shown in Fig. 5.a and Fig. 5.b, respectively, and the differences between the PetriNet$_{1.0}$ and PetriNet$_{2.0}$ metamodels. In particular, the new version of the PetriNet metamodel has been obtained by operating the following changes on PetriNet$_{1.0}$:

δ_1: pull up of the attribute `name` to the new abstract metaclass `NamedElement`
δ_2: renaming of the metaclass `Net` as `PetriNet`

Intuitively, all the rules of the transformation *PetriNet*$_{2.0}$*_to_PNML* that refer to the pulled up attribute `name` are still valid and do not require any adaptation. Concerning the rules of *PetriNet*$_{2.0}$*_to_PNML* whose source patterns refer to `PetriNet` elements can be still applied on `Net` elements after an adaptation phase that simply copies all the `Net` elements to target `PetriNet` ones. Thus the rule `PNMLDocument` in Fig. 5.b can be applied on `Net` elements generated by *Grafcet_to_PetriNet*$_{1.0}$ after an adaptation

```
 8⊖ rule PetriNet {
  9      from
 10          g : Grafcet!Grafcet
 11      to
 12          p : PetriNet!Net
 13          (
 14              location <- g.location,
 15              name <- g.name,
 16              elements <- g.elements,
 17              arcs <- g.connections
 18          )
 19 }
```

```
 7⊖ rule PNMLDocument {
  8      from
  9          e : PetriNet!PetriNet
 10      to
 11          n : PNML!PNMLDocument
 12          (
 13              location <- e.location,
 14              xmlns <- uri,
 15              nets <- net
 16          ),
 17          uri : PNML!URI
 18          (
 19              value <- 'http://www.informatik.hu-be
 20          ),
 21          net : PNML!NetElement
 22          (
 23              name <- name,
 24              location <- e.location,
 25              id <- e.location,
 26              type <- type_uri,
 27              contents <- e.elements.union(e.arcs)
 28          ),
```

a) PetriNet transformation rule of Grafcet_to_PetriNet$_{1.0}$ b) PNMLDocument transformation rule of PetriNet$_{2.0}$_to_PNML

Fig. 5. Sample transformation rules of Grafcet_to_PetriNet$_{1.0}$ and PetriNet$_{2.0}$_to_PNML

step that generates PetriNet elements from the generated Net ones. More precisely, the adaptation step can be performed by means of the *Adapter* transformation shown in Fig. 6.

The previous discussion relates to the coupled-evolution problem that has been intensively investigate over the last years [6]. For instance, in [7] the authors propose an approach to support the migration of models when the corresponding metamodels have been changed and it is necessary to recover the conformance relation with the new version of the metamodels.

In such contexts, according to [7,13] metamodel manipulations can be classified by their corrupting or not-corrupting effects on corresponding artifacts as

```
21⊖ rule Net2Petrinet {
22      from
23          s : PetriNetv1!Net
24      to
25          t : PetriNetv2!PetriNet
26          (
27              ...
28              name <- s.name
29          )
30 }
31 ...
```

Fig. 6. Fragment of the adapter transformation *Adapter$_{PetriNet1.0,PetriNet2.0}$*

- *non-breaking changes:* changes which do not break the conformance of models to the corresponding metamodel;
- *breaking and resolvable changes:* changes which break the conformance of models even though they can be automatically co-adapted;
- *breaking and unresolvable changes:* changes which break the conformance of models which can not automatically co-evolved and user intervention is required.

The synthesis of the adapters can be seen as the automated generation of migration rules for adapting models when metamodels undergo evolution. Thus, we have conceived the approach shown in Fig. 7: starting from a difference model [14] representing the differences between two incompatible metamodels, the approach is able to generate adapter transformations like the one in Fig. 6. The approach relies on the higher-order transformation we have developed to deal with the problem of metamodel/model

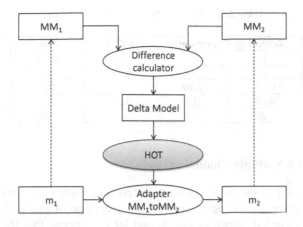

Fig. 7. Generation of the adapter transformation

coupled evolution presented in [7] and subsequently refined to deal with other related co-evolution problems [15,16,17,18].

The proposed approach can be applied in case of non-breaking and breaking and re-solvable changes. In fact, in such cases the adapter generation is completely automated without requiring user intervention. By considering the running example, since δ_1 is a non-breaking change, and δ_2 is breaking and resolvable, the approach in Fig. 7 can be applied and the output is the adapter shown in Fig. 6.

It is important to remark that *adapter transformations are generated when new transformations are added in the repository or deleted from it*. In particular, for each transformation addition, the corresponding source and target metamodels are taken as input by a similarity function [19,20,21] used to calculate a similarity value between such metamodels and all the others already stored in the repository. The used similarity algorithm has been borrowed from [21] that converts the input metamodels into graphs and apply on them the *similarity flooding algorithm* [20]. The similarity values are maintained in a table like the one shown in Table 1. If the similarity value between two considered metamodels is higher than a threshold (in our initial tests we have used 0,80 as threshold value) then an adapter transformation between them is generated. In particular, the metamodels found to be similar as previously said are compared and if the resulting delta model consists of non-breaking and breaking and resolvable changes, then corresponding adapter transformations are generated by means of the approach shown in Fig. 7. The similarity value is not calculated for those metamodels that are already related by a direct transformation. For instance, the similarity value between the *Grafcet* and *PetriNet*$_{1.0}$ metamodels is missing in Table 1, since the repository in Fig. 4 contains the transformation *Grafcet_to_PetriNet*$_{1.0}$. For explanatory reason in Fig. 4 we have reported only the adapter transformation *Adapter*$_{PetriNet1.0,PetriNet2.0}$. However, even though it is not shown in Fig. 4, the repository contains also the adapter transformation *Adapter*$_{PetriNet2.0,PetriNet1.0}$. When a model transformation is deleted from the repository, the similarity table has to be updated in order to add the missing values.

Table 1. Sample metamodel similarity values

	Grafcet	PetriNet$_{1.0}$	PetriNet$_{2.0}$	XML	PNML
Grafcet	1	0,2	0,30	0,29	0,26
PetriNet$_{1.0}$	-	1	*0,89*	0,2	0,28
PetriNet$_{2.0}$	0,30	*0,89*	1	0,3	0,3
XML	0,29	0,2	0,3	1	-
PNML	0,26	-	-	0,28	1

3.2 Dealing with Multiple Chains

The activity ❶ in Fig. 3 might give place to different possible chains and before going ahead with executing activity ❷, users have to select one of them. For instance, let us consider the situation shown in Fig. 8, and let us suppose that the user gives as input a *Grafcet* model and wants to generate a target *PNML*. According to the available transformations, such a request can be satisfied by two possible chains, i.e., $T_1 \rightarrow T_2$, and $T_1 \rightarrow T_3 \rightarrow T_4$. In these cases it is necessary to consider one or more evaluation

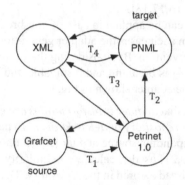

Fig. 8. Choosing among suitable chains

criteria that can be used to select one of the derived chains. By borrowing concepts from [22,23] in the implementation of the approach presented in the next section we support users by giving information about the following aspects:

- *Coverage of the source metamodels:* coverage is the measure regarding how many concepts of the metamodel have been covered by the transformation;
- *Usage:* we identified the usage of a transformation as one of the possible indicators of the trustworthiness of a transformation;
- *Number of transformations:* it refers to the number of transformations that are chained;
- *Execution time:* it refers to the time required to execute the whole transformation chain.

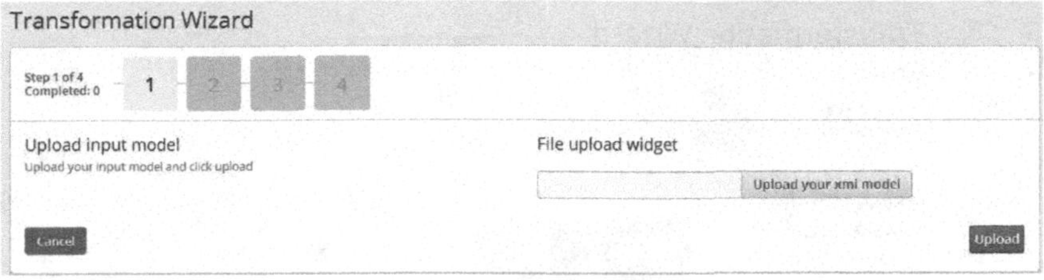

Fig. 9. Upload of the source model

It is important to note that the list of the aspects previously mentioned is not exhaustive and it is subject to extensions and refinements. We considered such a list in the current implementation of the system and we plan to extend it according to the outcome of a more extended validation of the approach as discussed in Section 5.

4   Implementation

In this section, we present a prototypical implementation of the approach discussed in the previous section. The implemented system consists of a J2EE application providing a Web-based front-end that users can conveniently adopt to *(i)* upload the source model, *(ii)* select the target metamodel among the available ones, *(iii)* select one of the proposed chains that are derived in a transparent manner for the user as discussed in the previous section, and *(iv)* remotely execute the selected chain. At the end of the process, the user can download the generated model. In the sequel, the front-end and the back-end of the developed system[6] are described separately.

4.1   Front-End of the Supporting System

The Web form to upload the source model is shown in Fig. 9. Once the model has been uploaded, the system is able to detect the metamodel the model conforms to. Afterwards, the user has to select the target metamodel as shown in the screenshot in Fig. 10. The list of metamodels shown to the user is retrieved from the repository used to store transformations and all the metamodels required to execute them. Once the target metamodel is selected, the whole activity ❶ of the process in Fig. 3 is executed.

In the third step, all the possible chains that satisfy the user request are shown. To help users in the selection, each chain is characterized by different attributes, like the number of single transformations that will be executed, the coverage with respect to the source metamodel, how many times the chain has been already executed, and its average execution time. Once the chain is selected, then the user can trigger its execution and wait for the generated model. Once the chain has been executed some statistical data are stored in the system and shown to the user as shown in Fig. 12.

---

[6] http://www.mdeforge.org

Fig. 10. Selection of the target metamodel

4.2 Back-End of the Supporting System

Figure 13 shows an overview of the architecture of the system back-end. A key role is played by the `Artifact Repository` which stores all the available transformations in a graph-based structured as presented in the previous section. The component `Transformations Discoverer` is able to retrieve the required transformations with respect to user requests. The `Adapter Generator` component is devoted to the generation of the adapter transformations as discussed in the previous section. Once the

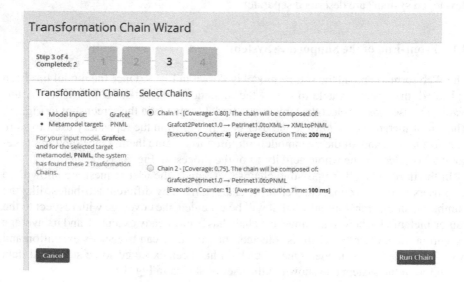

Fig. 11. Transformation chain selection

Fig. 12. Some information about the executed chain

required transformations are available, then all the possible transformation chains are derived by the `Transformations Chain Creator` component. The actual execution of the selected chain is performed by the `Transformation Chain Execution Engine` component.

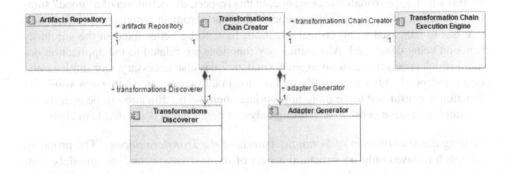

Fig. 13. Overview of the system back-end

5 Discussion

The main strengths of the approach proposed in this paper are related to the possibility of chaining transformations that would be discarded if only the notion of metamodel compatibility is considered. However, the approach as proposed in this paper can be enhanced in different directions as discussed in the following:

Management of Breaking and Unresolvable Changes: When the delta model of two considered metamodels contain at least one breaking and unresolvable change (BUR), the corresponding adapter transformation is not generated. We are aware that in this way we might exclude some feasible transformation chains. However, as also in the case of coupled evolution of metamodels and other related artifacts, managing BUR metamodel changes is complex and typically requires user intervention. This is why we decided to do not manage BUR changes at a first stage and investigate them as a future work.

Identification of Metamodels by Universal Resource Identifiers: Currently the identification of metamodels is performed by exploiting universal resource identifiers (URIs). This means that when a new transformation is added, if it is based on metamodels that already exist in the repository but that for some reason have different URIs, then such metamodels are added again. To avoid duplications of metamodels, we plan to improve the existence check of metmaodels in our repository by exploiting model differencing techniques. In this way, metamodels containing exactly the same elements but identified with different URIs will not be duplicated in the repository.

Metamodel Similarity Functions: The generation of adapter transformations strongly depends on the used metamodel similarity function. If it is not properly defined, we might end up with false positives (i.e., metamodels that are considered similar when they are not) and false negatives (i.e., metamodels that are not considered similar when they are). It is important to remark that the metamodel similarity problem is related to the problem of finding correspondences between two graphs [24]. Theoretically, the graph isomorphism problem is NP-hard [25] and the available approaches provides solutions which approximate the exact one. In this respect, the definition of a "good" similarity function relies on an iterative process that starts from an initial set of metamodels that has to increased when critical situations have to be better fixed in the similarity function being developed. Also, similarity functions are related to the application domain which means that cross-domain normalization is also necessary. Our implementation is independent from the similarity function in the sense that, when a new similarity function is considered to be more appropriate, then the modification to be operated in our implementation consists of refining only one method of a dedicated Java class.

Missing the Management of Semantic Aspects of the Transformations: The proposed approach is based only on structural aspect of transformations and metamodels. This means that users do not have semantic information about the derived transformation chains. However, dealing with semantics of model transformations and in MDE in general is complex [26] and represents an interesting and challenging research direction to pursue for extending the proposed approach. For instance, a first problem we should investigate to enhance our approach is related to semantics preservation of chained model transformations. Many approaches have been proposed to deal with such a fundamental aspect of model transformations (e.g., [27]) and we intend to rely on them.

Experimentation and Evaluation: The prototypical implementation of the approach has been validated by considering the transformations available in the ATL Zoo [7]. To better assess the validity of the proposed approach it is necessary to consider an extended set of data whose definition is a complex task per se.

6   Related Work

Increasingly, model transformation chaining has been a current topic of research and it has been treated from different perspectives.

---

[7] ATL Transformations Zoo:
  http://www.eclipse.org/atl/atlTransformations/

In the database community, the problem of generating adapters between databases with similar schemata has been studied for many years. There are several works studying this problem and many different implementations do exist. Some of them could be related to our approach by translating sequences of modifications of database schemata into sequences of transformations of related databases [28]. In [2] the authors present a convenient approach to design highly flexible chains from existing independent model transformations. The main difference with the presented approach is the *design* part that in our case is automatically calculated by the engine in discovery mode. They propose to artificially change the input and output of transformations in order to recover the compatibility of the involved metamodels. The work in [2] is an extension of what is presented in [1] where the authors address the problem of identifying conflicts between transformations, and checking if two transformations are commutative or not.

A language for defining composition of transformations is given in [3]. To support the concrete realization of transformation chains they propose a language to allow the concatenation of transformation components. A recent work [9] uses feature models to classify model transformations. Based on this feature models, automated techniques help the designer to generate executable chains of transformations. Another interesting work has been proposed in [29] where transformation chaining is called *orchestration*. This paper introduces a graphical executable language for the orchestration of ATL transformations, which provides appropriate mechanisms to enable the modular and compositional specification and execution of complex model transformations chains. The work presented in [4] describes an approach to designing large model transformations for large languages, based on the principle of separation of concerns. Chains are built by linking output parameters to input ones through connectors. Differently from such works we do not require the specification of transformation chains that in our approach are automatically derived with respect to the request of the user and to the transformations, which are stored in a dedicated repository.

In [30] the authors propose a mechanism of module superimposition to compose small and reusable transformations. The idea is to overlay several transformation definitions on top of each other and then execute them as one transformation. Differently from our work, the approach in [30] is specific for ATL and it is an internal composition approach. The work proposed in this paper is an external composition technique and it is independent from the used model transformation language.

Finally our work is related to the Electronic Tool Integration (ETI) Online Platform [31] complementing the STTT journal[8] by providing the opportunity to experiment interactively via internet with tools presented in STTT papers. Initially, the integration of such tools in the ETI platform was made by hand but the authors experience stated that this task was hard and error-prone. Then to partially automate the coding, and to ensure a uniformity in the programming style and result, an adapter specification language called MFI was introduced. From MFI specifications, the needed adapter code can be automatically generated similarly to the adapter transformations discussed in this paper.

---

[8] http://sttt.cs.uni-dortmund.de/

7 Conclusions and Future Work

In this paper we presented a novel approach to support the chaining of model transformations. Starting from a user request consisting of a source model, and the specification of a target metamodel, the system is able to calculate the possible chains satisfying the user request according to the transformation available in a proposed transformation repository. Interestingly, the approach is able to chain also transformations based on incompatible metamodels. To this end, adapter transformations are automatically generated in order to enable the chaining of transformations that otherwise would be discarded.

As said in the previous section we plan to extend the approach in different directions. Because of the key role played by the metamodel similarity function, we intend to enhance it by considering an extended set of metamodels. This will require also a proper validation of the approach by involving a significant number of model transformation experts. The current implementation of the approach is able to manage one-to-one ATL transformations only. However, since the chaining technique is transformation language independent we plan to support the derivation of chains consisting of transformations developed with different technologies. Finally, we will support also the off-line usage of the identified transformation chains. In particular, instead of uploading models and transform them on-line as discussed in the paper, we plan to provide users with the possibility to download a bundle containing the required transformation chains ready to be locally executed.

References

1. Etien, A., Aranega, V., Blanc, X., Paige, R.F.: Chaining Model Transformations. In: Proceedings of the First Workshop on the Analysis of Model Transformations, AMT 2012, pp. 9–14. ACM, New York (2012)
2. Etien, A., Muller, A., Legrand, T., Blanc, X.: Combining Independent Model Transformations. In: Proceedings of the 2010 ACM Symposium on Applied Computing, SAC 2010, pp. 2237–2243. ACM, New York (2010)
3. Vanhooff, B., Van Baelen, S., Hovsepyan, A., Joosen, W., Berbers, Y.: Towards a Transformation Chain Modeling Language. In: Vassiliadis, S., Wong, S., Hämäläinen, T.D. (eds.) SAMOS 2006. LNCS, vol. 4017, pp. 39–48. Springer, Heidelberg (2006)
4. Etien, A., Muller, A., Legrand, T., Paige, R.F.: Localized model transformations for building large-scale transformations. Software Systems Modeling, 1–25 (2013)
5. Wagelaar, D.: Composition Techniques for Rule-Based Model Transformation Languages. In: Vallecillo, A., Gray, J., Pierantonio, A. (eds.) ICMT 2008. LNCS, vol. 5063, pp. 152–167. Springer, Heidelberg (2008)
6. Di Ruscio, D., Iovino, L., Pierantonio, A.: Coupled Evolution in Model-Driven Engineering. IEEE Software 29, 78–84 (2012)
7. Cicchetti, A., Di Ruscio, D., Eramo, R., Pierantonio, A.: Automating Co-evolution in Model-Driven Engineering. In: Proceedings of the 2008 12th International IEEE Enterprise Distributed Object Computing Conference, EDOC 2008, pp. 222–231. IEEE Computer Society, Washington, DC (2008)
8. Rivera, J.E., Ruiz-Gonzalez, D., Lopez-Romero, F., Bautista, J., Vallecillo, A.: Orchestrating ATL Model Transformations. In: Proc. of MtATL 2009, Nantes, France, pp. 34–46 (2009)

9. Aranega, V., Etien, A., Mosser, S.: Using Feature Model to Build Model Transformation Chains. In: France, R.B., Kazmeier, J., Breu, R., Atkinson, C. (eds.) MODELS 2012. LNCS, vol. 7590, pp. 562–578. Springer, Heidelberg (2012)
10. Chenouard, R., Jouault, F.: Automatically Discovering Hidden Transformation Chaining Constraints. In: Schürr, A., Selic, B. (eds.) MODELS 2009. LNCS, vol. 5795, pp. 92–106. Springer, Heidelberg (2009)
11. Jouault, F., Kurtev, I.: Transforming Models with ATL. In: Bruel, J.-M. (ed.) MoDELS 2005 Workshops. LNCS, vol. 3844, pp. 128–138. Springer, Heidelberg (2006)
12. Rubin, F.: Enumerating all simple paths in a graph. IEEE Transactions on Circuits and Systems 25, 641–642 (1978)
13. Wachsmuth, G.: Metamodel Adaptation and Model Co-adaptation. In: Ernst, E. (ed.) ECOOP 2007. LNCS, vol. 4609, pp. 600–624. Springer, Heidelberg (2007)
14. Cicchetti, A., Di Ruscio, D., Pierantonio, A.: A Metamodel Independent Approach to Difference Representation. Journal of Object Technology 6, 165–185 (2007)
15. Di Ruscio, D., Iovino, L., Pierantonio, A.: Managing the Coupled Evolution of Metamodels and Textual Concrete Syntax Specifications. In: 2013 39th EUROMICRO Conference on Software Engineering and Advanced Applications (SEAA), pp. 114–121 (2013)
16. Di Ruscio, D., Lämmel, R., Pierantonio, A.: Automated Co-evolution of GMF Editor Models. In: Malloy, B., Staab, S., van den Brand, M. (eds.) SLE 2010. LNCS, vol. 6563, pp. 143–162. Springer, Heidelberg (2011)
17. Di Ruscio, D., Iovino, L., Pierantonio, A.: Evolutionary Togetherness: How to Manage Coupled Evolution in Metamodeling Ecosystems. In: Ehrig, H., Engels, G., Kreowski, H.-J., Rozenberg, G. (eds.) ICGT 2012. LNCS, vol. 7562, pp. 20–37. Springer, Heidelberg (2012)
18. Di Ruscio, D., Iovino, L., Pierantonio, A.: A Methodological Approach for the Coupled Evolution of Metamodels and ATL Transformations. In: Duddy, K., Kappel, G. (eds.) ICMB 2013. LNCS, vol. 7909, pp. 60–75. Springer, Heidelberg (2013)
19. Voigt, K.: Structural Graph-based Metamodel Matching. PhD thesis (2011)
20. Melnik, S., Garcia-Molina, H., Rahm, E.: Similarity flooding: A versatile graph matching algorithm and its application to schema matching. In: Proceedings of 18th International Conference on Data Engineering, pp. 117–128 (2002)
21. Falleri, J.-R., Huchard, M., Lafourcade, M., Nebut, C.: Metamodel Matching for Automatic Model Transformation Generation. In: Czarnecki, K., Ober, I., Bruel, J.-M., Uhl, A., Völter, M. (eds.) MODELS 2008. LNCS, vol. 5301, pp. 326–340. Springer, Heidelberg (2008)
22. Planas, E., Cabot, J., Gómez, C.: Two Basic Correctness Properties for ATL Transformations: Executability and Coverage. In: 3rd International Workshop on Model Transformation with ATL, Zurich, Suisse (2011)
23. Vignaga, A.: Metrics for Measuring ATL Model Transformations. Technical report (2009)
24. Read, R.C., Corneil, D.G.: The graph isomorphism disease. J. Graph Theory 1, 339–363 (1977)
25. Lin, Y., Gray, J., Jouault, F.: DSMDiff: A Differentiation Tool for Domain-Specific Models. 16, 349–361 (2007), (Special Issue on Model-Driven Development)
26. Bryant, B.R., Gray, J., Mernik, M., Clarke, P.J., France, R.B., Karsai, G.: Challenges and directions in formalizing the semantics of modeling languages. Comput. Sci. Inf. Syst. 8, 225–253 (2011)
27. Hülsbusch, M., König, B., Rensink, A., Semenyak, M., Soltenborn, C., Wehrheim, H.: Showing Full Semantics Preservation in Model Transformation - A Comparison of Techniques. In: Méry, D., Merz, S. (eds.) IFM 2010. LNCS, vol. 6396, pp. 183–198. Springer, Heidelberg (2010)
28. Sheth, A.P., Larson, J.A.: Federated Database Systems for Managing Distributed, Heterogeneous, and Autonomous Databases. ACM Comput. Surv. 22, 183–236 (1990)

29. Rivera, J.E., Ruiz-Gonzalez, D., Lopez-Romero, F., Bautista, J., Vallecillo, A.: Orchestrating ATL Model Transformations. In: Proc. of MtATL 2009, Nantes, France, pp. 34–46 (2009)
30. Wagelaar, D., Van Der Straeten, R., Deridder, D.: Module superimposition: A composition technique for rule-based model transformation languages. Software & Systems Modeling 9, 285–309 (2010)
31. Braun, V., Margaria, T., Weise, C.: Integrating Tools in the ETI Platform. STTT 1, 31–48 (1997)

Classification of Model Transformation Tools: Pattern Matching Techniques

Cláudio Gomes, Bruno Barroca, and Vasco Amaral

CITI, Departamento de Informática,
Faculdade de Ciências e Tecnologias,
Universidade Nova de Lisboa,
Portugal

Abstract. While comparing different model transformation languages (MTLs), it is common to refer to their syntactic and semantic features and overlook their supporting tools' performance. Performance is one of the aspects that can hamper the application of MDD to industrial scenarios. An highly declarative MTL might simply not scale well when using large models due to its supporting implementation. In this paper, we focus on the several pattern matching techniques (including optimization techniques) employed in the most popular transformation tools, and discuss their effectiveness w.r.t. the expressive power of the languages used. Because pattern matching is the most costly operation in a transformation execution, we present a classification of the existing model transformation tools according to the pattern matching optimization techniques they implement. Our classification complements existing ones that are more focused at syntactic and semantic features of the languages supported by those tools.

Keywords: Model Transformations, Languages Design, Pattern Matching Techniques.

1 Introduction

The immersion of computer technology in a wide range of domains leads to a situation where the users' needs become demanding and increasingly complex (the problem domain). Consequently, engineering successful software systems also becomes increasingly complex (solution domain). A promising "divide-and-conquer" idea to break down this increasing complexity, is to intensively use Models during all stages of software development.

In Model Driven Development (MDD), both the design and development of new software systems is done by having multiple levels of abstraction, where each level deals only with a particular aspect of the system (therefore decreasing its complexity), and assuring the consistency between them (e.g., translations, synchronizations, etc.). In practice, each level of abstraction can be formalized by means of a Domain Specific Modelling Language (DSML), and materialized by its respective supporting tools ,i.e., editors, simulators, interpreters, analysers and compilers [1,2,3].

J. Dingel et al. (Eds.): MODELS 2014, LNCS 8767, pp. 619–635, 2014.

In this context, Model Transformation Tools (MTTs) are specifically designed to transform models according to a transformation specification expressed in a Model Transformation Language (MTL) [4]. Model transformation specifications are expressed by means of a set of symbolic representations of the source languages syntactic structures (also known as patterns) that represent is to be transformed during its execution.

Meanwhile, there exist so many different MTLs, with so many different properties and features, that anyone using them, here denominated as Transformation Engineer, can have serious problems selecting which one is the most appropriate to be used in a particular model transformation task. Moreover, the level of abstraction used on these MTLs, in practice, impacts both the productivity, and the scalability. In the one hand, it is known that the high level of abstraction employed in declarative MTLs, implies that model transformations expressed on them are not only easier to read and maintain by the Transformation Engineers [5]. In the other hand, this high level of abstraction *still* imposes a considerable downside on the run-time performance of the execution of the model transformations expressed on these MTLs [6,7,8,9,10,11,12]. This can be explained by the fact that the operation of finding the specified pattern in an arbitrary input model of the source language (also called pattern matching) is equivalent to the problem of finding a graph isomorphism [13,14], which is an NP-Complete problem.

Run-time performance of MTLs is one of the aspects that can hamper the application of MTLs and consequently MDD, to industrial scenarios. In the general practice of software engineering, Transformation Engineers that use highly declarative MTLs in order to express their model transformations, can be forced to repeat themselves using imperative low-level programming languages, just because, it is still a major challenge for a declarative MTL to reach the point where its productivity outweighs its performance problems, at least compared with as imperative approach. We believe that research will continue to improve the performance aspect to the point where scalability will no longer be an issue. It is of utmost importance to provide the Transformation Engineer with a classification of the existing MTLs along with their supporting Model Transformation Tools (MTTs) in what matters to optimization techniques supported.

In this paper, we observe several Model Transformation Tools (MTTs), with particular focus on the implementation and optimization of the pattern matching techniques they employ.

This article contributes with the extensive collection of many different techniques ranging from the amount and kind of performance-related information required from the user, to the optimization techniques used on those tools.

In the next section, we present our methodology to select and classify existing MTTs. Then, in Section 3, we present some of the most used techniques, how they are organized according to our classification and which tools implement them. In Section 4, we explore our classification, how it can be used, and how it complements existing other existing classifications. Finally, we conclude in

Section 5 by relating the degree of optimization of each MTT with the syntactic features of the supported Model Transformation Language (MTL).

2   Methodology

In order to properly classify and compare the existing tools and their pattern matching techniques, we need to establish a common view and understanding of what is a model transformation environment and the execution process as a whole.

2.1   Transformation Environment Overview

A model transformation is "the automatic generation of a target model from a source model, according to a transformation definition" [15]. Fig. 1 establishes a common view of a generic MTL, its supporting tools and the involved models (input and output). Notice that all represented models are conforming to their respective metamodels.

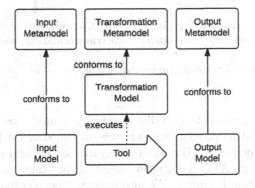

Fig. 1. Model transformation overview: language, tool and models

2.2   Transformation Execution Overview

In order to improve pattern matching, existing tools employ optimizations at multiple stages of the transformation process. This is very similar to what happens in database systems where, prior to any query execution, there is index creation so that, when a query is made, other techniques such as exploring different evaluation plans, are applied to get the most efficient execution of that query [16]. It is because of that, that in order to study each pattern matching technique, we need an high-level description of a typical transformation execution highlighting the multiple stages of the process.

Fig. 2 identifies the two most followed approaches to MTL execution: interpretation (left) and compilation (right). We stress the fact that the presented

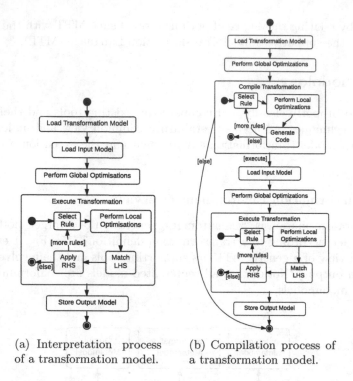

(a) Interpretation process of a transformation model.

(b) Compilation process of a transformation model.

Fig. 2. Execution process of a transformation model

diagrams are not supposed to describe exactly how model transformation tools operate, but instead to provide a clear view of the stages where optimization techniques can be employed. But these diagrams are general enough to fit even imperative tools (e.g., ATC [17]), where most of the stages are manually coded by the Transformation Engineer. We also assume that a transformation is comprised of a set of *rules*, each containing a Left Hand Side (LHS) pattern, that needs to be found in the input model, and a Right Hand Side (RHS) pattern which represents the model that will be output in the end of the execution. There is no loss of generality, since these *rules* (with the mentioned patterns) do not need to be explicitly represented in the MTL, but instead be explicit.

These Figures also show that an MTT always starts by loading the transformation and, in the particular case of interpretation, the input model. At this point, some existing MTTs perform **global** optimizations, such as the definition of indexes, refactorings, based on the analysis of the transformation specification. For instance, a **global** optimization may influence the order of rule selection, and even the information shared between different rules. Then the tool executes the transformation, selecting each rule and optionally performing some **local** optimizations. These optimizations are concerned with minimizing the search space while searching for the occurrences of the LHS pattern in a given input model, i.e., while executing one rule.

We define **global** and **local** optimizations in terms of the scope of their impact. While **local** optimizations are concerned with improving one particular pattern match operation, **global** optimizations can impact several ones. Furthermore, **global** optimizations handle information from the whole input model, or from a representative one while **local** ones rely on limited information, either about the pattern in execution, or from some kind of aggregation provided by some other **global** technique.

The main difference between a compilation and an interpretation, from the point of view of the pattern matching process, is when the information input model is available to the tool. The two approaches have advantages and disadvantages: in interpretation mode, an MTT has to spend some cycles gathering information about the input model before executing the actual transformation process; whereas while compiling a transformation, a MTT can only access to statistics about typical input models. However, in order to compensate for the lack of information available during the compilation process, some tools can still prepare the generated transformation code so that the actual input model can be analysed when it gets executed. This means that, in both execution modes, the information about the input models can always be retrieved so, in principle, each optimization technique can be applied regardless of whether we are talking about a compilation approach or an interpretation approach. Of course there are techniques that do not depend on the information about the input model.

In summary, the possible optimization techniques that can be employed do not depend on the execution mode of the transformation tools, and so we do not need to classify the optimization techniques according to the execution approach in which they are employed.

2.3   Classification Rationale

In order to identify most of the existing pattern matching techniques, we tried to cover as many and as diverse MTTs as possible. We achieved variety on the different observed MTTs, by taking into account their distinguishing syntactic and semantic features as identified in [18], namely: (i) imperative tools such as ATC [17] and T-Core [19]; (ii) declarative tools such as AGG [20], Atom3 [21]; (iii) programmed graph rewriting approaches such as GReAT [22], GrGen.NET [23], PROGReS [24], VMTS [25] and MoTif [26]; (iv) incremental approaches such as Beanbag [27], Viatra2 [9] and Tefkat [28]; (v) and bidirectional approaches such as BOTL [29]. Notice that there are many more MTTs but we had to restrict our search to MTTs that published at least one paper about its internal execution mechanisms and optimization techniques. For instance, we did not consider tools such as SmartQVT [30] because we did not find any paper about optimization techniques being used in SmartQVT.

We followed a systematic approach to classify the pattern matching techniques. We first paid attention to the degree of domain and tool knowledge the Transformation Engineer has to have in order to perform (and/or improve) the pattern matching execution of a model transformation. For instance, there are MTTs that require the Transformation Engineer to both manually code and improve the pattern matching procedure (these are called **manual approaches**). However, most of the existing MTTs do not require (or even allow) any intervention from the Transformation Engineer in the pattern matching procedure (**automatic approaches**). Yet, in an attempt to obtain the best of both worlds, there are MTTs whose languages introduce special syntactic constructs, so that if performance is at stake, the Transformation Engineer is able to interfere and optimize their execution (**semi-automatic approaches**).

We then organised the pattern matching techniques with respect to the scope of their impact. i.e., whether they are **global** or **local** optimizations.

We observed that some **local** techniques had a planning phase, were a cost model is used to perform the optimization, and some techniques rely on heuristics and hence, do not have a planning phase. These were classified in **planned** and **unplanned**.

These categories are just the foundation to classify most of the existing pattern matching optimization techniques. We found more categories while exploring a specific set of techniques. For instance, most **global** techniques are either **caching, indexing** or **overlapped pattern matching** techniques. In the next section we explore each of these categories and the concrete techniques with examples and referring to the state of the art MTTs that implement them.

3   Classification

Table 1 shows many MTTs and which pattern matching techniques they make use of. Since tools evolve very rapidly we have included the year next to the tool in which a paper was published concerning the tool's internal mechanisms to perform pattern matching. The header of Table presents the techniques we studied, organized according to the categories we introduced in the previous section. Notice that we do not include all the pattern matching techniques that we have found: we give special emphasis to those that are more pervasive across multiple MTTs.

We try to provide a simple and general explanation for each pattern matching technique with the help of the sample patterns shown in Fig. 4. We present each pattern as being matched against the input model shown in Fig. 3(a). Notice that, in the input model, the *id* attribute of each element appears to the left of its type.

3.1   Manual Techniques

MTTs that enable the Transformation Engineers to **manually** code and optimize the pattern matching process, usually do so by providing an API with the necessary imperative constructs to perform CRUD (Create-Read-Update-Delete) operations in the input model of the transformation. For instance, if the Transformation Engineer wants to match the pattern shown in Fig. 4(a) against the input model of Fig. 3(a), s/he could leverage his/her domain knowledge by manually coding the pattern matching process as shown in Algorithm 1.

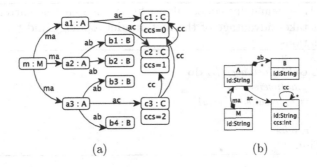

Fig. 3. Sample input model (left) and corresponding metamodel (right)

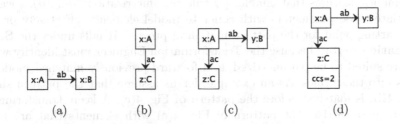

Fig. 4. Sample patterns

The Transformation Engineer combines two crucial bits of information: *(i) domain knowledge*, since s/he knows that any instance of B is always contained in an instance of A (as it is shown in the metamodel of Fig. 3(b)); and *(ii) tool knowledge*, since s/he knows that the underlying model storage framework keeps inverse associations (such as *y.abInverse* in Algorithm 1). Also note that the *GetAllInstances(B)* operation is part of the tool's API, and is used to fetch the set of all instances of B in the input model of Fig. 3(a).

ATC [17] and T-Core [19] are good examples of low-level, imperative languages that require the Transformation Engineer to manually code the pattern matching process.

Due to the imperative nature of these languages, there are no optimization techniques that fall under the **Manual** category: if we want optimization, we have to do it ourselves.

3.2 Semi-automatic Techniques

There is a wide array of **Semi-automatic** techniques such as the usage of *lazy rules* (as in ATL [31]), or the *user-specified strategies* employed to solve systems of equations involving several attributes (as in BOTL [32]). Most of the considered **Semi-automatic** techniques are exclusive of each individual tool but there is one that is pervasive in almost all the studied tools: **Pivoting**. It basically consists of reusing previously matched objects.

Algorithm 1. A manually coded algorithm to match the pattern shown in Fig. 4(a) that takes advantage of the metamodel topology and the existence of inverse associations

```
1: function MATCH
2:     for y ∈ GetAllInstances(B) do
3:         x ← y.abInverse
4:         results ← results ∪ {(x,y)}
5:     end for
6:     return results
7: end function
```

In order to support **Pivoting**, the MTL must include the necessary syntactic and semantic features that enable: *(i)* rule parametrization; and *(ii)* a way to instantiate those parameters with concrete model elements, effectively providing a starting point for the pattern matching process. It falls under the **Semi-automatic** category because the Transformation Engineer must identify which rules are suited to be parametrized, and forward previously matched model elements into those rules. As an example, let us assume that the pattern shown in Fig. 4(b) is matched before the pattern of Fig. 4(c). A keen Transformation Engineer parametrizes the pattern of Fig. 4(c) with elements that are to be matched in the pattern Fig. 4(b). Algorithm 2 shows the resulting generated code that matched the pattern of Fig. 4(c). For the sake of brevity, we omit the code generated to match the pattern of Fig. 4(b) as it would be similar to Algorithm 1. We also omit the generated code that calls the function defined in Algorithm 2 with the set of bindings collected during the matching process of pattern of Fig. 4(b).

GReAT [22,11] and MoTif [33] allow for semi-automatic **Pivoting**. In those MTTs, a transformation specification consists of a network of rules with a well defined interface of input and output parameters. The input interface declares the rule's incoming partial matches that serve as a starting point for the pattern matching. The output interface represents the bindings that will be propagated to the next rules in the network.

Algorithm 2. An algorithm to match the pattern of Fig. 4(c)

```
1: function GENERATEDMATCH(AacCOccurrences)
2:     for (x,z) ∈ AacCOccurrences do
3:         for y ∈ x.ab do
4:             results ← results ∪ {(x,y,z)}
5:         end for
6:     end for
7:     return results
8: end function
```

3.3 Automatic Techniques

Most of the identified techniques are automatic, i.e., they require minimal intervention and knowledge from the Transformation Engineer in order to be used. The MTTs that employ these techniques typically work with declarative rules and, optionally, provide imperative constructs in order to enable the control (or configuration) of the rule scheduling. In what matters to the pattern matching process, we distinguish **Local** techniques from **Global** techniques.

The **Local** pattern matching techniques are algorithms that have to *transverse* the input model (in the worst case), while checking if there is a match *for each* element in the pattern.

Since their execution involves the selection of multiple choice points (i.e., possible candidate nodes to be checked), and going back to those choice points to test further alternatives, these algorithms are said to be local search based [34]. Even MTTs that reduce the pattern matching problem to a constraint satisfaction problem (e.g., AGG [12]), or even a database query problem (e.g., Gr-Gen(PSQL) [35]) are indirectly performing local search [36,16]. Because of this, they all fall in the category of **Local** optimization techniques.

While studying these techniques, we found that some involved a planning phase in which they use special data structures (such as search graphs in Viatra2 [9], or pattern graph in PROGRES [37]); and some simply execute the search immediately using nothing but some global data structures (such as indexes, as is done in VMTS [25]). We classified the former kind of techniques as **Planned** and the later as **Unplanned**. The referred data structures in **Planned** techniques are typically built automatically from LHS patterns, and provide a representation of all possible ways of searching for a given LHS pattern. For instance, a possible way to represent the search graph for the pattern of Fig. 4(d) is represented in Fig. 5(a). Notice that from the starting point, represented as a smaller circle, the local search can begin at either A, or B, or C. Suppose it starts from C, as indicated by the bold arrows, it then can proceed to A elements (maybe taking advantage of inverse relations), and so on for B elements. The bold arrows represent one of the many search plans.

In order to be able to compare between search plans, and select a good one, MTTs use a cost model. We distinguish different **Planned** techniques according to the cost model used. Some cost models only use information about the metamodel (these are called **Metamodel Sensitive**); other cost models use statistical information about the input model (these are called **Model Sensitive**); or even explicit information about the tool's implementation (these are called **Implementation Sensitive**).

Metamodel Sensitive cost models employ a set of heuristics that make use of the match metamodel in a given model transformation—these were presented in [37], and used in the PROGRES tool. An example of such heuristics is the *first-fail* principle: a good plan should start the search in the most restricted pattern element, since it will have the fewest possible occurrences. Following this principle, a good plan to search for occurrences of the pattern shown in

Fig. 4(d) would be to start by searching all the z elements, given that they specify attribute constraints.

Model Sensitive cost models use statistical information about the current input model or, at least, of a representative collection of input models. As an example, we demonstrate the cost model used in the Viatra2 [9]. According to [9], the cost of a search plan is given by the potential size of the search tree formed by its execution. For instance, if we consider the search graph presented in Fig. 5(a), then the potential size of the search tree corresponding to a possible search plan shown in bold is given by $\bar{z} + \bar{z} * \bar{x}_z + \bar{z} * \bar{x}_z * \bar{y}_x$, where: $\bar{z}$ denotes the expected number of model elements that can be matched by the z element; $\bar{x}_z$ denotes the average number of model elements that can be matched by x after binding z to some model element; and $\bar{y}_x$ denotes the same for y after binding x to some model element. In Fig. 5(b), we show a weighted version of the presented search graph, but now considering the statistics of a given input model. Following the presented cost model (i.e., computing the potential sizes of the different search trees), it is clear that, in this case, the evaluation of a search plan that follows the order $z \rightarrow x \rightarrow y$ (shown in bold) yields a cost of 9.99, is preferable to a search plan that follows the order $y \rightarrow x \rightarrow z$, since its evaluation yields a higher cost of 12.

An **Implementation Sensitive** cost model such as the one presented in [6] and implemented in the GrGen.NET [23] tool, takes into account not only the size of the search tree, but also the cost of each individual operation such as the search for all the elements given some type. This allows the MTT to consider the existence of indexes and other characteristics of its own implementation in the cost model. This is similar to the cost model used in database systems since they typically take the indexes and other implementation features into account [16].

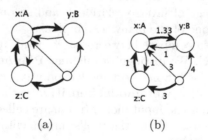

(a)   (b)

Fig. 5. Search graph (left) and weighted search graph (right). These graphs represent the pattern of Fig. 4(d).

In what matters to **Global** techniques, we identify three different types of optimization techniques: **Caching**, **Indexing**, and **Overlapped Pattern Matching**.

Most of the analysed MTTs allow the definition of variables and conditions composed of multiple expressions over elements in a match pattern definition. Depending on the number of times that the same expression is used in different match patterns, its repeated evaluation may degrade the overall performance of the transformation. To mitigate this problem, transformation tools such as ATL [31], apply **Caching** techniques, by evaluating all expressions once, and storing the resulting values so that they can be directly retrieved later.

All of the observed MTTs use indexes. Most of the indexes used keep model elements grouped by their corresponding type as described in the metamodel (**Type Indexing**). However, we have identified two additional kinds of indexes: **Attribute** and **Structural**. While the former allows the MTTs to efficiently find elements given a condition on one of their attributes, the later allows MTTs to index whole patterns that are matched often in the transformation. In order to perform indexing, the required intervention and knowledge from the Transformation Engineers range from minimal (as in PROGRES [37,24]), to none (as in Viatra2 [10,9]), where in the later case, the **structural** indexes are automatically created for all of the patterns defined in a transformation specification.

Finally, there are MTTs that try to automatically factorize two or more match patterns, in order to identify a common pattern that can be matched before them. In this technique, known as **Overlapped Pattern Matching**, the common (or overlapped) pattern occurrences are then passed as pivots in order to be matched by the remaining patterns of the two rules [38]. Note that the difference between this technique and **Pivoting** is in the common occurrences detection, which has to be fully automated. If the user is required to identify common occurrences, then it is just **Pivoting**, as is done in Great [22,11] and in Viatra2 [10,9]. To the best of our knowledge, only VMTS [25] implements this technique.

4   Discussion

Performance is one of the aspects that can hamper the application of MDD to industrial scenarios. Before undergoing a major project, the Transformation Engineer should study which tools are better suited for that project. S/He can not risk choosing a declarative and productive MTL and, at a later stage of the project, discovering that the transformations specified in that language, supported by that tool, do not scale well.

Our classification in Table 1 complements existing ones by looking at the optimizations employed in the implementation of the MTLs. Of course this is a moving target: in theory, a language is independent of its implementation, so we expect that more and more optimizations will emerge that will outdate Table 1. However, we do not expect the kinds of optimization techniques as identified in Section 2, such as **Manual** vs **Semi-automatic** vs **Automatic**, **Local** vs **Global**, **Planned** vs **Unplanned**, and so on... to change that much.

Perhaps the most widely applicable categorization of MTLs is presented in [18]. Their MTL categorization is done in a comprehensive way by means of a feature model that elicits the variability of MTLs w.r.t. both their syntactic constructs and their semantic features. However, they do not make explicit any features regarding the run-time performance of their transformation engines.

On a more pragmatic point of view of MTL's usage context, [39] provides a taxonomy that aims to aid Transformation Engineers in deciding which MTL is best suited to carry out a particular model transformation activity. They identify as important characteristics the degree of automation and complexity. This taxonomy was extended in [40] by grouping several model transformation purposes (e.g., simulation, synchronization, optimization), according to the models, metamodels and abstraction levels involved in a given transformation.

In the context of quality engineering, [41] proposes a comprehensive evaluation schema based on ISO 9126 [42]. The proposed evaluation schema aims to help the Transformation Engineers on choosing an appropriate MTL, by comparing different MTL's tooling support, implementation, syntactic features, community support and their future perspectives. In a similar line of research, [43] compares four different MTLs and corresponding MTTs using a common transformation problem. Their categorization is based on the following characteristics: the representation of models and metamodels, the constructs used to define transformation rules, rule scheduling constructs and formal analysis support. They also take into account the tooling support for each language such as: Editors, Transformation Simulation Support, Compilation, Debugging and Validation.

To our knowledge, only [9] provides a categorization of graph transformation tools based in their pattern matching strategies but with focus in the execution of individual rules.

In summary, there is no classification directed at the underlying techniques employed in the transformation engines of the existing model transformation languages across the whole transformation process. Instead, most classifications are directed at their usability w.r.t their syntactic and semantic features and usage scenarios. Knowing the optimization techniques supported by a given tool allows the Transformation Engineer to assess if that tool can be applied to industrial scenarios.

5   Conclusions

There is a wide variety of approaches to the pattern matching problem, having different outcomes, in what matters to the required amount of effort from the Transformation Engineer, and the end result in what matters to run-time performance. In this paper, we presented a classification of the different model transformation approaches w.r.t. the employed pattern matching techniques.

MTTs that focus on **Manual** approaches typically provide imperative (see Czarnecki's categorization [18]) constructs in their MTLs. Therefore, they require domain expertise and knowledge about the tool's internal pattern matching mechanisms. Their MTLs are powerful and expressive. However, the specified transformations are verbose and difficult to read, which hinders the productivity of the Transformation Engineer. Nevertheless, their execution can be extremely fast, since the Transformation Engineer is able to directly code any kind of optimizations using his/her knowledge about the domain. Therefore, these MTTs are ideally suited to perform critical model transformations, or even to implement higher-level MTLs, as is the case of T-Core [19], which was used to implement MoTif [44].

MTTs that support many **Automatic** pattern matching techniques require less amount of information from the Transformation Engineer and ease the creation and maintenance of the transformation specifications. The transformations are typically comprised of a set of rules declaring the manipulations in the input model without any information regarding the underlying required pattern matching process. Therefore, we can expect the maximum productivity of the Transformation Engineer. However, if the Transformation Engineer knows something about the domain that can be used to speed up the transformations' execution, he/she will not be able to use that knowledge because all the optimization decisions are made solely by the tool.

Finally, MTTs that support **Semi-automatic** techniques still require that the Transformation Engineer have some knowledge about their internal mechanisms, while enabling the expression of high-level declarative transformations. These tools typically focus on allowing the Transformation Engineer to modularize and parametrize rules (*Pivoting*) so that matched elements can be shared among them. The impact in the run-time performance is obvious: the initial bindings of a rule are automatically shared among the shared rules, decreasing (sometimes in several orders of magnitude) the amount of computation needed to match the remaining elements of a given pattern. However, in order to use this feature, the Transformation Engineer has to explicitly create the transformation with these features in mind in order to maximize the sharing of initial bindings between rules—i.e., this imposes a negative impact in the end productivity of the Transformation Engineer.

Ideally, one could expect that the problem of run-time performance of MTTs can be solved solely by **Automatic** pattern matching techniques. However, we observed that the approaches which invested more research in addressing the pattern matching problem tend to combine **Semi-automatic** and **Automatic** techniques. In the one hand, they allow the expression of model transformations as networks of rules, where the flow between rules represents shared LHS pattern occurrences; and in the other hand, they employ planned search in order to perform the pattern matching of the declared rules, while taking advantage of the shared LHS pattern occurrences.

We believe that further improvements on the state of the art regarding MTLs and their MTTs' run-time performance, will follow this research trend of powerful constructs to enable the tuning of model transformation specifications, and the configuration of the increasingly sophisticated pattern matching techniques.

Table 1. State of art tools and the pattern matching techniques in use

Tools	Manual	Semi-Automatic Local	Semi-Automatic Global (Pivoting)	Automatic · Local · Planned · Model Sensitive (Multiple)	Model Sensitive (Single)	Metamodel Sensitive	Implementation Sensitive	Unplanned	Caching	Global · Indexing (Type)	Attribute	Structural	Overlapped P.M.
PROGRES (1996)			X			X	X		X		X	X	
BOTL (2003)		X											
AGG (2004)			X		X	X		X		X			
Atom3 (2004)	X							X					
Great (2004)			X					X					
ATC (2006)	X												
Viatra2 (2006)	X		X	X	X	X				X		X	
Tefkat (2006)		X			X	X				X		X	
ATL (2008)	X	X							X				
GrGen.NET (2008)			X		X		X	X					
Motif (2008)			X					X		X			
BeanBag (2009)			X					X		X			X
VMTS (2010)	X		X					X		X			
T-Core	X												

References

1. Hailpern, B., Tarr, P.: Model-driven development: The good, the bad, and the ugly. IBM Systems Journal 45(3), 451–461 (2006)
2. Atkinson, C., Kuhne, T.: Model-driven development: a metamodeling foundation. IEEE Software 20(5), 36–41 (2003)
3. Van Gorp, P.: Model-driven development of model transformations. In: Ehrig, H., Heckel, R., Rozenberg, G., Taentzer, G. (eds.) ICGT 2008. LNCS, vol. 5214, pp. 517–519. Springer, Heidelberg (2008)
4. Sendall, S., Kozaczynski, W.: Model transformation: The heart and soul of model-driven software development. IEEE Software 20(5), 42–45 (2003)
5. Barroca, B., Amaral, V.: Asserting the correctness of translations. Electronic Communications of the EASST 50 (October 2011) ISSN=1863-2122
6. Veit Batz, G., Kroll, M., Geiß, R.: A first experimental evaluation of search plan driven graph pattern matching. Applications of Graph Transformations with Industrial Relevance, 471–486 (2008)
7. Larrosa, J., Valiente, G.: Constraint satisfaction algorithms for graph pattern matching. Mathematical Structures in Computer Science 12(4), 403–422 (2002)
8. Kalnins, a., Barzdins, J., Celms, E.: Efficiency Problems in MOLA Implementation. In: 19th International Conference, OOPSLA. Citeseer (2004)
9. Varró, G., Friedl, K., Varro, D., Schurr, A.: Advanced Techniques for the Implementation of Model Transformation Systems. PhD thesis, Budapest University of Technology and Economics (2008)
10. Bergmann, G., Ökrös, A, Ráth, I., Varro, D., Varró, G.: Incremental pattern matching in the viatra model transformation system. In: Proceedings of the Third International Workshop on Graph and Model Transformations. ACM (2008)
11. Zólyomi, I., Porkoláb, Z.: Towards generation of efficient transformations. In: Karsai, G., Visser, E. (eds.) GPCE 2004. LNCS, vol. 3286, pp. 266–282. Springer, Heidelberg (2004)
12. Rudolf, M.: Utilizing constraint satisfaction techniques for efficient graph pattern matching. In: Ehrig, H., Engels, G., Kreowski, H.-J., Rozenberg, G. (eds.) Graph Transformation, 1998. LNCS, vol. 1764, pp. 238–252. Springer, Heidelberg (2000)
13. Mehlhorn, K.: Graph algorithms and NP-completeness (1984)
14. Garey, M.R., Johnson, D.S.: Computers and Intractability. A Guide to the Theory of NP-Completeness. W H Freeman & Company (January 1979)
15. Kleppe, A.G., Warmer, J.B., Bast, W.: MDA explained: the model driven architecture: Practice and promise. Addison-Wesley Professional (2003)
16. Silberschatz, A., Korth, H., Sudarshan, S.: Database System Concepts. McGraw-Hill Science/Engineering/Math (January 2010)
17. Estévez, A., Padrón, J., Sánchez, V., Roda, J.L.: ATC: A Low-Level Model Transformation Language. In: The 2nd International Workshop on Model ... (2006)
18. Czarnecki, K., Helsen, S.: Classification of model transformation approaches. In: Proceedings of the 2nd OOPSLA Workshop on Generative Techniques in the Context of the Model Driven Architecture, vol. 45 (2003)
19. Syriani, E., Vangheluwe, H.: De-/re-constructing model transformation languages. Electronic Communications of the EASST 29 (2010)
20. Taentzer, G.: AGG: A graph transformation environment for modeling and validation of software. In: Pfaltz, J.L., Nagl, M., Böhlen, B. (eds.) AGTIVE 2003. LNCS, vol. 3062, pp. 446–453. Springer, Heidelberg (2004)

21. Lara, J.D., Vangheluwe, H., Alfonseca, M.: Meta-modelling and graph grammars for multi-paradigm modelling in AToM 3. Software & Systems Modeling 3(3), 194–209 (2004)

22. Balasubramanian, D., Narayanan, A., van Buskirk, C., Karsai, G.: The graph rewriting and transformation language: GReAT. Electronic Communications of the EASST 1 (2007)

23. Kroll, M., Geiß, R.: Developing Graph Transformations with Gr-Gen.NET. Applications of Graph Transformation with Industrial releVancE-AGTIVE 2007 (2007)

24. Schurr, A.: Progres, a visual language and environment for programming with graph rewriting systems. Technical report (1994)

25. Levendovszky, T., Lengyel, L., Mezei, G., Charaf, H.: A systematic approach to metamodeling environments and model transformation systems in VMTS. Electronic Notes in Theoretical Computer Science 127(1), 65–75 (2005)

26. Syriani, E., Vangheluwe, H.: A modular timed graph transformation language for simulation-based design. Software & Systems Modeling, 1–28 (2011)

27. Xiong, Y., Hu, Z., Zhao, H., Song, H., Takeichi, M., Mei, H.: Supporting automatic model inconsistency fixing. In: Proceedings of the the 7th Joint Meeting of the European Software Engineering Conference and the ACM SIGSOFT Symposium on The Foundations of Software Engineering. ACM (2009)

28. Lawley, M., Steel, J.: Practical declarative model transformation with Tefkat. In: Bruel, J.-M. (ed.) MoDELS 2005 Workshops. LNCS, vol. 3844, pp. 139–150. Springer, Heidelberg (2006)

29. Braun, P., Marschall, F.: Botl–the bidirectional object oriented transformation language. Technical report (2003)

30. Telecom, F.: Smartqvt: An open source model transformation tool implementing the mof 2.0 qvt-operational language (2007)

31. Jouault, F., Allilaire, F., Bezivin, J., Kurtev, I.: ATL: A model transformation tool. Science of Computer Programming 72(1-2) (June 2008)

32. Braun, P., Marschall, F.: Transforming object oriented models with BOTL. Electronic Notes in Theoretical Computer Science 72(3), 103–117 (2003)

33. Syriani, E., Vangheluwe, H.: Programmed Graph Rewriting with DEVS. In: Schürr, A., Nagl, M., Zündorf, A. (eds.) AGTIVE 2007. LNCS, vol. 5088, pp. 136–151. Springer, Heidelberg (2008)

34. Knuth, D.E.: The Art of Computer Programming, Combinatorial Algorithms, Part 1, vol. 4A. Addison-Wesley (January 2011)

35. Hack, S.: Graphersetzung für Optimierungen in der Codeerzeugung. Master's thesis, Universität Karlsruhe (2003)

36. Russell, S., Norvig, P.: Artificial intelligence: A modern approach 2003 (2003)

37. Zündorf, A.: Graph pattern matching in PROGRES. Technical report (1996)

38. Mészáros, T., Mezei, G., Levendovszky, T.: Manual and automated performance optimization of model transformation systems. International Journal on . . . (2010)

39. Mészáros, T., Van Gorp, P.: A Taxonomy of Model Transformation. In: Electronic Notes in Theoretical Computer Science ENTCS, vol. 152 (2006)

40. Syriani, E.: A multi-paradigm foundation for model transformation language engineering. PhD thesis. McGill University (2011)

41. Schubert, L.A.: An Evaluation of Model Transformation Languages for UML Quality Engineering. PhD thesis, Master's thesis, Georg-August-Universität Göttingen (2010) [cited at p. 101]

42. ISO/IEC: ISO/IEC 9126. Software engineering – Product quality. ISO/IEC (2001)

43. Ehrig, K., Guerra, E., Lara, J.D., Lengyel, L., Prange, U., Taentzer, G., Varro, D., et al.: Model transformation by graph transformation: A comparative study. In: Gheyi, R., Tiago (eds.) IN MTIP 2005, International Workshop on Model Transformations in Practice (Satellite Event of Models 2005), pp. 71–80 (2006)
44. Syriani, E., Vangheluwe, H.: Programmed graph rewriting with time for simulation-based design. In: Vallecillo, A., Gray, J., Pierantonio, A. (eds.) ICMT 2008. LNCS, vol. 5063, pp. 91–106. Springer, Heidelberg (2008)

Learning Implicit and Explicit Control in Model Transformations by Example

Islem Baki[1], Houari Sahraoui[1], Quentin Cobbaert[1,2], Philippe Masson[1,2], and Martin Faunes[1]

[1] DIRO, Université de Montréal, Canada
[2] Université de Namur, Belgium

Abstract. We propose an evolutionary approach that, in addition to learn model transformation rules from examples, allows to capture implicit and explicit control over the transformation rules. The derivation of both transformation and control knowledge is performed through a heuristic search, i.e., a genetic programming algorithm, guided by the conformance with examples of past transformations supplied as pairs of source and target models. Our approach is evaluated on four model transformation problems that require non-trivial control. The obtained results are convincing for three of the four studied problems.

Keywords: Model transformation by example, transformation control, genetic programming.

1 Introduction

Model transformation (MT) are a keystone of the model-driven engineering (MDE) paradigm, allowing to move from one model to another while keeping the overall consistency. As MT is the main mechanism that supports the MDE vision, much effort has been put into developing new approaches, languages and tools to improve model transformation writing and promote the adoption of MDE. However, writing MT remains a very difficult task and can thus compromise the benefits brought by MDE. In this regard, the automation of MT is critical to the success of an MDE-based project. There are many contributions that have been proposed to improve the automation of model transformations. Among them, learning model transformation by example (MTBE) is an appealing alternative to achieve automation in the absence of sufficient knowledge regarding the transformation.

During the last decade, the idea of learning MT using examples caught on. Numerous contributions have been proposed to learn model transformations from examples. Nonetheless, one common limitation of the existing approaches, is their inability to learn complex model transformations that require sophisticated mechanisms of control. Indeed, many transformations are complex and cannot be handled by separate pieces of knowledge. Target-model fragments to create must be arranged in a non trivial way to produce a consistent model [18]. Moreover, source-model constructs cannot be transformed in an arbitrary order.

J. Dingel et al. (Eds.): MODELS 2014, LNCS 8767, pp. 636–652, 2014.

To deal with these situations, MTBE approaches should also learn knowledge about the transformation control.

Recently, we proposed an approach to learn transformation rules from examples using a genetic programming approach [9]. We tested this approach on simplified model transformation problems that do not require sophisticated control. In this paper, we propose an enhanced approach that, in addition to learn transformation rules, allows to capture implicit control, i.e., control embedded within the transformation rules, and explicit control, i.e., in the form of meta-rules, over the transformations. Moreover, we broaden the spectrum of the learned transformations. The difference with our previous work includes, in addition to the control, the inclusion of navigation primitives, negative condition use (NOT), and the consideration of types and definition domains for the constants generation and constructs property setting. Similarly, to our previous work, the derivation of both transformation and control knowledge is performed through a heuristic search guided by the conformance with examples of past transformations supplied as pairs of source and target models. In our approach evaluation, we obtained precision and recall values higher than 75% for three out of four model transformation problems that require non-trivial control.

The rest of this paper is organized as follows. Section 2 reviews the related work on learning model transformations and on control in model transformation languages. Section 3 describes the transformation control mechanisms and learning problem. Our learning algorithm is detailed in Section 4, and its evaluation is reported in Section 5. Our findings are discussed in Section 6.

2 Related Work

To our best knowledge, there are no research contributions on the explicit control learning for model transformations. In this section, we briefly introduce the existing work on model transformation by example. Then, we give an overview on how the control is handled in the model transformation community.

In 2006, Varro [24] proposed a first approach to learn 1-to-1 model transformation rules by example. Transformation rules are derived semi-automatically from a prototypical set of interrelated source and target models. This initial contribution was improved in 2009 [1] by automating the approach using inductive logic programming (ILS) instead of the original ad-hoc heuristic. Similarly to the previous work, Wimmer et al. proposed in [26] a contribution to derive 1-to-1 transformation rules in the form of ATL rules. Later, Gacia-Magarino et al. [11] proposed an algorithm to generate many-to-many transformation rules presumably in several transformation languages (in the paper, rules are created in a generic tranformation language and are translated to ATL). Close to the above-mentioned work, Dolques [6] learn many-to-many transformation mappings organized in a lattice by means of relational concept analysis. Saada et al. [21] extended this work by producing executable rules from the mappings. With a different strategy, Kessentini et al. proposed in [14] an approach to transform a given source model by analogy with transformation examples. This approach, improved later in [15], does not produce knowledge (rules) but a concrete transformation of a given model. All these contributions need explicit mappings between the constructs of the source and target models given as examples. Faunes et al. [8] recently removed this constraint using genetic programming. Although the control was not considered in the learning process, this approach succeeded to learn complex transformations [9].

The only work that enforces the control in model transformation learning is the one on model transformation by demonstration [22,17]. The control is not learned per se. It is recorded from the order in which the operations are performed in the demonstration.

In the context of rule-based transformations, execution control [4], or rule scheduling, denotes the mechanisms responsible for determining the order in which the individual rules should be applied. Most of the existing model transformation languages offer such control mechanisms. However, the implementation and features differ greatly from one language to another. According to [2], those variations can be considered with respect to three rule scheduling aspects: rule selection, rule iteration and phasing.

Rule Selection. Rules can be selected by either implicit or explicit control techniques. There are languages such as BOTL [3] and OptimalJ that offer an implicit rule control, with which, the user can enforce a desired execution order by conditioning, for example, the execution of a rule to the presence of another rule's output. Hybrid transformation languages such as VIATRA [25] and ATL[13] use explicit control techniques. Explicit control techniques can be external (the control logic is decoupled from the rules) or internal. VIATRA offers external control through the basic set of Abstract State Machines (ASM) to support complex control flow. ATL, on the other hand, uses internal scheduling with the possibility for transformation rules to directly invoke other rules (called lazy rules). Other languages such as AToM3 [5] offer priorities based conflict resolution mechanisms as well as interactive rule selection. KERMETA [7] and SmartQVT [23] imperative approaches entail an explicit rules execution control where the rules are executed according to the flow of the transformation code. ModelMorf [19], which is an implementation of Relational QVT (and thus is fully declarative), allows both implicit and explicit scheduling. While a user cannot establish the execution order of the top-level rules explicitly, those rules can call others in *when* and *where* clauses.

Rule Iteration. This includes recursions, looping and fixpoint iterations. ATL, KERMETA SmartQVT supports recursion. VIATRA on the other hand, supports fixpoint iterations.

Phasing. A transformation may be organized into several phases. For each phase, a subset of rules is defined. ATL, OptimalJ, SmartQVT, and ModelMorf support phasing. For instance, OptimalJ has two distinct phases, one creates the containment hierarchy of the target model, and the other sets the attributes and references.

3   Problem Statement

3.1   Implicit and Explicit Control

To illustrate the notion of transformation control, let us consider the transformation of UML class diagrams into relational schemas. For this transformation, some constructs have to be transformed before others to produce a consistent relational schema. For instance, classes must be transformed into tables before transforming their attributes into columns of the corresponding tables.

The transformation control can be implicit or explicit or both depending on the transformation language. It is called implicit when it is embedded in the transformation rules themselves. For our example, we could ensure that classes are transformed before their attributes in different ways. If the language provides navigation facilities, we can define a single rule that, for each class, first generates a table and then iterates on its attributes to produce the corresponding columns. When the transformation language is fact-based like in Jess[1] [12], another way is to filter both an attribute and its class and then create a table and a column. The same table is created several times for the same class (one for each attribute of the class). However, as mentioned in [9], this is not a problem, since the creation of a table is a fact assertion, and the same fact can be asserted several times. Another possibility for defining implicit control is to test target model constructs in the left-hand side of the rules. For our example, one defines a first simple rule that generates a table from a class. Then, she adds a second rule that filters a class and an attribute from the source model, and a table from the target model. This rule tests if the attribute belongs to the class and if the table has the same name as the class. If yes, it creates a column with the same name as the attribute and attaches this column to the table. With this rule if a class is not transformed yet, its attributes cannot be transformed. This way of implementing the control works for transformation languages when the facts that trigger the rules could change during the firing process. This is possible in Jess because the rule firing is reevaluated each time after fact assertions using a Rete algorithm [10].

The control is explicit when it is possible to specify when rules should be fired. Many control strategies could be defined to explicitly state the control over the transformation rules [20]. In Jess, two strategies can be used. The first one consists in grouping rules into modules and defining an execution order for the modules. In our example, the rule that transforms a class is added to a module A and the rule for transforming an attribute is added to a module B. Then, module A is executed before B, i.e., rules in A are executed first and when no more rules can be fired, then rules of module B are considered. The second strategy available in Jess is rule salience. Each rule is assigned a priority level. When many rules can be fired, the one with the highest priority is executed. In our example, the class transformation rule will have a higher priority than the attribute one. This guarantees that classes are transformed before their attributes. In our approach, we consider both implicit and explicit control. For the implicit control, we learn

---

[1] In this work, we use the pure declarative generic language Jess to implement the transformations.

rules that, in addition to source constructs, filter target constructs. For the explicit control, we consider module or salience strategies offered by Jess.

3.2   Control Learning

Our learning process takes as input one example pair of models. This contains a source model sm_i and its corresponding target model tm_i. Each of the two models conforms to its respective metamodel (SMM or TMM). The goal of our process is to produce a transformation T (rules + control) such that $T(sm_i) = tm_i$. Note that T is not necessary the transformation Tr that allows to transform any model sm_k conforming to SMM into a valid model tm_k conforming to TMM. Indeed, generally, for a given input/output (sm_i/tm_i), there exist a family of transformations that allow to obtain tm_i from sm_i. By analogy, if we search for the program that produces as output the value 4 from the input 2, then, there exist a large number of programs that are valid for this input/output example pair (e.g., $b := a + 2$, $b := a \times 2$, $b := a^2$, ...). However, we conjecture that the more complete and complex is sm_i, the more probable that $T = Tr$.

Our goal is to learn both transformation rules and the control over these rules. Transformation rules, including the implicit control knowledge, are considered as the transformation knowledge fragments, whereas, the explicit control is seen as the control knowledge. Two alternatives could be explored to learn both types of knowledge: simultaneous and sequential learning. *Simultaneous learning* consists in learning simultaneously both types of knowledge. This alternative makes the hypothesis that transformation knowledge cannot be learned independently from the control. In *sequential learning*, we consider that, in a first step, the transformation knowledge fragments can be learned in the form of rules. Then, we explore how these fragments could be arranged (control) to produce consistent transformations. In the rest of this paper, we explore the first alternative, whereas, the second alternative is currently under investigation.

4   Transformation Rule and Control Learning

In our contribution, transformation rules are executable programs that analyze certain aspects of source models given as input and synthesize the corresponding target models. Learning complex and dynamic structures such as programs is not an easy task that can be handled by basic machine learning algorithms. Considering that we address an automatic program generation problem, genetic programming (GP) is a natural direction to explore.

4.1   Transformation Learning Using GP

Genetic programming is a learning technique allowing to solve automatically a programming problem, starting from high level statement on how the program should behave [16]. This statement usually takes the form of a set of input and output example values. Taking inspiration from the theory of evolution by means of natural selection, the learning process starts from a population of programs, obtained randomly or by means of another technique, and iteratively refines them by applying the genetic operators, crossover and mutation. At each iteration, the newly created programs are evaluated using a fitness function, which allows to rank them and to favor the fittest programs in the creation of the new ones. In general, to calculate the fitness of a program, this latter is executed with the provided inputs and its outputs are compared with the provided outputs.

The application of a GP algorithm to our transformation problem is not straightforward. In the majority of GP applications, the sought programs are imperative, and are modeled as abstract syntax trees. Consequently, the genetic operators are manipulations of trees (e.g., exchanging subtrees between programs or a random change of a subtree). Moreover, the inputs and particularly the outputs that are given to guide the learning have simple types and are then easy to compare. In our case, we are looking for declarative transformations with control mechanisms that cannot necessarily be encoded as trees. New genetic operators have to be defined according to the defined transformation encoding. Additionally, the inputs and outputs provided as examples are models, i.e., complex structures. This makes it difficult to define a cost-effective fitness function that compares the produced target models with the expected ones.

In the following subsections, we detail our adaptation of the general GP algorithm to the specific problem of model transformation and control learning. This adaptation concerns the candidate transformation encoding, the evaluation of a given candidate with the fitness function, and the derivation of new candidates by genetic operators. As the learning process requires that the candidate transformations are executed to determine their fitness, our adaptation is performed for the rule language and engine Jess.

4.2   Candidate Transformation Encoding

We encode a candidate transformation Tc as a vector of rules $Tc = \{r_1, r_2, ..., r_n\}$. Each transformation rule r_i is encoded as a triple $r_i = < LHS_i, RHS_i, cl_i >$, where LHS_i is the pattern to search for in a source model and possibly in the already-created fragments of the target model, RHS_i is the pattern to instantiate in the target model, and cl_i is the module or priority level of r_i depending on the (explicit) control strategy given as parameter to the learning process. Implicit control is achieved by allowing LHS_i to filter target model constructs.

LHS_i (**Left-Hand Side**) is the conditional part of a rule. When all the conditions of a rule r_i match the source or target model constructs, the rule is said fireable. LHS_i is composed of several interconnected "bricks". A brick is a generic model fragment (interconnected model constructs) which is self-contained, i.e., respects the minimum cardinalities of the references defined on the metamodel. For example, in a UML class diagram, a single class could form a brick (`class (name ?c)`) where `?c` is the variable to match with the names of the classes in the source model. However, an attribute should be associated to its class to form a valid brick, i.e., (`attribute (name ?a)(class ?c)`)

`AND (class (name ?c))`. Similarly, an inheritance relationship with two related classes (superclass and subclass) forms a valid brick with three constructs.

The bricks must be interconnected to be matched by concrete model fragments during the transformation execution. When two bricks belong to the same metamodel (source or target), the interconnection is made through a common construct. For example the superclass of an inheritance brick is the same as the class of an attribute brick. This is expressed in Jess by giving the same variable name to both construct names in the two bricks. When the two bricks to connect are respectively from the source and target metamodels, the connection is made through properties of the same type, e.g., class name and table name.

The example given in Listing 1.1 shows bricks (one from the source model and the other from the target model). The two bricks are connected through the variable `?c`. The presence of a brick from the target model enforces the implicit control that a column cannot be created before its table.

Listing 1.1. A rule example

```
(defrule Attribute2Column
  (attribute (name ?a)(class ?c))
  (class(name ?c))
  (table (name ?c))
=>
  (assert (column (name ?a)(table ?c))))
```

RHS_i **(Right-Hand Side)** is the action part of a rule. It consists of the creation (assertion) of target constructs, their initialization with property values from LHS_i. For example, the rule in Listing 1.1 creates a column and initializes its name with the attribute name `?a`. RHS_i allows also to connect a newly-created construct with an already-created one. In this case, the already-created construct is filtered in LHS_i. In Listing 1.1, the column is connected to the table by assigning to its *table* property the name `?c` of the filtered table.

cl_i **(Explicit Control Level)** is expressed in Jess by assigning the rule r_i to a module or by giving it a salience level. In the first case, for each candidate transformation, we create by default a fixed number of modules, {`Module1`, `Module2`, ..., `ModuleM`} using the primitive (`defmodule <module_name>`). Then, the rule r_i is inserted into the scope of the module corresponding to cl_i. When executing a candidate transformation, the modules are considered in the order of their definition. For the second control strategy, the salience is declared as an integer value inside the rule using the primitive (`declare (salience <value>)`).

Following this encoding, the initial population of candidate transformations is randomly generated. Each generated candidate transformation (rules + control) has to be syntactically correct with respect to Jess, and consistent with the source and target metamodels. A candidate is created by generating a random number of rules, bounded by a parameter nrs. For each rule r_i, we use a random combination of bricks from the source and target metamodels to define LHS_i. In addition to the interconnections explained in Section 4.2, we randomly generate conditions that combine three mechanisms: *construct property testing*, *Non-existence operator*, and *Navigation primitives*.

Construct property testing allows comparing the property of a filtered construct with a property of another construct, e.g., equality of names between two constructs, or with a randomly-generated and type-compatible constant, e.g., a cardinality of an association higher than a certain value. Non-existence operator (NOT) allows to check the absence of a construct type or constructs having a certain value for a property. For example, one can define a rule that merges two classes, having a 1-to-1 association, into a single table with the condition that none from the two classes has subclasses. Navigation primitives consist in creating sets by navigating into a model starting from one of the filtered constructs. Navigation primitives are not randomly created but used when creating candidate transformations. They are used in the transformation but their definition is independent from the transformation knowledge. For example, the following primitive, implemented as a query in Jess, produces the list of attributes of a class:

```
(defquery getAttributes
    (declare (variables ?c))
    ((attribute (class ?c)))
```

As the query results are sets, the random generation of rule conditions can include tests on the size of the returned sets. For example, a rule can test if a class has a single attribute as follows:

```
(class (name ?x))
(test (eq (count-query-results getAttributes ?x) 1))
```

The implicit control is generated in the initial rules by including bricks and conditions involving target model constructs. The explicit control is initially generated by randomly assigning a module/salience to the created rules.

4.3 Candidate Transformation Evaluation

The candidate transformations of each generation are ranked according to their quality by means of a fitness function. For each candidate Tc, this function compares, for the example pair (sm_i, tm_i), the target model $Tc(sm_i)$, produced by Tc with the expected model tm_i. Despite the complexity of comparing two models, the fitness function should perform the evaluation at a low cost. Moreover, to avoid a bias towards frequent but simple constructs, we first calculate the correctness f_t of transforming the constructs of each construct type t present in tm_i. f_t is defined as the weighted sum of the percentages of constructs that are respectively fully (fm_t), partially (pm_t), or non-matched (nm_t). Formally,

$$ft(mt_i, Tc(ms_i)) = \alpha fm_t + \beta pm_t + \gamma nm_t, \text{ with } \alpha + \beta + \gamma = 1 \qquad (1)$$

For each construct of type t in $Tc(sm_i)$, we first determine if it is fully matched by a construct in tm_i. As we are dealing with asserted facts, a construct cannot be matched to more than one expected construct (and vice versa). This allows us to calculate fm_t. For the remaining constructs of type t, we determine if they can be partially matched. A construct is partially matched if it exists in the produced model a construct of the same type that was not matched in the first step. Thus, pm_t is equal to the percentage of the partially-matched constructs of type t in tm_i. Finally, the last step is to classify all the remaining constructs of type t as non-matched and take their percentage as the value of nm_t. Regarding the weights α, β, and γ, we used the same range of values as for our previous contribution [9], with α usually set to a high value (typically 0.6) in order to favor the rules that produce the expected constructs. β is set to an average value (around 0.3) to give chances to rules producing the right types of the expected constructs. Finally, we set γ to a very small value (around 0.1). Although giving a small weight to the non-matched constructs seems counterintuitive, it promotes diversity, in particular, during the early generations, which helps avoiding local-optimum solutions.

The fitness f of a candidate transformation Tc is derived by calculating the average correctness of transforming the various construct types T_{tm_i} used in tm_i:

$$f(tm_i, Tc(sm_i)) = \sum_{t \in T_{tm_i}} \frac{f_t(tm_i, Tc(sm_i))}{|T_{tm_i}|} \tag{2}$$

4.4 Candidate Transformation Derivation

As mentioned earlier, the transformation learning consists in refining an initial set of candidate transformations. At each iteration, a new set of candidates is derived from the current set. This is done, by elitism, i.e., putting automatically the top fittest candidates into the next generation, crossover, i.e., deriving sibling transformations from existing ones, and mutation, i.e., randomly changing an existing transformation. Crossover and mutation should preserve the syntactic correctness and the consistency of the produced candidates. The process of creating the next population of candidates is as follows. First, the existing n candidates of the generation i ranked according to their fitness. Then, the l top-ranked candidates are injected automatically into the candidate population of generation $i + 1$. Until we complete the n slots of the new population, we iteratively and randomly select two parent candidates and using the crossover, when possible, produce two child candidates. These are possibly mutated and added to the population. Each time, we have to select a parent for reproduction, we use the roulette-wheel selection. This allows to assign, to each candidate, a probability to be selected proportional to its fitness. This selection strategy favors the fittest candidate transformations while still giving a chance of being selected to the others.

Crossover: The crossover operation consists of producing new rule sets (including the control) by exchanging the rules between the selected parents using the one-cut-point strategy. This operation is applied with high probability to each pair of selected parent candidates, i.e., by flipping a coin with a higher probability to obtain heads (accept the crossover). For instance, consider the two candidates $p1 = \{r11, r12, r13, r14\}$ having four rules and $p2 =$

$\{r21, r22, r23, r24, r25\}$ with five rules. If the cut-points are randomly set to 2 for $p1$ and 3 for $p2$, the offspring obtained are candidates $o1 = \{r11, r12, r24, r25\}$ and $o2 = \{r21, r22, r23, r13, r14\}$. The rules keep their control level (module name or salience), and the control for the obtained candidates is readjusted accordingly.

Mutation: After the crossover, the obtained offspring could be mutated with a certain probability, given as a parameter. Unlike the crossover where the existing transformation knowledge is only combined (rule exchange), mutation allows the introduction of new knowledge, which may or may not improve the transformations. This is achieved by randomly altering existing rules or by adding randomly-generated ones. Each time a candidate is selected for mutation, a strategy is randomly selected. Mutation strategies occur at different levels.

Rule-Set Level: Two strategies are defined at this level: adding a randomly-created rule to the rule set or deleting a randomly-selected rule. To avoid empty rule sets, deletion is not performed if the rule set has only one rule.

Rule Level: Seven mutations have been implemented at the rule level. The first one adds a brick in the LHS when the maximum number of bricks has not been reached yet. This additional brick has to be connected properly to the existing ones. The second strategy removes a brick from the LHS when the rule has at least two bricks. Conditions involving this brick are removed accordingly. The third strategy recreates a new LHS but conserves the RHS of the rule. The fourth mutation creates an additional construct in the RHS and initializes it. The fifth strategy removes a construct from the RHS. The sixth mutation recreates a new RHS while keeping the LHS. Finally, the last mutation changes the initialization of the created constructs in the RHS.

Control Level: The control could be mutated by assigning the rule to another module or by increasing or decreasing the salience of a rule depending on the chosen control strategy.

5   Evaluation

5.1   Setting

We assessed our approach on four transformation problems with different characteristics. In addition to the well known transformation of UML class diagrams to relational schemas (CL2RE), we selected three other transformations from the ATL database[2], namely, UML activity diagram to MS project diagram (AD2MSP), table to SVG bar charts (TB2BC) and finally simple process description language to petri nets (SP2PN).

The goal of **CL2RE** is to transform a class diagram into a relational schema. Unlike the version used in our previous contribution [9], we consider in this study a more complete version of the UML class diagram metamodel. The transformation we wrote is complex and considers many variations for the transformation

---

[2] http://www.eclipse.org/atl/atlTransformations/

of the constructs. For example, 1-to-1 associations between two classes could be transformed in many ways dependent on the presence of other associations involving these classes. The control here is very important because the chosen transformation impacts those of the other constructs. The expected transformation contains 20 rules organized into 7 modules.

AD2MSP aims to generate MS project diagrams from UML activity diagrams. The representation of the input activity diagram includes actions states, transitions, and pseudostates: initial, join, fork and final. The control here ensures that rules that generate MS project tasks are executed before those that establish the precedence between these tasks. The sought transformation contains 6 rules with two modules.

The purpose of **TB2BC** is to generate an SVG model containing bar chart representations that describe a data table. Roughly speaking, rectangle elements are created from the table to represent both the data and the table. These rectangles are grouped with their corresponding labels into group elements. A containment relation is defined between the group elements to allow to have the data rectangles (bars) inside the table rectangle. The dimension and positions of the rectangles are extracted from the cell values but also computed by means of the containment relationship. Indeed, the positions of the inner rectangles depend both on the outer rectangle and on the order in which the data is given in the table. Conversely, the dimension of the outer rectangle depends on the dimensions of the inner rectangles. The control in this problem enforces the constraints on the determination of positions and dimensions. This transformation involves 8 rules with two modules.

The goal of **SP2PN** is to build a petri net that describes the transitions between different states of the activities that form a process. A process is composed of work definitions, work sequences and resources. Each work definition is translated into four places characterizing the state (not started, started, in progress and finished) and two transitions (start and finish). The places are linked to their corresponding transitions. Work sequences, which denotes dependency between work definitions (activities), are translated into arcs of type 'read' that link the corresponding places and transitions. Resources are also transformed into places and are linked through regular arcs to the transitions (work definitions) that make use of them. One particularity of this transformation is that most of the target construct properties are not derived from source construct properties. Moreover some target constructs such as arc constructs depend highly on other target constructs (places and transitions). This dependency is expressed in the rules through the implicit control of filtering in the LHS the target constructs. This transformation is expressed with 10 rules.

After representing all the metamodels in Jess (as fact templates), we gathered/defined five prototypical examples as model pairs (source and target) for each transformation problem (20 example pairs in total). Table 1 shows the descriptive statistics of the size of the example models in terms of number of constructs SC in a source model (respectively TC in a target model). In our setting, we also wrote manually the transformations (rules + control) for the four problems and tested them on the corresponding examples. The choice of the four transformation problems allows us to explore various forms of control. For CL2RE, AD2MSP, and TB2BC, in addition to the implicit control, we used the module-based control strategy. For these problems module based and salience controls are equivalent. For SP2PN, implicit control was sufficient to write the transformation. The four transformations will serve later as references to which the learned transformations will be compared.

Table 1. Size of the example pairs in terms of source (SC) and target constructs (TC)

Transformation	Number of SC			Number of TC		
	Min	Max	Average	Min	Max	Average
CL2RE	12	28	18	18	38	26
AD2MSP	23	65	42	15	44	28
TB2BC	5	17	12	17	53	37
SP2PN	3	11	7	23	52	36

As our learning process is probabilistic by nature, we had to run it several times (five times in our validation) for each problem-example pair and select the transformation with the best fitness from the executions. Considering the size of the search space, the runs involved 100 candidate transformations per generation, with 1000 generations. We set both crossover and mutation probabilities to 0.9, and we included into each new generation the 10 fittest solutions (elitism). At the end of the five runs, the correctness of the best candidate is evaluated in two ways. First, we use the precision and recall to assess the target model produced by the candidate with respect to the expected model. The precision is measured as the ratio between the expected constructs that were produced and all the produced constructs, whereas the recall is the ratio between the expected constructs that were produced and all the expected constructs.

The second way to assess the learned transformations is by a manual qualitative analysis of the produced rules and control. Regarding the derived rules, we categorized them as correct, partially correct, or incorrect with respect to the transformation problem. In addition to the transformation knowledge contained in the rule, we also assess the implicit and explicit control.

5.2   Results and Interpretation

Table 2 gives descriptive statistics for the precision, recall, and fitness, obtained with the 5 example pairs considered for each transformation problem.

We observed the largest variability for the 5 examples in **CL2RE** with a precision ranging from 60% to 90% and a recall between 57.9% and 85.7%. We believe that these variations could be explained by the complexity of the transformation in terms of rules and control. Indeed, the search space for this problem is very large, and the fixed number of generations can be for some

Table 2. Fitness values, precision and recall for the 5 examples

Case	Value of the fitness function			Precision		Recall	
	Min	Max	Average	Min	Max	Min	Max
CL2RE	74.0% (14 rules)	93.1% (8 rules)	82.2%	60.0%	90.0%	57.9 %	85.7%
AD2MSP	92.5% (6 rules)	100% (4 rules)	95.7%	92.9%	100.0%	83.3 %	100.0%
TB2BC	86.7% (5 rules)	89.3% (6 rules)	87.8%	65.9%	76.5%	65.9%	76.5%
SP2PN	73.2% (4 rules)	80.6% (2 rules)	76.4%	36.8%	52.2%	34.1 %	52.2%

examples not large enough. This have been said, the maximal values obtained are very high considering the complexity of the transformation and the absence of knowledge other than the example source and target models. The derived rules were mostly partially correct. Some rules contained unnecessary conditions whereas others were less general than the expected ones. An example of this latter case is the rule in listing 1.2. This rule filters a 1-to-1 association and its related classes, and checks that the class to be merged (class ?c10) is not the superclass of another class. However, it does not check that this same class is not involved in other associations. The transformation control was mostly learned through explicit module mechanism. For instance, the rule in Listing 1.2 was, as expected, in the first module of the transformation plan. Similarly, rules that transform classes and attributes were in modules to execute before those containing rules dealing with associations.

Listing 1.2. CL2RE - Rule to transform 1-1 associations

```
1  (defrule R_5488581
2  (association11 (classa ?c00)(classb ?c10))
3  (class(name ?c00))
4  (class(name ?c10))
5  (not (inheritance(class ?c20)(superclass ?c10)) )
6  =>
7  (assert (table(name ?c00)(altername ?c10))))
```

Our approach obtained good results for the transformation **AD2MSP**. The precision was greater than 90% for all the examples, and perfect for one of them. The same observation can be made for the recall (from 83% to 100%). Regarding the produced rules, the genetic program derived between 4 and 6 rules. Most of the rules were ranked as partially correct because they contain unnecessary conditions in their LHS, which did not affect the outcome of the transformation (see listing 1.3 in which line 7 is always true). In most cases, rules were correctly scheduled, i.e., rules responsible for transforming states are scheduled before those transforming direct or indirect transitions.

TB2BC transformation gave good but less higher results than the previous ones with a maximum of 76.5% for the precision and 76.5% for the recall. The main reason is that the positions and dimensions of the rectangles require calculation primitives which increases dramatically the size of the search space. Concerning the rules that were derived, we obtained many partially correct rules.

The rules were unnecessary big and many constructs were created several times, which did not change the final results. Our algorithm was able to learn partially the control, as tables were transformed prior to cells. However rules that deal with positions and dimension constructs were not scheduled correctly because of the above-mentioned search space problem.

Listing 1.3. AD2MSP - Rule to transform two actions linked through a join or a fork

```
1  (defrule R_6382313
2  (actionState(name ?as00))
3  (actionState(name ?as40))
4  (pseudoState(name ?ps00)(kind ?ps01))
5  (transition(source ?as00)(target ?ps00))
6  (transition(source ?ps00)(target ?as40))
7  (not (relation(pred ?ps01)(succ ?ps01)) )
8  =>
9  (assert (relation(pred ?as00)(succ ?as40)))))
```

The results obtained for **SP2PN** for the five example pairs are average. The executions reached a maximum fitness score around 75%. However these results were mostly achieved by partial matches, the target models that were produced had average precision and recall (52.2%). Although the number of produced constructs was close to the number of the expected ones, many constructs, especially arcs, were incorrect. When inspecting the rules, those producing the arcs were incomplete. This is due to the fact that an arc construct contains 6 properties, most of which take constant values. As there is a large number of constants, this increases the search space and lowers the chances to reach the optimal solution. The implicit control works well except for rules dealing with arcs.

6 Discussion

After many contributions in the MTBE field [14,15,8,21,9], a main conclusion that we can draw is that if we seek to learn complex transformations, the search space is huge. This lowers the chance to learn complete correct transformations.

In our approach, we address both explicit and implicit control learning. The learning is only guided by the example models which makes it difficult to converge toward the optimal strategy. An aspect that may be worth studying to reduce the search space, is to help the learning process by injecting knowledge derived from the target metamodel specifications (minimal cardinalities and constraints). For example, one can conjecture that some target constructs should be connected to other already produced constructs when they are created, independently from the transformation program, e.g., in AD2MSP, the learning could use the information that tasks should be created before they are connected.

Another observation arose from the SP2PN transformation problem where the transformation uses many constants. In the current state of our approach, the sets of constants to use are provided per property type (integer values, a list of values for string properties, etc.). The search space could be reduced by specifying a domain definition for each construct property of the target metamodel.

Moreover, large domains such as integers could be partitioned into equivalence classes, which would reduce the number of possibilities to explore.

One of the important limitations of MTBE is the derivation of complex target property values from the source property values. In the TB2BC transformation, rectangle dimensions and positions are not set directly with values from source construct properties, but with calculated values. The trivial solution is to give all the possible operations allowed on source and target property values and let the learning algorithm explore their combinations. However, this results in an explosion of the search space size which reduces the convergence probability. Here again, a direction to investigate is to use knowledge about the target model to guide the combinations. In TB2BC, the learning process could use the constraint that an outer rectangle must be large enough to contain the bars.

As mentioned in Section 3, there are many possible transformations that can produce the given target model; the simplest is the example models, the largest is the set of possible transformations. To reduce the number of possibilities, we can either give large and complex example models or give many example pairs to the learning algorithm. However, this will increase dramatically the computation cost of which a substantial part is dedicated to compare target models (fitness). This can be circumvented by defining fitness functions with a good tradeoff between the comparison precision and the computation cost, and by providing input examples that balance the size with the source metamodel coverage.

Furthermore, many of the obtained rules are partially correct. After analyzing them, we noticed that many of them could be corrected automatically by a cleaning postprocessing task. For example, many conditions are subsumed by others, some conditions are contradictory or always false, which makes the rule useless, and finally, some conditions are always true, so they can be removed without changing the applicability of the rule.

Regarding the scalability, although the learning process may take up to 8 hours for the largest transformation, this could be acceptable in our context. Indeed, the transformation learning is not intended to be executed frequently.

7   Conclusion

In this paper, we presented an approach that aims to learn, simultaneously, the transformation rules and the control needed to perform the transformation correctly. To explore the large search space, we implemented our learning algorithm as an evolutionary process by means of genetic programming. We assessed our contribution on four transformation problems, three of which gave promising results. We believe that learning the transformation control is an important step towards making MTBE approaches more effective. Although our results are satisfactory, there is still room for improvement. In the future, we plan to investigate the option of learning the transformation and control knowledge in two separate phases. In addition to reduce the size of the search space, this strategy allows us to address the two problems with specific strategies (induction vs scheduling). We also plan to investigate the ideas sketched in the discussion section.

References

1. Balogh, Z., Varró, D.: Model transformation by example using inductive logic programming. Software and Systems Modeling 8, 347–364 (2009)
2. Biehl, M.: Literature study on model transformations. Royal Institute of Technology, Tech. Rep. ISRN/KTH/MMK (2010)
3. Braun, P., Marschall, F.: Transforming object oriented models with botl. Electronic Notes in Theoretical Computer Science 72(3), 103–117 (2003)
4. Czarnecki, K., Helsen, S.: Feature-based survey of model transformation approaches. IBM Systems Journal 45(3), 621–646 (2006)
5. de Lara, J., Vangheluwe, H.: Atom3: A tool for multi-formalism and meta-modelling. In: Kutsche, R.-D., Weber, H. (eds.) FASE 2002. LNCS, vol. 2306, pp. 174–188. Springer, Heidelberg (2002)
6. Dolques, X., Huchard, M., Nebut, C., Reitz, P.: Learning transformation rules from transformation examples: An approach based on relational concept analysis. In: Int. Conf. on Enterprise Distributed Object Computing Workshops, pp. 27–32 (2010)
7. Drey, Z., Faucher, C., Fleurey, F., Mahé, V., Vojtisek, D.: Kermeta language reference manual (2009)
8. Faunes, M., Sahraoui, H., Boukadoum, M.: Generating model transformation rules from examples using an evolutionary algorithm. In: Automated Software Engineering, pp. 1–4 (2012)
9. Faunes, M., Sahraoui, H., Boukadoum, M.: Genetic-programming approach to learn model transformation rules from examples. In: Duddy, K., Kappel, G. (eds.) ICMB 2013. LNCS, vol. 7909, pp. 17–32. Springer, Heidelberg (2013)
10. Forgy, C.L.: Rete: A fast algorithm for the many pattern/many object pattern match problem. Artificial Intelligence 19(1), 17–37 (1982)
11. García-Magariño, I., Gómez-Sanz, J.J., Fuentes-Fernández, R.: Model transformation by-example: An algorithm for generating many-to-many transformation rules in several model transformation languages. In: Paige, R.F. (ed.) ICMT 2009. LNCS, vol. 5563, pp. 52–66. Springer, Heidelberg (2009)
12. Hill, E.F.: Jess in Action: Java Rule-Based Systems (2003)
13. Jouault, F., Kurtev, I.: Transforming models with atl. In: Bruel, J.-M. (ed.) MoDELS 2005 Workshops. LNCS, vol. 3844, pp. 128–138. Springer, Heidelberg (2006)
14. Kessentini, M., Sahraoui, H.A., Boukadoum, M.: Model transformation as an optimization problem. In: Czarnecki, K., Ober, I., Bruel, J.-M., Uhl, A., Völter, M. (eds.) MODELS 2008. LNCS, vol. 5301, pp. 159–173. Springer, Heidelberg (2008)
15. Kessentini, M., Sahraoui, H., Boukadoum, M., Omar, O.B.: Search-based model transformation by example. Software and System Modeling 11(2), 209–226 (2012)
16. Koza, J., Poli, R.: Genetic programming. In: Search Methodologies, pp. 127–164 (2005)
17. Langer, P., Wimmer, M., Kappel, G.: Model-to-model transformations by demonstration. In: Tratt, L., Gogolla, M. (eds.) ICMT 2010. LNCS, vol. 6142, pp. 153–167. Springer, Heidelberg (2010)
18. Mens, T., Van Gorp, P.: A taxonomy of model transformation. Electron. Notes Theor. Comput. Sci. 152, 125–142 (2006)
19. ModelMorf, T.: A model transformer (2008)
20. Pachet, F., Perrot, J.-F.: Rule firing with metarules. In: SEKE, pp. 322–329 (1994)

21. Saada, H., Dolques, X., Huchard, M., Nebut, C., Sahraoui, H.: Generation of operational transformation rules from examples of model transformations. In: France, R.B., Kazmeier, J., Breu, R., Atkinson, C. (eds.) MODELS 2012. LNCS, vol. 7590, pp. 546–561. Springer, Heidelberg (2012)
22. Sun, Y., White, J., Gray, J.: Model transformation by demonstration. In: Schürr, A., Selic, B. (eds.) MODELS 2009. LNCS, vol. 5795, pp. 712–726. Springer, Heidelberg (2009)
23. Telecom, F.: Smartqvt: An open source model transformation tool implementing the mof 2.0 qvt-operational language (2007)
24. Varró, D.: Model transformation by example. In: Wang, J., Whittle, J., Harel, D., Reggio, G. (eds.) MoDELS 2006. LNCS, vol. 4199, pp. 410–424. Springer, Heidelberg (2006)
25. Varró, D., Balogh, A.: The model transformation language of the viatra2 framework. Science of Computer Programming 68(3), 214–234 (2007)
26. Wimmer, M., Strommer, M., Kargl, H., Kramler, G.: Towards model transformation generation by-example. In: Annual Hawaii Int. Conf. on System Sciences, p. 285b (2007)

IncQuery-D: A Distributed Incremental Model Query Framework in the Cloud*

Gábor Szárnyas[1], Benedek Izsó[1], István Ráth[1], Dénes Harmath[4],
Gábor Bergmann[1], and Dániel Varró[1,2,3]

[1] Budapest University of Technology and Economics,
Department of Measurement and Information Systems,
H-1117 Magyar tudósok krt. 2, Budapest, Hungary
{szarnyas,izso,rath,bergmann,varro}@mit.bme.hu
[2] DIRO, Université de Montréal
[3] MSDL, Dept. of Computer Science, McGill University
[4] IncQuery Labs Ltd.
H-1113 Bocskai út 77-79, Budapest, Hungary
denes.harmath@incquerylabs.com

Abstract. Queries are the foundations of data intensive applications. In model-driven software engineering (MDE), model queries are core technologies of tools and transformations. As software models are rapidly increasing in size and complexity, traditional tools exhibit scalability issues that decrease productivity and increase costs [17]. While scalability is a hot topic in the database community and recent NoSQL efforts have partially addressed many shortcomings, this happened at the cost of sacrificing the ad-hoc query capabilities of SQL. Unfortunately, this is a critical problem for MDE applications due to their inherent workload complexity. In this paper, we aim to address both the scalability and ad-hoc querying challenges by adapting incremental graph search techniques – known from the EMF-INCQUERY framework – to a distributed cloud infrastructure. We propose a novel architecture for distributed and incremental queries, and conduct experiments to demonstrate that INCQUERY-D, our prototype system, can scale up from a single workstation to a cluster that can handle very large models and complex incremental queries efficiently.

1 Introduction

Nowadays, model-driven software engineering (MDE) plays an important role in the development processes of critical embedded systems. Advanced modeling tools provide support for a wide range of development tasks such as requirements and traceability management, system modeling, early design validation, automated code generation, model-based testing and other validation and verification tasks. With the dramatic increase in complexity that is also affecting

* This work was partially supported by the CERTIMOT (ERC_HU-09-01-2010-0003) and MONDO (EU ICT-611125) projects partly during the sixth author's sabbatical.

J. Dingel et al. (Eds.): MODELS 2014, LNCS 8767, pp. 653–669, 2014.

critical embedded systems in recent years, modeling toolchains are facing scalability challenges as the size of design models constantly increases, and automated tool features become more sophisticated [17].

Many scalability issues can be addressed by improving query performance. *Incremental evaluation* of model queries aims to reduce query execution time by limiting the impact of model modifications to query result calculation. Such algorithms work by either (i) building a cache of interim query results and keeping it up-to-date as models change (e.g. EMF-INCQUERY [5]) or (ii) applying impact analysis techniques and reevaluating queries only in contexts that are affected by a change [10,21]. This technique has been proven to improve performance dramatically in several scenarios (e.g. on-the-fly well-formedness validation or model synchronization), at the cost of increasing memory consumption. Unfortunately, this overhead is combined with the increase in model sizes due to in-memory representation (found in state-of-the-art frameworks such as EMF [25]). Since single-computer heaps cannot grow arbitrarily (as execution times degrade drastically due to garbage collection problems), memory consumption is the most significant scalability limitation.

An alternative approach to tackling MDE scalability issues is to make use of advances in persistence technology. As the majority of model-based tools uses a graph-oriented data model, recent results of the NoSQL and Linked Data movement [20,1,2] are straightforward candidates for adaptation to MDE purposes (as experimented e.g. in Morsa [7] or Neo4EMF [3]). Unfortunately, this idea poses difficult conceptual and technological challenges as property graph databases lack strong metamodeling support and their query features are simplistic compared to MDE needs [15]. Additionally, the underlying data representation format of semantic databases (RDF [11]) has crucial conceptual and technological differences to traditional metamodeling languages such as Ecore [25]. Additionally, while there are initial efforts to overcome the mapping issues between the MDE and Linked Data worlds [13], even the most sophisticated NoSQL storage technologies lack efficient and mature support for executing expressive queries incrementally.

We aim to address these challenges by proposing a *novel architecture for a distributed and incremental model query framework* by adapting incremental graph pattern matching techniques to a distributed cloud based infrastructure. A main contribution of our novel architecture is that the distributed storage of data is completely separated from the distributed handling of indexing and query evaluation. Therefore, caching the result sets of queries in a distributed fashion provides a way to scale out the memory intensive components of incremental query evaluation, while still providing instantaneous execution time for complex queries.

We present INCQUERY-D, a prototype tool based on a distributed Rete network that can scale up from a single workstation to a cluster to handle very large models and complex queries efficiently (Sec. 3). For the experimental evaluation, we revisit a model validation benchmark (Sec. 2) from the railway systems domain and extend it to a distributed setup (Sec. 4). Furthermore, we carry out

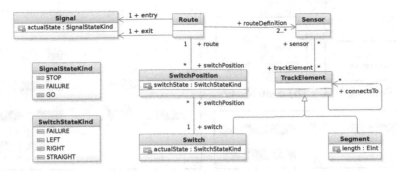

Fig. 1. The metamodel of the Train Benchmark

detailed performance evaluation in the context of on-the-fly well-formedness validation of design models (Sec. 4) which demonstrates that our distributed incremental query layer can be significantly more efficient than the native SPARQL query technology of an RDF triple store. Finally, we discuss related work in Sec. 5 and conclude the paper in Sec. 6.

2 Preliminaries

2.1 Motivating Example: A DSL for Railways System Design

In this paper, we use the Train Benchmark [15,29] to present our core ideas and evaluate the feasibility of the approach. The Train Benchmark is used in the MONDO EU FP7 [27] project to compare query evaluation performance of various MDE tools and it is publicly available[1]. It is built around the railroad system defined in the MOGENTES EU FP7 [26] project. The system defines a network composed of typical railroad items, including signals, segments, switches and sensors. The complete EMF metamodel is shown in Fig. 1.

2.2 Queries

The Train Benchmark defines four queries which have similar characteristics to the workload of a typical MDE application. The queries look for violations of *well-formedness constraints* in the model. The violations are defined by graph patterns. The graphical representation of the patterns is shown in Fig. 2. Opaque blue rectangles and solid arrows mark positive constraints, while red rectangles and dashed arrows represent negative application conditions (NACs). The result of the query (also referred as the *match set*) is marked with transparent blue rectangles. Additional constraints (e.g. arithmetic comparisons) are shown in the figure in text.

The queries contain a mix of join, antijoin and filtering operations. The two simpler queries involve at most 2 objects (PosLength and SwitchSensor), while the

---

[1] https://opensourceprojects.eu/p/mondo/wiki/TrainBenchmark

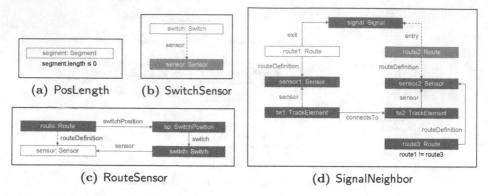

(a) PosLength   (b) SwitchSensor

(c) RouteSensor   (d) SignalNeighbor

Fig. 2. Graphical representation of the patterns in the Train Benchmark

other two queries involve 4–8 objects and multiple join operations (RouteSensor and SignalNeighbor).

For the sake of conciseness, we only discuss the RouteSensor query in detail. The RouteSensor constraint requires that all sensors that are associated with a switch that belongs to a route must also be associated directly with the same route. Therefore, the query (Fig. 2c) looks for sensors that are connected to a switch, but the sensor and the switch are not connected to the same route. This query checks for the absence of circles, so the efficiency of both the join and the antijoin operations is tested.

```
1  pattern routeSensor(Sen : Sensor) = {
2    Route(R);
3    SwitchPosition(Sp);
4    Switch(Sw);
5    Route.switchPosition(R, Sp);
6    SwitchPosition.switch(Sp, Sw);
7    Trackelement.sensor(Sw, Sen);
8    neg pattern noRouteDefinition(Sen, R) {
9      routeDefinition(R, Sen);
10   }
11 }
```

Fig. 3. The RouteSensor query in IncQuery Pattern Language

The textual representation of the RouteSensor query, defined in IncQuery Pattern Language, is shown in Fig. 3. This query binds each variable (Sen, Sw, Sp, R) to the appropriate type. It defines the three edges as relationships between the variables and defines the negative application condition as a negative pattern (neg find).

2.3 Transformations

The Train Benchmark defines a quick fix model transformation for each query. The graphical representation of the transformations is shown in Fig. 4. The insertions are shown in green with a «new» caption, while deletions are marked with a red cross and a «del» caption. In general, the goal of these transformations is to remove a subset of the invalid elements from the model. For example, in the case of the RouteSensor query, randomly selected invalid sensors are disconnected from their switch, which means that the constraint is no longer violated (Fig. 4c).

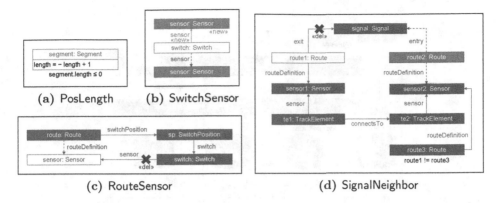

Fig. 4. Graphical representation of the transformations in the Train Benchmark

3   A Distributed Incremental Model Query Framework

The queries and transformations introduced in Sec. 2 represent a typical work-load profile for state-of-the-art modeling tools [15]. With current MDE tech-nologies, such workloads can be acceptably executed for models up to several hundred thousand model elements [29], however when using larger models con-sisting of multiple million elements (a commonplace in complex domains such as AUTOSAR [5]), the performance of current tools is often not acceptable [17]. Incremental techniques can provide a solution, however they require additional (memory) resources.

The primary goal of our approach is to provide an architecture that can make use of the distributed cloud infrastructure to scale out memory-intensive incre-mental query evaluation techniques. As a core contribution, we propose a three-tiered architecture. To maximize the flexibility and performance of the system, model persistence, indexing and incremental query evaluation are delegated to three independently distributable asynchronous components. Consistency is en-sured by synchronized construction, change propagation and termination proto-cols.

3.1   Architecture

In the following, we introduce the architecture of INCQUERY-D (see Fig. 5), a scalable distributed incremental graph pattern matcher. The architecture con-sists of three layers: (i) the *storage layer*, (ii) the *distributed indexer* with the *model access adapter* and (iii) the *distributed query evaluation network*.

Storage. For the storage layer, the most important issue from an incremental query evaluation perspective is that the *indexers* of the system should be filled as quickly as possible. This favors database technologies where model sharding can be performed appropriately (i.e. with balanced shards in terms of type-instance

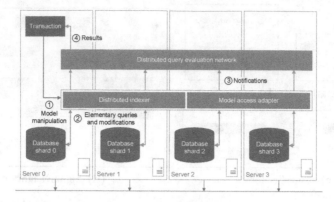

Fig. 5. The architecture of IncQuery-D, an incremental query framework (deployed in a sample four-node cluster configuration)

relationships), and elementary queries can be executed efficiently. Our framework can be adapted to fundamentally different storage back-ends, including triple stores, graph databases and relational database managements systems.

Model Access Adapter. In contrast to a traditional setup where the distributed model repository is accessed on a per-node basis by a model manipulation transaction, IncQuery-D provides a model access adapter that offers three core services:

1. The primary task is to provide a *surrogate key mechanism* so that each model element in the entire distributed repository can be uniquely identified and located within storage shards.
2. The model access adapter provides a *graph-like data manipulation API* (①) in Fig. 5) to the user. The model access adapter translates the operations issued by the user to the query language of the backend and forwards it to the underlying data storage.
3. *Change notifications* are required by incremental query evaluation, thus model changes are captured and their effects are propagated in the form of *notification objects* (③ in Fig. 5). The notifications generate *update messages* that keep the state of the query evaluation network consistent with the model. While relational databases usually provide *triggers* for generating notifications, most triplestores and graph databases lack this feature. Due to the lack of general support, notifications are controlled by the model access adapter by providing a façade for all model manipulation operations.

Distributed Indexer. Indexing is a common technique for decreasing the execution time of database queries. In MDE, *model indexing* has a key role in high performance model queries. As MDE primarily uses a metamodeling infrastructure, all queries utilize some sort of type attribute. Typical elementary queries include retrieving all vertices of a certain type (e.g. get all vertices of the type Route), or retrieving all edges of a certain type/label (e.g. get all edges of label sensor).

To support efficient query processing, INCQUERY-D maintains type-instance indexes so that all instances of a given type (both vertices and edges) can be enumerated quickly. These indexers form the bottom layer of the distributed query evaluation network. During initialization, these indexers are filled from the database backend (② in Fig. 5).

The architecture of INCQUERY-D facilitates the use of a *distributed indexer* which stores the index on multiple servers. A distributed indexer inherently provides some protection from exceeding memory limits.

Distributed Query Evaluation Network. INCQUERY-D constructs a distributed and asynchronous network of communicating nodes that are capable of producing the results set of the defined queries (④ in Fig. 5). Our prime candidate for this layer is the *Rete algorithm,* however, the architecture is capable of incorporating other incremental (e.g. TREAT [18]) and search-based query evaluation algorithms as well. In the upcoming section, we provide further details on this critical component of the architecture.

3.2 The Rete Algorithm in a Distributed Environment

Numerous algorithms were proposed for the purpose of incremental query evaluation. The Rete algorithm was originally proposed for rule-based expert systems [8] and later improved and adapted for EMF models in [4]. Our current paper discusses how to adapt the Rete algorithm in a distributed environment.

Data Representation and Structure. The Rete algorithm uses *tuples* to represent the vertices (along with their properties), edges and subgraphs in the graph. The algorithm defines an asynchronous network of communicating nodes (see Fig. 7).

The network consists of three types of nodes. *Input nodes* are responsible for indexing the model by type, i.e. they store the appropriate tuples for the vertices and edges. They are also responsible for producing the update messages and propagating them to the *worker nodes. Worker nodes* perform a transformation on the output of their parent node(s) and propagate the results. Partial query results are represented in tuples and stored in the memory of the worker node thus allowing for incremental query reevaluation. *Production nodes* are terminators that provide an interface for fetching the results of the query and the changes introduced by the latest transformation.

Construction. The system constructs the Rete network from the layout derived from the query specification. The construction algorithm may apply various optimization techniques, e.g. reusing existing Rete nodes, known as *node sharing* [4].

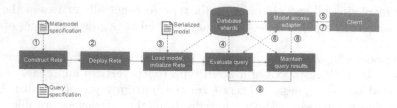

Fig. 6. The operational workflow of the distributed Rete algorithm

An efficient Rete construction is discussed in detail in [31], and it is out of scope for the current paper.

In a distributed environment, the construction of the Rete network introduces additional challenges. First, the system must keep track of the resources available in the server cluster and maintain the mapping between the Rete nodes and the servers accordingly. Second, the Rete nodes need to be aware of the current infrastructure mapping so they can send their messages to the appropriate servers. In our system, the Rete nodes are remotely instantiated by the coordinator node. The coordinator node then sends the infrastructure mapping of the Rete network to all nodes. This way, each node is capable of subscribing to the update messages of its parent node(s). The coordinator also starts the operations in the network, such as loading the model, initiating transformations and retrieving the query results.

Operation. The operational workflow of INCQUERY-D is shown in Fig. 6. Based on the *metamodel* and the *query specification*, INCQUERY-D first constructs a Rete network ① and deploys it ②. In the next step, it loads the model ③ and traverses it to initialize the indexers of the Rete network. The Rete network evaluates the query by processing the incoming tuples ④. Because both the Rete indexers and the database shards are distributed across the cluster, loading the model and initializing the Rete network needs network communication. The client is able to retrieve the results ⑤–⑥, modify the model and reevaluate the query again ⑦–⑨.

The modifications are propagated in the form of *update messages* (also known as *deltas*). Creating new graph elements (vertices or edges) results in *positive update messages*, while removing graph elements results in *negative update messages*. The operation of the network is illustrated on the instance graph depicted in the lower left corner of Fig. 7. This graph violates the well-formedness constaint defined by the RouteSensor query, hence the tuple ⟨3, 4, 2, 1⟩ appears in the result set of the query. The figure also shows the Rete network containing partial matches of the original graph.

To resolve the violation, we apply the quick fix transformation defined in the Train Benchmark and delete the sensor edge between vertices 4 and 1. When the edge is deleted, the sensor type indexer (an input node) receives a notification from the model access adapter ① and sends a *negative update* ② with the tuple

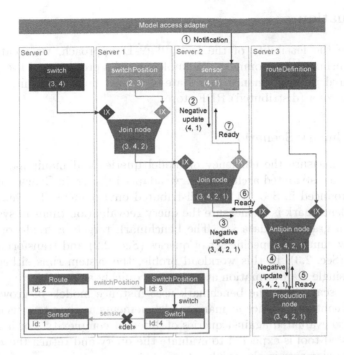

Fig. 7. A transformation sequence on a distributed Rete network

$\langle 4, 1 \rangle$. The subsequent join node processes the update messages and propagates a negative update ③ with the tuple $\langle 3, 4, 2, 1 \rangle$. The antijoin node also propagates a negative update message with the same tuple ④. This is received by the production node, which initiates the *termination protocol* ⑤–⑦. After the termination protocol finishes, the indexer signals the client about the successful update. The client is now able to retrieve the results from the production node. The client may choose to retrieve only the *change set*, i.e. only the tuples that have been added or deleted since the last modification.

Termination Protocol. Due to the asynchronous propagation of changes in Rete, the system must also implement a *termination protocol* to ensure that the query results can be retrieved consistently with the model state after a given transaction (i.e. by signaling when the update propagation has been terminated).

The protocol works by adding a stack to the update message propagated through the network. The stack registers each Rete node the message passes through. After the message reaches a production node, the termination protocol starts. Based on the content of the stack, acknowledgement messages (**Ready**) are propagated back along the network. When all relevant input nodes (where the original update message(s) started from) receive the acknowledge messages, the termination protocol finishes. The operation of the termination protocol can be observed in Fig. 7 (messages ⑤–⑦).

4   Evaluation

To evaluate the feasibility of the INCQUERY-D approach, we created a distributed benchmark environment. We implemented a prototype of INCQUERY-D and compared its performance to a state-of-the-art non-incremental SPARQL query engine of a (distributed) RDF store.

4.1   Benchmark Scenario

In order to measure the efficiency of model queries and manipulation operations over the distributed architecture, we adapted the Train Benchmark [15,29] (briefly introduced in Sec. 2.1) to a distributed environment. The main goal of the Train Benchmark is to measure the query reevaluation times in systems operating on a graph-like data set. The benchmark targets a "real-world" MDE workload by running a specific set of queries (Sec. 2.2) and transformations on the model (Sec. 2.3). In this workload profile, the system runs either a single query or a single transformation at a time, as quickly as possible.

To assess scalability, the benchmark uses instance models of growing sizes, each model containing twice as many model elements as the previous one. Scalability is also evaluated against queries of different complexity. For a successful run, the tested tool is expected to evaluate the query and return the *identifiers* of the model elements in the result set.

Execution Phases. The benchmark transaction sequence consists of four distinct phases. The serialization of the model is loaded into the database (load); a well-formedness query is executed on the model (initial validation); some elements are programmatically modified (transformation) and the query is reevaluated (revalidation).

Instance Models. We developed a generator that creates instance models. The instance models are generated pseudorandomly, with pre-defined structural constraints and a regular fan-out structure (i.e. the in-degree and out-degree of the vertices follow a uniform distribution) [15].

Transformations. In the transformation phase, the benchmark runs quick fix transformations (Sec. 2.3) on 10% of the invalid elements (the result set of the first validation phase), except for the SignalNeighbor query, where $1/3$ of the invalid elements are modified. The transformations run in a single logical transaction, implemented with multiple physical transactions.

Metrics. To quantify the complexity of the benchmark test cases, we use a set of metrics that have been shown to correspond well to performance [15]. The values for the test cases are shown in Fig. 8. The problem size numbers take the values of 2^n in the range from 1 to 4096. For space considerations, only every other

Problem size	Triples	Nodes	Edges	PosLength (2)		RouteSensor (4)		SignalNeighbor (8)		SwitchSensor (2)	
				RSS	MS	RSS	MS	RSS	MS	RSS	MS
1	23k	6k	17k	470	47	94	9	3	1	19	1
4	86k	23k	63k	1769	176	348	31	6	2	91	9
16	334k	88k	245k	6893	689	1301	126	19	6	326	29
64	1M	361k	1M	28239	2823	5324	511	69	19	1287	119
256	5M	1M	3M	110739	11073	21097	1996	254	74	5109	485
1024	21M	5M	15M	443458	44345	84107	8024	983	287	20716	1977
4096	85M	22M	63M	1769402	176940	336507	32051	–	–	81410	7730

RSS: result set size   MS: modification size

Fig. 8. Metrics of the instance models and queries

problem size is listed. The complexity of an instance model is best described by the *number of its triples*, equal to the sum of its nodes and edges. The queries are quantified by the *number of their variables* (shown in parentheses) and their *result set size* (RSS). The transformations are characterized by the number of model elements modified (*modification size*, MS).

4.2   Benchmark Architecture

Benchmark Executor. The benchmark is controlled by a distinguished node of the system, called the *executor*. The executor delegates the operations (e.g. loading the model) to the distributed system. The queries and the model manipulation operations are handled by the underlying database management system which runs them distributedly and waits for the distributed operation to finish, effectively creating a synchronization point after each transaction.

Methodology. We defined two benchmark setups. (1) As a *non-incremental baseline*, we used an open-source distributed triplestore and SPARQL query system, 4store. (2) We deployed INCQUERY-D with 4store as a backend database. It is important to mention that the benchmark is strongly centralized: the *coordinator* node of INCQUERY-D runs on the same server as the benchmark *executor*.

The benchmark executor software used the framework of the Train Benchmark to collect data about the results of the benchmark. These were not only used for performance benchmarking but also to ensure the functional equivalence of the systems under benchmark.

The precise execution semantics for each phase are defined as follows. (1) The load phase includes loading the model from the disk (serialized as RDF/XML), persisting it in the database backend, and, in the case of INCQUERY-D, initializing the Rete network. (2) The execution time of the initial validation phase is the time required for the first complete evaluation of the query. (3) The transformation phase starts with the selection of the invalid model elements and is finished after the modifications are persisted in the database backend. In the case of INCQUERY-D, the transformation is only finished after the Rete network has processed the changes and is in a consistent state. (4) The revalidation phase re-runs the query of the initial validation phase, and retrieves the updated results.

The execution time includes the time required for the defined operation, the computation and I/O operations of the servers in the cluster and the network communication (to both directions). The execution times were determined using the System.nanoTime() Java method.

Environment. We used 4store [12] (version 1.1.5) as our storage backend. The servers ran the Ubuntu 12.10 64-bit operating system with Oracle Java 7. For the implementation of the distributed Rete network, we used Akka [28] (version 2.1.4), a distributed, asynchronous messaging system.

The system was deployed on the private cloud that runs on the Apache VCL (Virtual Computing Lab) platform. We reserved four virtual machines on separate host machines, with each using a quad-core Intel Xeon L5420 CPU running at 2.5 GHz and having 16 GB of RAM. The host machines were connected to a dedicated gigabit Ethernet network.

4.3   Results

The benchmark results of our experiments are shown in Fig. 9. On each plot, the x axis shows the problem size, i.e. the size of the instance model, while the y axis shows the execution time of a certain phase, measured in seconds. Both axes use logarithmic scale.

First, we discuss the results for RouteSensor, a query of medium complexity. Fig. 9a presents the combined execution time for the load and initial validation phases. The execution time is a low order polynomial of the model size for both the standalone 4store and the INCQUERY-D system. The results show that despite the initial overhead of the Rete network initialization, INCQUERY-D has a significant advantage starting from medium-sized models (with approximately 1 million triples). Fig. 9b shows the execution time for the sum of the transformation and revalidation phases. The results show that the Rete maintenance overhead imposed by INCQUERY-D on model manipulation operations is low, and overall the model transformation phase when using INCQUERY-D is considerably faster for models larger than a few hundred thousand triples. Fig. 9c focuses on the revalidation phase. The performance of INCQUERY-D is characteristically different from that of the SPARQL engine of 4store. Even for models with tens of millions of tuples, INCQUERY-D provides close to instantaneous query re-evaluation.

Fig. 9d–9f are presented to compare the results for the PosLength, the Signal-Neighbor and the SwitchSensor queries, respectively. The PosLength query uses only a few variables but has a large result set. The SignalNeighbor query includes many variables but has a small match set. The SwitchSensor query uses a few variables and has a medium-sized result set.

The large result set of the PosLength query (Fig. 9d) is a challenge for incremental query evaluation systems, however, INCQUERY-D still provides reasonably fast load, transformation and query evaluation times, while outperforming 4store on the revalidation time. The results for the SignalNeighbor query (Fig. 9e) show INCQUERY-D has a characteristic advantage on both the transformation and the revalidation times. The SwitchSensor query also shows a clear advantage of INCQUERY-D for transformation and revalidation.

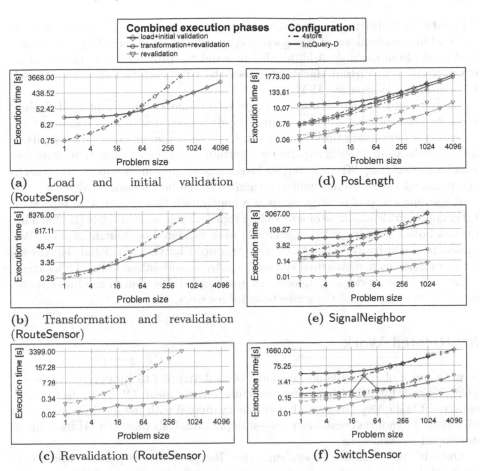

Fig. 9. Benchmark results

Summary of Observations. Based on the results, we can conclude the following observations. As expected, due to the overhead of the Rete construction, the *non-incremental approach* is often faster for small models. However, even for medium-sized models (with a couple of million triples), the Rete construction overhead already pays off for the first validation. After the Rete network is initialized, INCQUERY-D provides significantly improved transformation and revalidation times, with the revalidation times being consistently orders of magnitude faster due to the different characteristics of their execution time.

In summary, these observations show that INCQUERY-D is not just capable of processing models with over 10 million elements (pushing the limits well beyond the capabilities of single-workstation modeling tools), but also, it provides close to instantaneous query evaluation times even for very complex queries.

Threats to Validity. To minimize *internal threats to validity*, we turned off the caching mechanisms of the operating system to force rereading the serialized model from the disk. Additionally, to avoid the propagation of the warmup effect of the Java Virtual Machine between the runs, each test case was started independently in separate JVM.

As our cloud infrastructure was subject to minimal concurrent load during the measurements, we aimed to minize the distortion due to load transients by running the benchmark three times and taking the *minimum value* for each phase into consideration. We did experience a certain deviation of execution times for smaller models (Fig. 9f). However, for larger models (our most important target), the transient effects do not influence validity of the benchmark results.

Regarding *external validity*, we used a benchmark that is a faithful representation of a workload profile of a modeling tool for large-scale models [15,29]. The queries both for 4store and INCQUERY-D were validated by domain experts. We aimed to minimize the potential bias introduced by the additional degrees of freedom inherent in distributed systems, e.g. by a randomized manual allocation of the processing nodes of Rete network in the cloud. We plan to conduct a more detailed investigation of these effects as future work.

5   Related Work

A wide range of special languages have been developed to support *graph-based* querying over EMF [25] for a single-machine environment. OCL is a declarative constraint and query language that can be evaluated with the local-search based [6] engine. To address scalability issues, impact analysis tools [10,21] have been developed as extensions.

Outside the Eclipse ecosystem, the Resource Description Framework (RDF [11]) is developed to support the description of instances of the semantic web, assuming sparse, ever-growing and incomplete data stored as triples and queried using the SPARQL [33] graph pattern language. Property graphs [23] provide a more general way to describe graphs by annotating vertices and edges with key-value properties. They can be stored in graph databases like Neo4j [20] which provides the Cypher [24] query language.

Even though big data storages (like document databases, column family stores or MapReduce based databases) provide fast object persistence and retrieval, query engines realized directly on these data structures do not provide dedicated support for incremental query evaluation or efficient evaluation of query primitives (like join). This inspired Morsa [7] and Neo4EMF [3] to use MongoDB and Neo4j, respectively, as a scalable NoSQL persistence backend for EMF persistence, extended with caching and dynamic loading capabilities. The commercial Virtuoso binds relational and RDF domains into one universal database, supporting SQL and SPARQL querying, and distributed query evaluation. While Morsa and Virtuoso use disk-based backend, Trinity.RDF [34] is a closed source, pure in-memory solution, which executes a highly optimized local-search based algorithm on top of the Trinity distributed key-value store with low response time. However, the effect of data updating on query performance is currently not investigated.

Rete-based caching approaches have been proposed to process Linked Data (bearing the closest similarity of our approach). INSTANS [22] uses this algorithm to perform complex event processing (formulated in SPARQL) on RDF data, gathered from distributed sensors. Diamond [19] evaluates SPARQL queries on Linked Data, where the main challenge is the efficient traversal of data, but our distributed indexing technique is still unique wrt. these approaches.

The Train Benchmark framework was introduced in [29], where the domain and scenario were defined together with four queries, and an instance model generator. In [15], we extended the approach by characterizing models and queries with metrics, and introducing 30 new queries, and a new instance model generator. There are numerous graph and model transformation benchmarks [32,9] presented also at GRABATS and TTC tool contests, but only [16,30] focus specifically on query performance for large models.

The conceptual foundations of our approach are based on EMF-INCQUERY [5], a tool that evaluates graph patterns over EMF models using Rete. With respect to an earlier prototype [14], the main contributions of the current paper are (i) a novel architecture that introduces a separate distributed indexer component in addition to the distributed data store and distributed query evaluation network (which is key distinguishing feature compared to similar tools [19,22,34]) and (ii) the detailed performance evaluation and analysis of the system with respect to a state-of-the-art distributed RDF/SPARQL engine. Up to our best knowledge, INCQUERY-D is the first approach to support *distributed incremental query evaluation* in an MDE context.

6   Conclusion

We presented INCQUERY-D, a novel approach to adapt distributed incremental query techniques to large and complex model-driven software engineering scenarios. Our proposal is based on a distributed Rete network that is decoupled from a sharded graph database by a distributed model indexer and model access adapter. We presented a detailed performance evaluation in the context of quick-fix software design model transformations combined with on-the-fly wellformedness validation. The results are promising as they show nearly instantaneous complex query re-evaluation well beyond 10^7 model elements.

References

1. OpenLink Software: Virtuoso Universal Server,
   http://virtuoso.openlinksw.com/
2. Sesame: RDF API and Query Engine, http://www.openrdf.org/
3. Atlanmod research team. NEO4EMF (October 2013), http://neo4emf.com/
4. Bergmann, G.: Incremental Model Queries in Model-Driven Design. Ph.D. dissertation, Budapest University of Technology and Economics, Budapest (October 2013)
5. Bergmann, G., Horváth, Á., Ráth, I., Varró, D., Balogh, A., Balogh, Z., Ökrös, A.: Incremental Evaluation of Model Queries over EMF Models. In: Petriu, D.C., Rouquette, N., Haugen, Ø. (eds.) MODELS 2010, Part I. LNCS, vol. 6394, pp. 76–90. Springer, Heidelberg (2010)
6. Eclipse MDT Project. Eclispe OCL website (2011),
   http://eclipse.org/modeling/mdt/?project=ocl.
7. Espinazo Pagán, J., Sánchez Cuadrado, J., García Molina, J.: Morsa: A scalable approach for persisting and accessing large models. In: Whittle, J., Clark, T., Kühne, T. (eds.) MODELS 2011. LNCS, vol. 6981, pp. 77–92. Springer, Heidelberg (2011)
8. Forgy, C.: Rete: A fast algorithm for the many pattern/many object pattern match problem. Artificial Intelligences 19(1), 17–37 (1982)
9. Geiß, R., Kroll, M.: On improvements of the Varro benchmark for graph transformation tools. Technical Report 2007-7, Universität Karlsruhe, IPD Goos, 12, (2007) ISSN 1432-7864
10. Goldschmidt, T., Uhl, A.: Efficient OCL impact analysis (2011)
11. R.C.W. Group. Resource Description Framework (RDF) (2004),
    http://www.w3.org/RDF/
12. Harris, S., Lamb, N., Shadbolt, N.: 4store: The design and implementation of a clustered RDF store. In: 5th International Workshop on Scalable Semantic Web Knowledge Base Systems, SSWS 2009 (2009)
13. Hillairet, G., Bertrand, F., Lafaye, J.Y., et al.: Bridging emf applications and rdf data sources. In: Proceedings of the 4th International Workshop on Semantic Web Enabled Software Engineering, SWESE (2008)
14. Izsó, B., Szárnyas, G., Ráth, I., Varró, D.: Incquery-d: Incremental graph search in the cloud. In: Proceedings of the Workshop on Scalability in Model Driven Engineering, BigMDE 2013, pp. 4:1–4:4. ACM, New York (2013)
15. Izsó, B., Szatmári, Z., Bergmann, G., Horváth, Á., Ráth, I.: Towards precise metrics for predicting graph query performance. In: 2013 IEEE/ACM 28th International Conference on Automated Software Engineering (ASE), Silicon Valley, CA, USA, pp. 412–431. IEEE (November 2013)
16. Jouault, F., Sottet, J.-S., et al.: An AmmA/ATL solution for the grabats 2009 reverse engineering case study. In: 5th International Workshop on Graph-Based Tools, Grabats (2009)
17. Kolovos, D.S., Rose, L.M., Matragkas, N., Paige, R.F., Guerra, E., Cuadrado, J.S., De Lara, J., Ráth, I., Varró, D., Tisi, M., Cabot, J.: A research roadmap towards achieving scalability in model driven engineering. In: Proceedings of the Workshop on Scalability in Model Driven Engineering, BigMDE 2013, pp. 2:1–2:10. ACM, New York (2013)
18. Miranker, D.P., Lofaso, B.J.: The Organization and Performance of a TREAT-Based Production System Compiler. IEEE Trans. on Knowl. and Data Eng. 3(1), 3–10 (1991)

19. Miranker, D.P., et al.: Diamond: A SPARQL query engine, for linked data based on the Rete match. In: AImWD (2012)
20. Neo Technology. Neo4j (2013), http://neo4j.org/
21. Reder, A., Egyed, A.: Incremental consistency checking for complex design rules and larger model changes. In: France, R.B., Kazmeier, J., Breu, R., Atkinson, C. (eds.) MODELS 2012. LNCS, vol. 7590, pp. 202–218. Springer, Heidelberg (2012)
22. Rinne, M.: SPARQL update for complex event processing. In: Cudré-Mauroux, P., et al. (eds.) ISWC 2012, Part II. LNCS, vol. 7650, pp. 453–456. Springer, Heidelberg (2012)
23. Rodriguez, M.A., Neubauer, P.: Constructions from dots and lines. CoRR, abs/1006.2361 (2010)
24. Taylor, A., Jones, A.: Cypher Query Lang (2012)
25. The Eclipse Project. Eclipse Modeling Framework, http://www.eclipse.org/emf/
26. The MOGENTES project. Model-Based Generation of Tests for Dependable Embedded Systems, http://www.mogentes.eu/
27. The MONDO project. Scalable Modelling and Model Management on the Cloud, http://www.mondo-project.org/
28. Typesafe, Inc. Akka documentation (2013), http://akka.io/
29. Ujhelyi, Z., Bergmann, G., Hegedüs, Á., Horváth, Á., Izsó, B., Ráth, I., Szatmári, Z., Varró, D.: EMF-IncQuery: An integrated development environment for live model queries. Science of Computer Programming (accepted 2014)
30. Ujhelyi, Z., Horváth, Á., Varró, D., Csiszár, N.I., Szőke, G., Vidács, L., Ferenc, R.: Anti-pattern Detection with Model Queries: A Comparison of Approaches. In: IEEE CSMR-WCRE 2014 Software Evolution Week. IEEE (2014)
31. Varró, G., Deckwerth, F.: A rete network construction algorithm for incremental pattern matching. In: Duddy, K., Kappel, G. (eds.) ICMB 2013. LNCS, vol. 7909, pp. 125–140. Springer, Heidelberg (2013)
32. Varró, G., Schürr, A., Varró, D.: Benchmarking for graph transformation. In: Proc. IEEE Symposium on Visual Languages and Human-Centric Computing (VL/HCC 2005), Dallas, Texas, USA, pp. 79–88. IEEE Press (September 2005)
33. W3C. SPARQL Query Language for RDF, http://www.w3.org/TR/rdf-sparql-query/
34. Zeng, K., Yang, J., Wang, H., Shao, B., Wang, Z.: A distributed graph engine for web scale rdf data. In: Proceedings of the 39th International Conference on Very Large Data Bases, PVLDB 2013, pp. 265–276. VLDB Endowment (2013)

Translating OCL to Graph Patterns*

Gábor Bergmann

Budapest University of Technology and Economics,
Department of Measurement and Information Systems,
1117 Budapest, Magyar tudósok krt. 2
bergmann@mit.bme.hu

Abstract. Model-driven tools use model queries for many purposes, including validation of well-formedness rules and specification of derived features. The majority of declarative model query corpus available in industry appears to use the OCL language. Graph pattern based queries, however, would have a number of advantages due to their more abstract specification, such as performance improvements through advanced query evaluation techniques. As query performance can be a key issue with large models, evaluating graph patterns instead of OCL queries could be useful in practice.

The current paper presents an automatic mapping from a large sublanguage of OCL expressions to equivalent graph patterns in the dialect of EMF-INCQUERY. Validation of benefits is carried out by performance measurements according to an existing benchmark.

Keywords: Model query, OCL, graph pattern, incremental evaluation.

1 Introduction

Model queries are important components in model-driven tool chains. They are widely used for specifying reports, derived features, well-formedness constraints, and guard conditions for behavioural models, design space rules or model transformations. Although model queries can be implemented using a general-purpose programming language (Java), declarative query languages may be more concise and easier to learn, among other advantages. Popular modeling platforms (e.g. the Eclipse Modeling Framework *(EMF)* [1]) support various query languages.

OCL [2] is a standard declarative model query language widely used in industry. OCL queries specify chains of navigation among model objects in a functional programming style. However, query languages inspired by *graph patterns* [3,4] (such as SPAQL [5]) resemble logic programming, where the order of model exploration is freely determined by the query engine at evaluation time. Such more abstract query specifications have numerous advantages. The steps of graph pattern matching can be automatically optimized for performance in advance by a

---

* This work was partially supported by the European Union and the State of Hungary, co-financed by the European Social Fund in the framework of TÁMOP 4.2.4. A/-11-1-2012-0001 'National Excellence Program', and by the CERTIMOT (ERC_HU-09-01-2010-0003) and EU FP7 MONDO (ICT-2013.1.2) projects.

J. Dingel et al. (Eds.): MODELS 2014, LNCS 8767, pp. 670–686, 2014.

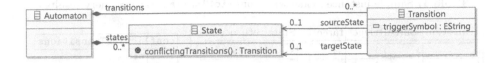

Fig. 1. Ecore Diagram of State Machine metamodel package

query planner [6,7] or during evaluation by a dynamic strategy [8]. For further performance gains in case of evolving models, incremental graph pattern matcher techniques [9] can deeply analyze the query to store and maintain the result of subqueries (as in EMF-INCQUERY [10], see Sec. 2.3). In search-based software engineering, if the goal condition is a graph pattern, its structure can be inspected to automatically guide [11] the design space exploration towards reaching the goal. When analyzing behavioural models, pre/post condition graph patterns can be inspected for efficient model checking [12,13] or to prove confluence [14]. It is possible to automatically generate instance models (e.g. for tool testing) that satisfy a given graph query [15] more efficiently than OCL [16].

Since the majority of declarative model query corpus available in industry appears to be OCL, the above mentioned benefits can only be reaped by translating OCL queries into graph patterns. This is not always possible, as OCL is more expressive. Nevertheless, by extending prior work [15], an automated mapping is presented in the current paper that transforms a large sublanguage of OCL expressions to equivalent graph patterns in the dialect of EMF-INCQUERY.

From the benefits listed above, query performance was chosen for validating the approach, as it can be a key issue with large models. This task is carried out by performance measurements according to an existing benchmark [10].

The running example and query formalisms are introduced in Sec. 2. The mapping is specified in Sec. 3. Performance measurements are presented in Sec. 4, Sec. 5 summarizes related work, and Sec. 6 adds concluding remarks.

2   Preliminaries

2.1   Running Example

Several concepts will be illustrated using a simple state machine modeling language. The metamodel, defined in EMF [1] and depicted by Fig. 1, describes how state automata contain states and transitions, where the latter have a source state, a target state, and a triggering input symbol. Model queries can support the application of this metamodel in many ways (such as simulation, model checking, code generation, etc.), two of which will be explored in greater detail.

A sample instance model containing a single `Automaton`, `States` $s_1 \ldots s_6$ and the `Transitions` listed by Table 1a will be used to demonstrate model queries.

Table 1. Sample instance model with `conflictingTransitions` query results

Transition	source	trigger	target
t_1	s_1	A	s_2
t_2	s_1	A	s_3
t_3	s_1	B	s_4
t_4	s_1	B	s_5
t_5	s_1	C	s_6
t_6	s_3	C	s_6

(a) Transitions

State	return value
s_1	$\{t_1, t_2, t_3, t_4\}$
s_2	$\emptyset$
s_3	$\emptyset$
s_4	$\emptyset$
s_5	$\emptyset$
s_6	$\emptyset$

(b) OCL results

conflictingTransitions	
self	t1
s_1	t_1
s_1	t_2
s_1	t_3
s_1	t_4

(c) Pattern match set

An instance model of this Ecore package is only considered *well-formed* if certain criteria are met. One such important sanity criterion is that the source and target states of a transition must both belong to the same automaton that contains the transition. A modeling environment could automatically validate instance models by issuing a model query that finds *violations* of this constraint.

Another use case of model queries is the definition of *derived features* - references or attributes that are not freely chosen, but are rather computed automatically from the values of other features (i.e. via a model query). The derived reference `conflictingTransitions` of class State identifies those outgoing transitions that are in conflict, i.e. share their triggering input symbol with one or more other outgoing transitions from the same state. Such a derived reference could be useful for exploring the nondeterminism of the behavioural model.

If the model is being continuously edited, the results of validation and derived feature queries have to be repeatedly updated. In case of large models, this could lead to performance problems unless incremental techniques are applied.

2.2   The OCL Language

OCL [17] is a pure functional language for defining expressions in context of a metamodel, so that the expressions can be evaluated on instance models of the metamodel. The language is very expressive, surpassing the power of first order logic by constructs such as collection aggregation operations (`sum()`, etc.). OCL queries taking a model element as input can be applied in use cases such as specifying well-formedness constraints (*invariants*).

Example 1. The OCL version of the derived feature is included as Lst. 1. When evaluated at a given `State` object, for each outgoing transition it collects the other outgoing transitions with the same trigger symbol, and the returns the accumulated set. The Set-valued expression is built by navigating from the `State` along references, and filtering the results according to attribute conditions. Results on the sample instance model are listed by Table 1b.

The rest of the section gives a basic overview of the most important characteristics of OCL expressions that will be necessary for understanding the paper; the reader is referred to the OMG standard [17] for more information.

Listing 1 OCL expression specifying the derived feature conflictingTransitions

```
1 context State def: conflictingTransitions: Set(Transition) =
2   let a : Automaton = self.automaton in
3     a.transitions->select(t1|t1.sourceState=self and
4       a.transitions->exists(t2| t1<>t2 and
5         t2.sourceState = self and t1.triggerSymbol = t2.triggerSymbol))
```

OCL Values and Types. OCL can express *values* of various *types*. *Primitive types* include character strings, integer and real numbers, etc.; Boolean is especially significant, e.g. for expressing well-formedness constraints. Classes in metamodels are OCL types; *instance model elements* are OCL values conforming to them, with subclassing. OCL allows constructing tuple types and collection types (Set, Bag, OrderedSet and Sequence) from any OCL type. In the current paper, primitive and metamodel types are collectively referred as *ground types*, while collection and tuple types are referred as *structured types*.

OCL Expressions. OCL expressions are functions expressed on a set of *input variables* (also known as *free variables*), each with an associated type. When a type-compatible OCL value is substituted for each of these input variables, the expression evaluates to a single result value, which is compatible with the type of the expression. For an OCL expression O taking input parameters $X_1, X_2, \ldots, X_n$, let $G \models y - O(x_1, x_2, \ldots, x_n)$ denote that expression O parametrized by actual parameter values $x_1, x_2, \ldots, x_n$ yields the result y if evaluated over model G.

Expressions are compositional: an expression may have sub-expressions whose results contribute to the result of the expression. Input variables of sub-expressions are often free variables of the whole expression as well.

OCL has *literal expressions* for various types. Primitive literals have no input variables and return constants. Collection or tuple literals contain zero or more sub-expressions yielding the elements of the collection or the tuple; note that such a structure literal may have input variables due to these sub-expressions.

A *variable reference* OCL expression returns the value of its input variable. The inputless allInstances() expression returns a Set of all instances of a given metamodel type; oclIsKindOf() tests membership of this Set. The constructs let-in and if-then-else combine the results of their subexpressions in the expected way. *Property call expressions* express *navigation* from tuples to their field values, or along (single- or multi-valued) model element features; the source of navigation is identified by a single sub-expression called *source*.

Example 1 demonstrates a derived feature specification as a let-in OCL expression taking a State as input and yielding a Set of Transitions as output. The first subexpression is navigation self.automaton, initializing variable a.

Operation call expressions evaluate operations associated with the type of their *source* sub-expression. The operation takes the result of the source as its argument, and in some cases the result of other sub-expressions as additional arguments. Some significant operations will be discussed in the following.

OCL Operations. Classes may declare *read-only model operations* (such as derived features) that OCL expressions can invoke on their instances. These operations can be specified as model queries (often written in OCL).

OCL also supports built-in operations on primitive types, including *arithmetic operations*, logical connectives, or comparisons (<> for inequality, <=, etc.).

Collection operations include membership testing, union, etc. of Sets. Operations that aggregate a collection into a single value include size() and sum().

Iterator expressions are a special kind of collection operations that take a lambda expression (the *body*) as their argument. When evaluating the iterator expression, the body is evaluated repeatedly, with collection members substituted for one or more of its input variables (called the *iterator*). The iterator expression select() will evaluate a Boolean-valued body predicate on each element of a collection, and form a resulting subset/subsequence/etc. containing those elements that evaluated to true. Similarly, exists() returns a Boolean indicating whether any members of the collection satisfy the body predicate.

Example 1 demonstrates operations =, <>, and, select(), exists().

2.3   Graph Patterns and EMF-IncQuery

Graph Patterns as a Query Language. The EMF-INCQUERY framework [10] aims at the efficient definition and evaluation of incremental model queries over EMF-based models, building on the idea of *graph patterns*. The query language is detailed in [18], only a brief overview is given here.

A basic graph pattern consists of *pattern constraints* expressed over *pattern variables* that represent model elements or primitive values. The *parameter variables* of a graph pattern are a subset of the pattern variables that are exposed to the query user. Pattern variables that are not parameters are called *local variables*. *Structural constraints* prescribe the existence and interconnection of graph nodes and edges of given types. *Attribute constraints* are defined by pure, deterministic *expressions* given in a Java-based language.

Basic patterns can be *composed* in numerous ways, thus the query language has the expressiveness [4] of first-order formulae over the model. *Disjunction* (OR) is expressed by several basic patterns (*pattern bodies*) defining alternative constraint sets (and local variables) for the same parameters. A *pattern call* reuses a pattern within another pattern as a single constraint expressed over its actual parameters (quantifying away the local variables of the called pattern). A *negative application condition* (NAC) is a pattern call constraint with negation, i.e. it is satisfied iff the called pattern isn't.

A *match* of a graph pattern is a value substitution of the parameters, so that the local variables of at least one pattern body can be assigned values to satisfy all pattern constraints of that body. The result of an (unbound) model query is the set of all matches, called the *match set*. Matches of a pattern are all tuples of the same format (one entry for each pattern parameter), and the result of pattern matching is the set of valid matches in the model, therefore the pattern essentially evaluates to a *mathematical relation* on elements of the model and primitive values, where the arity of the relation corresponds to the number of pattern parameters, and members of the relation are the matches of the pattern.

$P(X_1, X_2, \ldots, X_n)$ will denote a pattern P having parameters $X_1, X_2, \ldots, X_n$. The fact that the tuple $\langle x_1, x_2, \ldots, x_n \rangle$ is a match of the pattern P over model G will be denoted as $G \models \langle x_1, x_2, \ldots, x_n \rangle \in MatchSet^P$.

Example 2. The derived feature in the example metamodel can be specified by the pattern `conflictingTransitions` (Fig. 2). The single pattern body imposes 8 structural constraints (existence of connecting edges, inequality) on local pattern variables a, t2, str and parameters self, t1. Each pattern match means that transition t1 is included in the derived set `conflictingTransitions` of state self. See Table 1c for the match set on the sample model.

```
1  pattern conflictingTransitions (
2    // parameters
3    self : State , t1 : Transition
4  ) = { // constraints of single body
5    State.automaton(self , a);
6    Automaton.transitions(a, t1);
7    Automaton.transitions(a, t2);
8    Transition.sourceState(t1, self);
9    Transition.sourceState(t2, self);
10   Transition.triggerSymbol(t1, str);
11   Transition.triggerSymbol(t2, str);
12   t1 != t2;
13 }
```

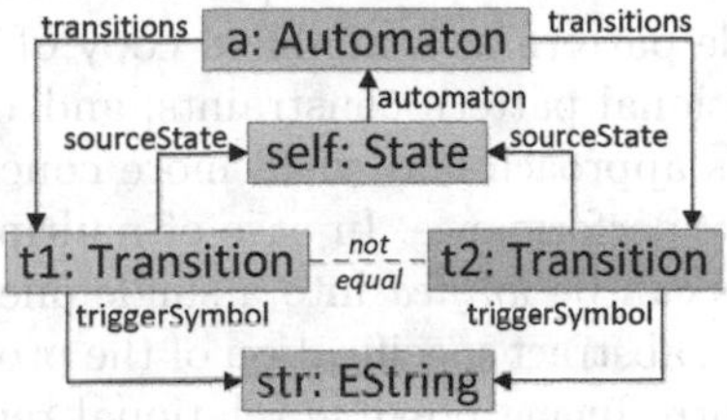

(a) Textual syntax   (b) Graphical form, parameters highlighted

Fig. 2. Graph pattern specifying the derived feature

Incremental Evaluation. A powerful feature of EMF-INCQUERY is its *incremental query evaluation*. This means that the match sets of graph patterns are cached and continuously updated as the model evolves. This choice increases memory consumption and imposes a run-time maintenance overhead on model manipulation; on the other hand, query results can be instantaneously retrieved without re-traversing the model. This characteristic can be beneficial in use cases including model validation, simulation and derived feature computation [19,20].

The particular algorithm used in EMF-INCQUERY is Rete [9], which caches match sets of subpatterns as well, with the benefit that maintenance cost is proportional to the change only, independently of model size (see [21]).

3 Mapping OCL Expressions to EMF-INCQUERY

An approach for constructing semantically equivalent EMF-INCQUERY graph patterns for certain kinds of OCL expressions is proposed in the following sections. Note that the graph pattern of Example 2, disregarding minor beautification, was automatically constructed from the OCL expression of Lst. 1 by a partial prototype implementation of this strategy (available at [22]).

3.1   Overview of the Approach

Graph patterns evaluate to match sets that are relations in the mathematical sense, while OCL expressions are typed functions. Thus the proposed approach aims to find relations that are equivalent to the original OCL functions, and then construct graph patterns that in turn express exactly these relations. For instance, the pattern of Example 2 is equivalent to the OCL expression of Example 1, as demonstrated on the sample instance model (Table 1).

One of the main challenges of defining such a mapping is making sure that relation domains (columns) are of ground types, as the graph pattern formalism does not support variables representing collections of model elements.

By structural recursion, the proposed approach first maps each OCL subexpression to a pattern; then these *helper patterns* are used for translating the whole expression. The helper pattern will often be included via pattern composition. In lieu of positive pattern composition, it is also possible to construct the whole pattern as a modified copy of the helper pattern, by *augmenting* it with additional pattern constraints, and/or modifying the set of pattern parameters - this approach may yield more concise output and potentially better run-time query performance. In case of multiple such subexpressions, several helper patterns can be *unified* into a single one that contains all their constraints.

An abstract specification of the proposed mapping will be provided in Sec. 3.2, by introducing possible relational representations for various kinds of OCL expressions. Then Sec. 3.3 provides the actual mapping of OCL language elements to graph patterns whose match sets will correspond to the appropriate mathematical relation specified in Sec. 3.2. The mapping is applicable to many graph query languages; only a few cases discussed in Sec. 3.4 require EMF-INCQUERY-specific constructs. For the sake of brevity, the complete coverage of the OCL Standard was only included in [22]. Limitations will be discussed in Sec. 3.5.

3.2   Abstract Mapping to a Relational Representation

Single-Valued Non-boolean Expressions. An OCL expression O with ground-typed inputs $X_1, X_2, \ldots, X_n$ and a ground-typed, non-Boolean result type will be mapped to a graph pattern P_O such that $G \models y = O(x_1, x_2, \ldots, x_n) \Leftrightarrow G \models \langle x_1, x_2, \ldots, x_n, y \rangle \in MatchSet^{P_O}$ for any instance model G and appropriately typed $x_1, x_2, \ldots, x_n, y$. Simply speaking, the function is mapped to a relation expressed on the function inputs and results. From Example 1, the OCL subexpression t1.triggerSymbol (a function that maps a transition to a string) is equivalent to the single-constraint pattern Transition.triggerSymbol(t1, str) that evaluates to a relation between transitions and strings. For the instance model of Table 1a, the relation is $\{\langle t_1, A \rangle, \langle t_2, A \rangle, \langle t_3, B \rangle, \langle t_4, B \rangle, \langle t_5, C \rangle, \langle t_6, C \rangle\}$.

Note that if at least one of $x_1, x_2, \ldots, x_n, y$ has a primitive type with practically infinite instance set (e.g. 2^{64} integers), the above definition of P_O may appear to yield a practically infinite match set size, making it unfeasible to apply fully incremental evaluation model query, where all matches have to be enumerated and stored. However, as we will see below, the value of these primitive-typed variables are in many practical cases either equated to literal values, or available as an attribute value of an instance model element, or (transitively) inferrable by expression evaluation from other primitive variables that have these properties. Augmentation also improves *finiteness*: even if a helper pattern for a subexpression does not meet this condition, its augmented version associated with the composite expression may do so. Therefore typically the match set will still be finite and computable by the query engine. The proposed approach does not support cases where this condition is violated. Another limitation is that the relation domains have to be of ground types, since domains of structured types would put the relation beyond the expressive power of graph patterns.

Boolean-Valued Expressions. An OCL expression O with ground-typed inputs $X_1, X_2, \ldots, X_n$ and a Boolean result type can be mapped to a graph pattern P_O similarly as above. Additionally, it can also be mapped to graph patterns P_O^+ or P_O^- that match those inputs for which the expression evaluates to true respectively false: $G \models true = O(x_1, x_2, \ldots, x_n) \Leftrightarrow G \models \langle x_1, x_2, \ldots, x_n \rangle \in MatchSet^{P_O^+} \Leftrightarrow G \models \langle x_1, x_2, \ldots, x_n \rangle \notin MatchSet^{P_O^-}$ for any instance model G and appropriately typed $x_1, x_2, \ldots, x_n, y$. From Example 1, let O be the OCL subexpression t1 <> t2 (a function that maps two transitions to a Boolean); then binary pattern P_O^+ has the constraint t1 != t2 (and implicit type restrictions) and no Boolean variables; while P_O^- has t1 == t2 and evaluates to $\{\langle t_1, t_1 \rangle, \langle t_2, t_2 \rangle, \langle t_3, t_3 \rangle, \langle t_4, t_4 \rangle, \langle t_5, t_5 \rangle, \langle t_6, t_6 \rangle\}$ for the model of Table 1a.

For each Boolean-valued OCL expression O, it is sufficient to define one of the three mappings P_O, P_O^+, P_O^-, as it can then be trivially transformed into the other two, unless a simpler mapping is known for them. P_O^+ (respectively P_O^-) can be synthesized from P_O by asserting y == true; (respectively y == false;) as an additional pattern constraint, and removing y from the pattern parameters. P_O^+ and P_O^- transform into each other via negative pattern call. Finally, P_O can be derived from P_O^+ (respectively P_O^-) by counting its matches, and then evaluating the Boolean expression that the number of matches is positive (respectively zero).

The reason for having three possible images P_O, P_O^+, P_O^- for a Boolean-valued expression O is that OCL often uses Boolean variables as conditions (e.g. in if, select(), or logical connectives), in which cases it is natural to include a pattern composition constraint of P_O^+ or P_O^- (or augment it, as discussed before). Thus the mapping result is simplified (potentially gaining run-time query performance benefits as well) in case P_O^+ or P_O^- are simpler to express than P_O.

Tuple-Valued and Tuple-Consuming Expressions. Since tuples consist of a statically known number of components, a tuple-typed variable can always be substituted with a set of variables, one for each tuple field. This principle can be applied to expression inputs and results in an analogous way; the latter case is elaborated in more detail below.

An OCL expression O with ground-typed inputs $X_1, X_2, \ldots, X_n$ and a k-ary tuple-typed result can be mapped to a graph pattern P_O such that $G \models \langle y_1, y_2, \ldots, y_k \rangle = O(x_1, x_2, \ldots, x_n) \Leftrightarrow G \models \langle x_1, x_2, \ldots, x_n, y_1, y_2, \ldots, y_k \rangle \in$

MatchSet^{P_O} for any instance model G and appropriately typed $x_1, x_2, \ldots, x_n$ as well as $y_1, y_2, \ldots, y_k$. Simply speaking, the function is mapped to a relation expressed on the function inputs and tuple components of the result.

If the result is a tuple of ground-typed fields, then the domains of the relation are of ground types. Tuples containing tuples can be trivially flattened before the mapping to tuples containing ground-typed values only. For tuples having one or more collections as components, see the following paragraphs.

Multi-valued Expressions. An OCL expression O with ground-typed inputs $X_1, X_2, \ldots, X_n$ and a collection result type will be mapped to a graph pattern P_O such that $G \models y \in O(x_1, x_2, \ldots, x_n) \Leftrightarrow G \models \langle x_1, x_2, \ldots, x_n, y \rangle \in$ *MatchSet^{P_O}* for any instance model G and appropriately typed $x_1, x_2, \ldots, x_n, y$. Simply speaking, the function is mapped to a relation expressed on the function inputs and elements appearing in the result, where each element of the result collection corresponds to a separate element of the associated relation. From Example 1, the OCL subexpression `a.transitions` (a function that maps an automaton to a set of transitions) is equivalent to the single-constraint pattern `Automaton.transitions(a, t1)` that evaluates to a relation between automatons and transitions, with one row for each transition. Similarly, the graph pattern of Example 2 evaluates to a relation (see Table 1c) that associates a `State` with individual `Transitions`, as opposed to a `Set` of transitions, which is what the equivalent OCL derived feature of Example 1 yields (see Table 1b).

If the element type of the collection is a ground type, then the domains of the relation are of ground types. Tuples can be dealt with as described in Sec. 3.2. Collections of collections (as well as tuples of more than one collection) are not supported by the approach due to the limitations discussed before.

Relations (pattern match sets) have set semantics, without multiplicity or ordering. Thus only `Set` collections can be faithfully mapped (and also `Bags` in case input and internal variables together make the output unique); other collection types are not supported in general. However, many collection operations (such as `isEmpty()`) and iterator expressions (such as `select()`) behave equivalently for the various collection types, in which case the collection can be implicitly cast to a `Set` by `asSet()` for the sake of the mapping.

The proposed approach does not support collection-typed input variables in OCL expressions, as collection operations are typically mapped to pattern composition constructs that call the pattern associated with the expression that defines the collection. Note that a collection can be used as an argument of an OCL operation, if it is provided as the result of a sub-expression (typically navigation along a multi-valued property); collection types are unsupported for free variables only. In practice, this limitation is not directly relevant for class invariants and derived features (due to single non-collection input); so OCL-defined model operations and preconditions are restricted only in their parametrization. The iterator input variable of an iterator expression body can be a collection only in case of a collection of collections, which is unsupported anyway. The only other way a new variable can be introduced is a `let` expression, in which case the initialization expression of the variable can replace the variable references in the in branch for the sake of the mapping, so once again it will not matter whether the type is a collection.

3.3   Concrete Mappings for Simple Expressions

The following paragraphs construct mappings of the simplest OCL expression into graph patterns according to the specifications in Sec. 3.1. The mappings result in single-bodied patterns unless indicated otherwise.

Navigation and Variable References. If O is a navigation expression along property *edgeType* and with source expression O^{source}, where O^{source} is mapped to pattern $P_{O^{source}}$ with parameters $x_1, x_2, \ldots, x_n, y^{source}$, then O is mapped to P_O with parameters $x_1, x_2, \ldots, x_n, y$. P_O is constructed by augmenting $P_{O^{source}}$ by a new structural constraint $edgeType(y^{source}, y)$ and replacing pattern parameter y^{source} with y. This works both for single-valued and multi-valued (collection-typed) properties. Mapping variable references is trivial.

For instance, self.automaton from Example 1 is translated in Example 2 to State.automaton(self, a); note the variable reference self as source expression. On the other hand, a hypothetical self.automaton.transitions, containing the former OCL expression as its source expression, would augment this pattern by a second pattern constraint Automaton.transitions(a, y).

Type Checks and Literals. If O is T.allInstances() for metamodel class T, it is mapped to the pattern P_O with parameter y and single pattern constraint $T(y)$; the same pattern is P_O^+ if O is y.oclIsKindOf(T). If O is a primitive-typed literal of value c, it is mapped to the pattern P_O with parameter y and the single pattern constraint $c==y$. For treatment of tuple literals, see Sec. 3.2. Set literals are mapped to a disjunction of helper patterns mapped from subexpressions.

Arithmetic Operations. If O is an arithmetic operation *op* on subexpressions $O^1, O^2, \ldots, O^m$, then O is mapped to P_O with parameters consisting of all input parameters of $P_{O^1}, P_{O^2}, \ldots, P_{O^m}$ in addition to y, and with the attribute constraint $y==\text{eval}(op(y^1, y^2, \ldots, y^m))$ (where y^i is the result variable of P_{O^i}) augmenting the unification of $P_{O^1}, P_{O^2}, \ldots, P_{O^m}$. For instance, OCL expression $p < q+r$ is mapped to pattern constraints $y^1==\text{eval}(q+r)$ and $y==\text{eval}(p < y^1)$.

If O is an equality, it can be more effectively mapped to P_O^+ using a pattern constraint $y^1==y^2$ and to P_O^- as $y^1!=y^2$ instead of the eval construct. Vice versa for inequality; e.g. <> from Example 1 is mapped to a != constraint in Example 2.

Similarly, many Boolean operations have simpler mappings. In case of and, the single body of P_O^+ is the unification of $P_{O^1}^+$ and $P_{O^2}^+$ (as applied repeatedly in the running example); while P_O^- would have two bodies: $P_{O^1}^-$ and $P_{O^2}^-$.

If-Then-Else and Let-In. In a let-in expression, the result of the let subexpression is used to parameterize the in subexpression. If O is a let-in expression with subexpressions O^{let}, O^{in}, then O is mapped to P_O with parameters consisting of y along with input variables of $P_{O^{let}}$ and input variables of $P_{O^{in}}$ except for the result variable of $P_{O^{let}}$; with the pattern body unifying $P_{O^{let}}$ with $P_{O^{in}}$. For instance, constraint State.automaton(self, a) in Example 2 is from $P_{O^{let}}$.

If O is an if-then-else expression with subexpressions $O^{condition}$, O^{then}, O^{else}, then O is mapped to P_O with parameters consisting of all input parameters of $P_{O^{condition}}$, $P_{O^{then}}$, $P_{O^{else}}$ in addition to y, and with two pattern bodies, one with $y^{then}{==}y$ augmenting the unification of $P_{O^{then}}$ and $P^{+}_{O^{condition}}$, the other with $y^{else}{==}y$ augmenting the unification of $P_{O^{else}}$ and $P^{-}_{O^{condition}}$. Can be simplified to Boole-logic if the result type is Boolean.

First-Order Collection Expressions. Many collection operations and iterator expressions are trivial to translate to first-order logic formulae, which are within the power of graph patterns [4]. A few cases will be briefly outlined below.

For instance, a collection is non-empty iff the mapped pattern has any matches with the given values of input variables. If O is an isEmpty() expression with subexpression O^{source}, then O is mapped to P^{-}_O, which is the same as $P_{O^{source}}$, with its result variable removed (quantified away) from the parameters.

If O is a select() expression with subexpressions O^{source}, O^{body}, then P_O is $P_{O^{source}}$ and $P^{+}_{O^{body}}$ unified, with the result variable of the former substituted for the iterator variable of the latter (and both removed from the parameters). For exists(), P^{+}_O is constructed similarly, but the result variable is removed from the parameters. Example 1 demonstrates both cases.

3.4   Mapping Higher-Order OCL Constructs

Some OCL constructs are not expressible using first-order formulae, but the EMF-INCQUERY language provides extensions over conventional graph patterns that may suffice in some cases. As above, details will be omitted here.

EMF-INCQUERY supports transitive closure [23], so a closure() iterator expression can be mapped by (1) mapping first the body expression to a graph pattern, (2) taking the transitive closure of this graph pattern, and (3) augmenting the graph pattern mapped from the source expression with the transitive call.

The simplest case of aggregation is the size() collection operation returning the number of elements of a set. A count find constraint in EMF-INCQUERY can aggregate matches of the graph pattern corresponding to the source expression defining said set. An analogous solution is proposed for OCL aggregation operations sum(), etc.; but the corresponding EMF-INCQUERY aggregators, while included in the language specification, are not fully implemented as of today.

3.5   Miscellaneous Cases and Limitations

Operation calls toward metamodel-defined custom (read-only) operations are trivial to support if they are defined as OCL expressions (or EMF-INCQUERY patterns, as in [20]). Operations implemented in a generic-purpose programming language are not supported in general, as there is no universal way to ensure that the incremental engine is notified of changes in the computation result, which is necessary for incremental maintenance. A solution [24] has been proposed which records all model reads during the computation to invalidate the result when these parts of the model are affected by a change, but this approach has its own practical limitations, as it would require wrapping all model processing - including the implementation of the metamodel-defined read-only operation - into a compliant model access layer.

As discussed throughout Sec. 3, the proposed approach has limitations. Due to the lack of support for ordering in the relational representation, iterator expressions `sortedBy()` and `iterate()` cannot be mapped, similarly to order-sensitive operations (e.g. `first()`, `at()`) on ordered collections. Representation of multiplicity (i.e. `Bag` collection) has limitations as well. Support for collections of collections is also lost due to the relational approach. As discussed before, the usage of collections of primitive types and primitive-typed top-level arguments is restricted due to finiteness / computability limitations of EMF-INCQUERY.

OCL has two special *undefined values*, `null` and `invalid`, which conform to (almost) all OCL types, but are not equivalent to each other. The proposed approach does not support them at the moment, partly due to type system incompatibility, and also due to semantic issues [25]; see [16] for a possible workaround.

Altogether it is clear that the mapped sublanguage is significantly weaker than OCL. Still, practice has shown that the supported OCL constructs are expressive enough to be useful in many cases.

4   Performance Measurements

The justification of the proposed mapping is that one can deliver efficient, incremental query evaluation for a subset of OCL expressions by transforming them to graph patterns of equivalent semantics, and applying EMF-INCQUERY. To demonstrate this, a subset of an existing performance benchmark for well-formedness (invariant) constraint checking was applied.

4.1   Measurement Setup

The Train Benchmark [10] defines a number of well-formedness constraints (of which only `SignalNeighbor` is used here) in a custom metamodel, and measures the constraint checking performance of various model query tools as they process automatically generated instance models of various sizes conforming to the metamodel. The goal is to provide near instantaneous feedback on constraint violations as the (simulated) user is editing a large model. The workload and measured performance indicators involve: (*phase 1*) reading the model, (*phase 2*) checking it for any inconsistencies as defined by the well-formedness constraint, (*phase 3*) simulating a transformation / manual editing of the model that performs a predefined sequence of modifications, and (*phase 4*) checking

Table 2. SignalNeighbor evaluation times for the instance model of 213K elements

Tool	Java	OCL	OCL-CG	OCL-IA	EIQ	OCL2IQ
Batch Validation [ms]	169 867	36 157	126 461	36 444	6 142	6 205
Continuous Validation Time [ms]	167 891	32 237	126 723	331 523	2	1
Memory Footprint [kB]	14 009	15 304	17 755	26 073	108 435	118 319

the updated model as well for inconsistencies. For fair comparison [10] of state-less tools against incremental ones, the most relevant performance indicators are *phase 1+2* ("Batch Validation") execution time and *phase 3+4* ("Continuous Validation") execution time (and of course the memory footprint). The workflow actually executes *phase 3+4* repeatedly; the reported values are the average time of one repetition (small modification + 1 query).

The run-time performance of the following solutions were compared[1]. **Java**: a naive Java implementation of the constraint check, as a hypothetical programmer would quickly implement it, without any special effort to improve performance. **EIQ**: hand-written graph patterns evaluated incrementally by EMF-INCQUERY. **OCL**: the OCL interpreter [2] of Eclipse, as it evaluates the OCL representation of the constraint check. **OCL-CG**: is Java code generated from the same OCL expression by Eclipse OCL [2]. **OCL-IA**: the OCL Impact Analyzer [26] toolkit, as it incrementally evaluates the same OCL expression. **OCL2IQ**: graph patterns automatically derived from the same OCL expression by a prototype partial implementation of the proposed mapping, likewise interpreted incrementally by EMF-INCQUERY (new contribution extending [10]).

4.2   Results

Results obtained from the input model of 213K elements (nodes+edges) are presented in Table 2; details and further experiments are reported at [22] along with instructions for reproduction.

The incremental strategy of EMF-INCQUERY performs extremely well in the "Continuous Validation" workload, delivering practically immediate feedback after model manipulation, at the cost of increased memory footprint. Furthermore, comparison against benchmark instances with different model sizes [22] confirms the theoretical result that this "Continuous Validation" time is practically independent of the size of unchanging parts of the model; EMF-INCQUERY memory consumption and "Batch Validation" time was found to scale approximately proportionally to model size, while OCL execution times are between a linear and quadratic proportion to model size. Finally, the graph queries automatically generated using the proposed transformation (OCL2IQ) perform similarly

---

[1] Experimental setup: Dell Latitude E5420 Laptop, Intel Core i5-2430M @ 2.4Ghz CPU, 16GB of DDR3-1066/1333 RAM, Samsung SSD 830; Eclipse Kepler on Java SE 1.7.0_05-b06 (with 2G maximum heap size) on Windows 7 x64; Eclipse OCL pre-release version 3.4.0.v20140124-1452, EMF-IncQuery 0.8.0 (nightly at 2014-03-05).

to manually written EMF-INCQUERY code (EIQ), outperforming pure Java as well as stateless or incremental OCL-based approaches.

The advantage of graph patterns at "Batch Validation" time likely stems from automatic query planning, while "Continuous Validation" times are a consequence of the deep caching of the Rete incremental evaluation strategy; these are two of the benefits of the proposed approach foreseen in Sec. 1. Thus translating OCL code to graph patterns is justified in this scenario.

4.3 Remarks and Threats to Validity

Diverging from [10] at the suggestion of Eclipse OCL leader Ed Willink, OCL evaluation was not invoked by substituting each model element as self, but only on a prefiltered list of instances of the context type of the constraint.

The performance of incremental techniques may depend on what kind of changes are performed in *phase 3*. The presented results were obtained from the *UserScenario* mode of Train Benchmark. The "Continuous Validation" times for OCL-IA are significantly worse in this case than with the alternative model manipulation workload *ModelXFormScenario* (see [22]), where OCL-IA re-evaluation is quick after a change, leading to efficient incrementality. EIQ and OCL2IQ are much less sensitive to this option, in line with theoretical predictions [21].

Note that the OCL query was produced by non-experts. Hand-optimized queries may perform better. However, the OCL2IQ approach received the same unoptimized query as input, so the comparison is fair.

The benchmark scenario was deliberately chosen as one where incremental approaches have potential advantages, and the selected query was complex to increase the role of automatic query optimization. Therefore the results do not show universal superiority of one tool over another, merely produce evidence that the proposed approach has legitimate use cases.

5   Related Work

5.1   Translating OCL to Logic-Based Languages

A similar translation procedure from OCL to graph patterns was utilized in [15], focusing on providing a means to automatically generate large instance models (e.g. for testing) that conform to a metamodel with OCL invariants. Compared to the proposed approach, [15] handles a smaller subset of OCL, translates it into a slightly different graph query language, and does not investigate query performance. Due to conceptual differences, the translation method proposed here is not a straightforward extension of theirs, even if there are some common elements. Particularly focusing on differences between the supported subsets of OCL, [15] has the following shortcomings: (i) support is focused on Boolean-valued OCL expressions only (though non-Boolean navigations can be used in certain ways); (ii) set operations such as select(), collect(), union(), etc. are not supported; (iii) aggregations such as sum() are not supported; (iv) the result of `size()` can only be compared against constants; (iv) the result of two paths of navigation can only be compared for equality. Thus e.g. the derived feature of Lst. 1 cannot be translated for multiple reasons.

Metamodel consistency checkers UML2Alloy [16] and UMLtoCSP [27] compile OCL to a constraint or logic language, similarly to the proposed approach; but without "flattening" collections to relational semantics (contrast Sec. 3.2). Thus the expressive power of OCL is preserved (at least for [27]), but the Rete algorithm (and some other benefits foreseen in Sec. 1) cannot be applied.

Mappings to formal semantic domains such as HOL (higher-order-logic) revealed [25] inconsistencies and ambiguities in the OCL standard. Fortunately, they have low impact on the OCL sublanguage supported in the current paper. Such transformations could not be directly reused for the same reason as above.

5.2 Incremental Evaluation of OCL

Due to the expressive power of OCL constructs, the Rete-based approach used in EMF-INCQUERY is not applicable for all queries formulated as OCL expressions. There are, however, alternative approaches for incremental evaluation of OCL queries, though they have a lower level of incrementality [21] than Rete.

Cabot's approach [28] and the Impact Analyzer [26] extension of the freely available query engine Eclipse OCL [2] rely on static analysis of OCL expressions when computing an over-estimate of query inputs that need to be re-evaluated from scratch for given elementary model change.

The Groher-Reder-Egyed approach [24] for incremental constraint checking is independent from the constraint language, but can be instantiated for OCL. The strategy is to wrap the model into a model access layer that records elementary model access operations, such as retrieving the value of an attribute, during the query evaluation; later the query can be re-evaluated for the given input if any of the recorded elementary queries are affected by a change. Some re-evaluations can be saved by language-specific maintenance [29] of a Boolean validation tree.

Case study-driven comparative performance benchmarking of incremental model query evaluation technologies is a currently ongoing effort [30,31,10].

6   Conclusion

The paper presented a general specification for mapping a large subset of OCL expressions to equivalent graph patterns, and provided concrete translations conforming to this scheme for numerous OCL constructs and Standard Library operations, while clearly indicating any limitations of the approach.

Experiments have demonstrated that query performance can be increased by evaluating the generated graph patterns (using EMF-INCQUERY) instead of the original OCL expressions, which was one of the benefits of the approach foreseen in Sec. 1. Although the measurements do not constitute a comprehensive performance assessment of the various tools, they suffice for proving the existence of cases where the proposed mapping can be directly useful.

The author wishes to thank Ed Willink for his advice on Eclipse OCL.

References

1. The Eclipse Foundation: Eclipse Modeling Framework, http://www.eclipse.org/emf/
2. Eclipse Model Development Tools Project: MDT-OCL website (2011), http://www.eclipse.org/modeling/mdt/?project=ocl
3. Ehrig, H., Engels, G., Kreowski, H.J., Rozenberg, G. (eds.): Handbook on Graph Grammars and Computing by Graph Transformation: Applications, Languages and Tools, 2nd edn. World Scientific (1999)
4. Rensink, A.: Representing first-order logic using graphs. In: Ehrig, H., Engels, G., Parisi-Presicce, F., Rozenberg, G. (eds.) ICGT 2004. LNCS, vol. 3256, pp. 319–335. Springer, Heidelberg (2004)
5. W3C SPARQL Working Group: SPARQL Query Language for RDF. Technical report, W3C (2008), http://www.w3.org/TR/rdf-sparql-query/
6. Horváth, Á., Varró, G., Varró, D.: Generic search plans for matching advanced graph patterns. In: Proc. of the Sixth International Workshop on Graph Transformation and Visual Modeling Techniques (GT-VMT 2007), pp. 57–68. Electornic Communications of the EASST, Braga (2007)
7. Veit Batz, G., Kroll, M., Geiß, R.: A first experimental evaluation of search plan driven graph pattern matching. In: Schürr, A., Nagl, M., Zündorf, A. (eds.) AGTIVE 2007. LNCS, vol. 5088, pp. 471–486. Springer, Heidelberg (2008)
8. Giese, H., Hildebrandt, S., Seibel, A.: Improved flexibility and scalability by interpreting story diagrams. ECEASST 18 (2009)
9. Forgy, C.L.: Rete: A fast algorithm for the many pattern/many object pattern match problem. Artificial Intelligence 19(1), 17–37 (1982)
10. Ujhelyi, Z., Bergmann, G., Hegedüs, Á., Horváth, Á., Izsó, B., Ráth, I., Szatmári, Z., Varró, D.: EMF-IncQuery: An integrated development environment for live model queries. Science of Computer Programming (0) (2014)
11. Hegedüs, Á., Horváth, Á., Ráth, I., Varró, D.: A model-driven framework for guided design space exploration. In: 26th IEEE/ACM International Conference on Automated Software Engineering (ASE 2011). IEEE Computer Society, Lawrence (2011)
12. Rensink, A., Distefano, D.: Abstract graph transformation. Electron. Notes Theor. Comput. Sci. 157(1), 39–59 (2006)
13. Baldan, P., Corradini, A., König, B.: Unfolding graph transformation systems: Theory and applications to verification. In: Degano, P., De Nicola, R., Meseguer, J. (eds.) Montanari Festschrift. LNCS, vol. 5065, pp. 16–36. Springer, Heidelberg (2008)
14. Heckel, R., Küster, J.M., Taentzer, G.: Confluence of typed attributed graph transformation systems. In: Corradini, A., Ehrig, H., Kreowski, H.-J., Rozenberg, G. (eds.) ICGT 2002. LNCS, vol. 2505, pp. 161–176. Springer, Heidelberg (2002)
15. Winkelmann, J., Taentzer, G., Ehrig, K., Küster, J.M.: Translation of Restricted OCL Constraints into Graph Constraints for Generating Meta Model Instances by Graph Grammars. In: Proceedings of the Fifth International Workshop on Graph Transformation and Visual Modeling Techniques (GT-VMT 2006), vol. 211, pp. 159–170. Elsevier Science Publishers B. V., Amsterdam (2008)
16. Anastasakis, K., Bordbar, B., Georg, G., Ray, I.: UML2Alloy: A challenging model transformation. In: Engels, G., Opdyke, B., Schmidt, D.C., Weil, F. (eds.) MODELS 2007. LNCS, vol. 4735, pp. 436–450. Springer, Heidelberg (2007)
17. Object Management Group: Object Constraint Language Specification, Version 2.4 (2014), http://www.omg.org/spec/OCL/2.4/

18. Bergmann, G., Ujhelyi, Z., Ráth, I., Varró, D.: A graph query language for EMF models. In: Cabot, J., Visser, E. (eds.) ICMT 2011. LNCS, vol. 6707, pp. 167–182. Springer, Heidelberg (2011)
19. Bergmann, G., Horváth, Á., Ráth, I., Varró, D.: A benchmark evaluation of incremental pattern matching in graph transformation. In: Ehrig, H., Heckel, R., Rozenberg, G., Taentzer, G. (eds.) ICGT 2008. LNCS, vol. 5214, pp. 396–410. Springer, Heidelberg (2008)
20. Ráth, I., Hegedüs, Á., Varró, D.: Derived features for EMF by integrating advanced model queries. In: Vallecillo, A., Tolvanen, J.-P., Kindler, E., Störrle, H., Kolovos, D. (eds.) ECMFA 2012. LNCS, vol. 7349, pp. 102–117. Springer, Heidelberg (2012)
21. Bergmann, G.: Incremental model queries in model-driven design. Ph.D. dissertation, Budapest University of Technology and Economics, Budapest (October 2013)
22. Bergmann, G.: Graph patterns from OCL: A performance evaluation (March 2014), https://incquery.net/content/graph-patterns-ocl-performance-evaluation
23. Bergmann, G., Ráth, I., Szabó, T., Torrini, P., Varró, D.: Incremental pattern matching for the efficient computation of transitive closure. In: Ehrig, H., Engels, G., Kreowski, H.-J., Rozenberg, G. (eds.) ICGT 2012. LNCS, vol. 7562, pp. 386–400. Springer, Heidelberg (2012)
24. Groher, I., Reder, A., Egyed, A.: Incremental consistency checking of dynamic constraints. In: Rosenblum, D.S., Taentzer, G. (eds.) FASE 2010. LNCS, vol. 6013, pp. 203–217. Springer, Heidelberg (2010)
25. Brucker, A.D., Doser, J., Wolff, B.: Semantic issues of OCL: Past, present, and future. In: 6th OCL Workshop at the UML/MoDELS Conference (2006)
26. Uhl, A., Goldschmidt, T., Holzleitner, M.: Using an OCL Impact Analysis Algorithm for View-Based Textual Modelling. In: Proc. 11th workshop on OCL and Textual Modelling (OCL 2011), vol. 44. ECEASST (2011)
27. Cabot, J., Clarisó, R., Riera, D.: Verification of UML/OCL class diagrams using constraint programming. In: Proceedings of the 2008 IEEE International Conference on Software Testing Verification and Validation Workshop, ICSTW 2008, pp. 73–80. IEEE Computer Society, Washington, DC (2008)
28. Cabot, J., Teniente, E.: Incremental integrity checking of UML/OCL conceptual schemas. J. Syst. Softw. 82(9), 1459–1478 (2009)
29. Reder, A., Egyed, A.: Incremental consistency checking for complex design rules and larger model changes. In: France, R.B., Kazmeier, J., Breu, R., Atkinson, C. (eds.) MODELS 2012. LNCS, vol. 7590, pp. 202–218. Springer, Heidelberg (2012)
30. Bergmann, G., Horváth, Á., Ráth, I., Varró, D., Balogh, A., Balogh, Z., Ökrös, A.: Incremental evaluation of model queries over EMF models. In: Petriu, D.C., Rouquette, N., Haugen, Ø. (eds.) MODELS 2010, Part I. LNCS, vol. 6394, pp. 76–90. Springer, Heidelberg (2010)
31. Izsó, B., Szatmári, Z., Bergmann, G., Horváth, Á., Ráth, I.: Towards precise metrics for predicting graph query performance. In: 2013 IEEE/ACM 28th International Conference on Automated Software Engineering (ASE), pp. 412–431. IEEE Computer Society Press, Silicon Valley (2013)

Author Index